AF673420

Islands Against Civilisation

Islands Against Civilisation

Anthropology, Nationalism, and the Politics of Scheduling, 1918–1950

SAAGAR TEWARI

Orient BlackSwan

All rights reserved. No part of this book may be (i) modified, reproduced or utilised in any form, or by any means, electronic or mechanical, including photocopying, recording or by any information storage and retrieval system, in any form of binding or cover other than in which it is published, without permission in writing from the publisher; or (ii) used or reproduced in any manner for the purpose of training, development or operation of artificial intelligence (AI) technologies and systems, including generative AI technologies, without permission in writing from the copyright holder.

ISLANDS AGAINST CIVILISATION: ANTHROPOLOGY, NATIONALISM, AND THE POLITICS OF SCHEDULING, 1918–1950

ORIENT BLACKSWAN PRIVATE LIMITED

Registered Office
3-6-752 Himayatnagar, Hyderabad 500 029, Telangana, India
e-mail: centraloffice@orientblackswan.com

Other Offices
Bengaluru, Chennai, Guwahati, Hyderabad, Kolkata,
Mumbai, New Delhi, Noida, Patna

© Orient Blackswan Private Limited 2025
First published by Orient Blackswan Private Limited 2025

ISBN 978-93-5442-648-3

040920

Typeset in
Adobe Jenson Pro 11/13
by Le Studio Graphique, Gurgaon 122 007

Printed in India at
Avantika Printers Private Limited, New Delhi 110 020

Published by
Orient Blackswan Private Limited
3-6-752 Himayatnagar, Hyderabad 500 029, Telangana, India
e-mail: info@orientblackswan.com

Dedicated to my Guru,
Professor Basudev Chatterji
&
My parents,
Shri Amar Nath Tewari and Smt. Kamala Tewari

Contents

Abbreviations

AICC	All India Congress Committee
AIEPEAA	All India Excluded and Partially Excluded Areas Association
BAJSS	Bharatiya Adimjati Sevak Sangh
CA	Constituent Assembly
CAD	Constituent Assembly Debates
CP	Central Provinces
CWMG	*Collected Works of Mahatma Gandhi*
GIPE	Gokhale Institute of Politics and Economics (digital archives)
ICS	Indian Civil Services
INC	Indian National Congress
NAI	National Archives of India
PCC	Provincial Congress Committee
PMML	Prime Ministers Museum and Library
RSS	Rashtriya Swayamsevak Sangh
RTC	Round Table Conference
SDA	Scheduled Districts Act
SIS	Servants of India Society
SR	Simon (Commission) Report
SWFA	South-West Frontier Agency
TAC	Tribes Advisory Council

Images, Maps and Table

Images

Maps

Table

Acknowledgements

This monograph emanates from two personal beliefs: that ideas have consequences and professional historians ought to generate verifiable truth claims. While critical reviews alone can assess whether the synthesis offered helps readers comprehend the 'hand of history' in constituting the present, a long quest has finally ended. To institutions and individuals who enabled my book to come into being, *tah-e-dil se, shukriya!*

My deepest remembrance is reserved for 'Sir', Professor Basudev Chatterji, a true humanist scholar of dizzying standards, who taught at the Faculty of Arts, University of Delhi. His lectures on Gandhi offered a breathtaking sweep of an India we have lost, perhaps irrevocably. In retrospect, it was his profound love of ideas which rubbed off and eventually led me to an intellectual history project. In Sir's absence, I can only wonder whether this book would have his approval. My Hindu College teachers Ratan Lal, Tripta Wahi, Nandita Sahai, and Manivannan helped to lay the foundations for an academic life. I was also influenced by Prabhu Mohapatra, Mukul Manglik, Sumit Sarkar, Rabindra Ray, Denys Leighton, Najaf Haider, Amar Farooqui, Partho Dutta, and Sanjay Sharma. Bibhu Mohapatra's 'story' was the crucial trigger which commenced this historian's *safar*. When education was still a 'public good', I found great friends (Pathania, Jordy Sir, and Santu) in the now bygone College Hostel. To Abhishek Detha, wish you were here!

After completing my Masters, I took a break, following which I joined the Centre for Historical Studies, JNU. Here, as co-supervisors, Neeladri Bhattacharya, Sangeeta Dasgupta, and Rohan D'Souza provided training in archival methods and theoretical rigour. Sangeeta, in particular, has offered the most far-sighted advice. At JNU, I have enjoyed delightful conversations with Avijit Pathak, Bimol Akoijam, Janaki Nair, Indivar Kamtekar, and the inimitable M. S. S. Pandian, who will remain etched in my memory. Auditing their courses and study circles honed my skills of presentation and critique. More recent conversations with Professor Madhavan Palat have been highly illuminating. Campus life forges friendships, lasting or otherwise; I will always remember Nabarun Da, Sourav, and Monish. To Uday, Ravindra, Gitika, Rajesh, Dhiraj, Kaustav, Neha, Bidisha, Prabodhan, Paulomi, Umar,

Dinesh, Arun, Khinvraj, Ashish Da, Dharmendar, non-teaching staff, and everyone else in the JNU of yore: you have all made this possible.

Collecting scattered evidence entailed many challenging journeys which would have been impossible without the help of staff from various libraries and archives. In Delhi, JNU and DELNET, the National Archives of India, Prime Ministers Museum and Library, Central Secretariat, Yojna Bhawan, and Bharatiya Adimjati Sevak Sangh (especially Sanjay Saxena) were instrumental to the book's framing. In Bhopal, the Tribal Research and Development Institute, Directorate of Archaeology, Archives and Museums (Padam Singh Meena), Vidhan Sabha, National Archives, and the Secretariat in Vidhyanchal/Satpura Bhawans were crucial. Special thanks to Roshini Chattopadhyay for sending the Starte Committee report from TISS, Mumbai. It provided the elusive key!

Outside India, I heartily thank the staff of libraries and archives in London, Oxford, and Cambridge. Special thanks are due to the Centre for South Asian Studies, University of Cambridge for permission to quote extensively from the Edgar Stanley Hyde papers. An exchange studentship to the King's College London opened my access to the British Library. I want to thank Jon Wilson, who gave me the touchstone question: 'What happens to a minority discourse which does not have its own elite?' To Timothy Riley and Priya Shankar, I am fortunate for your friendship and incomparable hospitality.

For the doctoral thesis, I received the Junior Research Fellowship from the Indian Council of Historical Research during the period 2012–2014. The thesis was examined by two stalwart historians, Mahesh Rangarajan and Crispin Bates, who continue to provide support. At the Centre for the Study of Developing Societies, a Visiting Fellowship helped me extend work in newer directions, for which Prathama Banerjee, Awadhendra Sharan, and Ravikant generously pooled their inputs. Abhay Kumar Dubey encouraged academic writing in Hindustani. I also found in Satendra a friend I deeply cherish.

At the Jindal School of Liberal Arts and Humanities (OPJGU, Sonipat), a small classroom offered the ideal setting to practice the vocation of teaching. I thank Kathleen Modrowski and Jayani Jeanne Bonnerjee for their consistent support. Dony, Amit, Mohsin, Deepanshu, Avinash, Vikash, Gargi, Jilani, John, Mani Sir, Matthew, Devyani, Arun, Kaushalya, Renu, Gagan, Gitanjali, Satya, Arpan, and Faisal have provided collegiality and friendship. Kriti Sharma's course on indigenous peoples' rights has added heft to the Epilogue.

Special thanks are due to Nishant Gokhale, whose careful reading of the entire manuscript cleaned major errors. Rakesh Ankit read one important piece and saved it from premature demise! I thank the anonymous reader who reviewed the manuscript; their comments were encouraging. Through her guidance, Professor Sudeshna Guha opened up the fascinating world of images. For permission to use photographs in the text, I am indebted to the Royal Anthropological Institute, London; Pitt Rivers Museum, Oxford; OUP Archives, PMML, and the Indian National Science Academy. Namita Wahi from the Centre for Policy Research, New Delhi kindly allowed me to adapt two very useful maps.

Words are insufficient to express what I owe to my parents; Papa and Maa have been the sheet anchors of our world. My brother Shekhar, Shikha, and Purab have been ever so loving and supportive. My sister Seema and Vinod Jijaji, along with their daughters Lori, Gehna, Medha, and Manogya, are all-weather allies who have provided joy, affection, and care. As intimate friends, Ritesh, Lalit, Razi, Varun, Pradyuman, Rajat, Mayank, Prachi, and Sameer have always kept their faith.

Meera's companionship is a blessing, without which this book would never have been written. Living in a better scholar's company and benefiting from her edits, I have discovered my voice as an author. Tied together in love for our children Uttara and Nandita, we have found delightful distraction, joy, and wisdom in times of ecological and political climate change. My in-laws, Shiv and Susan Visvanathan, have reminded us that scholarly credibility is sacrosanct, which authors must guard with their lives. Sir's reading of my doctoral thesis in 2019 helped to develop a polarity which it squarely lacked. Mum has read every full draft and, if this book succeeds in persuading the reader, it is due to her sagacity and wisdom. Sandhya, Mallika, and Anirudh have come into their own while this book was written, and will be most pleased to see the project conclude. To Suresh Uncle and Shobha Aunty, Mani Uncle and Ratna Aunty, we owe unqualified love and respect.

In Orient BlackSwan, I found the perfect publishing house. Hats off to Roopa Sharma, Nilanjana Majumdar, and Proteeti Banerjee for extracting the best that this author could offer. Finally, amongst the activists working for Adivasi rights, I am fortunate to know Ashok Chaudhary and the late Dr B. D. Sharma, whose lives serve as a testament of selfless service to the most marginalised sections of our national life. Academics can only feed ideas and inputs to the rights advocacy framework. Intellectuals remain in safe havens while the landless forest workers valiantly struggle for livelihood rights concerning *jal, jangal,* and *jameen*. It is to their indomitable spirit that I bow in reverence.

Dadri
January 2025

Introduction

In the second half of 1943, the Gokhale Institute of Politics and Economics, Poona published a pathbreaking book titled *The Aborigines—'So-called'—And Their Future*. Its author was the Bombay-based Indian sociologist Professor Govind Sadashiv Ghurye, who essentially rubbished the long established (and widely accepted) autochthonous status of Indian tribal people. Marshalling evidence from a variety of colonial sources, including the Census reports and various ethnographic accounts, Ghurye offered a trenchant critique of the colonial policy vis-à-vis aboriginal tribes. Moreover, he traced the dispossession and exploitation of the 'so-called' aborigines to the advent of British rule, and in particular to the revenue and judicial policies followed under the British masters. Thus, by placing the blame for the immense 'backwardness' suffered by aborigines squarely onto the shoulders of the British, the monograph provided the high-watermark of nationalist understanding of the tribal predicament in India.

There was, however, another main argument in the book, which was about the religious status of the aborigines. Claiming that the best description of the 'so-called Aborigines' was as 'Backward Hindus', Ghurye reasoned that 'the main problem of the aborigines ... is very similar to the problems of non-aboriginal agriculturists'.[1] As will become clear over the course of this book, Ghurye's powerful articulation summed up over two decades of administrative, anthropological, and nationalist discourse on aboriginal tribes. A lasting effect of *The Aborigines* lay in the attacks mounted on the class of colonial anthropologists such as Dr John Henry Hutton, the all-India Commissioner for the 1931 Census operations. Ghurye's choicest invectives, however, were reserved for 'Mr. Verrier Elwin'. The following extract offers a good representative example:

[1] G. S. Ghurye, *The Aborigines—'So-called'—And Their Future*, Publication No. 11, Gokhale Institute of Politics and Economics, Pune, 1943, p. 232.

> Lastly, Mr. Elwin's attitude toward the tribal reform movements, whether among the Hos or among the Gonds, is symptomatic of his keen interest in preserving tribal cultures as they are or as they were.... Mr. Elwin's whole attitude to tribal reform movements is thoroughly vitiated. Because some of the so-called reforms are obnoxious to one, either because one thinks, and rightly, that they are likely to affect the vitality of the tribe adversely, or because one's aesthetic sense, one's love for the quaint and the picturesque, is offended, it does not follow that the right of the people to mould their lives according to their light should be stifled by *creating a ring-fence around them* and by preaching through the schools stabilization of the tribal traditions and customs.... Mr. Elwin wants to see them not only protected in their interests, which need such protection, but also stabilized in their old tribal culture or cultures. Mr. Elwin is, in respect of them, a revivalist. He is thus both a no-changer and a revivalist.[2]

In a chapter titled 'So-Called Aborigines and Anthropologists', Ghurye took Elwin apart by repeatedly calling him a 'revivalist' and a 'no-changer'. Elwin's advocacy of the 'National Parks' for the Baigas and Gonds in the district of Mandla was particularly ridiculed. These ideas formed part of Elwin's first full-length ethnographic monograph, *The Baiga* (1939), following which he also published the famous pamphlet *Loss of Nerve* (1941). After the death of Rai Bahadur Sarat Chandra Roy in 1942, Elwin joined the editorial board of the most prestigious Indian anthropological journal, *Man in India*. Thus, in brutally attacking Verrier Elwin, Ghurye was taking on the most rapidly rising star in the world of Indian anthropology. In the academic understanding of Indian tribes, this moment marks the beginning of a misnomer, still standing in need of a scholarly revision.

Resetting the Terms of Discourse: Scheduling as the Tribal Question

This book is fundamentally about the late colonial debate on the territorial 'ring-fencing' or, to use an administrative category, 'scheduling'[3]

[2]Ibid., pp. 197–198, emphasis added.

[3]The root of this key word lies in the fourteenth-century Latin term *schedula*, which again is derived from *scheda*, meaning 'a strip of papyrus', a surface used since ancient times by Egyptians, Greeks, and Romans for recording of writing (*Chambers 21st Century Dictionary*, New Delhi: Allied Chambers (India) Limited,

of predominantly tribal areas in British Indian Provinces. In colonial statecraft, the instrument of scheduling was the act of committing certain areas to a written list or inventory of 'special administrative regimes', where the normal laws and regulations prevalent in the rest of British India were not applicable.[4] In an era of progressive constitutional reforms, the future of tribal communities inhabiting the Indian subcontinent became the subject of an intense polemical debate. Termed as the 'Tribal Question', it has largely been presented in scholarly literature as an ideological contest between Verrier Elwin[5] and G. S. Ghurye.[6] Their respective schools of thought have been dubbed as Isolation/Protection *versus* Intervention/Assimilation, wherein these two ideologues sparred over the most appropriate policy for safeguarding the interests of tribal communities residing within the British Indian empire.

2005 [2001], p. 1255). I thank Dr Sourav Kumar Mahanta, an ex-CHS peer, for his suggestion to include the etymology of this word.

[4]According to Nishant Gokhale, a legal historian, scheduling was a form of 'legal technology' through which a disparate group of areas could be clubbed together. The existence of this practice can be traced to the early period of the English East India Company's rule.

[5]On Verrier Elwin, see Ramachandra Guha's biography, *Savaging the Civilized: Verrier Elwin, His Tribals, and India*, New Delhi: Penguin, 2014 [first published by Oxford University Press, 1999]. This book has often been lauded for its empirical and intimate portrayal of Elwin. However, as Virginius Xaxa argues in his review of Guha's monograph, by glossing over the silences and erasures within the highly contradictory life of his muse, 'Guha comes across as Elwin's spokesperson through the book'. Virginius Xaxa, 'Elwin's Tribals', *Economic and Political Weekly* 36 (18), 5 May 2001, pp. 1519–1520. A few other notable studies on Elwin include T. B. Subba and Sujit Som (eds), *Between Ethnography and Fiction: Verrier Elwin and the Tribal Question in India*, New Delhi: Orient Longman, 2005; Archana Prasad, *Against Ecological Romanticism: Verrier Elwin and the Making of an Anti-Modern Tribal Identity*, New Delhi: Three Essays Collective, 2003.

[6]A number of scholarly studies have been done on Ghurye. For a critical understanding of Ghurye's work, see Nicholas B. Dirks, 'G. S. Ghurye and the Politics of Sociological Knowledge', *Sociological Bulletin* 62 (2), Special Issue on the Bombay School of Sociology: Stalwarts and their Legacies, May–August 2013, pp. 239–253; and Carol Upadhya, 'The Hindu Nationalist Sociology of G.S. Ghurye', *Sociological Bulletin* 51 (1), March 2002, pp. 28–57. For a somewhat hagiographic account, see S. K. Pramanick, *Sociology of G.S. Ghurye*, Jaipur: Rawat, 2020, revised second edition.

Within the evolving constitutional discourse, the Tribal Question signified the multifaceted debate on the pros and cons of scheduling as an instrument for providing protection to aboriginal tribes. Unfortunately, the core issue lying at the heart of the debate, that is, scheduling, has been given short shrift, while a barely existing one, that is, the Ghurye–Elwin debate, has reams written upon it.[7] Consequently, there is very little scholarly literature on the idea of scheduling. Therefore, it will be useful to survey some broad trends and misconceptions which have long persisted without any revision.

The term 'Tribal Question' was deployed in the Constituent Assembly Debates and has been used by sociologists like Nandini Sundar in secondary literature on the period.[8] While I have adopted the term for these historical and historiographical reasons, there are two crucial points of departure from Sundar. *First* is on the issue of the time-frame. While Sundar has situated the debate between 1927–1950, I contend that it actually commences with the Montague–Chelmsford reform proposals in 1918, stays within the colonial administrative apparatus, and by the mid-1930s, spills over to the political domain.[9]

---

[7]There is a series of publications which assume the centrality of the so-called 'Ghurye–Elwin Debate'. A few key ones are Anjan Ghosh, 'Whither Indian Sociology?', *Other Sociology* 1, 1989; Tiplut Nongbri, 'Tribe, Caste and the Indigenous Challenge in India', in Bengt G. Karlsson and Tanka B. Subba (eds), *Indigeneity in India*, London: Kegan Paul, 2006, pp. 75–95; K. S. Singh, 'G.S. Ghurye, Verrier Elwin and Indian Tribes', in A. R. Momin (ed.), *The Legacy of G.S. Ghurye: A Centennial Festschrift*, Bombay: Popular Prakashan, 2006, pp. 39–45; A. C. Sinha, 'Colonial Anthropology vs Indological Sociology: Elwin and Ghurye on Tribal Policy in India', in Tanka B. Subba and Sujit Som (eds), *Between Ethnography and Fiction: Verrier Elwin and the Tribal Question in India*, New Delhi: Orient Longman, 2005, pp. 71–85; Virginius Xaxa, 'Tribes as Indigenous People of India', *Economic and Political Weekly*, 18 December 1999, pp. 3589–3595, and 'Tribes in India', in Veena Das (ed.), *The Oxford Companion to Sociology and Social Anthropology in India*, Oxford: Oxford University Press, 2003, pp. 373–408.

[8]See the eponymous chapter in Nandini Sundar's *Subalterns and Sovereigns: An Anthropological History of Bastar, 1854–1996*, Delhi: Oxford University Press, 1997, pp. 156–190.

[9]Saagar Tewari, 'Tribe and Development: Nation-Making in Bastar, Central India (1930s–1980s)', Ph.D. thesis, Centre for Historical Studies, Jawaharlal Nehru University, New Delhi, 2014.

Second, following most established scholarship, Sundar has rather uncritically accepted the so-called Ghurye–Elwin debate.[10] As a discursive trope, this formulation remains ubiquitous and sadly unquestioned within tribal studies in India. On this count, it is my contention that no such debate ever took place, and especially after the departure of Hutton,[11] the real fault-lines emerged between Amritlal Vitthaldas Thakkar[12] and Elwin. Therefore, in the battleground of ideas on Indian tribes, Ghurye only made a proxy appearance and launched a blistering attack on Elwin's protectionist position through his book, *The Aborigines*. On his part, Elwin remained silent and quite uncharacteristically, never issued a single public or private response. Despite Elwin's deafening silence, it is at least amusing to acknowledge why no scholar has ever called into question the very idea of the Ghurye–Elwin debate. Additionally, a serious and often overlooked aspect of Ghurye's book was that, in the main, it was the high-watermark of the nationalist critique of the idea of 'ring-fencing' (or scheduling) of large territories away from the law-making powers of elected assemblies and councils. In the process, Ghurye undercut the protectionist argument of colonial anthropology and sharpened the nationalist one for the assimilation of tribes who were to be treated as 'Backward Hindus'.

Nevertheless, despite the obvious lack of focus on scheduling and a misguided one on the much vaunted but archivally ephemeral Ghurye–Elwin debate, there were indeed two opposing schools of thought that

---

[10]See Nandini Sundar's *Subalterns and Sovereigns*, pp. 180–183. For a relatively recent, if brief, reiteration, see 'Introduction', in Nandini Sundar (ed.), *The Scheduled Tribes and their India: Politics, Identities, Policies and Work*, New Delhi: Oxford University Press, 2016, p. 20.

[11]For a general overview of J. H. Hutton, see, P. K. Mishra, 'J.H. Hutton and the Colonial Ethnography of North-East India', in T. B. Subba (ed.), *North-east India: A Handbook of Anthropology*, New Delhi: Orient BlackSwan, 2012. For a brief and comparative account of Hutton's role in the very framing of the discourse on scheduling vis-à-vis W. V. Grigson, see Saagar Tewari, 'Spaces of Protection, Regimes of Exception: Anthropologists, Administrators and the Framing of the Late Colonial Discourse on Tribal Regions (1920–1950)', *Karatoya: North Bengal University Journal of History* 12, March 2019, pp. 114–130.

[12]For an overview of A. V. Thakkar's life and career, see (in Hindi) Saagar Tewari, 'Kasht Nivarak Thakkar Bapa: Samaj Seva ko Samarpit Jivan par ek Vihangam Drishti', *Pratimaan: Samay Samaj Sanskriti* 5 (2), July–December, 2017, pp. 278–296.

emerged in late colonial India. On the one hand stood the anthropologists, who viewed the Tribal Question primarily as an administrative problem. They held that the introduction of electoral democracy would harm the tribal people and that, consequently, there was a need to 'exclude' or 'partially exclude' the predominantly tribal areas of British India from the legislative powers of elected assemblies and councils. The nationalists, on the other hand, were vehemently opposed to such a policy of territorial segregation, viewing it as but another instrument of the British policy of 'divide and rule'. For them, the Tribal Question required a legislative solution as, arguably, it was the arbitrariness of the colonial administrative model that had led to the enduring backwardness of tribal communities. The Indian National Congress consistently maintained that the only way through which tribal people could be uplifted from their backwardness was by giving them guaranteed representation in the legislative bodies of the Indian nation.[13] In a nutshell, what has been termed as Isolation/Protection was the position of the anthropologists, who wanted scheduling of predominantly tribal areas. The nationalists opposed to scheduling were the advocates of Intervention/Assimilation, who wanted to jettison this colonial instrument lock, stock, and barrel. What has been dubbed as ideologies (Isolationism/Protectionism *versus* Interventionism/Assimilationism) with their key ideologues (Elwin *versus* Ghurye) in the debate on tribal futures was actually a pitched battle for and against the constitutional instrument of scheduling, respectively.

Consequently, what I have called the 'Politics of Scheduling' was a tug-of-war between the anthropologists and the nationalists. The contradictions within this dialectical framework sharpened after World War II. Thus, it was within the highly contingent unfolding of the politics of scheduling that the final leg of Constituent Assembly deliberations over the Tribal Question was played out. Given the staunch nationalist opposition to the very idea of scheduling, the formulation and enshrinement of the Fifth and Sixth Schedules within the Constitution of India remains a puzzle. Through a careful analysis of the discursive field, this book provides both an intellectual and a constitutional history of the politics of scheduling.

Much of the existing literature on the Fifth and Sixth Schedules assumes that these were modelled on the proposals for partially excluded

[13]See O. P. Gautam, 'The Indian National Congress and Nation Building', *The Indian Journal of Political Science* 46 (4), 1985, pp. 487–505.

and excluded areas of the Government of India Act 1935, respectively.[14] The British Indian Empire has historically had three large tribal belts, situated in the frontier zones of the North-West, the North-East, and what scholarship has termed as the 'internal frontier' running across the great Indian peninsula. After Independence and Partition, owing to the preponderance of Islamised tribes, the North-western frontier tracts went over to the new nation-State of Pakistan, while the latter two remained within the Union of India. This book provides a thorough mapping of the discursive terrain for predominantly tribal areas in British India. In the language of late colonial constitutional reforms, these were termed as either 'excluded' areas or 'modified exclusion'/'partially excluded areas' under the Government of India Acts of 1919 and 1935, respectively. Many of them were classed under the Fifth and Sixth Schedules of the Constitution of India.[15]

Literature Survey

Until recently, there were no scholarly works on the theme of scheduling.[16] An anonymous article summarising the late colonial deliberations, especially

[14]For the most recent reiteration of this formula, see 'Introduction', in Varsha Bhagat-Ganguly and Sujit Kumar (eds), *India's Scheduled Areas: Untangling Governance, Law and Politics*, London and New York: Routledge, 2020, p. 1.

[15]While most of the North-Eastern frontier region was indeed notified as 'excluded areas' since the enactment of the Government of India Act, 1919, areas in provinces outside Assam were also notified as 'excluded', in Madras (Laccadive Islands and Minicoy), Punjab (Spiti), Bengal (Chittagong Hill Tract), Bihar and Orissa (Angul), and Burma (all listed backward tracts). Hence, any straitjacketed formulation stating that excluded areas formed the Sixth Schedule while the partially excluded areas formed the Fifth Schedule is a misleading one.

[16]To the best of my knowledge, the only exceptions to this rule are three works by scholars trained in the US: Uday Chandra, 'Liberalism and its Other: The Politics of Primitivism in Colonial and Postcolonial Indian Law', *Law and Society Review* 47 (1), 2013, pp. 135–168; Poornima L. Paidipaty, 'Tribal Nation: Politics and the Making of Anthropology in India, 1874–1967', Ph.D. Dissertation, Graduate School of Arts and Sciences, Columbia University, 2010; and Ezra Rashkow, 'The Tribal Problem', in *The Nature of Endangerment in India: Tigers, 'Tribes', Extermination & Conservation, 1818–2020*, Oxford University Press, 2023, pp. 166–204. However, due to their own respective concerns and arguments, Paidipaty, Chandra, and Rashkow allude to, but do not address the issue of scheduling.

during the Constitution-making process, was published in 1977.[17] Since then, there have been a few reproductions of the Constituent Assembly archive on matters relating to the Fifth and Sixth Schedules. However, in recent years, there have been academic engagements on the excluded areas situated in the northeastern region.

In a thought-provoking article, Stephen Legg, a historical geographer, posed a grand question: What is constitutional history, and how might we write it? In his analysis of dyarchy in Assam and Darjeeling, which were both 'excluded' to varying degrees from constitutional reforms, Legg suggests that the British Provincial Governors' justifications were intended to 'pawing off the encroachments of democracy'. With this objective in mind, the excluded areas of varying hues were constituted into a network that embedded 'autocracy within putatively democratic frames of dyarchy'.[18] In a similar vein, Shaunna Rodrigues has argued from a political theory perspective that excluded areas acted as the 'limit of the political'.[19] Refreshingly, she has added the British Parliamentary debates in her analysis, which has enriched the meagre scholarly discourse on scheduling. Ornit Shani's work has similarly highlighted important tribal voices emanating from the North-East, which were demanding enfranchisement within the nation-State.[20]

Although Legg, Rodrigues, and Shani all provide valuable insights, their geographical focus is mainly on the areas constituting the Sixth Schedule in the northeastern part of the Indian subcontinent. While Legg's article does foreground how the creation of excluded areas within the constitutional regime of dyarchy produced specific arenas for political dynamics later, his analysis emanates from Foucauldian biopolitics, which occasionally provides

[17]'Background Notes I: The Scheduled and Tribal Areas', *Indian Journal of Public Administration* 23 (3), pp. 821–836.

[18]Stephen Legg, 'Dyarchy: Democracy, Autocracy and the Scalar Sovereignty of Interwar India', *Comparative Studies of South Asia, Africa and the Middle East* 36 (1), 2016, pp. 44–65, especially pp. 47, 54, 62.

[19]Shaunna Rodrigues, 'Excluded Areas as the Limit of the Political: The Murky Boundaries of Scheduled Areas in India', *The International Journal of Human Rights* 25 (7), pp. 1126–1147. Available at https://doi.org/10.1080/13642987.2021.1874359 (accessed May 2024).

[20]See Ornit Shani, *How India Became Democratic: Citizenship and the Making of the Universal Franchise* (Gurgaon: Penguin Viking, 2018), particularly Chapter 6, pp. 212–221.

good traction but by itself alone is inadequate to analyse the discourse on scheduling.

Shani's intervention is chiefly concerned with the preparation of electoral rolls in the first general elections. She has recovered several tribal voices demanding the power to vote, which shakes up the notion that tribes remained by and large silent in the constitutional discourse. On the contrary, tribal agency represented in groups and associations actively helped to create modern political institutions in the North-Eastern frontier. However, Shani's focus is squarely upon the electoral process, which constitutes only one aspect of the discourse on scheduling.

Rodrigues's analysis, on the other hand, while being persuasive on the point of the 'murky boundaries' of delineation leading to a palpable 'standoffish' character of the colonial State, suffers from two problems. *First*, such theoretical claims are almost always conceived in terms of a project of State-building, which disregards the contingent in historical time. This problem is especially palpable during visible moments of rupture. In Rodrigues's theoretical attempt, the chaos surrounding the sudden transfer of power (the Mountbatten Plan) leading to Indian independence and the Constitution-making exercise is given short shrift. The *second* problem with her formulation is that it plays upon a misconceived and false stereotype widely prevalent in the scholarship on Indian tribes. I am referring to the perception that the Scheduled Districts Act of 1874 marks the beginning of the phenomenon of scheduling in British India.[21]

Thus, it is my express contention that there is no truth behind the argument that the Scheduled Districts Act (SDA) of 1874 was the first all-India legislation which 'concretised the new colonial regime of direct rule in places identified as distinctly tribal'.[22] This is at best an erroneous impression, since there was absolutely nothing 'tribal' about the SDA, 1874. This misplaced notion was buttressed in scholarship because most of the later-day backward tracts and excluded/partially excluded areas also feature in the list attached to the SDA, 1874. However, there are also many other areas in the schedules of the SDA which do not even get a mention in the later constitutional discourse on scheduling. Such incongruities have been conveniently glossed over in tribal/Adivasi studies, and hence the resultant

[21] Rodrigues, 'Excluded Areas as the Limit of the Political', p. 4.

[22] Uday Chandra, 'Liberalism and its Other: The Politics of Primitivism in Colonial and Postcolonial Indian Law', *Law and Society Review* 47 (1), 2013, p. 144.

commonsensical notion about the SDA being a 'tribal' legislation codifying indirect rule is merely an assumption.

Further work is required to establish the broader framework of which the SDA was a part, but a perusal of the available files in the National Archives is enough to suggest that both later-day constitutional actors and scholars have been guilty of anachronistic understandings of this legislation. Historians/sociologists/anthropologists/political scientists, without exception, have failed to decipher the SDA of 1874 on its own terms, and have drawn a straight lineage with late constitutional discourse on scheduling. Perhaps this longstanding and unquestioned false genealogy stems from the word 'schedule', which has led scholars to consistently overlook a sister legislation called the Laws Local Extent Act, also passed in 1874 with exactly the same territorial inventory as in the Scheduled Districts Act. The Bill, originally introduced into Council on 25 March 1870, was titled 'A Bill to declare and consolidate the law relating to the local extent of the general regulations and Acts, and the local limits to the jurisdiction of the High Courts and chief controlling revenue authorities'.[23] Thus, the original legislation was only about placing certain territory-specific regulations away from the jurisdiction of the High Courts, and the legal term used in the early drafts was 'Excepted Districts'. These developments occurred in the post-1857 scenario when many far-reaching administrative changes and reforms were brought about in the wake of the transfer of power from the English East India Company to the British sovereign. This is a nineteenth-century story that has been surveyed in Chapter 1 of this monograph.

Why Do We Need a History of Scheduling?

In independent India, the discourse on tribal people has tended to centre on the 'politics of language, religion and identity'.[24] This has fed into the Union government's tribal policy, the cornerstones of which are the Fifth and Sixth Schedules of the Indian Constitution. These 'contain provisions for governance of tribal areas, enable devolution of power ... safeguard their

[23] Note by C. D. Field, Esq., dated 11 June 1874, in Proceeding No. 12–15, November 1874, Judicial Branch, Home Department, GoI, 1874.

[24] V. Xaxa, 'Politics of Language, Religion and Identity: Tribes in India', *Economic and Political Weekly* 40 (13), 2005, pp. 1363–1370.

traditions and practices [and], most importantly, guarantees protection of their land rights.'[25] While the colonial lineages of these schedules are well-known,[26] the processes after independence through which these schedules were incorporated into the Constitution has not been explained historically. This incorporation was meant to facilitate the integration of extremely disparate tribal populations into the body-politic of the Indian nation-State.[27] The reasons for this may have to do with the fact that scholarship surrounding the Constitution-making process has often focused on other issues.[28] When difference among groups and their rights in the apparatus of Indian democracy has been debated, it has tended to coalesce around the 'minorities' question' and its 'nationalist resolution'.[29] Further, the scholarship has relied largely on the Constituent Assembly (CA) debates to gauge the intents and motives of warring ideologues.[30]

Although there has never been a strictly defined yardstick for demarcating Scheduled Areas, this does not mean that there was no underlying logic governing their identification. In the statute books, the idea (although not the word) dates back to the late eighteenth century, and struck deep roots in the period of the Company's territorial expansion. Over its long career, several semantic shifts were noticeable in official classification, each

[25] S. G. Malhotra, 'Tribal Autonomy Undermined', *Economic and Political Weekly* 49 (13), 2014. Also see C. R. Bijoy, Shankar Gopalakrishnan, and Shomona Khanna (eds), *India and the Rights of Indigenous Peoples: Constitutional, Legislative and Administrative Provisions Concerning Indigenous and Tribal Peoples in India and Their Relation to International Law on Indigenous People*, Chiang Mai: AIPP, 2010, pp. 221–245.

[26] Rahul Sen, 'Tribal Policy of India', *Indian Anthropologist* 22 (2), 1992, pp. 77–89.

[27] V. Xaxa, 'Tribes, Tradition and State', *The Newsletter* 53, 2010.

[28] For a conglomeration, see Sujit Choudhry, Madhav Khosla, and Pratap Bhanu Mehta (eds), *The Oxford Handbook of the Indian Constitution*, New Delhi: Oxford University Press, 2016.

[29] See Rochana Bajpai, 'Constituent Assembly Debates and Minority Rights', *Economic and Political Weekly* 35 (21/22), 2000, pp. 1837–1845, and *Debating Difference: Group Rights and Liberal Democracy in India*, New Delhi: Oxford University Press, 2011.

[30] See Malvika Maheshwari, 'Collective Conservatism and the Constituent Assembly Debates: The Case of Free Speech in India', *Studies in Indian Politics* 5 (2), 2017, pp. 218–232.

having very specific connotations. Thus, at different conjunctures, terms such as 'Deregulation', 'Outlawed', 'Scheduled Districts', 'Backward Tracts', and finally, 'Excluded/Partially Excluded Areas' were used to denote the exceptional status of these areas in the legal and administrative framework.

By the turn of the twentieth century, as a result of nationalist demands, the British had begun a process of devolution of legislative and executive powers to Indian political representatives. The massive Indian participation in the British war effort surrounding World War I further bolstered nationalist calls for increasing the Indian element in colonial administration. In this context, administrative arenas were witnessing a steadily intensifying debate around what came to be known as 'excluded' and 'partially excluded' areas. Notifying tribal areas under these categories meant that they were excluded, totally or partially, from the legislative powers of the elected Provincial and Central Legislative Assemblies and Councils. The underlying principle behind these terms was that modern representative democracy (with its associated laws, courts, pleaders, and legal procedures), through the medium of elections, was highly unsuited to tribal communities. This principle also presumed that owing to their peculiar socioeconomic and cultural institutions and practices, tribes were unfit to responsibly exercise the power of the vote. The argument ran that while the aboriginal tribes could manage their lives well with the help of 'customary laws', if brought within the ambit of the Western legal framework, they would lose their distinctiveness and swell the ranks of the Depressed Classes.

In the twentieth century, at least, these special administrative frameworks were seen as legitimate instruments to 'protect' the tenurial rights of aboriginal tribes on land as well as shelter them from the impact of modern courts and legal codes. They aimed to preserve the distinctiveness of the socioeconomic and cultural systems of tribal communities. Often, the intention was to regulate infiltration by non-indigenous groups, who were seen as unscrupulous exploiters. Most votaries of scheduling were convinced of the unsuitability of modern representational democracy for tribal areas, and argued for providing a bulwark against rapid change. However, in an era of expanding nationalist politics, such exceptional provisions saw a rapid erosion of legitimacy and were increasingly seen as remnants of the paternal despotism of a bygone era.

Trajectory of the Nationalist Relationship with Indian Tribes

Although there is virtually no secondary literature on the history of scheduling, there is some scholarly literature on the interaction between tribal people and the forces of Indian nationalism. In this section, I will briefly engage with some important developments in this regard and survey the associated literature.

During World War I, the central and eastern Indian tribal belt witnessed several rebellions and movements. Apart from the British territories, some Princely States were also affected by this wave of rebellions. In 1914, Khonds arose in Daspalla State against intrigues connected with the succession of a childless ruler. This was suppressed by armed police from British India. In 1917, Mayurbhanj State was the site of a Santhal revolt over the recruitment of coolies for the Labour Corps in France, and various other economic grievances. This too was suppressed with help from the British Indian armed police and Gurkha Military Police. In 1918, there was an aboriginal uprising in Surguja State. The post-war period saw similar uprisings in Seraikella State (1925) and Kharsawan State (1931).[31] Given the small footprint of the Congress organisation in tribal areas, most of these rebellions did not have an intimate link with the Congress-led nationalist movement.[32] As World War I ended, a new framework of protest began to emerge. Under the leadership of Mahatma Gandhi, the Indian National Congress began attempts to expand its social base, seeking to ally with the rural populace.

It was the Congress nationalists of Gujarat who first reached out to the tribes from 1918 onwards. In 1919, Indulal Yagnik and A. V. Thakkar undertook to raise funds from some Bombay-based capitalists to distribute food among the Bhils of Panch Mahal, who were reeling under the effects of a failed monsoon and forceful land-tax exactions.[33] Subsequently, the Non-

[31]A. C. Lothian, *Report of the Constitutional Position of the States in Bihar and Orissa and the Central Provinces*, Simla: Government of India Press, 1932, p. 35.

[32]The only exception was the Tana Bhagat Movement, which could not be called a rebellion. For its linkage with the Congress, see Sangeeta Dasgupta, *Reordering Adivasi Worlds: Representation, Resistance, Memory*, New Delhi: Oxford University Press, 2022, Chapter 6, pp. 259–283.

[33]David Hardiman, *Gandhi in His Time and Ours*, New Delhi: Permanent Black, 2003, p. 138.

Cooperation Movement saw reasonably large participation from the tribal people of this region. Prohibition of liquor became a project of political work and social reform. A 'National Bhil Hostel' was established by Yagnik, modelled on similar institutions run by the government and Christian missionaries. A new 'Bhil Ashram' followed, which finally culminated in the establishment of the Bhil Seva Mandal by Thakkar, the pivot for his lifelong work among the tribal people.

David Hardiman's pioneering work on the 1922 Devi Movement of south Gujarat was the first full-length monograph on the influence of the national movement in tribal areas of western India.[34] The study focused on several talukas of the British-administered districts (Surat, Broach, Thana, and Nasik) as well as the princely state of Baroda (Navsari) and some minor principalities, where a new goddess of great power named Salabai was expressing her demands to the populace through spirit mediums. These included stopping the consumption of meat and liquor, living a clean and simple life, and boycotting the Parsis, who combined bootlegging with the lending of money at high rates of interest. Certain tribal communities, especially the Chodhris, enthusiastically followed suit, and the message spread rapidly. In time, the movement took a nationalist turn and Gandhian doctrines of wearing khadi, spinning the charkha, and attending nationalist schools were added to Salabai Devi's injunctions. As against earlier perspectives, which viewed the phenomenon as a product of ignorance and superstition, Hardiman argues that it was a major Adivasi initiative for far-reaching social reforms. It emerged organically, outside the domain of elite politics.

Almost simultaneously with the Devi Movement, a tribal protest movement amongst the Koya hillmen of the Gudem-Rampa region in Madras Presidency assumed the shape of a full-scale war with the colonial police and army.[35] According to Atluri Murali, restrictions on shifting cultivation and access to forest produce, combined with widespread resentment against the system of unpaid or underpaid forced labour or

---

[34]David Hardiman, *The Coming of the Devi: Adivasi Assertion in Western India*, New Delhi: Oxford University Press, 1987. Some important articles on this issue have been written by Vinita Damodaran, David Baker, David Arnold, Atluri Murali, Crispin Bates, and Biswamoy Pati.

[35]Atluri Murali, 'Alluri Sitarama Raju and the Manyam Rebellion of 1922–24', *Social Scientist* 12 (4), April 1984, pp. 3–33.

vetti, made British rule 'illegitimate' in popular perception.[36] The leader of this *fituri* was Alluri Sitaram Raju (a Telugu Kshatriya), and his genius lay in successfully linking popular grievances with his anti-colonial war. It is reported that Raju's 'austerity and his knowledge of astrology and medicine and his reputed ability to tame wild animals gained for him the respect and admiration of the tribal people who credited him with magical powers'.[37] Raju himself was influenced by Gandhi, adopted khadi, and began to preach temperance and the boycott of British courts. However, he was convinced that Indian independence could only be attained by force. This armed *sanyasi* carried on a tireless campaign of guerilla warfare against the British forces for close to two years, before being captured and shot on 6 May 1924.

But for its violent character, Alluri Sitaram Raju's uprising could be seen as an anomalous part of the Non-Cooperation Movement. While Raju made attempts to reach out to the Congress nationalists, he remained an unpalatable figure who did not receive Congress support. As David Arnold has shown, the Andhra Congressmen not only declined to join the *fituri*, but also threw their full weight against it.[38] The stated reason for this was their adherence to the Gandhian principle of non-violence. However, Arnold suggests that

> ...they (the Andhra Congressmen) represented precisely those interests—the traders, money-lenders, contractors, immigrant cultivators, and lawyers—whose hold on the hills the *fituridars* were fighting to overthrow. They had, moreover, the same contempt for the 'rude Koyas'.... To the nationalists of the plains the only useful function of the *fituri* was the opportunities it presented to make political capital from the government's blundering attempts to suppress it. For them Rama Raju's rebellion was an anachronism: it held no key to India's political future.[39]

Arnold's argument points to the class base of the Congress presence in the predominantly tribal areas. It also indicates that in the last three decades of

---

[36]Ibid., p. 8.

[37]M. Venkatarangaiya (ed.), *The Freedom Movement in Andhra Pradesh, Volume III, 1921–31*, p. 79, cited in David Arnold, 'Rebellious Hillmen: The Gudem-Rampa Risings 1839–1924', in Ranajit Guha (ed.), *Subaltern Studies I: Writings on South Asian History and Society*, New Delhi: Oxford University Press, 1982, p. 134.

[38]Ibid., p. 139.

[39]Ibid., pp. 139–140.

colonial rule, while the Congress was often ready to utilise the resentment of tribals against forest regulations or forced labour, as soon as the tide of mass civil disobedience subsided, these issues were usually and conveniently set aside.

Indeed, after the Non-Cooperation Movement petered out, the tribes and their issues were largely forgotten. Despite the obvious success of the movement in several tribal areas, Gandhi did not 'devote any great intellectual or political energy to them and their problems'. He had given the reins of political and welfare work among the tribals to his trusted lieutenants like Thakkar in Panch Mahal and Jugatram Dave in south Gujarat. According to Hardiman, Gandhi was content with the status quo, although he warned them against 'proselytizing their own values in a heavy-handed manner'.[40]

The Civil Disobedience Movement, launched in 1930, saw unprecedented tribal participation. This time, the stress was on disobeying forest laws, a characteristic that has led David Baker to class these acts as 'Forest Satyagraha'.[41] According to Baker, the Central Provinces (CP) (Hindi) Committee of the Congress raised the question of staging a forest satyagraha because, 'in the absence of a coastline they would be unable to mount the salt satyagraha envisaged by Gandhi'. Gandhi himself refused to grant sanction to these acts, but once he was jailed, Motilal Nehru gave his conditional permission that agitators must cut only grass, not wood, from the government forests.[42] The movement spread like wildfire across the Central Provinces and parts of Orissa, making it extremely difficult for the authorities to manage the situation.[43]

The forest agitations of the Civil Disobedience Movement far exceeded those of the early 1920s in terms of their 'size, extent, and the degree of accompanying violence'.[44] Grievances against the Forest Department and agrarian distress, coupled with the global economic crisis of the late 1920s, had created a situation ripe for agitations. While the Congress exploited these conditions for nationalist ends, its politicians often had little control over the agitating masses. Baker argues that the large-scale destruction

---

[40]Hardiman, *Gandhi in His Time and Ours*, p. 146.

[41]David Baker, '"A Serious Time": Forest Satyagraha in Madhya Pradesh, 1930', *Indian Economic and Social History Review* 2 (1), 1984, pp. 71–90.

[42]Ibid., p. 75.

[43]For the disturbances in Orissa, see Biswamoy Pati, 'Peasants, Tribals and the National Movement in Orissa (1921–1936)', *Social Scientist* 11 (7), July 1983, p. 37.

[44]Baker, '"A Serious Time"', p. 73.

of trees and repeated outbreaks of violence demonstrated 'how tenuously Gandhi, and hence the Congress, controlled the Civil Disobedience in different parts of India'.[45]

After the Gandhi–Irwin Pact, the Civil Disobedience Movement was gradually withdrawn. In the aftermath, the political energies of the nationalists came to be centred on addressing questions of 'communalism' and the 'Depressed Classes', as a result of which matters relating to tribes were again neglected. Gandhi himself 'continued to treat Adivasi issues as marginal to the movement as a whole'.[46] He insisted that Thakkar (who had been made the Secretary of Harijan Sevak Sangh) devote his energies to Harijan work rather than to the Bhils and other tribal people, despite the latter being Thakkar's chief interest.

Subsequently, the Quit India Movement in 1942 once again witnessed a considerable swell in tribal support for the Indian National Congress. Although there exists very little secondary literature on the issue of tribal participation in this movement, Biswamoy Pati's article on Laxman Naiko's revolt in the Malkangiri area gives us a good idea about the course of such events.[47] Despite the successful mobilisation that he conducted, Laxman Naiko was seen as a possible threat by local elites and the colonial administration. Thus, he was made the scapegoat for incidents of violence and sentenced to death. The remarkable thing about this movement was that it represented a convergence of local revolt with the all-India movement. While it incorporated elements from the earlier tradition of *fituri* (such as its messianic and millenarian aspects) in the area, it was also characteristically different. Pati suggested that there was a 'dialectical interaction of *swaraj* with the popular level'.[48] Pati's assessment seems to have a ring of truth in it, but such a general line of argument requires wider substantiation across several other tribal regions in the context of 1942. However, the relationship of the Congress and the tribals is a relatively under-explored theme in modern Indian historiography. Most certainly, many scholarly works remain to be written about the role that tribals played in the Congress movements of the 1930s and 1940s.

---

[45]Ibid., pp. 83–84.

[46]Hardiman, *Gandhi in His Time and Ours*, p. 147.

[47]Biswamoy Pati, 'Storm over Malkangiri: A Note on Laxman Naiko's Revolt (1942)', *Social Scientist* 15 (8/9, (August–September), 1987, pp. 47–66.

[48]Ibid., p. 59.

A Note on the Title, Protagonists, and Sources

Implicit in the book's title, my central argument is that the Neo-Diffusionist ideas articulated by W. H. R. Rivers constituted the ideological kernel informing constitutional protections that tribal communities in India were guaranteed under the Fifth and Sixth Schedules of the Constitution of India, 1950. It precisely captures the superimposition of an early twentieth-century anthropological imagination developed for the Melanesian Islands in the Pacific Ocean over the entire Indian subcontinent. In the primary title, 'Islands against Civilisation', the first word, 'Islands', stands for such areas in British India where 'Aboriginal Tribes' held numerical superiority. The second word, 'Civilisation', stands for the combined forces of law, democracy, and organised religions (chiefly mainstream Hinduism and, to a lesser extent, Christianity in North-East India), which were constantly impinging upon and trying to engulf the autonomous existence of tribal cultures in the hills and forests of the British Indian Empire. As indicated earlier, the sub-title 'Anthropology, Nationalism and the Politics of Scheduling' outlines the ideological friction between anthropologists and nationalists, which played itself out particularly in the last decades of British rule. The ultimate result of this churning was the incorporation of the Fifth and Sixth Schedule Areas in the Constitution of India, despite intense nationalist opposition.

To chart out the contours of this truly pan-India discourse, the book brings together the official anthropologists of Assam (John Henry Hutton and James Philip Mills) and Central India (Wilfrid Vernon Grigson) into conversation with archetypical characters like Thakkar and Elwin. Five chapters of the book are devoted primarily to analysing the ideas and activities of this main cast of ideologues. In doing so, this book has become, by and large, a prosopography of the main characters in the discourse. By using such a person-specific framework, this study seeks to bring into focus the enormous influence exerted by a few colonial administrators.[49] In a recent study on Herbert Hope Risley, C. J. Fuller has argued,

---

[49] There are very few full-length works on ICS officers. For a recent study, see Colin R. Alexander, *Administering Colonialism and War: The Political Life of Sir Andrew Clow of the Indian Civil Service*, New Delhi: Oxford University Press, 2019. Earlier studies include E. A. H. Blunt, *The I.C.S.: The Indian Civil Service*, London: Faber and Faber, 1937; L. S. S. O'Malley, *The Indian Civil Service, 1601–1930*, London: John Murray, 1931; and Philip Woodruff [Mason], *The Men Who Ruled India: The Founders*, London: Jonathan Cape, 1953, and *The Men Who Ruled India: The*

> The neglect of colonial officials by historians seriously undermines our understanding of politics, government and the state in British India. Of course, it is important to study local-level Indian politicians, or peasants, workers and the common people. But we must also recognize that the British Raj was an imperial despotism in which ICS officers wielded great power, so that a few men holding high office could act in ways that massively affected the lives of many millions of Indians belonging to both elite and subaltern groups.[50]

Moreover, my archival research suggests that up until the enactment of the Government of India Act, 1935, discourse on the aboriginal tribes was mainly administrative in nature. Ever since the Minto-Morley reforms scheme (1909), the colonial State had started devolving power and responsibility of administration onto the shoulders of the Indian political class. Simultaneously, the long-held demand for the Indianisation of higher civil services was also being addressed. Both these processes gained momentum after the Montague-Chelmsford reforms (1918) and the enactment of the Government of India Act, 1919.

Hence, this book engages with and analyses some key figures involved in the framing and conduct of the discourse on Indian tribes. These include J. H. Hutton, J. P. Mills, W. V. Grigson, E. S. Hyde, W. G. Archer, and the inimitable Verrier Elwin.[51] Some figures from Oxbridge, such

---

Guardians, London: Jonathan Cape, 1954. A few scholarly ones are Clive Dewey, *Anglo-Indian Attitudes: The Mind of the Indian Civil Service*, London: Hambledon Press, 1993; Roland Hunt and John Harrison (eds), *The District Officers in India*, London: Scholar Press, 1980; and Bradford Spangenberg, *British Bureaucracy in India: Status, Policy and the I.C.S. in the Late 19th Century*, Columbia, MO: South Asia Books, 1976. Perhaps the most acclaimed study is David Gilmour, *The Ruling Caste: Imperial Lives in the Victorian Raj*, London: John Murray, 2005.

[50]C. J. Fuller, *Anthropologist and Imperialist: H.H. Risley & British India, 1873–1911*, New Delhi: Social Science Press, 2023, p. 10.

[51]Despite their significance in shaping the discourse on aboriginal tribes, these ICS administrators-cum-anthropologists have remained little studied and are usually not even counted amongst the founders of Indian anthropology. For instance, barring Verrier Elwin, none of them feature in disciplinary histories of Indian sociology and anthropology. See Patricia Uberoi, Nandini Sundar, and Satish Deshpande (eds), *Anthropology in the East: Founders of Indian Sociology and Anthropology*, Ranikhet: Permanent Black, 2007. For a brief study on Hutton and Mills, see P. K. Mishra, 'J.H. Hutton and Colonial Ethnography of North-East India'; B. R. Rizvi, 'J.P. Mills and India's North East', both in T. B. Subba (ed.),

as W. H. R. Rivers and Henry Balfour are also discussed in some detail. However, it is with the former set of ideologues and protagonists that we would centrally engage in order to thrash out the similarities and differences between them and determine whether we can detect any shift in emphasis in the evolution of their ideas. However, before that, a few caveats are in order.

First, I would urge that the so-called 'ethnographic' works authored by these scholar-administrators should not merely be seen as monographs that contributed to the discipline of anthropology. This is a singularly limiting definition and assessment which misses out on a significant 'function' of these texts. I am suggesting that these works were products of their times and, consequently, they have to be seen as critical interventions in the ongoing political debate on the future of aboriginal communities. In the run-up to independence, a number of anthropological works were published at regular intervals from the 1920s onwards. Taken together, there is a remarkable unity in the ideas of this 'knot of men',[52] whose writings played a crucial role in the articulation of ideas and strategies designed for the protection of tribal communities in a future India. However, it must be mentioned that they were definitely not the founding fathers of this 'tradition', and were drawing their arguments from a much earlier lineage of administrators who also wrote anthropological treatises. Given that this period was also the twilight of the British Indian Empire, their contributions were extremely significant. Without analysing them, it is almost impossible to theorise the 'bridge' which connects the late colonial to the post-independence period as far as the discourse on the Indian tribal population is concerned.

Second, it must be remembered that the discourse on tribes was not a standard 'political' one, but rather had long-term 'constitutional' implications. Most of the debates took place in connection with the provisions for 'excluded' and 'partially excluded' areas under the Government of India Act, 1935. The same framework provided the basis and rationale for the Fifth and Sixth Schedule Areas under the Indian Constitution. However, the point that I

North-East India: A Handbook of Anthropology, New Delhi: Orient BlackSwan, 2012, pp. 57–78, and 79–98, respectively. For Mills, also see Chapter 4 by Angma Dey Jhala, 'The Administrator (as) Anthropologist: Reinventing Tribal Chiefs as Indian Princes in J.P. Mills's 1926–27 Tour Diary, Report and Proposals', in *An Endangered History: Indigeneity, Religion and Politics on the Borders of India, Burma and Bangladesh*, New Delhi: Oxford University Press, 2019, pp. 167–209.

[52] I have borrowed this term from Eric Stokes, *The English Utilitarians and India*, New Delhi: Oxford University Press, 1982 [1959], p. 9.

want to make here is that the aforementioned 'knot of men' were consciously crafting their ideas as active participants in this constitutional debate.

Third, I would suggest that when these actors were penning their ideas, the issue of the future of tribal communities was literally on the margins of the constitutional deliberations. The twin aspects of the 'communal' question, that is, Hindu-Muslim relations and the Depressed Classes issue, received the lion's share of attention. Additionally, in the virtual absence of an articulate and English-educated middle class amongst the tribals (a few notable exceptions being Jaipal Singh Munda, Rai Bahadur Dulu Manki, and Devendranath Samanta from Chota Nagpur or J. J. M. Nicholls Roy from North-East India), these handful of European men saw themselves as the only real 'representatives' of the interests of tribal communities. Their singular contribution lay in the explication of a minority politics articulated within a language of cultural distinctiveness and indigeneity. With important variations, their political vision was also imbued with a notion of a decentralised autonomous administration of predominantly tribal areas. This alternative was consciously articulated outside the hegemonic discourses of 'nation' and 'development'.

Among these archetypical characters, Hutton emerged as the first hinge of the discourse on tribal people. Although he considered culture-contact as something inevitable, he also held that its effects were largely detrimental to primitive tribal communities. In essence, Hutton was applying the Neo-Diffusionist views of Rivers, Balfour, et al. on culture-contact (which had been developed in the study of the Melanesian Islands) on the Naga Hills. The native communities in these island societies were geographically tucked away from the possibility of any massive intervention from mainland 'civilised' societies. However, with the onset of European colonialism, their 'isolation' was broken, which (it was claimed) resulted initially in a 'loss of interest' in life and ultimately led to the depopulation and virtual extinction of native societies. While this analysis was developed for the southern Pacific Islands, taking a cue from Balfour's juxtaposition of this framework over the Naga Hills, Hutton became a champion of this point of view in Indian anthropological circles.

Besides the 'official' archival repositories concerning the late constitutional reforms, this study is based on a wide variety of sources, viz., newspapers, private paper collections, parliamentary and legislative council debates. The fruition of many of the ideas contained in this book were impossible without the privilege of free archival access to the digital repository of the Gokhale Institute of Politics and Economics (GIPE), Pune. This is truly a national treasure house of first-rate primary sources pertaining to all parts of India, but especially rich for western India. Thanks to the GIPE digital repository, I have been able to add a new kind of primary source category emanating from socio-religious reform movements to the usual archival base for doing tribal history (missionary, anthropological, and bureaucratic).

In my effort to weave an all-India narrative, I have found the Census reports highly illuminating. The Census of 1931, in particular, holds several keys to understand the tribal predicament in India. Hutton, the Census Commissioner, devoted a substantial portion of the report to the need to differentiate 'Tribal Religions' from Hinduism. This was in part also a response to the discrediting of the category 'Animism', which originated in the 1921 Census report on the Bombay Presidency. The 1931 Census reports from the various local governments in the British Indian Empire also reflect wide-scale campaigns to claim Aboriginal tribes under the category of Hindus.

Structure and Chapterisation

The book is organised chronologically and thematically into two distinct halves, with four chapters each. While the first half focusses on the period between 1918–1936, the second concentrates on developments between 1936–1950. The evolution of the idea of distinct administrative regimes for hilly and forested tracts lies in the late eighteenth and early nineteenth century. Technically speaking, this is beyond our period of study. Nevertheless, two sections in Chapter 1 outline this history. Of course, there are obvious overlaps in the periods dealt with in individual chapters, but I have tried to maintain a linear chronological outline in the narrative.

Chapter 1 takes a broad-brush approach to developments in the long nineteenth century. It devotes a section to the making of the Scheduled Districts Act, 1874, and argues that the original intention of this legislation was to keep the newly acquired territories under the Company Raj, outside the powers of judicial review given to the newly constituted High Courts. This occurred in the post-1858 scenario when the British Crown took over as the sovereign authority. The legal term used in early drafts was 'Excepted Districts', and the word 'Scheduled' was introduced much later. Hence, in strictly legal terms, the period of this study underlines the transformation of these areas from 'spaces of exception' into what was legitimised as 'regimes of protection'.

Chapter 2 presents the intellectual milieu of the colonial anthropologists, who argued for providing a territorial solution to ensure cultural autonomy for the Indian aboriginal tribes. It engages with the Neo-Diffusionist school of thought dominant in British anthropology, and also provides an analysis of the ideas and activities of Hutton. Chapter 3 analyses the ideas of Mills, who served with Hutton in the Naga Hills for a large part of his career.

Chapter 4 deals with the evolution of ideas of the chief nationalist ideologue, A. V. Thakkar. It unpacks the religious imperatives behind the uplift and assimilation movements to which Thakkar subscribed. The social service effort pioneered by Thakkar amongst the Bhil tribes of Panch Mahal had a distinct Hindu ethos and sought to bring the tribes under a broadly conceived Hindu religio-cultural identity.

Chapter 5 seeks to understand the genealogy of the idea of 'Backwardness'. Much of the discourse owes its origin to the progress in the field of education in western India. The link between education and representation has been analysed through Census documents, legislative interventions, and official enquiries. This chapter also highlights the nationalist intervention in the politics of scheduling, after administrative ideas spilled over in the public domain and acquired political overtones.

Chapter 6 focusses on the ideas and policy interventions of Sir Wilfrid Vernon Grigson, who had a long administrative experience in Central India. In significant ways, his ideas marked a departure from the Huttonian paradigm on the tribal question. Also, the title of this book is inspired from Grigson's articulation.

Chapter 7 reexamines the Ghurye-Elwin debate and argues that the real debate was between Thakkar and Elwin. Ghurye entered the picture as a proxy for Thakkar, which changes the ideological balance between the anthropologists and the nationalists.

Chapter 8 moves away from discourse analysis and focuses on the rough and tumble of politics on aboriginal tribes, especially after the end of World War II, highlighting deliberations in the highest echelons of the colonial State. In this period, a number of Communist-led insurrections broke out, which politically challenged the Indian National Congress. Perhaps the greatest of these challenges was the Adibasi Mahasabha Movement in Bihar under the leadership of Jaipal Singh Munda. The chapter studies the Constituent Assembly deliberations and brings together all these disparate factors to explain why the Congress nationalists agreed to include provisions of the Fifth and Sixth Schedules in the Indian Constitution.

1

Spaces of Exception/Regimes of Protection

The Making of the Colonial Administrative Discourse on Scheduling Tribal Areas (1918–1936)

This chapter focuses on the late colonial administrative discourse of 'scheduling'. It will survey the gradual emergence of the practice of scheduling through the 1780s onwards. After laying out developments in the nineteenth century, it analyses the administrative and legislative discourse on the idea in the larger matrix of constitutional politics during 1918–1936.

Antecedents of Scheduling: The Internal Frontier of the Company Raj

Before charting the late colonial debate on scheduling, we need to understand its antecedents. The genesis of scheduling can be traced to the latter half of the eighteenth century, when military officials of the English East India Company first came in contact with communities settled in jungles, hills, and remote corners, away from the main lines of communication.

For the British ruling elite of the mid-eighteenth century, the nerve centre of their incipient Company State and civilisation lay in Bengal, the most prosperous Mughal *Suba*, whose control had passed into the hands of Company officers following the Battle of Plassey (1757) and the Battle of Buxar (1765). The revenue and prestige that accrued from ruling over Bengal provided legitimacy, as well as anchored the Company as a powerful actor in the political landscape of the Indian subcontinent. Administratively as well, pivotal decisions concerning the fortunes of the Company State were made in the bureaucratic corridors of the Fort William complex. Even as the Company State spread out in all directions, the map-obsessed British always imagined their frontiers with reference to this epicentre at Calcutta. In due course, three 'frontier' regions came into being: the 'North-East' and the 'North-West' frontier regions formed the outer limits of the Company State; these were transitional zones beyond which lay other centralised state-polities. In both these regions, the topography of the landscape was rough and mountainous, agricultural surplus was low, and they were populated by communities whom the State found difficult to control. But there was another frontier, closer home to Calcutta yet equally resistant to the Company Bahadur's control. This was dubbed as the 'South-West Frontier' by the early British rulers.

Lying towards the southwest of Bengal proper, this region, I argue, constituted an 'Internal Frontier' beyond which lay the territories of the Maratha Confederacy. To buttress its strategic interests in the region, the Company State first penetrated the Jungle Mahals/Tarai, thereby commencing its contact with the hill and forest-dwelling communities.

By highlighting from the beginning that Fort William constituted the core of the East India Company's Indian Empire, the distant peripheries were represented as frontier regions. Thus, this core-periphery model emerged as central to the Company's cartographic imagination of the territories it controlled. Frontiers were usually sparsely populated and meagre revenue-producing zones. Unlike the well-populated and revenue-yielding plains, the Company Raj was never too keen to bring frontiers under direct administration. Without sufficient revenue receipts from these areas, the financial costs of creating and maintaining a full-fledged legal and administrative apparatus were seen as prohibitive, and an avoidable item on the state's exchequer. As such, from the very beginning of the colonial period, frontier landscapes stoked anxieties about financing the Raj, and by implication, imposed clear and practical limits to the exercise of its sovereign authority.

Thus, to reiterate its significance: the internal frontier constituted a distant periphery of the 'core' controlled by the British, and helped the new rulers entrench their position in Bengal even further. Conceptually, the internal frontier was a form of territorial, political, geographic, and cartographic imagination. As such, the discourse on frontiers was always vitally concerned with the politics of annexations as it played out until the demise of the Company State.[1] Taken together with other main frontier regions of the North-East and the North-West, the internal frontier played a highly complex role in the long nineteenth-century story about what eventually became 'British India'.

Unlike the North-East and North-West Frontiers, which have been studied in greater detail, fewer works exist on the South-West Frontier. But this frontier is crucial to the story of this book. In what follows, I reconstruct on the basis of existing scholarship rudiments of the narrative for the nineteenth century. Although this scholarship does not foreground the internal frontier, it touches upon several aspects which are important and provide useful building blocks for the main narrative of this monograph. What follows is a reconstruction of the administrative developments in the South-West/internal frontier.

In her book *The Sepoys and the Company*, Seema Alavi shows how in 1772, the officials of the English East India Company first came in direct contact with the 'Jungleterry' (Jungle Tarai) region on the South-Western Frontier.[2] Initially, this heavily forested frontier was visualised in political and military terms, as it served as a crucial 'buffer' zone between the Company's dominions and the territories held by the Marathas. As a result, despite its extremely low revenue yields, the region acquired considerable importance in the Company's strategic calculus.

The earliest travel accounts of colonial officials framed the landscape of this internal frontier as spaces of 'wilderness', with their associated dangers to human life and endeavour. Administrative control of these areas was a source of constant anxiety as their recalcitrant inhabitants were seen as raiders, barbarians, and savages who posed a serious threat to the prospects of a lasting *Pax Britannica*. Such representations buttressed the depiction of forest/hill-dwelling people as essentially lawless and uncivilised.

K. Sivaramakrishnan's *Modern Forests* analyses the results of British intervention in the internal frontier. In marking out the trajectories of early 'British penetration into the forested areas of Bengal, the stabilization of colonial government in the region and the development of mechanisms of

[1]For a useful introduction and a selection of important primary documents, see Michael H. Fisher (ed.), *The Politics of British Annexation of India, 1757–1857*, New Delhi: Oxford University Press, 1993.

[2]Seema Alavi, *The Sepoys and the Company: Tradition and Transition in Northern India*, New Delhi: Oxford University Press, 1996, p. 155.

frontier administration',[3] he argues that political conquest of the forested frontiers of an emerging empire was lengthy and uncertain, especially in southwest Bengal and other central Indian forest regions. Over the course of the eighteenth and nineteenth centuries, the Company Raj eulogised a stable agrarian order and 'worked to dismantle forest polities and thus rid itself of the endemic problems that characterized frontiers'.[4]

In a period marked by the rapid disintegration of Mughal authority, the Company regularly experienced territorial gains as well as reversals in its battles against the Marathas and other regional powers. Partly owing to its involvement in these incessant military campaigns, it could not commit its limited fiscal resources towards creating a full-fledged governmental apparatus in the frontier areas. The British also recognised that maintaining the internal frontier—without directly administering it—was a strategically advantageous course of action that absolved the Company of the considerable fiscal, military, and logistical challenges they would have faced had these areas been annexed and ruled directly. Thus, treating the internal frontier as a 'buffer zone' allowed the British to entrench their position in Bengal.

As the early colonial State worked out its politics with a conception of an internal frontier on the edge of the territories it controlled in Bengal, a certain flexibility in administration became necessary, particularly in the domain of law. Initially, military officers in the service of the Company were regularly sent to these areas on various assignments. But in late 1773, Warren Hastings did away with the *ad hoc* nature of control, and reorganised the administration of 'the wild districts' (Nagpur, Ramgarh, Palamau, and the Jungleterry) on economic and administrative grounds. Hastings understood that prolonged military campaigns in forest regions were both expensive and hazardous as the prevailing tropical conditions often took a heavy toll on the health of Europeans. More army personnel succumbed to illnesses than to the battlefield, something that was to be avoided as far as possible. Guided by these practical imperatives as well as a strong intention to avoid 'disturbances', Hastings left the power to administer justice and collect revenue 'to the zamindars, to be managed in their own way'.[5]

[3]K. Sivaramakrishnan, *Modern Forests: Statemaking and Environmental Change in Colonial Eastern India*, New Delhi: Oxford University Press, 1999, p. 20.

[4]Ibid., p. 29.

[5]Vasudha Dhagamwar, 'Tribals and the Law', *India International Quarterly* 13 (3/4), December 1986, pp. 100–101.

Almost all colonial and independent Indian State records mention Augustus Cleveland as the progenitor of the idea of special administrative regimes for predominantly tribal areas.[6] Cleveland, a young officer in Hastings's favoured circle, was deputed to handle the situation that arose in the Rajmahal Hills as a result of the revolt of the Paharias (literally, 'residents of the hills') against their landlords. His enquiries convinced him that the application of ordinary Company law to the hilly tracts (which later became part of the Santhal Parganas) was the root cause of disorder. To blunt the Paharia resistance, Cleveland first co-opted local militiamen by creating a Hill Archers' Corps, which was endorsed by the Company authorities. The incorporation of these groups in the service of the colonial State effectively made them allies of the British.[7] Cleveland also convinced Hastings that the traditional Paharia 'Hill Assemblies' should be sanctioned with limited powers for the trial of civil and criminal cases. In this manner, he laid the foundations of the policy embodied in Regulation I of 1796, which was entitled *The Regulation for the Trial of Hill People in the District of Rajmahal and Boglepore for Crimes and Misdemeanours*.[8] This marked the first legislative attempt by the early colonial State to engage with the question of how to effectively administer hilly and forested regions situated away from 'civilisation' (read fertile and surplus revenue yielding alluvial tracts).

At just over twenty-nine years, Cleveland suffered an untimely death. However, the principles he established provided the edifice of Company administration in predominantly tribal areas. In the succeeding period, Cleveland's system enabled the entry of non-plain dwelling communities into the domain of colonial law. These interventions gradually legitimised the idea of a distinct model of administration for the hilly and forested tracts that constituted the core of the South-West/internal frontier. Thus,

[6]The following information on Augustus Cleveland has been gathered from a speech made by Sir Alexander Muddiman, Home Member of the Government of Bihar and Orissa, during a debate in the Bihar and Orissa Legislative Assembly on 10 February 1927, contained in F. No. P&J 689/1927 in IOR/L/PJ/6/1937, pp. 644–647. For a rich reproduction of colonial archival records on Cleveland and his contribution to the evolution of the Hill Assembly system of instituting judicial administration through customary laws, see Vasudha Dhagamwar, *Role and Image of Law in India: The Tribal Experience*, New Delhi: Sage, 2006, Chapters 2, 3, and 4, pp. 47–116.

[7]Alavi, *The Sepoys and the Company*.

[8]Dhagamwar, *Role and Image of Law in India*, p. 101.

Cleveland has a special significance in the history of colonial statecraft in general, and in the history of scheduling in particular.

Two decades later, after achieving success in the Third Anglo-Maratha war (1818), the East India Company acquired suzerainty over Cuttack and Sambalpur. The English now started positioning themselves as the paramount power. In eastern India, the Company authorities were now aiming to set up direct communications between Sambalpur and Bengal on one side, and between Cuttack and Benares on the other. For this purpose, control over the region of Singhbhum became necessary. As Sanjukta Das Gupta's work shows, in a bid to secure their strategic interests in the South-West Frontier, the British started pushing more deeply into the Chota Nagpur region.[9]

At first, the British were confronted with stiff military resistance in the Singhbhum region. But after suppressing the 1821 Ho rebellion, they brokered a political re-organisation with local forest polities like Seraikella and Kharsawan. Confronted with the defeat of the Marathas (to whom they had owed allegiance earlier), the local chieftains accepted the suzerainty of the Company. This brought the control of the Company State closer to these territories, especially with the stationing of the Governor-General's Political Agent on the South-West Frontier at Hazaribagh. Company troops were also posted at Chakradharpur under a Subedar of the Ramgarh Corps. According to Das Gupta, the British believed that such a policy would enforce a new conception of 'legality', which would enable the transformation of the Hos into 'useful subjects'. They also undertook to 'civilize' the 'savages' by initiating measures to curb 'barbaric' practices such as witch-killing.[10]

The limits of this policy became evident, however, with the Kol rebellion of 1831–1832, which brought to the fore the dissatisfaction of the Chota Nagpur tribals against the whole gamut of changes initiated by the Company Raj. In the wake of this rebellion, the British were circumspect when it came to intervening on behalf of their local collaborators. The Company officers

---

[9]See especially Chapter 3, 'British Intrusion and Administrative Reorganisation, 1820–1857', in Sanjukta Das Gupta, *Adivasis and the Raj: Socio-economic Transition of the Hos, 1820-1932*, New Delhi: Orient BlackSwan, 2011. pp. 89–132. The next few paragraphs are based on this work, especially pp. 89–101.

[10]See Shashank S. Sinha, 'Adivasis, Gender and the "Evil Eye": The Construction(s) of Witches in Colonial Chotanagpur', in Biswamoy Pati (ed.), *Adivasis in Colonial India: Survival, Resistance and Negotiation*, New Delhi: Orient BlackSwan, 2011, pp. 112–136.

increasingly 'conceded the futility of attempting to buttress a failing regime'.[11] As a result, a review of the policy in Chota Nagpur was initiated at the highest levels of the bureaucracy. The report of a detailed enquiry stressed the need for 'closer administrative and more effective control by British officers on the spot'.[12]

Captain Thomas Wilkinson, the Political Agent on the South-West Frontier, authored the new framework to be enforced in Ramgarh and the Jungle Mahals. This received legislative approval through Regulation XIII of 1833, which was popularly known as 'Wilkinson's Rules'. These rules became central to the reframing of the Jungle Mahals, Chota Nagpur, and Ramgarh into a special administrative entity called the 'South-West Frontier Agency' in 1834. Henceforth, in this territory, the operation of rules and regulations for the administration of civil and criminal justice and the collection of revenue were suspended. Authority on all matters vested in an officer, who was designated as the 'Political Agent to the Governor-General'. The powers vested in the Agent were equivalent to the Commissioners of Revenue and the Civil and Sessions Judges in Bengal.

The administrative reworking involved in the creation of this new Agency was a response to the logistical challenges faced by the Company State in this frontier region. This can be seen from the fact that two remarkable principles enunciated in 'Wilkinson's Rules' had a long afterlife in many parts of the British Indian Empire, with profound implications for the fate of millions of tribal people. Appearing as paragraphs 26 and 27 of Wilkinson's dispatch, they were as follows:

> 26—Vakils shall not be permitted to plead in any of the Courts within the jurisdiction but parties shall be allowed to conduct their business in the Courts, either in person or by Mukhtiars or authorized agents. But suits for the remunerations of the Agents or Mukhtiars shall not be heard in any Court.
>
> 27—No sale, transfer, or mortgage of any landed property, on account of claims for rent or on any other account, shall be legal until the

[11]Das Gupta, *Adivasis and the Raj*, p. 89.

[12]J. Reid, *Final Report on the Survey and Settlement Operations in the District of Ranchi 1902–1910*, Bengal Secretariat Book Depot, 1912, p. 26. This report was crucial in helping me to reconstruct the sequence of events leading to the formation of the South-West Frontier Agency. Subsequent details on the Agency provided in this section are from this report.

> authority of the Governor-General's Agent for such sale, transfer or mortgage shall have been obtained.[13]

In this period, what this meant was that the areas constituting the South-West Frontier Agency were to have courts devised on a completely different footing. Pleaders or Vakils were debarred and ordinary regulations enforced in other parts of British India were withdrawn from the area. Crucially, this led to the abolition of the *Dewani Adalat* (Civil Courts) from Ramgarh and the Jungle Mahals. Further, the appellate jurisdiction of higher court authorities would no longer apply to legal decisions taken by the Political Agent, which were now insulated from judicial review.

Also, through Rule 27, brakes were put on the 'commodification of land' vigorously taken up in the areas of Permanent Settlement in Bengal. Such legal exceptionalism privileged customs over code and signified a new theory of law, which gave credence to the supposedly autochthonous element in the local demography. K. Sivaramakrishnan's famous expression, 'zones of anomaly', was indeed applicable to this region, but its legal ramifications have not been studied in detail. Although in principle, as a part of Bengal, these areas came under the Permanent Settlement of 1793, Sivaramakrishnan specifically mentions that areas constituting 'zones of anomaly' were anomalous precisely in relation to the standardised system imposed by Lord Cornwallis.

Although these principles never found a uniform place in colonial statute books everywhere, they were remarkable on two counts. *First*, this enactment was amongst the earliest admissions on the part of the Company authorities that the penetration of the full system of colonial 'legality' (designed to make 'useful subjects') was not having its desired impact. Barring pleaders from courts was seen as a way to hold off 'vexatious litigation'. The rule points to the massive rift between intention and effect. *Second*, the protection being given to tribal land suggests that since the days of the late Company period of rule, the problem of land alienation was, as it still remains, the heart of the matter. Together, they constituted an early basis of what would exemplify the status of 'non-regulation' areas in the British Indian Empire.

As the British got more firmly entrenched, the period from 1770 to the 1830s witnessed the suppression of raids, an increase in settled agriculture, greater revenue, and the establishment of police and judicial infrastructure in Chota Nagpur. In such arenas, Company rule certainly

[13]Ibid., p. 28.

succeeded in modifying the nature of state-building processes in the South-West Frontier, which were characteristically slow in an earlier period. Also, the almost simultaneous and unbroken series of tribal rebellions suggests a stiff resistance, which necessitated a definite roll-back of the legal regime on the part of the Company State. This 'negotiated quality of state-making' is central in understanding the penetration of colonial power into these regions and the developments that followed. In a deeper sense, even while the internal frontier was being pushed back, this imagination continued to hold its ground in modifying British principles of exclusive sovereignty and the rule of law. These dynamics had long-term legal and administrative ramifications which will be discussed later.

Thus, the courts in the Agency exemplified a state of affairs where statutes and regulations applicable elsewhere were in a state of near-permanent suspension. In other words, a status of legal exceptionalism was steadily entrenched over a long period of time. This principle has been theorised as 'legal pluralism' in international law and provides an important key to understand the position of the large territorial entities termed as 'Agency' in the Company's lexicon of statecraft. Lauren Benton, a pioneering scholar of legal pluralism, writes,

> Empires did not cover spaces evenly but composed a fabric that was full of holes, stitched together out of pieces, a tangle of strings. Even in the most paradigmatic cases, an Empire's spaces were politically fragmented; legally differentiated; and encased in irregular, porous and sometimes undefined borders.[14]

In 1854, after the Nagpur state under the Bhonsles was escheated by Lord Dalhousie on grounds of the 'Doctrine of Lapse',[15] the Maratha territories were amalgamated into the North-West Provinces. In the same year, the system of governance put in place by Wilkinson's Rules was modified through Act XX of 1854. While many features of the earlier system were continued, the nomenclature changed, as the Political Agent of the South-West Frontier Agency now became the 'Commissioner' of the Chota Nagpur Division. From that year, the division was placed under the control

[14]Lauren Benton, *A Search for Sovereignty: Law and Geography in European Empires, 1400–1900*, New York: Cambridge University Press, 2010, p. 2.

[15]The doctrine stated that if the ruler of a native state died without a natural heir, then the dynastic line lapsed and the territories could be annexed by the Company State. Lord Dalhousie, as Governor-General, annexed several states on the basis of the Doctrine of Lapse.

of the Lieutenant Governor of Bengal and administered as a 'non-regulation' province, with Ranchi as its headquarters. Although the South-West Frontier Agency was relegated to oblivion in just two decades, its existence in the colonial administrative framework was significant for it heralded the emergence of distinct administrative regimes for predominantly forest landscapes with populations characterised as 'tribal'.

One interlinked and significant transformation was the change of the indigenous principle of shared sovereignty into exclusive sovereignty as understood by the British. Marked by a desire to standardise and erase fault-lines in the Indian political landscape, the rapidly expanding Company State, in a bid to establish dominance over native rulers (later termed 'Paramountcy'), pushed this logic to its limits. This process has been well-analysed by Ajay Skaria in the context of western India.[16] In a nutshell, the Company State's understanding of sovereignty was exclusive. Their ideologues and administrators held that political authority was unified and that there could be only one sovereign over a particular region. A gradual imposition of such a notion of exclusive sovereignty initiated a profound transformation of older relations of power. Now, under the British, the shift from frontiers to mapped boundaries, which, more than anything else, epitomised the creation of exclusive sovereignty, gained traction by the late nineteenth century.[17] An analysis of this process is beyond the scope of this work, but there are ample archival records on the tug-of-war over territories between the native rulers and the paramount power. Paradoxically, however, the consolidation of exclusive sovereignties further consolidated the internal frontier in the colonial imagination.[18]

Nevertheless, what happened in the South-West Frontier during the late Company period (1830s–1857) had distinct parallels in other parts of the subcontinent. In central and eastern India, too, one can argue that the earlier political system was based on a shared sovereignty prevalent over 'loosely defined frontiers'. It was a political landscape characterised by raids and shifting alliances, which underwent a profound transformation. Following Skaria, I would argue that the gradual displacement of Maratha

---

[16]Ajay Skaria, *Hybrid Histories: Forests, Frontiers and Wildness in Western India*, New Delhi: Oxford University Press, 1999.

[17]For a remarkable work on this phenomenon, published posthumously, see Ainslie T. Embree and Mark Juergensmeyer (eds), *Frontiers into Borders: Defining South Asian States, 1757–1857*, New Delhi: Oxford University Press, 2020.

[18]Skaria, *Hybrid Histories*.

authority until their territories were escheated in 1854 did not merely extinguish the Marathas as sovereigns; rather, this process could equally be seen as the subordination of forest polities since the British replaced the Maratha overlords as the new and exclusive sovereign. However, the Company strategists were not satisfied with the nullification of the Maratha challenge and were pushing equally for territorial claims in other theatres, using the appeal of the 'civilising mission'. Two relevant examples of how the paramount power staked sovereign claims under the garb of progressive values are the campaigns against human sacrifice and thugee. In both instances, separate 'Agencies' were created where military contingents ostensibly acted as boots on the ground in the civilising mission against these evil practices. However, this scaffolding was often merely a façade to legitimise the presence of Company troops in areas with porous frontiers.

As the Company State annexed more and more territories and the frontier was pushed back, they came into contact with other forest polities or 'Little Kingdoms'. In their ambition to dominate these hilly and forested landscapes, the British provided new dimensions to the internal frontier imagination. Legitimacy for its territorial ambitions in these new zones of engagement (for example, Bastar and the Ganjam/Vizagapatam tracts) was sought through the imperial project of civilising the savage. A distinctive aspect of the 'wilderness' as represented in the late Company period documents are the allegations of human sacrifice. The works of Nandini Sundar and Crispin Bates have provided a nuanced and detailed analysis of this aspect of the colonial discourse.

Thus, in 1836, the Madras government undertook its first expedition into the Khond zamindari of Ghumsur to exact the payment of land tax. After this mission, from about 1837, there were increasing rumours of ritual human sacrifice in Bastar. Further, the allegation that the kidnappers were acting on behalf of the king was a very serious one in the eyes of the British. This was perceived as a direct challenge to *Pax Britannica*. Subsequently, a special administrative unit called the Meriah Agency was established by the Government of India Act XXI of 1845. With Sir John Campbell as its head, the Agency was deputed to suppress and put an end to the rite of human sacrifice throughout the Khond territories of central and eastern India. Later, it was deputed the additional charge of preventing female infanticide.

Soon after, the Khond uprising of 1846–1847 erupted. This rebellion was represented as a response to the 'prevention of sacrifices and the famines that followed, although loss of land and payment of land tax were probably at least as important'.[19] The rebellion was suppressed by an expeditionary force, but the act of rebellion and the rite of human sacrifice became 'closely associated in the minds of British officials'.[20] Nevertheless, the final result of all these dynamics was 'the entrenchment of colonial rule'.[21]

In this context, Bates offers an explanation of the British 'civilising mission', which is both 'personal and imperial'.[22] He draws a parallel with the phenomenon of 'thugee', for whose suppression a special Agency was also created with William Sleeman as the Agent. As mentioned, the Meriah Agency[23] was similarly created, with complete administrative control over Ganjam, Vizagapatam, and Rajamundhry under Campbell. Bates writes,

> ... Campbell himself emphasizing the parallels between the two 'civilising missions'. Above all, the investigation of the agencies justified the drafting of considerable additional police and military forces in order to more firmly establish, or extend, British rule. Inevitably these expeditions were usually further associated with a more effective collection of land tax and/or a rise in the payments of tribute.[24]

In the nineteenth century, these areas were placed under the control of Madras Presidency, which administered them by special laws such as the Ganjam and Vizagapatam Act of 1839. These laws usually prescribed relatively simpler and elastic forms of judicial and administrative procedure for the hilly and forested tracts constituting the Madras Agency Tracts. It must be remembered that till their merger in the newly formed state of Orissa in 1935, the area of the Meriah Agency continued to be called the Agency Tracts.[25]

Here, I want to suggest a link between the use of the word 'Agency' and the imagination of the 'internal frontier'. The 'Thugee and Dacoity' Agency,

---

[19]Crispin Bates, 'Human Sacrifices in Colonial Central India: Myth, Agency and Representation', in Crispin Bates (ed.), *Beyond Representations: Colonial and Post-Colonial Constructions of Indian Identity*, New Delhi: Oxford University Press, 2006, p. 19.

[20]Ibid.

[21]Nandini Sundar, 'The Dreaded Danteswari: Annals of Alleged Sacrifice', in *Indian Economic and Social History Review* 32 (3), 1995, pp. 345–374.

[22]Bates, 'Human Sacrifices in Colonial Central India', p. 20.

[23]This specific Agency was in existence from 1845–1861.

[24]Bates, 'Human Sacrifices in Colonial Central India', p. 20.

[25]For a full-length study, see Felix Padel, *Sacrificing People: Invasions of a Tribal Landscape*, New Delhi: Orient BlackSwan, 2011.

the Meriah Agency, and the South-West Frontier Agency all seem to be in the parlance of Company administrators, tied together by an anomalous logic. In one way or another, they formed territories that were outside the ambit of colonial legality. Interestingly, a number of them evolved into categories of special administrative regimes, designed for predominantly tribal areas in central and eastern India. Variously called 'Scheduled districts', 'Backward tracts' and 'Partially excluded areas', and 'Fifth Schedule Areas' at different legislative and constitutional moments, I argue that they were crucial to the constitution of the 'internal frontier' in mid-nineteenth century colonial India.

Nevertheless, by the 1840s and 1850s, the Company (and later Crown) officials seemed to be slowly recognising that their earlier perception of the inhabitants of forests and hills as simply 'savages' or 'predatory raiders' was massively flawed. They now came to appreciate the distinctive character of the communities that lived in such geographically remote landscapes, far removed from forces of civilisation. Even the repeated tribal rebellions came to be seen as expressions of an indigenous community wronged by 'outsiders' or non-indigenous migrants.

Orientalist construction of knowledge about India played a significant role in this process.[26] Oriental scholars termed the forest and hill dwellers as 'Aborigine/Aboriginal', a term which ascribed to them the status of a true autochthon, a veritable 'son of the soil'. In this reading of India's long-term civilisational past, the Aryan invaders arrived and conquered the most fertile river-valley regions. The indigenous aborigines (referred to as 'Dasas' in Indo-Aryan literary texts), who lost this cultural conflict, retreated to the jungles and mountain fastnesses surrounding the fertile and surplus producing plains. Pushed to the margins of Hindu civilisation, these 'original' inhabitants continued to live a life of arcadian simplicity. Further ethnographic work by scholar-administrators highlighted the distinctiveness of aboriginal religious beliefs and value systems from their mostly caste Hindu neighbours. This intertwined set of geographical and cultural metaphors of imagination came to dictate the epistemological landscape for the entire subsequent period of colonial rule in India. In the iron grips of such a cognitive framework, the British colonial rulers refashioned

[26]For a classic study, see David Kopf, *British Orientalism and the Bengal Renaissance: The Dynamics of Indian Modernization, 1773–1835*, Berkeley: University of California Press, 1969. Also see Thomas R. Trautmann, *Aryans and British India*, Berkeley: University of California Press, 1997.

themselves as the 'guardians' and 'protectors' of aboriginal communities, now thought of as 'noble savages'. The 'sympathetic' European official insulated the aboriginal tribes from their caste Hindu neighbours, shielded them from complicated legal codes, and delivered quick justice at their doorsteps. He, as the redoubtable 'man on the spot',[27] was the sovereign's delegate, who cared and was (by all accounts) equally loved back.

Furthermore, with the consolidation of the Company's rule, the officials slowly realised and argued against the standardised enforcement of general regulations to all newly annexed territories, which they viewed as inappropriate. In such situations, the local authorities often applied to the Governor-General's Council for Acts to remove these areas from the ambit of unsuitable regulations. Such deregulation of Acts barred the application of the general statutes of colonial law. The stated intention in these cases was the removal of old regulations, thereby enabling more suitable legislation for such areas that would benefit the more 'primitive' sections of the population.

Thus, the overall picture until the mid-nineteenth century was that of a rapidly expanding British Indian Empire, wherein different sets of imperial interests operated in a highly variegated political landscape. The Company's logic of governance imperatives in the frontier regions was never uniform or standardised, let alone singular and cohesive, as it was not the unquestioned sovereign. Only after the Third Anglo-Maratha conflict did the East India Company start donning the mantle of the 'Paramount Power' in relation to other native Indian states. In the emerging equations that wove together issues of law, sovereignty, and territoriality, it is useful to highlight the distinctive role played by the 'Agency' tracts. We need to unpack precisely what this word meant in the lexicon of colonial statecraft. Nevertheless, I wish to emphasise that the internal frontier was central to the narrative of scheduling in the late colonial period. However, any analysis

[27]This was an East India Company-era term, which signified a tremendous concentration of executive and judicial powers in a single European official. In British India, everyday administration in predominantly tribal areas was often the responsibility of such paternalistic and sympathetic officers. The recurrent colonial trope was that an ideal 'man on the spot' provided rough and ready justice to simple and primitive people in accordance with their customary practices. Such a model was unencumbered by complicated courts and legal processes, and hence, by ensuring peace and tranquillity, was best suited to such areas. The other obvious but understated benefit was that it was a very economic mode of administration, as much of the costly paraphernalia of modern governance was absent in such areas.

of the scheduling process has to necessarily engage with the Scheduled Districts Act, 1874, which has long been misunderstood as the beginning of scheduling.

The Making of the Scheduled Districts Act, 1874

At the very outset of this study on scheduled areas, it must be emphasised that, contrary to a well-established impression, there was nothing 'tribal'/'aboriginal' about the Scheduled Districts Act, 1874. This enactment was, rather, a by-product of the wide-scale administrative and legal reforms introduced after the Revolt of 1857. While the Queen's Proclamation of 1858 marked the symbolic transfer of power from the Company to the Crown, the most meaningful reforms in the new colonial state apparatus unfolded in the early 1860s. These included the reorganisation of provinces, standardisation of civil and criminal codes, and the sweeping jurisdiction enjoyed by the new High Courts. Let me highlight in particular the role of the High Court. One of the established principles in the British state system was the separation of powers between the legislative, executive, and judicial branches. The three wings of Her Majesty's Government, with their clearly defined spheres of activity and power, were primarily designed to ensure checks and balances upon each other. In its bid to regain legitimacy and institute a new era of the rule of law, the governance model of metropolitan Great Britain was seen as a template from which certain elements were to be borrowed. Among the battery of far-reaching structural changes, an element of judicial review was introduced. Thus, as a colony, the reformed Government of India sought to replicate, in a limited manner, the principle of separation of powers between its executive and judicial arms of administration. Post 1858, the institution of the High Courts, with their sweeping powers to review and even reverse executive decisions, was potentially amongst the most far-reaching of the British Crown's reforms to restructure the Government of India.

While the clear-cut ramifications of these changes were not felt immediately, the ushering in of a separate and independent High Court (which in principle constituted an extremely powerful judicial wing) became a constant source of worry for the higher bureaucracy. Before this moment, there was very little supervision over the executive 'steel frame' (as it came to be known later). The senior ICS members constituted a powerful 'official block', responsible for both making laws and enforcing them throughout British India. Initially, not even the best legal and administrative minds within this supra-elite bureaucratic circle realised that there were many skeletons in the erstwhile Company's closet, threatening to burst forth. The enactment of the Scheduled Districts Act, 1874 should be seen as a pre-emptive strategy deployed by colonial bureaucracy against any adversarial judicial review by the High Courts. In other words, this legislation was part and parcel of a self-defensive armour devised for the protection of the ICS lobby manning the influential positions within the Government of India. How and why this bulwark was enacted deserves to be recounted, even if briefly for now.

Matters came to a head after the High Court discovered that a law which had been operating in Dehra Dun for thirty years was not legally in force there.[28] Thus began a frantic search for all laws enforced throughout 'British India'. However, given the geographical scale of the Empire, the task could not be completed satisfactorily. Moreover, an analysis of the legal position of the Deregulationising Acts revealed a potential minefield, primarily on two grounds. *First*, the legality of many of these enactments was doubtful. For the British jurists obsessed with standardisation of 'law'[29] could not see why such large areas were kept out of the normal operation of British Indian law.[30] *Second*, it was almost impossible to discover which Acts and Regulations were *de jure* in force in any given area, and which were not.

In its response, primarily intended to subvert the possibility of any further judicial intervention, the colonial bureaucracy decided to introduce a Bill specifying the areas to which Regulations and Acts extended. The Bill, originally introduced in the Council on 25 March 1870, was titled *A Bill to declare and consolidate the law relating to the local extent of the general*

[28] It was found that some officers had been deciding rent-suits under Act X, 1859, and some under the old Regulations which Act X, 1859 repealed. A reference to it is made in letter no. 369A, dated 2 July 1874, From Secretary, Government of North-West Frontier Province to Secretary, Government of India, Home Department in Proceeding No. 12–15, November 1874, Judicial Branch, Home Department, GoI, 1874.

[29] In philosophical terms, 'law' is a rule based on practice or observation, which says that under certain conditions, certain things will always happen. As such, a single exception disqualifies a phenomenon from being termed a 'law'. For instance, Newton's Law of Gravity, and the three Laws of Motion.

[30] Although I have not been able to sufficiently develop it in this chapter, this 'doubtful legality' of the Deregulationising Acts indicates the clash between the 'Universal' and the 'Particular' common to the History of Law. I thank Dr Sourav Mahanta for this insight.

regulations and Acts, and the local limits to the jurisdiction of the High Courts and chief controlling revenue authorities.[31] Thus, the original title of what mutated into the 'Laws Local Extent Bill, 1873' (and finally the Scheduled Districts Act, 1874) quite clearly outlines that the proposed law was drafted with the express intention of devising some mechanism to ensure that a High Court ruling could not undermine the legality of the Deregulation Acts. However, given the impossibility of obtaining complete information, the anxieties were emboldened. A solution had to be found, and this came through a legislative route.

Thus, the legal concerns of the colonial executive in India were laid to rest by a special enactment of the British Parliament. The Statute 33 Victoria, Chapter 3, Section 1 (The Indian Councils Act, 1870) was passed, which allowed the powers to make regulations 'otherwise than at meetings for the purpose of making laws and regulations held under the provisions of the Indian Councils Act, 1861'.[32] Under its provisions, the Secretary of State could declare that the Statute applied to a particular area, which was thus 'outlawed' (that is, placed outside the operation of the laws and regulations in force in the rest of British India). Following this, the local government had to submit a regulation for the governance of the specified area, which then had to be approved by the Government of India. The areas deregulationised under this Act of 1870 were called 'Excepted Districts' (and not 'Scheduled Districts').

To reiterate the central point, the basis for this exceptional status was not the tribal/aboriginal character of its population. In fact, the text of the Act does not mention any social group or category of human beings. The matter needs detailed investigation, which is beyond the scope of the current monograph. Nevertheless, evidence from a crucial file dealing with the Central Provinces (CP) throws important light on the imperatives governing this transformation in the legal character of the colonial State.

The Central Provinces was formed in the year 1861 as a result of the administrative redistribution of territories, in the aftermath of the Revolt of 1857. It contained vast geographical areas which were heavily forested and lay outside the main lines of road communication.[33] When the 'Laws Local Extent Bill' was being drafted and discussed with the various provincial

---

[31]Note by C. D. Field, Esq., dated 11 June 1874, in Proceeding No. 12–15, November 1874, Judicial Branch, Home Department, GoI, 1874.

[32]Ibid.

[33]The process of railway construction was just taking off in the 1860s.

governments, there was a proposal to include certain zamindari tracts in the Central Provinces among the 'Excepted Districts' listed in the Sixth Schedule of the Bill. These areas had not been deregulationised earlier on any occasion, and presented a formidable legal challenge. Such was their description and the problems they presented:

> They are as a rule the wild and remote zamindari areas, the difficulty of administering which properly under the law presents itself from time to time in one from [*sic*] or another, and indeed must continue to arise so long as the tracts are subject to an elaborate and technical system which it is impossible to adapt to their existing circumstances. In the first place these distant zamindary areas maintain their own Police, and are outside the range of [the] regular police system established under Act V of 1861. It would be impossible to bring them under the regular Police system without an expenditure so considerable as to place the question, independent of other strong objections, beyond discussion. Then the feudal relations which exist between the Zamindars and their people, and the remoteness of the local Courts, foster the additional feeling of constituting the Zamindars the arbiters of the various differences and disputes which occur, and the result is a number of unrecognized tribunals very convenient to the people and in consonance to their wishes, but unknown to the Law.[34]

In the above extract, the main imperatives for giving exceptional status to the zamindaris are clearly discernible. The foremost factor was fiscal considerations. In a tract that was 'wild and remote', the costs of maintaining a fully-fledged police force were prohibitive. Remember, this was a time before the passing of the Indian Forest Act, 1878, and the State was primarily dependent on the revenue generated from settled cultivation. These zamindaris were non-settled areas which paid, at best, a nominal revenue to the provincial administration. Thus, in effect, if the areas could not provide the fiscal resources needed for erecting and maintaining the entire paraphernalia of the colonial State apparatus, then it was better to keep them outside a fully operational legal regime. The consequence of

[34]Letter No. 2832/137, from J. W. Chisholm, Esq., Officiating Secretary to the Chief Commissioner Central Provinces, to Secretary to the GoI, Home Department, dated Nagpur, 11 August 1874, Proceedings No. 169–171, December 1874, Judicial Branch, Home Department, GoI, 1874, pp. 1–3. The next few paragraphs, including the extracts, on the Central Provinces case are based on this source.

such a state of affairs was that 'the requirements of the Law remain thus unapplicable to the facts as they exist'.

The local officials, too, unanimously opined that the zamindars exercised a jurisdiction that had no legal basis. However, 'supported by their people, the remote Zamindars continue to exercise their ancient powers'. Colonial rule, however, only ensured that this was 'done clandestinely instead of openly'. Although the zamindars were 'occasionally rudely handled' for their transgression of the foundational principles of British legal jurisprudence, the circumstances were 'too strong to be stemmed by a technical illegality'. In fact, so exceptional was the position of these zamindars in the Central Provinces that the Judicial Commissioner, in his notes on the proposed 'Central Provinces Laws Act', remarked that,

> these Zamindars at present exercise to an uncertain, but more or less limited extent both Police and Magisterial functions. In neither respect has the jurisdiction been constituted formally. But it has been exercised in a constant manner with the tacit sanction of the Local Government and I believe that the Chief Commissioner is not prepared to withdraw that sanction and provide for either the Police or Magisterial business which the Zamindars now perform in a way practically different from that now obtaining. So long then as the Zamindars are left to act as they do at present, it may not be necessary to raise questions as to the legality of their actions.

The Secretary to the Chief Commissioner of C.P. also referred to the Criminal Report for 1872, where the whole question of the criminal jurisdiction of such zamindars was raised. In his response, the Chief Commissioner remarked (in the third paragraph of his Review) that 'the Zamindars are simply doing what law and customs allowed them to do before the Nagpur Province became British Territory and a formal recognition of their position as guardians of order within their Zamindaris is alone wanting'. However, he went on to argue that,

> Now this formal recognition cannot assume the shape of investing them with powers as Honorary Magistrates, not only because such a course would be incomplete as dealing only with their criminal jurisdiction but because the authority exercised might be legally questioned owing to the police powers which they do now and have always exercised in their estates. The position then is that they cannot exercise under the law both Police and Magisterial powers for as stated by the Judicial Commissioner, if they discharge the duties 'of a Police Officer under the Act the legality of their magisterial action would, with reference

> to Section VI of the Police Act, at once be liable to question'. It is clear that under the law they cannot be made within the limits of their estates, both Magistrates and Police Officers, nor is it possible to find a legal basis for the Civil and Revenue jurisdiction which they exercise.

Thus, at least in the case of the zamindaris of the Central Provinces, large parts of which were acquired after the territories belonging to the Nagpur Bhonsles were escheated in 1854, the new principle of separation of police (executive) and magisterial (judicial) functions, enunciated after the Crown's takeover, presented seemingly insurmountable practical and legal problems. These problems could only be avoided by placing them in an exceptional state of legality. On these grounds, the Government of Central Provinces suggested that 'the only satisfactory solution of the difficulty which the administration experiences in efficiently managing these distant estates' was to place these zamindaris as 'excepted districts outside the operation of the regulations and Acts'. These large zamindaris would then stand in the future in the same position as the Cuttack and Chota Nagpur Tributary Mehals, and 'rules similar in scope to those in force in the Tributary Mehals would be prepared and submitted for approval'. These rules were to regulate the criminal, civil, and revenue procedures of the several excepted zamindaris, and would place their jurisdiction on a defined footing capable of systematic control.

Owing to the 'exceptional character of the tracts which it is proposed to treat exceptionally', the Government of India accepted the proposals of the Chief Commissioner of Central Provinces and, in total, fifty-four zamindari estates from three groups, viz., Chhattisgarh zamindaris (twenty-three), Chanda zamindaris (twenty), and Chhindwara jagirdaris (eleven) were notified as Part VI to the First Schedule of the Scheduled Districts Act (XIV of 1874) as well as Part VI of the Sixth Schedule of the Laws Local Extent Act (XV of 1874).

Nevertheless, it must be noted that not all the estates in this Central Provinces list were areas of high aboriginal preponderance. A careful analysis of the imperatives that informed the local government's recommendation on the notification of 'excepted' (or 'scheduled') districts reveals two chief challenges. The primary concern was fiscal/financial viability. In a State system still fiscally nourished by (and highly dependent on) the collection of land revenue, the challenge of 'financing the Raj' was supreme. The costs of erecting and maintaining a full-fledged governmental structure with distinct executive (police) and judicial (magistrates) branches geared to meet the requirement of ensuring the 'rule of law' were highly prohibitive in these C.P. zamindaris. A second related, but not insignificant, point was about legality. If the separation of the Executive and Judicial branches had been accepted as part of the reformed Government of India, then the same principle ought to have been reflected even at the local level. Since the zamindars were exercising *de facto* police and magisterial powers, that situation was *de jure* untenable and could open the doors to a plethora of litigation, which had to be avoided.

This evidence was illustrative of the factors that informed the notification of the Central Provinces areas in the consolidating enactment. Highly dissimilar conditions and factors were in operation in other territories acquired after 1818 in the regular Presidencies of Bombay, Madras, and Bengal. They included territories such as Assam[35] (acquired in Bengal during the late 1820s, after the First Anglo-Burmese War) and Sindh (acquired by Bombay Armies in the late 1830s). The details of these 'newly acquired territories' are lengthy, knotty, and merit a separate enquiry. This is only to foreground and illustrate that through this enactment, the bureaucrats at the Imperial Centre of Fort William were attempting to stitch together a highly disparate set of concerns from all parts of the British Indian Empire. Following various criticisms and altercations, it was decided that 'the main object of this Bill was to consolidate into a single enactment all the Acts and regulations by which particular portions of the Presidencies of Bengal, Madras and Bombay have, at different times, been withdrawn from the operation of the Regulations and Acts which would otherwise have extended to them'.[36] Subsequently, however, the principal object of the Bill became 'to remove doubts and difficulties existing in districts to which it is uncertain whether or not the general body of Indian Law has been extended'.[37]

The Bill had earlier been re-christened as the Laws Local Extent Bill, 1873. In its new avatar, the Bill was no longer intended to define the local limits of jurisdiction of the High Courts and the chief controlling revenue authorities. The Acts of the British Parliament were also withdrawn from

[35]Assam became a separate Chief Commissioner's Province in 1874, the same year as the passing of the Scheduled Districts Act and the Laws Local Extent Act.

[36]Letter No. 42A, dated 4 March 1874, from Judicial Commissioner to Secretary, Chief Commissioner, Oudh in Proceeding No. 12–15, November 1874, Judicial Branch, Home Department, GoI, 1874.

[37]Ibid.

the operation of the legislation now proposed. After further deliberations, it was decided to introduce a single Schedule in the Bill, specifying areas to which the laws did not extend as there was 'an obvious advantage in collecting in one Act the names of all the tracts to which the general Acts and Regulations do not apply'.[38] Therefore, on the supposition that the Laws Local Extent Bill was to become a law, the Scheduled Districts Bill became necessary, and was 'so drawn as to obviate all inconvenience'.[39] Hence, it was for the sake of convenience that a decision was taken to split this new Bill into two separate Bills. This entire process took four years and resulted in the Scheduled Districts Act (XIV of 1874) and the Laws Local Extent Act (XV of 1874). The two enactments were enforced together, and the latter declared certain Acts to be in force in British India as a whole or in particular provinces, but in each case 'excepting' the 'Scheduled Districts'. These areas were set out in the Sixth Schedule to the Laws Local Extent Act and were the same as in the First Schedule of the Scheduled Districts Act.

To highlight the salient features of this unique legislative moment again: the initial term for the areas with which the draft Bill was concerned was 'Excepted Districts'. It was later decided that 'Scheduled Districts' was a more apt and suitable legal term, as the Bill was now to have the list of deregulationised areas in its First Schedule. The Scheduled Districts Act gave no powers to remove any part of British India from the operation of ordinary law. It was essentially 'declaratory, extending, consolidating and permissive'.[40] It dealt only with written law and was not concerned with usage and custom. The First Schedule of the Act was a list of districts where certain laws were not in force at that time. An identical Schedule was attached to the Laws Local Extent Act, but the two Schedules were not modified *pari passu*.[41] Henceforth, no addition could be made to the list of

---

[38]Letter No. 369A, dated 2 July 1874, from Secretary, Government, North West Frontier Province, to Secretary, Government of India, Home Department, in ibid.

[39]Letter No. 4400, dated 1 August 1874, from Acting Under-Secretary, Government, Bombay, to Secretary, Government of India, Legislative Department, in ibid.

[40]J. P. Mills, 'Note on the Backward Areas of British India and their Position under the Government of India Act, 1935', in F. No. 4/III/35-G(B). and K. W., General (B) Branch, Reforms Office, Government of India, 1935, p. 1.

[41]*Pari passu* is a Latin adverb meaning *usually law* with equal place; together; proportionately.

'Scheduled Districts'[42] unless the area to be added was first deregulationised under 33 Victoria, Chapter 3, Section 1 (Indian Councils Act, 1870). In these districts, the local government, with the sanction of the Governor-General in Council, was empowered to declare which enactments were not in force. The local government could also extend any enactment in force in any part of British India to a Scheduled District (or a part of one), with or without modification. The powers conferred were not in practice in the whole area covered by the First Schedule. In many places, the ordinary enactments were allowed to remain or to come into force without any declaration.

Later, during World War I, the power to legislate for many of the areas classified as Scheduled Districts was provided by a Regulation under Section 71 of the Government of India Act, 1915. Initially, Scheduled District was defined as the areas included in the First Schedule of Act XIV of 1874. However, after the Government of India Act, 1915 came into force, the term also included 'any other territory in respect of which the power to make regulations has since the passing of the Act been created by virtue of a resolution by the Secretary of State under Section 71 of Government of India Act, 1915'. But, inasmuch as this Act did not contain a provision similar to that in Section 1 of the Scheduled Districts Act, by which any territory subsequently brought under Section 71 of the Government of India Act, 1915, also became 'a Scheduled District', the field covered by the two Acts could not remain identical. Thus, in time, the list of areas they contained no longer remained the same. This power could be exercised with respect to any territory to which the Secretary of State, by a resolution in council, applied the provisions of Section 71. Technically, these provisions could be applied to any part of British India, but in practice, the power to legislate by regulation was only given vis-à-vis backward areas. The application of this section could also be withdrawn in the same way.

'Backward Tracts' and the Framing of Limits: 'Exclusion' and 'Partial Exclusion'

The Montague-Chelmsford Report on Indian Constitutional Reforms (1918) marked a significant moment in the history of the idea of scheduling. Until then, this discourse lay purely in the administrative domain of the

[42] Appendix V of the Ninth Despatch on Indian Constitutional Reforms, IOR/L/PJ/9/23.

colonial bureaucracy. With the Report's publication, however, the issue was placed decisively in the Indian public domain for the very first time. A new term, 'Backward Tracts', was coined, which would characterise the areas to be scheduled. The Report stated:

> ... But even in the eight provinces which we have named there are included certain backward areas where the people are primitive, and there is yet no material on which to found political institutions. We do not think that there will be any difficulty in demarcating them. They are generally the tracts mentioned in the schedules and appendices to the Scheduled Districts Act, 1874, with certain exceptions and possibly certain additions which the Government of India must be invited to specify. Both the definition of these areas and the arrangements to be made for them will be matters for further consideration; but the typically backward tracts should be excluded from the jurisdiction of the reformed provincial Governments and administered by the head of the province.[43]

This semantic shift from 'Scheduled Districts' to 'backward tracts' is highly significant. If we do not mark out these differences in terminology, there is a very real possibility of slipping into colonial connotations without realising the subtle epistemological-cum-cognitive shift that the arrival of these new terms signified.[44] Essentially, by terming these areas as 'backward tracts', the late colonial administrative discourse acknowledged their distinctiveness from the predominantly non-tribal and settled plains areas. However, the exact contours of this backwardness were left undefined. In subsequent chapters, it will become clear how it was the yet undefined and continuously evolving character of tribal 'backwardness' that provided the framework in which the 'official block' within the local administration (that is, the provinces mainly manned by European officials supposedly 'sympathetic' towards the tribes) was coming in continuous conflict with the Congress nationalists.

Nonetheless, the bedrock of the Montague-Chelmsford Reforms scheme was the idea of the division of administrative subjects/departments

---

[43]Montague-Chelmsford Report on Indian Constitutional Reforms, 1918, Paragraph 199.

[44]I thank Dr Umar Khalid for this point. In this phase of colonial statecraft, 'backwardness' as an idea needs further enquiries. For a good scholarly article on the discourse of backwardness in western India, see Abhay Datar, 'Defining Backwardness: Debates in Bombay/Maharashtra', *Economic and Political Weekly* LII (51), 23 November 2017, pp. 89–96.

in the provinces into two categories of 'reserved' and 'transferred' subjects. The former was the exclusive domain of the colonial State (meaning thereby that the Governor, as the Agent of the Governor-General, was responsible for it), while responsibility for the latter was to be handed over to the popular ministries. This arrangement came to be known as 'dyarchy'. The subject of backward tracts was potentially contentious, as Indian politicians were expected to react negatively to the colonial State's policy of keeping the administration of these areas away from the control of popular ministries.

The debate on the future administration of predominantly tribal areas was initiated by the Government of India's detailed response, contained in its Ninth Despatch to the India Office.[45] The Governor-General's Council opined that if an area was wholly excluded from the scope of the reform scheme, it would inevitably follow that:

> (i) no legislation should be enacted, no question should be asked and no resolution should be moved, affecting such an area, in the legislative council. Legislation for such an area be effected, entirely by means of regulations made by the Governor-General in Council under Section 71 of the Government of India Act, 1915.[46]
>
> (ii) the administration of such areas, as regards both reserved and transferred subjects should be carried on either by the Governor, as proposed in the Report, or as we ourselves should prefer, by the Governor in Council.
>
> (iii) budget provision for the administration should be made separately and should not be subjected to the scrutiny of the legislative council.

These restrictions were formidable enough to confine their operations only to the 'typically backward tracts'. However, the Governor-General in Council held that the future constitutional status of 'intermediate areas ... not yet suited for the type of government' being proposed still hung in the balance. In the legal cartography of British India, these large areas occupied a liminal,

[45]Letter from Chelmsford, C. C. Munro, C. Sankaran Nair, W. H. Vincent, R. A. Maut, H. F. Howard, to Edwin Montagu dated Simla, 5 June 1919, Ninth Dispatch on Indian Constitutional Reforms (Assam and Backward Tracts), No. 7 of 1919 in IOR/L/PJ/9/23. Unless mentioned otherwise, this entire section is based on the Ninth Despatch.

[46]Except in the case of Darjeeling district (Bengal) and Lahaul (Punjab), to which that section did not apply.

undefined space between typically backward tracts and those proposed to be placed in the hands of elected ministries. What complicated matters even further was the fact that they sometimes also returned representatives to the councils, and hence any wholesale exclusion was likely to meet with objections from the increasingly vocal and confident Indian political class.

Anticipating difficulties, the Council remarked that the total exclusion of too many backward areas was not feasible and would lead to 'much avoidable confusion and friction in the administration'. In such grey areas, instead of enforcing the complete set of reforms, some modifications in the general scheme could enhance suitability. Consequently, it was recommended that the backward areas be divided into two categories, that is, wholly excluded areas and areas where a modified scheme should be introduced. The latter category came to mean that:

> (i) Acts of the Indian or provincial legislatures may be applied wholly, with modifications, or not at all, to any part of the area—by executive order: without such an order no Act will apply automatically.
>
> (ii) legislation by regulation under s.71 is to be constituted for those areas where it is now permissible—Sonthal Parganas and the Assam Hills Districts.
>
> (iii) it is to be recognized that the Governor is to be free to override the advice of his Ministers in transferred matters affecting these areas, in virtue of his personal responsibility for the best interests of backward classes.

The Government of India provided examples of areas to be 'wholly excluded' or 'excluded with modifications' from the province of Bihar and Orissa. Angul and Chota Nagpur Division provided the framing reference for both categories and were thus presented as the 'ideal types'.

Exemplifying the category of totally excluded areas, Angul comprised two territorial divisions separated from each other by Orissa state.[47] Putting forth a case for its 'wholly excluded' status and its administration by the Governor in Council, the Despatch stated:

> Each subdivision is a network of hills, valleys, ravines, and forests, with very little cultivated land. The density of population is less than in any other district of the province, and the inhabitants are mostly aborigines or low caste Hindus, of whom a very small percentage is literate. The district is a scheduled district and deregulationized by the Angul Laws

[47] Their respective headquarters were 90 miles apart.

> Regulation, 1913, that is, it is an area which is excluded from the operation of ordinary law. Legislation is effected by Regulation and the district is unrepresented in the legislative council.

Thus, the chief determinants for 'wholly excluded' status were a tough geographical terrain, which frequently also made it 'inaccessible', its agricultural backwardness, low density of population, high proportion of aborigines in the population, low literacy levels, its legal position (deregulationised or not), and finally, whether it had been represented in provincial councils.

The prototype for 'excluded with modifications', was the Chota Nagpur division. It consisted of five districts (Ranchi, Palamau, Hazaribagh, Manbhum, and Singhbhum) with an area of 27,000 square miles and a population of five-and-a-half million. The standard of cultivation varied considerably in different parts. The 'wilder' tracts of the area were inhabited almost exclusively by aboriginal and semi-aboriginal tribes. However, the division also comprised 'a certain number of towns, the most important coal-fields in the whole of India, and an area around the Tata Iron and Steel works which bids fair to become one of the most important industrial manufacturing centres in the country'.[48]

In legal terms, the whole division was notified under the Scheduled Districts Act, but was not deregulationised. Legislation could not be effected by regulation as the division, though scheduled, had not been the subject of a resolution under Section 71 (4) of the Government of India Act, 1915, or the provision which that section re-enacted. The districts of this division were represented in the provincial legislative council and the various enactments in force were of 'local application only and different in character from those in operation in other parts of the province'. Although ordinary Civil and Criminal Procedure Codes were in force in the entire division, in certain parts, the same officers administered both civil and criminal justice. In view of all these facts, the Government of India agreed with the local government's assessment that it was not advisable to wholly exclude this area from the scope of the reforms scheme. Moreover, a fear of tribal rebellion was also expressed. Thus, the government was also not prepared to recommend the inclusion of the division without some 'special safeguards'. Detailing what such safeguards should be, the Despatch recommended,

---

[48]This description presented an interesting imagery of Chota Nagpur as an aboriginal area dotted with 'industrial enclaves', where the extraction of natural resources was underway.

> … The Governor in Council should have the power to decide what legislation shall have force in the division, or any part thereof. We would give him a power by notification to exclude the whole or any part of the area from the operation of any Act or part of an Act passed by local legislature, and also power to apply any such legislation, with any restrictions or modifications that he considers necessary, to the division or any part of it. Except for these powers of exclusion, restriction or modification, the Lieutenant Governor in Council would have no positive powers of legislating for such areas otherwise than through his legislative council and if need be his grand committee.

On the administrative side, however, the Government of India suggested that it was undesirable that the Governor in Council be given the power to exclude any part of the division from the jurisdiction of ministers as this measure could be abused. The ministers would be given jurisdiction throughout the area, but the Governor would have wide discretion in varying their orders in these areas. Moreover, as an ultimate safeguard, the Governor was permitted to re-transfer any transferred subject in these tracts, should such an extreme measure become necessary.

The provincial governments responded to the reform scheme in different ways. The Government of Punjab said that Lahaul and Spiti were both scheduled districts, with Spiti being deregulationised as well, and hence both should be wholly excluded. The Government of Bombay and United Provinces did not propose the exclusion of any of their areas, a recommendation that was accepted by the Government of India. The Chief Commissioner of the Central Provinces also did not suggest any area for exclusion, but proposed that certain tracts should be represented in the legislative council by nomination rather than election. The Government of Bengal recommended the total exclusion of the Chittagong Hill Tracts and Darjeeling. The Government of Madras vociferously argued for the total exclusion of Agency Tracts and was not satisfied with mere partial exclusion.

The case of the frontier province of Assam was a peculiar one. The Chief Commissioner of Assam, Sir Nicholas Beatson, took strong exception to the suggestion contained in the Montague-Chelmsford Report that the 'schedules and appendices' of the Scheduled Districts Act, 1874, might form the criterion for the exclusion of areas from the scheme. Since the whole of the province of Assam was scheduled under this Act, such an interpretation meant that Assam would be totally excluded from the reform scheme. This was unacceptable to the Governor, who remarked that '(A)s Assam has been included in the report along with the seven major provinces of India, Assam must stand or fall along with them. The future constitution of Assam must follow the general lines of the constitutions of the other seven provinces.'[49] For Sir Nicholas, the primary consideration was to ensure that the hills were 'sympathetically administered and adequately financed'. He concluded that the whole of Assam province could safely be placed under the new administration of a 'Governor in Council'.[50]

Thus, at this early stage of policymaking with regard to the application of the proposals for 'exclusion' and 'exclusion with modifications', there were only a few issues open to argument: *first*, whether the 'total exclusion' of Darjeeling was preferable, and *second*, whether the modified exclusion of the Assam Hill Tracts was preferable. The first question was foregrounded by the fact that the electoral rules contained no provision for the representation of Darjeeling district on the Bengal Council. Hence, it would have been a 'contradiction in terms to allow the reforms Scheme even partially to affect an area whose inhabitants have no voice in the Council'. In the case of Assam, too, the Hill Tracts had no representatives (either elected or nominated) on the Council, thereby logically qualifying them for complete exclusion. The Government of India also recognised that complete exclusion of the Hill Tracts would mean setting up the paraphernalia of a reformed government for an area of just 27,000 square miles (of the total area of a province of 77,500 square miles, with more than 55,000 square miles being 'backward' Hill Tracts), thus saving itself enormous expenditure. The elevation of the Chief Commissionership of Assam to a 'Governor's Province' under the Government of India Act, 1919, further enabled the case for the complete exclusion of the Hill Tracts.[51]

Nonetheless, the Ninth Despatch finally recommended Angul, Chittagong Hill Tracts, Laccadive and Amindivi Islands, Spiti, and Lahaul as areas which were to be totally excluded. Chota Nagpur, Santhal Parganas, Sambalpur, Darjeeling, and the Agency Tracts in Madras were recommended for partial/modified exclusion. Of these, the last item, that is, the Madras

[49]Enclosure I (viii) Extract paragraphs 4 and 5 of a note by the Hon'ble Sir Nicholas Beatson Bell, Chief Commissioner of Assam, dated 24 October 1918 in the Ninth Despatch.

[50]Ibid.

[51]Assam's case is extremely interesting but very complicated, requiring detailed enquiries. It is bound to reveal very interesting genealogies of the Sixth Schedule. On the role of Assam administrators in the general project of scheduling, see Chapter 2.

Agency Tracts, led to a long tug-of-war between the bureaucrats of Simla and Madras. This issue opened up a significant and meaningful first debate on scheduling, which deserves analysis.

The Madras–Simla Controversy over the Agency Tracts

Arguably, the most remarkable early debate on scheduling occurred between the Imperial Government at Simla and the Government of Madras regarding the future status of the Agency Tracts in the districts of Ganjam, Vizagapatam, and Godavari. This highly argumentative correspondence was significant because it opened the discourse of scheduling in numerous ways. As a result of this locking of horns, a number of associated issues, such as the necessity of safeguarding the land tenures of aboriginal communities, their practice of customary law, and the potential administrative and financial implications of scheduling, were laid threadbare. Perhaps the sharpest differences of opinion between the two governments at Simla and Madras were displayed vis-à-vis the new upcoming class of representative-politician, who was often a trained lawyer.

The Agency Tracts[52] in Madras Province covered a total area of nearly 19,000 square miles and had a population of 1.5 million. Thickly forested and without many arteries for all-weather communication, these hilly tracts were inhabited by tribal communities, which were described as being 'most illiterate and ignorant of the ways of the world and yet ready to go on the war path, if any of their many particular susceptibilities are wounded'. Successive rebellions were supposedly a major reason for their exceptional legal status. Subsequently, they were placed under the direct administration of the Collectors as 'Agents' to the Governor, who were armed with special powers. The Agency tracts were notified under the Scheduled Districts Act, 1874, but it was doubtful whether they were completely deregulationised areas. At the onset of the Montague-Chelmsford reforms scheme, the tracts were administered directly by the Governor in Council, which periodically framed a few simple and elastic rules of procedure in virtue of the power conferred on the Governor by Acts XXIV of 1839 (Ganjam and Vizagapatam Act) and the SDA, 1874.

[52] The background information in this paragraph is based on the Ninth Despatch on Indian Constitutional Reforms.

While formulating its proposals for the Agency Tracts, the Government of India elicited the recommendations of the Government of Madras on the sort of 'exclusion' scheme most appropriate for the area. The latter responded that owing to their 'hilly and jungly character, the prevalence of malaria and the absence of communications', the Agency Tracts had 'remained almost completely undeveloped' and were generally exempt from the operation of the laws in force in the plains and the jurisdiction of the ordinary courts of justice. Explaining the character and traits of the aboriginal communities residing in the area and recommending total exclusion for the Agency Tracts, the Government of Madras wrote,

> The Agency Tracts are inhabited mainly by simple and ignorant jungle tribes whose education is still elementary and who retain their ancestral customs as to tenure of land, devolution of property, family or tribal organization and social observances. These tribes, are still in very early stages of civilization, use bows and arrows, wear little nothing, [*sic*] are timid, excitable and easily imposed upon and totally unfit for any form or degree of political advance.[53]

Thus, the Madras government was seeking to define the 'backwardness' of the tribes in terms that would justify total exclusion from the reform scheme. Also significant was the role of education as one of the chief markers of tribal backwardness. Moreover, the 'existing simple system of rules' provided a suitable administrative model and any attempt to bring them 'under the influence of complex codes' would adversely affect their future development.[54]

Despite the aforementioned reservations, however, the Government of India reiterated its original suggestion of applying the modified reform scheme to the Agency Tracts. It stated that large zamindars within the Agency Tracts shared franchise in the election of a member of the provincial council. Total exclusion of the Agency Tracts would therefore result in their disenfranchisement.

In its reply, the Governor in Council of Madras rejected the stance of the Government of India. *First*, it remarked that the Agency Tracts did not resemble Chota Nagpur in 'any material respect' as, besides having a far less dense population, they had 'no important industrial centres corresponding

[53]Letter No. 1024, dated Fort St. George, 9 November 1918; From Hon'ble Mr C. G. Todhunter, Acting Chief Secretary to GoM, Public Department; To The Secretary to the GoI, Home Department, as Appendix I in IOR/L/PJ/9/23.

[54]Ibid.

to the coalfields and the Iron and Steel works of Chota Nagpur'.[55] Instead, the Council outlined similarities of the Agency Tracts with Angul, as 'the area is undeveloped, largely covered with jungle, sparsely provided with communications and inhabited for the most part by tribes in a very primitive state of civilization'.[56]

Second, the Madras government argued that the tracts were adjuncts of districts and divisions, the greater parts of which lay in the plains. Hence, any attempt to introduce the whole statute book would necessitate a 'very large staff', thereby greatly increasing the cost of administration. Moreover, the revenue receipts from the Agency Tracts were nominal, meaning that the financial 'burden' of administration and development would be borne by the plains districts.[57]

After another rebuttal from the Reforms Office, the Government of Madras recommended a very interesting proposal to Simla. Madras argued that since the overarching policy of the government was the development of backward areas, selecting the 'most suitable form of administration' was a priority.[58] The developmental prerogatives of the Agency Tracts lay upon the government for two reasons. *First*, the Agency Tracts contained 'very valuable resources which are at present locked up in inaccessible places and the utilization of these resources for public benefit has already been too long delayed'. *Second*, the Government of Madras had an obligation of 'bringing forward the Agency peoples by some special form of administration until they are ready to take their place in an ordinary scheme of development and to join in the progress of the political movements of the times'. The problem for the Madras government was achieving a balance between these two aims. Thus, Madras argued that the Agency Tracts should be regarded as a *homogeneous whole*, and a single officer should be given the charge for developing it.

---

[55]Letter No. 2306–C–19–1, dated Fort St. George, 16 January 1920; The Hon'ble Mr E.S. Lloyd, I.C.S., Acting Secretary to the Government of Madras, Revenue Department, to Secretary to the GoI, Home Department) in IOR/L/PJ/9/23, p. 659, paragraph 3.

[56]Ibid.

[57]Ibid., paragraph 4.

[58]Reply No. 79–C–20–1, dated Fort St. George, 27 February 1920; The Hon'ble Mr E.S. Lloyd, ICS, Acting Secretary to GoM, Revenue Department, to Secretary, GoI, Home Department, in IOR/L/PJ/9/23. The following paragraphs and the long extract about this scheme are from this source.

This scheme was notable because it suggests that the same Agency areas which were, in legal terms in the nineteenth century, spaces of exception, were now being seen as potential spaces of extraction through an exploitation of their natural resources. A certain kind of discourse of underdevelopment was also being conducted in the wake of the constitutional reforms, which represented the 'Backward Tracts' as deficit areas with 'locked-up' resources. The solution to their underdevelopment, thus, was that they should be 'opened-up'.[59]

To fructify this scheme, the Government of Madras sought sanction from the Government of India and the Secretary of State. A superior post was to be created in the Indian Civil Service Cadre of the Madras Presidency and styled as 'Commissioner and Agent to the Governor in the Agency Tracts'. The post would encapsulate all branches of the Agency's administration with an overwhelming concentration of powers. In an era where the call was for responsible government, this arrangement was akin to the Agent of the South-West Frontier Agency devised almost ninety years earlier. Nevertheless, elaborating the contours of the proposed arrangement, the Government of Madras remarked,

> The proposed Commissioner should therefore rather be in a position of a Collector of [a] very large and very backward district. Departmental administration of the area should be the same as that of an ordinary district, and its budget should pass through the heads of department as usual. The Commissioner however should have, as is the case in Bombay, the final power of recommending to Government or otherwise any proposal put forward by the officers within the area over which he has charge. It is intended that the relations of the Commissioner with the Government should be direct. The aim being to secure a homogeneous policy of development, it is clear that the authority of the Commissioner must be very high and that the power of recommendation or deprecation proposed to be given to him is essential.

The proposal was sanctioned and a separate Agency Division was brought into effect on 6 November 1920. However, the amalgamation involved

---

[59]For the discourse of 'opening-up', see Ravi Ahuja, '"Opening up the Country"? Patterns of Circulation and Politics of Communication in early Colonial Orissa', *Studies in History*, New Series 20, I, 2004. For the developmental discourse in late colonial India, see Benjamin Zachariah, *Developing India: A Social and Intellectual History c. 1930–1950*, New Delhi: Oxford University Press, 2005.

increased expenditure, and barely two years later, the Madras Retrenchment Committee recommended reverting to the previous system. This was followed by a vote of the Madras Legislative Council reducing the allotment for the Agency Tracts by Rs 500,000 in token of its agreement with the Retrenchment Committee. The Madras government buckled under the Council's pressure and the Agency Division was abolished with effect from 16 October 1923.[60] Although the experiment folded up soon, it could be seen as a precursor to the formation of a distinct 'tribal/aboriginal region' for developmental planning and implementation purposes.[61]

The negotiations between Simla and Madras were leading to a meeting ground, but as the junior partner in the Empire's administrative hierarchy, the latter had to constantly jostle for space. Treading cautiously, Madras wrote that the Governor was willing to allow that the Agencies should come within the scope of the Legislative Council's authority. However, initially at least, the administration of the Agencies should be regarded as a 'reserved'[62] subject under the supervision of the Governor in Council. The Madras government based its appeal on paragraph 21 of the Government of India's Ninth Despatch, which had recognised (for Chota Nagpur) the 'need for special powers to meet the cases in which the application in the special tract of general ministerial policy might not be suitable or appropriate'. It argued that since Chota Nagpur 'as a whole represents a far more advanced civilization than that of the Agencies', the case for special powers in the Madras Agencies was much stronger. The government was,

> seriously apprehensive of the grave trouble which might arise in trying to enforce there a policy of a progressive minister in charge of such departments as Local Self-Government, Medical Administration,

[60]F. No. 19/27, Special Notes Branch, Reforms Office, GoI, 1927, p. 4.

[61]In independent India, such re-envisioning of predominantly tribal areas as highly industrial zones gained further traction, for example in the Dandakaranya region and the South-East Resource Region. See Saagar Tewari, 'Developing Bastar: The Dandakaranya Project', in Ravi Kumar (ed.), *The Heart of the Matter—Development, Identity and Violence: Reconfiguring the Debate*, New Delhi: Aakar Books, 2010, pp. 115–134.

[62]Letter No. 774–1–R dated Ootacamund, 9 July 1920; From A. R. Knapp, Esq, C.B.E., ICS, Secretary to the GoM, Public Department (Reforms), to The Secretary to the GoI, Reforms Office, Simla, Subject: Treatment of the Agency Tracts of this Presidency under the Reforms Scheme, in IOR/l/PJ/9/23, p. 652, paragraph 2.

> Public Health, Education or Excise. It may be hoped that as time goes on and the Agencies develop under the management of the Agency Commissioner and his new organization, conditions will be so modified as to admit of the agency administration.... But for the present the only safe course, in the opinion of the Governor in Council, is to keep the whole administration as a reserved subject.[63]

The Government of India shot down the proposal of the Madras government as impractical. It also opined that if all the subjects in the Agency Tracts were to be made reserved subjects, then

> officers of the transferred departments, whose jurisdiction extends into such tracts, will have to serve two superior authorities and officers required solely for the Agency Tracts will have to be borrowed from cadres controlled by ministers. Further it will undoubtedly be necessary whether there is an allocation of revenues between reserved and transferred subjects or not, to include in the reserved budget the receipts and expenditure on account of transferred subjects in these areas as the Legislative Assembly will insist on the two sides of the Government being shown separately.[64]

In its reply to Simla, the Madras government reported that the Governor was convinced that the experiment of immediately placing any part of the administration of the Agency Tracts' 'partially civilized and backward areas' under ministers who were not likely to have either 'personal knowledge of the areas or special sympathy with their inhabitants' involved a 'grave risk'.[65] It argued that although the powers under the Government of India Act were sufficient to stall inappropriate legislation, they were insufficient with regard to the 'extension into the Agencies of general executive policy which will require the most careful watching'. Disagreeing with the Government of India's proposal, the Governor in Council opined that it was

> undesirable thus deliberately to enter upon an arrangement under which the proper administration of the Agencies would depend to a large extent upon the use of the Governor's special powers or to

[63]Ibid.

[64]Telegram No. 772-F dated Simla, 27 July 1920; From: Secretary to GoI, Reforms Office, Simla; To: The Reforms Commissioner, Madras, Ootacamund in IOR/L/PJ/9/23, p. 653.

[65]No. 774-2-R dated Ootacamund, 9 August 1920; From: A. R. Knapp, Sec. GoM, Public (Reforms) Deptt.; To: Sec. GoI, Reforms Office in IOR/L/PJ/9/23, p. 654. This paragraph and the extract following it are based on this letter.

> contemplate a procedure which is likely to be so fruitful in disagreement and friction.

The Council foresaw that if the proposals were enforced, then there would be

> ...little safeguard against the application by departmental officers in the Agencies of the general policy which the minister is adopting elsewhere. It would be impossible to prevent an Inspector of Schools or an Abkari officer from raising a storm in the Agencies by merely introducing there the policy and practice to which he has been accustomed in the districts in the plains. The Government would know nothing about the matter until the trouble occurred and the power of *ex post facto* interference by the Government which alone would then be possible, would be neither an effective nor a desirable safeguard.

Hence, the Madras government stuck to its guns and recommended that all subjects in the Agency Tracts should be made reserved subjects. On its part, the Government of India replied in a manner that belied the assured air of imperial confidence. Brushing aside all objections raised by the Madras government, it observed that the inexperience of ministers was 'likely to predispose them rather towards timidity than towards rashness', and that it was 'very improbable that ministers would likely reject the considered recommendations of the Agent'.[66] It added that even if ministers did so, 'the Government of India feel sure that His Excellency would have no difficulty in making them realise the consequences of any rash policy upon which they might be tempted to embark'. It expressed confidence that future ministers would 'rarely, compel him [Governor] to resort to the use of his emergency powers'. With regard to the points raised by the Madras bureaucrats about departmental officers, the Simla counterparts replied that the officers who had served in the Agency Tracts would be cognisant of their conditions and it was not likely that they would be 'more prone to commit errors of judgment when working under ministers than they would be if placed under the administrative control of the Governor in Council'.[67]

To this rather haughty display of assuredness, the Government of Madras gave a stern reply. Until now, it had been firm but polite. However, in the last defence of its proposals, it dug deep and rather caustically replied that,

[66]No. 638-G, dated 23 September 1920; From: S. P. O'Donnell, Secretary to GoI, Reforms; To: Madras, A. R. Knapp, in IOR/L/PJ/9/23, pp. 655–658.

[67]Ibid.

> The Governor in Council regrets that he cannot share the confidence of the Government of India as to the attitude which ministers are likely to adopt towards the recommendations of the Agents.... It is probably from among the lawyers that a large proportion of the new council will be drawn: it is prima facie not unlikely that of the ministers of the future a good many will belong to that profession: and it seems to the Governor in Council not safe to assume that a policy which has taken such strong hold in the past on the lawyer politician will in the future be dropped merely in deference to the recommendations of the local officers.[68]

Here, the Madras government made no qualms about the absolute distrust it had for the class of representative lawyer-politician. Furthermore, with regard to the Government of India's reply on the point raised by Madras on officers, it remarked that senior departmental officers (for example, the Deputy Commissioner of Abkari or the Sanitary Commissioner whose jurisdiction would extend over areas other than the Agencies) would not necessarily have any experience of working in the Agency. Under the Madras scheme, however, 'such officers would be very much in the position of advisers to the Agent whose authority would be required for carrying out any particular measure'. In contrast, under the Government of India's proposals, such officers would be 'almost or entirely independent' of the Agent.[69] The future minister would be 'pressurized by his supporters to spend money in plains rather than hills', which would inevitably lead to a neglect of the Backward Agency Tracts.

The Simla bureaucrats seemed rather surprised at such stiff resistance from their Madras counterparts. However, their resoluteness did prompt a rethink in the ranks of the former and consequently, the guards were let down. Finally, in a telegram[70] to the Secretary of State, the Government of India replied that they were not convinced that the risks involved in the partial exclusion of the Agency Tracts were 'as great as the Government of Madras supposes'. Nonetheless, they admitted that the Agency Tracts were an exceptionally backward area, and they would not force upon the local

---

[68]Letter No. 774–3–R dated 22 October 1920; From: A. R. Knapp; To: Secretary, Reforms Office, GoI, in IOR/L/PJ/9/23, pp. 659–663.

[69]Ibid.

[70]Copy of Telegram 6046, From: Viceroy Reforms; To: Secretary of State; dated Delhi, 20 November 1920, Abbreviated correspondence in IOR/L/PJ/9/23, pp. 714–716.

government 'an experiment which they regard with such grave apprehension'. They also expressed hope that as the Agency Tracts developed, their administration would eventually be transferred to the ministers. Hence, finally, the bureaucratic tug-of-war was decided in favour of Madras. A recommendation for total exclusion was made, with a provision to review the case after two years of the reforms scheme. This proposal was accepted by the Secretary of State and the necessary notification was issued on 3 January 1921.

In later records, however, the Simla bureaucrats seemed to have turned the tables as the Agency Tracts are classified as a partially excluded area. The exact circumstances of its excision from the 'totally excluded' schedule are as yet unknown. Perhaps the status was revoked after the scheme for a separate Agency Division under the Commissioner was abolished. However, the face-off was interesting, and revealed various aspects of the knotty issue in the higher echelons of the colonial State's bureaucratic apparatus.

Backward Tracts after the Government of India Act, 1919[71]

At the end of the first reforms scheme, a number of notifications declaring certain areas as 'Backward Tracts' were issued under Section 52A(2) of the Government of India Act, 1919. They came to cover an area of 207,900 square miles and contained a population of about 13 million. Excluding Burma (which had the largest block of such territories), the backward tracts were to be found in five of the eight provinces, covered an area of 120,000 square miles, and had a population of 11.25 million. Almost all the tracts were Scheduled Districts under Act XIV of 1874, and by a notification made under Sections 5 and 5A of the Act, any enactment of British India, with restrictions and modifications, could be extended to them by executive order. In line with the recommendations of the provincial governments of Bombay and Central Provinces and Berar, no area within their territories was declared as 'backward tracts'. However, in the case of C.P. and Berar, the route of nomination over election was preferred for sending representatives to the legislative council.

[71]This section is based mainly on information contained in a note entitled 'Centralisation of Backward Tracts', in K.W. F.71/31–R, Reforms Branch, Reforms Office, GoI, 1931.

The tracts were classified according to their degree of backwardness. Some areas were considered so backward that they were wholly excluded from the reforms. These were the Laccadive Islands and Minicoy (Madras), Chittagong Hill Tracts (Bengal), Angul (Bihar and Orissa), Spiti (Punjab), and all the backward tracts of Burma Province.

The tracts which were excluded with modifications were the Agency Tracts (Madras), Darjeeling (Bengal), Lahaul (Punjab), Chota Nagpur (Bihar and Orissa), Santhal Parganas (Bihar and Orissa), Sambalpur (Bihar and Orissa), and all the backward tracts in the province of Assam.

The next important milestone in the late colonial administrative discourse on predominantly tribal areas was the enquiry conducted by the Indian Statutory Commission. Despite its wide mandate, the Simon Commission's engagement with the future arrangements for backward tracts in British India was not insignificant. It toured the length and breadth of British India, including remote corners of the Naga Hills, meeting frontier administrators such as J. H. Hutton, who were set to play a highly significant role. The Commission members also went to the Chota Nagpur plateau and recorded the evidence of a very wide range of witnesses, including Christian missionaries and Adivasi politicians who raised the demand for the separation of Chota Nagpur and Santhal Parganas from Bihar.[72]

The main recommendations of the Simon Commission were contained in its two-volume report, published in May 1930. The central pitch of its recommendations was for the near absolute centralisation of administration in territories earlier scheduled under the umbrella term 'Backward Tracts'. It coined a new category of 'Excluded Areas', which means that areas thus scheduled were to be entirely excluded from the reformed constitution for British India.[73] The Central government would assume the full charge and responsibility for their administration,[74] including the additional financial outlays.[75] The Governors would act as the Agents of the Central government for the administration of excluded areas.[76]

[72]Saagar Tewari, 'Framing the Fifth Schedule: Tribal Agency and the Making of the Indian Constitution', Special Issue of *Modern Asian Studies* 56 (5), 2022, pp. 1556–1594.

[73]*Simon Report* (henceforth, *SR*), Vol. II, para 128.

[74]Ibid., para 129–130.

[75]Ibid., para 132–133.

[76]Ibid., para 131.

The general principle laid down by the Commission was that where the bulk of the inhabitants of a backward tract were so little advanced that representative institutions could not be provided, complete exclusion must be adopted. On the other hand, in more developed backward tracts (such as Chota Nagpur, Sambalpur, and Santal Parganas), where aboriginals were still not fully equipped to participate in the normal constitutional politics, different arrangements were suggested to ensure their autonomy and freedom from unwarranted intervention, especially by the elected legislative councils.[77] In such 'partially excluded areas', the Governor, as Agent of the Governor-General in Council, would decide how far legislation enacted in the provincial council should apply.[78] In both cases, the revenues generated were to be spent in the area. The report also carried specific recommendations for Central Provinces, Bengal, Bihar and Orissa, and Madras.

At the centre, the Commission recommended that the Governor-General should nominate eleven members to represent people from the backward tracts to the Federal Assembly.[79] The Governor-General in Council would arbiter the extent of central legislation applicable to both excluded and partially excluded areas. Deficits in the budgets of both classes should be made good from the central revenues. In fact, the issue of financial outlay for the scheduled areas was the chief reason for the centralising impulse behind the Simon Commission's recommendations. The areas needed funds for their development in excess of the revenue that was generated within. Additionally, the backward tracts were often situated in provinces with revenue shortfalls. In a permanent state of deficit budget, the only feasible source of requisite funds for undertaking developmental tasks was the central revenues. The arguments and justification advanced by the Commission in support of its recommendations was succinctly put in the following terms:

> The stage of development reached by the inhabitants of these areas prevents the possibility of applying to them methods of representation adopted elsewhere. They do not act for self-determination, but for security of land tenure, freedom in the pursuit of their traditional methods of livelihood, and the reasonable exercise of their ancestral customs. Their contentment depends not so much on rapid political

[77]Ibid., para 132.
[78]Ibid., para 133.
[79]Ibid., para 144.

> advance as on experienced and sympathetic handling, and on protection from economic subjugation of their neighbours.
>
> The responsibility of the parliament for the backward tracts will not be discharged merely by securing to them protection from exploitation and by preventing those outbreaks which have from time to time occurred within their borders. The principal duty of the administration is to educate these people to stand on their own feet, and this is a process which has scarcely begun. It is too large a task to be left to the single handed efforts of missionary societies or of individual officers.[80]

In their responses, the Government of India and provincial governments criticised the Simon Commission's proposals for centralisation as unworkable and expressed their preference for maintaining the existing system. Among the provincial governments, only the Government of Assam was in agreement with the Simon Commission's recommendations for centralisation of administration for its backward tracts. Here, the problem was most extensive and hence the potential expense involved in development works was the greatest. Consequently, the 'prospect of transferring from the province to the centre the cost of administration of the areas was probably a considerable inducement'.[81]

In the early 1930s, an unprecedented feature of the administrative discourse on the problem of Indian aboriginal tribes was the constant reference to similar experiments on aboriginals conducted in other parts of the British Empire, especially Africa. It may be argued that an 'intra-empire flow of ideas' was reshaping the discourse, at least in the higher echelons of colonial power. Suggestions poured in that a 'solution of the problems incidental to the administration of "backward tracts" or "excluded areas" might be sought along the lines followed in administering of similar areas in South Africa and Southern Rhodesia'.[82]

For instance, Section 151 of the South African Act of 1909 provided for the transfer of any native inhabited territories by the Crown to the Government of the Union of South Africa. In the Schedule to the said Act, a description of the method of administration to be followed after such a transfer had taken place was also provided. Later, the plan for the administration of native/aboriginal areas was instituted in the Native

[80] *SR*, Vol. II, paras 128–129.

[81] Note titled 'Backward Tracts or Excluded Areas', in K.W. F.71/31–R, Reforms Branch, Reforms Office, GoI, 1931, p. 34.

[82] Note titled 'Backward Tracts' in ibid., pp. 22(B)–32.

Affairs Act of 1920, but this, too, was based on the arrangements prescribed in the aforementioned Schedule. However, as South Africa was a Union, the prescribed administrative machinery was central; but in India, where the ideal to be aimed at was a federal government, it had to be more appropriately local. In the case of Southern Rhodesia, the control of the 'Native Department' rested with the High Commissioner for South Africa. Here, all discriminatory legislation were to be reserved and laws affecting natives could be repealed only by the Crown. Despite these incongruities, the overwhelming opinion within the colonial bureaucracy seemed to be that the South African model was more suitable for India.

In these discussions, it was stated that the problem in India arose from two causes: *first*, that the protection of backward peoples was a responsibility of the British Parliament, and *second*, that the excluded areas were in general 'deficit' areas.[83] The totally excluded areas presented no real constitutional problem. However, as a slight modification, it was suggested that the Governor should act there as the Agent, not of the Governor-General in Council but of the Governor-General, as the responsibility of the Parliament for these areas would then be discharged through the Parliament's own Agents.

On the other hand, the proposals for partially excluded areas presented a formidable constitutional challenge. In a nutshell, how could the responsibility of the Parliament for these areas be discharged if the Governor, as the Agent of the Governor-General in Council or of the Governor-General, was to be guided by the advice of the Ministry? Conversely, how could the Governor administer these areas without consulting the Ministry when these areas were represented in the Legislature and when the way must be paved for their inclusion in the ordinary system of administration?[84]

Nevertheless, all such deliberations came to naught when the British Prime Minister Ramsay MacDonald, in a bold move, shelved the Simon Commission Report and its recommendations. Subsequently, the issue of the future administration of the Backward Tracts in British India was given a complete miss in the first session of the Round Table Conference. The consequences of the Round Table Conference were encapsulated in a Plenary Session speech delivered by MacDonald on 19 January 1931. In this speech, he declared the broad lines of the proposed future Constitution, but

[83]Ibid.

[84]Ibid.

did not utter a word on the issue of future arrangements for the Backward Tracts.

Taking note of these omissions and the contours of the Round Table Conference scheme as outlined in the Prime Minister's speech, the Government of India thought that no constitutional arrangements that would leave any area outside the jurisdiction of the proposed provincial governments could be contemplated. The silence on the issue of the Backward Tracts in MacDonald's speech was being interpreted as to imply that they might not be a part of the new constitutional scheme. Hence, in June 1931 the matter was referred again to the local governments, asking them to review the situation.

In reply, the Governments of Assam, and Bihar and Orissa registered strong protests against doing away with the special administrative regimes for the erstwhile Backward Tracts. The latter argued that since aboriginals were 'not vocal and (without a) political spokesman', the special arrangements had to continue. Also, the number of aboriginals ran into millions and hence, it was 'more incumbent on the British Parliament to embody in the Constitution necessary provisions for the protection of their interests'.[85] They also suggested that the problem of the Backward Tracts should be considered by a special Sub-Committee of the Round Table Conference.[86]

It was the Assam government, however, which led in raising such concerns. With the aid of a long and detailed historical appendix, it urged that any attempt to hand over the administration of the tribes to a popularly elected legislature without ensuring their effective representation would be disastrous. Staking their claim to the legacy of the British Empire in Africa, the Government of Assam argued,

> The British Empire is full of what may be considered instances repugnant to strict constitutional theory; and His Excellency in Council considers that if a workable scheme for the administration of these areas can be prepared, a continuity of policy ensured, and adequate financial arrangements made, it cannot be deemed contrary to the declarations of His Majesty's Government that in this portion of the Dominion a measure of Imperial responsibility should remain.

---

[85]Letter from Mr M. G. Hallett, Officiating Chief Secretary to the Government of Bihar and Orissa, to the Joint Secretary to the GoI, Reforms Office, No. 122–A.R.C., dated 9 July 1931 in F.71/31–R, Reforms Branch, Reforms Office, GoI, 1931, pp. 22–25.

[86]Ibid.

> He observes that within the outer territorial boundaries of the Union of South Africa there are two areas, British Bechuanaland and Basutoland, in which the responsibility of the executive to the Crown has been similarly preserved.[87]

Given such strong reactions from the provincial governments and consistent parallels being drawn with African versions of indirect rule, the Government of India decided to retain the provisions of protective ring-fencing for aboriginals in the upcoming reforms scheme. However, such a change in stance did not push the envelope much further. The issue of protection for aboriginal tribes never acquired more than a modicum of space in the ongoing discourse of constitutional reforms. The subject of Backward Tracts was yet again given a miss in the second session of the Round Table Conference. However, subsequently it did feature on the agenda list of the Consultative Committee.

The issue of the future of the Backward Tracts finally made its debut in the third and final session of the Round Table Conference. N. M. Joshi,[88] as an Indian delegate, took up the cause of increasing representation of the aboriginals in both the elected provincial councils and at the Centre. Joshi was ably assisted in this task by A. V. Thakkar of the Servants of India Society, Poona. As we shall see, Thakkar was emerging as the leading nationalist ideologue on the Aboriginal Tribes.

The 'Special Powers of the Governor-General and Governors' in relation to the Backward Tracts was another aspect which received some attention at the third session of the Round Table Conference.[89] Henceforth, the 'Special Responsibilities' of the Governor became an important part of the administrative discourse on Backward Tracts. This provision empowered the Governor-General and the Provincial Governors to intervene in blocking

---

[87]Government of Assam, The Governor in Council, Appointment and Political Department, No. 4533 A.P.; From: W. A. Cosgrave, Chief Secretary to the Government of Assam; To: The Secretary to the Government of India, Reforms Office, dated Shillong, 29 July 1931 in F.71/31–R, Reforms Branch, Reforms Office, GoI, 1931, pp. 26–36.

[88]A member of the Servants of India Society, Narayan Malhar Joshi was a tall spokesman on labour issues. This intervention was perhaps the earliest official nationalist intervention in the discourse on Scheduling.

[89]Under Head C—Special Powers of the Governor-General and Governors in Round Table Conference, Third Session Documents, IOR/Q/RTC/33, pp. 113–114.

or modifying legislations in the interests of the aboriginal tribes. This was a discretionary power which could be exercised even against the advice of the Indian ministers. In choosing to act in such a manner, they were to act exclusively as Agents of the British Parliament.

The sum total of deliberations in all three sessions of the Round Table Conference was encapsulated in a White Paper on Indian Constitutional Reforms released in March 1933.[90] Paragraphs 106–109 of this White Paper dealt with recommendations for the excluded and partially excluded areas. The administration of excluded areas was completely entrusted to the Governor, while that of partially excluded areas was deemed as one of his 'special responsibilities'. The White Paper contained the staple safeguards about the Governor's powers to repeal or amend any legislation to be applied in these areas. It also reiterated his powers to prohibit resolutions, discussion, or asking of questions in the provincial legislature on their administration. However, the White Paper was silent on the question of financing of the administration. In dealing with the working of the provincial executive, paragraph 70 of the Paper finally defined 'special responsibility'. The aboriginals and the Backward Tracts qualified on two counts:

> (b) The safeguarding of the legitimate interests of the minorities; and
> (f) The administration of areas declared in accordance with provisions in that behalf, to be partially excluded areas. It was left to the Governor's discretion to determine whether any of the 'special responsibilities' were involved by any circumstances.[91]

The publication of this White Paper was met with protests from Indian political interests. The proposals in paragraph 106–109 were deemed retrograde by the Indian National Congress, which upped its ante against the Government of India's policy of exclusion and partial exclusion. The next set of parleys on the issue began when the Joint Select Committee of the British Parliament took up the issue for discussion, and evidence was invited from the Indian representatives. This Committee's final report was supposed to provide the blueprint for the drafting of the Government of India Bill of 1935. This will be discussed in Chapter 2. Let us now turn to a

[90] The White Paper on Indian Constitutional Reforms (Author: Samuel Hoare); Memorandum by the Secretary of State for India; Printed for the Cabinet, March 1933, Most Secret, C.P. 49(33), CAB/24/238.

[91] Ibid.

debate which proved to be a turning point in the late colonial discourse on Indian tribal populations.

The Debate in the British Parliament

Arguably, the debate in the British Parliament on excluded and partially excluded areas was a watershed event in the discourse on Indian aboriginal tribes. In particular, the Cadogan Amendment, brought on the floor of the House of Commons in May 1935, initiated a process which culminated in an immense increase in the extent of areas notified under these categories.

Before we engage with details of the debate, it is important to delineate a few important points. *First*, around the mid-1930s, the issue of 'aboriginality' had gradually assumed some importance in the constitutional discourse on India. *Second*, the debate in the British Parliament could be seen as the theatre in which the differences which had emerged between the Government of India and the provincial governments on Backward Tracts were sought to be reconciled. Third, the British Parliament was concerned not only with the Indian Empire, but also brought together imperialist perspectives from across the spectrum of their colonial possessions, especially Africa. In a crucial way, the following debates provide us with a window to the larger picture in which the tribal question in India was being discussed.

The ball was set rolling on 10 December 1934, when the Secretary of State for India, Sir Samuel Hoare, put forward the draft Government of India Bill on the floor of the House of Commons.[92] In an introductory speech, Hoare expressed the hope that the Indians were being offered a scheme which contained 'in every chapter the seeds of future growth'.[93] Hoare's first reference to aboriginals was through the 'special responsibilities' and, defending them, he argued that 'we must keep in reserve powers to prevent these tribes and these remote districts [from] being exploited'.[94]

The first opposition to the proposals came from Wing-Commander James, who said that Hoare's strategy was 'not good enough'. Expressing hope that the enquiry to delineate aboriginal areas for protection was going

---

[92]House of Commons Debate, 10 December 1934, Vol. 296, Columns 45–168.

[93]Ibid., Column 59.

[94]Ibid., Column 53.

to be 'independent, unfettered and unprejudiced', he warned the British Parliament against accepting any 'bureaucratic substitute'.[95]

The second round of debate began in good earnest in late March 1935 when the specific clauses of the draft Government of India Bill were discussed on the floor of the House of Commons. The draft Bill's clause 91 had an attached Schedule Six, outlining four excluded areas and eleven partially excluded areas. Inaugurating the discussion, Colonel Josiah Wedgwood (Member for Newcastle-under-Lyme) commented that 'the backward tribes of India should remain under British control'. Wedgwood's ideal was that the tribals 'must be developed from themselves and not by being converted from good Nagas or whatever they are into bad Hindus'. Protection should mean ensuring them the 'right to retain their access to land and the opportunity of developing without the interference of civilisation'. Calling the aboriginals 'the original inhabitants of India before the Aryans and the Mohammedans came down and swamped the country', Wedgwood remarked that 'it is impossible to say that any other race on earth can look after them as well as we can'. He made a case for gradual change guided by anthropological principles, which would 'preserve all that is best in these native tribes'. He cautioned the House that if the aboriginal tribes were 'dragged into the competitive system of industrial organisation—into the mills and factories of India—they will be ruined'. Citing the example of the west coast of Africa, he argued that the Empire's administrative systems in Africa could serve as a model for India. Drawing a parallel between India and Kenya, Wedgwood said:

> The whole attitude of the settlers in Kenya, for instance, towards the population of Kenya is motivated by the same feeling that the more educated Indians have towards these backward tribes. They want to get them in as cheap labour. It is all part of the great labour problem all over the world, and, if these people are to be saved from the hell of civilisation as represented in more or less primitive countries, the only chance they have is British protection and British control, and to be free from the insidious advances of the rich people in the provinces to exploit and develop these natives.... It is not fair to put these tribes, for hundreds of years, I might almost say thousands of years, behind the

---

[95]House of Commons Debate, 11 December 1934, Vol. 296, Columns 214–348, 308–309. By this phrase, James meant recommendations from provincial governments. Subsequent paragraphs and extracts on pgs 72–74 have been reconstructed from this source.

> Indian to-day into the unrestricted hands of people whose object must be to exploit their labour and to sell them cheap goods at prices they are not worth.

African examples continued to inform the debate in the British Parliament. Valentine McEntee remarked that the British government in Uganda could serve as a model for aboriginal tracts in India, as it had ensured 'perfectly free access to the land in almost every part of the country'. This fostered their ability to grow food, and as a result the Ugandans were an independent and 'happy people'.

Until now, the main points raised in the debate were that 'civilisation' was a source of interference which grievously disrupted tribal societies. Many members advocated that anthropologists should have a major role in the administration of 'backward tracts'. One of the chief hallmarks of the discussion was the search for a model of 'sympathetic' administration within the British imperial domain, especially from Africa.

In his response, Hoare defended the Schedule Six proposals. Assuaging the fears raised earlier in the House, Hoare said:

> We realise ... that these backward people will only be victimised if we try to impose upon them institutions which, while they may be suitable for more advanced civilisations, will do nothing but lead to their exploitation. We realise the great danger of imposing upon them anything in the nature of representative Government as we understand it. We realise the great danger of imposing upon them criminal and civil codes, and all that is connected with them, which, while they may be admirable for civilised communities, are extremely dangerous and injurious to these backward races.

Regarding the identification of excluded and partially excluded areas, Hoare said the main problem was that the aboriginal people were 'scattered over the face of India'. Admitting that the scheduled areas did not cover the entire backward population of India, Hoare observed, however, that they did cover areas which were 'self-contained'. The important implication of this expression 'self-contained' (and, in later speeches, 'homogeneous') was that the areas to be scheduled had to display the demographic majority of aboriginal people. This was an important insight, as will become evident later.

On the future possibility of transferring the notified areas over to the provincial governments for regular administration, the Secretary of State replied that some change was inevitable as the people kept moving about. Future 'infiltration from one district to another' may prepare the grounds for such a transfer. However, Hoare promised the House members 'Parliamentary protection behind the transferred area. We ensure that the transfer can only be undertaken by an Order in Council, which has to obtain the approval of both houses. Therefore, I think that position is well protected.'

Although the House of Commons agreed on clauses 91 and 92 of the draft Bill, it was made clear by Alan Todd that there was a lobby intent on increasing the number of districts under the Sixth Schedule. There were clear and ominous signs for the Secretary of State that amendments with regard to the extension of the Sixth Schedule would be moved when it came up for debate in the House.[96] Upon receiving the notice of the amendment to be moved in the House, Hoare immediately sent the new list of areas proposed to be scheduled to the Indian and provincial governments for their reconsideration and with a view to extending the scope of the Sixth Schedule.

In its reply to the Secretary of State's anxious enquiries, the Government of India told him that the provincial governments were opposed to all suggestions for extending the scope of the Sixth Schedule, with the exception of Madras, which had agreed to the inclusion of Laccadive Islands and Minicoy in the list of Excluded Areas. It also informed that if pressurised, Assam would add North Cachar Hills and Punjab would include Spiti and Lahaul in the schedule of excluded areas.[97] In its response, the Government of India highlighted that while some excluded areas had a demographic preponderance of non-aboriginals, certain other areas displayed a mixed population, where 'advanced' sections coexisted with aboriginals and the latter did not require special protection. Thus, the letter presciently suggested that,

> To include these areas now in Schedule VI would excite political opposition on ground that a serious diminution of the scope of responsible government is being effected by this new method, and that we are turning our backs on what we have done in the past by including these areas in the general body politic. Our aim should be not to retain aboriginal areas concerned as picturesque survivals but to secure their

[96]Serial 1—Telegram from SSI No. 1103, dated 5 April 1935, in F. No. 4/I/35–G. (B), General (B) Branch, Reforms Office, Government of India, 1935.

[97]Serial No. 23, Telegram to the SSI No. 1031 dated 24 April 1935 in F. No. 4/I/35–G.(B), General (B) Branch, Reforms Office, Government of India, 1935.

> development by absorbing them with rest of the community. The process of assimilation has been going on and to put an obstacle in its way would be a retrograde step.[98]

In the last line, the appearance of the term 'assimilation' is significant. It marks a certain level of conceptualisation of the positions held by the different protagonists in the debate. The use of catch-all categories by figures like Elwin, Thakkar, and Ghurye is wrongly believed to be their own distinctive contribution to the discourse on aboriginal tribes. The chief debate that took place in the late colonial period on the future of tribal communities in India occurred in the administrative circles. Even the catch-all terms (Isolationism/Protectionism versus Interventionism/Assimilationism) which framed the 'Tribal Question' in the early 1940s had emerged in the administrative and constitutional deliberations under the Government of India Act, 1935. The later nationalists or even figures like Elwin did not coin them; they merely appropriated the terms, sometimes ascribing newer meanings to them. Exactly how this discourse 'spilled over' to other domains such as politics will become clear over the next few chapters.

On 12 May 1935, a day before the final charge of the Cadogan Amendment, Hoare replied to the Government of India that it was evident to him that 'I shall be most strongly pressed to do far more towards meeting amendment than making few concessions proposed by you. Great interest is taken in this matter in House and it is difficult to convince it that problem has been considered fully and without bias [*sic*].'[99] At this crucial stage, Hoare found it necessary to promise to amend clause 91, thereby giving power by Order in Council to add to the Sixth Schedule with provisions.[100]

In its reply, the Government of India insisted that the Secretary of State should 'make it plain to the House' that the government would not commit itself to adding new areas to the Sixth Schedule.[101] They said that the Government of India, provincial governments, and the Indian opinion were in 'complete unanimity' in their opposition to any enlargement of the

---

[98]Ibid.

[99]Serial No. 24. Telegram from the SSI No. 1471, dated 12 May 1935, in F. No. 4/I/35–G.(B), General (B) Branch, Reforms Office, Government of India, 1935.

[100]Ibid.

[101]Serial No. 25. Telegram to the SSI, No. 1256, dated 13 May 1935, in F. No. 4/I/35–G.(B), General (B) Branch, Reforms Office, Government of India, 1935.

Sixth Schedule. However, if it was impossible to maintain such a stand, the Government of India agreed to include new areas in it through an Order in Council.[102]

Interesting as the discussions were until April 1935, they were set to pale in comparison with the debate, at the Committee stage, in the House of Commons on the draft Sixth Schedule. Here, even the government ranks witnessed a back-bench revolt as they joined with the 'die-hards'.[103] The man of the moment was Edward Cadogan, whose amendment effectively brought about a paradigm shift in the discourse on Indian aboriginal people. Until this debate, the discourse was purely administrative, with little participation by the Indian political class. However, subsequent reporting in the Indian press generated righteous anger and more organised opposition by the Congress nationalists. They decided to oppose and delegitimise the British policy of protection towards the Indian aboriginal tribes. Effectively, the debate on the Cadogan Amendment proved the tipping point, after which the discourse could not remain confined to the realms of colonial bureaucracy and soon spilled over to the political domain. Thus, the Cadogan Amendment debate provided the critical threshold for the 'Politics of Scheduling'.

Edward Cadogan was a Member of the House of Commons from Finchley, and had visited India as part of the Indian Statutory Commission's peregrinations in the country. He had conversations with the 'head hunters of Kohima in their own jungle', visited the Sadiya Frontier Tract, and motored 100 miles across the plateau of Chota Nagpur district.[104] He submitted to the House that since there was no provision for bringing any areas under the Sixth Schedule in the future, it was expedient to take 'the risk of over-excluding rather than under-excluding'. Asking the House to accept his schedule of excluded (20) and partially excluded (31) areas, Cadogan claimed that it was based on the advice of 'men on the spot'.

Clement Attlee, future prime minister and a colleague of Cadogan on the Simon Commission, said there was 'overwhelming evidence that these people must be protected, and that they are far more liable to exploitation'. Supporting the Cadogan Amendment, Attlee said that 'we ought to err on

[102]Ibid.

[103]House of Commons Debate, 10 May 1935, Vol. 301, Columns 1343–1354, Column 1343. The subsequent paragraphs and texts quoted have been reconstructed from this source.

[104]Details of this long sojourn were later published in a book. See Edward Cadogan, *The India We Saw*, John Murray, 1933, pp. 199–205.

the side of inclusion and not on the side of exclusion'. He also pitched for the formation of a specialised cadre of officers for certain backward areas so as to ensure that 'the areas are dealt with by people who have a special interest in them'. As an ideal type of such an officer, Attlee heaped praise on Dr Hutton,

> Anyone who visited a man like Dr. Hutton must have been impressed by his great knowledge and ability, and the fact that his qualifications are entirely different from those which are found in the ordinary routine of Indian Government. He is really a highly skilled specialist and a scientific observer.[105]

In the course of the discussion, the amendment was receiving wider support than what its movers/advocates (later called the 'aboriginal party') or the government had themselves anticipated. Terming the subject of Backward Tracts and excluded areas 'a neglected garden', Lord Eustace Percy[106] remarked that they had never been 'dealt with the discrimination which their particular problems demanded'.[107] He observed that Parliament was dealing with two broad classes of areas: first, the areas which had a 'homogeneous primitive population', and second, a 'number of tracts where the aboriginal population exists side by side with, generally, an Hindu population'. The aboriginal tracts in the Central Provinces, where the aboriginal element ranged between 25 to 60 per cent, belonged to the latter category. In these pockets, Lord Percy raised the literary metaphor of Rudyard Kipling's famous novel and observed,

> We never get on to this subject without somebody talking about the 'Jungle Book'; but the chief impression left on my mind by the 'Jungle Book' is precisely that of an aboriginal population existing in a semi-settled, semi-nomadic condition in the midst of an ordinary agricultural population.

The chief defence of the government's policy and its opposition to amending the draft Sixth Schedule was made by the Under-Secretary of State for

[105]For details on Hutton, see Chapter 2.

[106]Chairman of the Sub-Committee of the Joint Select Committee on Indian Constitutional Reforms, which heard the evidence on the subject of excluded and partially excluded areas.

[107]House of Commons Debate, 13 May 1935, Vol. 301, Columns 1387–1449, Column 1389. The subsequent paragraphs have been reconstructed from this source.

India, R. A. Butler (known as 'Rab'). Disagreeing that the issue has been a 'neglected garden' for his government, Butler said that it was 'examined thoroughly' by the Statutory Committee, the Joint Select Committee, and the Government of India.

On the question of excluded areas, Butler said that out of the Cadogan Amendment list, the government was agreeable to excluding the Laccadive Islands (including the Amindivi Islands and Minicoy) in Madras, the North Cachar Hills District in Assam, and Spiti and Lahaul in Punjab. About the seventeen other areas proposed for total exclusion, Butler raised three chief objections. *First,* since total exclusion implied the direct responsibility of the Governor, a lot of 'administrative difficulty' was anticipated, especially in the case of small areas. It would also mean that such an area would not benefit from government-run programmes, like those in education. *Second,* some of the areas in Cadogan's wishlist (for example, Nallamalai Hills in Kurnool District of Madras, Dindori Tahsil of Mandla District and Garchiroli Tahsil of Chanda District in the Central Provinces, and Ranchi District in Bihar and Orissa) were already under the existing reforms since being brought into operation in 1919. As they had been under reformed administration for over twelve years, Butler anticipated 'intense dissatisfaction in India', making such a move extremely difficult. *Third,* Butler argued that purely in statistical terms, the proposals to exclude twenty areas lacked substance. He cited the characteristically small percentage of aboriginals in some of the areas proposed to be totally excluded by the Cadogan Amendment. Hence, Butler remarked that in view of the administrative difficulties, the past history of many areas as having been under reforms for some time, and the small percentage of aboriginals in a number of the areas, total exclusion would be very 'improper and invidious ... and that it would alienate the population in the surrounding districts.'[108]

The matter of partial exclusion was a knotty affair as the Cadogan Amendment desired thirty-one areas to be notified as such. Taking the cue from Lord Percy, Butler opined that the demographic character of partially excluded areas was 'partly aboriginal and partly the ordinary agricultural population.' Therefore, in many of the areas in Cadogan's list, there were 'small pockets of aboriginals whom it would be almost impossible to pick out and surround with a ring fence.' Using the garden metaphor again,

[108]In Butler's response on the debate on the question, Census figures exerted a great logical force, which was utilised by both pro and anti-exclusion lobbies to buttress their respective arguments.

Butler said that the 'aboriginals do not always stick to their own particular garden border; these blooms are to be found in every part of the garden, and it makes it difficult to pick out a particular bed of aboriginals and ring it round with a small fence'.

In the Under-Secretary's opinion, the case of Bombay and Central Provinces exemplified the difficulty of selecting areas for partial exclusion. In the latter, the unmixed aboriginal pockets were a rarity and one was likely to 'find a pocket here and a rather larger number there'. Therefore, the government had included in the Sixth Schedule only such areas as could be called a 'homogeneous unit'. Cadogan's recommendations in these provinces were not 'susceptible to the definition of being homogeneous units'.

Butler also supported the idea of appointing a special officer in the provinces who would keep a constant watch on the condition of aboriginals and thereby assist the Governor in fulfilling his special responsibility towards them. Summing up, Butler claimed to have 'shown to the Committee the great difficulties of total exclusion, the partial difficulties of partial exclusion and the impossibility of further defining, as we can see it at present, homogeneous areas which it is possible partially to exclude'. While concluding his speech, Butler outlined the general attitude of advisers and governments in India and the British government in the following terms,

> While we do not for a moment deny the importance of special measures for these areas, if we have to choose between assimilation or segregation, we go on as before with assimilation. Segregation, we feel, may not in every case meet the proper desires and needs of such areas.... But it would be disastrous at this stage to take any step which could alienate the public opinion of what may be called the advanced communities in India whom we wish to interest in the welfare of the backward areas. Let us look to the future. If at this moment we decide on a ring-fence policy and segregate as many areas as we can, we put off to a later date the chance of assimilating the backward areas in the general polity of India...

Butler's speech was a measured and well-articulated rejection of the Cadogan Amendment by the government. This was followed by Wing-Commander James's rebuttal; James ridiculed the government's concession of three additions to the excluded areas list—Lahaul and Spiti, Laccadives and Amindivi Islands, and North Cachar Hill District—as 'not worth anything'. According to James, the first was totally excluded by snow, the second by the Indian Ocean, and the third was too small and insignificant.

He supported the Simon Commission's recommendation for centralised administration of the erstwhile Backward Tracts. James also rejected the government's contention that a reversal of status for areas under reformed administration was not possible.

At this stage, Winston Churchill joined the debate. Churchill was a characteristically hard-hitting orator and an arch imperialist belonging to the conservative 'die-hard' lobby opposed to the passage of the Government of India Bill, 1935. Utilising the growing support behind the Cadogan Amendment, Churchill mounted a fierce attack on the basic principles of the proposed Bill. In what became a highly controversial and oft-quoted speech on the subject, Churchill lambasted the British government thus:

> I should be very glad indeed if the Under-Secretary were to accept the Amendment, and, even if my hon. and gallant Friend cared to add other districts to it, I should not object. I should not object indeed to including in it the entire scope of the great Indian peninsula.[109]

Colonel Wedgwood reminded Churchill that nearly three decades ago, the latter had advocated a very similar Bill for South Africa which excluded the three areas of Bechuanaland, Swaziland, and Basutoland from the South African settlement because under the South African Constitution, franchise was not extended for the Bechuanas, the Swazis, and the Basutos. Therefore, the solution was to 'exclude them and reserve the administration of those areas'. Wedgwood argued for a direct parallel with Indian territories as well, as 'these people have no votes, and, therefore, if they come under a Constitution with which they have no connection whatsoever, they should be excluded'. Godfrey Nicholson, in his response, focussed on the all-important economic dimension and its political implications, noting critically that,

> This is a political question rather than an anthropological question. The anthropologists are united in the sense of this Amendment. The answers must be political; the case is a political case.... The real basis of the case is not that there will be wilful neglect, but that inevitably economies will be made when it comes to spending more on an area.

[109]House of Commons Debate, 13 May 1935, Vol. 301, Column 1411–1412. This tirade from Churchill became a major rallying point for the nationalists in their opposition to the provisions for excluding and partially excluding predominantly tribal areas, and was often cited by them in print and speeches.

> Orissa is a deficit Province at the best of times. I cannot think that the future of a deficit area in a deficit Province will be particularly rosy.

At this stage, Cadogan extended a conciliatory hand to the government and said that his Amendment was merely a suggestion to improve the Sixth Schedule. Citing the support received from Members of the House of Commons, Cadogan said that the Under-Secretary should reconsider the matter. Suggesting that the government could 'retain some power of adding to the Schedule', Cadogan expressed willingness to withdraw his Amendment. The Members offered a few other suggestions and a consensus that local district officials or the veritable 'man on the spot' should be consulted in the final identification of the excluded and partially excluded areas seemed closer.

After all this commotion in the House, the government finally caved in to the tide of opinion that allied itself with the Cadogan Amendment. Nevertheless, the government's Attorney-General Sir Thomas Inskip said that the list of areas provided in the Amendment could not be accepted *in toto*. Also, if all the areas were to be discussed one by one, 'the Committee would have to sit as a sort of Royal Commission, a committee of inquiry, without any facilities for having papers and information'. Thus, calling for a truce, the government decided to withdraw the Sixth Schedule and offered to prepare an Order-in-Council to be later submitted to the House. This order was to act as the final settlement of the question and would be issued before the grant of provincial autonomy. An important part of the government's resolve was that no additional areas could be added to the list of excluded and partially excluded areas by any subsequent Orders-in-Council.

The immediate result of the debate in the House of Commons was that the draft Government of India Bill omitted the earlier draft Sixth Schedule. Clause 91 of the Bill was consequently amended by the House so as to give power to determine by an Order-in-Council the areas to be excluded and partially excluded after receiving Parliamentary approval.

The debate in the British Parliament over notifying excluded and partially excluded areas in the future Constitution of India proved subsequently to be a watershed event in many ways. Before this debate began, purely in terms of the number of entries, the original Government of India Bill had a draft Sixth Schedule, which proposed four areas for total exclusion and eleven areas for partial exclusion; the extension clause in the all-important Cadogan Amendment proposed twenty areas to be excluded and thirty-one to be partially excluded; and the final Order-in-Council notified eight areas in the excluded category while twenty-eight were partially excluded. The Cadogan Amendment thus initiated a process which resulted in an immense increase in the extent of the scheduled areas.

At an intellectual level, the debate dealt with a plethora of issues surrounding the aboriginal tribes and their future status in a reformed Constitution of India. Perhaps the biggest contribution of these discussions was the government's clear admission that the process of scheduling was ultimately guided by an area's demographic character. The principle of ring-fencing any area as excluded or partially scheduled was based on whether the territory was a 'self-contained' one or not. Many members, both from the government and the opposition benches, highlighted that the ideal area to be scheduled should be a 'homogeneous unit', meaning thereby that the aboriginal tribes must be in an absolute majority. Thus, the Census figures became extremely important in substantiating the case for either exclusion or partial exclusion. This made the most immediate figures of the 1931 Census operations (conducted under the supervision of J. H. Hutton) the litmus test for identifying the tribal majority areas for the purpose of scheduling. This was a straight acknowledgement of the centrality of cognitive paradigms as reflected in the Census documents while making administrative decisions, especially in dealing with special categories.

Furthermore, the difficulty with the scheduling process in Bombay and Central Provinces was due to the scattered distribution of their aboriginal population. In these large tracts, marking out specific zones of 'tribal preponderance' was extremely difficult. Through the long-term processes of population increase and agrarian expansion, caste Hindus had also percolated in large numbers into areas where aboriginal tribes traditionally resided. At the heart of it, it was perhaps the inability of these provincial governments to earmark such areas that instigated the proposals to schedule or reserve areas mentioned under the Cadogan Amendment. Nevertheless, the movers and supporters of this Amendment succeeded in turning the tables on the non-scheduling of areas within Central Provinces and Bombay. This, however, was preceded by an official enquiry which should be minutely analysed.

The First All-India Aboriginal Enquiry

After the embarrassment caused to the government on account of the Cadogan Amendment episode in the House of Commons, a rapid turn of events ensued. The Secretary of State for India, Sir Samuel Hoare, started rolling out a multi-pronged strategy to prevent any further loss of face. Above all, his moves were calculated to appease the British Parliamentarians who had put the government proposals on the Sixth Schedule on the docks.

First, Hoare directed the Government of India to immediately initiate a *de novo* examination by each provincial government to determine the areas to be excluded and partially excluded within their respective territories. The Secretary of State observed that the only relevant consideration was to ascertain the extent to which 'the areas in which such classes *predominate* can be brought, without administrative disadvantage or without countervailing disadvantage to the remainder of the inhabitants of the area'.[110] The Secretary was against the formation of any committee or commission and wanted the local governments to provide a 'full examination of the conditions of each district by the District Officer himself'.

As a *second* step, the India Office desired that an officer with 'special experience of the habits and needs of aboriginal people' be deputed for assistance in the final delineation of scheduled areas. James Philip Mills was eventually selected as Officer on Special Duty for two months in the Reforms Office of the Government of India.[111] Selecting an anthropology practitioner was designed to lend greater legitimacy vis-à-vis British Parliamentarians, who had repeatedly raised the argument that some form of expertise was required on board. The India Office wanted to leave no stone unturned, and Mills was an apt choice. He possessed a 'great deal of experience of backward

---

[110]Letter from the Indian Office to the Government of India, No. P. & J. (C) 5420, dated 7 June 1935, (and relayed through) Letter from the Government of India to all Local Governments (Except Burma) No. F.-4/35 G. (B.) dated 2 July in *Government of India Act 1935, Excluded and Partially Excluded Areas (Section 91) Recommendations of the Provincial Governments and the Government of India,* His Majesty's Stationery Office, London, 1936, pp. 1–14. It was this approximately 300-page printed document which the Secretary of State finally presented to the Parliament in January 1936. However, I found this published version towards the end of finishing my manuscript when it was too late to incorporate it. Hence, nearly all my subsequent references in this section are from the Reforms Office files kept at the National Archives, New Delhi.

[111]D.O. letter from Sir V. Dawson, KCIE, India Office, London (Whitehall), No. P & J(C) 5487/35 dated 28 June 1935; To: Sir James Dunnett, KCIE, Reforms Office, GoI, Simla in F. No. 4/II/35–G (B), General (B) Branch, Reforms Office, GoI, 1935.

tracts in Assam' and had published widely on the Naga tribes.[112] On the strength of his increasing recognition as an expert on hill tribes, Mills had also examined for the Anthropological Tripos at Cambridge. The Secretary of State thought that it 'might be politically of much assistance in dealing with the matter later on in the House of Commons if he is able to make it plain that a man with Mills' knowledge has, in fact, had a hand in framing the Government of India's recommendations'. Thus, clearly, the move to induct Mills was made to satisfy 'a considerable section in the House of Commons which was disinclined to be satisfied with any official inquiry and which wanted an independent commission largely manned by anthropological experts'.

These developments set the ball rolling on what was arguably the single largest enquiry on the aboriginal condition to ever be conducted by the British Indian administrative machinery. Its scale was truly remarkable as it encompassed the remotest nook and corner of British India. It also brought forth a variety of issues as well as various fault-lines within the official block. The most crucial issues that the enquiry addressed were the tenurial rights of aboriginals on land, the impact of courts/legal codes in aboriginal areas, practices of customary law, and the unsuitability of modern representational democracy in aboriginal areas. The identification and analysis offered in this enquiry provides a crucial window into official perceptions on the tribal question.

Some larger problematic areas were identified before the district officers began their respective enquiries. *First*, with respect to partial exclusion, the Government of India held that notification under the Scheduled Districts Act, 1874, could not be a criterion as this yardstick would mean a wholesale exclusion of entire provinces in Assam and Sind.[113] The Reforms Office remarked that this criterion was the result of an erroneous impression that a Scheduled District was a wholly or partially deregulationised area. In reality, comparatively few Scheduled Districts were deregulationised, and

[112]Mills was the Sub-Divisional Officer for the Mokokchung Sub-Division of Naga Hill Region between 1917 and 1924. He utilised his administrative experience to write two authoritative monographs, *The Lhota Nagas* (1922) and *The Ao Nagas* (1926), which were published by the Government of Assam and established his reputation as an expert on the Nagas.

[113]Serial No. 29, Telegram to the SSI, No. 1066 dated 2 July 1935, in F. No. 4/I/35–G.(B)., General (B) Branch, Reforms Office, Government of India, 1935.

it was only in respect of such areas that there was any real presumption in favour of partial exclusion.

Second, at the provincial level, fault-lines were clearly visible in the official ranks. For instance, on the total exclusion of the Garo and Mikir Hills, the Government of Assam admitted to a 'not insignificant divergence of opinion'. The Assam government observed that,

> there is definitely an 'aboriginal' and a 'progressive' view point on the matter—the 'aboriginal' party (to whom the present Commissioners and Dr. Hutton would claim allegiance) considering that the interests of the local people would best be protected by complete exclusion while the other party believes that progress in each static civilization as those in the Garo and Mikir Hills can only be brought about—as it has been brought about in the Khasi and Jaintia Hills—by gradual contact with a larger world and more advanced ideas.[114]

In the above extract, the terms used for pro ('aboriginal' party) and anti ('progressive') exclusion lobbies within the Assam officialdom are significant. Thus, there were major fault-lines on the question of exclusion and partial exclusion and a certain conceptualisation of their respective positions was already underway. These expressions provide further evidence that the subsequent catch-all categories had certainly not been first employed by Elwin in the early 1940s. The bracketing of positions into a distinctive oppositional binary had been going on in the colonial administrative bureaucracy. At least some years prior to the much vaunted Ghurye–Elwin debate, the question of exclusion and partial exclusion had drawn a wedge in the 'official block' itself.

Third, the financial argument of the plains providing revenues for the administration of Backward Tracts served as one of the most common grounds used by provincial governments to stave off total exclusion. In a typical case, the Government of Bengal had to provide a recommendation on the future status of the Chittagong Hill Tracts in the new Constitution. While material considerations such as 'primitive character and backwardness' would mean complete exclusion, the level of financial self-sufficiency could see a tilt in favour of partial exclusion. Thus, the Bengal province annually contributed Rs 2 lakh from general revenues towards the cost of administration of the Chittagong Hill Tracts. Based on this consideration,

[114]Letter from the Government of Assam, No. 3044–fr., dated 9 October 1935, in F. No. 4/I/35–G.(B)., General (B) Branch, Reforms Office, Government of India, 1935.

the government felt that there was an imperative to only partially exclude this area.[115]

Fourth, a substantial number of high-level bureaucrats in the provinces were extremely sceptical about introducing electoral politics and representational democratic institutions in areas inhabited by aboriginal communities. In line with this trend, the Government of Bengal, too, was firmly of the opinion that it was impossible to 'devise any system of representation for the Hill Tracts which would not have mischievous results in the present state of development of the inhabitants.'[116] So strong were its objections to introducing representative democratic institutions in the Chittagong Hill Tracts that the Bengal government went to the extent of writing to the Government of India that,

> ... whatever solution is adopted finally with respect to the classification of the area, it should be made clear that no system of representation can be introduced at present. The Local Government would prefer that the area should be classed as 'partially excluded'; they see no insuperable difficulty in classifying the area as 'partially excluded' and at the same time delaying the introduction of a representative system till such time as the local Government think the state of development of the Tracts justifies it. But if classification as 'partially excluded' does of necessity involve representation, then in spite of obvious difficulty which will follow if the money required for the administration of an 'excluded area' is to be found from Provincial funds although the Ministry and the Legislature will have no responsibility in respect thereof, the local Government recommend total exclusion.[117]

This was not a one-off instance where the provincial government was opposed to introducing representational democracy in predominantly tribal areas. Espousing similar concerns, the Government of Bihar and Orissa noted,

> The provincial Legislature, as a whole, has taken little interest in the backward tribes other than to press for the removal of existing forms of protection, the Congress has taken no interest in them except to exploit them for political purposes, and the local self-governing bodies

[115]No. 2606 A.R., dated Calcutta, 6 December 1933; From: R. N. Gilchrist, Esq., I.E.S., Reforms Officer to the Government of Bengal; To: Secretary to the GoI, Reforms Office in F. No. 4/I/35–G.(B), General (B) Branch, Reforms Office, Government of India, 1935, pp. 17–18.

[116]Ibid.

[117]Ibid.

> have usually been more anxious to provide for non-aboriginals than for aboriginal needs except in the few districts where the aboriginals themselves have effective representation on these bodies. The necessity for protection of the backward peoples has, therefore, become even more obvious in the fringe areas where they are in the minority than in the predominantly aboriginal core of the backward tracts. Further these fringe areas have a great importance as a buffer from the predominantly aboriginal tracts, a protection very necessary for the peaceful advancement of those areas.[118]

Such an attitude and scepticism towards representational democracy was not confined to Englishmen in the upper bureaucracy alone. Even Indian members of the Indian Civil Services (ICS) espoused similar concerns. For instance, S. N. Mozumdar, Deputy Commissioner of Manbhum, wrote in his report that,

> For adequate protection of the Backward tribes the proposed special powers of the Governor are essential. A minority is usually neglected. Their representatives or champions in the legislature will be an insignificant number. They will be completely out of the picture unless their cause has a powerful backing, which will be lacking in the legislature.... It will be unwise at present to leave the Backward tribes entirely in the hands of the legislature.[119]

In other instances, several District Officers also expressed their grave distrust of representational democracy for predominantly aboriginal areas. The Deputy Commissioner of Sambalpur wrote:

> But they are not in touch with modern political thought, and it will probably be some years before they understand a parliamentary system: or the desirability of securing a true representation of their interests in the provincial Legislative Assembly. The so called 'elected representatives of the people' are likely to be lawyers of the headquarter

[118]No. 7342–A.R. Government of Bihar and Orissa, Appointment Department; From: R. E. Russell, Officiating Chief Secretary to Government; To: The Secretary to the Government of India, Reforms Office; dated Ranchi, 18 October 1935, in F. No. 4/I/35–G.(B), General (B) Branch, Reforms Office, Government of India, 1935.

[119]Annexure D, No. 166–P.C., dated Purulia, 18 September 1935; From: S. N. Mozumdar, Deputy Commissioner Manbhum, to the Chief Secretary to Government, Bihar and Orissa, Ranchi, in F. No. 4/I/35–G.(B), General (B) Branch, Reforms Office, Government of India, 1935, p. 3.

> station. Our experience is that the latter have a singularly inadequate knowledge of the laws and customs of the district: and, if they were to attempt legislation, might make serious mistake.[120]

Perhaps one of the most stirring espousals of protection for aboriginals was made by the Government of Bihar and Orissa.[121] Even J. P. Mills waxed eloquent in his report on the memorandum submitted by the Government of Bihar and Orissa.[122] The Bihar government's position was that the aboriginal problem had altered materially since the Simon Commission enquiry as the 'federal' Constitution proposed through the Government of India Act, 1935, was fundamentally different from the strong Centre model suggested earlier. In this context, the only protection offered to backward peoples in areas which were not partially excluded was the 'negative power' vesting in the Governor-General and the Governor, who were responsible for safeguarding the legitimate interests of minorities. The powers to provide funds and to legislate would lie very largely with the legislatures. Given the new contours of the constitutional arrangements already in place, the Government of Bihar and Orissa raised an issue that lay at the heart of the matter, that is, land and the special tenancy laws operative in aboriginal areas. Their submission was:

> The special tenancy laws in Chota Nagpur, the Santal Parganas, Sambalpur and Angul are the bulwark of the backward peoples. The Legislatures of the future would have the power to amend, modify or even repeal these laws and the only safeguard against legislative action detrimental to the interests of the backward peoples is the power of the Governor to refuse assent. While that power may be effective to

[120] Annexure E, Report on the question of whether Sambalpur district should be 'partially excluded' under the new Constitution in F. No. 4/I/35-G.(B), General (B) Branch, Reforms Office, Government of India, 1935.

[121] Letter No. 7342–A.R. Government of Bihar and Orissa Appointment Department; From: R. E. Russell, Officiating Chief Secretary to Government; To: the Secretary to the Government of India, Reforms Office; dated Ranchi, 18 October 1935, in F. No. 4/I/35–G.(B), General (B) Branch, Reforms Office, Government of India, 1935.

[122] In his report, Mills wrote about the Government of Bihar and Orissa, 'Such is the attention they have long paid to the aboriginals under their charge that they may almost be said to have a cadre of specialists', 'Note on the Backward Areas of British India and their position under the Government of India Act, 1935', p. 28, in F. No. 4/III/35–G(B).& K.W., General (B) Branch, Reforms Office, GoI, 1935.

> prevent repeal, it will be more difficult to prevent repeated attempts at attrition. It may be difficult to get special legislation passed that may be required for the special needs of the aboriginals or to secure amendments of the tenancy Acts affording needed protection for their tenancy rights. The importance of these special tenancy laws to the aboriginals cannot be overstressed. The history of the Santal Parganas and of Chota Nagpur was one of continuous exploitation and dispossession of the aboriginals punctuated by disorder and even rebellion until special and adequate protection was given. In the fringe areas, such as Manbhum, where the non-aboriginals are in a majority, the aboriginal element would probably have been driven from the land long ago but for the protection given by the tenancy laws.... The fate of the aboriginal, where he has been unprotected, has usually been to lose his land and to be absorbed gradually into the depressed classes with the status of a mere labourer.[123]

In the above extract, the dangers of detribalisation and the fears of tribal rebellion are mentioned to justify partial exclusion. The District Officers also noted the necessity of the continuation of special tenancy laws, which, while not perfect, were nevertheless critical.

> Special measures to safeguard the interests of the backward tribes are essential. Such measures now exist, the principle being the Tenancy Act. But there are innumerable instances of how some of the provisions of this act too have failed in the desired effect. It is common knowledge how restrictions on transfer of holdings are circumvented by a surrender to the landlord and resettlement outside relationship, tribe and village. Cases are innumerable of instances of mortgagers kept out of possession, in spite of the law for years beyond the prescribed period. I do not pretend that in these cases there is no connivance of those who are sought to be protected. *But in the majority of the cases they arise out of the conflict between the economic interests of the non-aborigine and the aborigine,—the result of the acquisitive propensity of the former stimulated by the natural drawback of the aborigine character. But*

[123]No. 7342–A.R. Government of Bihar and Orissa, Appointment Department; From: R. E. Russell, Officiating Chief Secretary to Government; To: The Secretary to the Government of India, Reforms Office, dated Ranchi, 18 October 1935, in F. No. 4/I/35–G.(B), General (B) Branch, Reforms Office, Government of India, 1935.

> *for the special legislation regarding Khuntkatti and Korkar the aboriginal element would have long been wiped off the land.*[124]

Descriptions such as the one above brought the crucial issue of the displacement of aboriginals to the centre-stage of discourse. Several officers across British India raised similar concerns regarding this issue in the course of reporting on their respective districts or divisions.

The investigations also highlighted the unsuitability of modern legal codes in aboriginal areas, in opposition to their distinct customary laws. For instance, the officers reporting on Angul remarked,

> ... the district is still largely governed by local customs and recognized usages. These customs and usages are well understood by the people. Illiterate as they are, printed codes would not materially assist them, but would only tend to drive them into the hands of legal practitioners and touts. They probably have a better, and not worse, grasp of political laws which govern them than the equally illiterate people of some regulation areas have of *their* laws.... But the absence of codified law naturally gives to persons unacquainted with facts and local conditions the impression that the whole system is arbitrary, capricious and autocratic (though really, as we shall see, it is in many ways more democratic): and this impression might well lead to a spate of well intentioned but ill-designed legislation, if the district were placed under the control of Ministers responsible to a popular legislature.[125]

Some enquiry reports also indicated that many Backward Tracts or other aboriginal areas had evolved a distinct system of administration, aspects of which were designed to suit local conditions. For instance, the administrative system of Sambalpur had a 'special individuality' that rested on distinct systems of land tenure (which included the prohibition of land transfer outside the family) and village administration, the continuation of which, according to the District Officer, was a necessary 'condition of future advancement'. It was suggested that attempts, 'mischievous or well intentioned', to bring the district in line with the coastal tracts would

[124]Annexure D, No. 166–P.C., dated Purulia, 18 September 1935; From: S. N. Mozumdar, Deputy Commissioner Manbhum; To: The Chief Secretary to Government, Bihar and Orissa, Ranchi, in F. No. 4/I/35–G.(B), General (B) Branch, Reforms Office, Government of India, 1935, p. 3; emphasis mine.

[125]Report on the retention of Angul in the list of partially excluded areas in F. No. 4/I/35–G.(B), General (B) Branch, Reforms Office, Government of India, 1935, p. 7; emphasis in the original.

inevitably 'shake the foundations of those systems'. The District Officer forcefully argued that,

> ... the power of the Governor to frame regulations, based on the advice of experts and the opinion of the people concerned, is precisely what is wanted: and such a procedure will, one submits, be really far more in accordance with the principle of 'self-determination' than the enactments of Acts by the provincial assembly. Experience suggests that members of that body are not unlikely to rush forward with amateurish bills unsupported by a study of conditions: and it is much better that the Governor should frame regulations than that he should have to intervene to veto ill-considered Acts.[126]

Similarly, in the case of Angul, it was argued that the foundation of the system was not really autocratic. It rested

> upon the fact that in Angul the village communities have survived; and therefore many branches of administration, which could in coastal area be carried on only by public officials operating under codified laws and rules, can in Angul be conducted through Village Officials in accordance with customary usage.[127]

The village official (locally known as 'Sarbarkar') collected the rent of the village; was a police officer with duties of surveillance and powers of investigation; organised labour for the maintenance of village roads and tanks, etc.; and people could even approach him with their private grievances before taking recourse to the courts. Also, there were three notable features of the administrative system of Angul, in the form of *restrictions of lawyers, usury and transfer*.[128] *First*, the Angul Laws Regulation forbade the charging of compound rates of interest, restricted the simple interest charged on loans to 24 per cent per annum, and confined the total interest chargeable to the equivalent of the principal sum. *Second*, to prevent the people from being exploited by moneylenders and land-grabbers, the transfer and sale of lands without the permission of the Deputy Commissioner was prohibited.

---

[126] Annexure E, Report on the question of whether Sambalpur district should be 'partially excluded' under the new Constitution, in F. No. 4/I/35–G.(B), General (B) Branch, Reforms Office, Government of India, 1935.

[127] Report on the retention of Angul in the list of partially excluded areas in F. No. 4/I/35–G.(B), General (B) Branch, Reforms Office, Government of India, 1935, pp. 7–9. The next few paragraphs on Angul are based on this report.

[128] Emphasis in the original.

Last but not least, the Legal Practitioners Act was not in force, and hence the pleaders could appear before the courts only by permission.

The Report argued that in many respects, Angul was ahead of 'regulation districts'. Here, an attempt was underway to 'revive the community system, and by legal enactments (e.g., the Village Administration Act), propaganda and organization of rural welfare, to secure what Angul already possesses'. The reporting officer poetically invoked that,

> ... in the immediate present and probably for many years to come, changes—whether administrative or legislative—must be made with great caution and with a very full knowledge of the history and conditions of the district. It is not so much that the district is 'backward' as that it has an individuality of its own; and that its true needs can hardly be appreciated by a Legislative Assembly the great majority of whose members will have no acquaintance with it. It will not mean 'self-determination' for Angul if its affairs are to be decided by the votes of persons who have no knowledge of Angul.

Meanwhile, as the replies of provincial governments and their district officers poured into the Reforms Office, J. P. Mills, the Officer on Special Duty, was busy sifting through them. However, the India Office, in apprehension of the pro-exclusion views of Mills, clipped the wings of his enquiry somewhat when it directed the Government of India that,

> We had not understood ... that there was any intention to proceed on basis that Mills would produce an independent 'report' which would be forwarded by Government of India with their comments. While Secretary of State is anxious that Mills should be given every opportunity to work up case and make recommendations to Government of India, he would hesitate to agree to his recommendations being treated in any other way than those of any other member of Government of India Secretariat or being published among papers presented to parliament as a report by an independent expert. He would therefore request that Government of India frame their own Despatch as a self-contained document which, while naturally taking very fully into account Mills' views, will contain no reference to Mills himself as responsible for them.[129]

[129]Telegram No. 3811 from V. Dawson, India Office, to Mr W. H. Lewis, Additional Secretary, Reforms Office, dated 29 November 1935, in F. No. 4/I/35–G. (B), General (B) Branch, Reforms Office, Government of India, 1935, p. 12.

As far as the selection of areas for partial exclusion was concerned, the Government of India claimed to have kept prominently in mind the general distribution of aboriginal and primitive peoples through the uplands and forests of the Indian subcontinent, and to 'define them as closely as we can, and to select boundaries capable of being expressed in simple and easily intelligible terms'.[130] As seen in the previous section, the movers and supporters of the Cadogan Amendment in the House of Commons were mainly interested in increasing the number of partially excluded areas in Bombay, and Central Provinces. Both provinces featured quite centrally in the debate that took place at the Committee stage in the House of Commons. Ultimately, in the category of partially excluded areas, the proposals of the Cadogan Amendment enjoyed a greater measure of success as the eleven areas mentioned in the Sixth Schedule swelled to twenty-eight in the final Order-in-Council. Several new areas in the Bombay Presidency, and the Central Provinces and Berar featured in this expanded list. This was quite significant as no areas from these provinces had earlier been declared as 'Backward Tracts' under the 1919 reforms scheme. Despite having a substantial tribal population, the local governments in both Bombay and Central Provinces had steadfastly refused to recommend any of their areas for exclusion or partial exclusion. Owing to their sustained opposition, these provinces had not been featured in the Draft Sixth Schedule of the Government of India Bill, 1935. While conducting enquiries for his report, J. P. Mills, too, was baffled at the attitude of the provincial governments of Bombay, and Central Provinces and Berar, and remarked that both provinces involved 'very important and complicated' areas.[131]

In fact, the Government of India devoted a special segment of its recommendation report to the problem posed by aboriginal areas in Bombay, and Central Provinces and Berar.[132] The government stated that while in Assam, and Bihar and Orissa a large aboriginal population occupied well-defined, extensive areas with a long history of special protection, in

---

[130]Ibid., p. 2.

[131]Note by J. P. Mills, dated 23 November 1935, in F. No. 4/III/35–G(B) and K. W., General (B) Branch, Reforms Office, GoI, 1935, pp. 3–4.

[132]No. 1 of 1935, General (B) Branch, Reforms Office, Government of India; To: the Most Hon'ble the Marquess of Zetland, Secretary of State for India, New Delhi, 24 December 1935, in F. No. 4/I/35–G. (B), General (B) Branch, Reforms Office, Government of India, 1935, p. 15. The rest of the section is based on this source.

Madras and Bengal, the aboriginal population was predominant in only isolated areas and did not constitute a considerable proportion of the total population of the provinces. In all these provinces, the Government of India opined that the representation of aboriginal tribes in the local legislature would be relatively unimportant. However, in Bombay (excluding Sind) the aboriginal population was roughly 22,00,000 out of a total population of 18 million (that is, 12 per cent). Similarly, in C.P. and Berar, out of a population of 16 million, 3 million (or 19 per cent) were aboriginals. It was clear in both cases that the aboriginal representation in their respective local legislative councils would be less than their proportionate share in the total province. Consequently, on account of the large aboriginal population, the effective representation of aboriginals in the legislatures became 'cogent', and hence the problem assumed a new aspect.

The Government of India provided a brief assessment of the administrative disadvantages of treating selected areas under the special provisions of Section 91. If a large number of areas were selected for special treatment in the matter of legislation in a province, some challenges were bound to accrue; however, the government noted that these would not be 'insurmountable'. It observed, though, that the disadvantages accruing from a provision requiring the Governor to personally scrutinise the 'administrative proposals of general application to the province in order to satisfy himself of their effects upon a large number of great or small areas' could be significant.

The Government of India contended that these two lines of argument, that is, the degree of representation and the measure of administrative disadvantage, led to two conclusions. *First*, there was 'no justification for the partial exclusion of areas occupied by aboriginals in Bombay and the Central Provinces in such a sweeping manner and in such large blocks as to practically cover the whole of the aboriginal population'. Special protection under Section 91 could only be given to a portion of the aboriginal population. The government expressed hope that in practice, the partial exclusion of areas, coupled with a 'fair and possibly increasing representation of the whole aboriginal population in the local legislature', would afford protection to the aboriginals staying in other areas.

Second, the Government of India concluded that 'the administrative disadvantages attendant upon a multiplicity of partially excluded areas of differing local characteristics and necessities within a province' could make protection through scheduling ineffective. In such a mosaic landscape requiring meticulous and complex description, it would have been administratively impossible for the Governor to exercise individual judgement on tracts that were not immediately recognisable. Hence, the government saw that necessarily, a 'judicious selection of areas' involved choosing only such as could be defined 'in terms of easily intelligible boundaries'.

As far as the province of Bombay was concerned, the Government of India, in its final recommendations, echoed J. P. Mills and selected several aboriginal areas in Bombay for partial exclusion. It also rejected the suggestion of the Government of Bombay that 'protection of this limited kind would involve isolation or segregation or would ... cut off the Bhils from the sale of their produce or credit facilities'. The Government of India remarked that the broad effect of partial exclusion was 'simply to subject the normal legislative and executive jurisdiction of the province in selected areas to a degree of personal control by the Governor'. While recommending areas for partial exclusion in Bombay, the Government of India proposed special protection over a wide area in the western portions of the West Khandesh district, as it was the chief home of the Bhil tribes. They also recommended partial exclusion for areas in the East Khandesh, Nasik, Thana, and Panch Mahals districts.

At the end of this monumental enquiry, the Government of India accepted the recommendations of the Government of Assam, Bihar and Orissa, Madras, the United Provinces, the Punjab, and the North-West Frontier Province *verbatim* and without any changes. To the proposals for partial exclusion of the Government of Bengal, it added two parganas in the Mymensingh district for better protection of the Garos living on its northern boundary. In the case of the Government of Central Provinces and Berar, the Government of India only expanded two of the five areas recommended for special treatment. However, in the case of Bombay, it 'departed somewhat extensively from the limited recommendations of the local Government'.

Conclusion

The core of this chapter traced the evolutionary journey of special administrative regimes for predominantly tribal areas. In the long period of colonial rule, discursive practices underwent many shifts which are impossible to cover in the current work. Nevertheless, I have outlined the administrative transformation of 'spaces of exception' into 'regimes of protection'.

The rapid expansion of British power in eighteenth and nineteenth-century India inevitably brought its early military officials in contact with forest/hill-dwelling communities. In their written representations, these jungle spaces, situated away from the civilisation of settled plains and full of unknown dangers, were enframed using tropes of wilderness. As the Company Bahadur strengthened its territorial control, a need to establish authority over many such frontier landscapes became imperative in their strategic calculus. However, the chief challenge lay in co-opting the local inhabitants without incurring enormous expenditure on administration. In this context, Augustus Cleveland's innovative approach in the Rajmahal Hills (pensions to the Tappa and Hill Manjhis; creation of the Hill Archers' Corps; dispensation of justice through Hill Assemblies) laid the foundation of the idea of a territorial ring-fencing of areas predominantly inhabited by hill and forest dwellers. In essence, this formula underlined the need to provide local autonomy to these communities in the hilly and forested regions.

The chapter also highlights the emergence of a distinct 'internal frontier' in the South-West part of Bengal. British military strategists dubbed it as the South-West Frontier, beyond which lay the territories of the Maratha Confederacy that still held sway over large parts of the great Indian peninsula. To secure their military and strategic interests, the early Company rulers reinforced the buffer mentality which legitimised the logic of maintaining the status quo in the internal frontier. However, even after the Maratha challenge had weakened considerably, there was a renewed push to control these forested landscapes. This offensive faced a severe backlash and following a number of local revolts, the Company rulers were forced to step back and allow the development of a new administrative framework in contra-distinction to the established principles of a standardised regime undergirded by the rule of law. Thus, the 1830s and 1840s witnessed the emergence of 'de-regulation' areas that placed certain territories outside the statutes and enactments in force elsewhere. Through Wilkinson's Rules (1833), for instance, pleaders were banned and severe checks were placed on the commodification of land, which was being vigorously pushed in other parts of the Empire. The emergence of the South-West Frontier Agency perhaps marks the birth of the first extensive non-regulation area within the Company's Indian Empire. Simultaneously, the 'civilising mission' to establish *Pax Britannica* took the form of campaigns to control and eliminate savage and barbaric practices like human sacrifice. In this phase, 'Agency' administration (under an Agent who bypassed the appellate jurisdiction of higher bureaucratic and judicial personnel) in the internal frontier came to acquire new meanings and was constituted over fairly large areas. Consequently, the word 'Agency' in the vocabulary of colonial statecraft also came to be applied to territories outside the ambit of legality.[133] Interestingly, a number of them subsequently evolved into distinctive categories of special administrative regimes, designed to 'protect' tribal communities in central and eastern India during the late colonial period.

This chapter has argued against the widely held, yet erroneous impression that the Scheduled Districts Act 1874 was a law that brought together into a single schedule most tribal/aboriginal areas in British India. Perhaps this myth stems from a later impression that all Scheduled Districts were wholly or partially deregulationised on account of the largely aboriginal character of their respective populations. On the contrary, I have demonstrated that the said enactment, along with the Laws Local Extent Act, 1874, constituted a legislative solution devised by the colonial executive. As the original term 'Excepted Districts' (used in earlier versions of legislative discussions) implied, the intention behind these twin enactments was to keep certain areas outside the potential powers of judicial review by the High Courts introduced as a result of the post-1858 administrative reorganisation. Earlier, the division of powers between the legislative, executive, and the judiciary was at best nominal and seldom substantive.[134] The virtual absence of this principle in the actual practice of governance was especially pronounced in large parts of the Empire (for example, in Sindh, Assam, and Punjab) acquired after the Maratha challenge was finally brought under control. Even the chief Presidencies of Bengal, Madras, and Bombay had several areas whose rulers had acknowledged the Company Bahadur's suzerainty in the last three decades of its rule. Taking the case of zamindaris in the Central Provinces, I have outlined the fiscal and legal considerations that qualified these zones as 'Excepted Districts'. Hence, in effect, these areas were 'spaces of exception' in the colonial legal framework,

[133]This is an understudied area and has immense research potential, with most records readily available in the National Archives of India.

[134]For an exception, see Rahul Govind, 'The King's Plunder, the King's Justice: Sovereignty in British India, 1756–1776', *Studies in History* 33 (2), 2017, pp. 151–186.

where normal laws and regulations applicable elsewhere in the British Indian territories were not enforced for a variety of reasons. In the earlier stages of empire-building in India, the terms that came to denote their exceptional status in the colonial legal and administrative paradigm were 'deregulation' and 'outlawed' areas. However, after the passage of power to the British Crown in the aftermath of the Great Mutiny of 1857, the desire to collate all such areas into a single 'schedule' (under the Scheduled Districts Act, 1874) created the false impression that this moment marks the beginning of the idea of scheduling.

The rest of the chapter analysed the administrative and constitutional deliberations from 1918–1935. In much of this phase, the tribal question occupied, at best, a marginal space in the overall picture. It was repeatedly not discussed in the Round Table Conferences as most Indian politicians were preoccupied with other pressing concerns such as the future of Muslims and the Depressed Classes. The nature of discourse in this period was purely administrative and stemmed from the anxiety that the 'official block' of sympathetic Europeans was set to wither away. The ICS members rued the possible consequences of leaving all aspects of aboriginal administration in the hands of representative Indian politicians, and, most often, trained lawyers with little understanding of their way of life. The results could be disastrous, for the aboriginals were uneducated, lacked an English-speaking middle-class elite, and hence could not give voice to their interests. These deficits, in tandem with their characteristic silence, invisiblised tribal concerns in the constitutional deliberations. The official block thus argued that aboriginal tribes were politically unfit for representative electoral democracy. Hence, the best alternative was to territorially separate the predominantly tribal areas from the areas of reformed administration under the new Constitution.

A few yardsticks determining the areas to be scheduled as excluded or partially excluded were tough geographic features, agricultural backwardness, low density of population with a high proportion of aboriginals (making them 'self-contained' or 'homogeneous'), low literacy levels, and their respective position in the legal cartography of British India (whether deregulationised or not). At a later stage of the discourse, it also mattered whether some form of representation was extended to them in the Government of India Act, 1919. Serious discussions were conducted on the permanently 'deficit' nature of their respective economies, to subvent which the Indian Statutory Commission recommended a completely centralised system of administration for all the Backward Tracts. In the early 1930s, several parallels were drawn with African examples of indirect rule, which suggests that an intra-Empire flow of ideas had shaped the reconstitution of the discourse on aboriginal tribes. Participants in the discussions also referred constantly to a fear of tribal rebellion if too rapid an influx of outsiders was allowed in these regions. Many of these ideas made a significant appearance in the House of Commons debates in relation to the Government of India Act, 1935. As the protection of backward people was the responsibility of the British Parliament, it reached a feverish pitch at the Committee stage reading of the draft Sixth Schedule in May 1935, when Cadogan pressed his list of twenty excluded and thirty-one partially excluded areas. After detailed arguments and counter-arguments, the Government of India agreed to subject the final decision on scheduling to an enquiry, to be conducted by local officers throughout British India, at the end of which there was a sudden boom in the number of areas scheduled for special administrative treatment.

The late colonial debate on scheduling stemmed from a deep anxiety caused by a rapid Indianisation of the higher civil services. Moreover, it was also foreseeable that the sympathetic European 'official block' would wither away and be replaced by the class of Indian lawyer-politicians acting as civilian ministers in the reformed government. This new representative politician had little common interest with the aboriginal people, who would be placed at their mercy. Since the aboriginals were, so to speak, silent and lacked an ability to voice their interests, the suitability of elections as a means to send their representatives to the legislative bodies of the reformed Constitution of India was extremely doubtful. The colonial bureaucracy had a long tradition of confidence in the ability of the 'man on the spot', in whom executive and judicial powers were concentrated. The official block sought to maintain these, with no checks and balances by the elected assemblies and councils.

In the British Parliamentary debate, the centrality of the demographic character of the area to be scheduled emerged very clearly. As the supreme sovereign authority in the British Empire, the Parliament's voice and decisions mattered above every other institution. At the time of the debate in the House of Commons, many serving Parliamentarians had personally been involved in devising the new constitutional framework for India. In these deliberations, Census figures played a prominent role. The guiding principle seems to be that areas with a 'homogeneous' population of aboriginals were to be classed as excluded areas. Other parts of India, primarily Bombay and Central Provinces, where aboriginal people existed as 'self-contained' pockets surrounded by other groups (of primarily Hindu agriculturists), were to be selected for partial exclusion. The underlying logic was to identify and ring the territory so that the majority character of an area's population could be maintained. Within this ring-fence, land could not pass to non-aboriginals, disputes would be settled through custom rather than codes, and modern electoral democracy would be debarred. The logic was buttressed by Hoare's comment that even future de-scheduling would be shaped by the movements and migrations of people, which in time was bound to change the demographic character of an excluded or partially excluded area. However, in any case the final arbiter of the fate of Indian aboriginals was the British Parliament, and not the representative politician of the Congress. Such appropriation by Englishmen, including statements by the likes of Churchill and the territorial ring-fencing of vast areas outside the reformed Constitution, led the administrative discourse to spill over into the political domain. This process will be analysed in a later chapter.

Lastly, by the late nineteenth century, the legitimacy of Anthropology as a discipline that could inform and provide guiding principles for the sympathetic treatment of aboriginal people had begun to take shape in metropolitan Britain. It was presented as a 'reformer's science' by early pioneers such as Sir Edward Burnett Tylor. These new epistemological currents had been reshaping the administrative discourse in India. Increasingly, a new breed of administrators influenced by such anthropological theories had come to helm constitutional discussions pertaining to the future policy vis-à-vis aboriginal tribes. Foremost among them were Hutton and Mills, both of whom spent the bulk of their respective ICS careers as administrators of the Naga Hills in the frontier province of Assam. Hutton, in particular, owing to his role as the 1931 Census Commissioner, played a pivotal role in the discourse on Indian tribal populations in this period till 1935. It is towards this fascinating intellectual and constitutional history that we shall now turn our attention.

2 

Anthropology and Administration

J. H. Hutton and the Formulation of the Tribal Question

This chapter will reconstruct how a set of ideas dominant in the British anthropological discourse around the Great War came to exert a shaping influence on the constitutional debates on the scheduling of predominantly tribal areas in India. While this discourse was vitally framed by a select group of anthropologically-oriented administrators hailing mainly from the Indian Civil Service, they were essentially adapting and purveying ideas developed in the Melanesian Islands located in the Pacific Ocean. Drawing upon such ideas from the 1920s, a number of them, viz., J. H. Hutton, J. P. Mills, W. G. Archer, and W. V. Grigson, published ethnographic works at regular intervals and gained a reputation in the British metropolitan academic circles. As anthropological experts of the Neo-Diffusionist persuasion, they advocated that certain principles should inform the official government policy for the protection of tribal communities in India. In the late 1930s, the group expanded a little with the inclusion of non-official (but still White European) figures like Verrier Elwin and Christoph von Furer-Haimendorf, who shared ideological affinities with the ICS cohort. Taken together, there is a remarkable unity in the ideas of this 'knot of men',[1] whose writings and activities played a crucial role in the discourse as well as the politics of scheduling.

As is clear from Chapter 1, these individuals were not the founding fathers of the rather long tradition of Europeans 'sympathetic' towards Indian aboriginal tribes. However, their arguments certainly built upon the legacy of similarly predisposed colonial administrators. In the relief of the

[1] I have borrowed this phrase from Eric Stokes, *The English Utilitarians and India*, New Delhi: Oxford University Press, 1982 [1959], p. 9.

ongoing constitutional deliberations, the aforementioned group certainly sharpened the arguments of their predecessors by grounding the policy of protection in the ideas then fashionable in British anthropological circles. Crucially, such a theoretical padding also provided an epistemological veneer to the understanding of Indian aboriginal tribes, which helped to amplify concerns about saving them from the forces of civilisation, democracy, and modern law. Given that the period of efflorescence for this bunch of scholar-administrators was also the twilight of the British Empire in India, these contributions were extremely significant. Without a thorough analysis of these figures, both individually and in relation to each other, it is impossible to theorise the bridge that connects the late colonial to the period after Indian independence as far as the discourse on the tribal population is concerned.

In the absence of an educated tribal middle-class elite capable of articulating its interests to the colonial rulers in the English language, the scholar-administrators sought to provide them with a voice in the constitutional deliberations. In essence, the knot of men, by speaking on behalf of the Indian tribes, was attempting to prolong the centralised and paternalistic 'man on the spot' model of administration in predominantly tribal areas that had been followed through much of colonial rule. However, in an era of increasing nationalist demands for representative democratic institutions, this was a rather tall order. These policymakers demanded a territorial solution to the tribal question by segregating predominantly tribal tracts as excluded and partially excluded areas. By such territorial ring-fencing, the knot of men tried to carve out enclaves (or islands) where they and others of similar persuasion could regulate the 'culture-contact' with civilised Indians. Their main argumentative plank stemmed from the overall numerical inferiority of tribals in the Indian population, which predisposed addressing of their concerns, both economic and cultural, by future legislative bodies. The inability of aboriginals to use the power of the vote to their advantage was a further disability that exaggerated these concerns. Consequently, scheduling gained legitimacy as an instrument of protective state policy, which would enable tribal majority areas to maintain a demographic status quo and save individual tribes from potential cultural genocide.

In its essence, this chapter attempts to retrace the intellectual trajectories of the late-colonial discourse on the constitutional protection to be provided for the tribal population in British India.

Evolutionism vs. Diffusionism: British Anthropology and the Ideas of W. H. R. Rivers

A synoptic overview of the incipient discipline of anthropology in metropolitan Britain is essential to understand the intellectual discourse that has had a lasting impact on the future of Indian tribal populations. The word 'anthropology' or the study of man had come into existence in the English language by the early nineteenth century.[2] Before this neologism emerged, the wider field of human cultural enquiry itself was highly amorphous and fluid. The journey towards the formation of a distinctive discipline was predicated on the increasing contact of Europeans with the natives of the New World, Africa, Asia, and Australasia through trade, commerce, and forms of colonisation. As the early modern colonies grew in number and size, businessmen, professionals, military personnel, and missionaries from Western Europe found greater avenues to work in different regions of the world. Aside from their duties, the steady streams of new migrants were also introduced to exotic landscapes, people, and the flora and fauna of non-European cultures. Slowly, buoyed by their experiences and explorations in unknown parts of the world, many amongst them decided to record their impressions. Convinced of the civilisational supremacy of Europe, this new gaze upon the rest of the world provided important inputs into the ongoing attempts at providing a rational, 'scientific' explanation of naturally occurring phenomena.

With a burgeoning publishing industry, this body of amateurish (written and artistic) contribution to Europe's rapidly expanding horizons found a large audience in Great Britain. A degree of antiquarian interest in objects and textual materials from the non-West had long been in existence. However, the steady inflow of fresh eyewitness accounts of different geographical regions into the metropolitan centre provided an impetus to generate a certain synthesis of knowledge about them.

A growing humanitarian-cum-evangelical concern for the variety of human cultures vanishing off the face of the earth due to ever-deeper European penetration also inspired some gentlemanly scholars to engage

[2]Henrika Kuklick, *The Savage Within: The Social History of British Anthropology, 1885–1945*, New York and Cambridge: Cambridge University Press, 1991, p. 6. Kuklick traced the very first mention of the word 'anthropology' to an 1805 issue of *Edinburgh Review*, a journal for the cultivated upper-middle class.

in comparative studies of religion, customs, and philosophy. In later years, a heavy dose of racism also followed, which profoundly affected anthropology by legitimising the differences between the West and the non-West. This was the heyday of armchair scholarship which collected and collated a variety of data and information without ever venturing into the 'field'. Thus, the emergence of anthropology followed the post-Enlightenment intellectual, religious, and philosophical ferment and was part of the wider swell of modern social sciences. Broadly categorised under 'Natural History', it was slowly recognised as a distinct branch of knowledge about the non-industrialised world. Nevertheless, nineteenth-century positivistic claims about its impartiality and 'scientific' nature have to be taken with a heavy dose of salt. At the least, the hierarchy within anthropology between the civilised West and the savage non-West has been implicitly accepted amongst its amateur and professional practitioners through a large part of its mytho-history.

Within the emerging anthropological domain, there were two main lines of causative explanation of human diversity across the world: evolutionism and diffusionism. Classical evolutionism was founded on the idea of a 'psychic unity' or psychology common to all of humankind. This intellectual trend interpreted cultural similarities in different parts of the world as the product of 'independent origin and development'. They offered a polygenist (that is, multiple origin) view of races in largely static physical terms. For them, every race was aboriginally adapted to distinct climatic conditions, which accounted for their differences with other racial stocks.

Standing in contrast to evolutionists were the diffusionists. Until the eighteenth century, the Biblical tradition of mapping world historical change exerted a heavy influence in Western speculative attempts to explain the bewildering variety of human cultural forms. In this monogenist (or single origin) paradigm, Noah's three sons, Shem, Ham, and Japeth, were seen as the progenitors of all of humanity, whose descendants repopulated the earth after surviving the Great Deluge. It was this set of ideas inspired by Biblical diffusionism that paved the way for the emergence of ethnology or the science of races. The monogenist ethnologist argued that all existing races were the 'historical products of movements through differing environments'. They established physical, cultural, and linguistic connections in order to trace the relationships of present human groups back through time and space to a single original source.

According to George W. Stocking, Jr., diffusionism was 'one of the ur-forms of anthropological speculation in the western European intellectual tradition'. He adds, '(I)f evolutionism can be traced to early Greek speculations, "Diffusionism" is as old as the Old Testament.' Taken together, evolutionism and diffusionism were 'the two major traditional paradigmatic alternatives structuring speculation about human differences which were characteristically seen as products of change in time'.[3]

The 1850s and 1860s witnessed great theoretical changes that shook the foundations of Mosaic ethnology. In pre-historic archaeology, the discovery of Swiss lake dwellings and the bones of Neanderthals had led to a rethinking of Biblical time-scales. The most conclusive moment was when human artefacts were found *in situ* with extinct animals at the Brixham Caves. Gradually, a range of irrefutable evidence piled up. Finally, Charles Darwin's book, *On the Origin of Species* (1859), greatly altered the Biblical notion of human history and gradually delegitimised the diffusionary explanation of ethno-linguistic differences resting on the myth of the Tower of Babel.

Nevertheless, for about three decades, evolutionism and diffusionism had a parallel co-existence. Then, in 1871, the monogenists and the polygenists buried their hatchets and decided to amalgamate their respective associations under the common banner of the Anthropological Institute. It became an umbrella organisation where practitioners of all persuasions engaged with anthropological research being conducted across the British Empire. With the establishment of the Anthropological Institute, the ideas of Biblical diffusionism were finally discredited and classical evolutionism emerged triumphant. However, despite the delinking of religious explanations from historical understandings of the human world, the hold of the racial explanation for human diversity and personality traits in specialist discourse persisted for several decades. Only after World War I did anthropologists become insistent that race did not determine culture. Nonetheless, an important result of this intellectual struggle was that classical evolutionism was established as a widely accepted anthropological paradigm, albeit briefly. At the turn of the nineteenth and early twentieth century, however, the Neo-Diffusionists reclaimed the leadership of the anthropological domain and became highly influential around World War I.

[3]George W. Stocking, Jr., *After Tylor: British Social Anthropology, 1888–1951*, Madison: University of Wisconsin Press, 1995.

To sum up this process of intellectual history in Stocking's famous argument, the master image of branching trees was replaced by a staircase model of incremental civilisational fulfillment, where Western Europe stood at the apex and 'primitive' savage societies at the bottom. This staircase was strictly evolutionary and viewed savage societies as the remnants of humanity's past. A discourse centred on diffusionary migration and tracing the original Biblical tribes (mosaic ethnology) slowly took up the language of science. Thus, nineteenth-century ethnology established the legitimacy of race as a concept and used it to divide humanity in a rigid hierarchy. This paradigm was teleological, and the Anglo-Saxon race achieved the hallmark of civilisation.[4]

One abiding assumption that proponents of both evolutionism and diffusionism shared was that human behaviour could only be explained historically. Their methodology was diachronic and, according to Kuklick, both schools 'expected their research to yield laws of historical change'. While the evolutionists emphasised 'steady and gradual development', the diffusionists' scheme eulogised 'an episodic past—periods of stasis intermittently punctuated by moments of drastic change'.

The turn of the twentieth century in British anthropology saw the rise to prominence of the Neo-Diffusionist school of thought. Approximately three decades after monogenist explanations by diffusionists had yielded intellectual ground to the polygenist evolutionists, leading, quite literally, to the former's eclipse, the phoenix rose up again!

Interestingly, the new adherents of diffusionism brought back the earlier monogenist paradigm, albeit with a twist in their tale. This time, the source of all 'civilisation' was different. Their inspiration rested not on the Holy Bible and/or Noah's Ark, but rather on Egyptian hieroglyphs and the pyramids of Giza. The new school of speculative anthropological thought traced the global spread of civilisational values and technologies to ancient Egypt. The early Egyptians, worshippers of the Sun, were the fountainhead of all civilisational values. They spread the 'heliolithic culture' across the earth via long sea voyages. The key notion of the Neo-Diffusionist enterprise was 'culture contact'. Whenever a higher culture came in contact with a lower one, a certain amount of transference or diffusion took place, and this explained the spread of civilisation. Important scholarly figures

[4]George W. Stocking Jr., *Victorian Anthropology*, New York: The Free Press, 1987.

of this resurgent school were W. H. R. Rivers, W. J. Perry, and Grafton Elliot Smith.

A near contemporary work by R. H. Lowie summarised the basic ideas of the Neo-Diffusionists as follows:

1. Man is uninventive; hence cultures arise only in exceptionally favourable circumstances, and almost never twice independently.
2. Such circumstances existed only in Egypt; hence elsewhere, culture (except some of its simplest elements) must have spread from Egypt with the rise of navigation.
3. Civilisation is naturally diluted as it spreads to the outposts; hence decadence has played a tremendous role in human history.[5]

Thus, the Neo-Diffusionist theoretical framework was premised on a distinctive core *versus* periphery model of understanding. The superior culture of Egypt spread out from a civilisational core situated along the River Nile. Gradually, its sphere of influence increased once it came in contact with lower cultures. Thus, technological innovations as well as theological belief systems were transferred in this process of 'cultural contact'.

Convinced of the validity of their explanatory framework, the Neo-Diffusionists had much to say about India as well. For instance, Perry's famous book, *The Children of the Sun*,[6] supposedly provided evidence that the carriers of Egyptian culture frequented Indian shores from about 2600 BCE. Similarly, Smith published another Neo-Diffusionist classic, *The Migrations of Early Culture*,[7] which stated his belief that

> sea-farers from the West from the Third millennium and especially in the period about 800 BC carrying heliolithic culture, mainly evolved in Egypt, far and wide along the coast of the Old world and the New, mingled their blood with the aboriginal pre-Dravidian population and the result was the 'Dravidians'.[8]

---

[5] R. H. Lowie, *The History of Ethnological Theory*, New York: Rinehart and Company, 1937, p. 161.

[6] W. J. Perry, *The Children of the Sun: A Study in the Early History of Civilisation*, London, Methuen and Co. Ltd., 1923.

[7] Grafton Elliot Smith, *The Migrations of Early Culture*, Manchester: Manchester University Press, 1929 [1915].

[8] Quoted in W. H. Shoobert, *Census of India, 1931, Volume XII, Central Provinces & Berar, Part I—Report*, Government Printing, C. P., Nagpur, 1933, p. 346.

Nevertheless, amongst the Neo-Diffusionists, neither Perry nor Smith rose to such prominence as W. H. R. Rivers, who also engaged substantively with these ideas only in the last decade or so of his career. After an early training in medicine, Rivers came under the influence of neurologist John Hughlings Jackson, and went on to study experimental psychology in Germany. After his return, Rivers joined the University of Cambridge and introduced the first ever course on experimental psychology in Britain. Between April 1903 and December 1907, Rivers conducted a series of celebrated experiments on his collaborator, Henry Head. A surgeon had severed the nerves in Head's left forearm, and Rivers took thousands of precision readings on the gradual recovery of 'epicritic' feeling in the affected part.[9] The findings were published in a leading neurological journal and quickly established his reputation.[10] Subsequently, it earned him the prestigious title of F.R.S. and the award of a Royal Society Gold medal in 1915. It is because of this legacy that today, Rivers is primarily remembered as one of the fathers of experimental psychology in Britain. However, Rivers was essentially a polymath whose eclectic and unorthodox imagination pushed him towards ethnology from the end of the nineteenth century. His contributions to the field were made in an important period of both domestic and global turmoil in the British Empire. As such, they deserve keen assessment by historians and anthropologists.

According to Stocking, Rivers came to ethnology from experimental psychology, 'one of the more methodologically explicit areas of the human sciences—Rivers brought with him a high degree of self-consciousness about problems of method; but also possessed an uninhibited (Mauss said "intrepid") explanatory imagination (1923), and was quite capable of pursuing a pet hypothesis well beyond the limits to which rigorous method

---

[9]Pursuing an evolutionary explanation for instinctive behaviour, Rivers proposed that all instincts are derived from the 'protopathic' sensations. Rivers and Head equated the more highly evolved nervous system with 'epicritic' and the more primitive one with the 'protopathic'. See Stocking, Jr., *After Tylor*; also see Tim Bayliss-Smith, 'Colonialism as Shell-Shock: W.H.R. Rivers' Explanations for Depopulation in Melanesia', in Edvard Hviding and Cato Berg (eds), *The Ethnographic Experiment: Rivers and Hocart in Island Melanesia, 1908*, New York and Oxford: Berhahn, 2014, pp. 179–213.

[10]W. H. R. Rivers and H. Head, 'A Human Experiment in Nerve Division', *Brain* 31, 1908, pp. 323–450.

Image 1: Professor William Halse Rivers Rivers

Copyright: Copyright © Royal Anthropological Institute, London. Reproduced with the kind permission of the RAI, 400_037010.

could carry him'.[11] He went on to work in physiology, psychology, psychiatry, sociology, folklore, and social anthropology. In the decade of the Great War, he also became the leading proponent of Freudian ideas in Britain. His intellectual evolution and contribution to the history of anthropology in India has so far not received adequate appraisal. However, as will be evident in this chapter and the book at large, the legacy of his ideas (largely posthumous) had an immense bearing on the fate of the millions of people classified as aboriginal tribes in the Indian subcontinent. I would argue that Rivers' ideas constitute, without any exaggeration, the edifice upon which the policy of 'Protection' advocated by the ICS knot of men was based.

[11] George W. Stocking, Jr., "The Ethnographer's Magic: Fieldwork in British Anthropology from Tylor to Malinowski', in George W. Stocking, Jr. (ed.), *Observers Observed: Essays on Ethnographic Fieldwork*, History of Anthropology Vol. 1, Madison: The University of Wisconsin Press, 1983, p. 85.

In 1898, Rivers hesitantly accompanied a group of evolutionary natural scientists from Cambridge University, led by A. C. Haddon, on an expedition to Torres Strait. Perhaps one of the most significant aspects of this mission was the introduction of trained experimental psychologists into the fledgling anthropological domain. Being a field naturalist, Haddon was aware of his own limitations and the need for technical elaboration in gauging 'the mental and sensory capacities of primitive peoples'. Rivers fitted the requirements perfectly and proved his selection correct by devising the 'genealogical method'.[12] Indeed, Rivers' device proved to be a methodological milestone in kinship studies.[13] The 'vital statistic' that was generated as a result of Rivers' pioneering approach also greatly enabled the discipline of historical demography. The psychologist in him had begun thinking about population changes in island ecologies. This was a key line of enquiry which culminated in a remarkable argument, taken up by anthropologically-minded administrators in the Indian context.

In 1901–1902, Rivers developed a strong India connection during a five-month stint of fieldwork amongst the Todas, a primitive tribe of the Nilgiri Hills, which was published as the eponymously titled book, *The Todas*.[14] In both the Torres Strait and the Nilgiri Hills, Rivers came across the phenomenon of population decline. In 1908, he proceeded to Melanesia and conducted extensive fieldwork in the islands of Simbo and Vella Lavella. Here, too, the 'genealogical method' was employed to collect data of the population change as well as gather insights into the prevalent social organisation. Its results were published in his widely acclaimed two-volume work, *The History of Melanesian Society*.[15] However, there was no mention of demographic changes in this work, and the links between psychology and demography were to clearly emerge only in Rivers's Fitz Patrick Lectures.[16]

---

[12]W. H. R. Rivers, 'A Genealogical Method of Collecting Social and Vital Statistics', *Journal of the Royal Anthropological Institute* 2, pp. 80–81.

[13]I. Langham, *The Building of British Social Anthropology: W.H.R. Rivers and his Cambridge Disciples in the Development of Kinship Studies, 1898–1931*, Dordrecht: D. Reidel Publishing Company, 1981.

[14]W. H. R. Rivers, *The Todas*, London: Macmillan, 1906.

[15]W. H. R. Rivers, *The History of Melanesian Society*, 2 vols, Cambridge, UK: Cambridge University Press, 1914.

[16]Posthumously published by Rivers's literary executor, G. E. Smith, as W. H. R. Rivers, *Medicine, Magic, and Religion*, London: Kegan Paul, Trench, Trubner & Co., 1924.

An important development after Rivers' return from Melanesia was his increasingly palpable tilt towards theories of the unconscious, dreams, and Freudian psychoanalysis. Until Rivers' own endorsement, the bulk of British academia displayed a strong resistance to the Freudian explanation of human psychology. Eventually, however, Rivers became the leading advocate of neo-Freudian theories of psychology and played a role in their acceptance within British academic circles. This influence was fundamentally linked to the outbreak of the Great War and Rivers' own involvement in it.

From 1915–1919, Rivers joined the Royal Army Medical Corps and served as an army psychotherapist. Here, he was 'treating soldiers and airmen for neuroses that came under the popular heading of "shell-shock"'.[17] This experience of four years of clinical practice amongst the survivors of the Great War's mass slaughter formed the kernel of Rivers's theoretical work after the war ended. In contemporary parlance, this was the Post-Traumatic Stress Disorder (PTSD) which, according to Bayliss-Smith, qualified Rivers 'to mount a formidable critique of Freudian emphasis on repressed sexuality as the key to psychic disturbance, and to suggest instead a more comprehensive understanding of psycho-neurosis'. At the height of success and confidence, Rivers started amalgamating the various strands in his thinking as an experimental psychologist, self-taught ethnologist/anthropologist, and most recently, a neo-Freudian theorist. He decided to revisit the data from Melanesia in the light of his new-found interest in colonialism and cultural diffusion, and published at least six papers on the subject. Essentially, Rivers was seeking to now understand and theorise on the 'psychological basis for population change in Melanesia'.[18]

According to Bayliss-Smith, in this late phase of Rivers' career, he propounded the theory of 'Colonialism as Shell Shock'. For the people in the island ecologies of Melanesia, the multiple impacts of colonial 'contact', after long centuries of isolation, had been extremely traumatic. In a comparatively short time span, the administrators, missionaries, and traders from European colonial powers had unleashed enforced pacification, labour-trade, and a highly interventionist set of policies. This large-scale 'disturbance' adversely affected the psychic equilibrium of the Melanesians, thereby hampering the ability of the native population to replenish and sustain a stable level of population. More than a high death rate, it was low fertility that was failing to replace the worn-out and aged populace of the islands. Rivers invoked

[17]Tim Bayliss-Smith, 'Colonialism as Shell-Shock', pp. 179–213.

[18]Ibid.

'psycho-neurosis' as having a severe impact on the parental instincts of the Solomon Islanders. The Islanders had succumbed to hysteria/neurasthenia or, to use Rivers' preferred term, 'anxiety-neurosis'. They were victims of 'shell-shock' caused by colonialism. In a yet unpublished piece, Bayliss-Smith opines that in taking this line, Rivers was following

> more popular writers like Robert Louis Stevenson in regarding the cultural impacts of colonialism in the Pacific as leading to fatalism, despair and the loss of will to live. Invoking 'suggestion' as the way in which such feelings could affect whole societies, he saw population decline as the inevitable consequence.[19]

With some variations, this was the core idea that an entire generation of administrators 'sympathetic' towards Indian aboriginal tribes subscribed to. Although neither the term 'shell-shock' nor (obviously) 'colonialism' was used in the explanatory framework designed for India, the territorial ring-fencing of tribal majority areas against forces of civilisation became the standard argument for protecting tribal communities. Nevertheless, what did come to exert a tremendous influence on the minds of frontier administrators like J. H. Hutton and J. P. Mills appeared in a book edited by Rivers, titled *Essays on the Depopulation of Melanesia*.[20] In this collection, members of the Melanesian Mission run by Rivers contributed their analysis of the decline in population of several Pacific Islands after their isolation was broken by European contact. The last article in the book was titled 'The Psychological Factor' and was penned by Rivers himself. Here, he argued that the 'discouragement and destruction of native institutions' was the chief cause of the depopulation of primitive communities in the Melanesian Islands. Rivers wrote,

> The point I wish to emphasize is that through this unintelligent and undiscriminating action towards native institutions, the people are

[19]Tim Bayliss-Smith, 'Population Decline in Island Melanesia: Aphrodisian Cultural Practices, sexually Transmitted Infections and Low Fertility'. Paper presented at a conference on 'Sex, Disease and Fertility in History', University of Cambridge, September 2015, p. 13. Available at https://www.researchgate.net/profile/Tim_Bayliss-Smith/publication/308952902_Population_decline_in_Island_Melanesia_Aphrodisian_cultural_practices_sexually_transmitted_infections_and_low_fertility/links/57ff489808aeaf819a5d3e82.pdf (accessed June 2024).

[20]W. H. R. Rivers (ed.), *Essays on the Depopulation of Melanesia*, with a Preface by Sir Everard im Thurn, Cambridge, UK: Cambridge University Press, 1922.

> deprived of all that gives interest to their lives. I have now to suggest that this loss of interest forms one of the reasons, if it be not the most potent of all the reasons, to which the native decadence is due.... It is the loss of interest in life underlying the more obvious causes which gives them their potency for evil, and allows them to work such ravages upon life and health.[21]

In Melanesia, the increase in the death rate coupled with a decline in the birth rate produced the phenomenon of depopulation. The former was assisted by a 'loss of interest in life' because the native, 'when ill loses heart at once, shows little resistance to disease, and soon succumbs', while the latter occurs 'even when the causes to which depopulation is usually ascribed are absent'.[22] This argument about the 'loss of interest in life' would become the core belief of the knot of administrators in India. Later, Elwin took a cue from this and coined his famous phrase, 'loss of nerve'.

From Melanesia to Naga Hills and Beyond: J. H. Hutton and the Paradigm of Territorial Segregation

For a critical understanding of the late colonial debate on the appropriate administrative arrangements for tribal populations in India, it is necessary to evaluate the ideas of John Henry Hutton.[23] Hutton became the leading ideologue of the British policy of territorial segregation of areas predominantly inhabited by tribal communities, whose policy interventions led to the passage of the Order-in-Council of March 1936 that declared large parts of British India as either excluded or partially excluded areas under the Government of India Act, 1935.

Born in England in 1885, Hutton took his B.A. degree from Worcester College, Oxford in 1908. In 1909, he entered the Indian Civil Service as an Assistant Magistrate and Collector in the Eastern Bengal and Assam cadre. Initially, Hutton was posted at Dacca, Khasi and Jaintia Hills, Mymensingh,

---

[21]W. H. R. Rivers, 'The Psychological Factor', in W. H. R. Rivers (ed.), *Essays on the Depopulation of Melanesia*, pp. 84–113. Also quoted in E. A. P. Review Essay on 'Essays on the Depopulation of Melanesia by W.H.R. Rivers', *The Geographical Journal* 62 (2), August 1923, p. 147.

[22]Ibid.

[23]The lion's share of the chapter is dedicated to the study of Hutton's ideas and policy interventions on the Indian 'Tribal Question'.

Image 2: Dr John Henry Hutton

Courtesy: B. Mukerji and P. K. Bose (eds.) *Indian Science Congress Association (with Life-Sketches of General Presidents), 1914–1963*, Calcutta: Indian Science Congress Association, 1963.

and Bakarganj. In 1912, he was made Assistant Commissioner and sent to the Naga Hills. Hutton was promoted to Deputy Commissioner in 1920 and continued to serve with distinction in the Naga Hills. In 1929, he was made the All-India Census Commissioner for the 1931 Census operations.[24] Thus, barring the final phase of four years (1929–1933) as Census Commissioner, Hutton was based in Assam for the bulk of his service.

Hutton came to Assam at a very interesting anthropological moment. In his Presidential Address to the Anthropology Section of the Eighth Indian Science Congress 1921, S. C. Roy remarked about this intensely prolific

[24]The biographical information in this paragraph and elsewhere has been mainly taken from B. Mukerji and P. K. Bose (eds), *Indian Science Congress Association (with Life-Sketches of General Presidents), 1914–1963*, Calcutta: Indian Science Congress Association, January 1963, pp. 64–65.

phase of anthropological research in Assam. In 1903, the Government of India sanctioned a scheme for the preparation of a series of monographs on the tribes and castes of Assam. This was first proposed by Assam's Chief Commissioner, Sir Bampfylde Fuller, who laid down a detailed scheme for monographs dealing with the habitat, economic and domestic life, tribal and social organisation, laws and institutions, religion and folklore, language, racial affinities, and traditions of the selected communities. Under Major Gurdon's editorial watch, a series of excellent monographs was produced on several Assam tribes.[25]

Surrounded by colleagues, seniors, and missionaries who were part administrators and part scholars writing detailed anthropological works, the young Hutton was smitten by the newly emerging discipline of social anthropology and eventually took his M.A. in the subject from Oxford in 1919. Hutton's long stay in the Naga Hills formed the basis for his first anthropological endeavour—an account of the Angami Nagas, completed in 1915. On account of World War I, its publication was deferred by seven years. Further, Hutton's administrative duties saw his involvement in Kuki operations (1917–1919),[26] and for services rendered, he was awarded with a C.I.E. Simultaneously, from 1915–1920, he was also preparing a monograph on the Sema Nagas. With the publication of both his books on the Nagas in 1921, Hutton's star witnessed a meteoric rise. Positions and accolades quickly followed: in 1922, he was made the Honorary Director of Ethnography for Assam, a position he continued to hold until 1929, when he was made the Census Commissioner. In 1923, his *alma mater*, Oxford University, conferred a D.Sc. on him. On his part, Hutton utilised his new-found position deftly. In the 1920s, several of his articles were published in prestigious journals in both India and Britain. These included the *Journal of the Royal Anthropological Society, Man, Man in India, Journal of the Asiatic Society of Bengal, Modern Review, Assam Review,* and *Folklore.*[27]

---

[25]In S. C. Roy, 'Anthropological Research in India', *Man in India* 1, pp. 43–44.

[26]In recent years, groundbreaking research has been published on the Kuki operations. For two seminal volumes, see Jangkhomang Guite and Thongkholal Haokip, *The Anglo-Kuki War, 1917–1919*, New Delhi: Routledge India, 2019; and Ngamjahao Kipgen and Doungul Letkhojam Haokip (eds), *Against the Empire: Polity, Economy and Culture During the Anglo-Kuki War, 1917–1919*, New Delhi: Taylor & Francis, 2020.

[27]A detailed but incomplete list can be found in the Bibliography in P. K. Misra, 'J.H. Hutton and Colonial Ethnography of North-East India', in T. B. Subba (ed.),

In order to understand and fully appreciate the positions Hutton came to take in the Indian constitutional discourse on the tribal populations, it is necessary to understand the intellectual milieu which shaped his ideas. From the 1920s onwards, the constitutional debates on the scheduling of predominantly tribal areas were influenced by currents in British anthropology, especially the work of W. H. R. Rivers and Henry Balfour. Much secondary literature exists on the subject,[28] and here I will only raise a few points that have a bearing on the evolution of Hutton's ideas.

It was most likely while completing his Masters in Anthropology that Hutton encountered Rivers's ideas on culture contact. While the above work by Rivers had not yet been published, the roots of these ideas were available in the 1911 Presidential Address to Section H (Anthropology) of the British Association of Advancement of Science. Two other articles by Rivers on the same theme (cited by Balfour, Hutton, and Mills) were published in 1917[29] and 1920,[30] respectively.

It was also at Oxford that Hutton encountered Henry Balfour, the curator of the Pitt Rivers Museum, whose knowledge about the cultural aspects of primitive communities was formidable. In 1921, Balfour contributed a Foreword to Hutton's book on the Sema Nagas. In July 1922, at Hutton's invitation, he spent three months in the Naga Hills, travelling on foot through numerous villages along with Hutton and his protégé, James Philip Mills. Hutton also cemented his position in the Oxbridge network of anthropologists by making a generous donation of a large part of his own 'very fine and valuable ethnographical collection'[31] to the Pitt Rivers Museum.

North-East India: A Handbook of Anthropology, New Delhi: Orient BlackSwan, 2012, pp. 77–78.

[28]George W. Stocking Jr., *Victorian Anthropology*, New York: The Free Press, 1987; Thomas R. Trautmann, *Aryans and British India*, New Delhi: Yoda Press, 2004; Henrika Kuklick, *The Savage Within: The Social History of British Anthropology, 1885–1945*, Cambridge: Cambridge University Press, 1991.

[29]W. H. R. Rivers, 'The Government of Subject Peoples', in A. C. Heyward (ed.), *Science and the Nation*, Cambridge, UK: Cambridge University Press, 1917.

[30]W. H. R. Rivers, 'The Dying Out of Native Races', *Lancet* 98, 1920, pp. 42–44 and 109–111.

[31]'Foreword' by Henry Balfour in J. H. Hutton, *The Sema Nagas*, Bombay: Oxford University Press, 1968 [1921], p. xvii.

Image 3: Henry Balfour

Image courtesy: Pitt Rivers Museum, University of Oxford, 1998.356.17.1.

Balfour's contribution to the evolution of Hutton's ideas came in the form of a lecture where he applied the theoretical framework developed by Rivers to the Naga Hills. In 1922, when Rivers died at the age of fifty-eight, Balfour was chosen to succeed him as President of the Folklore Society. In March 1923, Balfour delivered his Presidential Address on the subject of 'The Welfare of Primitive Peoples'.[32] Acknowledging his predecessor's contribution to the discipline of anthropology, Balfour said that Rivers's work had shown that 'the past history of the effects of the contact of indigenous savage populations with exotic civilized invaders, is not reassuring and gives little grounds for complacency'. In the light of experience from Australia, South Africa, North America, Melanesia, and the Polynesian group of islands, it was difficult to say that the effects of 'contacts with civilization'

[32]Henry Balfour, 'The Welfare of Primitive Tribes', *Folklore* 34 (1), March 1923, pp. 12–24. The following few paragraphs on Balfour's ideas on protection, and the quotes attributed to him on pgs 116–118, have been reconstructed from this source.

had been beneficial for the primitive native populations. Instead, the effects had been deleterious, as observations proved that the native populations had dwindled, were marked by restlessness and apathy, and even their physiques had deteriorated.

The two main themes which Balfour juggled through the course of his address were 'culture' and 'environment'. He sought to establish that the 'primitive outlook' was fundamentally different from the 'civilised' one. Consequently, the administrators responsible for the well-being of primitive communities had to tread cautiously while trying to reform their traditional lifestyles. 'Tampering with or suppressing certain special practices and observances' without understanding the relationship between culture and environment was bound to have 'serious consequences'. In a strongly worded plea for caution in governmental actions, Balfour said,

> The inter-relationship and interdependence of the various important elements in that culture should be ascertained *before* and not *after* governmental prohibitions are imposed and time-honoured practices are abolished....
>
> A higher culture may be introduced to the backward races provided that the assimilative process is gradual one spread over a prolonged period of time. Civilization is like arsenic—an admirable tonic if administered in small successive doses, which can act cumulatively with beneficial results. But, as with arsenic, an *overdose* of civilization is likely to have disastrous effect. Being incapable of assimilation in large doses it usually induces a state, to put it mildly, of mental indigestion, which may easily lead to worse conditions.
>
> ... A disheartened savage who feels that the odds are heavily against him may, however healthy he may be physically, die in a few days. The statistics from Melanesia bring home to us these facts all too clearly. Depopulation is the surest indication of flaws in the administrative machinery.

Echoing Rivers' arguments on Melanesia, Balfour created an island imagery of culture contact wherein a 'higher' culture, in its bid to 'civilize' a geographically isolated 'lower' one, led to a 'lack of interest ... in life' amongst members of the latter. The inevitable result was 'depopulation' and, to avert it, the remedy was *gradual* change. This articulation was again to have a shaping influence on colonial anthropologists and administrators in India.

In his lecture, Balfour referred to his recent trip to the Naga Hills and noted that the 'indigenous culture of the Naga Hills is undergoing inevitable changes under the influence of a stable government'. At the same time, he appreciated the 'keen interest' shown by successive administrators in studying the Naga 'native customs, beliefs and general culture-phenomenon', resulting in an 'intimate knowledge which alone can render administration effective'. Although the British had done good work in administering the area, Balfour felt that the gradual 'imposition of systematic government upon hitherto independent natives involves changes of a drastic and far-reaching nature'. The one similarity between the Melanesian Islands and the Naga Hills was the tradition of head-hunting, which the British administration had suppressed in both cases. Balfour argued that the suppression of this practice had completely unintended consequences, for it was a

> typical instance of a practice whose associated ritual is deeply rooted in the social structure of many primitive peoples. So completely involved is it in the general culture-complex of some native tribes, that its sudden eradication is liable seriously to affect the organization, cohesion, general outlook and the interest in life, and indirectly even the physical efficiency of the natives.

Applying these observations to the Naga Hills, Balfour divided the region into two culture zones: the eastern districts, which were outside the administered area and largely unsurveyed, and the western districts, which were under the British government that practices a sympathetic administrative regime. In Balfour's analysis, the 'relatively uncontaminated' 'primitive pagan' of the central and eastern districts was superior to the Nagas, whose culture had been exposed to infiltrations from the plains. If the 'untouched' Nagas were taken as a yardstick, different levels of advancement in 'cultural-metamorphosis' could be carefully studied and the agents of negative change could be checked and identified. Such an anthropological approach would not only help in 'avoiding the mistakes of the past', saving the Nagas from the fate of 'backward peoples in the South Pacific', but also ensure that they developed 'into an efficient ethnic unit, enjoying a stable organization—a race equipped to play a useful part in the world and with an undeniable claim to a "right to exist"'.

As Deputy Commissioner of the Naga Hills, Hutton was inspired by the ideas of Rivers and Balfour. In 1922, the year of Rivers's last major publication, *The Depopulation of Melanesia*, Hutton published a review of the book in *Man in India*.[33] He thought the book contained important lessons,

[33] J. H. Hutton, 'Depopulation of Primitive Communities', *Man in India* II, 1922, pp. 220–227.

> for all those who, as missionaries, doctors or administrators have to deal with tribes or races of primitive culture, who have been comparatively recently brought into contact with the outside world. The result of such contact in Melanesia has been very rapid and far-reaching decay, and there is every reason to suppose that a similar contact will entail similar results in other parts of the world, if the lesson is not learnt; and indeed in Assam, at any rate, already shows signs that the same mischief is at work, and that similar results will follow, if the danger is not taken in hand in time.[34]

In this article, as in subsequent works, Hutton became almost obsessed with establishing a connection between the Nagas and the people of the Pacific Islands. He agreed that any racial affinity between these two groups of people was difficult to establish, but in terms of cultural features and the effect of culture contact on their primitive societies, the similarities were striking.[35]

---

[34]Ibid., pp. 220–221.

[35]In 1924, Hutton published an article in *Man in India* which was a paper he had read in the Anthropological Section of the eleventh meeting of the Indian Science Congress in Bangalore that year. Here, Hutton argued against the then widely held view that populations migrated from India to the Pacific Islands and propounded a new theory of migration. He found that Naga customs were much closer to those of the Pacific Islands, which were 'exemplified by the similarity in the use of stone and in the practices and beliefs connected with death'. He believed that there were indications to show that these existing cultural traits amongst the Nagas 'reached Assam from the south', as a result of some trans-marine migration. This led Hutton to argue that the centre of dispersal was Indonesia, rather than India. Subsequently, Henry Balfour published a paper in the March 1925 issue of *Man* on 'Thorn-Lined and Their Distribution'. Here, Balfour described the varieties of conical fish-traps lined with *calamus* thorns which were used by Naga tribes and went on to trace the geographical distribution of similar traps in the Indonesian archipelago down to the southern Pacific Islands. This linked the geographical distribution of the same kind of traps, and Balfour believed that this evidence 'affords one of the most convincing chains of concrete evidence helping to prove an affinity between the cultures of Naga Hills at one end of the range, and Melanesian culture at the other end'. For Hutton, this must have been a major encouragement and in the next few years, he would completely adopt the diffusionist line pioneered by Rivers and Balfour. See J. H. Hutton, 'Assam and the Pacific', *Man In India* IV (1 & 2), 1924, pp. 1–9, and 'Anthropological Notes and News', *Man in India*, p. 92, quoted in 'Indian Ethnology in Current Periodical Literature', *Man in India* V, 1925, p. 277.

One of the most extended explications of Hutton's views on culture contact can be seen in his Presidential Address to the Anthropology Section of the Fourteenth Indian Science Congress. Titled 'Anthropology and Administration', it outlined the importance of following certain key principles of 'scientific' anthropology in the administration of 'primitive' races. Hutton utilised his administrative experience in the Naga Hills to illustrate the form of administration that would suit the needs of tribal communities. He viewed contacts with deep suspicion and wrote, 'it has not been [by] blood and thunder alone that primitive races have been exterminated. Ignorant and arrogant attempts to "improve" have probably done almost as much to destroy native races ..., possibly even more.'[36] However, an anthropologist who was willing to understand the primitive 'point of view' was well placed to assist in the task of good administration. Influenced by Balfour's formulation of civilisation as 'arsenic', to be administered in small doses, Hutton wrote,

> Civilization is, as it were, a drug, which however harmless or even beneficial to the hardened and immune, is a rapid poison to those unaccustomed to its use. It is no less destructive than opium or alcohol, and like them needs to be controlled, and that straitly [*sic*], in the interest of the weak.

For Hutton, the importance of anthropology to administrators lay 'in informing them and warning them of the evil effects which follow universally the contact between a lower and a higher culture'. It was the absence of such intimate knowledge that generated ignorance and misunderstanding between the rulers and the ruled. Sometimes this manifested itself in rebellions or disturbances, but the end result usually was 'apathy, depression and degeneracy', which had caused many primitive tribes to 'decay under administration'. The similarity of Hutton's argument with those of Rivers and Balfour remains apparent.

Drawing on his experience in the Naga Hills, Hutton viewed the effect of British administration on the Nagas as harmful. He spoke harshly about the imposition of an alien system of justice upon the primitive communities,

---

[36]J. H. Hutton, Presidential Address to the Section of Anthropology on 'Anthropology and Administration', *Proceedings of the Fourteenth Indian Science Congress, Lahore, 1927 (Second Circuit)*, Asiatic Society of Bengal, Calcutta, 1927, pp. 286–299. The next two paragraphs, and texts/quotes attributed to Hutton on pp. 120–121, are based on this source.

often at the expense of their own customs, which were better suited to local conditions. He also criticised the missionaries, saying that 'they are apt to destroy more than they create, and in so far as they do that, they do more harm than good'. Before the British administration was established in the Naga Hills, Hutton commented that it was necessary for everyone to live in a state of alert, which fostered 'active habits of mind and body'. These had been lost under the peaceful conditions imposed by the new administration. As a result, diseases like small-pox, measles, influenza, and syphilis, which were previously unknown in the hills, began to spread, causing 'far more loss of life in a short time than head-hunting ever did in a long one'.

Hutton made a case for the need to control the contact between 'civilization and wild tribes, so that progress is very slow and that the wild man may have time to accommodate himself gradually to new conditions'. Suggesting a protective regime that could counter 'introducing change too fast', Hutton concluded by saying,

> Among other things much greater freedom is needed in regulating the communications between primitive tribes and the more civilized world. Enlightened countries like Australia have gone so far as to prohibit the entry of any persons whatsoever into their native reserve except occasional scientists and the administrator of the tribe. Even schools and missions have been barred, as this appears the only way at present of protecting the remnant of their aborigines from extermination. There is no reason why legislation on somewhat similar lines should not be applied to these primitive areas of India and Burma, and it would vastly improve the present position with regard to the acculturation of aborigines if the entry of civilized foreigners and of their trade goods into such areas was put under much severer control than it is at present.... Anthropologists know that haste in civilizing, educating, and acculturating is likely to do more harm than good. The difficulty is that other people do not believe it. The facts are at variance with political and philanthropic tradition, and therefore unwelcome. It is not an easy thing to induce a large number of persons to discard the familiar and comfortable ideas of a lifetime in reluctant exchange for new and unaccustomed views, but it is our duty to keep trying even though we feel, as I so often do myself, like a sparrow disconsolate on the house top or a voice crying in the wilderness.

It is interesting to note that almost twelve years before the publication of Verrier Elwin's *The Baiga* (which became notorious for its idea of 'National Parks' for central Indian tribes), Hutton was already pushing the idea of establishing 'aboriginal reserves' in India and Burma along the lines pioneered in North America and Australia. In these territorially segregated spaces, all kinds of contact with civilisation, such as schools, missions, and even business, would be strictly regulated, if not entirely debarred. Taking a cue from Hutton's imagery, I would argue that such enclaves were to become, in effect, 'islands against civilisation'. The imprint of Rivers's geographic field area (the Melanesian Islands), where he had developed the theory of colonialism as shell shock, was set to colour the resolution of the Indian tribal question in the years to come.

In his memorandum of evidence to the Simon Commission, Hutton once again suggested that the colonial State formulate a 'policy of reservation as effected in Australia ... in order to prevent the decimation' of the tribes.[37] In addition to this, through a binary reading of history, he framed the hostility between the inhabitants of the hills and the plains as a long-term phenomenon.[38] Hutton argued that the hillmen had been driven to their present abodes by better organised invaders who occupied the plains. However, the hostility between them continued unabated as the 'hillmen rarely ceased to harry the plains' through regular raids. It was only due to British military interference that they were finally subjugated. The hill-plain binary could be seen on three levels: those of religion, society, and culture. The religion of the hillmen did not relate to either Hinduism or Islam, but could instead be described as 'Animism' and centred around ancestor worship. At the sociological level, too, the caste system characteristic of the plains was unknown amongst the hill people. Also, tribal societies were marked by a considerable degree of gender equality. Culturally and linguistically, too, the hill society was clearly distinct from that of the plains. On this basis, Hutton urged the Simon Commission to separate the administration of the

[37]Indian Statutory Commission Memoranda, Assam—57–1033, E-Assam-126, Note by Mr J. H. Hutton, C.I.E., D.Sc., Deputy Commissioner, Naga Hills, dated 17 March 1928 (Part of Memoranda of the Government of Assam on the working of the reformed government prepared for the Indian Statutory Commission), Appendix B to Chapter II, Assam Government Press, 1928, IOR/13/1/1. This paragraph is based on this source.

[38]For a very good recent work on the nineteenth-century discourse surrounding the hill *versus* plains distinction in the Garo, Khasi, and Jaintia Hills region (now constituting the state of Meghalaya), see Reeju Ray, *Placing the Frontier in British North-East India: Law, Custom and Knowledge*, Oxford: Oxford University Press, 2023.

hills from that of the plains. He also advocated an entirely separate budget, consisting of all the receipts from the 'Backward Tracts' plus an annual grant to cover the difference between receipts and expenditure. This grant was expected from the Imperial government, as the 'security of the frontier was in the paramount importance to the whole of India'. Many of Hutton's demands were endorsed by the Simon Commission Report. However, as shown in Chapter 1, the Commission's proposals for the Backward Tracts elicited a lot of negative reactions, from both the Government of India and the respective local governments. For a variety of reasons that fall beyond the scope of this work, the Indian Statutory Commission's Report was shelved and nothing substantive came out of its proposals. In effect, the hills were the islands that had to be cordoned off from the pernicious influence of the plains, which housed the forces of civilisation.

Hutton, the 1931 Census, and the Paradigm of Tribal Religion

The apex of Hutton's career as an ICS officer was the 1931 Census report, of which he was (as mentioned earlier) the presiding all-India Commissioner. In the opinion of K. S. Singh, the 1931 Census reports are 'easily the most comprehensive of all such reports complete with maps, statistics, ethnographic accounts and the provinces reports together with a three volume all-India report'.[39] This extensive format owed a lot to Hutton who, unlike previous Census Commissioners/Superintendents, was 'not an administrator-turned-academician but ... an administrator who was formally trained as an anthropologist'.[40]

As is well-known, the 1931 Census was the last colonial census which undertook an enumeration of individual castes and tribes. What is also important, but less well-known, is that this Census was the last one to use the category of 'religion' to define the concept of 'tribe'. While the study of the British Indian Census has attracted considerable scholarly attention,[41]

---

[39]K. S. Singh, 'Foreword', in J. H. Hutton, *Census of India 1931: With Complete Survey of Tribal Life and System*, New Delhi: Gian Publishing House, 1989 reprint, p. i.

[40]K. S. Singh, 'Foreword', p. 1.

[41]The essay by Bernard Cohn, 'The Census, Social Structure and Objectification in South Asia', has attained canonical status. A useful collection of articles on the

most existing studies have focussed on issues of religion, caste, and labour migration. Critical studies on the notion of the 'tribe' in censuses of the colonial period are missing.[42] Scarcer still are studies on the use of census data in the constitutional discourse during the last phase of British rule in India. In this section, I will provide a limited analysis of the 1931 Census, showing how it is an important milestone for understanding the tribal question in the constitutional politics of late colonial India.

One aspect of the 1931 Census was that it strove to accurately enumerate the primitive tribes. The results of Hutton's efforts were significant for, as compared to the 1921 Census, the population figures of primitive tribes rose steeply by 8 million in the 1931 Census. According to official figures, including Burma and Ceylon, there were 24.6 million inhabitants belonging to the 'primitive tribes', which made for 6.9 per cent out of a total of 352 million for the entire British Indian Empire. If the figures for princely territories were included, then their numbers swelled even further, touching 27.50 million.

A point that Hutton emphasised on several occasions within this document was the phenomenon of 'Hinduisation'. He noted that out of the 24.6 million people belonging to primitive tribes, only 8.28 million returned themselves as adhering to 'tribal religions'.[43] When compared to 1921 figures, this was 15.3 per cent lower, and this decline in numbers could be explained 'primarily due to losses by conversion to Hinduism or Christianity'. Some of the decline could also be attributed to the 'arbitrary classification of Tribal religion as Hindu', and to propaganda by Hindu and Christian zealots who insisted that primitive tribals return themselves as adherents of their respective creeds.[44] Conversely, the increase in the number of Hindus from the 1921 Census could be explained as a result of accretion from tribal religions.[45] Further, 'the numbers of Tribal religion have also suffered depletion owing to the decay, which attacks so many primitive

Census can be found in N. Gerald Barrier (ed.), *The Census in British India: New Perspectives*, New Delhi: Manohar, 1981.

[42]Possibly the only exception is Chapter 2 in Sangeeta Dasgupta, 'Reordering of Tribal Worlds: Tana Bhagats, Missionaries and the Raj', unpublished Ph.D. thesis, Centre for Historical Studies, Jawaharlal Nehru University, 1998.

[43]K. S. Singh, 'Foreword', in Hutton, *Census of India 1931*, p. iii.

[44]Hutton, *Census of India 1931*, p. 391.

[45]Ibid., p. 392.

tribes when brought into contact with civilisation'.[46] In these articulations, some of Hutton's ideas came to bear an encoded meaning where 'civilisation' was equated with Hinduism in the Indian context. Thus, I would argue that 'islands against civilisation' were land enclaves designed in the main to bar the infiltration of Hindu migrants inside tribal territory. This was supposed to preserve the economic self-sufficiency, cultural autonomy, and most significantly perhaps, the demographic majority of tribal communities. These issues should become clear in the discussion ahead.

In the first instance, Hutton's attempt to mark out followers of 'tribal religions' as distinct from Hinduism was perhaps evolved to quantify the loss in tribal ranks. However, his motives were far more complicated, as we shall shortly see. Also, he was responding to a serious intellectual challenge emanating in the 1921 Census exercise, which had delegitimised the earlier category of Animism.

A Challenge to 'Animism': Bursting Borderlines of Faith

According to H. H. Risley, the 1901 all-India Census Commissioner, the word 'Animism' was coined by Georg Ernst Stahl. It was essentially a metaphysical concept used in ancient times for the 'identity of the vital principle and soul'. In his book *Theoria medica vera* (1707), Stahl revived the idea 'in scientific form' and used it to challenge Hoffman's theory of purely mechanical causation by attributing all organic action to the functioning of *Anima*. Subsequently, E. B. Tylor, the great Victorian scholar, used it in his book, *Primitive Culture*. This marks the transference of a metaphysical concept into the domain of ethnology.[47] Tylor wrote:

> It is habitually found that the theory of Animism divides into two great dogmas forming parts of one consistent doctrine; first concerning souls of individual creatures, capable of continued existence after the death or destruction of the body; second, concerning other spirits, upward to the rank of powerful deities. Spiritual beings are held to affect or control the events of the material world, and man's life here and hereafter; and it being considered that they hold intercourse with men, and receive pleasure or displeasure from human actions, the

[46] Ibid.

[47] H. H. Risley, *People of India*, Calcutta: Thacker, Spink and Company, 1908. The next few paragraphs and quotations attributed to Risley are based on this book.

> belief in their existence leads naturally, and it might be said inevitably, sooner or later to active reverence and propitiation. Thus Animism, in its full development, includes the belief in souls and in a future state, in controlling deities and subordinate spirits, these doctrines practically resulting in some kind of active worship.

In 1901, H. H. Risley accepted Animism without reservation, calling it 'the best name that we are likely to get'. For him, the term embodied 'a precise conception of the confused bundle of notions wrapped up in savage religion'. Having served in Chota Nagpur, he had 'enjoyed some special opportunities of studying Animism in those forest solitudes which are its natural home'. The idea at the root of primitive religion was that of '*power*, or rather of many powers', including spirits, ancestral ghosts and sacred groves, etc. The entity was not a person they feared and attempted to propitiate. Rather, Risley wrote,

> What the animist worships, and seeks strange ways to influence and conciliate, is the shifting and shadowy company of unknown powers and tendencies making for evil rather than for good, which reside in the primeval forest, in the crumbling hills, in the rushing river, in the spreading tree, which give its spring to the tiger, its venom to the snake, which generates jungle fever, and walks abroad in the terrible guise of cholera, small-pox or murrain.... Some sort of power is there, and that is enough for him.

Summing up the leading features of Animism in India, Risley noted:

> It conceives of man as passing through life surrounded by a ghostly company of powers, elements, tendencies, mostly impersonal in their character, shapeless phantasms of which no images can be made and no definite idea can be formed. Some of these have departments or spheres of influences of their own: one presides over cholera, another over small-pox, and another over cattle disease; some dwell in rocks, others haunt trees, others again are associated with rivers, whirlpools, waterfalls, or with strange pools hidden in the depths of the hills. All of them require to be diligently propitiated by reason of the ills which proceed from them and usually the land of the village provides the ways and means for this propitiation.... The essence of all these practices is magic.

Risley speculated that since, at the time of Tylor, the distinction between religion and magic was not clearly defined, the term may never have come into existence. However, the works of James George Frazer had shifted the focus away from belief, dreams, spirits, and soul, and instead foregrounded magical practices as the defining feature of the daily life of semi-civilised men. Hence, going along with the assumption that Animism was an 'exceedingly crude form of religion where magic is the predominant element', Risley sought to outline the ambiguous contours of the relationship between Animism and popular Hinduism.

Unsuccessful as Risley was, this issue had been a constant challenge for Census authorities since the 1880s. The starting point of such enquiries was, of course, an attempt to arrive at an acceptable definition of Hinduism itself. If a comprehensive answer could be given to the central question, 'What is a Hindu?', then its relationship with Animism, accurately defined, could be arrived at. Numerous attempts had been made to address the central issue. Within the colonial Census apparatus, a significant effort was made by E. A. Gait, who succeeded Risley as the all-India Census Commissioner in 1911. However, Gait too failed to provide conceptual clarity, and the challenge continued to exist. Almost every Census report accepted the term as well as the fuzziness of boundaries between Hinduism and Animism.

Nevertheless, this intellectual stalemate was about to break open. The catalyst emanated from a section highly critical of Animism and found a place in the chapter on Religion in the Bombay Census Report of 1921. Written by L. J. Sedgwick, the Superintendent of Census operations in the Bombay Presidency, it constituted the most vociferous frontal attack on the concept of Animism. These few pages in a Census volume portended a remarkable intellectual ferment in official State categories, which would continue until the making of the Indian Constitution. Essentially, Sedgwick lambasted the use-value of Animism as an official Census category and argued for jettisoning it. For him, Animism was an outdated concept which had failed to keep abreast with developments in the discipline of anthropology. Sedgwick argued:

> Since the time of Tylor much research has been done among savage and primitive peoples, and it has been found that belief in spirits or entities dwelling in natural objects is by no means the most primitive of beliefs. The most primitive savage does not distinguish between spirit and matter. The danger from the tree is not from the tree spirit, but simply from the tree itself, which, as an object sways about and makes a noise, is necessarily possessed of a vague potency, a 'mana' (to use a Polynesian word which has become the technical term among Anthropologists for the primitive idea outlined above). Nor does he distinguish natural from artificial objects. The attitude of such peoples

> is that of a child, who, when it knocks its leg against a chair, exclaims, 'naughty chair' and kicks it. When we hang up over our door a horseshoe to bring luck we are unconsciously reverting to the most primitive savage beliefs. The belief in 'mana' of natural and artificial objects has been called by some writers as 'Animatism' though this word is perhaps not generally accepted. This 'Animatism' can, and does, in the case of some peoples, continue to exist side by side with a belief in spirits and even gods. The extent to which it exists among the jungle tribes of this Presidency, either by itself or in combination with Animism or other forms of primitive religion, is possibly not fully known.[48]

Quoting the work of R. E. Enthoven (in charge of the Ethnographic Survey of Bombay and author of *The Tribes and Castes of Bombay Presidency*), Sedgwick ascribed to the mentality of the Bhils 'a stage of religious development considerably beyond Animatism'.[49] Thus, Sedgwick argued that the use of the category was unsuitable for a population such as the Bhils, who were the most numerous aboriginal community in Bombay Presidency.

Sedgwick also raised certain glaring procedural issues related to the information gathering exercise during the Census. He pointed out that barring the Hindu–Animist dilemma, the enumerator was duty bound to accept the answer provided by the individual. In this instance, however, if the enumerator thought that the question was misunderstood, he was 'left to decide whether any member of a jungle tribe is a Hindu or an Animist'. This was to be further corroborated by whether such a return was 'accepted by the villagers'. The impossibility of calling and questioning the villagers together regarding the religious status of every Bhil meant that it was 'almost a matter of luck what the numbers returned as Animists will be'. In addition to the subjective interpretation of individual enumerators, there was further uncertainty regarding classification 'on the ground of caste by the head of the Abstraction office'. Sedgwick referred to one such important case in 1911, when all-India Census Commissioner E. A. Gait, on tour of the Bombay Presidency, 'converted 70,000 Bhils in Reva Kantha from Hindus to Animists by a stroke of the pen'.

[48] L. J. Sedgwick, *Census of India, 1921*, Vol. VIII, Part I, Bombay, p. 62.

[49] Sedgwick wrote, 'They worship female deities known as Matas represented by symbols rather than images, by wooden posts, earthen pots, toy horses, wicker baskets, and winnowing fans. Originally perhaps the wicker basket was an animated and potent object possessed of "mana".'

Focussing on the sociological background of the actual enumerators working on the ground, Sedgwick gave a powerful explanation for the numerical inconsistency apparent in successive Censuses about Animistic followers. Citing Enthoven again, Sedgwick writes:

> ... when the Bhil worships a big tree or a stone, he is only doing what the Hindu of the plains does, when he girds the pipal tree with the sacred thread or paints red lead on a *lingam* stone. Moreover, Hinduism of to-day is not the Vedic religion; nor is it the Puranic religion; nor is it the philosophic pantheism of the highly educated Brahman. It is a vast mixture, in which the Vedic worship of the great forces of nature, the Puranic *avatars*, the philosophical doctrine of karma, and be it noted—the pre-Aryan reverence of trees, stones, animals and tribal *totems* are inextricably interlmingled [*sic*]. Consequently most enumerators would regard the Bhil, whose persona-objects of worship are his ancestors, a particular tree, a particular stone, the boundary god, the small-pox mother and a winnowing fan, as no less a Hindu than the *Kunbi* of his own village, who worships his ancestors, the *pipal* tree, the circle of stones known as *Vetala*, the boundary deity, the small-pox mother, and a plough even though the latter may be told *puranic* stories a few times a year by his *guru*, have some vague ideas of the doctrine of *karma*, and employ a Brahman to perform his ceremonies.... Mr. Farquar, who makes Hinduism depend on 'birth and conformity'. By birth he means birth into one of the recognised Hindu castes. But if some Bhils are Hindus then Bhil is a recognised Hindu caste. It is particularly to be noted that a Bhil does not enter any new caste when he gradually passes into a Hindu and worships *puranic* gods.[50]

Thus, on the basis of these objections and critiques, Sedgwick introduced a class angle into the Hindu–Animism distinction. He was not only mounting a frontal attack on the epistemological/ontological consistency and robustness of Animism, but he also brought out the arbitrariness behind the Census data generated in its wake. Sedgwick's critique was the most serious challenge to the decades-long validity and legitimacy enjoyed by Animism as a taxonomical category within the colonial Census grid.

In addition to exposing the hollowness of Animism, Sedgwick's argument presented an extraordinarily sharp and logical challenge to anthropologists within the colonial bureaucracy. In essence, Sedgwick argued that in line with other great religious traditions of the world, the

[50]Sedgwick, *Census of India, 1921*, pp. 63–64.

'Hinduism of the highly educated Brahman is something totally distinct from the Hinduism of the lower strata of Hindu society'. If this were true, then:

> the jungle tribes being, as it were, non-Puranised Hindus (one cannot use the term 'primitive Hindus' since Hinduism is not derived from the pre-Aryan cults, but has absorbed them), no justification for continuing to treat Animism as a distinct religion exists, *unless we can obtain figures which show rational changes from Census to Census.* (emphasis in the original)

Using statistics derived from the Census operations, Sedgwick also pointed out the great divergence between different districts in the caste-heads clubbed together under the category of Animists.[51] Also significant was the trivial number of persons under certain group terms. Such low figures suggested that 'a single energetic enumerator of pronounced views' was probably responsible for such returns. Sedgwick also used the discrepancies and inconsistencies within colonial documents about Animistic communities like the Chodhras, Naikadas, Gamta or Gamit. If the various accounts of the religious practices followed by these numerically significant 'Animists', generated by the colonial bureaucracy itself, were often contradictory, then the rationale behind the category itself was questionable. He pointed out that groups such as Kolis were 'certainly Hindus' and the Mes were followers of a mixed Hindu–Mussalman cult. Of all the groups, only the Katkaris were 'possibly the least Hinduised', and whose religious practices were worthy of separate treatment. In a powerful indictment of the futility behind the Census category of Animism, Sedgwick summed up his argument without mincing words:

> In short I suggest that our returns of Animists are *absolutely worthless.* They represent nothing and are entirely a matter of chance. The vast decrease between 1891 and 1901 and the vast increase between 1901 and 1911 cannot be attributed to losses by and recovery from famine. Any such idea is completely disproved by the regional figures. The Bhils, who contribute most to the figures are practically Hindus, and the other castes seem to be so also. I have therefore no hesitation in

---

[51]Sedgwick wrote, 'Thus Reva Kantha and the Panch Mahals between them return Animists under 19 different castes, Surat and Surat Agency 14, Satara 7, Cutch 4, Palanpur and Broach 3 each and no other district more than 2. In the case of 19 names from the Panch Mahals and Reva Kantha only 3 are common to each. Seven districts and a number of States returned no Animists at all.'

> saying that Animism as a religion should be entirely abandoned, and that all those hitherto classed as Animists should be grouped with Hindus at the next Census, Hinduism being defined as including the religious or semi-religious beliefs of those jungle tribes who have not actually embraced Islam or Christianity. In saying this I am of course to be taken as discussing the conditions of this Presidency only. There may be regions such as Chota Nagpur where the boundary between Hinduism and Animism is clear and definite.[52]

Although limited to only the Bombay Presidency, Sedgwick's diatribe was a milestone moment. Perhaps for the first time in over four decades, such a systematic onslaught was launched on the very idea of the essential difference of Animistic beliefs from Hinduism, and especially their *worthlessness* in the decennial census.[53] To corroborate his argument, Sedgwick also marshalled other kinds of ammunition emanating from non-official circles, including the academia and Christian missionaries.

In an attached footnote, Sedgwick recounted the presentation of the above thesis at a meeting of the Anthropological Society of Bombay. A 'learned Sanskrit scholar' present there claimed that 'this very question was really settled long time ago at the time when the Atharva Veda, which is nothing but a mass of Animistic magic, was received into the canon of "Sruti"'. Sedgwick contended that if 'Animistic mantras' were a 'recognised portion of the Hindu Canon', there was 'very little justification for excluding Animists from the definition of Hinduism'. He also referred to a belief that 'the relegation of the Bhils and other similar tribes to the head of Animism ... (was) more or less an artificial classification of the early census authorities, and was not dictated by any strong feeling on the part of educated Hindus'.

To further buttress his argument, Sedgwick published a note, titled 'The Bhils—Are they Hindus or Animists?' in the 1921 Bombay Census volume. This piece was written by Rev. Enoch Hedberg, a Christian missionary in the West Khandesh district who had first-hand experience of the Bhils. Hedberg argued that there were two tests applicable to the issue: *first*, whether they call themselves Hindus, and *second*, whether they conform to Hindu practices. On the first yardstick, Hedberg claimed that 'all Bhils', including 'the most wild and backward, with the exception of a small

[52]Ibid., p. 67; emphasis in the original.

[53]However, Sedgwick's assault was not limited to Census figures and elsewhere in his report, he goes on to develop the idea of a 'Hinduistic Scale' of social groups. This will be analysed in a later chapter on the idea of 'backwardness'.

number which has turned Muhammadans or Christian, declare themselves to be Hindus'. The surrounding native Christians, Muslims, and Hindus alike refer to those who 'stick to their ancestral religion' as 'Hindu-Bhils'. Even the 'very wild Bhils of the Akrani' would regard the non-Hindu tag as an insult. About the second criterion, that is, the level of Bhil conformity to the tenets in Hinduism, Hedberg provided three reasons: (*i*) observation of prohibitive caste rules on inter-dining and intermarriage; (*ii*) celebration of Hindu festivals such as Holi, Dasera, Divali; and (*iii*) worship of the Hindu pantheon of gods and goddesses. Hedberg acknowledged that a certain 'difference between a common Bhil and an ordinary Hindu' was noticeable. However, in his opinion, such distinctions were 'more of a racial and ethnological nature than a religious one, and is (were) rapidly disappearing'. Summing up his argument, Hedberg wrote that the Bhils should be accorded the same rights as other Indians, and their own word in religious matters should be final. The Census authorities should classify them as Hindus if they profess it themselves.[54]

Sedgwick's forceful arguments enabled a quick dismantling of the category of Animism from the decennial Census operations. It was a defining moment in western India at least, for it gladdened the hearts of Hindu social reformers, one of whom reported that Sedgwick had 'done a useful public service in exposing the Animist "stunt" which had obsessed Census Commissioners for nearly a generation'.[55] The ideological and utilitarian legitimacy of a longstanding official Census category, which had created a basis for distinguishing the aboriginal tribes from their Hindu neighbours, was severely dented. At the level of anthropological knowledge, too, Sedgwick's challenge was deeply theoretical. The fact that it emanated from within the higher echelons of bureaucracy provides one more proof that the colonial State was not a monolith, especially in its ideological orientation. Using the apparent contradictions existing in the colonial records, gazetteers, and published documentation on tribes, Sedgwick's attack questioning the meaningfulness behind the utility of Animism itself must have ruffled many feathers. After all, in the next edition of the 1931 Bombay Census, the writers came out in opposition to Sedgwick's

---

[54] Appendix N, Rev. Enoch Hedberg, 'The Bhils: Are They Hindus or Animists?', in L. J. Sedgwick, *Census of India, 1921, Bombay Presidency, Vol. VIII*, Bombay: Government Central Press, 1922, p. xxxiii.

[55] 'Animism and Hinduism', *The Indian Social Reformer* XXXIII (42), 16 June 1923, p. 677.

argument.[56] However, unlike the detractor, they were unable to produce any sharp facts or figures in support of their contention. For nationalists like Thakkar, the efficacy of Sedgwick's attack was further bolstered by his formulation of educational backwardness, caste, and the Hinduistic scale, which have been dealt with in a later chapter.

The efficacy of his attack became apparent in the 1921 edition of the Census itself when J. T. Marten, the all-India Census Commissioner, accepted the bulk of Sedgwick's argument. He decided to drop Animism as a Census category, substituting it with a new one, christened as 'Tribal Religions.' Marten opined that a 'natural inference' generated by the Census category of Animism was that the head 'contained all those who held animistic beliefs', which, however, would be 'entirely misleading.'[57] Marten explained his decision to jettison Animism in favour of the new category of 'Tribal Religions'; concurring with the class-lens devised by Sedgwick, the head of the 1921 Census apparatus wrote:

> Animism, frequently associated with the worship of the souls of ancestors and of rudimentary deities representing the larger forces of nature, forms to some extent a substantial influence among the less enlightened adherents of most religions; and in India, where the original beliefs of the indigenous population were essentially of this primitive character, the introduction under foreign influences of the more philosophical religions has not radically changed the religious attitude of the lower illiterate classes. There is little to distinguish the religious attitude of an aboriginal Gond or Bhil from that of a member of one of the lower Hindu castes. Both are essentially animistic and the difference lies in the fact that the one has identified his chief objects of worship with those in the Hindu pantheism and has, to a greater or less extent, brought his social and personal life into line with the requirements of the recognized Hindu system. It is obvious, therefore, that the term Animism does not represent the communal distinction which is the essence of the census aspect of religion and that, as a description of a definite religious category distinct from the other religions returned, it is distinctly misleading both in its content and its extent. For this reason I have decided to change the heading of this category to 'Tribal Religions.' The title at least covers with some

[56] A. H. Dracup and H. T. Sorley, *Census of India, 1931, Vol. VIII, Part I, Bombay Presidency, General Report*, Government Central Press, p. 356.

[57] J. T. Marten, *Census of India, 1921, Vol. I, India, Part-I, Report*, Superintendent Government Printing, Calcutta, 1924, p. 110.

> accuracy the information which was actually obtained in the schedule, though it is inconvenient in that it cannot be resolved into a compact substantive which will describe the person whom it includes.[58]

Thus, Marten acknowledged the seriousness of Sedgwick's argumentative challenge by citing the latter's reasoning in his own decision. Despite the decision to drop Animism as a Census category, the Census Commissioner had not abandoned the idea of the distinctiveness of tribal religious belief systems. However, this decision marked the end of official recognition of an important ethnological idea coined half-a-century ago. The wind was taken out of the sail of Animism and its advocates were left high and dry.

Further on, Marten qualified the decision by adding that merely a change in nomenclature in the heading of this category would not ease the interpretation of associated Census figures. The vagueness behind Animism was not obliterated by the new term 'Tribal' as it, too, was an indefinite idea. The term was certainly generic in nature, showing a tripartite division. *First,* there were 'aboriginal tribes, denizens for the most part of the hills and jungles' scattered across the Indian subcontinent, who stood largely outside 'even the fringe of any of the systematized religions'. *Second,* there were those groups who in recent times had lived in constant and close interaction with 'more sophisticated neighbours of the plains and open country'. Such tribals had 'partially adopted their practices and methods of life'. *Third,* there was a large mass of tribes who, through long association, had 'acquired an indefinite position' on the outskirts of Hinduism. Many of them had 'obtained a kind of negative recognition as Hindu outcastes'. Years later, Marten's articulation was perhaps re-hashed by Verrier Elwin to splinter the category of the 'aboriginal'.[59]

Thus, when the Census enumerators were out for counting, they had to face individuals from all these categories 'with little equipment except his local knowledge and his own personal inclinations and prejudices'. Having first ascertained the caste or tribe of the subject, a member of any of the 'undoubted Hindu castes' would be returned as Hindu. For 'more doubtful classes', the enumerator would receive some 'suggestion from those whose ambition to take a higher place in the social scale has prompted them to range themselves definitely as Hindus'. Otherwise, he would record them

---

[58]Ibid., pp. 110–111.

[59]This tripartite formula was reiterated twenty years later by Verrier Elwin in his famous 1941 tract *Loss of Nerve,* without, however, any acknowledgment. That story forms the penultimate chapter of this book.

either as Hindus or under their tribal name according to his local knowledge and the personal view he was inclined to take. In the record of the schedule of this class, the personality of the enumerator, then, was a major factor.

As is clear from the above discussion, Sedgwick's intervention in the context of Bombay Presidency had all-India ramifications. It literally shook up the ontological foundations of the Hindu *versus* Aboriginal distinction. In most previous decennial Censuses, especially from 1891 onwards, attempts were made, albeit unsuccessfully, to encompass communities classed by colonial officials as 'tribes' under catch-all categories such as 'Animism' and 'Tribal Religions'.

In the 1931 Census operations with Hutton at its helm, there was a sustained attempt to resurrect the meaning, legitimacy, and distinction of 'Tribal Religion' vis-à-vis Hinduism. Using his scholarly credentials as an anthropologist of repute, Hutton made every effort to philosophically set up 'Tribal Religions' as a belief system different from Hinduism, although, as he himself admitted, 'the line is hard to draw between [them]'.[60] In 1989, decades after the publication of the 1931 Census, the uniqueness of Hutton's effort was best described by K. S. Singh:

> Though like many other census officials, Hutton was prone to describe tribal religions as being inevitably absorbed into Hinduism, unlike them he used the formidable power of his scholarship and rich anthropological imagination, to identify such elements of the tribal material being absorbed into Hinduism as unmistakably bore the impact of primitive religion and the 'foreign elements'. These were possibly the Negrito reverence for the *pipal* tree and practice of a primitive phallic fertility cult; the Proto-Australoids' totemism; the Mediterraneans' mother goddess and megalithic cultures; the Mundas' theory of life-essence that developed into that of reincarnation; the Aryans' personified deities, practice of sacrificial propitiation and a formalised worship, and institutions such as that of the deva-dasi from Asia Minor (?) and the priestly class. Hutton goes on to describe how the theory of soul-matter influenced fertility cults, the practice of head-hunting, human sacrifice and cannibalism, and the institutions of the memorial to the dead, totemism and witchcraft. These elements are described as the survivals not of 'mere vague imaginings of superstitious and untaught minds', as described in the census report of 1911 but as 'the debris of a real religious system, a definite philosophy' which testify to 'the one time widespread prevalence from Europe to

[60]Hutton, *Census of India 1931*, p. 397.

> Australia outside India, of a great tribal religion,' hagiolatory. Many of the assumptions of this mind-boggling conceptualisation are now open to question, though a few regarding 'oceanic intrusions' of people and culture from the Pacific are being explored further.[61]

The above description is an almost perfect précis of the 'mind-boggling conceptualisation' that Hutton attempted in the 1931 Census. As suggested by Singh, Hutton used several tropes simultaneously to argue that the tribal religions 'represent, as it were, surplus material not yet built into the temple of Hinduism.'[62]

A crucial theme in Hutton's formulation of tribal religion was 'soul-substance'/'soul-matter', which he borrowed from W. H. R. Rivers. In 1920, Rivers wrote an article in which he juxtaposed the concept of 'soul-substance' as found in Indonesia to similar ideas in the primitive communities of New Guinea and Melanesia.[63] The idea was that life itself was a 'transferable and material substance', and Hutton argued that there was remarkable similarity between the beliefs of primitive communities in India on this count.[64] In this formulation, cultural practices such as fertility cults, cults of the dead, headhunting, erection of monoliths, foundation sacrifices, ideas of reincarnation, totemism and witchcraft, etc., all coalesced into a definite religious philosophy of 'hagiolatory', which bound together all the disparate sets of beliefs found among various primitive tribes in India.

The belief in a tribe-caste continuum (although the term 'continuum' was not used until the 1950s) and that tribes provided the stock for an increase in the number of Hindus was common amongst colonial officials. Hutton, too, held on to this theoretical paradigm. He was not alone in subscribing to this argument; such a viewpoint was held by a number of ICS men interested in the primitive tribal communities of India. For instance, T. C. Hodson,[65] Hutton's senior in the Assam cadre who had been

---

[61] Singh, 'Foreword', in Hutton, *Census of India 1931*, p. iv.

[62] Hutton, *Census of India 1931*, p. 399.

[63] W. H. R. Rivers, 'The Concept of "Soul-Substance" in New Guinea and Melanesia', *Folklore* 31 (1), 30 March 1920, pp. 48–69.

[64] Hutton, *Census of India 1931*, p. 398.

[65] Hodson wrote several books in the early twentieth century and contributed to anthropological journals. Some examples are *Thado Grammar* (1906), *The Meithis* (1908), *The Naga Tribes of Manipur* (1911), and *The Primitive Culture of India* (1922). For more details on Hodson, see Edmund Leach, 'Notes on the Mythology

appointed as the first occupant of the newly created William Wyse Chair of Anthropology at Cambridge University, wrote,

> The facts are insistent and decisive—The 'untouchables' are constantly recruited from the Hill and Forest tribes, some of whom have shown signs of political consciousness and have fostered the purification of tribal religion from within. Others are worked by Christian Missions with some success. Others—perhaps the majority—move more and more towards Hinduism. We are told that Hinduism does not proselytize but it is certainly acquisitive. Its numbers are kept up by accessions from the Hill and Forest tribes and by the superior fertility of the depressed classes which to a considerable extent consists of groups which quite recently were definitely tribal groups. Hinduism has been described as magic tempered by metaphysics, it is also metaphysics tainted by magic, because its converts bring their traditional ideas and their tribal deities into the common stock and pass their colour through the whole polity.... The Hill and Forest Folk are numerous enough to deserve consideration. They are important, because they are moving into and refreshing the ranks of Hinduism. They are full of potential value, and are an integral element in the dynamics of the Indian polity.[66]

The distinction that Hodson draws out between the proselytising *versus* acquisitive forms of the Hindu religion deserves greater attention of scholarship. It is important to highlight that Hutton agreed with the notion of acquisitive Hinduism completely. In a lecture delivered before the Indian Section of the Royal Society of Arts on the 1931 Indian Census operations, Hutton referred to 'considerable acquisitions from tribal religions', which had benefitted Hinduism and Christianity.[67]

In Chapter 3 on A. V. Thakkar, these trends will play out in much greater detail. Thakkar's ideas of 'uplift' and 'assimilation' became the pivot of the nationalist position on Indian aboriginal tribes. For now, we must turn our attention to a debate that Thakkar conducted with Hutton, which brought out several important issues in the early 1930s.

---

of Cambridge Anthropology', *The Cambridge Journal of Anthropology* 9 (1), 1984, pp. 1–12.

[66]T. C. Hodson, late Indian Civil Service officer, writes to the *New Statesman* (On the C.P. Award Question), Ritavada, dated 20 November 1932, The Backward Tribes of India—Franchise Question, IOR/Q/IDC/45.

[67]J. H. Hutton, 'Census of India, 1931', *Journal of the Royal Society of Arts* 80 (4154), 1 July 1932, p. 794.

The Thakkar–Hutton Debate

To understand Hutton's policy interventions, it is necessary to have a sense of the impact that the 1931 Census figures on primitive tribes had on the constitutional deliberations about their future position. In 1932, The Indian Franchise Committee headed by Marquis Lothian was given the task of recommending the parameters of the elective system to be put in place in British India upon the inauguration of the new Federal Constitution. In March 1932, when the Committee organised its first public meeting in New Delhi, Hutton, then Census Commissioner, deposed before it. Hutton's deposition was a rare example of evidence heard by the Committee on the issue of representation to the aboriginal tribes. Hence, it is important to take a critical look at it, which will be done a little later.

However, for Thakkar, who continued to keep an alert eye on constitutional developments around the issue of aboriginal tribes, the recommendations of the Lothian Committee presented a definite advance over that of the Southborough Committee, which had earlier enquired into the franchise question.[68] Thakkar was an old proponent of providing representation to the aboriginal tribes.[69] He expressed happiness that the Lothian Committee had recognised 'the necessity of special representation by some method of election (and not nomination) at least in the provinces of Bihar and Orissa, Assam, the C.P., and possibly Madras'.[70] However, Thakkar picked on an anomaly, which raises important questions about Hutton's role as Census Commissioner, for he wrote,

> But what is almost an enigma to us may be clearly stated here. As stated above, the total aboriginal, i.e. forest and hill tribes population in the whole of India was calculated at 16 millions in 1921. This number must have surely grown to 18 millions in 1931, taking into account the greater fecundity of these tribes. Deductions have to be made from this figure for those residing in Indian States, separate figures for which are

[68]Formed in 1919, to recommend steps to be taken on the issue of providing franchise to the Indian population, the Southborough Franchise Committee had, for the first time ever, recommended representation to the aboriginal tribes. However, this was to be done only in the provinces of Bihar and Assam, and that too, through a system of nomination.

[69]See Chapter 3 on Thakkar.

[70]A. V. Thakkar, 'Representation of the Aborigines', *The Servants of India Society* XV (23), 23 June 1932, p. 192.

> not given in the census report of 1921. But making a liberal allowance for their numbers resident in the States, a greater deduction than 50% need not be made; thus their number resident in British India cannot be taken as less than 9 millions at the least. But we are now told by the Lothian Committee that their number is a little above only 5 millions, which is a figure much less than 9 millions, which is by itself an underestimated figure. This requires to be explained by Mr. Hutton, the Census Commissioner for 1931, who is known to be a great well-wisher and lover of the aborigines. But to the ordinary student this abrupt drop in the total aboriginal population in unintelligible.[71]

This astute observation by Thakkar had a ring of truth to it. As K. S. Singh had pointed out, by making 'all kinds of adjustments', Hutton had indeed arrived at a figure of 24.6 million aboriginals for entire British India. This was much higher than the figure of 18 million anticipated by Thakkar. Then how did Hutton, as the all-India Census Commissioner, provide the figure of 5 million to the Lothian Committee? While it is important to highlight the fact that this quibbling over numbers became extremely important at a time when the British were in the process of conferring 'responsible' representative democracy upon Indians, the key to the aforementioned anomaly lies in the correspondence between Thakkar and Hutton. After this particular article was published, Thakkar actually wrote to Hutton and sought an explanation for the riddle.[72] Hutton's reply presents an interesting clue to a historian putting the puzzle together. Hutton replied in a 'purely private capacity' and wrote,

> The actual number of aboriginal tribes who returned their tribal names for their religion in 1931 was 8,280,347 and the number in British India was 5,779,709. This of course does not represent the population of the tribes themselves, as owing in part to the natural process of the substitution of Hinduism for their tribal religion, and the idea of social superiority attaching to a return of Hinduism in addition to a very vigorous propaganda by the Hindu Mahasabha at census time, directed presumably to abtaining [*sic*] as large as possible a return of Hindus as might be, there has been a very considerable transfer at this census from 'Tribal Religions' to 'Hinduism'.[73]

---

[71]Ibid.

[72]Letter No. 1, dated 8 September 1932, From: A. V. Thakkar; To: J. H. Hutton, IOR/Q/IDC/45.

[73]D.O. No. 18, dated 10 September, Office of the Census Commissioner, From: J. H. Hutton; To: A. V. Thakkar, IOR/Q/IDC/45.

Hutton said that this 'transfer' was very considerable in the Central Provinces (C.P.) and Assam. This explained why the figure of 8 million in the 1931 Census represented the 9 million of a decade earlier. Hutton further wrote, 'I am not quite sure what your 16 millions refers. It cannot be to "Tribal Religions" and must be to primitive tribes including those who returned themselves as Hindu and as Christian.'[74]

At this point, it is necessary to take a step back in time by a few months. In March 1932, the Central Provinces Franchise Committee had recommended that two seats provided for the representatives of aboriginal tribes in the provincial legislative council should be filled by nomination.[75] Now C.P. and Berar had one of the highest proportionate populations of aboriginal tribes in the entire British India. Out of its 18 million inhabitants, the aboriginal tribes constituted nearly 3 million, making it a sixth of the total population. In this respect, the C.P. Franchise Committee award was quite minimal. However, in the August 1932 declaration of the Communal Award, this figure was further reduced to just one seat. Interestingly, the term used for the representation of aboriginal tribes was 'Representative from Backward Areas'. Predictably, Assam had the highest number (nine), which was closely followed by Bihar (eight). The provinces of C.P., Madras, and Bombay received one representative seat each. However, no provision was made for aboriginal representation in the Federal Assembly.

Thakkar was quite upset at this diminution of aboriginal representation and wrote to Hutton that the allocation was unreasonable. He also remarked that Hutton's provision to the Lothian Committee of only the number of tribal religionists, and not the total number of aboriginals, meant that the Committee made 'no distinction between the two, though the former figure is only half, or less than one-half of the latter'. In an indirect way, Thakkar protested this move and wrote to Hutton: 'A Gond or a Santhal remains a backward or a primitive type of man, all the same, whether he professes tribal, Hindu, Christian or even Muslim religion.'[76]

Hutton wrote back to Thakkar, agreeing that the case of C.P. aboriginals 'will be more prejudiced ... than anywhere else'. He also informed Thakkar that during his evidence to the Lothian Committee, he 'inferred from the questions asked that there was a distinct feeling against giving aboriginal

[74]Ibid.

[75]*The Times of India*, 3 March 1932, p. 10.

[76]Letter No. 3 from A. V. Thakkar to J. H. Hutton, dated Bhil Seva Mandal, Dohad, 12 September 1932, IOR/Q/IDC/45.

separate representation on the central body'. Hutton added that the term 'animist', as applied to tribal religion, was misleading, and he thought that 'the great many of them are more or less animistic in their belief than the followers of most other religions'.[77] In his reply, Thakkar agreed that the C.P. aboriginal situation was 'already prejudiced and that too very badly'. He further wrote,

> They are not vocal. Though a separation, I mean a separate electoral roll, may not be liked by the C.P. representatives on the Lothian Committee, they cannot surely object to a large number of seats being reserved for them in general (or Hindu) electorate. They should be given the same number of seats as in Bihar and Assam i.e. 8 or 9 if not more.
>
> I would add that the same seats should be reserved for them at least for the first 5 or 10 years in the Central Legislature, the composition of which is not yet settled. It is in this connection that I want to make a representation, more so as the Lothian Report is silent over this point.
>
> Yes, the word 'animist' as applied to tribal religion is no doubt misleading, but the word has been used for long time past and it would be a pity to change it in favour of any other term. No doubt the phrase 'tribal religion wala', may be used and 'animist' dropped.[78]

From the last line in particular, it can be inferred that Thakkar was being sarcastic about Hutton's laboriously constructed notion of 'tribal religion'. Subsequently, Thakkar roped in N. M. Joshi, the veteran trade union leader from Bombay Presidency, to raise the issue at the third session of the Round Table Conference, which he did in good earnest. Rightly sceptical about Hutton's questionable move, Thakkar wrote to Joshi that he must take up the matter with Lord Lothian, who was a 'fair minded man', so that the error may be rectified.[79] Casting aspersions on Hutton, Thakkar wrote,

> In fact, the Census Commissioner gave him (Lord Lothian) and his Committee a wrong figure. He gave the figure of 'Followers of Tribal Religions' in place of 'Primitives' or the 'Aboriginal and Hill Tribes', a

[77]Letter No. 5, D.O. No. 18, dated 19 October 1932; From: J. H. Hutton, Office of the Census Commissioner for India, Simla; To: A. V. Thakkar, IOR/Q/IDC/45.

[78]Letter No. 6 from A. V. Thakkar to J. H. Hutton, dated Delhi, 26 October 1932, IOR/Q/IDC/45.

[79]Letter from A. V. Thakkar to N. M. Joshi, dated Delhi, 24 November 1932, IOR/Q/IDC/45. The following paragraphs and quotes are based on this source.

> majority of whom have returned themselves as 'Hindus' or 'Christians', and not 'Animistic'.

Thakkar further said that 'to be quite fair to them, they ought to have 7% of Hindu or "general seats" in the Central Legislature'. His desire was that the aboriginals must be given ten reserved seats in the Centre (Assam, Bihar and Orissa, and C.P. and Berar two seats each; Bombay and Madras one seat each; and two aboriginal members would be co-opted as members of the central Legislative Assembly). He urged Joshi to raise the issue at

> the proper time in the Round Table Conference and not let the case of my and your Aboriginal Tribes go by default. I did not go before the Lothian Committee as a witness and I then failed in my duty to those friends. I do not wish to repeat that error, especially as they are far from vocal like our Depressed Classes.

Coming from a leading nationalist social worker interested in aboriginal tribes, these ideas clearly convey the nationalist line about the role of tribals in a future representative democracy in India. They were to be given seats in proportion to their total population in the Central Assembly, and even in the provinces the same principle was to be maintained. The stress in Thakkar's correspondences that the tribes were not 'vocal' also reveals the nationalist idea that the aboriginal tribes were 'silent' and had to be spoken for.

With regard to the part played by Hutton, it is difficult to understand his motives. Perhaps it is worth posing a related question: What would have happened if Hutton had provided the all-India figures of 'Aboriginal and Hill Tribes', and not the followers of 'Tribal Religion', to the Lothian Committee? Perhaps denying 24.6 million inhabitants any genuinely representative voice in the Federal Assembly would have been difficult and they would have received a greater representation even in the provincial assemblies. It is important to note here that eventually, Hutton and Grigson were nominated as officials to the Federal Assembly in 1935–1936, and there is evidence to suggest that Hutton intervened on the questions raised in the House on aboriginal tribes in general, and nationalist attempts to delegitimise the instrument of scheduling in particular.[80] Also, perhaps if the larger figure had not been mooted, the notion of the territorial segregation of predominantly tribal areas through the mechanism of exclusion and partial exclusion would have gained much less traction than it did in the years leading to the Cadogan

[80] 'The Reforms to Backward Areas', 18 February 1936, *The Indian Annual Register*, January–June 1936, Vol. I, p. 117.

Amendment debate in the House of Commons. Nonetheless, the question of 'if' can only be asked by a historian with great reservations in this case, as the evidence cannot corroborate any alternative thesis. However, it is clear from this narrative that the Census figures played a key role in the period before and during the events leading up to the passage of the Government of India Act, 1935.

The Argumentative Logic of 1931 Census Reports: Detribalisation under Acquisitive Hindu Civilisation

At the time of the 1931 Census operations, there was an unprecedented nationalist surge accompanying the Civil Disobedience Movement. Although the British government was able to control the mass movement, it did so with difficulty.[81] Thus, there was no possibility of returning to an absolutely centralised model of administration of the Backward Tracts as proposed by the Simon Commission. Consequently, the British were forced to engage with Indian opinion on the future constitutional model for India. The results were the Round Table Conferences, where the Imperial government held intense deliberations with Indians on a variety of issues.

As indicated earlier, a point that Hutton emphasised on several occasions in the 1931 Census volumes was the phenomenon of 'Hinduisation'. He noted that out of the 24.6 million people belonging to primitive tribes, only 8.28 million returned themselves as adhering to 'tribal religions'.[82] When compared to 1921 figures, this was 15.3 per cent lower, and for Hutton, this decline in numbers was 'primarily due to losses by conversion to Hinduism or Christianity'. As a qualification, Hutton remarked that undoubtedly, some of the decline could be attributed to the 'arbitrary classification of Tribal religion as Hindu'. He also highlighted the fact that some of this decline owed itself to propaganda by Hindu and Christian zealots, who insisted that the primitive tribals return themselves as adherents of their respective creeds.[83] Hutton used comparative figures from the 1921 Census to suggest,

---

[81]Intending to swell the numbers of Hindus, several organisations were conducting 'Shuddhi' campaigns to return tribal subjects as Hindus in large parts of Assam, Bihar, and Bengal. There is substantial evidence of these activities in the volumes of the 1931 Census report. See also Chapter 3.

[82]Hutton, *Census of India 1931*, p. iii.

[83]Ibid., p. 391.

> ... the extent to which the Hindu community is indebted to accretion from tribal religions for its growth at this census. With the exception of Baluchistan, where the Hindus are generally speaking immigrants and their number easily influenced by the composition of military units in Quetta, no province has shown any proportionate increase of Hindus to the general population except where there have been tribal religions to draw from.[84]

Hutton clearly disliked this trend and took up cudgels against nationalist politicians in the discussion on tribal religion. He gave the following set of reasons behind his argument that 'very ancient and primitive beliefs continuing(ed) under the guise of Hinduism':[85]

> ... it is not difficult to understand the claim of certain politicians that the term Hinduism should cover all religions having their origin in India, even though we hold that the original impulse came from the Mediterranean or Asia Minor, since Jainism, Buddhism and Sikhism are all offshoots of the same root. The claim is less logical when applied to tribal religions which have not yet reached the stage of accepting the Brahmanas as priests or of attaching any sanctity to the cow or of worshipping in Hindu temples in their own villages. An occasional visit to Hindu temples away from home is not quite a safe test since many such shrines undoubtedly occupy sites dedicated originally to more ancient indigenous deities and subsequently Hinduised, and in any case it is typical of primitive religion to propitiate the gods of any locality they may visit. Admittedly however the line is hard to draw between Hinduism and tribal religions. The inclusion of the latter within the Hindu fold is easy and wherever hill and forest tribes live in permanent daily contact with Hindus their religion rapidly assimilates itself to that of their neighbours though the old method of thinking is unchanged. Thus it is that religious or quasi-religious beliefs and practices among Hindus appear very frequently to be used on the principles of magic, *mana* or other ideas common in primitive religion. The very word *brahma* itself seems to have probably connoted originally supernatural power or influence of the nature of *mana*—a view apparently supported by Atharva Veda, and these beliefs and practices survive and operate with all their primitive qualities alongside the loftiest heights of asceticism and philosophy.[86]

---

[84] Ibid., p. 392.
[85] Ibid., p. 397.
[86] Ibid.

The above formulation is a good example of how Hutton (for instance, in invoking the *Atharva Veda*) was responding to the challenge thrown up by Sedgwick in the 1921 Bombay Census report. Essentially, the followers of tribal religions were in danger of rapid depletion precisely in the areas where the aboriginal tribes were in 'permanent daily contact' with Hindus. On the contrary, wherever their location was deeper in the hills and forests that prevented such everyday interaction, the threat of cultural and demographic decline was less palpable. Significant in this respect was Hutton's comment that 'the numbers of Tribal religion have also suffered depletion owing to the decay, which attacks so many primitive tribes when brought into contact with civilisation.'[87]

As a top bureaucrat of the British Indian Empire, Hutton was well aware that the impending constitutional changes in India could sound a death knell to the system of special administrative regimes in predominantly tribal tracts. This anxiety permeated the text of the 1931 Census report. He used the culture contact paradigm of the Neo-Diffusionists widely while arguing for a protective policy towards Indian aboriginal tribes. The key to this protectionist policy in the Huttonian worldview was limiting contact with civilisation. With this logic, Hutton repeatedly argued against the 'opening up' of tribal tracts and wrote,

> The rapid opening up of communications involving contact at many points and often the practical settlement of tribal country, generally speaking, substitutes conflict for contact, not necessarily a conflict of arms but of culture and material interest. Attempts to develop minerals, forests or land for intensive cultivation can only be made at the expense of the tribe whose isolation is thus invaded; tribal customs which regulate the ownership, usufruct or transfer of land are normally superseded by a code of which the tribe is deprived of its property, generally in the name of law, either by alienation to foreigners or by transferring the trusteeship of a tribal chief into absolute ownership of a kind quite foreign to the customs of the tribe.[88]

Thus, the effects of 'opening up' were often disastrous and contact usually translated into conflict, especially in cultural terms. Hutton drew upon the colonial traditions and stereotypes to outline the negative impacts that the imposition of systematic administration had had on tribal communities. These communities were crushed by excise laws, and as the power visibly

---

[87]Ibid., p. 392.

[88]Ibid.

passed to Hindus and Muslims, and as both were pro-prohibition, the future looked bleak. While alien civil laws had pushed the tribals into a hopeless debt trap that frequently led to land alienation, the criminal laws of civilised communities were often 'entirely at variance with what is felt to be just and proper by tribal custom'. Similarly, Hutton illustrated through examples how the traditional rights of primitive tribes on land and forests were being severely curtailed. The colonial State had banned shifting cultivation, and although Hutton agreed that this method of cultivation was 'frequently extremely wasteful of forest land', he also highlighted that it was 'very often the only known means of subsistence'. Likewise, the exploitation of minerals deprived the tribals of their land and introduced an alien population in their midst, which impinged upon their lives in many ways. Missionaries had also created havoc by breaking the unity of the tribal communitarian spirit. Echoing his past masters, Rivers and Balfour, on culture contact, Hutton raised an alarm when he wrote,

> It is easy to see how combination of anti-tribal forces is likely to create a condition of excessive discomfort in tribal life, the most serious aspect of which is the complete breakdown of the communal organization. A tribe living in comparative isolation will usually be found to have developed an adaptation to its environment which within certain limits approaches perfection, an adaptation which may have taken millennia to accomplish, and the breakdown of which may be the ruin of the tribe, for it is likely to proceed at a far greater rate than either the gradual change in physical environment or than the still slower process of adaptation to that change.[89]

Hutton noted that by declaring the predominantly tribal areas as 'non-regulation districts', the colonial State had provided a mechanism through which the adverse impacts of contacts with civilisation could be effectively managed. The administration was 'in a position to tamper the conflict of interest', which was potentially ever-present. The results were special laws such as the Chota Nagpur Tenancy Act, which provided a bulwark for the tribal communities' control over land as a resource. Another example of a wise policy was banning the appearance of pleaders in courts and hearing the tribals' cases in accordance with their customs. However, he admitted that there were loopholes in the functioning of such exceptional mechanisms, for they had not worked very well. As a warning sign against the possible erosion of protective legislation, Hutton wrote,

[89]Ibid., p. 506.

> It seems more than likely that the incorporation of tribal areas into regulation areas, when such areas are governed by more or less democratic forms of government on the constitution of which the tribes will be placed in an insignificant minority, will bring their interest into direct conflict with the interests of their neighbours under conditions in which the administration of the tribal area will have very little power to modify the severity with which it will react on the tribes. Tribes occupying such an area realize little or nothing of the method in which laws are administered outside it; if they do they have no means of making themselves heard. The consequence is that a few alien settlers who are able to do so and are wishful to live under the ordinary codes, which give tremendous advantages to traders and others dealing with simple and unlettered men, are likely to succeed (it has under existing conditions often been done) in getting a method of administration extended to a tribal area the disadvantages of which to the tribesmen are completely unappreciated by them until they find themselves irrevocably within its grip. In the process of accommodation it is only too likely that a previously nonhinduised tribe may become a depressed caste.... In the alternative they may retain a sort of emasculated tribal life, deprived of the customs and festivals that gave it meaning and cohesion, and fall into that physical apathy and physical decline which has decimated so many tribal communities in the Pacific and elsewhere; and this decline is accelerated in another way by opening up of communications. Many new diseases are imported against which no immunity has been evolved, since they do not form part of the environment to which the tribe is adapted, and the result is a staggering mortality from which there may be no recovery.[90]

Coming at the very end of Hutton's all-India report, these lines are indicative of the ideological argument that permeated the entire text of the 1931 Census report. *First,* by formulating the religio-philosophical definition of 'Tribal Religions,' Hutton established the disparate group of 142 communities of 'primitive tribes' as a minority element of the Indian population, distinct from 'Hindu' society. *Second,* he suggested that the comparative isolation of tribal habitats had enabled them to evolve and maintain a culture which was highly suited to their environment. The impact of colonialism on these isolated communities had been debilitating, but because of the special administrative regimes operative in these 'non-regulation' areas, they could still hold their own. This tribal culture, however, was increasingly coming

---

[90] Ibid., pp. 506–507.

under threat due to the ever-growing intrusion of missionaries, adventurers, and traders, who came from outside and introduced a number of evils that had spread disease and degeneration amidst them. *Third*, Hutton suggested that the impending new constitutional scheme, whatever it may be, was set to increase this outside intervention on a scale unknown earlier as under the democratic form of governance, the special laws for these tracts were set to wither away. Furthermore, the rapid 'opening up' process was geared to infuse new industries such as mining which, besides being highly exploitative, would increase the unwanted 'outsider' element. Hence, *finally*, Hutton argued that the possible outcome of such exacerbated 'contact with civilisation' could only be either 'detribalisation' accompanied by 'Hinduisation', followed by a loss of interest in life, which eventually culminated in the depopulation of communities. He predicted that if the former happened, then the tribes would be converted to Depressed Castes among the Hindus.

Hutton's Policy Interventions in the Constitutional Discourse

Once Hutton had established his argumentative logic in the 1931 Census, he set out on a related mission with his usual zeal. This was to oppose, tooth and nail, the extension of legislative powers of the provincial and federal assemblies over areas primarily inhabited by tribal communities. According to K. S. Singh, Hutton did this because, as an anthropologically trained administrator, he believed that the tribals 'formed a distinct element in the Indian population which was not amenable to normal constitutional processes but which required a strategy of intervention by the government to protect their rights and promote their welfare'.[91] However, any analysis of Huttonian strategies of protection leading up to the passage of the Government of India Act, 1935, has to begin from his memorandum submitted to the Indian Statutory Commission. It is significant for the hill *versus* plains binary which Hutton put his weight behind. Without an understanding of this ideological edifice, Hutton's later strategy cannot be made sense of.

In his evidence to the Simon Commission, Hutton emphasised that unlike the plains, where a 'regular routine of standardized and codified administration' was in force, the prevailing system of administration and policing was completely different in the hills. Most significantly, the land

[91]K. S. Singh, 'Foreword', in Hutton, *Census of India*, 1931.

revenue system, various forms of which operated across India, had 'never been and probably never could be introduced'.[92] While the hills were definitely 'an unprofitable possession', Hutton argued that they had been occupied by the British 'to protect the plains but we have no moral right to accomplish that end at the expense of the hills themselves'.[93] The hill tribes were remarkable for 'decentralization and individuality' in their own indigenous systems of administration, which also provided an alternate vision for the future in the creation of autonomous tribal areas.[94]

Further, in the case of Assam, it was undesirable to place the hill districts under the Assam Legislative Council since this would not suit the needs of the hills and would also impede the development of the plains. The hills already possessed 'a great measure of local self-government' and any future reform should be attempted through the agency of tribal councils. Elaborating his concerns, Hutton wrote,

> Politically they [the hillmen] are at present lacking in cohesion among themselves and with no common basis for the election of representatives; even in restricted areas they have little unity of sentiment such as would enable them to work for a common end. They can produce no leaders of education suitable to represent their interests on an elected body, and they have no community of interest whatever with the people of the plains, which would enable them to obtain suitable sponsors from the more educated communities of the province and their present representation on the Legislative Council is farcical.... A fair representation would mean at least one representative from every tribe, and more than one from some tribes. It is to be doubted that the Council would accept such a proposition with equanimity, but even if it did, the difficulty of finding representatives who could understand

---

[92]Indian Statutory Commission, Memoranda Assam, 57–1033, E-Assam-126, Note by Mr J. H. Hutton, C.I.E., D.Sc., Deputy Commissioner, Naga Hills, dated 17 March 1928 (Part of Memoranda of the Government of Assam on the working of the reformed government prepared for the Indian Statutory Commission), Appendix B to Chapter II, Assam Government Press, 1928, IOR/13/1/1.

[93]Ibid., p. 5.

[94]Ibid. 'The true solution of the question of their administration is the gradual creation of self-governing communities, semi-independent in nature, secured by treaties on the lines of the Siemships in the Khasi Hills or the Shan States of Burma, for whose external relations alone the Governor of the province would ultimately be responsible.'

> one another and the President would be insuperable for a generation at least.[95]

Here, we can see that even Hutton was drawing a link between education and a capacity to represent the interests of a tribal community. Since the hill tribes lacked an educated class of representative politicians, it was better that their areas be kept away from the elected councils, which would be flooded by such characters from the plains. If the hills were brought under the scope of reformed councils, not only would the Council become a 'battle ground of religious contention', but under a popular government, the hill vote would also be of no importance and the interests of the hillmen were bound to suffer. Finally, large financial concerns with vested interests in the exploitation of oil and coal would further harm the interests of hill societies.[96]

As apparent in Chapter 1, Hutton was one among many in the colonial bureaucracy who believed that the predominantly tribal tracts should be territorially segregated spaces where laws passed by Indian legislators should not apply. In this context, scholars like Poornima Paidipaty have highlighted Hutton's position that complete exclusion was the only way forward and partial exclusion was an insufficient remedy.[97] I shall deal with this issue shortly. However, an unknown aspect of Hutton's views is that he recommended a system of separate electorates for aboriginal tribes.

As mentioned in an earlier section, in March 1932, Hutton deposed before the Lothian Committee. The Committee heard only two others[98] on the issue of representation to the aboriginal tribes. Hence, Hutton was the chief 'expert' on whose arguments the Committee could ultimately rely. This limited deliberation on the issue of tribal representation was linked to the fact that the British were only extending franchise rights, and not making them universal. Only provincial subjects who met certain financial (land revenue, chowkidari tax, etc.) or educational qualifications were included in the voters' roster. Consequently, franchise was restricted to only a small and relatively privileged section of the Indian population. Given their poor

[95]Ibid., p. 3.

[96]Ibid.

[97]Poornima L. Paidipaty, 'Tribal Nation: Politics and the Making of Anthropology in India, 1874–1967', Ph.D. Dissertation, Graduate School of Arts and Sciences, Columbia University, 2010.

[98]These were the Chota Nagpur Improvement Society and W. H. Shoobert, the 1931 Census Superintendent for the Central Provinces.

economic and educational status, most tribal subjects could not even hope to enter the domain of representative politics. Even in large administrative units such as the Central Provinces, which had a significant tribal demographic, their absence from the electoral rolls was obvious.

In his written statement submitted to the Lothian Committee, Hutton urged that the aboriginal tribes be given definite representation. He contended that the millions of hill and forest tribes were a distinct element of the Indian population. They were not Hinduised, followed their own unique set of beliefs that constituted but one form of the Indian 'tribal religions', and 'occupied a social position which was certainly not that of the depressed classes'.[99] Therefore, he declared that they should be 'somehow represented on any body which had the right of legislating for them'. The problem of tribal representation could best be solved through nomination, but he realised it would be extremely difficult 'to find suitable representatives to nominate from the tribes to be represented'. The remedy for this was to be found among colonial officials. Hutton asserted that by far 'the best representative from most of the hill tribes was some official, who had had long administrative experience of the people he had to represent'. Additionally, he asked for 'absolute freedom' for such official representatives 'to vote in the interests of the people they represent', since 'the interests of the Government might frequently be antagonistic to those of the tribes represented'.[100]

Appearing before the Committee, Hutton argued that by making no reference to the question of tribal representation during the Round Table Conference, the Government of India indicated that it 'was not very much interested in them', and he feared that their case would 'go by default'. When a Committee member asked whether he thought that the aboriginal tribes were capable of exercising franchise, he replied that 'many of them are most capable and not all'. Hutton opined that at least in the excluded areas, the tribes themselves should elect their representatives.[101] He was also of the opinion that seats should be allotted to the tribals on the basis of their

---

[99] *The Times of India*, 24 March 1932, p. 5.

[100] Ibid.

[101] Evidence of Dr J. H. Hutton, D.SC., I.C.S., Census Commissioner for India, Selections from Memoranda submitted by Individuals and Oral Evidence (Punjab, Bihar and Orissa, Central Provinces, Assam, North-West Frontier Province, and Delhi), *East India (Constitutional Reforms), Indian Franchise Committee, 1932 Vol. V*, Published by HMSO, 1932, Printed in India, pp. 495–503, Question 29.

proportion in the total population, with a minimum guarantee of one seat. On being asked whether a plural constituency (that is, where more than one representative was sent to the legislatures) was a suitable system of representing its people, Hutton remarked that unless 'special representation' were given to the aboriginals, they would not get any representation.[102]

Hutton made the case for the clan system of the tribes to be used as the basis for enfranchisement.[103] However, any utilisation of the clan system to elect a tribal representative had to be carefully worked out, with different details for different areas. Reproduced below is a particularly crucial part of Hutton's oral evidence,

> Q22: Assuming it is impossible to hold elections in these areas, what system would you suggest for their representation?
> Hutton: I would mention a concrete example; In Kolhan in Bihar and Orissa there is the clan organization still existing. It is known to all aboriginals there. According to it, the village headman elects representatives of several villages and they again meet together and elect tribal representatives. There you have got a complete system already. It is, however, quite absent in Bombay.
>
> Q23: Will you suggest any special franchise by which a certain number of these people could be put on roll?
> Hutton: I think you should have a separate roll.
>
> Q24 (Mr Chintamani): Would you be satisfied if there was a recommendation that the Agency tracts in Madras and the other areas in other provinces which you have mentioned in your note are constituted into separate electorates instead of being mixed up with contiguous areas or the plains portion of Vizagapatam, Ganjam and Godavari in Madras?
> Hutton: I should be satisfied if it also stipulated that the representative should be one of the tribes of the area.
>
> Q25: Could you not trust the members of those tribes to elect one among themselves, if available?
> Hutton: If there is one among them they will elect.
>
> Q26: They will have discretion to do that?
> Hutton: I would trust them.
>
> Q27: I think you will get carpet-baggers?

[102] Ibid., Question 37.

[103] *The Times of India*, 24 March 1932, p. 5.

> Hutton: They can be trusted to turn such people out. They will realize what is involved in electing an outsider, though in some cases it might work against them. In Ajmer-Merwara, however, Mr. Sarat Chandra Roy, who was chosen to represent their interests, did so fairly well. I think there should be a stipulation that no outsider should be chosen as their representative.[104]

A perusal of the above evidence suggests that at the time of the Round Table Conferences, Hutton was vouching for an award of separate electorates for the election of aboriginal representatives. In doing so, he was clearly following the lead provided by the most vocal segments of 'minorities' recognised by the colonial State, that is, Muslims and Depressed Classes. Although he continued to hold on to the belief that the excluded areas should be outside the purview of elections, Hutton's position had become more nuanced since the time of the Simon Commission. His suggestion that officials with a long administrative experience of tribal areas be allowed to function as representatives suggests that he also wanted the 'official block' to stay and provide a bulwark against any depletion of protective mechanisms by the predominantly nationalist Legislative Councils and Assemblies.

When a member asked Hutton if the aboriginal question was an all-India matter or a provincial one, he replied, 'It depends entirely on the Constitution to be conferred on India.' While Hutton was keen that the aboriginals be represented in the Federal Assembly, he was against a uniform and standardised solution to the representation of aboriginals across British India. He remarked that although the prevalent social and political system ignored the tribals and kept them outside of it, he was not sure whether 'they feel oppressed by that at all'. On the contrary, he thought that the tribals would 'prefer to remain outside'.[105]

At the end of Hutton's evidence, a member asked for his clarification on an apparent contradiction: 'You say effective representation is required for aboriginal tribes, but you say that the hill and forest tribes should be excluded.' Hutton answered, 'I did not mean any distinction. I would exclude all the people I could for the time being. Wherever I could get a homogeneous area I would exclude it and treat it as a native state.'[106] This line is significant because, in essence, Hutton sought to exclude the tribes

---

[104]Evidence of Dr J. H. Hutton, *East India (Constitutional Reforms), Indian Franchise Committee, 1932 Vol. V*, pp. 495–503.

[105]Ibid.

[106]Ibid.

completely from the workings of the reformed Constitution and treat all 'homogeneous' territories as a potential autonomous area. This aspect of Hutton's policy line will become more apparent shortly when we come to the evidence he gave before Sub-Committee D of the Joint Committee on Indian Constitutional Reforms.

Hutton's imprint on the Committee's report was apparent in its very short chapter on the 'Aboriginal and Hill Tribes'.[107] Numbering five million (a key statistic which Thakkar thought was fraudulent), such groups were found mainly in the 'highlands and hills' of various provinces, living 'a life entirely apart from the rest of the population of India'. Since, under the franchise scheme being recommended by the Committee, 'only a negligible number' amongst them would be brought to the electoral rolls, their 'interests' should be 'protected by effective representation in the councils, or, if this is not possible, by some other arrangement in the new constitution'. The Committee strongly recommended the adoption of some method of election by the local village headmen, which was far more preferable to the earlier system of nomination. However, a serious obstacle in such an electoral path was the lack of suitable tribal candidates. The Committee suggested and hoped that 'an electorate formed of headmen would be sufficiently intelligent to see that their representative, even if not an aboriginal himself, would be capable of looking after their interests in the legislatures'. The evidence providers (chiefly Hutton and Shoobert) highlighted to the Committee that the aboriginals were 'an entirely distinct community from the depressed classes, and under no circumstances should the two communities be amalgamated for purposes of representation'. The Lothian Committee accepted this argument. It is significant to state here that Dr B. R. Ambedkar, who too was a member of this Committee, did not submit any dissenting note. Hence, we may infer that he did see the two categories as indeed quite distinct from each other in matters of identity, interest, and representation.

Thus, Hutton nearly succeeded in achieving some of his key demands. The Lothian Committee report put its weight behind the idea that at least in the provincial councils, aboriginal interests should be protected by providing them with 'effective representation' (which was the prevalent term for separate electorates). However, a spanner was thrown in Hutton's plans by three Indian members of the Lothian Committee who resolutely

[107] *Indian Franchise Committee, Vol. I, (Report)*, Central Publication Branch, Calcutta, 1932, pp. 135–136.

opposed the Committee's proposal to provide separate electorates to Aboriginal and Hill Tribes. These were S. B. Tambe, C. Y. Chintamani, and R. R. Bakhale, the last two being Members of Legislative Council. Coming from a staunchly nationalist vantage point, the three jointly submitted a detailed rebuttal of many of the Committee's recommendations. In the context of the Committee's stance vis-à-vis the issue of representing the tribes in Legislatures, their dissenting statement included the following:

> We are strongly opposed to separate electorates for any class or community and cannot subscribe to any proposal to create a fresh class or caste electorate. We therefore do not agree with our colleagues in recommending that seats should be set apart for aboriginal tribes. The reason advanced for special representation of these tribes is that they live a life entirely apart from the rest of the population and therefore their interests and welfare should be protected by efficient representation. The implication is that the future governments will not look after their interests; but the experience of the past ten years shows that more attention has been paid by Ministers to the welfare of the backward classes than before the reforms. More persons from these classes are likely to be brought on the electoral roll under the proposed extension of the franchise, and their advancement will be more rapid by being brought into closer association with the general population than by being kept aloof. Undoubtedly the uplift of these tribes should be an active concern of the legislatures. The areas they inhabit should no more be relegated to the position of 'excluded areas'. There is at present a number of non-official agencies working for their uplift, and with the extended franchise now proposed one or more of them will not find it difficult to secure election to the legislatures, and they will make the welfare of the tribes their special concern.[108]

The above extract should count amongst the earliest formal expressions of nationalist opposition to the colonial policy of carving out 'excluded areas' in British India. Its appearance in a high-level official document about the future constitutional arrangements marks a watershed moment. These Indian members expressed an unambiguous and vehement criticism of the idea of granting separate electorates to the Aboriginal and Hill Tribes. The trio's reference to 'non-official agencies' working for the 'uplift' of Aboriginal and Hill Tribes also suggests, in all probability, a close link with organisations

---

[108]Minute of Dissent by Messrs. S. B. Tambe, C. Y. Chintamani, and R. R. Bakhle, in ibid., p. 225.

such as the Bhil Seva Mandal under A. V. Thakkar, a theme that will be explored in Chapter 3. Thakkar himself jumped into the debate and, in a piece severely critical of Hutton, vociferously opposed any move to provide separate electorates to the aboriginals on the lines demanded by the Muslims and the Depressed Classes. Hutton's suggestion of resorting to nomination in certain cases was also rejected by Thakkar, on the grounds that it was 'objectionable under any system of responsible government because it gives the Governor, in some degree power to make or unmake a Ministry'.[109]

The majority members of the Lothian Committee issued a rejoinder to the dissenting minute in which they expressed displeasure at the trio's suggestion that the system of joint electorates be given a free hand in predominantly tribal areas.[110] The Committee did not recommend any seats for the aboriginal tribes in the Federal Assembly, but suggested that in the provinces, certain seats should be reserved. Consequently, they deferred any final recommendations on the question and remarked that the issue should be re-examined by local governments at a later date when the delimitation of electoral constituencies was finalised.

The fruit of the Indian Franchise Committee's recommendations was the announcement of the Communal Award of August 1932. The British government agreed to provide separate electorates to Mohammedans, Sikhs, Indian Christians, Anglo-Indians, and Europeans in the enactment of the future Government of India Act.[111] However, it did not recognise the principle advocated by Hutton—that the followers of 'Tribal Religions' were a distinct religious minority who should be given separate electorates. Thus, the official dissenting note by the joint nationalist trio of Tambe, Chintamani, and Bakhale had successfully torpedoed Hutton's suggestion of separate electorates for Aboriginal and Hill Tribes. Hutton's labours had received their first major setback. His arguments had failed to cut ice with the top brass at the India Office as well as the British Cabinet. Regardless, he was to put up a valiant fight in the final round of constitutional politics that followed the declaration of the Communal Award.

The sum total of all negotiations and policy deliberations was encapsulated in a White Paper of the British government released in March

---

[109] A. V. Thakkar, 'Representation of the Aborigines', *The Servants of India Society* XV (23), 23 June 1932, p. 192.

[110] 'Brief Note by a Majority of the Committee', *Indian Franchise Committee, Vol. I (Report)* Central Publication Branch, Calcutta, 1932, p. 234.

[111] *The Times of India*, 17 August 1932, p. 9.

1933. This document put forward the official British view on the various aspects of the constitutional solution to be offered to Indians. These were guidelines and broad contours along which the final set of deliberations before the drafting of the Government of India Bill were to take place. A Joint Committee of both the House of Commons and the House of Lords was formed to decide on the broad framework of the future Federal Constitution of India. Paragraphs 106–109 of this document outlined the mechanism of total exclusion and partial exclusion. At this stage of constitutional deliberations, Hutton changed his strategy and asked for a much expanded territorial solution for the Indian aboriginal populations.

In his memorandum and evidence to the Joint Committee on Indian Constitutional Reforms, Hutton recorded his fundamental reservations and opposition to the proposals contained in the White Paper. While expressing satisfaction with the provisions of total exclusion, '*provided* exclusion is widely and freely resorted to at the outset', he opined that the scheme of partial exclusion was not a useful tool.[112] Hutton reiterated throughout his evidence proceedings that the aboriginal 'interests' were not adequately protected under the White Paper proposals, and felt that they 'should go further'.[113]

Hutton's ideal scheme for predominantly tribal areas was the one recommended by the Indian Statutory Commission or the Simon Commission Report.[114] It is important to highlight here that it was the Simon Scheme for 'Backward Tracts' that changed their nomenclature to 'Excluded' and 'Partially Excluded' Areas. The totally excluded areas were to be centrally administered and financed by the Central government, and the provinces could not interfere in their administration at all (including raising questions in the respective Legislative Councils). This aspect of the Commission's recommendations was vehemently opposed by the Government of India, as well as by most local governments. Nevertheless, such stringent provisions for the total exclusion of tribal areas from processes

[112]Memorandum of Evidence to be given by Dr J. H. Hutton, C.I.E., I.C.S. to Joint Committee of Indian Constitutional Reform, IOR/Q/IDC/45, p. 1, emphasis in the original. Also reproduced in *Joint Committee on Indian Constitutional Reform, Minutes of Evidence taken before sub-committee D, Die Lunae 16 Octobris, 1933*, His Majesty's Stationary Office, London, 1933, pp. 6–13. Henceforth, *HE (Hutton's Evidence)*.

[113]*HE*, p. 25.

[114]Ibid.

of modern representative democratic politics had greatly pleased Hutton. He wished more areas to be 'added to' such a list.[115]

In this regard, Hutton advocated a massive expansion in totally excluded areas. In the province of Assam, he asked for total exclusion to be extended to the North Cachar Hills, Mikir Hills, Garo Hills, and part of the Jaintia Hills. In other provinces, Hutton suggested that the Chittagong Hill Tracts of Bengal; Palamau and Ranchi districts, Damin-i-Koh in Santal Parganas, and Kolhan in Singhbhum in Bihar; Lahaul and Spiti in the Punjab; and certain parts of Orissa, Central Provinces, Bombay, and Madras Agencies, as well as the Andaman Islands and some parts of Burma, be totally excluded.[116]

Despite his view about the inadequacy of the White Paper's provisions on partial exclusion, Hutton still advocated its application to certain areas where it was 'impracticable' to impose total exclusion. Thus, Hutton's wish-list of partially excluded areas comprised the hill tracts in Madras, south of the Godavari River, and certain tribal majority parts of northern Bengal, Bihar and Orissa, and the Central Provinces. However, he insisted that in order to ensure good administration, the officer in charge should have the power to remove any person from the area deemed undesirable by him.[117]

According to Hutton, partial exclusion was an 'unsatisfactory expedient' as it placed the 'Governor of a Province in a difficult position in which his special responsibility for the interests of the aborigines may be found at issue with the views of both his Ministers and his Council'. He argued that the experience of Bihar and Orissa as well as Assam had shown that 'pressure will undoubtedly be brought upon the Government ... to extend the regime of ordinary law to the hill and forest areas where it is a curse and no blessing'.[118] Thus, his chief objections were against the interference of legislative bodies and the jurisdiction of the High Courts. In effect, Hutton argued that the legislature and judicial functions of the State should remain permanently suspended until the areas themselves chose to integrate themselves in the Provinces. In the Huttonian paradigm, ideal exclusion would mean that all power would be concentrated in the executive or the proverbial 'man on the spot', who was usually a 'sympathetic' European officer.

[115]Ibid., p. 26.
[116]Ibid., p. 13.
[117]Ibid.
[118]Ibid., p. 17.

A careful look at the Memorandum of Evidence supplied by Hutton to the Joint Parliamentary Committee on Indian Constitutional Reforms proves that the imagination of a perpetual and irreconcilable opposition between hillmen *versus* plainsmen undergirded his argument. For instance, Hutton stressed that the 'primitive hill and forest tribes in all parts of India differ from their neighbours in the plains in race, in social organisation, in communal and domestic habits, in religion (very largely) and in their general attitude towards the philosophy of life'. Therefore, Hutton argued that both groups (the aborigines of the hills and the civilised of the plains) could not be 'conveniently included in the same system'. Referring to the irreconcilable differences between the two, Hutton argued that the aborigines were numerically insignificant, and hence their 'representation in an elected body will carry no effective weight'. Hutton argued that since aboriginal interests were 'commonly alien if not antagonistic to the interests of their more civilised neighbours', it was extremely likely that the former would be sacrificed as the latter enjoyed numerical majority. Hutton also reiterated the theme that was becoming commonplace in the late colonial constitutional deliberations, viz., the 'silence' of the aboriginal tribes. Articulating the tribals' wish for autonomy, he wrote, '(T)he aboriginals themselves although unvocal, are in several cases conscious of the dangers to themselves of inclusion in the autonomous provinces and are definitely wishful for self-determination and for the preservation of their traditional culture and manner of life.'[119]

Hutton also argued that the administration of hill and forest tracts was a 'specialised' domain and pleaded for the establishment of a special cadre of servicemen in order to avoid serious 'mistakes'. He contended that the 'interests of the aborigine is often alien to or antagonistic to the interests of the plainsmen', and consistently resorted to the hill *versus* plains binary. His illustrations covered broadly the aspects of the (*i*) ownership of land; (*ii*) administration of forests; (*iii*) exploitation of the land for minerals; (*iv*) administration of excise; (*v*) provision of education; and finally (*vi*) administration of justice. The dominant trope of Hutton's objections was based on the issue of the application of law. His memorandum outlined in detail many of the stock arguments of administrators as to why tribal areas should be kept out of the ambit of the proposed provincial legislatures.

Predictably, the first issue raised by Hutton was that of land alienation. He argued that tribal law generally did not recognise forms of realisation

[119]Ibid., p. 6.

of debt through dispossession. However, the law courts based on alien principles of justice had aided the 'civilised' outsiders in forcing tribals to part with their land. Similarly, forest laws had been disastrously inimical to tribal interests. Tribal communities generally subsisted on hunting-gathering and shifting cultivation which, as livelihood practices, required large stretches of forested land. By limiting the tribal communities' exploitation of forest products, the colonial policy of creating forest reserves had gradually illegitimised their way of life.[120] Similarly, policies of mineral exploitation often dispossessed these communities from the vast stretches of land previously in their possession.[121]

It was in the 'administration of justice' that Hutton saw the main flaw in extending systematic administration to predominantly tribal tracts. Outlining the disadvantages of applying normal law to tribal areas, Hutton wrote,

> The methods of the plains courts and the legal procedure is completely unsuited to the hillmen and the errors of High Courts particularly the Calcutta High Court, have resulted in serious injustices in the past. Where the Hillman is in contact with the plainsman and the two frequent the same courts with the same procedure the Hillman very soon learns that truth and a straight-forward statement of his case does not pay. Consequently, he resorts to chicanery in which he is no match at all for his more sophisticated neighbour. In non-regulation district, however, the rules of the procedure code are not strictly adhered to, and the more common method is, as in the Assam Hills, to follow the lines indicated by tribal methods. Distances are great and communications bad, and the first essential of justice in the hills is that it should be speedy. Consequently a form of summary procedure is generally found most suitable for all but really serious cases. Generally, owing to the difficulties raised by languages and customs entirely alien to the plains, lawyers are useless. They are only allowed with the permission of the court, which would be given wherever their interference would be of any value, but generally the employment of lawyers merely complicates cases, and if they once took to practicing in the Naga Hills, for instance, the administration of justice would probably become impossible. At best it would become a mere gamble instead of as at present, a generally effective dispensation of tribal customs qualified by equity. It should be added that the presence of legislative bodies is always towards

[120]Ibid., p. 7.

[121]Ibid., p. 9.

> introducing the lawyer. This is shown by experience (of Bihar and Orissa).[122]

To supplement the above argument, Hutton gave the examples of the hill districts of Assam and the Damin-i-Koh of the Santal Parganas, where policing was 'generally both absent and unnecessary'. It is here that the change in Hutton's argument first becomes pronounced, for he wrote,

> The clansmen themselves, when not interfered with, are their own courts and their own police. A small civil police force is maintained to deal with the foreign population, ... but is not normally allowed to interfere at all in tribal cases. For sophisticated people probably both police and lawyers are necessary evils, but where neither is found to exist, or to be needed, it seems a mistake to introduce them.[123]

No longer did he resort to the religious distinctiveness of primitive tribes, which he so carefully sought to define in the 1931 Census. Instead, from now onwards, the preservation of 'tribal custom' became the pivot of his thesis for the territorial protection of predominantly tribal tracts. This significant change in Hutton's argumentative strategy is buttressed by few other pieces of evidence.

The articulation and defence that Hutton mounted in person before Sub-committee D of the Joint Committee on Indian Constitutional Reforms was perhaps the climax of his policy intervention on the future of Indian aboriginal tribes. On 16 October 1933, he appeared before the committee, which also had Indian members like Hari Singh Gour, B. R. Ambedkar, and Shafa'at Ahmad Khan. This episode was also probably the only instance when Hutton was confronted by hawk-eyed legal minds like Gour and Ambedkar. As will be apparent shortly, their critical examination revealed inconsistencies and problems within the Huttonian paradigm.

In Hutton's oral examination by the Sub-committee, it was the issue of local tribal custom being at variance with normal law that was stressed upon. In his Memorandum, Hutton had cited the instance of a Bhil who was sentenced by the High Court for carrying out marriage by capture, 'which would undoubtedly have been acquiesced in by the society in which he lived'. When H. S. Gour enquired if this was an incorrect decision by the

[122]Ibid., pp. 12–14.
[123]Ibid.

Court, Hutton replied that, 'The trouble arises when you do not allow such a case to be settled by local custom.'[124]

During Hutton's oral examination, he suggested that nomination alone was an appropriate method for the representation of backward areas in the provincial legislature. Inside the Backward Tracts, however, Hutton thought it was feasible to hold a 'Tribal Durbar'. Offering his reasons for abjuring elections completely, Hutton said,

> No, because it seems to me that the real representatives of the areas are the older men, who are familiar with custom, and who are recognised by the younger people as representing them, but who are quite incapable of coming forward in anything like a legislative assembly. That is the great difficulty. The man who really represents the feelings of his village is not the educated man who can come forward in an Assembly and play a part, but one of the old men of the village who retains the traditions of his tribe. For that reason, I would urge total exclusion wherever possible.[125]

The minutes of the evidence also reveal that on this issue of custom, Hutton was critiquing the entire edifice of colonial jurisprudence as practised in India. In reply to a question by Sir Reginald Craddock, Hutton said that 'part of the evil is that the Civil and Criminal Courts recognise Hindu and Muslim law and never recognise tribal law'. This made it useless for the tribes to plead their respective case in any court of appeal.[126] In contrast to other parts of British India, Hutton proudly proclaimed that in the Naga Hills, 'my courts often administer the customary law'. He added, 'What I am afraid of is that once the district is regularized the administration of the customary law will be prevented.' Hutton also wanted an absolute ban on lawyers and the High Court. He approvingly cited Sir John Simon, who had reportedly told him upon visiting the Naga Hills, 'Whatever you do, do not let the lawyers come in. They will only ruin the place.'

---

[124] *The Times of India*, 18 October 1933, p. 9. The Bhil case is also referred to in J. H. Hutton, *Census of India 1931*, p. 506.

[125] Memorandum of Evidence to be given by Dr J. H. Hutton, C.I.E., I.C.S. to Joint Committee of Indian Constitutional Reform, IOR/Q/IDC/45, p. 1, emphasis in the original. Also reproduced in *Joint Committee on Indian Constitutional Reform, Minutes of Evidence taken before sub-committee D, Die Lunae 16 Octobris, 1933*, His Majesty's Stationary Office, London, 1933, pp. 6–13.

[126] Ibid., p. 15.

As an astute legal authority,. Hari Singh Gour picked up the logical thread running through Hutton's memorandum, which was the hill *versus* plains binary. Gour's probing revealed cracks in the Census Commissioner's argumentative paradigm. He asked Hutton 'whether the conditions he has described in Assam apply all over India and in Burma, the Shan States, and so on?' Gour clarified that by using the word 'conditions' he meant whether the aboriginal tribes in Assam occupied certain 'localities', that is, geographical features such as the hills. To this query, Hutton replied in the affirmative, adding that this was 'partially true of other parts of India, certainly'. Upon being asked for examples in 'other provinces', Hutton replied,

> I should say it occurred in the Agency Tracts in Madras; in certain districts of Chota Nagpur, not all over, but in the Palamau and Ranchi districts; the Damini Koh in the Santal Parganas; the Kolhan in Singhbhum; Lahaul and Spiti, undoubtedly in the Punjab; and probably in areas in southern Madras with which I am not acquainted; Nicobar Islands and Laccadives islands; parts of Central Provinces. I do not know Central Provinces well enough to give any areas; the Chanda Zemindari.

This exchange provides the clearest expression in the archive that Hutton juxtaposed the hill *versus* plains understanding he had developed in Assam to almost the entire Indian subcontinent. Gour pressed on and said that the application of Hindu law to all non-Muslims was mandated by Warren Hastings through the British Parliament's Regulation Act of 1776. Hence, he asked Hutton if he was objecting to a process which had been 'going on for about a century and a half', to which Hutton again replied in the affirmative. The following is a particularly interesting excerpt from their exchange:

> Gour: Your complaint is therefore of the past?
> Hutton: And the present.
>
> Gour: The difficulty has now arisen that that law has now become stereotyped in the case of many aboriginal types who have been following *nolens volens*, the family law, and accepting it.
> Hutton: In some cases, that is true; in many cases not. I do not think it applies among the Gonds of the Central Provinces at all.
>
> Gour: Many of them claim to belong to the Kshatriyas, the ruling classes?
> Hutton: Some of the sophisticated Gonds do.
>
> Gour: And the rest would belong to the Hindus?
> Hutton: Many of them; not all of them.

Gour: Have you noticed that these tribes are gradually becoming assimilated to Hinduism?
Hutton: In some cases, certainly. In one case, at any rate, to Muhammadanism.

Gour: But in the bulk of them the tendency is to gravitate towards Hinduism?
Hutton: Yes.

Gour: For how long has this process been going on?
Hutton: I imagine for 2,000 years.

Gour: Therefore, if you were to lock them up in compartments of their own, do you not think this process of evolution would be retarded?
Hutton: Not necessarily. Nobody wants to interfere with their religion; at least, I do not.

Gour: At the present moment, every member of the aboriginal tribe when he leaves the village and comes to the town becomes a member of the Hindu community (I am speaking of the bulk of them; some of them became members of the Muslim community as well) and they take part in the daily life of the Hindus and mix with them, and they are not regarded as depressed classes at all?
Hutton: They are usually regarded as depressed classes when they become Hindus.

Gour: Not the Gonds?
Hutton: In Bihar and Orissa, certainly.

Gour: That may be so, but in the Central Provinces the Gonds and the Bhils are not regarded as depressed classes?
Hutton: Are they not?
Sir Reginald Craddock: They governed the country for four centuries.
Sir Hari Singh Gour: Quite so. As a matter of fact they are proud of the fact that they were the rulers of the country?
Hutton: In Madras, certainly they are treated as depressed classes.

Gour: So the observations you have to make would be qualified to the extent that conditions throughout India are not the same and a generalisation dealing with the aboriginal conditions might be true as regards one province or locality, but would not be true of another province or another locality?
Hutton: It might not be equally true as regards all province. I admit that you cannot generalise completely for India. It is a very large place....

Gour: Do you think that in spite of the Act [Scheduled Districts Act], the aboriginal tribes have suffered?
Hutton: I do.

> Gour: To what you would ascribe their suffering?
> Hutton: There are various causes in different places.
>
> Gour: So you cannot generalise even on that ground?
> Hutton: No.
>
> Gour: If, therefore we do not know what are the causes which lead to these sufferings on the part of the aboriginal tribes, we cannot lay down one general rule as to how to deal with them?
> Hutton: I would not say that. One may not know the cause of an illness, but one may know the general rule for applying a cure.[127]

In the above cited extract, it came out quite clearly that the pivot of Hutton's argument was that the aboriginal was a quintessentially hill/forest dweller who had to be protected from the civilised plainsmen. His experience in Assam coloured Hutton's diagnosis and prognosis of the tribal question across the subcontinent. When Gour questioned him, the contradictions within Hutton's argument were made apparent, and Hutton himself admitted the inapplicability of a one-size-fits-all formula that he had been advocating before Sub-Committee D of the Joint Committee on Indian Constitutional Reforms.

Another very interesting exchange which Hutton had in the very same meeting was with the illustrious Dr B. R. Ambedkar. Also an astute logical and legal mind, Ambedkar first made Hutton accept the central tenets of his own position, explicit and implicit in Hutton's written and oral evidence. In doing so, Hutton agreed that the tribes should 'under no circumstances come within the purview of the new constitution'. When Ambedkar asked Hutton to succinctly articulate his ideal solution to the tribal predicament, the latter replied, '(T)he minimum of interference by anybody'. In some future time, however, Hutton thought that the areas in question should 'become part and parcel of civil society and outgrow the tribal conditions'. Having said that, he qualified the statement that the time was not yet ripe for such a change, and there was a possibility that 'in some cases you might never be able to achieve that ideal'. Reiterating his core belief, Hutton added, '(What) troubles me is that unless they are separated they are likely to be destroyed by too abrupt contact. That is what has happened nearly everywhere else in the world.' In interrogating Hutton further, Ambedkar, perhaps deliberately, pulled out the central issue, that is, protection of land,

[127] *HE*, pp. 22–23.

on to the Committee's table. A lengthy exchange followed, which deserves to be reproduced in detail:

> Ambedkar: My suggestion is this, that if these primitive people are brought under the same constitution as the rest of India they would not be quite alone in their demand for keeping the moneylender out and seeing that the land remains in the hands of those who cultivate it. There would be many others who would have a similar demand to make in the Legislature. The point I want to make is that they would not be isolated?
> Hutton: The point that I should be inclined to make is that the proof of the pudding was in the eating, and, as far as experience went, it has shown that they always have been done out of their land.
>
> Ambedkar: But, Dr. Hutton, would you mind making this distinction, that the Legislatures, as they were composed some time ago, are not going to be the same as the legislatures that will be composed under the White Paper?
> Hutton: Yes.
>
> Ambedkar: You would have a certain amount of representation of the depressed classes in the various legislatures. You would have certain amount of representation assigned to labour, and you would have, I am sure a certain amount of representation drawn from the general electorate who would favour the poorer classes. The experience of the last Legislature would be no safe guide in a matter of this kind?
> Hutton: I would sooner be on the safe side and exclude them.
>
> Ambedkar: I do not know, but you are not prepared to deny the fact that they would have many friends in the Legislature?
> Hutton: I would not admit that. I should like to be convinced first that they would have many friends. There may be others with similar interests, but they would have very little in common with them individually.
>
> Ambedkar: Yes, but I mean so far as the general question of protection for a class similarly situated is concerned?
> Hutton: I can conceive that a Musselman cultivator in Silhat would demand the maximum of protection for himself and the maximum of non-protection for his neighbour.
>
> Ambedkar: Do you think the Legislature would go to the length of saying that certain laws which are necessary in the interests of Indians are not to be extended, and that the protection of those laws is not to be given to the primitive classes?
> Hutton: No, I do not think they would go as far as that.

Ambedkar: How would the discrimination arise?
Hutton: I think the primitive classes might have extreme difficulty in obtaining the necessary protection. There is no guarantee with the depressed classes that the cultivator will obtain the necessary protection under the new constitution.

Ambedkar: Quite true; I agree with you. There can be no protection that the other classes probably would not club together and prevent protection being given to some other minorities? The fear is legitimate, but taking into calculation all the forces on the one side and all the forces on the other, the point I want to make to you is that the fear, that one or two, or a few representatives of the primitive classes in the Provincial Council will feel that they are overwhelmed by the forces on the other side, is not quite justified by an analysis as I am presenting it to you of the composition of the future Legislature as it will be under the White Paper proposal?
Hutton: In view of the difference of race, I think it is possibly justified, at any rate in certain places....

Ambedkar: Therefore, as I say, taking their educational need, in the Legislative Council, they would not find themselves isolated?
Hutton: They might do.

Ambedkar: You would desire that they should be completely excluded, and their need, such as education, which I think is the greatest need of these people myself, should be met entirely by revenues supplied by the Governor under his special responsibilities?
Hutton: Yes.

Ambedkar: I want to put this to you: whether a Governor would at all go to the length of providing what he thought was a sufficient amount of funds for the education of the primitive classes if his Ministers did not support him?
Hutton: That is a serious difficulty.

Ambedkar: If there is something in the point that I have put to you, would not it be desirable that some representatives of these people should be in the Legislative Council so that a member may be dependent upon their votes, and may be amenable to their wants?
Hutton: An odd vote or two would not be likely to affect a Minister.

Ambedkar: I do not say one or two. You may have a small number, but assuming they have adequate representation in the Legislature, would not the Ministers be dependent upon their votes, and, therefore, he might be more amenable to their wants?

> Hutton: Theoretically, but not in practice. Their numbers would be so small.
>
> Ambedkar: In politics a single vote might turn the balance....
> Ambedkar: But my point is that the Minister would have a word, because there would be other rival claims for expenditure, and a Minister cannot be expected to be interested in primitive peoples who are not part of the legislature.
> Dr Shafa'at Ahmad Khan: Would not the representatives of the primitive people in the Legislature generally combine with the depressed classes?
>
> Ambedkar: That is what I am visualising, and, therefore, they would have many friends?
> Hutton: I do not think the representation would be affected.
>
> Ambedkar: If I felt as pessimistic as you feel I should at once say: 'I do not want this constitution at all'?
> Hutton: But I do not, for the primitive tribes.[128]

I have chosen to reproduce the official exchange *in extenso* because this is the only piece of archival evidence I have found in which the two leading ideologues of the Depressed Classes and the Aboriginal Tribes were exchanging ideas. One crucial undercurrent that permeates this debate is the polar opposite views of the political process. For Ambedkar, speaking a full year after the Poona Pact with Gandhi, was propounding a politics of the marginalised where disparate groups were likely to come together on issues of common interest. He was hopeful that a common ground could be found and an alliance between representatives of the Depressed Classes and Aboriginal Tribes could function as an effective antidote to untrammelled governmental power in the hands of civilised elites, who were mostly caste Hindus.

In stark contrast stood Hutton, who saw no hope for the aboriginal tribes in the future nationalist political framework. Although he never directly criticised either the Indian National Congress or any other political party, Hutton's silence on the effect of nationalism on aborigines was suggestive. As a career 'man on the spot', Hutton was a quasi-military figure who had spent two decades in the North-eastern frontier. As such, he clearly equated nationalists with representatives of the forces of 'civilisation', who were bound to have a debilitating impact upon the tribes. As the exchange with Ambedkar indicated, Hutton placed no value on the possibility of exploited

[128] Ibid., pp. 28–30.

sections forming alliances inside the Legislative Assembly or councils. For him, hill tribes were numerically insignificant everywhere and their support to run the government could never be substantial enough to merit any real negotiations by the powers based mainly in the plains. Elsewhere in the oral evidence and memorandum, Hutton's argument is clear: that any failure to protect the tribes from legislative interference and jurisdiction of the High Courts would certainly mean their cultural extinction. The forces of civilisation (and Hindu civilisation in particular) could not be let loose upon tribes who were ill-prepared to survive what Hutton foresaw as Hindu civilisation's formidable economic and cultural onslaught. Hence, he argued that the best course of action would be to totally exclude as many tribal areas as possible because the instrument of partial exclusion was insufficient. Once such scheduled areas were identified, they should be completely shut off from all contact with civilisation. Thus, in a nutshell, Hutton's ideal solution was to create 'islands against civilisation'.

After giving evidence to the Joint Committee, Hutton started developing this argument further by taking into cognisance practices of 'indirect rule', as they had developed in the African colonies of the British Empire. An instance of this was provided in his Presidential Address to the 22nd Indian Science Congress in 1935. Explicating on the 'practical value of a study of anthropology', Hutton stated,

> Thus in Africa the substitution of Indirect Rule for the older system of direct administration is the immediate result of applied anthropology. Indirect Rule is an educative system and its objective is to evolve by a natural process an indigenous system of administration which shall conform to civilized standards without jettisoning what is good and environmentally suitable in the native systems which direct rule must completely obliterate. To quote the Report of the Kenya Land Commission: 'The principle is that it is better to take the native customs as they stand and build from them as a basis, than to rely upon some novel but imported pattern which would not be understood.' Such a principle involves of course not only the knowledge of what is but of what has been the knowledge of the origin and *raison d'etre* of customs and belief, since no complete understanding of these is possible without the knowledge of how and why they came into existence and developed as they did. The experiences of Africa have an important bearing on the administration of the more primitive parts of India, and it would be wise in our administration of tribal areas to look for light not from the east but from the dark continent.... [A]lthough the

> system of Indirect Rule has lately incurred much criticism and may in some cases have been carried too far, we have had only too little of it in India.[129]

Thus, Hutton advocated a massive expansion in the areas to be totally excluded from the new Constitution. Despite his dislike for partial exclusion, Hutton still advocated its application to certain areas which had already been penetrated by plainsmen to varying degrees. He insisted that even in the partially excluded areas, the officer in charge must be given powers to remove any undesirable person if this was unavoidable for good governance. Finally, Hutton suggested that while deliberating upon the boundaries of excluded or partially excluded areas, 'regard should be given to tribal rather than to political boundaries'.[130]

The selection and training of officers, too, was a necessary aspect of Hutton's scheme to territorially protect aboriginal areas. He proposed that a separate 'Department for the Protection of Aborigines' be established by the Government of India, with its headquarters in either Delhi or Calcutta. It should be headed by a Director with twelve provincial officers working under his command and supervision.[131] While the Director's duty would be to supervise and co-ordinate the efforts of the provincial officers, the latter were assigned the following tasks: advising the Governor-in-Council on the welfare of aborigines; touring for 200 days every year; advising on all legislation; acting as Deputy Governor should any such appointment be made for any Scheduled District as provided in the Montague–Chelmsford reforms; sitting as Assessors in cases where aborigines were being tried for serious offences; collecting specimens for provincial museums.

Hutton recommended that each of these provincial officers be given a seven-year contract and be chosen from 'men of anthropological training and practical experience'. They were to inculcate a knowledge of tribal languages and must be willing to engage in serious research work amongst the tribal

---

[129]J. H. Hutton (Congress President), Presidential Address, 'Anthropology and India', *Proceedings of the 22nd Indian Science Congress, Calcutta, 1935*, Asiatic Society, Calcutta, 1935, p. 31.

[130]Ibid., p. 21.

[131]Note by Dr Hutton: Suggestions for a Department of Protection of Aborigines, IOR/Q/13/2/83. (Bengal & Assam—2 each, Madras and Andaman—2, one each for northern India, Bombay, Central Provinces, 3 officers would provide surplus reserves for leave and special duty.) The rest of this section is based on this source.

communities. Elaborating upon the other important aspects of his scheme, Hutton wrote,

> It is essential that the officers recruited should be men of high education ability and character, able and not reluctant to propound and defend their own views, since any innovation of method or outlook is always treated with suspicion or hostility by bureaucracies. The service should probably be European, or mainly so, until it can be replaced, as it should be, by officers remitted from the aborigines themselves.

The above extract makes it eminently clear that Hutton did not put an iota of trust in the ability of Indians to benevolently administer his beloved aboriginals. Rather, he believed that in the absence of tribals administering themselves, only 'sympathetic' European officials were capable of protecting them.

After a detailed explication of Hutton's views and role in the constitutional discourse on tribal areas, I now move to an analysis of his successor, James Mills, who, in one form or another, continued Hutton's argumentative line in the period after Hutton retired from service. Mills succeeded Hutton in administrative positions on several occasions, which allowed for a certain level of continuity in terms of both ideology and administrative policies. For these reasons, it is important to outline and analyse Mills' contributions to the discourse on Indian aboriginal tribes.

3

J. P. Mills and the Huttonian Paradigm

James Philip Mills (1890–1960) was educated at Winchester College and Corpus Christi College, Oxford. In 1913, he entered the Indian Civil Services and served for many years in the Naga Hills of Assam. In official positions, he succeeded Hutton three times: *first*, as the Assistant Commissioner of Mokokchung Sub-Division; *second*, as the Deputy Commissioner of Naga Hills; and *finally*, in 1930, as the Honorary Director of Ethnology, Assam. After two years at this position, Mills was promoted as the Secretary to the Government of Assam. In the final phase of his India career, he served as Advisor to the Governor of Assam for Tribal Areas and States (1943–1947).[1] After his retirement from active service, Mills returned to England and was appointed as Reader in the Department of Anthropology at the School of Oriental and African Studies, University of London.

As Hutton's immediate junior in the Assam cadre, Mills became his closest associate. Both were simultaneously posted in the Naga Hills District, a large administrative charge divided into two sub-divisions—Kohima and Mokokchung. Mills succeeded Hutton as the Sub-Divisional Officer for the Mokokchung Sub-Division of Naga Hill Region, and remained at this position from 1917 to 1924. Subsequently, he utilised this administrative experience to write two authoritative monographs, *The Lhota Nagas* (1922) and *The Ao Nagas* (1926), which were published by the Government of Assam and established his reputation as an expert on the Nagas. It is clear from Hutton's introduction to *The Lhota Nagas*[2] that he had encouraged

[1]The information in this introductory paragraph has been taken from David R. Syiemlieh's 'Introduction', in David R. Syiemlieh (ed.), *On the Edge of Empire: Four British Plans for North East India, 1941-1947*, New Delhi: Sage, 2014.

[2]J. P. Mills, *The Lhota Nagas (with an Introduction and Supplementary Notes by J. H. Hutton, C.I.E., Hon. Director of Ethnography, Assam)*, Published by direction of the Government of Assam, Macmillan and Co., London, 1922.

Mills to undertake a study of this tribe for 'they, more than any other tribe in the Naga Hills District, were beginning to lose their distinctive features' under the influence of the American Baptist Mission or the Hinduism practised by settlers from Nepal or Assam.[3] Hutton expressed satisfaction that Mills had 'put them on record while there was yet time'.[4] The book followed the standard format adopted by most ethnographic studies done by colonial officers: a general introduction, followed by details of the tribe's domestic life, laws and customs, religion, folk tales and songs, and finally, the language of the tribe along with a few short pieces attached as Appendices.

Like Hutton, Mills too was increasingly influenced by W. H. R. Rivers' work on the debilitating effect of culture contact on primitive tribes. Building on Rivers' thesis, Mills began to articulate a set of administrative arrangements for ensuring the protection of the tribes. For instance, he wrote in his book:

> While it would be far from true to say that all customs of all races are good, yet suddenly to sweep away the entire culture of a race is to ruin it. To expect a race to adjust itself immediately to a new social scheme is like trying to turn a tank fish into a sea fish by putting into salt water; it dies, and so does the savage. The late Dr. Rivers has shown that races deprived of their old interests tend to dwindle and become extinct.[5]

Also, in a review of a book on the 'Red Indians' by G. E. E. Lindquist, published in *Man in India*, Mills noted the failure of the American government's policy of creating 'Reservations' for Native American tribes. Drawing an analogy with the Naga hillmen, Mills wrote,

> It is not yet too late to apply the moral of this melancholy story to this situation in parts of India today. There are still in places such as Assam primitive hill tribes living the life which centuries of experience have shown to be best suited to their environment. But two dangers threaten them. Some are unlucky enough to live where coal and oil are found, and there is grave risk that the land which now grows rice may some day be taken to produce dividends for share-holders. If the demands of commercial progress are too imperious to be denied, the tribesmen should, if possible, be given suitable land near the few places where it is available, and the mistakes of the Reservation policy of the United States avoided. I emphasise that the land must be near,

[3]J. H. Hutton, 'Introduction', in ibid., p. xi.

[4]Ibid., p. xii

[5]Ibid., p. 20.

Image 4: James Philip Mills at his study, 1935
Image courtesy: Pitt Rivers Museum, University of Oxford, 1998.266.11.

> to plant the village of one tribe on the land of a distant and alien tribe is to court disaster. Failing suitable land in the same tribal area, adequate yearly compensation from royalties is the only alternative. But it is a bad one, which is almost bound to tend to idleness and degradation [*sic*]. The second danger which threatens these primitive folk is a greater, more insidious one. Under the pretext of 'civilizing influences' certain organizations are pursuing towards the hill tribes a policy of denationalization and assimilation very similar to that which is being carried out towards the Red Man in the United States. Not only is it unnecessary, for there are still ample areas left which are never likely to be taken from them where the hill tribes can live their own lives undisturbed, but its results are likely to be even more disastrous than in America.[6]

Here, we see Mills beginning to form a set of ideas that would define his career for the next three decades or so. 'Segregation' was preferred to 'assimilation', and a modified 'Reservation' policy was advocated for protecting the 'hill tribes'. The success of such a policy was based on ensuring the possession of 'suitable land'.

---

[6]J. P. Mills, 'The Lesson of the Red Man', *Man in India* III, 1923, pp. 221–222.

Mills' second book, *The Ao Nagas,*[7] contained a Foreword by Henry Balfour, and hence even here, the line of patronage/endorsement continued. Several photographs, sketches, and supplementary notes were provided by Hutton, in addition to a long bibliography on the Nagas. A significant aspect of this book was the attack launched by Mills on the Christian missions working in the Naga Hills. A careful perusal of his footnotes and text, especially the pieces in Appendix III and IV, titled 'Administration' and 'The Effects of Mission Work Upon the Aos', gives us a fair idea of Mills' ideological position. Mills accused the missionaries of breaking the unity of village life and provoking non-converts on everyday matters concerning village rituals and practices. The result was a total disruption of the social life of the Aos, which was now marked by strife rather than harmony.[8] The converts began seeing the beliefs of their forefathers as vestiges of the past which must be shunned.

Mills argued that tribal life was built on the 'subordination of the individual to the community', but the spread of Christianity had inculcated the novel conception of the 'communion of the individual's soul with God and its eternal salvation as objects of far greater importance than the prosperity, or even the existence of the State'. This resulted in a 'general disintegration of the body politic' of the Aos:

> The non-Christian Ao is far from being unselfish ... but he thinks much of the welfare of his village. He hates to live away from it, he works for it, he helps to run it, he subscribes to its worship, he readily shares in presents which it gives to guests, he feasts it and in the old days, he fought for it. Though the Christian still retains some of this love for his village and willingness to serve it, the feeling is undoubtedly less strong in him. Christians are often quite willing to live elsewhere than in their villages, and converts frequently refuse to take any part in its government. Attempts are often made to avoid little acts of social service on the most trivial excuses.... In matters where their religion is concerned Christians will work together, but in secular matters they are inclined to rate the welfare of the individuals far above that of the body politic, and if the process continues their villages will become

---

[7]J. P. Mills, *The Ao Nagas (with a Foreword by Prof. Henry Balfour and Supplementary Notes and Bibliography by Prof. J. H. Hutton)*, Second edition, Published by direction of the Government of Nagaland, Delhi, Oxford University Press, 1973 (First edition published by Macmillan & Co., London, 1926).

[8]Ibid., p. 412.

> mere collections of houses instead of highly-organized social units in which every man shoulders his burden of service and responsibility.[9]

The imposition of an alien Western culture was detrimental in other ways as well. For instance, Mills argued that Western dress was 'entirely unfitted to the Naga mode of life', and had contributed to the spread of pulmonary disease in the Naga Hills. More dangerous was the fact that a Naga who adopted foreign dress also 'adopts with them a foreign outlook'.[10]

The next important public statement by Mills came with the publication of the 1931 Census. Hutton gave a lot of space to Mills, as a result of which the third volume has a total of nine articles by Mills, two of which he co-authored with A. H. Fletcher. While eight of these pieces were ethnographic notes on various tribes, the ninth article, on 'The Effect on the Tribes of the Naga Hill District of Contacts with Civilization', provides an explication of his views on culture contact.[11] Mills argued that while improved communications had led to improved trade (in which the Nagas were taking an active part), this had had unintended consequences on the local society and economy. New diseases such as tuberculosis and venereal disease had been introduced, and 'epidemics spread more quickly'; the scourge of tuberculosis, he feared, might eventually lead 'the Nagas and Kukis of these hills [to] follow other primitive peoples into oblivion'. Following the British colonisation of the region, it had become common for gangs of Naga men to go and work in the tea gardens. Such men were 'apt to waste money on rubbish they see displayed in the shops, and for distilled liquor for which they acquire a taste'. The casual labourer ('himself the product of contact with civilization') was most affected by such changes as he had 'no wife with him to brew his rice beer and buys spirits instead'. Another related evil was the rise in the numbers of opium addicts among the detribalised Nagas living in Kohima bazaar. Mills ended his article with a grim view of the future:

> Will the time come when these hills will be inhabited by scattered families, without pride in the past or hope for the future, without arts and without recreation, dressed in non-descript garments as drab as

[9]Ibid., pp. 419–420.

[10]Ibid., p. 422.

[11]J. P. Mills, 'The Effect on the Tribes of the Naga Hill District of Contacts with Civilization', in J. H. Hutton, *Census of India (With Complete Survey of Tribal Life and System), Vol. III*, New Delhi, Gian Publishing House, 1991 (reprint), pp. 147–149. The next few citations are from this source.

> their lives, and busy only to win from the steep, rocky slopes enough sustenance to enable them to beget children and die?

In Chapter 1, I have discussed how Mills' anthropological reputation earned him a short appointment as Officer on Special Duty in the Reforms Office of the Government of India following the Cadogan Amendment episode in the British Parliament. The final report that Mills submitted at the end of his appointment (titled 'Note on the Backward Areas of British India and their position under the Government of India Act, 1935') was a remarkable document in many ways.[12] In this note, there were clear signals that Mills was beginning to think of Central India. Unlike the north-eastern region which he was familiar with, and where a binary of hills and plains could work, Central India exhibited mixed populations.

The report starts with a brief yet clear explanation of the idea of devising special administrative regimes for predominantly tribal areas since the early days of colonial power. It also explains the reasons why the Scheduled Districts Act and the Laws Local Extent Act, 1874, became necessary. He also took objection to the statement that Indian opinion was unanimously opposed to the full application of that policy, arguing that 'apart from the opinion of the seventeen million voiceless aboriginals of British India, Indian scientists are overwhelmingly in favour of it'.

Mills went on to chart the lines of argumentation of the opponents of the policy of exclusion and then critiqued several of their key arguments. *First*, he took on the notion that the primitive tribes were bound to be absorbed into the general population and that the adoption of special measures for their seclusion was to uselessly 'postpone the inevitable'. He remarked that such an argument was fallacious as,

> Absorption, in any true sense of the word, can only come about by intermarriage. The Danes, Saxons, Normans, and so on were absorbed into the general population of England because they intermarried with it. In India caste is the bar to absorption. In purely Moslem areas, where intermarriage has taken place, the 'tribal problem' is either non-existent or negligible; in the far greater Hindu area it is urgent. No one can foretell when, if ever, inter-caste marriage will become normal. Till

[12]J. P. Mills, 'Note on the Backward Areas of British India and their position under the Government of India Act, 1935', in F. No. 4/III/35-G(B). & K.W., General (B) Branch, Reforms Office, GoI, 1935. The rest of the section is based on this source.

> it is the fifteen million Brahmins and the twenty million aboriginals of India will alike remain unabsorbed.

Second, Mills questioned the notion that the 'aboriginals must and should be assimilated to the general population' because,

> Assimilation is not only possible, but inevitable, if no steps are taken to prevent it. But it can only be with the Depressed Classes ... the disabilities of the Exterior Castes and the mental and moral effects of these disabilities are still serious. The Depressed Classes were primitive tribes once and no one could wish the remaining tribesmen to join them.

The above extract shows that Mills viewed the tribe-caste continuum in terms very similar to those articulated by Hutton. By stating that 'caste is the bar to absorption', Mills argued that the only manner in which the tribes could be absorbed in the socio-religious fabric of Hinduism would be as Depressed Classes.

Mills advocated an alternative and highly decentralised political imagination for India, which could be created along tribal 'clan' lines. Applauding the customary law practices of tribal communities, he viewed them as great repositories of legal principles which could be drawn upon when India tried to evolve a legal system of its own. 'These laws will be needed in the future,' he wrote, 'for a growing body of opinion holds that the day will come when the complicated procedure of English law will either disappear from India or be modified and simplified beyond recognition.' Mills' argument for the protection of tribal customary laws was double-pronged: on the one hand, he attacked the uniform standardised Western law and legal institutions as unsuited to the complex and variegated Indian social conditions, while on the other hand, he presented tribal customs as an invaluable repository of traditional wisdom evolved through many generations of living in a particular environment. In doing so, Mills espoused the theoretical paradigm advocated by W. H. R. Rivers, Henry Balfour, and his mentor-cum-predecessor, J. H. Hutton, who undoubtedly was the leading ideologue of scheduling in the discourse on Indian constitutional reforms.

Arguing in favour of special protection for predominantly tribal areas, Mills wrote that experience had shown that the admirable qualities of tribal communities could only survive if they were 'given time and space to develop on their own lines'. To deny these factors to the tribes would be to 'oppose the world-wide demand for self-realisation, the strongest movement of our generation'. He also thought that it would be 'inconsistent and unfair' to deny the primitive tribes the 'chance of working out *their* salvation in their own way'.

While making recommendations on the individual areas in provinces, Mills claimed to have 'used every scrap of reliable information I could find to make what might be called an aboriginal survey of the whole of India'. However, while dealing with such a large expanse as the Indian subcontinent, Mills encountered several problems, since India was divided into Provinces and States whose boundaries had been fixed without taking into account factors of 'race, culture or outstanding geographical features'. Since administrative boundaries were not congruent with tribal clan organisation, Mills took a case-by-case approach. Since it was 'not races but areas' which had to be excluded or partially excluded, he acknowledged that such areas 'must be of reasonable size and have easily recognizable limits'. Due to these administrative considerations, Mills recognised that his recommendations failed to include a very high percentage of the aboriginals of India who ought to fall within them. Like Hutton, who openly regarded total exclusion as preferable to partial exclusion, Mills indicated his preference for the former, although never stating this position unequivocally in the report itself.

For the most part, Mills suggested criteria based on numerical strength to the provincial governments while recommending areas for exclusion and partial exclusion. In his own survey, however, he used the categories 'tribalisation' and 'detribalisation', borrowed from African sociological literature. Outlining the logic of this distinction, he wrote:

> My criterion is that if a body of aboriginals still retains a tribal organization it retains with that organization qualities which make special protective measures desirable; if, on the other hand, a body of aboriginals is detribalised it generally for all practical purposes forms part of Depressed Classes and must share their fate, be it good or bad. Where to draw the line between tribalised and detribalised is a matter which has to be decided on the merits of each case.

One of the most interesting proposals that Mills made in this report was the provision for 'Special Officers'. In Chapter 2, we saw that Hutton too had mooted a proposal for a Department of the 'Protection of Aborigines', which had to be manned by such Special Officers. Mills developed these ideas in greater detail in his report, arguing that the effective fulfillment of 'special responsibilities' that the Government of India Act, 1935, had entrusted upon the Governors of the provinces where aboriginals were present in any significant numbers could only be achieved through the agency of Special

Officers. The situation required that the Governor be 'fully and constantly informed of their condition and needs'. In the absence of a 'Special Officer', it was the District Officer, the veritable 'man on the spot', who kept tabs on the state of affairs in aboriginal areas. However, they were very often 'busy men', who 'found it difficult to get away on long tours on foot through hills and jungles'. Also, the forest tribes often lived away from roads and any tours of the District Officers usually followed such routes in cars, making it difficult for them to accurately assess the conditions under which the tribals lived. Consequently, unless the District Officer was truly sympathetic and interested in the primitive people, the tribals were prone to be 'neglected or left to the care of subordinates'.

Hence, Mills recommended that in certain provinces, a Special Officer should be appointed, and claimed that this was 'as essential to the welfare of primitive people as the exclusion and partial exclusion of areas'. Elaborating upon the duties of these officers, Mills wrote,

> The duties of the Special Officer are bound to vary somewhat from Province to Province and only experience will reveal them all. It is only possible now to suggest what some of them may be. He will have to examine every Bill that comes before the Local Legislature and see whether it contains anything harmful to those under his care. If it does, he will inform his Government of the fact and suggest provisos or amendments required to put the matter right. Equally important will be his duty of examining all existing provincial laws, regulations and rules, and of pressing in the proper quarter for such amending Bills and alterations as he considers necessary. When it is desirable that an Act passed by the Local Legislature should apply to totally or partially excluded areas only with certain omissions or modifications, it is on him that the Governor will rely on advice as to what those omissions or modifications should be. Similarly he will assist the Governor in framing any Regulations which may be required for the better government of totally or partially excluded areas. Lastly, and most important of all, he will have to tour constantly in order to gain first hand knowledge, especially of the remote areas which District Officers find it hard to visit. He will consult and be consulted by the District Officers till he is a reservoir of experience from which all can draw.

Further, in the report, Mills emphasised the legal aspects of the protective regime required for tribal areas. For one, he remarked that it was essential to find 'suitable pleaders for aboriginal litigants'. He also emphasised that the knowledge generated by the work of Special Officers should not be lost after their death or retirement. Hence, it was important that these be preserved by encouraging the Special Officers to write monographs on the tribes they had experience of. Mills waxed eloquent on such monographs as produced in Assam and Bihar and Orissa, and appealed to the other provincial governments to provide 'the small amounts of funds necessary for the production of similar detailed studies in their own jurisdictions'.

Mills' proposals are quite similar to Hutton's, who had argued for a seven-year contract for Special Officers to be employed in the Department for the Protection of the Aborigines. Mills, however, did not confine the selection to just the European members of the ICS, but was open to other services. However, nowhere in the report does he mention that Indians too were fit to man such positions, which indicated his closeness to Hutton's view on the matter. Perhaps one can also see in the proposal of a Special Officer a last-ditch attempt by Hutton and Mills to preserve the 'official block', as the final arbiter between elected Legislatures of the future and tribes who were not fit to use their votes intelligently.

Last but not least, in a provocative concluding segment, Mills raises questions about the future of the excluded and partially excluded areas in India. He also questioned whether this official policy would imply the 'everlasting separateness' of the aboriginals from Indian society and polity. For Mills, the answer was an emphatic 'No'. Explaining his preferred blueprint for future policy on tribals, he wrote,

> The tribesman has three needs greater than all others—land, health and education. He needs land because from land ultimately all food comes. He must have security of tenure, even to the extent of protection against himself by Land Alienation Acts. Without ample food he cannot resist the diseases prevalent in the unhealthy regions to which he has in general been forced to retreat. Health too is the best cure for his admitted insobriety. To cut off his legitimate supplies of liquor now is both cruel and useless. He will only distill illicitly, as the records show. It is admitted that he drinks primarily to drown his miseries. Reduce his miseries and his drink will reduce itself. Land, and hence food, has an intimate bearing on education. Even if the children of the parents hard put to it to get their next meal can be spared to go to school at all, it is next to useless to send them. Their starved little brains absorb nothing. Only a well fed child can learn.

Mills' recommendations about the actual carving out of excluded and partially excluded areas were only partly accepted by the Government of

India. Nonetheless, his stress on the Bombay and C.P. and Berar territories did bear some fruit, and while none of their areas were earlier mentioned in the draft Sixth Schedule (which was abandoned after the debate on the Cadogan Amendment), the final Order-in-Council of March 1936 contained many areas recommended by Mills.

Although it cannot be convincingly argued that this report was the sole basis upon which the areas were finally selected for inclusion in the Order-in-Council, it did, perhaps, succeed in making a major impact on official thinking about the aboriginal problem. With regard to the partial exclusion of areas in Central India, particularly the Bombay Province, Mills' recommendations went a long way and were decisive in the case of this province. His other major target area was Central Provinces and Berar, where his recommendations achieved a rather limited success. However, some of his ideas, for example concerning 'Special Officers', were far ahead of their times, and subsequently became an important part of the policy framework for 'tribal development' which emerged after independence.

So far, we have seen that both Hutton and Mills were frontier administrators posted for long years in the Naga Hills, and both of whom played an extremely important part in the constitutional discourse on the tribal population. They maintained a remarkable ideological unity and a certain consistency as policy framers of the protectionist regime devised in the form of excluded and partially excluded areas, as provided in the Government of India Act, 1935. Both believed in the existence of the hill *versus* plains binary, privileged tribal customary laws over British codes, viewed representative democracy with suspicion (if not contempt), and opposed the activities of Christian missionaries in predominantly tribal areas. They laid special stress on the necessity of maintaining a specialised corps of European officers 'sympathetic' towards the aboriginals. Hutton and Mills wanted to totally exclude large parts of the Indian subcontinent from the workings of a reformed Constitution. In Chapter 1, we saw how, despite tough opposition from the local governments at Bombay and Central Provinces, the final schedule included many territories within these two provinces under the category of 'partially excluded areas'. This was chiefly due to the efforts of and active lobbying by Hutton and Mills. Without their intervention, it was improbable that the Cadogan Amendment debate could have taken place, which eventually led to an all-India enquiry and culminated in the scheduling of large, predominantly tribal territories of Central and western India. It is useful to highlight here that of the two,

Hutton was undoubtedly the archetypical personality who left an indelible imprint on the conceptual journey of the 'aboriginal tribe'. However, despite the important positions he held, Mills only played a secondary role in the shaping of the discourse.

In Conclusion

In Chapters 2 and 3, I have tried to show that the ideological framework of the late-colonial constitutional discourse on the future of Indian aboriginal tribes was informed by a distinct anthropological worldview called Neo-Diffusionism. The leading ideologue of this theoretical framework was W. H. R. Rivers, who argued that the depopulation of the Melanesian Islands stemmed from rapid changes in the wake of European contact with these long isolated and self-sufficient human cultures in the Western Pacific region. Led by J. H. Hutton, a select group of anthropologically-minded administrators took up Riversian ideas and applied them in the Indian context to demand a territorial ring-fencing of 'homogeneous' tribal areas throughout British India. They highlighted the similarities between experiences in Melanesia and India to predict a demographic and cultural genocide if the rapid pace of changes was not stemmed in time. They collectively argued that the need of the hour was to save Indian aboriginal tribes from the triumvirate of civilisation, democracy, and law.

In 1929, Hutton became the all-India Commissioner for the upcoming 1931 Census exercise. In this position, he emerged as the leading ideologue of the British policy of 'protection' for aboriginal tribes in British India. In addition to policy interventions, Hutton also sought to respond to a serious delegitimisation of a key Census category, that is, 'Animism', in the 1921 Census report of the Bombay Presidency. To buttress the idea of the distinctiveness of tribal belief systems, Hutton spent considerable energy to erect 'Tribal Religions' as a philosophically coherent set of beliefs, and hence as a valid Census category. The several references embedded in the 1931 Census reports bear testimony to Hutton's attempt to show that the disparate set of tribal beliefs possessed a theological unity and stood absolutely distinct from Hinduism. It is in these articulations that certain of Hutton's ideas reveal an encoded meaning, which equated the word 'civilisation' with Hinduism in the Indian context. Thus, the British policy of scheduling excluded and partially excluded areas would create territorial enclaves in such a manner that they could be seen as 'islands against civilisation'. Their express purpose was to bar the infiltration of Hindu migrants inside tribal territory. This policy was supposed to preserve the economic self-sufficiency, cultural autonomy, and perhaps most significantly, the demographic character of tribal majority areas.

Hutton's penchant for binaries is reflected in the 1931 Census volumes where he tried to conceptually distinguish aboriginal tribes vis-à-vis the Hindu population. In doing so, Hutton widely deployed the hill-plains binary to distinguish tribal areas from non-tribal ones and argued that the interests of the two were at loggerheads with each other. This worldview was derived from his long experience of service in the Naga Hills, which had earlier found expression in his evidence before the Simon Commission. In juxtaposing the hill-plains binary over the entire Indian subcontinent, Hutton had in reality pushed the island imagery to its absolute limits. This theoretical imposition highlighted the essentially geographic nature of the metaphors which distinguished tribes from non-tribes (or caste) in the colonial discourse. Hutton's motives were revealed when he recommended separate electorates for the representation of aboriginal tribes. Here, he was following the lead provided by Muslims and the Depressed Classes, whose leaders had demanded and received the gift of separate electorates from the British ruling elites.

Thus, in the Huttonian paradigm, plains provided the seats of the civilisational 'core' while the hills constituted the outlying periphery. Essentially, Hutton changed the Riversian idea of 'colonialism as shell shock' and blamed 'civilisation' for the uncertain future that the Indian aboriginal tribes were staring at. In contrast to his ideological guru Rivers, Hutton (and later Mills) projected sympathetic European officials as the last remaining bulwark against forces of civilisation in India.

Thus, Hutton and his associates played a vigorous role in the constitutional deliberations by pitching their argument for the territorial segregation of predominantly tribal tracts to maintain a demographic status quo. Thus, 'excluded areas' were to act as a buffer against the potential exploitation of tribal communities. Their main argument was that aboriginals needed protection from the legislative powers of an elected body, where they will remain in a state of perpetual minority. Because of their numerical inferiority, tribals were set to lose the battle of culture contact, and hence the Governor (who would inevitably be British) would be the final arbiter in the application of any laws passed by the central or provincial legislature.

For Hutton, the best government for tribal areas was one that governed the least. He repeatedly emphasised the need for a gradualist approach to changing the social fabric of primitive tribal communities, and portrayed tribal elders as the keepers of tradition and hence as the only real 'representatives' of tribal interests. His contribution lies in his explication of a minority politics for a constituency that could not boast of an English-educated, middle-class elite. Locationally not an aborigine himself, Hutton nevertheless used a language of cultural distinctiveness and indigeneity.

Hutton's position on Tribal Religion as well as his stiff resistance to the introduction of representative democratic institutions in predominantly tribal areas was challenged only by some Indians. Some of them, like Hari Singh Gour and B. R. Ambedkar, were part and parcel of the constitutional committees where such issues were being probed. Social workers like A. V. Thakkar tried to point out the fallacies in the Census figures that Hutton had provided to the Franchise Committee. Their interventions in Hutton's assiduously constructed argumentative paradigm inside and outside the Joint Select Committee revealed vital flaws. In the Huttonian quest to carve out a distinct and monolithic pan-Indian tribal identity, the local variations were largely ironed out. Hutton's obstinate preference for an absolutely centralised and European controlled mechanism of tribal administration reveals his disdain for nationalism and any other form of modern associational politics. However, these were finer points of the debate which had little bearing in the 1930s, as in that period, the tribal question stood at the margins of constitutional deliberations.

Nevertheless, there was one figure who cultivated a strong inspiration to 'uplift' and 'assimilate' the Indian tribal people into mainstream national life. He was a man who preferred to work behind the scenes and played an extremely important role in the discourse on the future of aboriginals. The story of Amritlal Vitthaldas Thakkar deserves serious assessment if an understanding has to be developed about the evolution of a distinctively nationalist position on the politics of scheduling. Essentially, Thakkar argued that the tribal areas scheduled as excluded and partially excluded should not remain islands against civilisation. Doing so would shut them off from the larger changes happening elsewhere. It is his nationalist model of understanding aboriginal tribes that we must now turn our attention to.

4

Uplift, Assimilation, and Socio-Religious Reform

A. V. Thakkar and the Aboriginal Tribes

The nationalist historiography generated after independence has had a major side effect. With the notable exception of Muslims and Depressed Classes, the narratives have emphasised, for the most part, the rise and growth of Gandhian non-violent mass movements. Such an uncritical and narrow commissioning of research agendas has largely eclipsed the other fault-lines of representational claims.

Another unfortunate result of this tendency has been a lack of understanding about the social reformers active in the late nineteenth and early twentieth century. The idea of social reform in most history books lies confined to the nineteenth century, with emphasis on Rammohan Roy,[1] Ishwar Chandra Vidyasagar,[2] and Keshub Chandra Sen[3] in Bengal and Jyotiba Phule[4] in western India. However, the impulse to 're/form' society did not die with the demise of these pioneering figures.[5]

---

[1]There are a number of studies on Raja Rammohun Roy. For a recent one, see Shomik Dasgupta, *Ethics, Distance and Accountability: The Political Thought and Intellectual Context of Rammohun Roy*, New Delhi: Oxford University Press, 2021.

[2]For a book-length but dated account, see Subal Chandra Mitra, *Isvar Chandra Vidyasagar: A Story of His Life and Work*, New Delhi: Rupa, 2008 [1902].

[3]For a recent study, see John A. Stevens, *Keshab: Bengal's Forgotten Prophet*, New York: Oxford University Press, 2018.

[4]For a classic account, see Rosalind O'Hanlon, *Caste, Conflict and Ideology: Mahatma Jotirao Phule and Low Caste Protest in Nineteenth Century India*, New Delhi: Permanent Black, 2011.

[5]For a historical survey of socio-religious reforms, see Kenneth W. Jones, *Socio-Religious Reform Movements in British India* (The New Cambridge History of India, Vol. III-1), New York: Cambridge University Press, 1989.

Consequently, an entire generation of social reformers active in the twentieth century has either simply been left out of being recorded, or their contributions have been inadequately contextualised. Chronologically, many of these reformers' activities shared crucial overlaps with the constitutional reforms that the British unfolded at the end of every decade since the Minto-Morley reforms of 1909. Their efforts were not only instrumental in creating a generation of educated leaders well-suited to represent their respective communities, but also enabled Gandhi to expand the impact of nationalist ideas amongst various groups hitherto oblivious to them. In the context of Tribal/Adivasi Studies, specifically, this lacuna in understanding becomes even more critical, because more often than not, the various tribal movements are seen at best as local insurgencies/rebellions without a pan-Indian consciousness.

A significant part of this problem owes itself to the nature of the primary sources used to reconstruct the histories of tribal communities. In the context of such histories, there are three broad categories of actors/agents whose written documents have been utilised as archives by modern historians: (*i*) the scholar-administrators; (*ii*) the Christian missionaries; and (*iii*) the anthropologists. This chapter proposes to open up a new arena of archival sources which were generated by social reformers at the turn of the twentieth century. As such, my focus will be on the ideas and practices of social, economic, educational, and religious reform advocated by A. V. Thakkar. His work for the welfare of aboriginal tribes, particularly the Bhil community in western India, constituted a significant watershed moment in the annals of twentieth-century Indian history. There are perhaps many such figures who crucially shaped the discourse, not only on tribal futures but also on the fate of marginalised communities across the spectrum during the late colonial and independent India. This is a humble attempt to historically resurrect the career of someone who I believe emerged as the fulcrum of nationalist understanding and response in the late-colonial politics of scheduling territories inhabited predominantly by aboriginal tribes. As will be apparent later in the book, Thakkar, more than any other nationalist figure, also emerged as the key arbiter of the Fifth and Sixth Schedules of the Indian Constitution.

Background

The narrative must begin in western India where the first two decades of the twentieth century have to be viewed as a period when the educational efforts of nineteenth-century social reformers had started bearing fruit in the arena of political representation. The most celebrated figure of this ferment is Dr B. R. Ambedkar, about whom reams of historiographical literature have been written. However, his political fortunes rose only around 1917–1920 when communitarian mobilisation accelerated around the issues of representation raised by the Montague–Chelmsford Report. In this context, Ambedkar's wide education in reputed universities of the Western world, skills of sharp articulation in the English language, training as a lawyer, as well as knowledge of the British system of representing interests in front of statutory committees became significant.

Here, it is necessary to state that from the days of Jyotiba Phule's Satyasodhak Samaj, there had been a strong anti-Brahmin party in the Bombay Presidency, especially in Poona. In fact, the city became the nerve centre of reform movements, both of caste Hindus and of the non-Brahmin party inspired by Phule.[6] The former group organised its educational efforts amongst the Depressed Classes under the aegis of organisations such as the Deccan Educational Society. Other bodies in the Presidency, such as the Bombay Prarthana Samaj and the Social Service League, also undertook similar reform activities. Together, these caste-Hindu controlled bodies were aiming to create articulate representatives amongst the Depressed Classes, and ultimately bring them into the fold of nationalism of the moderate variety. In this respect, the nineteenth-century efforts towards social and educational reform by figures like Justice Ranade, Gopal Krishna Gokhale, and many others await historical enquiry.

Vitthal Ramji Shinde

A pioneering social reformer whose role (especially in non-Marathi academia) remains little known is Vitthal Ramji Shinde.[7] In the eyes of

[6]This remains a major gap in historical knowledge, which deserves to be bridged. A very useful archive can be accessed at www.gipe.ac.in.

[7]A notable exception is a competent and award-winning biography of Shinde in Marathi by Professor G. M. Pawar, which was published in 2000 by the Sahitya Akademi. In 2013, an English translation was also published by the institution. See G. M. Pawar, *The Life and Works of Maharshi Vitthal Ramji Shinde*, (translated Sudhakar Marathe (trans.), Sahitya Akademi, New Delhi, 2013.

contemporaries such as V. S. Srinivas Shastri,[8] A. V. Thakkar, and many others, Shinde played a particularly significant role through his organisation, the Depressed Classes Mission. Thakkar considered him the 'Father of the Depressed Classes Welfare Movement' and, more personally, a Guru who offered valuable lessons in how to conduct schools for 'untouchable' children.[9]

The work against untouchability was carried on in different parts of India by a few religious and philanthropic bodies. However, such efforts remained *ad hoc* as there was no systematic effort to have a regular organisation till Shinde's intervention. Shinde was a graduate of Bombay University who became a member of both the Prarthana Samaj and the Brahmo Samaj. After graduation, he volunteered to serve the Brahmo Samaj and was sent to Manchester College, University of Oxford, to study Comparative Religion.[10] Upon his return, Shinde began working as a missionary and educator with the Bombay Prarthana Samaj. Later, in 1906, with the help of Sir N. G. Chandavarkar, he established the Depressed Classes Mission, which was formally registered in 1910. He was also a key organiser of the Theistic Movement in western India and considered the 'vast numbers of untouchables and intermediate caste-groups of Marathas as part of the Hindu society' who needed social 'elevation/uplift'. A contemporary observer called Shinde the pioneering figure of the Uplift Movement in India. Some two decades after Shinde started the Depressed Classes Mission, an assessment ran as follows:

> The cause of the depressed classes appealed to him and he made a noble venture in organising a Society for promoting the intellectual, moral and spiritual condition of those people. The Prarthana Samaj lent its full support to his scheme. The Samaj had already opened a number of night schools and was too ready to do something for improving the lot of the so-called low caste. When Mr. Shinde made his proposals, help came from all quarters.... The Society has grown

[8]V. S. S., 'The late Mr. V. R. Shinde', *The Indian Social Reformer* (henceforth, *TISR*) LIV (19), 15 January 1944, p. 150.

[9]A. V. Thakkar, 'V.R. Shinde', *TISR* LIV (31), 8 April, 1944, pp. 246–247.

[10]In September 1900, the sudden unfortunate death of Moti Bulasa, the scholarship winner from the Bombay Prarthana Samaj *en route* to England, created the immediate context for Shinde's departure to study comparative religion. For details of his selection, see Chapter 15 in G. M. Pawar, *The Life and Works of Maharshi Vitthal Ramji Shinde* (translated by Sudhakar Marathe), New Delhi: Sahitya Akademi, 2013, pp. 121–134.

> up gradually since 1906. It intends to elevate the social and spiritual condition of the depressed classes by promoting education, providing work, remedying their social disabilities and by preaching to them principles of liberal religion, with a view to improve their personal character and to teach them the lessons of good citizenship. It is not the policy of the Society to make converts but to impress upon the people the beauty and necessity of a belief in the Fatherhood of God and Brotherhood of Man.[11]

Shinde's chief mission was to advance the educational capabilities of the marginalised groups in Maratha society. His team of committed social reformers ran several schools throughout the Presidency. Here, it is necessary to state that the vocabulary of social reforms in early twentieth-century western India was largely shaped by Shinde and his followers. The effect of the Mission's efforts was such that the category 'Depressed Classes' became synonymous with 'untouchables'. According to Gail Omvedt, Shinde was

> the most prominent of the 'nationalist Marathas' who opposed the non-Brahman party and attempted to draw the Maratha community into the Congress movement. His Depressed Classes Mission performed the same function for the Dalit community, and drew them not only into the Congress but into Hindu revivalist associations such as the Hindu Mahasabha.[12]

While this view has a grain of truth in it, other Marathi intellectuals would rather place Shinde within the non-Brahmin tradition that allied with forces of nationalism.[13]

Even when Ambedkar launched his political career with the support of Shahu Chhatrapati of Kolhapur and challenged Shinde's leadership, he had to acknowledge the political potency of the term 'Depressed Classes'. Despite his opposition to Shinde's pro-Hindu ideas, when Ambedkar started organising the Akhil Bhartiya Bahishkrit Parishad, he stuck to the category popularised by Shinde and called it the 'All India Depressed Classes Conference'.[14] In a way, Shinde had prepared the field which Ambedkar

---

[11]'The Uplift Movement II', *The Indian Social Reformer* XXXVII (8), 23 October 1926, pp. 118–120.

[12]Gail Omvedt, *Dalits and the Democratic Revolution: Dr. Ambedkar and the Dalit Movement in Colonial India*, New Delhi: Sage, 1994, p. 143.

[13]Personal communication with Dr Prabodhan Pol.

[14]For some interesting details of the Shinde–Ambedkar relationship, see Omvedt, *Dalits and the Democratic Revolution*, pp. 143–147.

reaped and took over through his deft manoeuvres in the 1920s and 1930s. Despite his antipathy, Ambedkar stuck to Shinde's term for a long time and only in the 1942 session of the All India Depressed Classes Conference did he float a new category. He called this new political entity the 'Scheduled Caste Federation'.[15] Nevertheless, any analysis of the discourse on scheduling necessitates a mention of Shinde because of the intellectual influence that he exercised on the chief nationalist ideologue on Indian aboriginal tribes, A. V. Thakkar, who extended Shinde's reformist agenda towards the tribal communities of western India. Thakkar's own identity was synonymous with Servants of India, whose contribution to the growth of Gandhian mass politics awaits assessment.

Gandhian Nationalism and Servants of India

In the annals of nationalist historiography, there has been a eulogisation of Gandhi's leadership, especially as witnessed during the three chronologically successive mass movements officially titled Non-Cooperation (1921–1923), Civil Disobedience (1930–1933), and Quit India (1942). Perhaps owing to the anti-imperialist nature of the demands expressed therein, the historians of Indian nationalism have ploughed well the field of both provincial and pan-Indian political dynamics during these key movements. Nevertheless, between returning from South Africa in January 1915 and his assassination in January 1948, Gandhi spent almost the entirety of those thirty-three years on Indian soil. The sum total of Gandhi's political campaign period

[15]Ambedkar's antipathy to the inclusion of Depressed Classes within the joint electorate system of representation led to an iconic standoff with Gandhi. Gandhi's epic fast in Yeravada prison and the resultant Poona Pact are very well-known. However, as will be clear in a later chapter, Ambedkar's own position regarding the place of untouchables within the Hindu fold remained ambivalent till 1930. Only in the context of the Round Table Conference deliberations, where the British made it clear that while the electoral college would be expanded, Indians would still not be extended universal adult franchise, did Ambedkar take a clear position: he wanted 'special representation' for communities defined on the basis of religious and social distinctiveness. Although he had to step back after the Poona Pact, which provided a guaranteed number of seats for the Depressed Classes in a system of joint electorate, from 1935 onwards Ambedkar continued to argue that his followers amongst the untouchables should be regarded as non-Hindus. Just prior to his death, along with lakhs of his followers, Ambedkar converted to Buddhism.

in the three movements that he led does not even account for a decade.[16] Gandhi knew well that the masses were incapable of sustaining non-violent movements indefinitely. Historians such as Bipan Chandra have explained the Gandhian strategy of intense struggles followed by a long fallow period before recommencing the fight for freedom through the chronological model of Struggle-Truce-Struggle (S-T-S). From a staunch nationalist perspective, this sounds plausible and even convincing as the masses recouped their strength, resources were mobilised, fresh batches of Congress workers were trained, and eventually newer groups were recruited in the succeeding rounds of struggle for independence. However, the flaw in Chandra's model of explanation lies in its narrow outlook for a decade-long period of 'truce', which merely constituted an interregnum for the political fight against foreign masters. This presents a misplaced notion of Indian nationalism, in which political rights are privileged over sustained attempts to 'reform' the socio-religious life of the underprivileged classes.[17]

As is well-established in academic circles, Indian nationalism differed in significant ways from its classical form in Western Europe of the eighteenth and nineteenth centuries. To put it simply, classic nationalism (which Benedict Anderson has famously called 'imagined communities') was predicated on three key shared features characterising the nationalist bond between disparate groups of people, viz., a common language, a common religion, and a common enemy.[18] To take an example, England and France were separate nations because of (*i*) the linguistic difference (English *versus* French); (*ii*) religious difference (Protestantism *versus* Roman Catholicism); and (*iii*) the age-old enmity between the neighbours separated by the English Channel. In contrast, for Gandhi, India was, above all, a civilisational entity, a subcontinental landscape marked by linguistic, religious, and cultural differences where a narrow form of Western nationalism was neither feasible nor desirable. Hence, the Gandhian idea of Indian nationalism was non-exclusivist in nature and also predicated on unity in diversity.

It is well-known that Gandhi utilised a wide array of religious idioms and symbolisms to create a mass form of nationalism that welded together

---

[16]I would like to thank Professor Awadhendra Sharan, CSDS, for this insight.

[17]For a brilliant exposition of this dialectic, see B. R. Ambedkar, *Ranade Gandhi & Jinnah*, Bombay: Thacker & Co., 1943.

[18]Professor Ramachandra Guha's lecture on 'Patriotism versus Jingoism' at the 23rd Justice Sunanda Bhandare Memorial Lecture in New Delhi. Available at https://www.youtube.com/watch?v=YpvoxlKHpZ8 (accessed June 2024).

disparate communities and mutually antagonistic groups. For Gandhi, religion was foremost an ethical code of conduct. He believed that all religions ascribed to a distinct ethical philosophy and the only difference within and between them was one of emphasis. In the Gandhian philosophical framework, every religion was perfect from the viewpoint of its followers and imperfect from that of the followers of other faiths. Over time, however, certain of the ethical aspects of religious communities became corrupted, leading to the rise of social evils such as untouchability and communal hatred against other social groups. The overtly non-political aspects of Gandhi's interventions in India, such as the adoption of khadi, removal of untouchability, famine/flood relief, and promotion of communal solidarity between Hindus and Muslims, enabled him to mask over the existing fault-lines between socio-religious groups. He chose to call a variety of such tasks that his band of followers undertook as 'constructive programmes'. A careful look at this array of activities, especially in the first two decades of Gandhi's avatar in India, is enough to reveal the significance of the role played by an organisation of social workers under the banner of the Servants of India Society.

The Servants of India Society (henceforth SIS) was established by Gandhi's self-professed political guru, Gopal Krishna Gokhale, in 1905 in Pune.[19] As is well-known, Gokhale belonged to the moderate faction of the Indian National Congress and represented a distinct branch of Indian liberalism. However, his contributions in the field of social service, especially the role played by the SIS, awaits historical enquiry. Gokhale's farsightedness in establishing this august body of social workers proved to be a milestone in the history of professional social service in India. His intention was to collect a committed group of professional social service personnel who would engage, deliberate, and act upon the whole gamut of challenges facing the Indian masses and encourage nation-building activities. Interested people had to apply to become a life member of the SIS. Once admitted, members were given a full five years of comprehensive training in social, economic, and political issues. The senior members supervised and guided the new recruits under an apprenticeship model. The training effort was also directed to develop expertise on a few interrelated issues. Even during

[19]There is hardly any secondary literature on this remarkable organisation. The information gathered here has been gleaned from the study of primary sources available at the digital space of Gokhale Institute of Politics and Economics. See https://dspace.gipe.ac.in/xmlui/ (accessed 11 July 2024).

the training period, if a call for help came from a corner of the country, members were deputed to reach the spot to organise relief activities. Thus, it was a complete training module, combining both theoretical rigour and strong practical welfare work experience. The Society took on the financial responsibility for ensuring the livelihood of individual members, making it a committed professional band of men who abjured narrow individualistic ends. One golden rule of the SIS was an annual month-long fallow/retreat period, where everyone assembled at the Pune campus to reflect upon the experiences of the year gone by. A stock-taking of the emerging political situation in the country also provided members with a new perspective and enabled the organisation to update its understanding on the burning issues facing the country.

Amritlal Vithaldas Thakkar: A Pioneer Begins his Second Innings

A key figure destined to play a major role in the late colonial discourse on the Indian tribal population became a member of the SIS on 6 February 1914. Amritlal Vithaldas Thakkar[20] was forty-five years old at the time and had resigned from a high position in the Bombay Municipality to commit himself to a life of social service. Born on 29 November 1869 in a Lohana[21] caste family of Bhavnagar city in the Saurashtra region, Thakkar was a holder of a Licentiate in Civil Engineering from Pune. Before joining Gokhale's organisation, Thakkar had had an eventful working life and had served in several Princely State administrations. He had also served on a railway project in Africa. Always motivated towards social service for the downtrodden, Thakkar's transformation accelerated during his nine-year stint (1905–1913) in the Bombay Municipality. Here, he came in contact

[20]Much of the information in the current and subsequent paragraphs has been gleaned from a biography written in the Hindi language. See Kantilal Shah, *Thakkar Bapa*, New Delhi: Bharatiya Adimjati Sevak Sangh, 1955. Another great source for both writings of and reminiscences on Thakkar was a festschrift volume presented to him on his eightieth birthday. See T. N. Jagadisan and Shyamlal (compiled and edited), *Thakkar Bapa: Eightieth Birthday Commemoration Volume*, Madras: Diocesan Press, 1949 (henceforth, *TBCV*).

[21]Traditionally classed as Kshatriyas, Lohanas had made a name as traders and exerted a strong commercial influence in Saurashtra and Kathiawad.

with scores of workers from the Depressed Classes, living in sub-human and highly exploitative conditions right in the heart of colonial India's most cosmopolitan city. Most of these workers had come from the Gujarat-Kathiawad region, and his linguistic affinity with them enabled Thakkar to understand the grim realities of their perilous living conditions.

Image 5: Amritlal Vithaldas Thakkar, Servants of India Society

Source: WikiCommons, https://upload.wikimedia.org/wikipedia/commons/b/b5/A_V_Thakkar.jpg.

In the squalid workers' quarters at Chemboor, Thakkar also came under the influence of Vitthal Ramji Shinde, who gave him his first lessons in public service. Shinde's Depressed Classes Mission was operating a school for the children of sanitation workers under Thakkar's supervision. His personality and method of selfless service touched Thakkar deeply. He gradually imbibed a lifelong commitment to provide education for the children of the underprivileged and marginalised sections of society.

Around 1910–1911, Thakkar also came in contact with Gopal Krishna Devdhar of the SIS, who was the head of the Society's Bombay Branch. Like Gokhale, Devdhar belonged to the moderate party and disliked the extremist wing of the Congress led by Bal Gangadhar Tilak. He was also carrying on social welfare activities amongst the Depressed Classes communities of Bombay. Devdhar was amongst Gokhale's first set of recruits to the organisation. He commanded a deep knowledge of economics and was a key figure in the Cooperative Movement in India. Devdhar was also an active member of the Seva Sadan, the highest body for the service of women in the city of Poona. At this time, Thakkar was trying to understand the problem of 'Dasturi' (indebtedness leading to bonded labour) amongst the municipal workers from the Depressed Classes. He had also begun donating half his salary towards social work. Impressed by Thakkar's commitment, Devdhar agreed to supervise his researches. Thakkar too was deeply affected by Devdhar's altruism as well as work ethic, and started considering him his guru. Devdhar seems to have been a key figure in Thakkar's transition into social service, and also facilitated the latter's entry into the SIS fold. Soon enough, Thakkar made up his mind to resign from his government job and join his mentor's organisation. However, his father (whom Thakkar considered his first guru) objected and, in deference to his dying wishes, Thakkar postponed the decision. In the month following his father's death, Thakkar put in his papers and applied for life membership to the SIS.

In a fortunate chance of events, Thakkar's entry into the SIS and Gandhi's re-entry into India were less than a year apart. Gandhi returned after spending more than two decades in South Africa, which had served as a laboratory for the development of *Satyagraha* or the Gandhian method of non-violent political protest. Unfortunately, Gokhale himself died on 19 February 1915, barely a month after his protégé's return to Indian shores. The vacuum left by Gokhale's demise was filled by figures like C. F. Andrews, S. K. Rudra, and Rabindranath Tagore, who stepped in and served as his interlocutors.[22] No doubt, these individuals were crucial intellectual/spiritual companions and interlocuters for Gandhi. However, he also required close associates who could execute such plans with character, honesty, and commitment. Being an excellent appraiser of useful and committed allies, Gandhi drew upon his intimacy with Gokhale to rope

[22]Susan Visvanathan, 'S. K. Rudra, C. F. Andrews and M. K. Gandhi: Friendship, Dialogue and Interiority in the Question of Indian Nationalism', *Economic and Political Weekly* 37 (34), January 2002. pp. 3532–3541.

in the SIS group, whose professional social service credentials were well-established. The men of SIS gladly took the lead offered by Gandhi. They formed the initial nucleus of Gandhi's socio-political activities and played a critical role in establishing his moral legitimacy not only in the Bombay Presidency, but also as a pan-Indian leader.

In Gandhi's oeuvre, we find evidence of his growing closeness with A. V. Thakkar from his first year in India. At first, Gandhi established the Kochrab Ashram in Ahmedabad. On 26 September 1915, an outcaste person named Dudabhai was admitted to the Ashram on the recommendation of Thakkar.[23] In November, Thakkar himself began staying in the Ashram.[24] However, this was only a stop-gap arrangement as Gandhi was in search of a larger campus which would house 'a workshop for weaving, living rooms, kitchens ... and a building for the national school'. Finally, a 55-bigha plot of land was selected on the banks of the Sabarmati River where the eponymous Ashram came up, which served as his headquarters for several years. It is a little-known fact that while Gandhi was leading his debut Champaran Movement against the indigo planters, he entrusted A. V. Thakkar, a lapsed civil engineer, with the responsibility of supervising the construction of the now iconic Sabarmati Ashram.[25]

Subsequently, Gandhi included other members of the SIS in direct political interventions, although they were, strictly speaking, investigative enquiries leading to reportage published in newspapers and periodicals. For instance, in early 1918, a team of SIS life-members, comprising Devdhar, Thakkar, and N. M. Joshi,[26] was sent to Kheda to assess the conditions of agrarian distress.[27] They verified that the season's *Kharif* crop in the area 'practically came to nothing', and in a 'majority of cases were (valued at) under

---

[23]*Collected Works of Mahatma Gandhi, Vol. XIII (Jan. 1915–Oct. 1917)*, 1965 edition (henceforth, CWMG), p. 127. This is a footnote entry and says, 'The event caused a stir in the socio-religious life of Ahmedabad and people thought of even boycotting the Ashram.'

[24]Ibid., p. 137.

[25]Circular Letter for funds for Ashram from Motihari, Champaran, July 1917, ibid., p. 457. The initial drawing up of plans for the construction were thus handled by Thakkar, see ibid., pp. 516, 538, 552.

[26]Narayan Malhar Joshi was also a life member of the SIS. He specialised in issues concerning industrial labour in Bombay city.

[27]G. K. Devdhar, N. M. Joshi, and A. V. Thakkar, 'Conditions in Kaira: A Ness Investigation', *The Times of India*, 23 February 1918, p. 10.

four annas'.[28] Such reports written by experts adept at the collection of data and analysis were then published widely, including in SIS newsletters. As the propaganda spread, it slowly legitimised the demand of Kheda cultivators for the remission of rent and prepared the grounds for intervention by Gandhi. Ultimately, these were meaningful interventions and outreaches in the public affairs of Bombay Presidency, and added to the growing stature of Gandhi.[29]

Thus, the bond between Gandhi and Thakkar slowly deepened. Both shared the affinities of age, language, and a highly disciplined work ethic. Thus, their relationship was a symbiotic one of equals, where each complemented the other. Thakkar was a silent worker who chose to stay away from the limelight, but was always available at Gandhi's call. Early into their association in 1920, he was sent to Orissa by Gandhi to organise famine relief work.[30] Over time, this became a pattern and Thakkar went wherever Bapu deputed him. Once in the field, Thakkar would send detailed reports to his master, portions of which Gandhi would publish in an article on the issue, along with a call for charity. Donations would pour in and the money thus collected would then be sent to Thakkar. He would supervise the expenditure and prepare detailed accounts, which would finally be published to maintain transparency. This was their model of work, which continued unabated in campaign after campaign till the end of Gandhi's life.[31] Later, Thakkar undertook other aspects of Gandhian constructive programmes, such as the spread of weaving of Khadi and removal of untouchability.

Until the end of World War I, Thakkar's chief interest continued to be the spread of primary education. In 1919, arguing for more funds to be dedicated to the spread of compulsory education, he wrote,

> Elementary education is as necessary for the good government and for the prosperity of the country, as protection by the army, by the police and by the navy. It is as necessary as the post and telegraph, the railway and irrigation works. All these departments are conducted as national as all-India, concerns. If expenditure voted for the construction of new railways or for the building of houses for the police or for prodigal expenses on the army, etc., be treated as national burden, one cannot

---

[28]*CWMG, Vol. XIV (Oct. 1917–July 1918)*, pp. 212–213, 281, 289.

[29]See Judith Brown, *Gandhi's Rise to Power*, Cambridge University Press, 1972.

[30]*CWMG, Vol. XVII (Feb.–June 1920)*, pp. 404–405, 420.

[31]The high point of this association was the long period of work under the banner of the Harijan Sevak Sangh.

> understand why education, and primary education at that, should be an exception and a local matter.[32]

These were early days for Thakkar the social worker. Although fifty years of age, he had only spent five years with SIS. Fortunately, however, Thakkar had just stumbled upon the real mission for his boundless reformist energies. This mission was for 'Aboriginal Uplift', which would characterise Thakkar's social service career and also seal his place in the annals of Indian nationalism. It is to an analysis of this trajectory that we shall now turn.

Beginning of A 'Hindu Mission' among the Bhils

To his longstanding interest in the education of the Depressed Classes, Thakkar added the cause of 'Aboriginal uplift' in March 1919 when he visited the famine-stricken district of Panchmahal (Godhra) and came face-to-face with the conditions of its largely Bhil tribal populace.[33] The ball was set rolling by Indulal Yagnik, a Gandhian social worker and a close associate of Thakkar. The two had cooperated to organise the Gujarat Educational Conference in 1916.[34] In its successful aftermath, Thakkar guided Yagnik in the opening of schools in villages (including for children belonging to the Dalit castes) constituting the backward areas of east Gujarat. On Gokahle's second death anniversary, 19 February 1917, Gandhi, along with Thakkar and some other social workers, landed in Godhra for a memorial meeting. After Gandhi's departure, the duo spontaneously decided to undertake a 'quick visit to all the talukas of this backward district'. They organised a meeting in Dohad with the help of local leaders and made an appeal to the townsmen to educate their children. Thakkar and Yagnik were moved by the begging Bhil men, women, and children and opined that they 'appeared to be the poorest and most destitute in the whole of Gujarat'. Finally, 'thinking of their uplift', the two returned to Bombay.[35]

---

[32]A. V. Thakkar, 'Compulsory Education', *The Servant of India* (henceforth, *TSI*) II (44), 4 December 1919, p. 519.

[33]A. V. Thakkar, 'Famine Tour in Panch Mahal', *TSI* II (10), 10 April 1919, pp. 117–118.

[34]Indulal Yagnik, *The Autobiography of Indulal Yagnik*, Vol. I, New Delhi: Manohar, 2011, pp. 235, 243, 250–251.

[35]Ibid., pp. 259–261.

Yagnik subsequently opened several schools in the Panch Mahal District for the Depressed Classes and Bhils. Then, in 1918, the monsoon rains failed miserably in the district and the Bhils, along with the cattle, faced dire famine conditions. Most of the approximately 200,000 Bhil tribesmen were indebted to a handful of Banias and Bohras. The governmental apparatus was not doing much to ameliorate famine in the area. Yagnik's informant, a Brahmin mason named Sukhdev Vishvanath Trivedi, helped him to make an extensive tour of the area. Having worked there for a decade as a government servant, Trivedi knew the region, its Bhili dialect, and hence its problems first-hand. He decided to quit his job and dedicated himself to welfare work amongst the Bhils. Using the information collected via Trivedi's help, Yagnik wrote a series of articles in his own periodical journal *Navjivan ane Satya*,[36] and subsequently also in the *Bombay Chronicle*. As a result of the public attention they generated, Thakkar was deputed by the Bombay Presidency Famine Relief Fund to ascertain the relief work done and the extent of philanthropic help required from the well-off provincial subjects.

Thakkar's experience of touring in the Jhalod and Dohad talukas of the district undergoing widespread starvation melted his heart and he 'came away with a great liking for the Bhils'. He wrote the following description in the SIS newsletter:

> The Bhil is a very good fellow. Improvident by nature, he does not spend much labour on his farm. Besides he is addicted to drinking. But he is a brave, honest and straight forward [*sic*] man. He does not reside in congested villages with crooked and insanitary lanes, but in the open in his farm house. A village is a number of hamlets spread over a few square miles.... He is not regarded as an untouchable but still even the Sudra may not drink water touched by him perhaps because the Bhil does not cherish the same reverence for the cow as other Hindus do. The Salvation Army and other Christian Missionaries befriend him, but no Hindu religious or social organization has yet given a thought to the amelioration of his condition, for he is in a tight economic bondage to his Sowkar.[37]

[36] Yagnik voluntarily handed over the reins of this Gujarati journal to Gandhi. Subsequently, it became a mouthpiece for Gandhian ideas.

[37] A. V. Thakkar, 'Famine Tour in Panch Mahal', *The Servant of India* (henceforth, *TSI*) II (10), 10 April 1919, p. 118. The following paragraphs and quotes are based on this source.

The above extract is revealing for, in addition to repeating the colonial trope of an honest aboriginal in love with his freedom and alcohol, Thakkar here highlights their spatial/cultural distinctiveness from the surrounding Hindu population. Beef-eating was common amongst the Bhils, because of which even the Depressed Classes considered them lowly. Also, the spatial imagery of a Bhil village which Thakkar invoked here was completely at odds with the other villages that he had seen. A traditional village in western India was compact, but the predominantly Bhil villages were much more spatially scattered as the tribals lived on the farm houses that made each household an autonomous unit. The insanitariness characteristic of traditional villages was also absent in the tribal ones.

His observation on Christian missionaries was also mixed with a certain disdain for their methods. Later in the article, Thakkar expresses 'great admiration and respect for the Salvation Army, which is doing meritorious work.... The Army officer goes out in the villages with bundle of clothes to cover the naked and arranges to send the poor man's lean bullocks to his cattle kitchen.' As a devout Vaishnava Hindu, beef-eating was certainly unpalatable for Thakkar. Hence, his praise of the Christian missionaries working amongst aboriginals was also interwoven with a lament on the lack of a similar spirit from the Hindus, which would 'elevate' the life conditions of Bhils. Outlining his future plans, Thakkar provides a succinct worldview which he would propagate with a dedicated band of followers:

> The workers are being selected from among college students who are prepared to spend their days of vacation among the Bhils and their children, trying to help them, instruct them in the three R's and elevate them, preaching abstinence or moderation in drink and giving them a wider outlook on life. About a dozen such workers will it is hoped, be living in famine camps, befriending the Bhil and sowing the seeds of a Hindu Mission for the Bhils in the near future. Let even the illiterate Bhil feel that he forms a part of the Indian nation and that he too is not a mean citizen of the British Empire.

This is the earliest write-up by Thakkar on the tribal people and the penultimate line, with its emphasis on a 'Hindu Mission', highlights their distinctiveness from the surrounding Hindus, a theme which was to assume critical significance from the 1930s onwards.

Another remarkable fact that emerged in this piece was the educational efforts made by the Bombay government amongst the aboriginal communities. Thakkar acknowledged that a large number of Bhil teachers had been sent out from the Bhil Boarding Schools at Dohad (Panch Mahals) and Godsamba (Mandir Taluka of Surat District). Such a supply pipeline of aboriginal teachers had 'made it possible to start a number of primary schools for Bhil children and thus to elevate the younger generation'. The Bombay government was making a lot of effort towards enhancing the literacy and education of children. Even during World War I with its financial constraints, the Education Department was opening 500 new primary schools every year.

In the annals of twentieth-century literacy campaigns in India, the Bombay government was, by far, not the only entity undertaking such educational work amongst the aboriginals and Depressed Classes. In 1920, an enormous enterprise was started by the Labour Department in the Madras Presidency, where 'a couple of thousand such schools' were opened in 'very backward districts'.[38]

Even in the case of princely orders, from the late nineteenth century onwards Baroda State under Sir Sayajirao Gaikwad provided a massive push to literacy by opening schools. Many of them were open to Depressed Classes and aboriginals as well. These were significant milestones and need further enquiry. Despite some criticism concerning the neglect of educational efforts amongst aboriginals, Thakkar called the Baroda ruler 'a pioneer of free and compulsory primary education in the country'.[39]

After his brief exposure to the Bhil landscape, Thakkar decided to take on the responsibility of representing the interests of Bhils. Soon after his famine tour, Thakkar wrote a letter of complaint to the Editor in *The Times of India* when he heard about the closing down of primary schools in Panch Mahal.[40] Apparently, as a measure to save money on clerks' wages, which had shot up during World War I, the official famine relief team had decided on the 'strange device of ... converting teachers into clerks on famine work'. The Famine Relief Committee comprising prominent civil society

[38] A. V. Thakkar, 'How are the Backward Classes?', *Hindustan Times*, 26 December 1948, reproduced in *TBCV*, p. 337. It is generally presumed that the colonial State was doing precious little in regard to the education of the underprivileged masses, but these instances provide a counterpoint which need further enquiries.

[39] A. V. Thakkar, 'Education in Baroda: Neglect of the Aborigines', *TSI* IX (8), 25 March 1926, pp. 98–100.

[40] A. V. Thakkar, 'Famine in Panch Mahal: Closing of Primary Schools', Letter to the Editor of *The Times of India*, 10 June 1919, p. 8. The following extract is from this source.

personalities of Bombay, who had deputed Thakkar to conduct the March enquiry, had offered a sum of Rs 4,000 to the Collector to ensure that the education of school-going children continued. Nevertheless, with the closure of schools imminent, the prospects of Bhil children gaining primary education became rather bleak. Thakkar wrote:

> ... a set-back has been given to this unfortunate district peopled by a most backward community, the Bhils. A Central School exists in this town to train Bhil Teachers for schools here, but some officers think that this is a waste of public money and that the Bhil could never be educated and brought into line with the rest of humanity. Your readers will shudder to hear that a certain high official pleaded with me like this in a conversation in all seriousness. The sooner such men are removed from office, the better it will be for the ignorant mass who are living as if it were in the fifteenth century in this twentieth century.

As mentioned earlier, the efforts of Indulal Yagnik had resulted in the opening of schools in Panch Mahal district. There was an English school at Dohad; Anglo-Vernacular schools at Godhra, Dohad, Jhalod, and Nadisar; a primary Gujarati school and an exclusive English school for girls (both at Godhra). Thakkar publicly appreciated Yagnik's efforts, albeit without naming him.[41] The schools ran successfully, with Yagnik and Sukhdev Trivedi doing the bulk of the pioneering work. Subsequently, a Bhil Ashram was opened at Mirakhedi, whose management was entrusted to Dayabhai Nayak.[42] Nayak became a close associate of Thakkar in the years to come. However, the young Yagnik was a tempestuous nationalist who could not stick to the stable and patient missionary spirit necessary for the growth of education amongst the Bhils. When the Non Co-operation Movement was launched under the leadership of Gandhi, Yagnik threw caution to the wind and gave in to his innate nationalist enthusiasm. He participated in political agitation and courted arrest. In his memoirs, Yagnik wrote,

> I had written to Thakkar Bapa even from jail that if nothing else in the world would suit, in the end I would lay down my bed in the Bhil Ashram of Mirakhedi.... But usually in such Ashrams, there was a tradition of looking after the life of the students, keeping one's head down and concentrating only on agitation and not coming to collision

---

[41] A. V. Thakkar, 'Education in Panch Mahals,' Letter to the Editor of *The Times of India*, 5 April 1919, p. 9.

[42] Indulal Yagnik, *The Autobiography of Indulal Yagnik, Vol. II*, New Delhi: Manohar, 2011, p. 203.

> with the government. This I could not possibly accept without some perspective on the future progress of the entire peasant community, and with doing some daily activity I could not possibly join such institutions. Thus there was no place for me in the institutions started by me, not to talk of making even a small entry in others.[43]

Hence, after running these institutions successfully for about three years, Yagnik had entrusted their charge to Thakkar Bapa.[44] This was a turning point in Thakkar's life as he was now in command of a chain of institutions which had done some pioneering work in Panch Mahals. This became the kernel of a major aspect of his life as a professional social servant. He could now realise his dream of starting a 'Hindu Mission' for the social 'uplift' of the Bhils. His key associates in this endeavour were Sukhdev Bhai, Dayabhai Nayak, and Sumant Mehta of Vadodara.[45] Together, they began their activities under the banner of the Kali Paraj Seva Mandal (Adivasis Service Association), whose name was subsequently changed to Bhil Seva Mandal. They all became key members of this association. While Yagnik was in jail, Thakkar came to meet him periodically and described the activities of the Mandal. All the institutions were now provided economic support by the Provincial Congress Committee. Hearing about the healthy state of his erstwhile institutions, Yagnik's 'heart felt proud and satisfied'.[46]

Socio-religious Reforms at the Bhil Seva Mandal

Once Thakkar was in charge of the Bhil Seva Mandal, he continued Yagnik's educational activities amongst the Depressed Classes and Bhils. However, he also began realigning the ideological core of social reform activities amongst the Bhil community. Thakkar began by deeply investigating their

---

[43]Ibid., p. 251.

[44]Indulal Yagnik, *The Autobiography of Indulal Yagnik, Vol. III*, New Delhi: Manohar, 2011, p. 246.

[45]Yagnik, *The Autobiography of Indulal Yagnik*, Vol. II, p. 251. A medical professional, he was a leading citizen of Baroda who played an important role during the Devi Movement in south Gujarat. He questioned the use of the term Kaliparaj for its pejorative nature and suggested that Raniparaj be used instead. See David Hardiman, *The Coming of the Devi: Adivasi Assertion in Western India*, New Delhi: Oxford University Press, 1987, pp. 186–188.

[46]Yagnik, *The Autobiography of Indulal Yagnik*, Vol. II, p. 126.

living conditions, reached several conclusions, and made interventions in accordance with the training he had received at the Servants of India Society. In an article published in the Society's newsletter, Thakkar pointed out that the bane of the Bhils' economic plight was their servility to the greedy *sahukar* or moneylender. They served as an important source of credit for the Bhils but charged exceptionally high rates of interest on the money loaned out. Thakkar argued that a 'large land bank is a great necessity to assist him to escape the very kind attentions of a class of men who live on the labour of the over-trustful and illiterate Bhil'.[47] He had started twenty-five Co-operative Credit Societies for the Bhils, but the problem was severe and the effort insufficient. Thakkar also pointed out the exploitative nature of governmental machinery in the Bhil areas and wrote:

> The Bhil is in very great fear of the 'Mehtas' (officials) of the all-powerful Government and of the thousand and one regulations of the Sarkar. He will allow himself to be subject to any zoolum on the part of the petty officials. Though daring and physically powerful, he will not grumble in the least against the illegal exactions or corporal punishment inflicted by a peon or a talati.

For Thakkar, the essential way out was to guide the Bhils to break the chain of exploitation in which a campaign for literacy and education were to be instrumental. He wrote that 'Illiteracy is his (Bhil's) great enemy and he does not know how much power lies behind the art of reading and writing'. Thakkar considered the efforts of missionaries and the government to spread literacy 'a very small beginning'. The Bhils were indeed interested in sending their children to schools, but the 'proper class of teacher, one with a missionary zeal were not coming forward'. Thakkar looked to his own experience of supervising a free boarding school and a day school for Bhil boys, which had yielded results 'much beyond ... expectations'. Finally, he emphasised the 'great necessity' for 'an organization exclusively devoted to the service of the Bhils in Gujarat.' Thakkar's truly missionary enterprise emphasised '(I)ntensive work for their social and economic betterment in a small area'. He issued an appeal for a band of 'steady and disinterested social workers from the educated and advanced classes' who would carry out 'such missionary work for the uplift of a section of our countrymen'. The

---

[47] A. V. Thakkar, 'Social Work Amongst the Gujarat Bhils', *TSI*, 22 June 1922, reproduced in *TBCV*, pp. 297–298. The following citations and paragraphs are based on this source.

workers who would sign up were required 'to work there for about ten years, if not for life'. To those who seriously considered his call for social service (or better yet, a 'Hindu Mission'), a succinct manifesto was also provided by Thakkar. The devoted workers would live among the Bhils and conduct the following activities:

(a) By personal contact inculcate in them the habit of cleanliness and abstinence from drink. To teach the children of both sexes the art of reading and writing in schools to be started and to adults the habits of industry and hard work.
(b) To give them protection from the greed of the sowkar and to start co-operative credit and stores societies. To secure him against petty tyrannies of the police, forest and land revenue subordinates.
(c) To hold periodical informal meetings and to read to them stories from the *Ramayana* and other religious books and also to give them a certain amount of general information from the newspapers.
(d) To reform their customs in respect of marriage, birth, death and guide their caste meetings.

This landmark manifesto by Thakkar was an overt admission of the 'Hindu' nature of his social service amongst the Bhils. I would argue that the sum total of this manifesto points out quite clearly that the Bhils were to be converted to (or brought into the fold of) Hinduism. Here, the word 'uplift' appears for the first time in Thakkar's writing (the earlier term he had used was 'elevate'). It never left the arsenal of Thakkar and his associates, and became a part and parcel of the vocabulary of professional social service amongst the aboriginals, up to independence and beyond. A little later, we shall see how Thakkar himself added other meanings to the term. Nevertheless, the power of the word 'uplift' lay in the specific imagery it invoked. Remember, the word is a 'verb' and signified resolute action by Hindu missionaries, who would adopt the Bhil and carry on educational activities, temperance work, ameliorate their economic conditions, reform their customs, and spread the word of Lord Ram amongst them.

Interestingly, the word 'caste', appearing in the last point of the manifesto, also signified that the nature of these social workers' task was to uplift the aboriginal in the scale of the Hindu social order. At least in this stage of Thakkar's intellectual evolution, his motives were not merely philanthropic but were driven by a not-so insignificant dash of religious imperatives as well. Rather like his guru, Vitthal Ramji Shinde, who envisioned the inclusion of the 'Depressed Classes' into the fold of the Hindu socio-religious hierarchy,

Thakkar too had come to view the aboriginals as essentially a part of the Hindu belief system. Not only were the living conditions of the Bhils to be ameliorated, but their uplift also meant that they were to be absorbed into the Hindu fold.

The Bhil Seva Mandal was not operating in a vacuum of social reform action. Already in the neighbouring Kaliparaj areas of Surat district and the Navsari Prant of Baroda, the Devi Movement had gained considerable strength. Even prior to this there had been a certain Guru Govind Giri, himself a Banjara nomad, who had led his Bhil Bhaktas in an effort to bring about social reform.[48] We also have a fascinating reference to an event in the first quarter of 1923.[49] This was at an early stage of the Bhil Seva Mandal's social service career amongst its target population, and provides remarkable insights into the kind of activities being conducted by Thakkar and his associates.

Just before the Hindu festival of Holi, a large gathering of about 1,000 Bhils was organised in a village near Jhalod town on 27 February 1923, 'in the open air under huge banyan trees in the best of the day'. The reporter communicated that 'some educated men and influential Patels from among the community itself are moving their own people for solid social reform'. Together, the attendees 'made rules regarding standardizing their marriage customs and expenses, abstaining from liquor even on festive occasions and slaughter of cattle, taking a daily bath and the removal of inconvenient leg ornaments of their women and other matters'. It was claimed that the 'large scale' movement was 'spontaneous', without the assistance of any outside agency. However, a closer examination of the resolutions passed at this conference, organised in the heart of the operational area of the Bhil Seva Mandal, reveals a clear imprint of Thakkar's core ideas:

---

[48]David Hardiman, 'Assertion, Conversion and Indian Nationalism: Govind Giri's Movement Amongst the Bhils', in R. Robinson and S. Clarke (eds), *Religious Conversion in India: Modes, Motivations, and Meanings*, New Delhi: Oxford University Press, 2003, pp. 255–284; also see Alf Gunvald Nilsen, 'Subalterns and the State in the *Longue Durée*: Notes from "The Rebellious Century" in the Bhil Heartland', *Journal of Contemporary Asia* 45 (4), 2015, pp. 574–595.

[49]'Letter to the Editor, The Indian Social Reformer, From A Correspondent, dated Dohad 3 March 1923', titled 'Reform Among Bhils', *The Indian Social Reformer* XXXIII (28), 10 March 1923, p. 450. This paragraph and the following long citation on p. 208 stems from this source.

(1) The bride's father shall not receive more than Rs. 101 from the bridegroom's father, out of which Rs. 50 will be utilised for making ornaments for the bride. The penalty in case of breach will be twice the excess amount paid.
(2) At the time of the betrothal 'Gool' should be distributed instead of liquor as at present.
(3) The custom of elopement by girls should no longer be recognised as marriage and those who assist the parties will also be penalised by the Caste *Punch*.
(4) The man who keeps as wife a woman who is married to another but not divorced with the sanction of the Caste *Punch* will be fined upto Rs. 200 and the woman at fault will be returned to her first husband.
(5) Divorce on the application of a woman may be granted if the *Punch* sees valid reason for the separation and in that case the second husband, if any, will pay the first husband the sum of Rs. 101 and some other expenses.
(6) The period of '*Ghar Jamai*' or resident son-in-law's compulsory stay with his father-in-law is reduced from 7 years to 5.
(7) Use of liquor on occasion of death, dinner, marriage and other social functions is prohibited. The Patel or the 'Bhagat' of every village to report the head-quarters breaches if any occur.
(8) No cattle or goats should be killed in any death ceremony or in cases of sickness or on any other occasion.
(9) Water should be used after answering nature's call and a daily bath is prescribed for all adults male and female.
(10) Women shall remove from their legs brass ornaments called 'jhanjharia'. These are tapering pieces of brass cylinders from the knee down to the ankle and cause great discomfort while at work in the fields.
(11) A committee of leading Patels was appointed to go round the villages, acquaint all the people with the rules made by representative *Punch* and appoint local committees to watch the working of these rules and to deal with the defaulters.

We can clearly discern that besides the usual stress on ideals of 'uplift' in matters relating to cleanliness, vegetarianism, and temperance, the conference's resolutions constituted a clear attempt to institute practices amongst the Bhils of Panch Mahal that were consonant with other caste groups. This, of course, would have meant that the traditionally prevalent 'customs' amongst Bhil tribesmen were to be radically altered. In structural terms, these throw up a number of issues which have to be studied in greater depth. For instance, the proposed injunctions, especially in relation to marriage customs, seemed to have been re-designed along patriarchal lines by Hindu social reformers working under the guidance of Thakkar. Thus, the holy grail of customary practices were also being Hinduised, in the process altering the gender roles amongst the Bhils. This provides just one example among many potentially fascinating aspects of reform work in the 1920s.

Thakkar was thus seeking to recast the Bhils in civilisational terms through reformist work. Soon after Thakkar's own 'civilising mission' had come into being, a further crisis knocked on the doors of the Bhils of Panch Mahal district. The famine of 1918–1919 had already broken the back of the peasant economy in the region. In 1922, when the Bhils had not yet recovered sufficiently, the rains failed once again. The resulting conditions of scarcity were not as dire as earlier, but they were bad enough to put a fresh set of challenging relief work before Thakkar. He toured the area again, collected donations to conduct relief activities, and pulled together associates to help the Bhils. After coming in 'pretty close contact with the Bhils', Thakkar opined,

> The Bhil is to be found in every stage of civilization; from the wild hunter to the orderly and hardworking peasant, the Bhil of the Panch Mahals very nearly approximates to the latter description.... To the police, every Bhil is a potential thief, and truly so, because he is so often starving. As the Sanskrit proverb runs, 'Which sin is not capable of being committed by a starving man? ... on the whole he is an honest, simple, manly fellow and capable of hard work, but he needs to be lifted up above the primitive state in which he now is.[50]

In November 1922, after winding up the famine relief work, he converted the relief centre at Dahod into the headquarters of the Bhil Seva Mandal.[51] This is a milestone in the history of tribal communities in India, as this site continued to act as the nerve-centre of the nationalist social workers conducting welfare work amongst them. In the years to follow, the Bhil Seva Mandal emerged as a modular nationalist organisation dedicated to reform work amongst aboriginal communities. It borrowed from the 'seva/service' vocabulary of the SIS and the Gandhian Constructive Programme and

---

[50] A.V. Thakkar, 'The Bhil', *TSI*, 14 December 1922, reproduced in *TBCV*, p. 296.

[51] The year 2022 marked the centenary celebrations of the Bhil Seva Mandal's establishment.

became the prototype whose programmatic agenda and mode of functioning were replicated in other parts of British India.[52]

Soon, Thakkar prepared the blueprint of the organisational structure and in SIS newsletters and other monthly journals such as *Yugdharma*, an appeal was made for funds and dedicated personnel. A few young activists such as Laxmikant Srikant,[53] scion of a wealthy Bombay family and also a Congress member, and his friends Pandurang Vanikar, Ishwarlal Vaidya, Rupajibhai Parmar, Maganlal Mehta, and Ambalal Vyas joined the team of Hindu missionaries that Thakkar had envisioned. Together, they opened new schools, boarding houses, and co-operative credit societies, and conducted medical relief work. By its first anniversary, the Mandal had seven centres (five free day schools and two free boarding schools) in the Jhalod and Dohad talukas and two dispensaries that were visited by a *vaid* every fortnight, where medicines were distributed free of cost. There were five volunteers, four probationers, two vaids, and a number of teachers. D. K. Karve, whom Thakkar regarded as his mentor, spoke on this occasion and 'expressed joy at the remarkable success which the Mandal had achieved in a short period.'[54] Luckily, we have the first annual report of the Bhil Seva Mandal that was published in *The Indian Social Reformer*. Penned by Thakkar himself, it provides a number of very interesting details.[55]

---

[52]Many significant late-colonial figures in the discourse on tribal communities, like Verrier Elwin, were introduced to the field of social service by A. V. Thakkar. Although Elwin had distinctive ideas on Indian aboriginal tribes and later tried to engage Thakkar in a full-length debate, he chose to style his own organisation as the Gond Seva Mandal. Later, Elwin changed the nomenclature to Bhumijan Seva Mandal, but in both cases, he followed (at least) the vocabulary enunciated by Thakkar's organisation.

[53]Owing to his education and familial connections with the Congress nationalists, Srikant emerged as a key figure in the Bombay Presidency. Subsequently, he became a member of the Legislative Council and took a lead role in lambasting the excluded and partially excluded policy of the Government of India when the matter was discussed in the House in 1936. Post-independence, Srikant was appointed as the first all-India Commissioner of the Scheduled Castes and Scheduled Tribes, a portfolio he continued to hold for almost a full decade.

[54]'Education for Bhils: Work of Seva Mandal, *The Times of India*, 17 December 1923, p. 13.

[55]A. V. Thakkar, 'Bhil Seva Mandal Dohad', *The Indian Social Reformer* XXXIII (47), 21 July 1923, p. 763. The next few paragraphs, including the quotes, are based on this single source.

Thakkar called the enterprise an 'indigenous mission for social work among the Bhils of Panch Mahals'. A deep involvement in famine relief efforts since 1919 had convinced him 'of the necessity of such a mission'. The Bhils were an 'aboriginal community' who had 'partly adopted themselves to their Hindu surroundings', but who also held 'themselves as far aloof as possible'. Living in scattered settlements, their connection with the townspeople was the 'meagrest'.

The Bhil Seva Mandal's organisational units for conducting social work were 'settlements' or 'working centres'. Owing to scarce monetary resources, the village centres were no more than inexpensive makeshift structures constructed from wood or bamboo. Usually, such temporary buildings were erected on plots of land donated by sympathetic Bhil cultivators. The activities in each unit consisted of 'a school, a few common medicines, occasional readings from religious books, material help with clothes and grains in cases of extreme poverty and preaching abstinence from drink'. Five such centres had been opened, of which three (at villages Garbada, Jesawada, and the headquarters itself) were located in Dohad taluka and two (in the villages of Gultora and Mudaheda) in Jhalod taluka of the Panch Mahal district. Each centre was put in the charge of a 'devoted worker, who does duty both as a *teacher* and a *preacher*, with the aid of a Bhil assistant'. Additionally, one of the centres (Jesawada) had a boarding house for 20–25 primary school boys and a 'dispensary in charge of a competent and devoted *Vaid*'. The majority of the workers committed themselves to a minimum of three years of work.

The imprint of the Christian missionary model (teaching and preaching) was clear on Thakkar's reformist enterprise, with its focus on education and health. In all the schools run by the Bhil Seva Mandal, instruction was free of charge. In addition to teaching, the students were provided 'free clothes, slates and books'. In order to enable them to internalise the ethics of personal hygiene, once every week they were also given 'soap for washing their clothes in the presence of teachers'. At some sites like Garbada, the schools were 'overflowing'. However, it was not all easygoing and Thakkar reported that the boarding school for primary boys at Jesawada was facing constant desertions as '(C)oming from a wild tribe, they find it irksome to submit to the discipline of a boarding school and do occasionally run away to their villages'. Nevertheless, they were becoming 'steadier day by day'.

In the field of health, too, the opening of the dispensary at Jesawada, run by a devoted and competent Vaid, had proved to be a 'great boon'. People from the surrounding villages visited it for treatment and the numbers rose further as news of successful treatment spread. Guineaworm was the most common disease, caused by drinking water from *kucha* or stepped wells. Indoor patients were also kept occasionally at the dispensary, even though it lacked proper arrangements. The Mandal intended to buy a plot of a few acres of land and develop *pukka* buildings to house them.

The headquarters was at Dohad, where a worker was permanently stationed. He was in charge of office work, safekeeping of the money-cum-accounts, and ensuring timely and logistical supply of materials to all village workers. On paper, Thakkar himself was stationed at the Dohad headquarters, but in effect, he was seldom present there. Thakkar kept a watchful eye on all the Mandal centres and workers. Given the scattered landscape of the operational area, constant touring was the only possible way. Consequently, most of his time was spent visiting the different centres in a bullock cart. The tall figure of Thakkar visited each centre about once a month, and stayed there for a night or two. Other activities of the working centres included temperance propaganda and the establishment of co-operative credit societies. At Garbada, a weavers' society had also been formed.

One constant source of weakness and worry for the Bhil Seva Mandal and Thakkar was its financial and funding model. It neither possessed a heavy corpus of seed capital nor did it receive any government money. Hence, from its inception, the organisation's philanthropic activities were completely dependent on donations and charity. Thakkar informs the readers that 'Our urgent needs' were funds required to meet the recurring expenses on (*i*) the allowances of workers; (*ii*) boarding charges of the Jesawada Ashram; (*iii*) cost of clothing, soap, and school material in all schools (*iv*) cost of medicines; and (*v*) cost of land and buildings for the Ashram and dispensary. The organisation's monthly expenditure exceeded Rs 700. The total contributions in the first year of its existence amounted to Rs 2,748/-, but had left 'practically no balance'. Thakkar added, 'We are thus living from hand to mouth and every new month must bring in new contributions, if expenses are to be met'. Desperate for continuing and expanding the welfare work of the Bhil Seva Mandal, Thakkar appealed for generous donations in the following manner:

> Now I appeal to the numerous souls in cities and mofussil who feel the need of ameliorating the lot of the lowly and down-trodden. The Bhil is numerous and has great potentialities, but is almost unconscious of

> being human. This great sturdy community is an asset worth winning back to the country and to humanity. The work of winning is not light. It requires patient application of human energy. At the same time it requires *money*. The fortunate few hold in their palms and through it the means of the uplift of the down-trodden. Will they not open their palms? Will they fail to provide the open sesame to those who yearn for it? I am confident my appeal will not go in vain.[56]

Thus, of all the many challenges Thakkar and his associates had to encounter, the chief one pertained to finance. As these institutions were free of charge for the students, their economic model was based on philanthropy and generous donations, which were not always forthcoming. Bhil Seva Mandal's literacy campaigns also directly challenged the privileged position of the local vested interests groups, which had perennially exploited the Bhils. They had thrived on exactions of forced labour, bribery, and the debt trap of high-interest loans. These lobbies were keen to ensure the failure of Thakkar's socio-educational reform effort as much of their exploitative apparatus depended on the ignorance and illiteracy of the aboriginals. They ganged up to create all kinds of logistical and legal hassles: the availability of land for the establishment of new ashrams was forestalled; workers found it hard to rent accommodation; and false litigation was resorted to by these local groups keen to unsettle the philanthropic ventures of Thakkar Bapa.[57] Under such trying conditions, he gave solace to and boosted the sagging morale of his committed cadre, who continued their Hindu missionary work amongst the Bhils of Panch Mahal. Thakkar was to spend the better part of the following decade in the district, extending and closely supervising the work of the Bhil Seva Mandal.

---

[56]Bhil Seva Mandal Dohad, 15 July 1923, A. V. Thakkar of the Servants of India Society. *The Indian Social Reformer* endorsed Thakkar's appeal and wrote:

> We invite the attention of our readers to the report of the solid work which the Seva Mandal at Dohad is doing for the Bhils of the district, under the sagacious guidance of Mr. A.V. Thakkar of the Servants of India Society. It is precisely this kind of work that, undertaken in numerous centres in the country, will help the growth of the Indian people into a single social and cultural unit. We cordially support Mr. Thakkar's appeal for funds, to carry on the Mandal's work. (Ibid., pp. 755–756)

[57]Hindi article entitled 'Kasht Nivarak Thakkar Bapa: Samaj Seva ko Samarpit Jiwan par ek Vihangam Drishti', *Pratimaan: Samay Samaj Sanskriti* 5 (2), July–December 2017, pp. 278–296.

Nationalising the Aboriginals: A. V. Thakkar and a New Anthropology

As Thakkar's involvement deepened in the Panch Mahal region, he also started reading colonial anthropological literature surrounding the category of the aboriginal tribes. He realised the immense scope for social work (of the kind started by him), which could be replicated amongst aboriginal groups similar to the Bhils who were spread across the Indian subcontinent. The colonial ethnographies clearly influenced Thakkar's notions of the aboriginal past, and his writings in the early 1920s exhibit an acceptance of the Aryan race theory.

Thakkar gave concrete shape to many of these budding ideas in a paper that he prepared, to be read at the fourth session of the annual All India Social Service Conference.[58] This was published in the SIS newsletter where Thakkar wrote,

> A large part of our people, found in all parts of India, are known by the name of forest tribes or aboriginals. They apparently are the remaining non-Aryans who were driven to hills and forests by successive Aryan invasions. Originally they were the owners of this land, until our Aryan forefathers dispossessed them of it.

Notice the stress in the very first line on 'our people'. However, while Thakkar could accept the colonial theory of India's civilisational history, the nationalist in him critiqued the long-established colonial policy of doing little for the aboriginal communities. He lamented the lack of literacy among them and lambasted the role of 'Aryans, especially the so-called higher castes', who, in collusion with the government official, 'have all combined to keep them down, and to treat them not like human beings but like wild beasts or, at the best, like cattle'. He had realised that because of a lack of any elite, well-educated group amidst the aboriginals, they were staring at a bleak future unless a vocal class emerged from within to represent their interests in an era of developing constitutional and electoral politics. In the years to follow, Thakkar was to increasingly stress this fundamental requirement of giving the aboriginals a voice in the public domain. In this paper, he wrote:

---

[58] A. V. Thakkar, 'Social Work Among the Aboriginals', *TSI*, 6 December 1923, reproduced in *TBCV*, pp. 299–300. This paragraph and the following quotation have been taken from this source.

> Yet I am afraid I am not exaggerating when I say that our national conscience towards these tribes has still not awakened—not even to the extent that it has towards the untouchable classes. There is a greater and stronger barrier between these aboriginal tribes and ourselves than between the untouchable classes and ourselves. We do take service from the untouchables; we do let them live, though in locations, in our villages: but there are hardly any points of contact between the forest tribes and ourselves except the money-lending and purchasing their forest and other produce at very cheap rates. Very few, if any, social workers of note have worked amongst them, except Christian missionaries. The Hindu has completely neglected them, though, by slow degrees, the aboriginal is willing to, and does as a matter of fact, assimilate himself to him. His religion is described in census reports as animistic, but very large numbers from them are enumerated as Hindus in this Presidency.

This is a remarkable passage for very significant reasons. *First*, it is here that Thakkar ascribes an even greater marginality to the aboriginal than to the Depressed Classes amongst whom social reformers had worked for over half-a-century in Bombay Presidency. Although the word 'isolation' does not yet appear in print, the idea itself was embedded in this articulation. *Second*, Thakkar was also lamenting the lack of 'points of contact', which suggests that he was becoming familiar with the anthropological vocabulary associated with Neo-Diffusionism.[59] *Third*, he was clearly marking out the aboriginals as a field of social service with a distinct Hindu motif. While the Christian missionaries had been active amongst them, the Hindu missionary had shown an absolute neglect, despite the willingness of the aboriginal to 'assimilate' himself within the larger pantheon. To my knowledge, this provides the first evidence of the usage of the word referring to the process of 'assimilation', which was again evoked in the aftermath of the Thakkar–Elwin debate in the early 1940s. *Lastly*, the mention of the Census and animism is significant because it shows that the Hindu mission taking shape under Thakkar's tutelage was conscious of the need to swell the numbers under the Hindu fold. Certainly, the mission was not merely philanthropic and altruistic, but had political motives as well. Thakkar's endeavour was therefore pregnant with implications that unfolded in the years to follow.

In the same piece, he referred to the social service activities being conducted under the auspices of the Bhil Seva Mandal. The Dohad and

[59]For details, see the first section of Chapter 2 on J. H. Hutton.

Jhalod talukas had seven centres carrying out the Mandal's work, 'each having a school with an agricultural bias for their children' (including two boarding schools). Two dispensaries were being run, which brought in the much appreciated medical relief. Here, we can clearly see that Thakkar's notion of social service, of a distinctly Hindu variety, was clearly modelled along the lines of Christian missionaries. However, it differed as well for Thakkar added a strong concern for protecting the Bhils from the tyranny of subordinate officials and sahukars. Also added to the programme was a 'religious turn ... given to their daily life and their songs'. The biographer of Thakkar Bapa has mentioned that under the latter's supervision, the *Ramayana* was translated into the local Bhili language. This was significant for, by doing this, Thakkar was once again following the Christian missionary model, whereby The Holy Bible had been translated into several indigenous languages of India.

A singularly important aspect of Thakkar's reformism was the centrality of temperance work to his scheme of social service. Being a staunch Vaishnava and Gandhian, Thakkar's ideal was total prohibition as, from his point of view, the love for drink was economically as well as socially harmful for the Bhils. It is important to mention that Thakkar and his associates were involved in the Kaliparaj Movement, which has been historicised by David Hardiman.[60] However, in his narrative, Thakkar's role is confined to popularising the term 'Adivasi' in the 1940s. Nevertheless, this lacuna concerning the role played by the Bhil Seva Mandal in the Devi Movement needs to be filled. The key to this lock seems to be the anti-liquor campaign, conducted much on the lines of the Tana Bhagat Movement amongst the Uraons of Chota Nagpur.[61] In newspaper reports of the Presidency, there is clear evidence that Thakkar and his team of social workers were part of the temperance campaign to discourage alcohol consumption amongst the Bhils of the Princely States and Bombay Presidency.[62]

[60]David Hardiman, *The Coming of the Devi: Adivasi Assertion in Western India*, New Delhi: Oxford University Press, 1987.

[61]Sangeeta Dasgupta, 'Reordering a World: The Tana Bhagat Movement, 1914–1919', *Studies in History* 15 (1), February 1999, pp. 1–41.

[62]A. V. Thakkar, 'Social Work Among the Aboriginals', pp. 299–300. Thakkar wrote letters during the course of the movement, which were published in the newspapers. For evidence of this sustained campaign against alcohol, see A. V. Thakkar, 'Kaliparaj Movement': To the Editor The Times of India, *The Times of India*, 17 July 1923, p. 11, and 'Reader's Views: Kaliparaj Movement Community's

In this connection, Thakkar referred to the Kaliparaj Movement of Surat and Baroda where the aboriginal and forest tribes were 'recently awakened in an astonishing manner to a sense of self-respect. He has cast off, as if by a miracle, his vice of drink, and now leads a hygienic and clean life and refuses any longer to serve the bullying landlord.' Thakkar called it a self-purifying movement, setting out a wider appeal to more advanced classes for the 'uplift' of all the forest or aboriginal tribes of Gujarat, and wrote:

> Their numbers are very large, their ignorance stupendous, their degradation unthinkable. Our treatment of them in the past has been nothing short of criminal. No doubt the work amongst them, living as they do, not in settled villages, but each one in his own farm, on hills and in jungles, is more difficult than that in ordinary villages and towns, much more so than in industrial cities like Bombay, Calcutta or Cawnpore. Their habits are different, their mode of living strange, their language difficult to master and their religious ideas very crude. But we can no longer afford to neglect them. Their number is several times greater than the Factory Labour of the whole country, and the call of duty towards them is really more urgent than that towards the industrial worker. Our neglect of them in the past has been scandalous and compensation to them for our sins is long over-due. May the Almighty God give us strength to make amends for the past!!

While Thakkar read the paper at the conference, he also brought along a Kaliparaj delegate named Amersing to the gathering. The SIS newsletter reported that Amersing 'gave a graphic description of oppression and exploitation under which his people suffered'. A Parsi delegate stopped him in the middle by shouting 'Question', whereupon the speaker, who was 'little used to public meetings', became nervous and could not again gather courage to complete his narrative.[63] Nonetheless, Thakkar's paper and Amersing's presence seemed to have an impact on the occasion. The delegates passed a resolution which stated that 'This Conference views with concern the deplorably backward condition of the aboriginal communities of India and calls upon all social workers, the public and Government to devote serious

---

Grievances to the Editor of The Times of India', *The Times of India*, 28 June 1923, p. 10.

[63]'Social Workers in Conference—II. 4. The Outcast C. Aboriginals', *TSI* VI (46), 13 December 1923, p. 545.

attention towards their uplift.'[64] The Bhil Seva Mandal were now receiving wider recognition and accolades for their pioneering work amongst the Bhils. The resolution advocating 'uplift' was proof of his rising stature in the field of social service amongst the aboriginal communities. In this context, Thakkar's network of colleagues and associates at SIS and his links with Vitthal Ramji Shinde were proving quite helpful.

For instance, in October 1924, a public meeting was held under the auspices of the Social Service League in the compound of the Prarthana Samaj, Bombay. With his SIS colleague and guru G. K. Devdhar as Chair of the meeting, Thakkar delivered a lecture on 'Social Work among the Bhils and Other Aboriginal Tribes'. The newspaper reported the following:

> Mr. Thakkar said that the outstanding characteristics of the Bhils and other aboriginal tribes were illiteracy and intemperance. Their level of civilisation was very low. Although the Bhils in this Presidency were slightly advanced than those in other parts of India, yet a great deal more had to be done to elevate them. The higher and more advanced classes in India should feel it their duty towards those tribes to ameliorate their condition. They had till recently pursued the trade of the huntsman and the little benefit they derived from their present day crude agricultural operations was squandered away on drink. Their passion for that vice and their conservatism prevented them from appreciating any intervention for their good, so the reformers had to contend against great odds. The Christian Missionaries had braved any amount of obstacles and had pushed on their noble mission undaunted; but a great deal remind [*sic*] to be done. They had to be saved from themselves, a proof of which was the grave suspicion with which they looked upon a law passed in 1900 making their lands inalienable. It was, therefore, evident that those who felt for their brethren in the lower rungs must lose no time in persistently exerting themselves to elevate those tribes, may be against their own will. Government, too, had contributed their share by opening schools for those tribes. For that purpose, Mr. Thakkar concluded, the present as well as the future workers could with advantage take the Christian Missionaries as models 'par excellence'.[65]

---

[64]Ibid. Also see *All-India Social Service Conference (4th Session: Report, Proceedings & Papers submitted to the Conference)*, Servants of India Society, Bombay, 1924, p. 217.

[65]'Social Work Among the Bhils: Missionaries' Contribution', *The Times of India*, 13 October 1924, p. 5.

In the above extract, Thakkar's ideas on aboriginal welfare seem to be finding their theoretical underpinnings. The chief impediments were illiteracy and the drinking habit. The discourse of uplifting the Bhils propounded by Thakkar resoundingly emphasised the need to extricate them from their love of liquor. On this count, the Bhils had to be 'saved from themselves', and this task ought to be done even 'against their own will'. Also, despite his admiration for Christian missionary activities, Thakkar's views on their impact in the field of education was set to change a little while later.

Meanwhile, Thakkar had also started organising political meetings amongst Bhils, at which he raised demands for political representation for them in the Legislative Council of the Bombay Presidency. In May 1924, a 'representative conference of Bhils and their sympathisers' met at Dohad under the Presidentship of C. F. Andrews and resolved:

> This conference is of opinion that a special representative, by nomination, of aboriginal and hill tribes, such as Bhils, Kaliparaj, Chowdharas, Dhodias, etc. be appointed to the Bombay Legislative Council to watch their interest, similar to the representative of Depressed Classes nominated by Government.[66]

Citing this conference and the resolution, Thakkar wrote a letter to the Editor of *The Times of India*, where he articulated what can be construed as probably the earliest nationalist opposition to the British colonial policy of designating predominantly tribal areas as 'Backward Tracts'. Thakkar pointed out that the population of aboriginal tribes in Bombay Presidency was about 800,000, which was distributed over several districts like West Khandesh, Panch Mahal, Nasik, and southern Sind. Therefore, in his assessment, the protection offered by Section 52A (2) of the Government of India Act, 1919, was not conducive to the aborigines of Bombay, as 'these semi-civilised tribes are distributed over a large area and are not restricted to one compact area'. Making a strong pitch for the resolution passed by the conference of Bhils, Thakkar wrote,

> Fresh under the present constitution these tribes do deserve to have a representative either from among themselves if one can be found or one best fitted by sympathy and knowledge of the tribes to speak for them. Nothing is heard in the Councils about the special grievances and disabilities they are suffering under, and they are so appallingly

[66]A. V. Thakkar, 'Representation of Hill Tribes: To the Editor of the "*Times of India*"', *The Times of India*, 27 May 1924, p. 11.

> ignorant and silent. They are the most illiterate community in the Presidency returning only 4 males out of 1,000 and a very small fraction of one in 1,000 females as literates even in their mother-tongue.[67]

In essence, Thakkar the social worker was simultaneously involved in a double action. On the one hand, he was closely supervising the work of his 'Hindu Mission' under the auspices of the Bhil Seva Mandal, and on the other hand, he was reading, touring, lecturing, and occasionally writing on a variety of issues concerning the future of administration, democracy, and local self-government amongst the aboriginal people. Evidence of such wider detours and canvassing began appearing in 1926, when he went out on a prolonged tour of central India as well as Assam.

Thakkar's Tour of the Central Provinces

In the first leg of his 1926 sojourn, Thakkar stopped at several aboriginal areas in the Central Provinces (C.P.), then considered 'the most backward among the provinces of India'. In the Chhattisgarh region, which he described as 'the backwoods of the Central Provinces', Thakkar saw small aboriginal groups of Savaras, Binjwars, and Halbas. Their respective descriptions provide us with clues about the *modus operandi* and ideological lenses through which Thakkar was developing a pan-India understanding of the aboriginal tribes.

For instance, writing about the Savars of the Oriya country found on the eastern boundary of C.P., Thakkar observed that they became Oriya speakers after having 'lost their tribal language'. The Savars, Thakkar continued,

> ...(had) adopted several of the Brahmanical marriage customs and other ceremonials. In parts of Madras, however, they still retain their tribal Kolarian speech. According to the census of 1911, they numbered about six lakhs, five lakhs of whom were met with in Oriya-speaking areas. The census of 1921 shows their number to have decreased to 4¾ lakhs, a fact worth inquiring into detail. The word Savar is said to have been derived from the Seythian word *Sagaris*, meaning an axe. As they are rarely seen without an axe in their hands, it is quite possible that this derivation is the correct one. In the Aiteraya Brahman, they are spoken of as the descendants of Vishwamitra, while in the Mahabharata they are said to have been created by Kamdhenu. It was from a woman of

[67]Ibid.

> this tribe that Sri Ramchandra accepted wild berries, first tasted by her as being sweet and worth offering to a man of rank like Ramchandra. Their place of pilgrimage even at the present day is Seori-Narayan in Bilaspur district, where Ramchandra is said to have passed some time during his exile. Having lived amongst the priest ridden Orissa, they have dropped the custom, prevalent among many primitive tribes, of the bride being taken to the bridegroom's home for the purpose of celebrating their marriage. I found that a large number of them have a daily bath, and have abjured drinking at weddings and funerals. They not only do not yoke the cows to the plough, as the Gonds do, but never eat beef and have gone to such a length in their respect for the cows that if by neglect or even accident a bullock in harness or one tethered in a shed dies, the owner thereof has to undergo expiation and thereafter to give a feast to his castemen as a penance.[68]

This extract is a good representative example of Thakkar's descriptive method vis-à-vis tribal communities. He laid great emphasis on the demographic numbers as generated in the decennial Census returns, often comparing them with previous ones. Literacy figures also featured prominently in his descriptions. A notable place was given to sacred Hindu scriptures. At this stage of familiarising himself with non-Bhil tribesmen, Thakkar was actively using mythology to claim a certain historicity in the place of such communities in the Hindu civilisational order. Ram to him was a historic figure, and the pilgrimage sites (Seori Narayan) were the actual spots where Sabri had offered the avatar of Narayan her proverbial *Shabari ke ber*. Also noteworthy was the Vaishnavite Thakkar's appreciation of the adoption of Brahmanical purity/pollution norms such as personal hygiene, temperance, vegetarianism, reverence for cows, and even changes in marriage customs that reinforced patriarchy.

Further on, Thakkar's treatment of the Binjhwars and Halbas follow similar observations about the Hinduisation process at work amongst them. Writing of the Halbas as 'a (military) caste of considerable influence', Thakkar wrote that 'I have noted social awakening even amongst them due to the recent wave of self-purification coming in the wake of non-co-operation'. He expressed hope that the construction of railways (then underway to tap the forest resources) would spur 'greater self-consciousness among them and that they will rank with what may be called middle Hindu castes'. This

[68] A. V. Thakkar, 'In the Land of the Aborigines: Savars, Binjhwars and Halbas', *TSI* IX (6),11 March 1926, pp. 69–71. The rest of the section is based on this source.

provides significant evidence that the incorporation of groups considered aboriginal in the Hindu caste structure was the desirable road ahead.

Perhaps the most noteworthy comments were the ones on the educational scenario among aboriginal communities in the Central Provinces. Whenever Thakkar wrote on matters of education and aborigines, his language and articulation assumed their sharpest form as both were his chief interests as a social worker and reformer. His first observation was: '(A)s in other parts of the country, so in the C.P., the education of the aborigines lags much behind even that of the depressed classes.' The Mahars of Berar, who had been 'in contact with advanced Deccan Brahmins', were ahead of the Chamars of Chhattisgarh. Nevertheless, insofar as literacy levels could be compared, the aborigines, only a small proportion of whom had 'come down from their habitation in hills and forests to the plains', were 'very much behind' the Mahars or Mehras of C.P.

The Gonds were numerically the biggest aboriginal community of the C.P. With a number of 21 lakhs, they formed two-thirds of the aboriginal population. According to Thakkar, while the Gonds were 'a little more advanced than the Chamars ... they (had) trudged on only a third of the distance travelled by Mahars on the path of literacy'. Unfortunately, however, both the government and the 'advanced section of the people' had neglected their plight. The former was so apathetic that no representational claim on behalf of the aborigines was forwarded, which had been done for the depressed classes. Comparing this neglect with Bihar, Thakkar poignantly wrote,

> The Bihar Government, on account of their possibly greater alertness or of the 'Tana Bhagat' movement which created a commotion some time before the enquiry was undertaken, were able to secure two seats in the reformed Legislative Council, with a much smaller percentage of aborigines than the C.P. No doubt the Mahars were more vocal than the dumb Gonds and Kawars and were able to secure what they claimed. But Gonds could not speak for themselves and their Government did not think it necessary to speak in their b half [*sic*].

Thakkar's emphasis on the inability of the Gonds to speak for their interests was an evocative expression of the sorry state of affairs, whereby the quintessential aborigine remained dumb and silent. In Thakkar's view, such debilitating silence had to be broken and corrected in an era of constitutional reforms, when power was slowly being handed over to Indians. In such pregnant times, aboriginal inaction stood in sharp contrast to other backward communities like the Mahars, who were leaps and bounds ahead in raising a well-pitched demand for political representation in the legislative bodies. Thakkar rightly pointed out the case of Bihar, where the visibility gained during the Tana Bhagat Movement, along with the activities of the Christian aborigines, had successfully galvanised the government to grant a couple of seats in the Legislative Council. Essentially, Thakkar was slowly coming to terms with the reality of Central India where, despite the strength of numbers as depicted in the decennial Census returns, the absence of an articulate, English-educated elite amongst the aborigines had meant their inability to participate in the political processes at all levels of locality, province, and finally the nation.

In a nutshell, Thakkar was witnessing the phenomenon of a numerically significant minority being edged out of representative politics because it had failed to parade an elite of its own. Thus, to ameliorate any further marginalisation of aborigines, Thakkar was eager for and focussed on gaining two-fold results: *first*, securing political representation, and *second*, the provision of special educational facilities for them. He rued the condition in C.P. where the provision of resources for the educational advancement of the aborigines was left to the discretion of district councils.

In the same piece, Thakkar raised the very pertinent issue of the classification of aborigines, which was set to have tremendous implications for the unravelling of the politics of scheduling in late colonial India. He wrote:

> From the reports of the Director of Public Instruction, it is rather difficult to know under what 'race or creed' the aborigines are classed. Other provinces with a much smaller aboriginal population consider them sufficiently numerous to be classed by themselves along with Hindus, Muslims, Buddhists, Parsis etc. This province (C.P.), however, though it has over 20 per cent of its population as aborigines or forest and hill tribes, does not think that number large enough to deserve a separate classification. Hindus have been subdivided into (1) higher castes and (2) depressed classes. A list of depressed classes is given in a footnote under General Table 41, in which Gonds and other tribes are not included. They are therefore either classed with the higher castes of Hindus or altogether forgotten by the Education Department; in either case it is a cruel mockery.

This was perhaps the earliest instance where Thakkar was questioning the official classificatory scheme of aboriginal tribes in government documents. Here, the lacuna was pointed out in the Education Department's records for the Central Provinces. However, a careful scrutiny of the article shows that the underlying claim that Thakkar was making was the demand for state recognition of 'aborigines or forest and hill tribes' as Hindus. If the depressed classes had found a place in the statistics of Hindu society, why were the aboriginal tribes kept out? As shown in Chapter 2, this key question was to assume far greater significance after the 1931 Census.

Making a further appeal to the C.P. government and the Council members, Thakkar reminded them of the existence of a 'vast mass of their countrymen going by the name of Gonds or other similar tribes, which they can no longer afford to forget or neglect'. His main pitch was for their educational advancement through the provision of free studentships, a generous number of scholarships, and free hostels across all stages of schooling. Raising a moral imperative, Thakkar wrote,

> The grievous apathy of the past must be amended and amply amended. It is not enough to say that they are not coming forward to make a demand for such facilities. The facilities must be given and proclaimed from the housetop before they clamour for them. They are too shy, made too timid and left too ignorant to ask for them. Their tradition has not been that of persistent demand, much less of begging. They would rather die of starvation than beg for anything, much less for the fruit of knowledge, which they have not yet tasted. I do not consider our legislators, who are supposed to represent the masses of the people, less blameworthy than the C.P. Government, who boasts of safeguarding the interests of the 'dumb millions'.

Thakkar's View of the Aboriginal Tribes in Assam

After visiting the aboriginal areas in the Central Provinces, Thakkar moved to the North-eastern part of the British Indian Empire. He spent a considerable period visiting the Assam Hill Tribes, which opened his eyes to the bewildering variety of tribal cultures in that region. Reporting in the SIS mouthpiece, Thakkar wrote, 'Assam is thus an ethnographical museum of races among whom there is a perplexing variety of languages, dialects and customs.' Besides the staple administrative and statistical information on population, education, and the number of Christians in the province, Thakkar noted that there existed real differences between the inhabitants of the hills and those of the plains areas, as they shared very few 'points of contact'. Additionally, the 'natural barrier of hills and forests and the great linguistic and dialectical variety' had facilitated isolation, not only between hill and plains people but also between one hill tribe and another.[69]

The vast influence of Christian missionary organisations was palpable to Thakkar's eyes. He noted the work of the Welsh Calvinistic Presbyterian Church in the Khasi and Jaintia Hills, which had spent a 'very large amount in conducting educational and medical institutions'. It boasted of a large network of schools and had even received a substantial governmental grant. The Educational Manual of Assam also pointed out that the Mission directly controlled the management of education in the Khasi and Jaintia Hills, while the government was only indirectly involved.

Thus, the effect that Christian missionary activities had on tribal solidarity left a strong impression upon Thakkar. For instance, he noted that the non-Christian Khasis widely complained that 'Christianity alienates the Khasi convert from his social and cultural contact with the Khasi people as a whole'. As a potential counterpoint to such missionary control and propaganda, Thakkar mentioned the existence of Seng-Khasi of the Khasi Association, which 'may prove a very useful institution under proper guidance'. This body maintained a 'negative attitude inasmuch as it is animated by the counter-evangelical motive'. However, Thakkar thought that it was 'not enough ... to continue in a posture of protest; and to be useful, it must undertake positive and constructive work of educational and social reform'.

After the Khasi country, Thakkar stepped into the Sadiya frontier tract where he encountered the Abors and the Mishmis. Here, too, Thakkar closely observed the activities of the American Baptist Mission amongst the Abors. He mentioned a boarding school for boys maintained by the Mission, where they were being 'prepared' for conversion. As if to provide proof of his allegations, Thakkar rather sarcastically noted, '(T)hey read Abor texts consisting of Bible stories and sing Christian hymns in the Abor language. The great devotion and steadiness with which the Mission works for the hill tribes is admirable.' Thakkar noted that these Missions also had plans for the future expansion of their activities amongst tribals where they had no influence. The same Mission was contemplating opening a station at Lumding junction to serve the Mikirs.

[69]A. V. Thakkar, 'In the Land of the Aborigines—Assam Hill Tribes', *TSI* IX (11), 15 April 1926, pp. 137–139. The following paragraphs and extracts in this section are based on this source.

After Sadiya, Thakkar went to the Naga Hills District whose headquarters, Kohima, he described as a 'semi-military post'. The Deputy Commissioner was invested with large powers of extradition of any outsider. Several Missions were actively running schools, even in this landscape. Thakkar noted that although each Naga tribe spoke a different language, the students of these schools were learning the Angami Naga language. In the government schools, Assamese was taught, and some institutions were also imparting artisanal skills to the Naga students.

Thakkar also visited two Angami Naga villages and noticed that the Naga 'eats almost any animal that he can kill or catch'. They proudly displayed the heads of Mithun[70] as trophies in front of their houses and were extremely fond of rice beer. Their 'houses were full of foul smell and are very dirty'. Thakkar also witnessed Jhum cultivation, in the course of which forest tracts were burned, and found it 'wasteful'. He preferred terrace cultivation and found that the Nagas showed 'great skill in cutting the terraces and irrigating them from hill streamlets'. Interestingly for a historian, he noted in this piece that it was 'not uncommon to meet officials and Missionaries in Assam who heartily wish to save the tribes from "civilization"'. He added that this was understandable, as the 'first fruits of contact between the "civilized" persons and primitive tribes' were drunkenness and exploitation. Such a rationale, Thakkar noted, 'may easily be made an excuse for withholding from the backward tribes all that is best in civilization either of the eastern or western type'. As always, Thakkar reserved his most astute comments on the matter of education. He wrote,

> The teaching of languages to pupils of the hill tribes is a very complicated question. The variety is well-neigh baffling and a great impediment to educational progress and inter-tribal contact. The language walls also shut out from the tribes the civilizing influences of Assamese and Bengali. The present educational policy of the Government is to recognise the tribal language or dialect of the area in which the school is situated. The text books are written in Roman characters and mostly prepared by the missionaries. Normally they contain Bible stories and sometimes a translation of the Gospel is also taught. Assamese forms the third language, English being the second.

Here, we can clearly see that for Thakkar, the Assam tour opened up the extent of Christian missionary activity in the region. Despite his qualified admiration towards them, Thakkar's views about their impact in the

[70] *Bos frontalis*, a bovine found mainly in North-east India.

field of education were changing. Further on, he ripped apart the Assam Educational Department's claim that the 'object' of the school in the Hills District was 'To civilize the inhabitants and to develop their intelligence'. His chief objection was on the grounds of language; he wrote,

> Assamese would be of far greater help than the tribal languages and dialects pedestalled on Roman script with a written literature consisting of a few biblical primers and hymn-books. Language is a great civilizing and unifying force. A perpetuation of the tribal language and erection of dialect barriers, therefore is tantamount to condemning the province to a babel of tongues. It may well serve to-day's purpose; but those who think of the future of Assam and its progress cannot approve the present policy. In the larger interests of the province, it is desirable to establish increasingly greater contact between the different tribes and the Assamese population. The present administrative and educational policy of the Assam Government tends to accentuate the existing differences and keep them apart for ever.

This was a remarkable admission of the ideological underpinnings of Thakkar's still budding nationalist linguistic policy towards tribal languages. In another article written and published during the same trip, Thakkar had advocated that the government should (*i*) open schools under its own direct management; (*ii*) gradually take over the responsibility for education from missionary control; and (*iii*) ensure that the grant they provided to the Missions was not utilised for evangelical purposes. Thakkar declared that 'Imparting of education like defence of life and property is a primary duty of the State and cannot be contracted out to those who offer the lowest tender'.[71] Also, the issue of tribal dialect/language and its scripts caught the now veteran social worker's imagination. The issues that he raised here remain a very significant matter, on which there is huge scope for primary historio-linguistic research.[72]

Until now, the chapter has focussed on reform action vis-à-vis aboriginal tribes in western India, where Thakkar emerged as the pioneering figure. I

---

[71] See A. V. Thakkar, '"Farming out" of Education in the Assam Hills', *The Servant of India* IX (9), 1 April 1926, pp. 109–110.

[72] This is a fascinating area of study where new work is emerging again. For a relatively recent example, see Nishaant Choksi, 'From Language to Script: Graphic Practice and the Politics of Authority in Santali-Language Print Media, Eastern India', *Modern Asian Studies* 51 (5), 2017, pp. 1519–1560. Available at https://doi.org/10.1017/S0026749X16000470 (accessed 11 July 2024).

will now proceed to analyse the process of Hinduisation as discernible from the 1931 Census reports. The focus of the following analysis will be on the states of Assam, Bengal and Bihar, and Orissa.

The Uplift Movement in Eastern India: The 1931 Census Reports and Hinduisation of Aboriginal Tribes

The 'Uplift Movement' of the 1920s has to be situated in the contemporary context of the worsening communal situation in the country. The decade began with the Moplah rebellion in Malabar, followed by the ignominious collapse of the Khilafat agitation. It was also marked by periodic widespread communal riots in different parts of the country. This had placed Hindu–Muslim relations under immense strain, which, towards the end of the decade, led even staunchly secular figures like M. A. Jinnah to a 'parting of ways'. The gradual decolonisation which began with the Minto-Morley reforms (1909), with their grant of separate electorates, had already sowed the seeds of dissension and the aforementioned events merely added fuel to the fire. The decade also witnessed an increasing pitch by Indian social reformers against the activities of the Christian missionaries. All these processes set the stage for religious mobilisation across the board. Some of these have been captured very well in the 1931 Census reports.

By the early 1920s, social reform mouthpieces had started envisioning a 'Hindu Renaissance'. Such articulations eulogised a redemptive Hinduism, which had again 'opened its doors to all those who want to be admitted in its fold'.[73] Earlier in the chapter, a brief analysis was provided of the term 'uplift'. A legacy of caste Hindu reform movements at the turn of the nineteenth century and the advent of the Gandhian constructive programme added both personnel and resources to the idea, enabling it to gather further momentum in western India.[74] However, by the mid-1920s, these ideas had found widespread resonance in eastern India as well, and the broader developments were now being conceptualised as an all-India Uplift Movement.

---

[73]'The Hindu Renaissance' (from *Prabudh Bharat*), *The Indian Social Reformer* XXXIII (42), 16 June 1923, pp. 684–685.

[74]'Throughout the 1920s, Gandhi's preferred term for the target groups subject to uplift activities was *Antyaj*, meaning 'the last born'.

The main feature of this assemblage of ideas around the Uplift Movement was its articulation in Hindu civilisational terms. The bewildering variety of groups inhabiting the Indian subcontinent was classed primarily in terms of religious denominations (Hindus, Muslims, Sikhs, Christians, Jains, Buddhists, and Animists), and secondarily in terms of racial categories like Aryan and non-Aryan. The proponents of the Uplift Movement claimed that the 'vast bulk' of Indian people were Hindus, which was a denominative term for 'a variety of social classes' organised on the principle of *Varnasrama* or the caste system. The basis of this social complex was 'exclusiveness', which prohibited inter-dining and intermarriage between various castes.[75]

The largest group outside of this socio-religious system was that of the Depressed Classes, who numbered in excess of 45 million. Also outside the Hindu fold were the 'mostly illiterate and uncivilised' aborigines. Some tribes also lived by following 'criminal practices', with scant regard for 'laws of morality and good living'. Thus, it was this very large group of downtrodden people (in official terms, the Depressed Classes, Aboriginals, and Criminal Tribes) outside the pale of Hinduism that provided the 'ready disciples' for the 'proselytising religions of Islam and Christianity', as neither recognised caste. The Christian missionaries, in particular, had done 'splendid service in imparting education among the aborigines and the depressed classes'.[76] Expressing a 'fear of small numbers',[77] these reformers claimed that successive Census reports had shown that the Hindu numbers were declining, while those of Muslims and Christians were rising. There was often a conflation of religion and nation in the reformer's appeal. A characteristic example would be as follows:

> The existence of these untouchables and backward people clogs the wheels of progress. So long as they are not placed on the same footing with the other citizens and are not taught to demand their rights as fellow creatures, all idea of progress and national advancement will be a myth. A progressive nation must have as its watch-words: equality, fraternity, and liberty. It must weld into a homogeneous whole all the divergent elements and must be able to *assimilate any, absorb everybody who will come into its contact.* The vitality of the Indian nation was

---

[75] 'The Uplift Movement in India', *The Indian Social Reformer* XXXVII (7), 16 October 1926, pp. 104–105.

[76] Ibid.

[77] I have borrowed this term from Arjun Appadurai, *Fear of Small Numbers: An Essay on the Geography of Anger*, London: Duke University Press, 2006.

> present when the Greeks, the Mongolians, the Kushanas and the Hunas were absorbed into it.... Modern India has set up barriers against not only foreign inroads, but has lost her ability to bind together the diverse types of her peoples and to inspire them with the message of hope and unity.[78]

A feature of the Uplift Movement that is clearly visible in the above extract may be called the 'acquisitive thrust' on the part of social reformers to stake a new claim upon these sections in order to get them enumerated in the Census as 'Hindus'. The terms that signified this process were 'absorption' or 'assimilation', which were couched in the quasi-diffusionist terms of culture contact. Often, the propagandists would go on to argue that the '*problem is not only social and economic but it is mainly religious*' (emphasis mine). A major aspect of the assimilationist project was the Hinduisation of the aboriginal or animistic tribes, and it is to this phenomenon, evident in the 1931 Census reports of Assam, Bengal, Bihar, and Orissa, that we should turn our attention to.

While these reports loudly resonate and agree with Hutton's argument about the 'borderline of faith' between Hinduism and tribal religions, they add a new twist to the tale. This was the widespread prevalence of a new phenomenon of Hindu propagandists, who were actively encouraging the tribals to return their religion as Hindu during the 1931 Census operations. Often designated as 'Hindu Sabha' or 'Hindu Mission', these groups acted like proselytising bodies whose members had internalised a distinct ideological formulation that will be discussed below. The beginning seems to have been made in Bengal.

The Census authorities in Bengal highlighted that the 1920s had been a decade during which 'communal feeling had been more bitter between Hindus and Muslims'.[79] This had alerted leaders and members of the respective communities to the 'importance in Bengal of the numerical strength of his co-religionists in view of the impending constitutional changes and the question of communal electorates'. One of the significant results during the decade was the establishment, in 1925, of an institution of missionary activity amongst the Hindus of Bengal. It was called the 'Hindu Mission' and its professed aims were (*i*) to preach and propagate Hindu religion and culture; (*ii*) to reform and readjust orthodox Hindu

[78]'The Uplift Movement in India', pp. 104–105; emphasis mine.

[79]A. E. Porter, *Census of India, Vol. V, Bengal & Sikkim, Part I, Report*, Central Publication Branch, Calcutta, 1933, p. 384. Henceforth, *BR (Bengal Report)*.

society in the light of Hindu ideals; (*iii*) to reclaim all those who, or whose ancestors, had once wandered away from the parent faith of Hinduism. The mission adopted a very wide definition of 'Hindu', that is, 'all persons who follow a religion or doctrine which had its origin in India or in good faith call themselves as Hindus and generally follow or try to follow the fundamental principles, usages and customs of the Hindus as enjoined in the Hindu scriptures'.[80]

In Bengal, the principal contention arising out of the Mission's definition was that the members of primitive tribes were Hindus, 'whether or not they conform to Hindu belief and practice'. According to Census authorities, 'considerable effort was expended by the mission and its workers in order to secure the return of primitive peoples as Hindus'. To broadcast their views, a number of pamphlets were issued and disseminated during the course of the enumeration. One such pamphlet in the Bangla script, with an English translation, was published in the 1931 Bengal Census Report. Titled 'Census and Hindu Society in Bengal', it goes as follows:

> From the days of the Ramayana and the Mahabharata there have been living in Bengal, Bihar and Assam, thousands of Santhals, Garos, Dalus, Banais, Khasias, Oraons, Mundas, Mikirs, Miris, Lushais, Kukis, Lalungs, Kacharis, Rabhas and Meches. These inhabitants of Hindustan are fundamentally Hindus. In the census of 1921 they were returned as Animists instead of as Hindus. By this a wrong has been done to our simple religious brothers and sisters.
>
> We hope that during the forthcoming enumeration in January 1931 the above Hindus, men and women, will rectify the mistakes made at the previous census. They should record 'Hindu' as their religion, 'Kshattriya' as their caste and 'Sinha' or 'Ray' as their family name. Special propaganda should be undertaken to see that these instructions are carried out uniformly in all places.
>
> Each member, supporter, devotee and disciple of the Hindu Mission wherever he may be should devote himself to giving this matter publicity amongst all his Hindu neighbours.
>
> The sympathy and help of every Hindu is required for the success of this enormously extended undertaking.
>
> *Dated, the 6th Ashwin 1337.*[81]

[80] Ibid., p. 394.

[81] Ibid., p. 395.

Interestingly, the Hindu Mission's claim that the primitive people in India were 'really Hindus who have lost sight of their religion' was termed as a 'non-political' line. The Hindu Mission distanced itself from the idea of 'conversion'. Instead, it used the vernacular term '*Suddhi*' or purification to refer to the 'ceremonial inclusion within the Hindu fold of any person of Indian origin'. Particularly directed towards Muslims and primitive tribal converts, the word 'Suddhi'[82] indicated that their 'reception into orthodox Hinduism merely involves a cleansing away of objectionable practices and by inference the least possible interference with accepted tribal belief'.

The *Report* also talks about the 'other main non-political activity of the mission', called '*Sangathan*', that is,

> the unification or integration of Hindu society by such reforms as the abolition of untouchability, remarriage of widows, the encouragement of inter-caste and international marriages, the spread of female education and the encouragement of such festivals (*pujas*, *utsavs* and *kirtans*) as may be participated in by all classes of the Hindu community.

Thus, Suddhi and Sangathan formed the core non-political activities. This suggested that the propaganda towards the enumeration of tribes as Hindus in the Census figures had worked successfully.

The Hindu Mission's reports regularly recounted the number of conversions carried out amongst primitive tribes, Indian Christians, and Bengali Muslims. Also mentioned in these documents were the celebrations of '*sarvajanin*' or '*Durga Utsavas*', aimed at consolidating the Hindu community. The Bengal report acknowledged that the figures for tribal religion had shown a pronounced decline since 1921, despite a marked increase in the population of primitive tribes, and hence the attrition rates were worrisome indeed.[83]

The 1931 Assam Census report exhibited notes and arguments that were very similar to those of neighbouring Bengal.[84] In terms of respective strength in geographic regions, Hindus dominated the Assam Valley;

---

[82]For a scholarly study, see, J. T. F. Jordens, 'Reconversion to Hinduism, the Shuddhi of Arya Samaj', in G. A. Oddie (ed.), *Religion in South Asia: Religious Conversion and Revival Movements in South Asia in Medieval and Modern Times*, New Delhi: Manohar, 2020, pp. 145–162.

[83]*BR* [Bengal Report], pp. 395–396.

[84]C. S. Mullan, *Census of India, 1931, Vol. VIII, Assam, Part I—Report*, Government of India, Central Publication Branch, Calcutta, 1932. Henceforth, *AR* (*Assam Report*).

Muslims, the Surma Valley; and the followers of tribal religions were most numerous in the Hills. Here, the nodal body for a Bengal-like intensive propaganda campaign was the 'Hindu Sabha' of Assam. The report claimed that its inspiration came from outside the province and was confined to the plains districts of the Assam Valley. The campaign in the Nowgong district was particularly effective, and was

> conducted with considerable skill by the distribution of leaflets in Mikir, Lalung and Kachari villages and by propaganda work among Hindu census supervisors and enumerators as well as among Hindu *Mauzadars* and influential local gentlemen. Tours were made by officers of the Sabha to propagate the new faith that all tribesmen were really Hindus. Mikirs were told that they were descendants of Raja Bali and hence genuine Hindus of ancient lineage.[85]

Despite many similarities, and perhaps common propaganda authors, the parallels with Bengal were not absolute. The prime anxiety of Hindu propagandists vis-à-vis Assam was not focused on Muslims, but rather the Christian missionaries. Despite their low overall numbers, the Indian Christians were almost doubling their numbers in successive Census enumerations. Over a thirty-year period, their numbers had increased by a factor of eight. Thus, the chief aim of the Hindu propagandists in Assam was to put a stop to the highly organised and well-funded activities of various Christian missionary denominations. The Assam Census Report reproduced the following extracts from a pamphlet titled 'The Hindu Mission—Aims and Activities':

> In order to stem the tide of conversion to Christianity we commenced work amongst the aboriginal people of Bengal, Bihar and Assam since the beginning of 1926. These people who are mentioned in the census reports as Animists form an important part of the population in these three provinces. Their number may be roughly estimated as no less than four million—i.e., two millions in Bihar and one million each in Bengal and Assam. These are regarded as the chief recruiting centres of the different Christian Missions. At present there are more than fifty different Missionary Societies of different countries of Europe, America and Australia who have concentrated their energies in spreading Christianity amongst the simple men and women of the hill tracts of Bengal, Assam and Bihar. These people may be considered naturalised Hindus by long and close contact with their Hindu

[85]Ibid., p. 188.

> neighbours. But owing to the prevailing rigour of untouchability amongst the caste Hindus and partly owing to difference in language, taste and race the Hindus took very little interest about these people. But as soon as the Hindu Mission organised propaganda parties, opened centres and took up the work of introduction of simple Hindu rites amongst these people and the removal of the vice of untouchability to bring them closer to the caste Hindus the success was phenomenal. During the year ending in March 1928 over sixty thousand Santals, Oraons, Khasis, etc. were absorbed into the Hindu fold after a very simple ceremony of initiation. Amongst this number there are a few thousands of Christians also.[86]

The Mission's pamphlet hailed the quick success of its propaganda over all of Bengal, Assam, and parts of Bihar. For several months leading to the 1931 Census enumeration exercise, a large number of workers of the Hindu Mission conducted intensive propaganda. A rough estimate by the organisation suggested 'a substantial increase of Hindu population in these provinces in consequence of the *absorption of Animists*'.[87] The published Census figures only buttressed the Hindu Mission's achievement, as the decrease in Animists and proportionate increase in Hindus in Bengal and Assam 'clearly assert that at least a million of Animists has been absorbed into the Hindu society'. Examining the cause of their stupendous success, the Hindu Mission acknowledged a broader solidarity with other Hindu organisations like the Hindu Mahasabha and the Ramakrishna Mission in the following terms:

> Incessant propaganda amongst these people since 1926 carried the message of this mission to the remotest corner of the hills and plains of these two provinces. Lakhs of people have been formally initiated and lakhs of others have been automatically absorbed by the initiated ones as well as by the local Hindus who felt interested in this work. Other local organizations such as the branches of the Hindu Mahasabha and the Ramkrishna Mission have also added their contributions to this number. The mission has created an active and intensive enthusiasm for the assimilation of those who stand outside the fold of Hindu society and the expansion of Hinduism on all sides in the path of love and toleration.

[86]Ibid., p. 189. The rest of the discussion on Assam as well as the extracts are based on this source.

[87]Emphasis mine.

In fact, the Hindu Mission claimed that the actual absorption was far more than that 'testified' by the Census reports. The 'newly initiated Animists wanted to be returned as Kshatriyas', a request that was declined by the authorities. This resulted in a form of mild non-cooperation with the enumerators at many places, and such 'Hindus' were returned as Animists as in 1921. The Hindu Mission put forward a demand to the Census Superintendent of Assam that such corrections should be made. Moreover, the Mission opined that despite the success of its campaign, about four million Animists remained in the Bengal, Bihar and Orissa, and Assam provinces, 'who may be easily assimilated into the Hindu society. All that is required is a little propaganda, humanitarian services, and social liberalism'.

Similar references to the Hindu Mission's activities appear in the Bihar and Orissa Census Report. Citing the Mission's definition of 'Hindu' (almost verbatim as the Bengal example cited above), the Census authorities noted that such efforts 'makes short of the old time theory that a Hindu must be born of Hindu parents. It recognises no fine distinctions between the processes of reclamation, absorption and conversion'. On the contrary, the Hindu Mission propagandists insisted that there was 'no rule laid down by the Rishis or the Shastras that the Hindu religion must be confined to India and to men born in that faith.... From the Vedic days upto the Muhammadan invasion the Hindu religion has been a proselytizing religion.'[88]

Thus, a rather radical recasting of Hinduism was taking shape which, despite its avowed 'non-political' line, was quite literally proselytising. In the era of competitive identity-based politics, its character was certainly political. The rapidly evolving framework visualised India as a Hindu nation with its ever-expanding brood of new 'castes' and 'aboriginal tribes', which were constantly being added to the new social and political imaginary. Such an enormous expansion of millions and millions of subjects of the British Indian Empire was bound to shake up well-established official classificatory schemes, including the ones foundational to the decennial Census documents.

A further aspect of great importance was raised in the 1931 Census reports, most prominently by Hutton, the all-India Census Commissioner himself. This was the issue of the fuzzy nature of the boundary between Depressed Classes and followers of tribal religion. As noted in Chapter 2, one of Hutton's main contentions was that the detribalisation/Hinduisation of

[88] W. G. Lacey, *Census of India, 1931, Vol. VII, Bihar and Orissa, Part I—Report*, Government Printing Bihar and Orissa, Patna, 1933, p. 247.

primitive tribes had meant a swelling in the numbers of Depressed Classes. In the chapter on 'Race, Caste, Tribe' in the 1931 Bihar and Orissa Census Report, the authorities acknowledged 'some overlapping between the totals for the depressed classes and aboriginal communities, in as much as nearly two million Hinduized aboriginals have been included in both categories'.[89]

This points to the problems faced by the colonial State's cognition of these categories through the decennial Census exercise.[90] Given the veritable ocean of statistics and anthropological literature contained in the all-India Census reports from 1871–1931, it is too daunting a task to attempt within the parameters of the present monograph. However, one important point needs to be made here. At least from the 1890s onwards, the intensive thrust given to the ethnographic survey by Risley and many others had meant that a large measure of 'anthropological bias' had crept into the Census operations. In crucial ways, the 'cognitive legacy' of nineteenth-century ethnological and ethnographic understanding of the categories of 'race', 'caste', and 'tribe' loomed large over all the twentieth-century colonial Census operations. For instance, the failure of Risley himself to define 'caste' and 'tribe' in an academically sound manner was a reflection of the inability to break out of that legacy. As far as its effect on the official categories is concerned, until the 1931 Census operations, all reports had a single chapter, titled 'Race, Caste, Tribe'. It was, quite literally, impossible to treat them separately within the statist framework of the decennial Census documents.[91]

An understanding of the classificatory lenses deployed by the colonial State is perhaps the Gordian knot of modern Indian social history. To solve this puzzle, a plausible approach perhaps lies in the work of social reformers

[89]Ibid., p. 270.

[90]For two excellent articles on the colonial State's cognition of caste in decennial Census exercises, see Rashmi Pant, 'The Cognitive Status of Caste in Colonial Ethnography: A Review of some Literature on the North West Provinces and Oudh', *IESHR* 24 (2), 1987, pp. 145–162, and Padmanabh Samarendra, 'Classifying Caste: Census Surveys in India in the Late Nineteenth and Early Twentieth Centuries', *South Asia: Journal of South Asian Studies*, n.s., XXVI (2), August 2003, pp. 141–164.

[91]Some of this chaos was related to the battle being waged in British anthropology in places like Oxford and Cambridge. We must remember that even stalwarts of nationalist sociology like G. S. Ghurye and M. N. Srinivas were trained in this tradition, and hence such forces continued to shape the sociological understanding of caste and tribe for decades to come.

like Vitthal Ramji Shinde and his protégé, Amritlal Vitthaldas Thakkar. As a result of their efforts in the first quarter of the twentieth century, initially the 'Depressed Classes' and subsequently the 'Aboriginal and Hill Tribes' started to be counted under the expanded notion of 'Hindu'. The result was evident in the 1931 Census report of Bombay Presidency, where the 'Hindu community' was separated into (*i*) Hindu-Advanced; (*ii*) Hindu-Intermediate; (*iii*) Hindu-Primitive; (*iv*) Hindu-Other Backward; and (*v*) Hindu-Depressed.[92] This is a fascinating tale that necessitates an intellectual enquiry into the concept of 'backwardness'. As will become evident in Chapter 5, it is crucially linked to the spread of education, which was the key area of reform for both Shinde and Thakkar.

Conclusion

Like most arguments raised in this chapter, only further enquiry can establish the distinct Hindu leanings of Thakkar's reformist efforts, the nature of the Uplift Movement, or the truth behind the Hindu Mission's claims made in the 1931 Census documents. Nevertheless, certain broad trends are clearly visible over the decade of the 1920s.

First, an academic understanding, which was necessary to step out of the view of 'politics' narrowly defined within nationalist frameworks in terms of the mass mobilisation activities of the Indian National Congress under the leadership of Gandhi. Serious attention must be paid to the sphere of social reform action, which contributed substantially to the vibrant constitutional politics of interest-representation. To bring to fruition his idea of a constructive programme, Gandhi himself recruited personnel from these increasingly professionalised networks and added his substantial fund-raising abilities to various causes. This staggered process slowly broadened the appeal and legitimacy of Indian nationalism, with Gandhi as its political and spiritual head.

Second, some of the most far-reaching reformist tendencies were visible in western India. The twin cities of Poona and Bombay emerged as the nerve centres of social reform, and were the seats of many important institutions and patronage networks. Vitthal Ramji Shinde of the Depressed Classes Mission and Gopal Krishna Gokhale of the Servants of India Society are

[92] A. H. Dracup and H. T. Sorley, *Census of India, 1931, Vol. VIII, Part I, Bombay Presidency: General Report*, Government Central Press, 1933, p. 380.

a couple of significant names awaiting historical enquiry. Their respective roles in professionalising social service and providing an expanding network of workers for the Gandhian mass movements remains to be contextualised.

Third, the emergence of Thakkar as the first nationalist ideologue of aboriginal tribes has to be established within the context of the Gandhian constructive programme. In this chapter, I have provided an analysis of the first eight years (1919–1926) of Thakkar's dense involvement with the Bhils of Panch Mahal district, which continued until the mid-1930s. The Bhil Seva Mandal established by Thakkar was perhaps the first nationalist organisation dedicated to the amelioration of aboriginal tribes. Until he assumed charge of the Harijan Sevak Sangh, established after the Poona Pact between Gandhi and Ambedkar, Thakkar's chief focus of reformist activity remained the aboriginal tribes of western India.

In this phase, some crucial evolutionary strands in Thakkar's ideas on the aboriginal condition have been outlined. The chief way to 'uplift' the aborigines was through a multi-pronged socio-religious and cultural reform, consisting of the propagation of education, temperance, cleanliness, and standardisation of tribal customs. He also began opposing the colonial policy of delineating predominantly tribal areas as Backward Tracts and demanded that the aboriginal tribes be included in the scheme of devolution of powers to the Indians. However, above all, Thakkar's reformist impetus was geared to facilitate their absorption into the Hindu fold.

Towards the end of this phase, Thakkar was sufficiently rooted in the Bhil locality to start expanding his gaze to other predominantly tribal areas in both the Princely States and British India. In his tour notes, we find him expressing a dawning awareness of the vast potential of the 'Hindu Mission' for other parts of India. In a long exposure visit to the North-East corner of the subcontinent, Thakkar also displayed an antipathy to Christian missionary welfare work. Nevertheless, this unease was mixed with a fair amount of appreciation about their role in the spread of education. He also began to articulate ideas about State-led interventions in the educational advancement of the aboriginal tribes. Some interesting ideas on the place of tribal languages were put forward with honesty and candour.

Fourth, figures like Thakkar, directly or indirectly, contributed to a Hindu mobilisation campaign aimed at admitting the hitherto excluded/marginalised groups of the Depressed Classes and aboriginal tribes within the fold of a reformed Hinduism. In this scenario, the terms 'absorption' and 'assimilation', widely used throughout the 1920s by the votaries of uplift, had a distinct connotation in the removal of fault-lines that weaken the Hindu national identity.

Fifth, the impending constitutional changes to be brought in after the decade-long experience of the Government of India Act, 1919, initiated political mobilisation along communal lines. In the charged political climate, the 1931 Census became a site of efforts to increase the Hindu numbers, which took the shape of intensive propaganda in the provinces of Bengal, Assam, and Bihar and Orissa. Lakhs of people belonging to the 'Primitive Tribes' were persuaded to return themselves as Hindus, and not as followers of 'Tribal Religion'. An unintended result of this massive expansion in Hindu numbers in several British Indian provinces was the revising of official classificatory frameworks. This phenomenon perhaps also acted as a catalyst for scholar-administrators like Hutton, who pushed for a territorial solution to the tribal question in India. The rapid spread and success of the Hindu Missions in predominantly tribal areas became the basis for Hutton's argument in favour of ring-fencing such areas away from all outside influences. In the Huttonian framework, once cordoned off, the hills and jungles would serve as safe havens for followers of tribal religion. Eventually, then, territorial segregation though scheduling would save the Indian aboriginal tribes from the threat of extinction which Hindu civilisation posed for them.

Lastly, in Bombay, the new classificatory framework splintered the category of 'Hindu Community' into five sub-divisions: Advanced, Intermediate, Primitive, Other Backward, and Depressed. This was supposed to reflect the changed social reality brought about as a result of the spread of education, which was not uniform and affected social identities differentially. Thus, the yardstick for measuring the 'literacy' levels of groups became the basis of the new social taxonomy. This novel scheme lacked any anthropological baggage and sought to classify the Hindu social order in a graded manner, according to educational attainment. However, one of its unintended consequences was the ascription of extreme 'backwardness' to certain social groups which lay outside the caste Hindu social order.

Nationalists like Thakkar saw great merit in the scheme of 'backwardness' derived from the differential levels of literacy among Hindu social groups. Such a measurable and non-anthropological basis provided the ideological edifice for a nationalist social and political imaginary. It also placed the respective caste groups in a core-periphery model for ameliorative State action. Targeted State intervention in the arena of education could thus potentially remove the disabilities of peripheral social groups. Through the three decades of late colonial rule, nationalists like him sought to frame backwardness on their own terms, free from the diffusionist jargon of culture contact. This constituted the chief nationalist ideological response, both before and after the administrative discourse on the scheduling of predominantly tribal areas spilled over into the arena of popular politics. It is to this fascinating story which had (and continues to have) immense ramifications that we shall now turn.

5

Framing 'Backwardness'

Nationalist Responses to the Tribal Question

After providing an overview of A. V. Thakkar's intellectual evolution on the question of aboriginal tribes in the 1920s, this chapter seeks to understand the wider set of nationalist interventions and responses to the question of backwardness. In the annals of Indian nationalism, the twin issues of education and representation were deeply intertwined, but as of now, the interrelationship between their respective trajectories remains to be fully worked out. In an attempt to understand this connection, this chapter will primarily focus on the discourse of educational backwardness in western India by tracing its genealogy in the emerging official 'schedules' of communities. Additionally, this intellectual *sangam* (or confluence) should enhance our understanding of the political trajectory of Congress-tribal interaction.[1]

As the debate on scheduling gradually came to frame the background for visualising the future of tribal people in an independent and sovereign India, a related development in the intellectual domain was the foregrounding of the educational backwardness of aboriginal tribes. This was seen as a prerequisite towards ensuring their genuine representation in the political domain. Here, once again, Bombay Presidency provided the main battleground for the debate as some of the most catalytic ideas were generated in the domain of law as well as in the Census Reports of 1921 and 1931. Taken together, these ideas added to the ferment in official taxonomies. Moreover, the mapping of these shifts in the administrative and legislative discourse during the 1920s and the nationalist response it generated in

[1]Crispin Bates, 'Congress and the Tribals', in Mike Shepperdson and Colin Simmons (eds), *The Indian National Congress and the Political Economy of India, 1885–1985*, Dartmouth Publishing, 1988, pp. 231–252.

western India led to changes in the official cognition and classification of the various communities clubbed under the very broad and generic category of 'Hindu'. Educationally 'advanced' groups became the yardstick by which the quantum of 'backwardness' that others suffered from could be measured. In the process, backwardness emerged as a relational category and the State its chief arbiter.

Literacy, Census, and the Backward Classes

As outlined in Chapter 4, the Government of Bombay was making impressive strides in the field of education. Undoubtedly, a part of this initiative stemmed from the pressure generated by the late nineteenth and early twentieth-century social reformers in western India, like Jyotiba Phule, Savitribai Phule, Justice Ranade, Gopal Krishna Gokhale, and Vitthal Ramji Shinde. It would not be an exaggeration to say that intervention in the field of education became the central pivot for both social reformers and affirmative State action in the first half of the twentieth century.

Another factor adding valuable synergy to the Bombay government's educational impetus emanated from its neighbourhood. In every stage since 1893, the neighbouring Princely State of Baroda had been providing funds and initiatives to bolster both mass and higher education.[2] Under its ruler Saiyaji Rao Gaikwad, in 1907, the State also enacted the Compulsory Education Act (5th of Samvat 1983), in accordance to which all boys (between 7–14 years) and girls (between 7–12 years) were to compulsorily attend schools. The Kaliparaj population (the term given to members of aboriginal tribes) was not exempt from the ambit of this Act. However, '(E)xperience proved that teachers from the towns were disinclined to go and work in the out of the way and often malarial places' where these tribal communities dwelt. Generally illiterate, the tribes could not boast of teachers amidst themselves. Additionally, their 'custom of living in small scattered groups, very seldom in villages of appreciable size' made it difficult to find suitable locations for schools where children could conveniently attend them. These and many other difficulties (not adequately understood)

[2]Manu Bhagwan, *Sovereign Spheres: Princes, Education and Empire in Colonial India*, New Delhi: Oxford University Press, 2003.

made the Baroda State exclude the tribal villages from the ambit of the Compulsory Education Act in the year 1926.[3]

In the Presidency's administrative capital of Bombay, the increased impetus placed on education by the governmental apparatus was gathering momentum in the closing years of World War I. On 5 December 1917, the Legislative Council enacted the Bombay Primary Education (District Municipalities) Act. Popularly called the Patel Act (as it was introduced by Vithalbhai Patel), this legal statute made Bombay 'the first British Indian Province to take up legislation for the introduction of compulsory primary education'.[4] Its scope, however, was limited as the provisions applied only to Municipal areas, excluding the city of Bombay. Thakkar actively assisted Vithalbhai Patel by conducting enquiries that fed into the making of the Act. In Thakkar's view, while this law was a definite advancement over the previous situation, it stopped shy of making primary education compulsory for the masses.[5] In the first five years after its enactment, only five Municipalities (Bandra, Surat, Satara, Dakore, and Byadgi) had introduced compulsion and only the first two included girls in its ambit.[6]

By the early 1920s, however, public opinion had begun demanding more than what the Patel Act provided for. The Non-Cooperation Movement and the educational propaganda undertaken by the Indian National Congress had greatly increased the demand for education. Leaders had started arguing that 'it was the duty of Government rather than that of Local Bodies to take initiative in the matter and introduce compulsory education all over the Province within a prescribed time limit, say ten years'. It was also argued that 'compulsion was more urgently needed in rural areas than in urban ones'.

---

[3]*Report by Mr L. Littlehailes, M.A., C.I.E., Educational Adviser to Baroda State*, Baroda State Press, 1934, pp. 16, 44–45.

[4]J. P. Naik, *Compulsory Elementary Education in the Province of Bombay: A Historical Review*, First Published in the Progress of Education, Poona, December 1940, p. 1.

[5]A. V. Thakkar, 'Compulsory Education', *TSI* II (44), 4 December 1919, p. 519.

[6]J. P. Naik, *Compulsory Elementary Education in the Province of Bombay: A Historical Review*, First Published in the Progress of Education, Poona, December 1940, p. 3. The rationale behind this decision (although unstated here) might have been the impact of the Devi Movement.

Thus, the demand caught on for another Act, which would be 'broader in scope and more thorough in execution'.[7]

As a result, in July 1921, the Bombay government appointed a Committee to carefully investigate the 'growing popular demand for primary education'. The chief concerns of this enquiry were to ascertain the 'desirability and practicability' of introducing compulsory primary education in both Municipality and rural areas; suggest new sources of taxation to meet the cost; and finally, the creation of a necessary machinery for enforcing compulsion.[8] This eleven-member Committee was headed by Sir Narayan G. Chandavarkar, a former judge of the Bombay High Court.[9] After collecting a good deal of statistical information and replies from Presidency divisions as well as the Princely States, the Committee submitted its report in March 1922.

The report stated that the population of the Bombay Presidency, excluding Sind, was 160 lakhs. In terms of percentage, the main divisions were: Brahmins (4 per cent), Non-Brahmin Hindus (84 per cent), Musalmans (8 per cent), and others (4 per cent). Amongst the Non-Brahmin Hindus, about 30 per cent, or close to 40 lakhs, belonged to the Depressed Classes and jungle and criminal tribes,[10] who had made 'little or no progress in education'. The Committee reported the literacy figures of the 1911 Census to show the gap between Brahmins and Non-Brahmins. The figures stated that 635 male Konkanasth Brahmins per mille (1,000) were literates, as against 46 Marathas, 10 Mahars, and 2 Bhils per mille. This disparity was much higher in secondary school classes. The report noted that 'the main problem is to develop primary education among the non-Brahman Hindus in the Presidency proper'. The Chandavarkar Committee

[7]Ibid., p. 6.

[8]Press Note No. 3319, dated 15 July 1921, cited in *Report of the Committee appointed by the Government of Bombay to consider and report on the question of the introduction of free and compulsory primary education into the Bombay Presidency*, Yeravda Prison Press, Poona, 1922, p. 1.

[9]Ten were Members of Legislative Council and the Director of Public Education was an *ex-officio* member. Chandavarkar was once a close associate of Vitthal Ramji Shinde, and the Depressed Classes Mission had been started by them together.

[10]Press Note No. 3319, dated 15 July 1921, cited in *Report of the Committee...*, p. 7.

termed these groups 'Backward Communities', with no identification of the specific groups that were to be clubbed as such. However, even without direct evidence it is plausible to argue that by characterising several communities as 'backward', the Chandavarkar Committee was taking its cue from the Census reports of 1911 and 1921.

Thus, in this period the Bombay Presidency was marked by a rapid evolution in the administrative classification of caste and tribe groups. There were three important milestones in this journey, which we shall now look into.

1. 1921 Census Report and the 'Hinduistic Scale'

Chapter 2 on J. H. Hutton has shown that the 1921 Census report of Bombay Presidency contained a rigorous indictment of the category of Animism. Its Superintendent, L. J. Sedgwick of the Indian Civil Services, had made a radical conceptual departure by jettisoning the category in the enumeration of the aboriginal tribes and had argued that they should be located within the umbrella category of 'Hindu' religion. This had profound implications on the fate of the underprivileged and marginalised sections of the Indian population.

A chapter on Literacy had become a standard part of the colonial decennial Census exercise. In the 1911 Census, the Bombay Provincial Tables had a distinct categorisation for 'Hindu, Jain and Animistic Caste'. According to Sedgwick, this umbrella group was divided into three 'classes', viz., Learned, Backward, and Rest. Thus, clearly the principle behind this tripartite categorisation was education and literacy. Learned communities that were educationally ahead were the obvious beneficiaries, and most government jobs were monopolised by them. All non-literate others were deemed as 'Backward'. Of course, members of overwhelmingly non-literate cultural groups like the Animistic tribes were even beyond the pale of the Backward in terms of formal education.

Nevertheless, almost half-a-century of sustained educational effort by Christian missionaries as well as reformers amongst the caste Hindus and non-Brahmins alike had changed the picture considerably. The entry of the Gandhian Constructive Programme with its ever increasing number of social workers and institutions such as the Gujarat Vidyapith was also making rapid inroads in the educational sector and gaining broader legitimacy in western India. In all this, Gandhi's own remarkable ability to raise funds for 'uplift' activities had acted as a catalyst, adding further momentum to changes in the educational landscape of Bombay Presidency.[11]

Perhaps as a result of these combined pressures, the Census authorities needed to move beyond the principle of the Brahmin/Non-Brahmin binary upon which the tripartite division of Learned/Backward/Rest based itself. A new classificatory schema was required which could accurately provide a conceptual grid to map the changed socio-educational reality of the Bombay Presidency. Yet again, it was Sedgwick who provided the impetus towards such a new classification.

In the chapter on Literacy, Sedgwick made a comparison of the literacy figures of Baroda State (to juxtapose the effects of the experiment in compulsory education) with the contiguous British districts (of the Gujarat region) in the Bombay Presidency.[12] His reading of the figures suggested that they 'show possibly a more progressive state of things in Baroda'. The two zones were neck and neck in literacy rates across most age groups. However, the radical re-interpretation that Sedgwick made was to link educational advancement with economic conditions, and consequently with caste. In a remarkable paragraph, he wrote:

> It is desirable to ascertain how far compulsory education in Baroda results in enhanced literacy among those strata of Hindu society which otherwise usually remain uneducated. In Gujarat generally any boy of certain castes, such as Brahmin, Vani, Soni, etc., can secure education if his father is willing to send him to school. There are hardly any persons of those castes who require their small sons to help them in business. On the other hand in the middle strata, such as Leva Kanbi, Kadava Kanbi, etc., some fathers can well afford and some can ill-afford to spare their sons from their farms or shops, while when we come to the lowest strata, such as Dhed, Bhangi and other untouchable castes, depressed

[11]One of the primary target groups of the Constructive Programme in western India was the category of *Antyaja* or the 'Last Born'. Caste groups like Dheds, Bhangis, and Bhils were included in this group and Thakkar Bapa was doing extensive work among them. For useful references, see *The Collected Works of Mahatma Gandhi* at www.gandhiheritageportal.com.

[12]Subsidiary Table No. 82—Comparison of literacy in Baroda with literacy in British Districts of Gujarat by age-groups, 1921, in L. J. Sedgwick, *Census of India Volume VIII Bombay Presidency, Part I, General Report*, Government Central Press, Bombay, 1922, p. 136. The next couple of paragraphs are based on this chapter on Literacy.

> castes such as Vaghri and jungle tribes such as Chodhra, Dubla, etc., it may be said that almost all small boys have to be turned out on to earn money as soon as they can scare birds from the crops, or take the cattle out to graze. Free and compulsory education would be of little value if it merely enables the upper strata to get their sons educated for nothing, and leaves the lower strata as ill-educated as before, but with pockets depleted by paying fines for the non-attendance of their children.

In essence, Sedgwick was arguing that if the provision of compulsory education was to act as an effective door for emancipation, or in other words, facilitate upward social mobility, its potential was being thwarted by the socioeconomic background of the children's parents. By and large, this backdrop was dictated by the caste groups into which the students were born. This factor of birth fundamentally determined whether the literacy or education they gained would be utilised further to change the traditional occupations inherited from their fathers. In most cases, the imperative to add to the household's income forced the students to revert to agriculture or animal husbandry upon reaching adolescence. Thus, a status quo was maintained in terms of the future occupations of young adults, which further reinforced caste hierarchies and, by implication, reinforced the overall architecture of the Hindu social order. As a result of this imbalance in the system, even the smattering of literacy gained by students, or even the 'education is wasted, and in after life they are not really able to "write a letter to a friend and read his reply"'.

From this perspective, Sedgwick observed that Baroda State areas depicted 'certainly a tendency for the lower strata to be better educated than in British Territory'. Sedgwick developed this logical line, which led further to a very interesting argumentative terrain. In the chapter on 'Caste, Tribe and Race',[13] he mentioned that the stalwart scholar-administrator, R. E. Enthoven, Superintendent of the Bombay Ethnographic Survey, was of the opinion that the concept of caste was so 'hopelessly vague that our figures are useless'. Enthoven strongly urged that the 'recording of castes at the Indian Census should be abandoned, or, as an alternative, should be carried out every twenty years instead of every ten years'. However, Sedgwick opposed this because,

[13] L. J. Sedgwick, *Census of India Volume VIII, Bombay Presidency, Part I, General Report*, Government Central Press, Bombay, 1922.

> In contradistinction to language, Caste has an economic value. In this country more than in any other that I know of, children that are born into the world are born with unequal chances. This is due to the Caste system, and can best be seen from a consideration of educational facilities. To the Deshasth Brahman boy education is his birthright, and if he fails to go to school he is more or less of an oddity. On the other hand, the Mahar boy enters upon life with long odds against his going to school, and if he does go, his birthright is to be segregated off from the other boys and sit outside on the verandah, or even in the sun and dust of the road. Consequently as long as the Caste system survives such Departments as the Educational will need to have Caste figures.[14]

Having established the need for caste figures in the Census in order to gain a sense of the social disparity in the field of education, Sedgwick undertook a comparative analysis of the literacy figures between various caste groups. This comparison depicted clear inequalities from caste to caste, which were 'emphatically not proportionate to the *capacity of the particular castes to receive instruction* but (mainly due to) ... *the peculiar structure of Hindu Society, which keeps all Castes at a definite and unalterable social and economic level*'.[15] The Education Department's work had shown that boys from the Mahar and other depressed castes were 'as quick to learn up to the age of 16 as the boys of higher castes'. The introduction of education amongst the Chodhras, Dublas, Dhodias, and other Kaliparaj tribes in south Gujarat had shown that these boys were 'the intellectual equals of the boys of the highest castes'. Sedgwick explicates:

> It would be most interesting if some educationalist would collect statistics to prove the degree of 'capacity to learn' in the case of each caste. Complete incapacity could be called 0, and the absolute extreme capacity 100. These limits and the intermediate values could be fixed on some such basis as the percentage of boys who, commencing school attendance at any age below 10, and not leaving in the interval, pass some given standard within three years. This ought not to be very difficult to ascertain. We would then be able to make a classified list of castes according to their position in the 'Scale of Capacity to Learn.' The advantage of this would be twofold. First, similar positions in the scale would be a small but not negligible argument in favour of possible

[14]Ibid., p. 178.

[15]Ibid., p. 140; emphasis added.

> common racial origin; and secondly, by comparing the percentage position in the Scale with the *per mille* ratio of literates in Table IX we could ascertain the extent to which education is available in the case of each Caste.... No one except an imbecile is unable to learn to read and write a letter; so the Scale of Capacity and the Ratio of Literates are possibly not mathematically commensurable. Nevertheless, even though exact mathematical treatment were impossible, the comparison of the two scales would be of interest, and would go far to combat the view (seldom expressed but often held) that Mahars and Bhils are not educated because they are not worth educating.[16]

Thus, Sedgwick's conception of a 100-point scale depicting 'Capacity to Learn' stemmed from his wish to challenge the established stereotypes, biases, and notions of both orthodox Hindu society and the anthropological belief in racial differences. The logic inherent in the above extract became the basis on which Sedgwick constructed an idea of the 'Hinduistic Scale' of castes. He argued for the production of detailed statistics on Literacy by Castes, which could be extremely useful in breaking up the unscientific biases against the educational advancement of backward communities. On one end of this Hinduistic scale stood the higher Brahmanical castes, whose children had much better chances to receive education, while on the other end stood those caste groups whose living conditions made it virtually impossible for their children to receive any valuable education. Thus, an uneasy and exploitative status quo was maintained. According to Sedgwick, once constructed, this Hinduistic scale would also exhibit a 'vast mass of literacy (which) remains to be broken down'. He added that it was 'obvious that the Brahmanic and other higher castes *can look after themselves*. It is the lower strata that require organised effort.'[17]

Apart from this theoretical explication, Sedgwick introduced an administrative innovation never before attempted in the annals of the Indian Census operations. He developed a tripartite classification (based on educational figures) within the broad religious rubric of 'Hindu, Jain and Animistic Castes'. These three divisions were Advanced (24 castes), Intermediate (157 castes), and Backward (145 castes).[18] This was also perhaps the first time that three separate schedules of castes, based on their respective degrees of educational status, were produced in the Indian

[16]Ibid., p. 141.

[17]Ibid., pp. 140–141; emphasis in the original.

[18]Sedgwick, *Census of India, 1921, Bombay Presidency, Vol. VIII*, pp. ix–x.

Census. This was also perhaps the very first example of scheduling of castes across the spectrum of Hindu religion anywhere in the British Indian Empire. In less than a decade, this same classification was adopted by the Starte Committee recommendations, which have had a strange afterlife in independent India.

In this rapidly evolving administrative saga of backwardness, we must now move to the domain of legislation, where an enactment marked the beginning of a new era of administrative classification, which was to have immense implications for the future of representative politics.

2. Bombay Primary Education Act, 1923, and its Rules, 1924

Based on the recommendations of the Compulsory Education (Chandavarkar) Committee, the Bombay Legislative Council enacted the Bombay Primary Education Act, 1923 (No. IV of 1923) after much debate and discussion. The law repealed the Patel Act, superseded it, and made a few changes of far-reaching importance. *First,* it laid down that the government would bear the entire expenditure incurred by the local authorities on primary education. *Second,* it proposed a definite timetable for the expansion of universal compulsory education in the next ten years. *Finally,* this Act became one of the earliest statutes in British India where the category 'backward classes and depressed classes' was inserted. This was done in Clause 3 (1) regarding the constitution of School Boards, in which these groups were to be represented along with women and minorities like the Muslims. The Act also declared that the category 'shall mean classes so declared by the Government'.[19]

For a variety of reasons, the Act did not result in heralding an era of compulsory primary education in Bombay. Owing to the revenue and administrative challenges created by the Great Depression and the subsequent political unrest, the government could not provide unlimited resources to enforce the overall objectives of the law. However, the third aspect, that is, the creation of a legal category of 'Backward Classes and Depressed Classes', proved to be a milestone of sorts. Prior to the Bombay Primary Education Act, only Madras had compiled a list of Depressed Classes, a number of which were scheduled under the Madras Local Boards

[19]Later in 1934, through an amendment of the Act (IV of 1934, s.2 [1]), there was a change in nomenclature, and the new category was called 'Intermediate and Scheduled Classes'.

Act, 1920.[20] Hence, this was possibly the debut moment for the category 'Backward Classes' in a legal statute emanating from a major Presidency in the British Indian Empire.[21]

After any enactment is finalised and the Gazette Notification enforces the law, the next step is to formulate rules that would determine the functioning of the Act. The Bombay Primary Education Rules, 1924 were framed a year later. In this document, the 'Backward'[22] and 'Depressed' Classes were defined as those 'mentioned as such in schedule A and shall include such classes as Government may in consultation with the local authority from time to time declare to be "backward" and "depressed" classes'.[23] An added implication was that the Depressed Classes and Backward Classes were now statutorily part of the Hindu community. Earlier, the Chandavarkar Committee had already provided a similar interpretation of the category 'Non-Brahman'. The document of rules further elucidates that 'a local authority shall pay special attention to the needs of Muhammadans, backward and depressed classes and may make special provision for such classes by opening separate schools, by instituting scholarships, or by employing and training teachers belonging to these classes'. Once started, local authorities had to also maintain 'special facilities' for the aforementioned classes. These may include central schools for Muhammadans and backward communities, scholarships for depressed classes, and similar objects for which special grants would be made by the Bombay government.[24] In the constitution of School Boards and Committees, too, due representation was to be provided for the Backward Classes, Depressed Classes, women, and religious minorities like the Muhammadans.[25] Finally, the document contained Schedule A towards

[20]Franchise Committee 1932: I, 112 cited in Marc Galanter, *Competing Equalities: Law and the Backward Classes in India*, New Delhi: Oxford University Press, 1991, fn 10, pp. 121–122.

[21]For a historically informed and detailed discussion on the journey of the term 'Backward Classes' through the late nineteenth and twentieth century in Bombay, see Abhay Datar, 'Defining Backwardness: Debates in Bombay/Maharashtra', *Economic and Political Weekly* LII (51), 23 December 2017, pp. 89–96.

[22]The Bombay Primary Education Rules, 1924 (as amended upto 1 September 1933), p. 4.

[23]It was made clear that these words did not include Muhammadans. Clearly, at this time, the word 'minority' was equated with religious connotations in general, and the Muslim community in particular.

[24]Ibid.

[25]Ibid., pp. 10, 33.

the end, which comprised two columns of Backward Classes and Depressed Classes. The former listed 174 social/caste groups, while the latter had 146 entries. The list of Depressed Classes also contained many of the Aboriginal and Hill Tribes. This co-mingling of 'untouchables' and tribals under the single administrative category of 'Depressed Classes' was to create much confusion in the following years. This admixture came in for severe criticism from an official Committee, largely consisting of Indian members and delegated the task of enquiring into the conditions of Depressed Classes and Aboriginal and Hill Tribes. It is to this report that we must turn.

3. Starte Committee: Nationalist Redefinition of the 'Backward Classes'

In August 1928, in the Bombay Legislative Council, a resolution by Purushottam G. Solanki was moved and adopted by the House. It called for an enquiry into the 'educational, economic and social conditions of the Depressed Classes and of the Aboriginal Tribes and to recommend measures for their uplift', and was duly passed by the Council. Consequently, on 5 November 1928, the Educational Department of the Bombay Presidency constituted a ten-member Committee, headed by O. H. B. Starte, I.C.S., and including five members of the Legislative Council (prominent among whom were Solanki and B. R. Ambedkar[26]), A. V. Thakkar of the Servants of India Society, Lt. Col. Burfoot of the Salvation Army, and the Dangs[27] Diwan. Sindh was kept outside the scope of this enquiry.[28] Despite being chaired by

[26]For the terrible experiences of Ambedkar, who travelled on this enquiry committee, see a short chapter titled 'Fights in & around the Legislative Council: The Starte Committee and Bhikaji Gaikwad', in Gail Omvedt, *Building the Ambedkar Revolution: Sambhaji Tukaram Gaikwad and the Kokan Dalits*, Mumbai: Bhashya Prakasham, 2011, pp. 37–41.

[27]Dangs was a heavily forested region in the Bombay Presidency, inhabited by the Bhil tribes.

[28]*Report of the Depressed Classes and Aboriginal Tribes Enquiry Committee, Bombay Presidency*, March 1930, Government Press Kolhapur (reprint, 1950), p. 1 (henceforth, *SCR*). From the beginning of my research, this has been the most difficult report to obtain. Fortunately, a later-day reprint exists in the library of the Tata Institute of Social Sciences, Bombay. I am most grateful to two research scholars, Roshni Chattopadhyay at TISS and Nishant Gokhale at the University of Cambridge, who made a copy of this very crucial document and posted it to me.

a British colonial civil servant, the Committee was overwhelmingly Indian in composition. As far as the future of the Backward Class population in Bombay was concerned, the result of the enquiry conducted can legitimately be called the first official nationalist policy document, which provided a crucial window to assess the evolution of distinct governmental taxonomies for marginalised and backward communities. Perhaps before analysing this report, a little should be said about another state category, viz., 'Criminal Tribes', as the Chairman of the Committee, O. H. B. Starte, was intimately connected with state-sponsored welfare work amongst them.

A number of scholarly studies have been conducted on the Criminal Tribes Act, 1911.[29] However, none concern the workings of the law and the associated official mechanism in the Bombay Presidency. The Chairman, O. H. B. Starte, was a member of the Indian Civil Services who had been deputed in November 1919 to oversee the Special Settlement at Bijapur for reforming members of the communities legally designated as Criminal Tribes. He had worked as the Criminal Tribes Settlement Officer for a decade, first at Bijapur and then subsequently supervising such work for the entire Presidency.

In 1924, Starte read a paper at the fourth session of the All-India Social Service Conference organised by the Servants of India Society.[30] Here, he outlined a history of the kind of work being done in such settlements and traced the governmental efforts to reform the Criminal Tribes[31] in settlements from the year 1910. These endeavours began at first with the United Provinces, with Bombay and Punjab joining in a little later. By 1924, fourteen such settlements were in existence in the Bombay Presidency

[29]Meena Radhakrishna, 'The Criminal Tribes Act in Madras Presidency: Implications for Itinerant Trading Communities', *The Indian Economic & Social History Review* 26 (3), September 1989, pp. 269–295, and 'Surveillance and Settlements under the Criminal Tribes Act in Madras', *The Indian Economic & Social History Review* 29 (2), June 1992, pp. 171–198; Andrew J. Major, 'State and Criminal Tribes in Colonial Punjab: Surveillance, Control and Reclamation of the "Dangerous Classes"'. *Modern Asian Studies* 33 (3), 1999, pp. 657–688.

[30]H. Starte, 'Criminal Tribes Settlement', *All-India Social Service Conference (4th Session): Report, Proceedings & Papers Submitted to the Conference*, Servants of India Society, Bombay, 1924, pp. 36–41.

[31]For the purpose of law, Starte said, 'a criminal tribe is defined as a tribe, gang or class of persons addicted to the systematic commission of non-bailable offences. In most cases this history of crime goes back many generations, and is interwoven into their traditions and customs' (ibid., p. 36).

alone. However, only some of them were under the direct control of the government, while others were run by mission agencies such as the Salvation Army.[32] In a way, Starte, although an elite member of the colonial State apparatus, was also active in the field of social service. His participation in this conference was indicative of the dialogue that non-State organisations such as the SIS were forging with State agencies, thereby contributing to the development of a distinct vocabulary and discourse of welfare amongst marginalised groups in western India. This is again an underexplored theme that requires careful archival work.

Returning to the Starte Report, its first remarkable set of comments was on the nomenclature of official categories. The Committee derided the word 'untouchable' as an 'offensive term'. It deliberated on various alternatives such as Adi-Hindu and Adi-Dravidas, which would be 'sufficiently definitive and yet not so offensive'. However, ethnologically speaking, they could not be 'accurately applied to all untouchable Classes'. Hence, the Report concluded that the term 'Depressed Classes' should be retained to designate the untouchable castes included in its Schedule I, Appendix II. This decision was taken on the grounds of 'existing common practice'. In official reports emanating from Bombay as well as most other Provinces, the phrase 'Depressed Classes' was used as a 'synonym for the untouchable classes'. For Vitthal Ramji Shinde, it was a double victory of sorts when the term '*Bahishkrit*' was decided as the vernacular equivalent for the Depressed Classes—both were his coinages.

Ambedkar, who was a signatory of this report, did not submit any minute of dissent either. Hence, we may conclude that by this time in 1930, Ambedkar had not yet adopted a vehemently anti-Hindu stance. In fact, the preceding years were marked by his leadership of the iconic Mahar Satyagraha (1927) and several attempts to enforce the entry of the Depressed Classes into Hindu temples. However, despite his acquiescence to the Starte Committee's decision to retain the practice of referring to 'untouchables' as Depressed Classes, he was never very fond of this official

[32] Again, there is a huge lacuna in the academic understanding of the role played by the Salvation Army, which managed settlements for reforming Criminal Tribes not only in Bombay but also in other British Indian Provinces. Some published pieces include J. Lally, 'Crafting Colonial Anxieties: Silk and the Salvation Army in British India, circa 1900–1920', *Modern Asian Studies* 50 (3), 2016, pp. 765–807; and Rachel J. Tolen, 'Colonizing and Transforming the Criminal Tribesman: The Salvation Army in British India', *American Ethnologist* 18 (1), 1991, pp. 106–125.

term. A little later, during the 1931 Round Table Conference, Ambedkar and R. Srinivas (another Depressed Classes representative) together opined that the term was 'degrading and contemptuous', and proposed its substitution with alternatives such as 'Non-caste Hindus', 'Protestant Hindus', or 'Non-conformist Hindus'. Ambedkar's iconic clash with Gandhi is too well-known to recount here. However, it is worth mentioning that the term Depressed Classes was used in the text of the Yeravada Pact. Talking about the post-Poona Pact scenario, Marc Galanter writes:

> But events took a different course. Shortly afterwards, Gandhi began to popularize 'Harijan' and then the Government of India Act, 1935, denoted those who would enjoy the special electoral arrangements for untouchables as 'Scheduled Castes' a term destined to remain the official designation for untouchables down to the present. Just as 'Harijan' fossilized the evangelical fervour of Gandhi's anti-untouchability campaign, so 'Scheduled Castes' summons up the bureaucratic rigidification and torpor that overtook Ambedkar's measures for secular improvement.[33]

To turn back to the recommendations on official nomenclature, the report expressed that 'great confusion' had been caused by the Schedule to the rules of the Primary Education Act (Government Notification Educational Department, No. 2534 of 10 October 1924). Here, the phrases 'Backward Classes' and 'Depressed Classes' had been given an altogether new and wider meaning than in the established practice of Bombay Presidency's Education Department. In ordinary usage, the phrase 'Depressed Classes' meant the untouchable castes. However, in its new meaning, the category included 'besides the untouchable classes also the Aboriginal Tribes and the Criminal Tribes, and some other wandering and backward Castes'. Such a classification was 'very unfortunate and has resulted in much confusion of thought' because numerically, the untouchables did not even constitute 'half of this new and enlarged grouping of Depressed Classes'.[34]

To prevent further confusion, the Committee therefore proposed that the nomenclature of the classifications made in the rules under the Primary Education Act should be changed. In the new scheme, the Backward Classes should be re-named as 'Intermediate Classes'. Similarly, the Depressed Classes should be re-named as 'Backward Classes'. In effect, the Committee recommended reverting to Sedgwick's tripartite scheme of nomenclature

[33]Marc Galanter, *Competing Equalities*, fn 46, p. 34.
[34]*SCR*, p. 8.

(Advanced, Intermediate, and Backward) proposed in his Bombay Census Report of 1921. However, the Starte Committee went a step further by recommending that the 'Backward Classes' itself should be sub-divided once again into (*i*) 'Depressed Classes' (untouchable classes only); (*ii*) the 'Aboriginal and Hill Tribes'; and (*iii*) 'Other Backward Classes'. Perhaps this classificatory ferment was a result of a new kind of claim-making on identities as far as representative politics was concerned, and further research needs to be conducted on this aspect. Interestingly, the Committee made the following remarks:

> An exact definition of 'Aboriginal and Hill Tribes' is not possible. It cannot be done wholly on ethnological lines. Our attempt at the classification of 'Aboriginal and Hill Tribes' has been based on the consideration as to whether a large proportion of the caste inhabit or did inhabit until recent times the forest areas. However as we do not propose any separate treatment for the 'Aboriginal Tribes and Hill Tribes' than that proposed for the 'other Backward Classes', the distinction between the two classes is not important. As far as we are concerned we would prefer that the 'Aboriginal and Hill Tribes' and 'other Backward Classes' should be grouped into one category called 'Primitive Classes', but we fear this classification might involve difficulties in the Government of India Statistics for Educational purposes.[35]

The above remarks by the Starte Committee about 'Aboriginal and Hill Tribes' were significant and, historically speaking, even downright startling. By calling the 'Aboriginal and Hill Tribes' a caste (albeit one residing in 'jungles'/forests away from traditional villages), there was a definite move to disclaim their cultural distinctiveness from the surrounding Hindu society. At an intellectual level, it also indicated an understanding of tribal society as similar to the Depressed Classes, whereby no strict ethnological yardsticks could be pointed out in the delineation of both groups (see the earlier discussion of alternative terms for Depressed Classes). For the nationalists, tribal distinctiveness was derived from the geographical landscapes (primarily jungles and hills) that these groups inhabited. In turn, these geographical metaphors and a core-periphery imagination of tribal habitats were part of a long tradition of colonial anthropological thinking. Almost thirty years ago, H. H. Risley had attempted to define the tribes, but that attempt too had failed. Even in the hands of a Committee

[35]Ibid., p. 9.

composed largely of Indians, the situation had not been considerably altered. Only some crucial strands of religio-cultural (Hindu/Thakkar) and radical-political (non-Brahman/Ambedkar) imperatives seem to have been amalgamated within the geographical imagination of tribes. Hence, much like the 'Depressed Classes', the category of 'Aboriginal and Hill Tribes' also continued to successfully evade both official and non-official/nationalist attempts at strict definition. In the eyes of the Committee, there were key similarities and differences between Aboriginal and Hill Tribes vis-à-vis Depressed Classes:

> To a certain extent the problem of Aboriginal and Hill tribes is not essentially different from that of the Depressed Classes. In both cases the difficulty arises from the fact of isolation from the main body of the community. But the problem of the Depressed Classes becomes different because in their case the evils of isolation are aggrevated by the fact of untouchability, and the result is that while in the case of the Depressed Classes the problem is due to denial of opportunities, in the case of the Aboriginal Tribes the problem is due to the geographical difficulties combined with a lack of desire to avail themselves of such opportunities.[36]

Thus, the Aboriginal and Hill Tribes emerge as a geographically determined category living in jungles and hills away from the settled village community. Their social situation was better than that of the Depressed Classes as they were not subject to the practice of untouchability by caste Hindus. The Report acknowledged two notable differences between the issues concerning the Depressed Classes and Aboriginal and Hill Tribes. *First,* while the former had attracted wide attention from the public, the latter groups had largely escaped any notice in the public discourse. *Second,* the sense of servility among Depressed Classes was absent in the Aboriginal Tribes; '(R)ather they are characterised by a pride of race despising the culture of the other Communities.'[37]

The report then took three representative examples (amongst the twenty-four groups mentioned in Schedule II of their consolidated list of 'Backward Classes') and gave short descriptions of each. The first were the Bhils, who were the most numerous aboriginals in the Bombay Presidency. They were expert 'Bowmen' and were described in largely martial terms. The second were the Varlis of Thane district, 'a backward section of the Aboriginal

[36]Ibid., pp. 4–5.

[37]Ibid., p. 5.

Tribes.'[38] The Varlis were also 'slightly influenced by Hinduism.'[39] The third and last group was the Dhodias, who were described as a 'community on the borderline between the Aboriginal Tribes and Intermediate Classes'. Educationally, the Dhodias were ahead of the other aboriginal tribes of Gujarat and the Deccan. It was observed that if adequate encouragement was given to the Dhodias, they would 'easily come into line with Hindu "Intermediate Classes"'. The report points to Erthoven's volumes on 'The Tribes and Castes of Bombay' and the 1911 Census volumes for further information on the Bombay tribes. Interestingly, the section culminated with the following quotation, which suggests a strange amalgam of nationalist and diffusionist ideas:

> Whatever their own desires may be, the march of civilization inevitably brings the Aboriginal Tribes into contact with others. If they remain in their present condition they will become more and more the prey of the unscrupulous from among the more educated communities. The problem for them is to implant a desire for education, to break down their exclusiveness and to enable them to take a part in the national life befitting their numbers. Yet one fears for them in this closer contact with other communities which is inevitable, lest they lose some of the characteristics of cheerfulness, hardihood and truth-loving, which binds them to the hearts of all those who come into close contact with them.[40]

In dealing with the problem of education amongst the Aboriginal Tribes, the Report argued that it differed 'vitally' from that of the Depressed Classes. The latter lived in villages as a 'minority', and removal of the 'special disabilities attached to their position in relation to the Hindu Society' would accelerate their educational advancement. On the other hand, the Aboriginal Tribes 'lived originally in forest areas', although the majority had started living in the plains, 'especially in the areas adjacent to the forest'. They lagged far behind the Depressed Classes and stood at the very bottom compared to any other group in the Bombay Province. The Aboriginal Tribes despised 'education as being a useless and cramping thing which unfits them for their free life in the jungle, and for agricultural pursuits, if they are leading a settled life.'[41]

[38]Ibid., p. 6.

[39]Ibid., p. 7.

[40]Ibid.

[41]Ibid., pp. 18–19.

The Committee opined that the children of the Aboriginal Tribes who lived in villages presented a different set of challenge vis-à-vis those who were 'scattered in forest hamlets'. The former group could be enlarged by attracting them to the common village school and by 'opening more schools where none exist', as there was 'no serious objection on the part of other communities in admitting them'. Given their impoverished economic condition, most students required scholarships, and the Committee recommended increasing their numbers. Another problem the Aboriginal children encountered was a lack of 'relatives in places where there are full primary schools'. The Committee recommended building and running hostels where such students could live and pursue education.

The indifference or even downright hostility of parents towards the education of Aboriginal children was a major challenge. The Committee felt that the key lay in making small one-teacher schools in forest areas 'as efficient and attractive as possible'. An Achilles heel of such schools was the 'reluctance of the ordinary teacher from the plains to remain in such forest areas'. Often, it was found that once posted in a forest school, they would use 'every excuse and influence to get away, and failing that to reduce the attendance so that the school may be automatically closed'. The Committee argued that the only solution lay *'in the recruitment of more teachers from the Aboriginal Tribes'*, who would be prepared to 'live in such villages and take their share in the uplift'.[42]

Along with the opening of primary hostels for Aboriginal children, the Committee recommended that voluntary agencies (Hindu and Christian) be assisted in similar endeavours through the provision of grants. Interestingly, it also recommended changes in curriculum for the Aboriginal children, with a view to turning them into good field cultivators/peasants in general and potentially channelising the finer minds amongst them towards the educational advancement of their own brethren:

> [A]t least for the primary schools attended mainly by the Aboriginal Tribes the curriculum should be that of the Agricultural bias and at an earlier period of a boy's career than that given in the present curriculum. We would however urge that the course be made more practical than is the case in the average agricultural bias school at present. This will help them in after life to take a more intelligent interest in the cultivation of their fields, and those who pass the Agricultural Vernacular School Final, and become teachers will have a better back-ground for their

[42]Ibid., p. 19, emphasis in the original.

> teaching in forest villages than those who pass the ordinary Vernacular School Final can possess.[43]

The Committee expressed the view that educating the Aboriginal Tribes was the 'hardest problem which the educationalist has to solve in this Presidency'. Therefore, it was necessary to think outside the box in a search for appropriate methods and curriculum. There was a strong case for experimental areas, with the provision of special assistance amongst the Katkaris and Varlis, and Bhils of the hilly areas.

In the Committee's assessment, 'compulsion forms the final solution for the education of these people'. However, its implementation was not feasible on financial grounds. It agreed that 'very valuable experience might be gained ... by introducing it into limited areas populated mainly by Aboriginal Tribes'. The report recommended the adoption of an integrated approach by the staff in experimental areas, who would not limit themselves to questions of education. Instead, they should also start co-operative societies amongst the people and 'preach sanitation and temperance' amongst tribals.[44]

Other important issues concerning the problem of educational advancement, upon which recommendations were made, included education for girls from the Backward Classes, hostels for girls from the Aboriginal Tribes, as well as addressing the alarming dropout rates. While 33 per cent of all students attained literacy, the corresponding figures for children belonging to the Backward Classes was a paltry 17 per cent. The Committee called this an 'appalling waste of public money'.

The Committee also highlighted the importance of providing secondary education as it was 'from this group, and in particular from those who ... proceed to College or to some technical training, that the future leaders of the Backward Classes must be drawn'. To ensure the uplift of their brethren, it was imperative for a few educated ones to 'obtain a fair footing

---

[43] Ibid., p. 20.

[44] Amongst the witnesses it examined, the Committee found a 'great desire for complete prohibition' and opined that 'Prohibition is the only solution to many of the economic ills of their classes'. About the effect of liquor on Aboriginal Tribes, the report stated

> ... the temptation to drink is too great to be resisted by them at every minute of their life with so many facilities placed next door to them. This is specially so with the child races like Bhil or Varli. Where drink shops are reduced in number or the quantity rationed to them in a Taluka or a District, the total consumption goes down, and the people concerned are benefitted materially and morally. (*SCR*, p. 54)

in all Government Departments', and secondary and college education was therefore a necessity. The reality of secondary education amongst Backward Classes was, however, chilling. As on March 1927, the total number of Depressed Classes and Aboriginal Tribes students studying in secondary schools in the entire Presidency was 730 and 54, respectively.[45] At the college level, too, there were only nine students from the Depressed Classes and none from the Aboriginal and Hill Tribes or the other Backward Classes in the entire Presidency. Calling the figures of the Aboriginal Tribes 'very disappointing', the Committee opined:

> In particular it seems to us that if secondary education spreads more amongst these classes, useful recruits for executive and clerical works in the Forest Department could be obtained who would not shrink from the life in the jungles. This increase is also needed for another reason. As a class they are taking no part in the political life of the country. To a restricted extent persons of other communities become their leaders, but they have raised no leaders of their own and as a result, to a much greater degree than is the case with the Depressed Classes, they have little or no influence on the local politics of the district, or on the broader politics of the Presidency. Had the Aboriginal Tribes any educated representatives of their own in the Councils, and more representatives in the Local Boards and the School Boards their interests would not be so easily overlooked as they often are at present when the interests of different communities conflict.[46]

Besides the obvious utility of trained and educated tribals in forest administration, owing to their familiarity with their surroundings, the above extract explicates several aspects of the emergent nationalist thinking on the tribal predicament. The chief points were: (*i*) the Aboriginal Tribes were a silent community with no leaders of their own; (*ii*) their geographical isolation and educational backwardness had rendered them incapable of taking care of their own interests; and (*iii*) the need of the hour was to ensure them a representative voice at all levels of the governmental machinery, from School and Local Boards all the way to the Legislative Councils. The hope behind this diagnosis and prognosis by the likes of Thakkar was that once the tribes had developed the requisite capabilities, they would take part in national life on an equal footing with the other communities.

---

[45] *SCR*, p. 27.

[46] Ibid. This seems to have come straight from Thakkar's pen. Ambedkar, too, was a complete teetotaller. On this issue, the twain did meet.

Taking the link between higher education and the potential for representative leadership even further, the Committee also recommended making available one scholarship for a Backward Class student for 'study abroad in technical or literary subjects'. The rationale given was the following:

> It is very important that there should be a few men among these communities of wide views and experience. The existence of such men, though they will necessarily be very few, will give greater confidence to these communities that they are not forever doomed to be the underdog of Society, but that they too can rise and take an honourable and important place in the life of the nation.[47]

The Committee also stressed the issue of representation of Backward Classes on public bodies such as the Legislative Council, Municipalities, Local Boards, and School Boards.[48] The resultant benefit would be two-fold: *first,* the representatives would safeguard the interests of their respective groups; and *second,* the experience of serving in such institutions would provide valuable training in leadership and administration. Not insignificant was also the benefit of 'intermingling with other communities' in Council or Board meetings, which would provide 'an object lesson of the equal rights of these Classes with the rest of the community'.

The Committee noted that the question of increased representation of the Depressed Classes in the Legislative Council had been put before the Simon Commission. However, a similar move regarding the need for representation of the Aboriginal Tribes and other Backward Classes had attracted 'practically no notice, though they too need spokesmen in the Council and under the present constitution they are practically unrepresented'. Drawing attention to this need, the Committee noted:

> Owing to the confusion of thought in the dual use of the phrase Depressed Classes it is sometimes not clear, whether the special representation is meant only for the Depressed Classes (untouchables) or if it is meant for all the Backward Classes as defined by us, of which the Depressed Classes form only 38 per cent. In our view however the interests of the Depressed Classes are so divergent from that of the other Backward Classes (the Aboriginal Tribes and Hill Tribes and the 'other Backward Classes') *that separate representation is required for them.* Whether that be by separate election, reservation of seats or by nomination or by any other method we do not feel ourselves

[47]Ibid., p. 33.

[48]Ibid., p. 64.

> competent to judge. But that it should be secured by them in some way seems to us very necessary, and this must not be at the cost of the Depressed Class representatives.[49]

The Starte Committee also argued that the representation of Backward Classes across all levels, that is, in Legislative Councils, Municipal Boards, District Local Boards, Taluka Local Boards, and School Boards, was:

> ... inadequate in view of the proportion of their population to the rest of the community and to the fact that in practice they stand no chance of election in a general electorate. Adequate representation on these Boards is the more important because exceedingly wide powers especially in relation to Primary Education have been given to them. It becomes very important therefore that the interests of the Backward Classes especially in education should be watched and this can be best done by their own representatives.[50]

The Starte Committee considered it necessary to ascertain the needs of the Backward Classes as a whole, and also that there should be 'some one definitely charged with the duty of seeing that their progress is continuous and their rights upheld'. Undoubtedly, help was required by them primarily in the field of education, but 'Education alone will not solve the problem'. Their overall 'uplift' was dependent on many other allied fields. It was a question of the rights of the Backward Classes, which, if not addressed, would mean a 'grave danger to the rest of the community'. There was a 'growing sense of bitterness of the Depressed Classes, especially the younger and more educated members, who are realizing their inherent rights as human beings and the injustice under which they now labour'. Similarly, the interests of the Aboriginal Tribes were 'specially liable to be overlooked', as they were 'very unorganized, and have no effective means of making their grievances and needs known and redressed'. To meet such massive challenges, the Starte Committee finally recommended '*that it is very necessary that a Backward Class Board with a Backward Class Officer working with it should be appointed to watch over their interests*'.[51]

In essence, on grounds of economy, the Starte Committee recommended the adoption of the Madras model of conducting uplift work. In 1920, the Madras government had created a designated post of Labour Commissioner.

[49]Ibid., emphasis in the original.

[50]Ibid., pp. 64–65.

[51]Ibid., p. 65; emphasis in the original.

He was a senior permanent officer of the Collector grade, whose main duty was 'to look after the interests of the Depressed Classes and Aboriginal Tribes'. Additionally, he was also responsible for the Criminal Tribes Settlements.

For Bombay, the Starte Committee also recommended changing the designation of the Criminal Tribes Settlement Officer to 'Backward Class Officer', as the Criminal Tribes formed a branch of the Backward Classes. The Backward Class Officer should always be of a Collector's grade, and with not less than twelve years of service. Some of his duties, as recommended by the Committee, were investigation and reporting; making policy suggestions to the government; collection of the reported facts and figures; preparation of a short Annual Report; drawing the attention of any Department to their needs; allocation of the Trade Apprenticeship scholarships; providing assistance to the Backward Classes in obtaining employment under the government; preparation of suitable simple pamphlets on health, temperance, and co-operation, explaining 'in simple language the orders of the Government in relation to entry into schools, buses, dispensaries etc'; keeping in touch with the various Depressed Classes and Aboriginal Tribes Societies; and finally, investigating the need for house sites for the Backward Classes, emigration, etc. The Backward Class Officer was also to be given a small staff to assist him. Two officers of the Deputy Collector rank were to assist him in working out these schemes throughout the Bombay Presidency.[52]

In addition to the Backward Classes Officer, another far-reaching implication of the Starte Committee report was its recommendation to constitute a Backward Classes Board. While the Officer would belong to the bureaucracy with a knowledge of the governmental machinery in order to provide meaningful benefits to the target population, these efforts would need guidance. True representatives of the Backward Classes themselves, who could 'spare the time to study the subject in more detail' would assist the Backward Classes Officer. Hence, the Board would be a platform for people's voices to emerge. Made up of the Legislative Council members, the Backward Classes Board was to be constituted for consultative and directive purposes on important problems relating to the Backward Classes. The Board was to enable the officer to keep in touch with current public opinion,

[52]Ibid., p. 68.

and then direct that opinion towards the removal of the disabilities afflicting the Backward Classes.[53]

The ideal composition of the Backward Classes Board was three Legislative Council members, each as representatives from the Depressed Classes, Aboriginal Hill Tribes, and the General classes, plus a government servant or social worker, 'co-opted for the purpose of explanation or guidance, but having no vote'.[54] The Backward Classes Officer was to act as Secretary of the Board, and collect all the required information. The resolutions of the Board were to be forwarded to the government for its consideration and appropriate action.[55]

Thus, the recommendations of the Starte Committee constituted a significant moment not only in the discourse of Aboriginal Tribes, but also for the Depressed Classes as the report ruminated on the ways to bridge the wide educational gap between Advanced and Backward Classes. It was the first official enquiry on the question and only two of its ten members were non-Indians. This report remains a watershed document for several reasons. To begin with, an understanding of the official classification enshrined in the Starte Committee report becomes necessary as it was here that a clear category of the 'Backward Classes' emerged, with very far-reaching implications for State policy discourse. It was a generic and an umbrella term that included Depressed Classes (Untouchables), Aboriginal Hill Tribes, and Other Backward Classes. Hence, the report was the first official document to outline the three separate schedules, with a number of communities, castes, or *jatis* clubbed together under these three sub-headings (Schedule I: Depressed Classes, 36; Schedule II: Aboriginal and Hill Tribes, 24; Schedule III: Other Backward Classes, 95).[56] This is amongst the first official consolidated inventories of its kind, based on a tripartite division which later became the basis for the affirmative action framework of the independent Indian nation-State, with the new nomenclature of Scheduled Caste (SC), Scheduled Tribe (ST), and the Other Backward Classes (OBC, the last letter of which, since the Mandal Commission, 1980, has now become 'Caste[s]').

---

[53]Ibid.

[54]In case the MLCs were insufficient to provide their quota, the government would choose the member of the Board.

[55]*SCR*, p. 69.

[56]Appendix II, Classification of Castes, *Backward Classes*, *SCR*, pp. 77–79.

Any history of reservation in India will have to acknowledge the Starte Report as a milestone document for these three communitarian schedules contained therein. Nonetheless, it remains an act of scheduling of communities which was to have immense implications for the discourse of backwardness in general, and the fate of tribes in particular. However, the focus of the Committee's efforts was on the first two categories of Depressed Classes and Aboriginal Hill Tribes, and their enquiries largely by-passed the category of Other Backward Classes which lay outside their terms of reference. Finally, the constitution of the Backward Class Board out of the Members of Legislative Council of Bombay probably served as an inspiration for a similarly envisioned Tribes Advisory Council in provinces with large tribal populations and also with Scheduled Areas. Later in 1949, this provision was vigorously debated in the Constituent Assembly of India.[57]

Beginnings of Nationalist Associational Politics

By the mid-1930s, the general apathy on the part of the nationalists vis-à-vis the tribal question was changing. As we saw in Chapter 1, following a tumultuous debate in the British Parliament, large parts of British Indian territories were declared as 'excluded' and 'partially excluded' areas under Sections 91 and 92 of the Government of India Act, 1935. The carving out of large tracts away from the purview of a reformed Constitution jolted the Indian National Congress. The Congress nationalists now began organising a sustained opposition to this extra-constitutional framework, arguing that it was motivated by the British policy of 'divide and rule'. Resolutions against exclusion and partial exclusion were passed at the Faizpur (1936) and Haripura (1938) sessions of the INC, and attempts were made to fashion an organised resistance to these policies.

Following the All India Congress Committee (AICC) session at Haripura in February 1938, a number of Congressmen came together to form the All India Excluded and Partially Excluded Areas Association with its headquarters at Rajahmundry in the Madras Presidency.[58] The second Article of the Association's Constitution stated that its objective was,

[57]See the final chapter of this book.

[58]The 1934 report by P. Kodanda Ramaiah (typed in the form of a mimeograph in 1937) in the AICC papers takes the name of this association with its office at Swaraj Ashram, Polavaram via Kovvur, M.S.M. Railway. It is likely that the

> [S]afeguarding the political, economic and social interests of the residents of the Excluded and Partially Excluded Areas all over India, by peaceful and legitimate means and the ultimate merging of these Areas into normally administered Areas, so as to enjoy the same democratic rights as are enjoyed by the latter.[59]

The Association was to 'organise the residents of the said Areas on the basis of their immediate demands and shall carry on the day to day struggle'.[60] The Executive Committee of the Association was constituted with N. G. Ranga as President and P. Kodanda Ramaiah as its Secretary.[61] Ramaiah had been a member of the Servants of India Society, as a result of which he became closely associated with A. V. Thakkar. In 1934, he was given the task of undertaking a study of the Partially Excluded and Excluded Areas in Madras Presidency. This was just prior to the separation of Orissa in 1936, after which the whole of the Ganjam Agency and the major portion of Vizagapatam Agency were transferred to the new Orissa province. Ramaiah's report drew upon material from the Census reports and the Gazetteers, but was also based on his own fieldwork in these areas. It throws important light on the nationalist critique of the British policy of exclusion and partial exclusion of predominantly tribal areas prior to the watershed moment of the controversial Cadogan amendment.

One of the benchmarks of the Madras Agency system was that the Collectors of Ganjam, Vizagapatam, and East Godavari were given special powers in their respective agency areas in their capacity as government agents. The functions of the Collector, District Magistrate, and District and Sessions Judge were combined in the office of the Agent. Ramaiah

---

association was formed earlier and this same body was expanded after the Haripura Session of the AICC in February 1938, F. No. 10—Miscellaneous, 1938, AICC Papers, PMML.

[59]Pamphlet of All India Excluded and Partially Excluded Areas Association, Rajahmundry, 1938, Published by P. Kodanda Ramaiah, General Secretary, in IOR/P/T/2845, p. 1.

[60]Ibid., Article III.

[61]The other office-holders were P. Lakshmi Narayan Mishra (Joint Secretary) and Liladhar Barooah (Joint Secretary). Members included Mohan Lal Saksena, Kuladhar Chaliha, Sarat Chandar Bose, E. M. S. Namboodripad, M. V. R. Anaharachariar, N. V. Gadgil, Ram Narayan Singh, Laxmidas M. Shrikant, Sardar Amar Singh, and Virendra. Not a single man in this all-Congress organisation was a tribal.

argued that it was 'highly necessary that the Civil and Criminal powers in one man should be separated as soon as possible.'[62] He also criticised the 'high-handedness' of the police in the Agency areas, which was popularly called '"Jabardasti" or the Jungle-Rule.'[63] In addition, he flagged the forest administration, public health, excise policy, and education as areas that needed substantial improvement. Critiquing the Simon Commission recommendation of nominating eleven members from the excluded and partially excluded areas to the Central Legislature, he advocated sending elected representatives instead, arguing that although '[the] Moderates may say that the backward tracts are not in a position to send their elected representatives but it is only the voting capacity which gives them political education.'[64]

As the 1940s unfolded, the All India Excluded and Partially Excluded Areas Association became the front organisation of the Congress for conducting activities and propaganda along its anti-exclusion line. Although there exists a relative paucity of material on this association, such archival material as we possess reveals an interesting picture of the strategies used by the Congress to mobilise support for its position in the tribal regions. Given that the tribal areas had aroused little or no political or public interest in India until the 1935 British Parliamentary debates, responses by Indians on the question of scheduling are relatively scarce. However, one area where the spilling over of the scheduling discourse has left a significant archival trail is the debates of the Legislative Assemblies and Councils.

Debates in the Legislative Assemblies and Councils

The earliest nationalist political response to the discourse on scheduling dates back to 7 December 1922 when Rai Bahadur Dvarika Nath moved a resolution in the Bihar and Orissa Legislative Council, demanding the withdrawal of the notification which declared the Santal Parganas to be a 'Backward Tract' under Sections 52 (A) and 71 of the Government of India Act, 1919.[65] Similar resolutions were moved in the Central Legislative Assembly (in 1927), and a few times in the Bihar and Orissa Legislative

---

[62]F. No. 10—Miscellaneous, 1938, AICC Papers, PMML, p. 53.

[63]Ibid., p. 54.

[64]Ibid., p. 62.

[65]IOR/L/PJ/9/23, p. 594.

Councils (in 1922, 1927, 1933, and 1935). In 1927, the Indian Legislative Assembly passed the following resolution:

> This Assembly recommends to the Governor General in Council that he may be pleased to take immediate steps to bring about the withdrawal of the Chota Nagpur Division, the districts or divisions of Angul, Sambalpur, and the Sonthal Parganas in the province of Bihar and Orissa from the operation of section 52A of the Government of India Act 1919, and to amend the schedule to the Act accordingly.[66]

These resolutions were episodic at best, and did not translate into sustained political activism for the removal of scheduling from the colonial statecraft. However, after the British Parliament took upon itself the role of final arbiter on the fate of the excluded and partially excluded areas (after the Order-in-Council expanded the list, none of the areas could be 'de-scheduled' without the British Parliament's final approval), the nationalists woke up to the issue. In particular, Winston Churchill's statement in support of scheduling the whole Indian peninsula caught the Indian political imagination by storm. Since that moment, nationalists across political persuasions joined hands to oppose the instrument of scheduling. One of the chief ways in which they set out to do this was by introducing resolutions in the central and provincial Legislative Assemblies, demanding the abolition of the distinction between normally administered areas and excluded/partially excluded areas. Often, these discussions generated animated debates which were widely reported in the nationalist press as well. This section will outline a few of these debates and discussions in order to identify the major planks of the nationalist attack on scheduling. Since my objective is to get a sense of the reasons why the Indian nationalists were against British posturing, I have not included the statements (mostly by Englishmen, but a few by Indians as well) defending the colonial policy of exclusion and partial exclusion.

The first major discussion on the issue of scheduling began on the floor of the Central Legislative Assembly in Delhi, on 11 February 1936. It was just a few days before the final Order-in-Council declaring excluded and partially excluded areas was released by His Majesty's Government in Britain. The resolution was drafted by S. Satyamurti but finally moved by Ram Narain Singh, a Congress member from Bihar. It demanded that the Governor-General in Council take steps to extend 'the same level of

[66]Quoted in 'Extract from the Council of State Debates, Vol. I, No. 8', 20 February 1939, F. No. 89/1/39-G, 'G' Branch, Reforms Office, GoI, 1939, p. 2.

administration' to the people of the excluded areas, partially excluded areas, and the Chief Commissioners' provinces, including British Baluchistan, from 1 January 1937.[67] Ram Narain Singh argued that 'special treatment' for these areas had effectively meant a system of 'one man rule'.

The nationalists' attack was reinforced by N. V. Gadgil, another Congressman from Poona, who argued that the British were not motivated by the desire to confer any benefit upon the tribals, but rather 'with a view to preserving these areas for the exploitation of British capitalists'.[68] Similarly, taking examples from Orissa, Pandit Nilkantha Das alleged that the provisions of exclusion and partial exclusion provided a shroud under which 'companies are cropping up there to loot the mineral wealth in the dark'.[69]

N. M. Joshi was a close associate of A. V. Thakkar and a life member of the Servants of India Society. He worked as a trade-unionist in Bombay and, at the instance of Thakkar, was the only person to have represented the concerns of the aboriginal people during the Third Round Table Conference, attacking the autocratic rule of the civil servants. Joshi did not spare the anthropologists either, calling them 'most wickedly selfish', who wanted 'all the primitive people in India to remain uncivilized', so that they 'could indulge in their intellectual pursuits'. The main plank of Joshi's attack was that the Round Table Conference had failed to guarantee effective representation to the tribals. Out of the total 1,500 seats in the provincial councils, only twenty had been awarded to the aboriginal and hill tribes, whereas in proportion to their overall population they deserved seventy-five seats. There was also not a single member in the Central Legislature who was a tribal, and it was left to 'poor me!' to raise the matter. Joshi said he could not 'approve of a scheme which encourages autocracy without giving any protection to these people, either in the matter of education or in the matter of their land or protection against the usurers'.

N. B. Khare and M. S. Aney were the other speakers who supported the resolution. Khare spoke on the partially excluded areas in the Central

---

[67] *The Legislative Assembly Debates (Official Report), Volume I, 1936 (3 February to 14 February 1936), Third Session of the Fifth Legislative Assembly, 1936*, Government of India Press, Delhi, 1936, p. 600.

[68] Ibid., p. 611.

[69] 'Extract from the Legislative Assembly Debates, Vol. II, No. 2', in F. No. 2/1/36-Public, Public Branch, Reforms Office, GoI, 1936, pp. 4–5. The following paragraphs, including the quotes extracted, have been reconstructed from this source, especially pp. 18–19 and 22.

Provinces (C.P.) and attacked the colonial bureaucracy's reluctance to hand over power to the future ministers. Aney criticised the secrecy around the inquiry and the lack of attempt by the colonial State to invite Indian public opinion on the subject of excluded and partially excluded areas. He alleged that the real motive of this British policy was to create a 'permanent cleavage' between the people of the excluded areas and the civilised Indians. Aney thundered,

> And what is the reason for that? What is the theory underlying all this? What are the implications of an exclusion of this nature? When we consider these implications, I believe, there cannot be any self-respecting man in this House whose blood will not boil with indignation. It means that the civilized people of India are incapable and shall for ever remain incapable, perpetually remain incapable, of looking after the interests of their backward people in this country. There is that arrogant assumption also along with it which will be resented from every quarter in this House, no doubt, *viz.*, that the foreigner coming from 7,000 miles has got an inherent capacity to look after the interests of these men. The capacity of the foreigner is prodigious!

A second discussion on a similar resolution in a central legislative body occurred on 20 February 1939 in the Council of States. This resolution was introduced by Ramdas Pantulu, a member from Madras province, and appealed to the Governor-General in Council to convert all excluded and partially excluded areas in British Indian provinces into 'normal areas governed by the normal administrative machinery of the respective provinces'.[70]

Referring to the vigorous debate on the issue in the British Parliament, Pantulu suggested that there were 'imperialistic and exploitary motives' behind the policy. He refused to believe that this could be for the benefit of the tribal populations living in the excluded and partially excluded areas:

> If that is so, the easiest thing to ascertain is whether these areas have improved politically, socially or economically during the last 150 years during which they have been administered under the special powers of the Central and Provincial Governments. Far from being so, we find that they are in a much worse position today. Sir, I can quote any

[70]'Extract from the Council of State Debates, Vol. I, No. 8', 20 February 1939, F. No. 89/1/39-G, 'G' Branch, Reforms Office, GoI, 1939, p. 1. The following paragraphs are based on this source, especially pp. 4–5, 11–14.

> number of authorities to show that the position of these people is rapidly deteriorating. Educationally they are ignored and economically they are exploited.

Pantulu also cited several extracts from the 1931 Census report authored by J. H. Hutton as well as from the Simon Commission report to argue that 'protection by the Government has not resulted in these people being prevented from exploitation by middlemen and moneylenders'. Instead of benefitting the tribals, colonial laws on forests, gaming, etc., had deprived them of the traditional rights which they enjoyed earlier. They received neither any educational measures nor any medical relief. The people were further oppressed by official orders demanding supplies and forced labour to cater to the needs of the authorities.

B. N. Biyani from Berar alleged that the colonial policy was motivated by the maxim of divide and rule. Besides encouraging communal passions, the British had divided the country into three political compartments: the British Indian Provinces, the Indian States, and finally, the Excluded and Partially Excluded Areas. He condemned the exploitative forest and game laws and claimed that 'the lives of these people in these tracts is on verge of barbarism and they are kept under a form of military occupation'. Discussing the increase in the areas falling under special administrative regimes, N. K. Das, a member from Orissa, held:

> Progressively, therefore, as the period of British administration in this country increased, the number and area of the tract that must be denied the normal administration and advancement increases in geometric progression, until a day may come, Sir, when perhaps the whole of the country is designed by our present administrators to be thrown into the abyss of darkness and classed as a backward continent!

In the years 1938 and 1939, resolutions condemning the colonial policy of exclusion and partial exclusion were also moved in the Provincial Legislative Assemblies of Bihar, Orissa, and Bombay. One of the most hard-hitting speeches on the subject was given in the Bombay Legislative Assembly by L. M. Shrikant, an MLA from Panch Mahals East. Shrikant was the scion of an affluent family, but after coming under the influence of Gandhi and Thakkar, he had committed himself to a life of public service. Shrikant's speech is of importance also because he went on to become the first Commissioner of Scheduled Castes and Scheduled Tribes in independent India, and remained in that important constitutional position for nearly a decade.

On 10 November 1938, Shrikant moved a resolution in the House to 'abolish the division of India into Excluded Areas and Partially Excluded Areas and the rest of the country with a view to encourage the growth of uniform democratic institutions throughout India.'[71] In particular, he took issue with the suggestions put forward by Wing Commander James and Hutton before the Joint Select Committee of the British Parliament. James had proposed that the tribes should be administered by forest officers, and ICS officers who should be recruited specially by the Secretary of State for India, insultingly adding that 90 per cent of them should be Europeans. Hutton, too, had suggested that it would be safer for the aboriginal areas to be entirely excluded from the purview of the provincial government, instead of just partial exclusion, and mooted the idea of having a special cadre of officers to administer the excluded areas. In his attack, Shrikant alleged that,

> He [Hutton] would remove the areas entirely from the influence of the legislatures. No nomination—because they have their own councils; they carry on through a *panch*. They do not want any democratic institutions. It is arranged like this: if they are made into small States, they will preserve their traditions, just like the anthropologists who want these people as exhibits in a museum for all times to come! You will see a Bhil as he was in the 17th or the 18th century, because somebody wants to study his old traditions, customs and habits!

Shrikant also spoke at length about the role of Christian missionaries. Acknowledging their good work among the tribals, he nevertheless remarked that it was done for the sake of encouraging conversions. Given that the British rulers were disparaging the entire class of Indian politicians as inimical to the interests of the aboriginals, it was essential to define a politician. In his opinion, missionaries were politicians as well, but their politics was silent. Speaking out against the conversion activities of the missionaries, Shrikant gave the example of Verrier Elwin, who, having become disgusted with such propaganda, shunned it and began doing humanitarian work instead. Emphasising that the tribals were Hindus, Shrikant said that they understood Hindu customs and believed '... in Hindu Gods. They say "Ram Ram" when they meet each other and when they are on the death bed.' The remarkable aspect of Srikant's articulation

[71]Bombay Legislative Assembly debates, Official Report, Vol. 4, Part 56, Thursday, 10 November 1938, F. No. 137/38-G, 'G' Branch, Reforms Office, GoI, 1938. The following paragraphs are based on this source, especially pp. 3993–3995, 4002–4005.

was its chronological location, for it followed Hutton's notion of tribal religion in the 1931 Census while preceding both Elwin's *Loss of Nerve* and Ghurye's 'backward Hindu' argument.[72]

Lastly, while discussing democratic institutions, Shrikant argued vociferously that the Bhils had started coming into their own. The Congress had proudly given them the power to vote and had also introduced a provision to give the Bhils representation in the district local boards in proportion to their population. The Congress did it because 'we know that it is only by bringing these people into contact with the other civilized people that culture and civilization can be spread among them'.

From a perusal of the evidence, a few planks of the nationalist attack on exclusion and partial exclusion can be ascertained. *First,* while agreeing that these areas were 'backward' in every manner, the nationalists put the blame for this state of affairs squarely upon the colonial State. After all, they argued, the British had been administering these areas for more than a century: if they had been unsuccessful in ameliorating the living conditions of the tribals, they had no right to stop these areas from being normally administered by the nationalists. *Second,* the nationalists held that the British attitude smacked of their time-tested policy of divide and rule: by creating yet another minority within the body politic of the emerging Indian nation, the British were trying to bolster fissiparous tendencies. *Third,* the nationalists alleged that the policy of excluding and partially excluding large tracts of areas from normal provincial administration suggested a deep-rooted mistrust of both the civilised Indians' ability to govern themselves and their aboriginal brethren's ability to take their rightful place in the emerging body politic. *Fourth,* the system of administration prevalent in these areas was highly autocratic and discretionary, resulting in the exploitation of the simple-minded tribals by landlords and officials alike. The paternal despotic model espoused by the colonial administration was a relic of the past, and could have no place in the future Constitution of the Indian nation.

Moreover, the nationalists launched a vitriolic attack on the anthropologists and administrators such as Hutton and others who were interested in keeping the aboriginals in isolation. They lambasted the policy of creating tribal reservations, and insisted that contact or assimilation with the surrounding 'civilised' population was the only way through which the tribals could be 'uplifted'. The participants argued that the colonial policy was driven by vested interest lobbies, such as mining companies and plantation

---

[72]See Chapter 7 on Verrier Elwin.

owners, who wanted to exploit the mineral wealth of these areas and treat the tribal inhabitants as a source of cheap labour. Finally, in mounting a virulent attack on the role of the Christian missionaries in tribal areas, the Congress was also articulating its own narrative of 'culture' and 'civilisation'.

A lasting effect of this incessant propaganda generated through Assembly resolutions and the work of the All India Excluded and Partially Excluded Areas Association was that in the period of provincial autonomy (1937–1939), there was not a single instance where the special powers of the Governor were exercised in any of the provinces having partially excluded areas. The Congress had made it politically impossible to do so.[73]

Provincial Enquiries Conducted by Congress Ministries

An important step taken by the elected Congress Ministries in Bombay and Orissa was to order enquiries into the partially excluded areas of their Provinces. It is to an analysis of these reports that we shall now turn.

Symington's Report on the Partially Excluded Areas of Bombay Province

In 1937, David Symington, an ICS officer of the Bombay Province, was assigned to report on measures for the improvement of conditions of the Bhils and other aboriginals in the partially excluded areas. Symington's *Report on the Partially Excluded Areas of Bombay Province*, the first of its kind for a British Indian Province, became a benchmark in the discourse on the future of these areas.

The choice of Symington, an English ICS officer, by the newly elected Congress ministry was an interesting one. Its roots lay in the developments following the Cadogan Amendment in the British Parliament, when an all-India review was conducted of predominantly tribal areas for the purpose of incorporating them in the Excluded or Partially Excluded Areas list. At this time, Symington was the Backward Class Officer of the Bombay Presidency, a post established as a result of the Starte Committee recommendations. When asked to report on the matter, he replied that he had 'no first hand knowledge of the aboriginals and backward people concerned', and except

[73]See G. S. Ghurye, *The Aborigines—'So-Called'—And Their Future*, Pune: Gokhale Institute of Politics and Economics, 1943, pp. 152–153.

for a short stint at Nasik, he had not served in any of the districts which contained the areas proposed to be partially excluded.[74] In what would become a favourite quote among the nationalists, Symington wrote,

> Now it is easy to point out the backwardness and poverty of the Aboriginal and Hill tribes, but it is quite another thing to say that their condition is due to 'existing administration'. Perhaps more could and ought to have been done for them by Government in the days when there was more money to spend; if so, the blame if any must attach to Government and cannot be attributed to the introduction of the democratic system under the periodical Reforms. There is no reason to think that the Legislative Council and Ministers have been less sympathetic towards the aboriginals than the old bureaucracy. That being so there seems to be little logic in pressing the proposal to set up partially-excluded areas in this Presidency.

Symington held that partial exclusion 'might result in a tendency to leave the responsibility for progress on the Governor's shoulders as his special responsibility, and the Governor is likely for many reasons to be reluctant to exercise his individual powers except on special occasions', which would be a 'real danger'.

Subsequently, the Government of India sidelined the objections of the Bombay government and went for a massive expansion in the size of the partially excluded areas in the Presidency. In 1937, following the first elections held in accordance with the Government of India Act, 1935, a Congress ministry came to power in the (new) Province of Bombay. No doubt influenced by Symington's earlier expressed views on the question of partial exclusion, the Congress ministry under Premier B. G. Kher appointed him as the Special Officer to report on the partially excluded areas in the Province.

To prepare his report, Symington undertook an in-depth tour to enquire into the special problems faced by the aboriginal and hill tribes inhabiting the partially excluded areas of Bombay Province. What he saw on this tour seems to have led to a change in his earlier stance. At the beginning of his report, Symington wrote that he 'profoundly disagreed' with the

---

[74] Letter No. B.C.-1016 of 1935, dated 1 August 1935; From: D. Symington, Esq., ICS, Backward Class Officer, Bombay Presidency, Poona, To: The Chief Secretary to Government, Political and Reforms Department, Bombay, in F. No. 4/I/35-G. (B)., General (B) Branch, Reforms Office, GoI, 1935, NAI. The following extract and paragraph are based on this source.

Starte Committee's stance that the problem of the aboriginal and hill tribes arose from their isolation from the main body of the community. Instead, rephrasing the culture contact arguments used by the anthropologists and scholar-administrators, he argued that the problem

> lies not in their isolation from but in their contacts with the main body of the community. Where their geographical position keeps them beyond the reach of the outside world, as in Akrani *mahal*, they are happy and independent; but in the places, now all too many, where they are in constant contact with more educated people, they are degraded, timid and exploited.[75]

Evoking the image of the aboriginal as an innocent child, Symington wrote,

> My position is that, at any rate for the next generation, we must regard the aboriginal as being in the nursery. Like a child he must be protected from outside interference and victimization, and like a child he must be taught how to hold his own. In short, the State's attitude must be paternal.[76]

Given his changed outlook, Symington now supported the provisions of partial exclusion under Section 92 of the Government of India Act, 1935, and remarked that 'whatever the origin of the sections, they offer an extremely convenient vehicle, from administrative point of view, for Government's policy of placing backward classes and backward areas on their feet'.[77]

The first part of Symington's report dealt with 'Agriculture and General Economic Conditions'. He held that the Bhils in partially excluded areas, despite possessing good land, lived 'near the starvation line'[78] due to their 'inextinguishable debt'. The problem of indebtedness was created by unscrupulous *sowcars*, *as a result of which* 'entire profits of agriculture are taken out of the villages and put into the pockets of non-agriculturists'. While the government's policy of reserving these areas for the Bhils had saved them from becoming landless labourers, they had instead become 'a kind of serf, working on their own fields on a bare maintenance for the profits of others'.[79]

---

[75]D. Symington, *Report on the Partially Excluded Areas of Bombay Province*, 1939, p. 1. Henceforth, *SRB*.

[76]Ibid., p. 2.

[77]Ibid., pp. 2–3.

[78]Ibid., p. 11.

[79]Ibid., pp. 7–8.

Symington recommended that all new lands should be reserved for the backward classes. Interestingly, he argued that economic conditions should determine backwardness and the Vanjaris, Mahars, and other Scheduled Caste groups should be eligible for land on equal terms with members of the aboriginal and hill tribes. He further suggested that Bhils who had converted to another religion should not be debarred from getting the benefits of this scheme. Hence, Christian and Muslim Bhils should be equally eligible, 'since their change of religion has not affected their economic status.'[80]

Symington was convinced that any long-term solution to the economic plight of the tribals was impossible without strictly regulating the moneylending profession. He advocated making moneylending in these areas a licensed activity, where only a certain number of license-holding moneylenders could extend loans to members of backward classes.[81] As a substitute source of credit for tribal cultivators, Symington suggested that a co-operative purchase and sale society 'should be set up within reach of every village which will perform on fair terms the same functions as are now performed by the sowcars on unfair terms.'[82]

The report's other major suggestions were for ensuring proper wage rates for the tribals employed in forest work, through either the government department or forest contractors. It also dwelt on some length on the system of forced labour (*veth*) prevalent in these tracts, which 'entails conditions of life hardly distinguishable from slavery on the bulk of the aboriginal population.'[83] Symington advised the government to confer the right of permanent tenancy on all members of the Backward Classes who had cultivated the same fields for three successive years, including the 1937 season.[84]

The second part of Symington's report dealt exclusively with the problem of alcohol consumption. In a clear departure from the scholar-administrators, Symington remarked that the tribals 'do themselves untold damage by their addiction to drink.... Drink causes him to waste money which ought to be spent on food or clothes, makes him idle and neglectful of his fields, and careless of the future.'[85] The prevalent excise policy based

[80]Ibid.

[81]Ibid., p. 18.

[82]Ibid., pp. 18–19.

[83]Ibid., pp. 34–36.

[84]Ibid., p. 37.

[85]Ibid., p. 63.

on cheap alcohol had fuelled an increased consumption of liquor in these areas. Recommending complete prohibition, Symington advocated a policy of absolute control of the *mhowra* flower, which was the 'root of the evil'[86] as it was the base used in 90 per cent of illicit distillation. In a suggestion that would surely have brought smiles to the faces of staunch Gandhian Congressmen, Symington wrote, 'if the present liquor-shops could be replaced by tea and sweetmeat stalls, where gramophone music or radio programmes could also be provided, I believe they would constitute a strong counter-attraction to drink.'[87]

With regard to Local Board activities in the partially excluded areas, Symington showed that the aboriginal tribes had had hardly any representatives elected to these boards from the time of the passage of the Bombay Local Boards Act, 1923. In certain *taluka*s such as Umbergaon, Dahanu, Wada, and Shahapur, despite constituting the majority of the local population, not a single member of the aboriginal tribes had ever been elected.[88] Linking this situation to a lack of education, Symington wrote,

> But Aboriginal and Hill Tribes people are not sufficiently educated and advanced either to use their votes sensibly, or to produce among themselves enough representatives capable of looking after their interests intelligently on local boards. They are not only illiterate but also ignorant of everything outside their immediate daily round. They are contemptuous of education which they regard as a degrading and senseless waste of time. They have more faith in witch-doctors than in any pharmacopoeia. They live near the border-line of starvation. They are inveterate drunkards. It is not surprising that they take no interest in such matters as local board elections or local board administration.... If left entirely to themselves they will not vote at all, and very few will even stand for election.[89]

Symington called for drastic reforms to mend this sorry state of affairs. Through detailed statistics, he showed that the partially excluded areas enjoyed 'far less than their proper share of the educational facilities.'[90] Even such facilities as were provided in these areas were mostly utilised by children of the advanced classes. In the Dhadgaon, Nandurbar, and Taloda

[86]Ibid., p. 66

[87]Ibid., p. 69.

[88]Ibid., p. 76.

[89]Ibid.

[90]Ibid., p. 77.

areas, hostels had been built for Bhil boys studying in primary schools since the time of government control. The objective behind setting up these hostels was to 'provide teachers for the schools in the forest areas, where high caste hate to serve and often try to keep attendance down in order to get the schools closed and themselves transferred'. In practice, however, this potential source of Bhil teachers willing to work in those areas was neglected, as the School Boards did not recruit many of them to teaching positions. As a result, among the Bhils of East and West Khandesh, only 0.5 per cent were literate.[91] Symington asked for the Starte Committee recommendations for compulsory education in these regions to be taken forward. The government should resume their control over primary education in the partially excluded areas and manage the educational efforts through its Education Department.[92]

Finally, the Symington Report recommended a number of miscellaneous measures for the Bombay government, ranging from increased medical help to propaganda for agricultural, financial, and social services. Symington insisted that most of the suggested measures were mutually interdependent, and was convinced that 'social and economic reforms cannot be undertaken piecemeal. If we tackle one, we must tackle the whole field.'[93] Given the size of the aboriginal population in Bombay Presidency, tackling the issue at the level of a whole administrative unit was cumbersome. Hence, he regarded the provisions for the partial exclusion of certain areas (thirteen talukas) in Bombay, which covered 39 per cent of the total aboriginal population in the Presidency, as 'exceedingly fortunate'.[94] Explaining his point of view, Symington wrote,

> In dealing with these jungle peoples it is necessary to avoid most carefully any doctrinaire adherence to the theories of representative government. We must face the facts boldly and realize that socially and politically these tribes are centuries behind even the intermediate castes of the Presidency; as witness the fact that most of them have not yet reached the stage of living together in a village community; and that what they need above all things is strong Government action to protect them from exploitation, and to supply in as full a measure as possible their educational, social and economic needs thus gradually

[91] Ibid., p. 78.
[92] Ibid., p. 81.
[93] Ibid., p. 3.
[94] Ibid., p. 100.

> bringing them up to the general level of their neighbours. That is enough for one generation both to accomplish and to receive, and if such a policy can now be put into operation with sufficient firmness the next generation of Bhils, Warlis and others will grow up better educated, more intelligent, and less hag-ridden by poverty and sowcars than their fathers. They may then perhaps be able to manage their local affairs, a task which is like beyond the powers and aspirations of the present generation. If so, the time will *then* have come to experiment with local democratic institutions for jungle tribes. Meanwhile our past experiments on these lines should be regarded as premature and a failure, and should be abandoned.[95]

In retrospect, Symington's *Report on the Partially Excluded Areas of Bombay* was a remarkable document in many ways. It was the first in a series of such provincial enquiries commissioned by the nationalist Congress governments that came to power after their electoral success in 1937. As suggested earlier, given Symington's earlier opposition to partial exclusion, the Congress government probably miscalculated the recommendations that would be finally enshrined in the Bombay report. Had an English ICS officer critiqued the provisions of partial exclusion for the Bombay Province, a serious split in the ranks of the 'official block' would have been established. The Congress was surely eyeing the political capital which such a split in the bureaucratic ranks would beget. However, as it turned out, Symington did a *volte face* on his earlier position, and his report gave full support to the provisions of partial exclusion and lauded the delimitation of the thirteen talukas in the province which were partially excluded. Consequently, in Orissa, A. V. Thakkar was made the head of the Committee to report on the conditions of the partially excluded areas of that province. It could be argued that the Congress was once bitten, twice shy of appointing ICS officers for future enquiries.

Much of the Bombay report followed the tropes of land alienation, indebtedness, forced labour, exploitative forest regulations, etc., and on these issues Symington agreed with the group that came to be known as the 'Protectionists'. Again, Symington's affinity with the Protectionist position was evident in his criticism of the functioning of the District Local Boards, as well as of the way that representative democratic institutions, through elections, excluded any effective aboriginal participation in these areas. In

[95] Ibid., p. 83; emphasis in the original.

these respects, the report dealt a body blow to the Congress position on the issue.

Nevertheless, on a contrary and more pro-Congress ministry line, a novel feature of this report (where Symington differed from the group of scholar-administrators and anthropologists) was the strong support he lent to the argument for massive State intervention in these areas, especially in the field of education, which he considered the prerequisite to any meaningful experiment in local self-government. Another major deviation from the Protectionist position was Symington's recommendation of the imposition of a strict excise policy prohibiting alcoholic beverages in the partially excluded areas inhabited by the Bhils. It was possibly this stance which led Verrier Elwin to remark that he was 'disappointed'[96] by Symington's report on the Bhils, as it had 'played into the hands of the Bombay Ministry'.[97] Elwin was worried to see that after the publication of the report, an agitation had begun 'to extend prohibition to the Gonds'.[98]

A curious aspect of the Symington Report was the fact that it was kept under wraps by the Kher Ministry for a long time. The report was submitted on 31 March 1938, but was published only fifteen months later, during which period its contents were kept secret (and the resulting suspense created some political flutters). Upon its publication in July 1939, the Bombay government welcomed the author's efforts and approved some of its recommendations, while giving an 'in-principle' nod to many others.[99] However, with the resignation of the Congress ministries at the outbreak of World War II, most of these recommendations were never put into action.

An issue that needs further research is the impact of the Symington Report upon the discourse on the future of the tribal communities in India. Being the first report of its kind, it set the tone and agenda for future enquiries. It was also possibly the most widely quoted document in debates over the subsequent decade. In an early 1940 tour of partially excluded areas in Mandla and Balaghat districts, Sir Francis Wylie, the Governor of Central Provinces and Berar, observed remarkable similarities between

---

[96]Personal Letter from Verrier Elwin to E. S. Hyde, dated 7 August 1939, Box III, Hyde Papers, CSAS, Cambridge.

[97]Personal Letter from Verrier Elwin to E. S. Hyde, dated Mandla, 21 September 1939, Box III, Hyde Papers, CSAS, Cambridge.

[98]Personal Letter from Verrier Elwin to E. S. Hyde, dated 7 August 1939, Box III, Hyde Papers, CSAS, Cambridge.

[99]*The Times of India*, 13 July 1939, p. 11.

what Symington had described and what he saw in his tour, during the course of which he became 'aboriginal-conscious'.[100] The result was a detailed enquiry (in the C.P. and Berar) on the 'Bombay-model', conducted by the anthropologist-administrator W. V. Grigson, which followed the Orissa report by A. V. Thakkar.

The Orissa Partially Excluded Areas Enquiry Report

The Province of Orissa was created in 1936 by separating its territories from the earlier conjoint Province of Bihar and Orissa. None of its territories were declared as excluded areas. However, 20,836 square miles (almost two-thirds of the new Province) were declared as partially excluded. This covered the Sambalpur and Angul districts, the Agency tracts of Ganjam district, the Khondmals, and most of the new Koraput district.[101] The total number of inhabitants living in these areas was 26,09,424 (including 11,18,356 aboriginals), which comprised about one-third of Orissa's population. [102] Having such a large area under partial exclusion was a problem, since most of these districts were financially deficit areas. The provincial government of Orissa was severely strained as only three (Puri, Balasore, and Cuttack) of its six districts were normally administered areas that paid sufficient revenues to the state coffers.

Orissa's first Chief Minister, Bishwanath Das, was vocal in his demand for subvention from the Central government, repeatedly stating that while the partially excluded areas needed communications, public health, medical aid, and education, it was difficult for his government to provide these services given the lack of funds.[103] During a debate in the Orissa Legislative Assembly on the annual budget of the Province for the year 1937–38, the subject of the Backward Tracts came up for discussion. In his reply to the Assembly, Das promised to examine the special regulations enforced in these areas. Accordingly, in December 1938, the Governor of Orissa

---

[100]Personal Letter from Verrier Elwin to E. S. Hyde, dated Mandla, 12 April 1940, Box III, Hyde Papers, CSAS, Cambridge.

[101]*The Times of India*, 21 May 1936, p. 14.

[102]*Report of the Partially Excluded Areas Enquiry Committee (Orissa)*, Superintendent, Government Press, Cuttack, Orissa, 1940, p. 7 (henceforth, *OR* [Orissa Report]).

[103]*The Times of India*, 20 January 1938, p. 11.

appointed a committee headed by A. V. Thakkar to enquire into the general administration of the partially excluded areas of Koraput, Ganjam Agency, the Khondmals, and Angul.[104] Subsequently, the scope of the enquiry was extended to the partially excluded areas of Sambalpur district as well.[105] The terms of reference of the committee touched upon every branch of administration and concerned 'problems of social, moral and economic uplift' of the inhabitants of the partially excluded areas.[106]

The Thakkar Committee Report held that the poor financial position of the partially excluded areas of Orissa presented the main challenge in their development. While the needs and revenues of the coastal plains were flexible and could be increased, there were 'constitutional, legal and practical difficulties' in raising revenue demands from the partially excluded areas. The sparse population of the Jeypore, Khondmal, and Ganjam areas prevented land revenues from being raised in this region. Only forests offered a lucrative revenue resource, but that too depended on opening up the means of communication. The excise head did yield significant revenue, but the Committee was in favour of recommending prohibition. As Thakkar viewed it, 'Development of these areas will require heavy cost at the initial stages, though it might ultimately pay its way.'[107]

With regard to land-revenue administration, both the *raiyatwari*[108] and *mustajari* systems were prevalent.[109] The Committee observed that conditions of life were comparatively better in the raiyatwari areas, since the mustajari system had degenerated into an exploitative one where illegal exactions and forced labour services (*bethi*) were the order of the day. Hence, the Committee recommended that all mustajari villages be converted to

[104]Resolution No. 12513—Poll., dated 19 December 1938, *OR*, pp. 1–2.

[105]Resolution No. 3622—Poll., dated 24 May 1939, *OR*, p. 3.

[106]*OR*, p. 5. For details of the terms of reference, see *OR*, p. 2.

[107]Ibid., pp. 13–14.

[108]Under the raiyatwari system, first devised by Thomas Munro in the early nineteenth century, the State collected land revenue directly from the individual peasants.

[109]A Mustajar was an agent or contractor, appointed by the Jeypore Maharaja to collect rent from a single village or a group of villages and pay the agreed amount to the estate. His remuneration consisted of a certain piece of rent-free land or a percentage of the rents realised. For all practical purposes, a Mustajar was the master of the village.

raiyatwari ones within a period of ten years.[110] It also recommended that the prevalent systems of both 'plough tax' and commutation dues be abolished.[111]

Another major state intervention that was suggested was the suppression of bonded labour, locally known as the *goti* system. Under this, a person taking a loan from a *sahukar* pledged himself by written agreement to labour for the creditor so long as his loan remained unpaid. In practice, the system had 'degenerated into serfdom'. The committee acknowledged the havoc which the *goti* system had caused in these tracts, leading to migration as well as agitations. Since the problem arose from rural indebtedness, it recommended that immediate and efficient steps be taken to check malpractice by the *sahukars*.[112] It also praised the recently passed Madras Government Regulation (III of 1940), which had abolished debt bondage and made strict provisions for the performance of certain kinds of labour in the partially excluded areas of Madras Province.[113]

The report vehemently criticised the practice of *podu* or shifting cultivation as 'wasteful' and causing immense damage to the forests. The committee opined that '*podu* cultivation is itself inherently defective and economically unsound'.[114] However, it also recorded that the people 'insist that they have a right to remain in the hills as their ancestors have never done any kind of cultivation except Podu'.[115] Notwithstanding such resistance, the committee came to the unanimous decision that podu cultivation should be abolished as early as was practicable. It suggested a scheme of sedentarisation, to be implemented over the next ten years, where cultivable lands would 'be given to these people free of assessment for the first five years and thereafter by graded assessment'.[116]

On expected lines, the Thakkar Committee recommended strict control over the *mahua* flower. It adopted a strictly Gandhian approach and recommended prohibition, arguing that:

> Drink causes the average aborigine to waste money which might be spent on other necessarirs [*sic*] of life. Drink makes him indolent and neglectful of his field work. Women and children are also encouraged to

[110]*OR*, pp. 17–18.
[111]Ibid., p. 30.
[112]Ibid.
[113]Ibid., pp. 46–47.
[114]Ibid., p. 23.
[115]Ibid., pp. 24–25.
[116]Ibid., pp. 25–26.

> indulge in this evil ... we are of the opinion that prohibition of distilled liquor, ganja and opium in Koraput district should be enforced as early as possible in view of the fact that the bulk of the population are aborigines, who though now addicted to drinking ought to be weaned off for reformation. There may be some opposition at present from the peoples' side, but by education and propaganda the people will be convinced of prohibition.[117]

On education, the committee held that expenditure was insufficient and the functioning of schools was ill-supervised. Since the majority of primary schoolteachers came from other parts of the Province and did not know the aboriginal dialects, it was suggested that all serving teachers be induced to learn Kui or Savara, while for new entrant teachers a working knowledge of these languages should be made compulsory.[118] No fee should be charged from tribal students in secondary schools and scholarships/stipends should be provided to them. The report also advocated a strongly vocational aspect, calling for the setting up of an industrial and residential school where, in addition to academic learning, the boys should be trained in making agricultural implements, ordinary household furniture, and metalwork.[119] This aspect followed from the paradigm of the Gandhian Constructive Programme and Thakkar's own educational welfare work model in the Bhil Seva Mandal.

The introduction of reforms in local self-government was a major concern for the Thakkar Committee. In any scheme for democratic representation in Orissa's partially excluded areas, the interests of the aboriginals vis-à-vis the non-aboriginals had to be finely balanced. While outlining the case of Koraput district, the report remarked that there were far too few aboriginals in the entire district who possessed the educational or other qualifications required 'to represent the hill tribes in the Board and to exercise the franchise in an intelligent manner'. It also raised the apprehension that 'if certain backward tribes are enfranchised and others excluded from voting it might give rise to inter-tribal jealousy and consequent unrest'.[120] The committee recommended abolishing the system of cent per cent nominations in the District and other Boards. Instead, half the seats should be filled by elections and the other half would be nominated by the government, in order to

[117] Ibid., pp. 20–21.
[118] Ibid., p. 35.
[119] Ibid., p. 36.
[120] Ibid., p. 55.

represent the aboriginals and other minority interests. Here, Thakkar was not towing the official Congress line for he did not insist upon elections as the only means to ensure aboriginal representation.

Another significant recommendation of the Thakkar Committee was the formation of a 'Backward Classes Welfare Department'. The committee argued that their recommendations for the welfare of the aboriginal population would fall flat unless a *special agency* was created to 'carry these into successful operation'.[121] Such an agency should be charged with 'continuously thinking and planning of the necessary measures to enable the backward people to come to the level of the advanced population of the coastal districts'. This department was to be manned by a special officer, assisted by an Advisory Board.

The Thakkar Committee Report was marked by an increasing awareness that the partially excluded tracts of Orissa were repositories of not only forest products, but also vast amounts of mineral resources. The Geological Survey of India had recently conducted a preliminary survey of some places in Koraput district to ascertain the possibility of establishing mining industries, and the committee hoped that the agency would take these measures forward.[122] The committee remarked candidly,

> The main obstacles to development are want of proper communications, shortage of labour and the existence of malaria. The first requisite for the development is the completion of the system of roads, we have recommended in this report. That is only a question of money. There is no great difficulty in importing labour from adjoining districts. No attempt at colonizing the country, specially the district of Koraput, has yet been made, nor at systematically utilizing the labour of hill-men. With the development of communications and earnest attempt of the authorities for the eradication of malaria, the question of colonization will be solved to a great extent, and we have evidence before us that large areas of waste lands are available for settlement and cultivation at comparatively low rates of assessment. The hill-men are good workers, but they are ignorant of the new type of work that will be required of them. It should be the duty of the authorities to utilize their labour as far as practicable in preference to outsiders.[123]

---

[121]Ibid., p. 153, emphasis in the original. This recommendation was implemented in 1946 when the Congress Ministry returned to power.

[122]Ibid., p. 104.

[123]Ibid., p. 105.

In the above extract, it is clear and quite remarkable how the word 'colonisation' was now being used by the nationalists so nonchalantly. Also, the 'internal frontier' imagery is quite apparent. The Thakkar report was replete with arguments for opening up the partially excluded areas, for colonisation at first, but the ultimate vision of an industrial economy replacing that of the hill tribes was apparent. In this context, increasing the accessibility of these areas was a prime necessity. But this required the utilisation of vast financial outlays in the construction of roads and bridges. Consequently, the Thakkar Committee suggested a 'system of taxation by toll gates of all conveyances' so that taxes could be levied on both agricultural commodities and major/minor forest products such as timber, sunari bark (wattle), tamarind, myrobalans, nux-vomica, mohua, lac, bamboos, and siali leaves, kendu leaves, etc.[124]

Interestingly, one of the hallmarks of the Thakkar Report was the drastic changes it suggested in the management of forests in partially excluded areas. It strongly recommended that the prevalent Madras Forest Act (V of 1882) be replaced by the Indian Forest Act (XVI of 1927), as the provisions of the former were not sufficient to preserve the 'invaluable national assets'.[125] This would have meant a complete takeover of all rights to exploit the natural resources of these areas. The Thakkar Committee was visualising the forest wealth of Orissa state as a source of revenue, not only in terms of the minor forest produce mentioned earlier, but also through the extraction of wood and minerals, etc. This imperative to monetise the forest land in an effort to transcend the deficit and precarious nature of the new state's financial position indicated a desire to centralise the management of natural resources as per the logic of 'eminent domain'. That this stricture came from the pen of a lifelong dedicated Gandhian was even more remarkable! As part of an enticing pronouncement of what the new Congress dispensation would do to the forests and the tribals inhabiting it, the Committee strongly advocated reserving large tracts of forests.[126]

When the Thakkar Committee was formed, it was expected that the report would come down heavily on the system of excluded and partially excluded areas. As against this expectation, the Thakkar report was marked by a guarded acceptance of the principles behind partial exclusion.

[124]Ibid., p. 41.
[125]Ibid., p. 31.
[126]Ibid., p. 68.

In making its recommendations, the Committee preferred a case-by-case approach, wavering between 'modified continuation' and 'complete change' in the existing system.[127] Like Symington, Thakkar's tour experience in the tribal areas had changed his outlook significantly. The reasons for his retreat are spelt out clearly in the following portion of the Orissa Partially Excluded Areas Committee report:

> So long as the hill people were isolated, they developed their own manners of life without any interference from outsiders. With the march of time ... [t]he tribes are no longer isolated and their contact with the men of the plains has brought into existence several new problems which threaten to wipe out or completely absorb the aborigines into the general mass of population.... Drink, disease, malnutrition and debt are at work to handicap their development.... If adequate protection is not given to them and beneficial schemes to help them are not put into action early, the aborigines will sink still lower and become a drag on the society.... It is the sacred duty of the present generation to protect them and to help them to improve themselves in every direction and to become efficient and useful citizens in the economic and social structure of the country.[128]

Thus, Thakkar came to acknowledge that increased contacts between the hill tribes and the plainsmen had broken the former's isolation. This culture contact had to be controlled if the aboriginals were to be protected. Superficially, the above articulation seems like a reiteration of the Neo-Diffusionist rhetoric. However, Thakkar's terms for regulating culture contact differed significantly from those espoused by figures such as Hutton, Mills, and Elwin. For Thakkar, 'development', rather than territorial 'protection' through exclusion or partial exclusion, would be the magic wand that would protect the interests of the aboriginals. The desire to convert the tribals into citizens of India was in keeping with the ideological bent of the Congress nationalists. Thakkar viewed partial exclusion as only an interim measure and held that the proper course would be to 'reduce the partially excluded areas to a minimum',[129] for,

---

[127]Ibid., p. 7. It is to be noted that the committee did recommend the delisting of Sambalpur and Angul from the partially excluded areas of the Province, as well as the Chokpad Khandam and Pondakhol Muttah areas of the Ganjam Agency tracts.

[128]Ibid., p. 90

[129]Ibid., p. 58.

> The customs, beliefs and manners of the aboriginals are bound to change under the impact of civilization and within a short time it should not be difficult to obtain a fair amount of homogenity [*sic*] between the partially excluded areas and the plains. The policy should be one of blending and levelling by stages rather than of isolation, segregation and maintenance of '*status quo*'.[130]

From Chapter 4, it should be clear that A. V. Thakkar's reading of the term 'civilisation' in the context of India was a strictly 'Hindu' idea. From the stress laid on 'homogeneity' in the above extract, it follows that the terms of inclusion for tribes living in the partially excluded areas were also similarly conceived. In a nutshell, the 'plains' were viewed as the gold standard and the quintessential 'mainstream' of national life. The pattern of life followed by the tribal Indian citizens residing in the partially excluded areas of Orissa was to be homogenised and made barely distinguishable from that in the coastal plains. By implication, this mainstream was again orthodox Hindu in orientation.

Furthermore, it will be a useful exercise to compare the two reports of Thakkar and Symington owing to their different vantage points, and the arguments that each offered to resolve the tribal question in India. Perhaps the most significant link between Symington and Thakkar was the idea of backwardness of certain communities. Right from the Starte Committee (1930), the continuation of the generic phrase 'backward classes', encompassing both the depressed classes and aboriginals/hill tribes, suggests that in the logic of colonial governmentality, certain social groups were ascribed 'backwardness', measured in similar educational, economic, and social terms.

While Symington was the incumbent Backward Classes Officer in the Bombay Presidency when the Congress ministries took charge, the Thakkar Report expanded the idea of a single special officer looking after the Depressed Classes and aboriginals by recommending the formation of an entire Backward Classes Welfare Department for their upliftment. Aside from the loss of the central figure of a sympathetic European officer in the new framework, the introducing of the word 'welfare' marks a different governmental logic. Although it was couched in a democratic rhetoric, the new establishment was as paternalistic in its conception. Both in Orissa and in Bombay, Thakkar's recommendations were implemented in 1946 when the Congress returned to power. The similarities continued as both reports

[130]Ibid.

gave their wholehearted support to the idea of prohibition and the need to spread education amongst tribal communities.

Nevertheless, there were significant differences between the two reports. Symington was in favour of retaining the provisions of partial exclusion, while Thakkar was arguing for the 'mainstreaming' (in effect, 'Hinduising') of such areas. Despite being commissioned by a Congress government, Symington accepted the position of the anthropologically-minded administrators and denounced the possibility of having true aboriginal representatives in the absence of an educated section amongst the aboriginal and hill tribes. On the contrary, representative democracy through elections was a sacred maxim for Thakkar, and although he recognised the inadequate educational levels amongst the tribal communities, the committee recommended that at least half of their representatives should enter local and legislative bodies through the electoral route. By recommending elections, Thakkar was also overturning the central idea behind scheduling, that is, insulating these areas from democratic forms of governance.

Although the Thakkar Committee did recommend the delisting of certain partially excluded areas, the higher echelons of the colonial bureaucracy were very relieved that the provisions for partial exclusion had not been rejected *in toto* by a committee dominated by Congress nationalists. In a letter to Lord Linlithgow, the Viceroy of India, John Hubback, the then Governor of Orissa, expressed satisfaction that Thakkar had agreed to keep Koraput and the Ganjam Agency tract, including Khondmals, as partially excluded areas. On the recommendations of the committee, he wrote, 'On the whole they are not nearly so radical as I had feared, and I think a good deal of them can be accepted.'[131]

Figures such as Verrier Elwin were unhappy with many aspects of the Orissa report. Elwin was particularly taken aback by Thakkar's intense opposition to the practice of shifting cultivation and his recommendation to ban it altogether. Almost a year after its publication, when Thakkar pressed Elwin for his opinion on the Orissa report, the rising star of Indian anthropology wrote,

> I must admit that the Orissa report caused me great disappointment and very real pain.... For years I have been striving to get the Imperialist Government to allow a few human rights to the aboriginals. First and foremost among those rights is that of shifting cultivation. Just

[131] P&J 2729/1940, D.O. No. 281 G.O., dated Governor's Camp Orissa, 10 May 1940; From: John Hubback, To: Lord Linlithgow, IOR/L/PJ/7/2309.

> as certain impression had been created, the fruit of hour after hour of patient and often very weary work, you come and cut the ground underneath my feet.... And in whose interest would you stop bewar? The forest belongs to the aboriginals. I should have thought anyone who was a Nationalist would at least advocate swaraj for the aboriginal![132]

The Ambedkar-Thakkar Debate

The second quarter of 1945 witnessed the eruption of a public debate on the pages of the prominent Bombay-based daily, *The Times of India.* The protagonists of this debate were B. R. Ambedkar and A. V. Thakkar. At this time, Ambedkar was the serving Labour Member of the Viceroy's Executive Council while Thakkar was the *de facto* head of the Harijan Sevak Sangh.

Before entering into the details of the debate, it may help to provide a brief background of the relations between these two public figures. Ambedkar and Thakkar shared an uneasy relationship that went back a long way. They had both served as members of the Starte Committee formed by the Bombay government in 1928 to enquire into the social and educational conditions of the Aboriginals and Depressed Classes of the Province. Subsequently in 1932, when the Communal Award controversy erupted over the issue of granting separate electorates to the Depressed Classes (as demanded by Ambedkar for the community), Mahatma Gandhi went on a fast unto death. This episode, which ended with the famous 'Poona Pact', saw Ambedkar retreating from his position and agreeing to a system of joint electorates with seats reserved for the Depressed Classes. Much work has been done on this historic event, but few people know of the key role that Thakkar played in it. G. D. Birla, a trusted lieutenant of Gandhi, recounted the same in the following words:

> I entered into a deep bond with Thakkar Bapa in 1932. When Bapu had taken a vow of fast-unto-death and was lying on his death-bed, then a few of us were talking with Mr. Ambedkar, deeply thinking to figure out a way to solve the Harijan question. As time went by, Bapu's body was slowly and gradually drowning towards an inert state. A few people were engaged in a tug-of-war over the seats which greatly irked us. At that time, the responsibility of calculating the justifiable

[132]Copy of Elwin's Letter to A. V. Thakkar, dated Mandla, C.P. 7 July 1941, Subject File No. 8, P. Kodanda Rao Papers, PMML.

> number of seats for the Harijans was given to Thakkar Bapa which he fulfilled without any prejudice whatsoever. The life of the 'Poona Pact' is the right to vote provided to the Harijans and this is the creation of Thakkar Bapa. We signed on this document with our eyes closed.[133]

After the Poona Pact, Gandhi formed the Harijan Sevak Sangh and gave over its charge to Thakkar Bapa, who hesitantly took over its reins as he considered aboriginal welfare his 'first love'. Both Thakkar and Ambedkar spent the subsequent decade working on the Depressed Classes issue, albeit along divergent trajectories.

On 6 May 1945, Ambedkar made an elaborate speech before the Third Conference of the All India Scheduled Castes Federation in Bombay. The title of his talk was 'Communal Deadlock and a Way to Solve It', which he later published as well. His scheme dealt with the Central Legislative Assembly and all the eleven provincial assemblies. In a situation where partition seemed imminent, Ambedkar hoped to avert it through his proposals, which 'do not ask Hindus to abandon the principle of majority rule' but asked that they be 'satisfied with relative majority'.[134]

The hallmark of Ambedkar's scheme was that guaranteed representation would be given to several communities, both in the Central and provincial legislatures. The formula that Ambedkar suggested was a proportionate one. The following details appeared in the press reports (the percentage figures in parentheses denote the population percentage): of the 100 seats in the Central Legislative Assembly, Hindus (54.68 per cent) would get 40 seats; Muslims (28.5 per cent) 32 seats; Scheduled Castes (14.3 per cent) 20 seats; Indian Christians (1.16 per cent) 3 seats; Sikhs (1.49 per cent) 4 seats; and the Anglo-Indians (0.05 per cent) 1 seat. Likewise, Ambedkar also gave figures for all the major provinces. In arriving at these numbers, Ambedkar deducted the population of the Aboriginal Tribes from the available 1941 Census figures and made no provision for any seats to them at all.[135] In fact, Ambedkar referred to this anomaly in his speech, but the major press reports omitted the following part of his address, where he said,

> It will be obvious that my proposals do not cover the Aboriginal Tribes, although they are larger in numbers than the Sikhs, Anglo

[133]Ghanshyamdas Birla, 'Thakkar Bapa' (in Hindi), T. N. Jagadisan and Shyamlal (compiled and eds), *Thakkar Bapa: Eightieth Birthday Commemoration Volume*, Madras: Diocesan Press, 1949; translation mine.

[134]*The Times of India*, 7 May 1945, p. 1.

[135]Ibid., p. 5.

> Indians, Indian Christians and Parsees. I may state the reasons why I have omitted them from my scheme. The Aboriginal Tribes have not as yet developed any political sense to make the best use of their political opportunities and they may easily become mere instruments in the hands of either a majority or a minority, and thereby disturb the balance without doing any good to themselves. In the present state of their development it seems to me that the proper thing to do for these backward communities is to establish a Statutory Commission to administer what are now called the 'Excluded Areas' on the same basis as was done in the case of South African Constitution. Every province in which these 'Excluded Areas' are situated should be compelled to make an annual contribution of a prescribed amount for the administration of these areas.[136]

This extract remarkably captures the protectionist logic at work in Ambedkar's mind. He perhaps took this stance as, at this time, he was the Labour Member in the Viceroy's Executive Council, and his position could be seen as allying with that of the British on the tribal question in India. An astute constitutional thinker, Ambedkar's views on the tribal predicament remains to be worked out fully in scholarship. However, in Chapter 2, it is clear that in 1933, Ambedkar's view of the political process for aboriginal tribes was similar to that of his own constituency, that is, the Depressed Classes. The reference to the South African Constitution is also noteworthy. The official archive does display instances which suggest a discursive exchange of ideas and experiences regarding administering the 'tribal' areas in Africa.

Nevertheless, in an India on the cusp of political independence, Ambedkar's omission of representation for tribals from his proposed constitutional scheme was astonishing to the nationalists. On 12 May 1945, Thakkar wrote a letter to the Editor of *The Times of India*, which was published in its issue of 17 May 1945. In it, he pointed out that even the British government had recognised aborigines as eligible for some representation in the Government of India Act, 1935,

---

[136]A. V. Thakkar, 'Education among Tribal People very backward: State's responsibility for their Advancement', *Leader*, 11 July 1945, reproduced in *Aboriginals' Cry in the Wilderness: Controversy between Dr. Ambedkar and A.V. Thakkar with Facts and Figures regarding Aborigines and Hill Tribes, Their Education and Representation in Legislature*, Published by A. V. Thakkar, Servants of India Society, Bombay, n.d., p. 11.

> It is somewhat surprising that this doughty champion of the oppressed and depressed and exploited should have so completely ignored the Aboriginal tribes who are worse off than the Harijans. He would even take away what was given them already! Some Champion indeed of the lowly![137]

Thakkar argued that Ambedkar seemed to favour the principle of providing weightage to all communities 'in inverse ratio to social standing, economic position and educational conditions of the community'. Perhaps that was why he suggested that the Harijans receive a larger weightage than the Muslims. Thakkar pointed out that since there were about one crore and sixty-seven lakh aborigines in the British Indian Provinces alone, '(I)f his principle be applied to Aborigines the weightage for them would be very much larger than for the Harijans; in fact, it may justify an absolute majority!' Thakkar remarked that the only principle of Ambedkar which stood out in his scheme was his 'excessive favouritism for the Harijans and contemptuous denial of justice to the Aborigines'.[138]

Ambedkar was evidently stung by Thakkar's attack, for he drafted a response the same day in which he wrote,

> I have never claimed to be a universal leader of suffering humanity. The problem of the Untouchables is quite enough for my slender strength, and I should be very happy if I could successfully rescue the Untouchables from his clutches and those of Mr. Gandhi.[139]

Ambedkar pointed out that Thakkar had criticised him on the 'basis of such extracts as have appeared in the papers'. Had Thakkar read the full text of his speech, it would have been clear that 'far from excluding the cause of Aboriginal Tribes, I had made what, according to my belief, I thought was a far better and a far effective proposal for their protection'. Rejecting Thakkar's charge of 'partiality and small mindedness', Ambedkar explained his position thus,

> The reason why I did not include the Aboriginal Tribes in the scheme of distribution of seats in the Legislature is not the result of my

---

[137] A. V. Thakkar, Letter to the Editor, 'The Times of India', dated Poona, 12 May 1945, *The Times of India*, 17 May 1945, p. 6.

[138] Ibid.

[139] B. R. Ambedkar, Letter to the Editor, 'The Times of India', dated Bombay, 17 May 1945, *The Times of India*, 18 May 1945, p. 6. The following paragraphs are based on this source.

> antipathy to them, but is entirely due to my belief that these Aboriginal Tribes do not as yet possess the political capacity which is necessary to exercise political power for one's own good.

Ambedkar asked Thakkar what he had done to raise the educational standard of the tribals, 'so that they may know their own aspirations to rise to the level of the highest Hindu and be in a position to use political power as a means to that end'. He went on to state that the inability to produce a single graduate from the aboriginal tribes was a sorry commentary on Thakkar's two-decade-old career as a professional social servant. For Ambedkar, the absence of educated graduates among the aboriginal tribes was an impediment which disqualified them from participating in modern representative democratic institutions such as the legislative assemblies of future India. Ambedkar added to the protectionist logic the argument that a virtual 'absence' of education constituted the chief handicap of the aboriginal populations and the prime reason for their being 'backward'. Right through the Starte Committee proceedings and then through the Symington Report, Bombay had emerged as the chief site of the discourse of educational backwardness.

Last but not least, Ambedkar argued that although Thakkar desired to provide representation to the aboriginal tribes in proportion to their population, he would know that in order to give them some sort of weightage, it would be necessary to scale down the representation of the Muslims. In a final salvo, Ambedkar posed the following challenge,

> Is Mr. Thakkar prepared to fight with the Muslims his battle for the Aborigines? Mr. Thakkar does not prove his love for the Untouchables by cutting into their representation. Mr. Thakkar is not proving a hero by raising his sword against a weak community like the Untouchables which has not received in the past even its fair share of representation. He would prove himself a lover of the aborigines and their hero if he fought to get something out of the weightage enjoyed by the Muslims.

In less than a week, Thakkar was back with a rejoinder on the editorial page of *The Times of India*. He denied the charge of malice towards Ambedkar and pointed out that in the speech in question, Ambedkar had not confined himself to the status of the Scheduled Castes alone. Instead, what was propounded was a 'constitution for India based on principles of general application'. Thus, Thakkar was rather amused that Ambedkar had concerned himself only with the Scheduled Castes, and sarcastically commented that 'I had credited him with a wider and juster out-look'.[140] He came down heavily on Ambedkar for denying 'not only weightage, but any representation' to the aboriginals, calling it the 'unkindest cut of all'.[141]

Subsequently, when this correspondence was published as a booklet, Thakkar provided the following table (see Table 5.1), asking readers to compare the figures in the fourth column to that of the last:

Table 5.1: Percentages of Aboriginal Population and their Representation to Total Population and Total Representation[142]

Province	*Total Population in Lakhs (1941)*	*Aboriginal Population in Lakhs (1941)*	*Percentage of Aboriginal to Total Population*	*Total No. of Seats in the Provincial Assembly*	*No. of Seats Reserved for Aborigines*	*Percentage of Aboriginal Seats to Total Seats*
Madras	493.4	5.62	1.13%	215	1	0.45%
Bombay	208.4	16.14	7.74%	175	1	0.57%
Bengal	603.0	18.89	3.11%	250	Nil	Nil
Bihar	363.4	50.56	13.91%	152	7	4.60%
U.P.	550.2	2.89	0.05%	228	Nil	Nil
C.P. & Berar	168.1	29.37	17.47%	112	1	0.89%
Assam	102.0	24.85	24.36%	108	9	8.33%
Orissa	87.2	17.21	19.73%	60	5	8.33%

To simplify his argument, Thakkar broke down the numbers proportionately. Hence, in Bihar, Assam, and Orissa, the representation of tribes was one-third to one-half of what should be due on the basis of population. In Orissa, four out of five seats were nominated ones and of these four, only one member was actually a tribal. Also, he pointed out that in the provinces of Bombay, Bengal, and C.P. & Berar, their representation was negligible, the greatest 'injustice' having been done in C.P. & Berar.

[140]From: A. V. Thakkar, Letter to the Editor, 'The Times of India', dated 23 May 1945, *The Times of India*, 26 May 1945.

[141]Ibid.

[142]*Aboriginals' Cry in the Wilderness: Controversy between Dr. Ambedkar and A.V. Thakkar with Facts and Figures regarding Aborigines and Hill Tribes, Their Education and Representation in Legislature*, Published by A. V. Thakkar, Servants of India Society, Bombay, n.d., p. 17.

In a further attack on Ambedkar published in the newspaper *Leader*,[143] Thakkar termed his proposals 'unjust and reactionary'. This is the first known public piece by A. V. Thakkar in which he abandoned the use of 'Aboriginal/Aborigine' and started using the word 'Tribe/Tribal people' instead. In this particular piece, he also made a strong pitch for massive State intervention in the task of educating the tribal people. The educational backwardness of the tribes was an incontrovertible fact, a result of neglect by the colonial State for the past one-and-a-half centuries. Additionally, the geographical isolation of these communities in 'remote hilly and jungle parts of the country, as well as in their own colonies in the plains' was a major factor in creating this deficit. Only in some areas like the Ranchi district and the Chota Nagpur plateau had the work of Christian missionaries resulted in the educational advancement of tribal people.

In response to Ambedkar's jibe that the aboriginals do not have a single graduate amongst them, Thakkar wrote that he had been able to collect a list of 112 graduates. Of these, seventy-two were from the Mundas, Oraons, and Santals of Bihar, even though most of them were Christians. A number of these were professors in colleges or employed in the judicial and educational services of the Province. Next came Madras, which accounted for twenty-one graduates, mainly from the Badaga tribe of the Nilgiris, but also from the Yerukulas and Enadis of the East Coast. Most of them were Hindus who had 'advanced considerably through their own efforts'. Assam came third with eleven graduates, who were mostly Hindus and practising lawyers. Mavis Dun, a Khasi law graduate, had been a minister in the provincial government. Another law graduate, Rupanath Brahma, had been a minister for the past six years. Among other Provinces, C.P. accounted for five and Bombay for four graduates, respectively. These numbers led Thakkar to argue that 'even now there is an appreciable intelligentsia from these tribes, who may be drawn upon to represent them in the Legislature, the Executive, as well as the Services'.[144] Thakkar expressed the hope that the 'very large number' of tribals receiving a college education would soon 'come out and rub shoulders, not only with Harijan graduates, but also with advanced communities in the country'. However, he reiterated the need for State-sponsored 'schemes of special measures of advancing their education

[143] A. V. Thakkar, 'Education among Tribal People very backward: State's responsibility for their Advancement', in *Leader*, dated 11 July 1945, reproduced in *Aboriginals' Cry in the Wilderness*, pp. 9–13.

[144] Ibid., p. 12.

and social betterment'. A consequence of the debate with Ambedkar was that education came to be a defining aspect of tribal backwardness in the nationalist imaginary.

In April 1946, the Congress took over the reins of power in the Central Provinces and Berar. Upon its behest, A. V. Thakkar drew up a five-year plan for the backward areas of the province. In this short report, Thakkar emphasised the need for a comprehensive welfare plan that would 'embrace along with economic betterment, the improvement questions of … education, health and communications' for the tribals of the Province.[145] For the purposes of administrative convenience, he divided the backward areas of the entire Province into ten contiguous zones with roughly equal population levels. He proposed that every year, five schools should be started in every zone, each of which would be manned by at least two teachers. 'Aboriginal conditions' would be taken into account while framing the syllabus. Half of the total school hours would be utilised to impart education in the three Rs (Reading, Writing, and Arithmetic), while the rest would be devoted to manual work such as 'agriculture, gardening, some handicrafts suited to the locality, physical training and outdoor games'. If the scheme was to run smoothly, Thakkar envisaged that about 250 new schools had to be opened and run by the newly established Welfare Department of the Government of C.P. and Berar.

These educational policies were soon to have an impact on tribal regions within the Princely States as well. In December 1947, four months after the State of Bastar acceded to the Indian Union, Thakkar Bapa reached the newly formed district. He addressed a public meeting at Jagdalpur Public Library, where he announced scholarships for aboriginal girls who attended the primary schools. When the Social Education scheme was launched in Jagdalpur town for the education of adults, it was Thakkar who inaugurated it on 1 May 1948: he gave his blessings and 'the first word taught in his presence in each of these centres was the beloved word of the Hindus, i.e. "Ram"'.[146]

[145] A. V. Thakkar, *Five Year Plan for the Betterment of the Condition of the People in the Backward Areas of Central Provinces & Berar*, n.d., p. 3.

[146] S. P. Shrivastava, 'Bapa's Work for the Murias and Marias of Bastar District, C.P. and Berar', T. N. Jagadisan and Shyamlal (compiled and eds), *Thakkar Bapa: Eightieth Birthday Commemoration Volume*, Madras: Diocesan Press, 1949, p. 132.

Conclusion

This chapter charted out an evolutionary journey of 'Backwardness' vis-à-vis 'Aboriginal and Hill Tribes' in western India during the late colonial period. Until World War I, both concepts were ill-defined and offered no clear-cut yardsticks. However, the constitutional reforms promised by the British unleashed a variety of representational claims. Beginning with the 1921 Census reports, vigorous dynamics followed in the search for who was backward (and on what grounds). This process precipitated several changes in the official taxonomies of the colonial State, some of which were inspired by the reformist movements. Thus, a far-reaching classificatory ferment catalysed semantic shifts in official and non-official terminology/ nomenclature. For instance, in the Bombay Primary Education Rules, 1924, the category of Depressed Classes clubbed together both the 'untouchables' and Aboriginal Tribes. However, while the former had an Ambedkar, the aboriginal interests were represented only by nationalists like Thakkar. This pointed to the deep chasm in representative politics when many groups did not have elites to voice their interests. Each of these cognitive categories held deep implications for the constitutional politics that played itself out later. Perhaps the most profound imprint of this politics of ideas was on the exploited and marginalised sections of the Indian population in general and the tribal communities in particular.

Conceptually, this chapter argues that 'backwardness' emerged as a relational category for the groups seen as 'Backward' occupied that position in relation to others deemed 'Advanced'. The respective status of the various caste/tribe groups on this teleological spectrum could be traced by foregrounding achievements in the realm of 'education'. Hence, the discourse of backwardness was primarily informed by this criterion. In the 1921 Bombay Census report, Sedgwick proposed the notion of a caste-based 'Hinduistic Scale' in the realm of literacy and education and placed different communities into schedules of Advanced, Intermediate, or Backward. The idea was soon reflected in legislation on educational matters and other official enquiries. With the publication of the Starte Committee report in 1930 and the subsequent institutionalisation of a dedicated officer and board for 'Backward Classes', notions of backwardness in educational terms as well as the legitimacy of massive State intervention to ameliorate the deficit was further entrenched in Bombay. In this process, the participation of nationalists like Thakkar further crystallised the immense educational backwardness of 'Aboriginal and Hill Tribes' in the administrative discourse.

Nevertheless, in contra-distinction to educationally 'Advanced' groups such as Brahmins, the tribal groups embodied the other extreme end, that is, 'Backward', in the educational spectrum. Their educational status was compared to a black hole, a near hopeless situation that was very hard to remedy. This directly affected the potential emergence of true tribal representatives who could represent their interests in legislative and administrative bodies. Thus, their extreme educational backwardness was seen as a factor limiting their participation in a future Indian democracy. This idea is exemplified in all provincial enquiry reports and found a climax in the public debate between Ambedkar and Thakkar in 1945.

This chapter is also an attempt to chart out the intellectual and political trajectory of nationalist intervention in the tribal question during the last three decades of colonial rule. During this phase, the debate on the idea of scheduling gradually, but increasingly, came to frame the background for visualising the future of aboriginal tribes. In the beginning, the resolution of the tribal predicament was quite clearly marginal to the Gandhian mass movements. My evidence also suggests that until the Cadogan Amendment episode in the British Parliament resulted in a massive expansion in the number and size of partially excluded areas, the Indian National Congress lacked a definite strategy towards the instrument of scheduling. It will not be an exaggeration to argue that until this threshold moment, the anthropologically-minded British administrators appeared far more concerned with the aboriginal tribes than the Congress nationalists. However, following the rapid expansion in the list of scheduled areas in March 1936, the issue spilled over to the political domain, whereby nationalists organised themselves into associations such as the All India Excluded and Partially Excluded Areas Association, which periodically raised issues concerning tribal people. They also carried out effective propaganda inside Central and Provincial legislative assemblies, demanding that the categories of excluded/partially excluded areas be abolished. In a manner of speaking, it was the nationalists' claim that the tribes were silent as the British had deliberately kept them uneducated and tucked away in inaccessible geographic regions. This political line remained virtually unchanged until the Constitution-making exercise began in early 1947.

6

The Challenge of Backwardness

W. V. Grigson and the Aboriginal Tribes of Central India

Both conceptually and politically, the 1940s provided the temporal stage for perhaps the most important period of debate on the 'tribal question' in India. This decade demands a careful perusal as it gave rise to the catch-all terms 'Isolationists/Protectionists' *versus* 'Assimilationists/Interventionists', which began to make an appearance. In time, this binary gained such force that it continues to reverberate even today. An extremely important figure in this discourse was W. V. Grigson, who provided a very peculiar middle of the road approach to the tribal question and the politics of scheduling. It is to an analysis of his ideas that this chapter is dedicated.

The publication of reports on Bombay (1939) and Orissa (1940) was followed by Grigson's *The Aboriginal Problem in Central Provinces and Berar* in 1944. Thus, it was the third in the series of provincial reports published in the last decade of colonial rule.[1] Interestingly, this enquiry was not commissioned by a Congress government in power, and hence remains the only provincial report penned by a key member of the 'knot of men'.

It was undoubtedly J. H. Hutton who led the advocacy group arguing for a protectionist policy vis-à-vis Indian aboriginal tribes. However, following his appointment at the University of Cambridge (1937), Hutton left India. The timing was significant as it coincided with the spilling over of the administrative discourse onto the domain of popular politics, with the nationalists taking up cudgels against the instrument of scheduling. Even

[1] A. Aiyappan, *Report on the Socio-economic Conditions of the Aboriginal Tribes of the Province of Madras*, Government Press, Madras, 1948. I have chosen not to analyse the Aiyappan Report because it was produced in independent India under very different discursive conditions and imperatives.

Image 6: The front cover of W. V. Grigson's book on the Maria Gonds of Bastar
Source: Internet Archive.

within the elite group of scholar-administrators, the uniform application of the Huttonian paradigm throughout the British Indian Empire did not go unchallenged. In this sense, Grigson, with his extensive administrative experience of the central Indian tribes, drew upon but also differed from his ideological predecessor. Grigson occupied a middle position on the spectrum between Hutton, who preferred total exclusion, and Thakkar, who rejected scheduling and sought the full-scale 'uplift' and 'assimilation' of the Indian aboriginal tribes. Grigson's ideas thus provide a counter-poise to both the Neo-Diffusionist anthropologists and the nationalists. Another novel aspect of his articulation was the emphasis he placed on the spread of education and development of communication in meeting the 'challenge of backwardness'.

Grigson joined the Indian Civil Service and served in the Central Provinces (C.P.) cadre. Between 1927–1931, he was the Administrator of the Bastar state and developed a lifelong passion for tribals. He chose to focus on the groups clubbed under the generic term 'Gonds', and even wrote an authoritative monograph on one such tribal group in Bastar.[2] In examining Grigson's approach to the wider tribal question in India, our narrative must begin in 1935. Grigson, then the Deputy Commissioner of Hoshangabad, submitted a memorandum to the Reforms Office, titled *The Moral and Material Elevation of the Aboriginals of the Central Provinces*.[3] In this argumentative piece, Grigson expressed a preference for partial exclusion vis-à-vis total exclusion. Articulating this position, he wrote,

> There is in total exclusion the danger of further blinding educated Indian opinion to the extent of the problem. The country rapidly approaches full self-government, and as Indians are to govern themselves, it would be fatal not to attempt from the beginning to associate them in the fullest way with all attempts to solve the problem and not to do all possible to arouse the Indian conscience to its duties in this respect. Total exclusion therefore might be a mistake.... So long as the administration was run on paternal despotism such an attitude did much to safeguard the aboriginal. Now however the aboriginal is face to face with a Hindu and Mohammadan electorate which will be actuated mainly by the self-interest of its most influential landholders and businessmen....

The winds of nationalism were sweeping the country and, being a political realist, Grigson foresaw the major objections that Indians would have to the continuation of the earlier 'man on the spot' administrative model. Hence, he saw in partial exclusion a useful expedient that, while providing effective

[2] W. V. Grigson, *The Maria Gonds of Bastar*, Oxford University Press, 1938.

[3] Memorandum by Mr W. V. Grigson, I.C.S., Deputy Commissioner, Hoshangabad, dated 1 May 1935, *The Moral and Material Elevation of the Aboriginals of the Central Provinces*, in F. No. 4/III/35-G(B). & K.W., General (B) Branch, Reforms Office, GoI, 1935, pp. 5–10. The following extracts and paragraphs are from this source.

cover to the aboriginals, would not alienate nationalist opinion. Grigson argued that partial exclusion would ensure that the aboriginal problem would remain the 'concern of the whole province and of the ministry responsible to the legislature'. Additionally, this intense polemical debate might propel 'enlightened Indian public opinion' into becoming fully engaged with the problem. Grigson did anticipate local outcry as partial exclusion was likely to amount to 'emasculation of the powers of the legislation or dismembering of the province'. However, he remarked that it would be desirable to focus public opinion on the problem beforehand by having it investigated by a Commission.[4] Grigson categorically stated that

> unless there is partial exclusion and legislation compelling separate measures and expenditure for the aboriginal areas, I fear that the Legislature will never prove independent enough of the clamour of influential constituents to devote to the aboriginal the heavy expenditure which will be needed on any real uplift measures.

Grigson recommended partial exclusion for the tracts in which 'aboriginal islands exist in the middle of a predominantly Hindu populace'.[5]

Elsewhere in the memorandum, Grigson firmly opposed elections and preferred the nomination of aboriginal representatives in the Provincial Legislature of Central Provinces and Berar. This was once again in marked similarity to the position forwarded by Hutton and Mills, who preferred nominations to elections. However, by choosing to send aboriginals themselves to the Legislatures, Grigson was negating Hutton's principle: that the best representatives of aboriginal interest were sympathetic European officials.

Now let us return to the 1944 report *per se*. Unlike the reports on Bombay and Orissa, we have a very good source in the Edgar Stanley Hyde papers at Cambridge with which to reconstruct the backdrop against which the report was written. The genesis of Grigson's enquiries lay in a note by the Governor of the Central Provinces and Berar, Sir Francis V. Wylie,[6] who, in March 1940, conducted an intensive tour of the partially excluded

[4]By this, Grigson meant a Royal Commission on the future of aboriginal communities on the lines of similar enquiries that had been conducted on the issues of labour and agriculture.

[5]It is this expression of Grigson's which has inspired the title of this monograph.

[6]'Note by the H.E. The Governor on the Condition of Aboriginal Tribes in the Balaghat and Mandla Districts' by F. V. Wylie, dated 27 March 1940, Box II, Hyde Papers, CSAS, Cambridge.

areas of the Baihar Tahsil of Balaghat and the Dindori Tahsil of Mandla districts. Proceeding on the assumption that 'our aboriginal problem is an administrative and not a legislative problem',[7] Wylie drew considerably on D. Symington's report on the partially excluded areas of Bombay Province, with which the conditions in Mandla and Balaghat had significant parallels. Touching upon fields such as medical aid, education, agriculture, excise, stock-raising, and water, Wylie suggested several ameliorative measures to rectify the state of tribal affairs. Evidently moved by what he saw during his tour, he wrote,

> The truth is that our aboriginal tribes get no concerted attention from the administration. Some of our officers are interested in them others are not. The aboriginals of the Central Provinces and Berar again belong to a number of different tribes ... we have no considered policy as regards these areas. Again their needs tend to get crowded out by the more clement demands of the developed parts of the Province.... I propose therefore that we hold a full dress enquiry on the Bombay model at once.[8]

Following this tour, Wylie appointed Grigson as the Aboriginal Tribes Enquiry Officer with effect from 1 May 1940. This was a serendipitous occasion for two reasons. *First,* the entire district of Mandla, which had revealed fascinating information throughout the course of this enquiry, had been declared a 'partially excluded area' under Section 92 of the Government of India Act, 1935. *Second,* Edgar Stanley Hyde, who had served as the Administrator of Bastar State for six years (1933–1939), was specially posted in June 1940 as the Deputy Commissioner of Mandla district. Since 1932, the district had also been home to a rising star of Indian anthropology, Verrier Elwin, who contributed enthusiastically to Grigson's enquiry. In effect, three prominent ideologues of anthropologically guided administration were spun together in an enterprise dear to them. Of course, it helped that all three were very good friends as well. The enquiry led to the publication of three documents.[9] However, instead of sifting finely through

[7]Ibid., p. 1.

[8]Ibid., p. 10.

[9]W. V. Grigson, *Notes on the Aboriginal Problem in the Mandla District,* Government Printing, C.P. & Berar, Nagpur, 1940; *The Aboriginal Problem in the Balaghat District: A Preliminary Report,* Government Printing, C.P. & Berar, Nagpur, 1941; *The Aboriginal Problem in the Central Provinces & Berar,* Government Printing, C.P. & Berar, 1944.

the reports, I will outline some of the overt and covert ideological positions embedded in their narrative structure and highlight their differences with the Huttonian paradigm.

Spanning more than 500 pages, Grigson's report was the single largest document concerning the partially excluded areas in British India.[10] However, the author himself was able to continue as the Aboriginal Tribes Enquiry Officer for only a few months. The rapidly changing political conditions and the outbreak of World War II meant additional responsibilities for the civil servants of Central Provinces and Berar. Being an able, efficient officer who was much in demand, Grigson was at the same time made Joint Secretary to the Government in Police, Jail, General, Administration, Political, and Military and Ecclesiastical departments.[11] Although he continued as the Aboriginal Enquiry Officer, these responsibilities compounded pressures on the time available to him for conducting tours in the partially excluded areas. In April 1941, he was appointed Secretary to the Governor of the Province, a post he held until February 1942. After a brief furlough, Grigson returned to Hyderabad State as the all-important Revenue Member of the Nizam's Executive Council. Such frequent changes meant that the full report was finally completed only in November 1942, that too under the pressure of heavy administrative charges, both in Nagpur and Hyderabad. Grigson realised that he had been unable to devote the required effort towards the enquiry, and admitted that the report was 'somewhat disjointed and deals with certain terms of reference more fully than with others'.[12]

Nevertheless, to a historian working on Central Indian tribes, this is a fascinating document precisely for its *ad hoc* character and intermittent writing spread over a tumultuous period of two-and-a-half years in the middle of World War II (1940–1942). Seen along with Grigson's two other published reports on Mandla and Balaghat, the output was not inconsiderable at all.[13] It remains an important document for our purposes

[10]W. V. Grigson, *The Aboriginal Problem in the Central Provinces & Berar*, Government Printing, C.P. & Berar, Nagpur, 1944 (Vanya Prakashan, Bhopal, 1993).

[11]Grigson, *The Aboriginal Problem*, p. 4.

[12]Ibid., p. 5.

[13]Governor Wylie, who appointed Grigson as the Aboriginal Enquiry Officer, wrote a few years later that this enquiry report was 'a little undigested' but was 'a mine of information', D.O. No. D.5523-P/44, Political Department, New Delhi, 23 November 1944; From: F. V. Wylie; To: P. J. Patrick, India Office, Whitehall, IOR/L/P&J/7/6787, p. 107.

as it establishes the shift in emphasis that was taking place in the discourse on the tribal population earlier framed by Hutton and Mills. We must also remember that Grigson's report was published three years after Elwin's *Loss of Nerve* and a year after the publication of Ghurye's influential volume on the aboriginals. Furthermore, it was in Hyderabad that Grigson's passionate quest for the welfare of aboriginal tribes materialised in a series of extremely well thought out and implemented experiments, especially in the fields of education and land reforms. Hence, Grigson's C.P. and Berar reports require extremely delicate handling as they are rare historical documents and products of multiple intellectual, administrative, and political trends.

An illustration in this respect would be Grigson's attitude towards 'Tribal Religions', which was once the central tenet of Hutton's approach to the aboriginal question. With one exception, Grigson completely jettisoned the figures given for tribal religions in the statistical information provided in the report. Grigson explained this omission in the following manner,

> ... I have omitted all reference to the figures of tribal religion. They are meaningless. It is impossible to say when a man's religion ceases to be tribal or begins to be Hindu. Fluctuations in the percentages of aboriginals returned as animists, or tribal by religion occur in different districts at different censuses and are no true index even of the degree to which the tribal religion is becoming hinduised. Much depends upon the approach to this question made by individual enumerators. If I were myself an enumerator, I could guarantee to make almost all aboriginals except the super-hinduised Raj-Gond landlord answer that they were tribal by religion.[14]

Another instance in the report that indicated Grigson's ideological evolution was the breaking up of the notion of the aboriginal as the 'original son of the soil'. Instead, the new paradigm indicated a shift towards a notion of 'backwardness', which included other, non-aboriginal communities as well. Illustrating this trend as well as his justification for State intervention through the territorial segregation of tracts predominantly inhabited by aboriginals, Grigson wrote,

> In the really backward aboriginal tracts the aboriginal way of life is largely shared by all the villagers whether aboriginal or members of backward Hindu castes or the Scheduled Castes. Many officials and others answering the questionnaires in this enquiry have protested against special treatment for aboriginals as unfair, there being no reason

[14]Grigson, *The Aboriginal Problem*, pp. 7–8.

> in their view why they should be specially selected from amongst their fellow Indians for remedial measures. The special reason is that though they constitute 3,000,000 of the population of the province they have been neglected in the past and are educationally and politically unfitted to hold their own and protect their interests in the provincial legislature and local bodies, or against the exploiter. Not a tenth of the special steps that have been taken for the Scheduled Castes or harijans has been taken for the aboriginals. Moreover in the Partially Excluded Areas at least, probably also in the other backward areas, it will be impossible to exclude members of the backward and menial castes from the benefits of the measures designed for the aboriginal.[15]

Many such curious instances abound in Grigson's report of the newly emerging ideas concerning the 'tribal question'. However, I will concentrate only on a few aspects of the report itself and juxtapose them with the correspondences between Grigson and Hyde. Both British civil servants had served for a considerable stretch of time in Bastar, where they pioneered a new administrative policy for 'aboriginal welfare' which has now been largely forgotten. Another theme dealt with briefly in this section is Grigson's stance on the effectiveness of modern representative institutions through the medium of elections in predominantly tribal areas. It is through these expressions that Grigson was articulating a distinct approach towards the amelioration of educational backwardness amongst aboriginal tribes in Central India.

In a letter to Grigson dated 6 July 1940, Hyde emphasised the need for total exclusion in the tribal areas in C.P. and Berar. He completely espoused the Hutton–Mills framework of protective policies, including not allowing outsiders to operate without a license.[16] He also wanted a personalised administration with a high level of centralisation of powers in the office of the District Officer, the redoubtable 'man on the spot'. Hyde's letter elicited an extremely interesting reply from Grigson, who remarked that although he sympathised with Hyde's suggestions concerning the 'drastic reorganization of aboriginal administration', the aboriginal problem in the Central Provinces was characteristically different from the one in the North-East Frontier. Grigson remarked, '(O)*ur aboriginals live, broadly speaking,*

[15]Ibid., p. 10.

[16]Letter No. 94-C/40, dated Mandla, 6 July 1940; From: E. S. Hyde; To: W. V. Grigson, Box II, Hyde Papers, CSAS, Cambridge.

as large or small islands in a sea of Hindus.'[17] Also, the kind of isolation experienced by the Assam tribals was not evident in Central India, as the '(M)ain lines of communication by road and rail across India pass through aboriginal areas'. As a case in point, Grigson used population statistics to highlight the fact that even the 'most "advanced" districts include primitive patches'. In Grigson's mind, the main challenge in aboriginal protection was the issue of protecting the tenancy rights of the aboriginals. Outlining the recent spillover of the administrative discourse onto the domain of popular politics, Grigson wrote,

> The psychological mistake ... was that the suspicious politicians have been able to misrepresent Sections 91 and 92 of the Government of India Act as typical of the British distrust of Indian self-government, instead of Indians themselves being in any way associated with the policy that lies behind the Sections. The Sections have been valuable in opening the eyes of Indian public opinion to the aboriginal problem, but had there been a Royal Commission on the subject before or immediately after the Act was enacted, the result might have been better.[18]

We shall now return to a few notable features of the C.P. and Berar report. Grigson divided the document into four main parts. After the introduction, the second part of the report dealt with the 'Loss of Aboriginal Land and Debt'. This was the largest section, dealing with land alienation, bond-service, and indebtedness, and constituted more than half the text of the report. The third section dealt with 'Nation Building other than Education', and the main themes in this section were the works of various government departments (Agriculture, Veterinary, Co-operative, and Industries), Excise Policy, Forest Policy, and Public Health. The fourth and final section was titled 'Political and General Education and Conclusion'. Although Grigson does not state it anywhere, it is clear from the aforementioned classifications that in his scheme, aside from economic and welfare measures (dealt with in Parts II and III of the main report), 'Political and General Education' were the prime 'nation-building' activities. It is to these issues that I shall now turn.

---

[17]D.O. No. 185, dated Chhindwara, 12 July 1940; From: W. V. Grigson, Aboriginal Tribes Enquiry Officer, C.P. & Berar; To: E. S. Hyde, Deputy Commissioner, Mandla, Box II, Hyde Papers, CSAS, Cambridge; emphasis mine.

[18]Ibid.

Like his predecessors, Hutton and Mills, Grigson, too, was decidedly against elections in tribal areas. Explaining his stance, he wrote,

> There is a general tendency on the part of the educated public to assume that if the aboriginal be given the vote, all his troubles will ultimately disappear. At present, however, there is little sign of either the aboriginal understanding the power of the vote and of his own numbers to secure representation, or of the non-aboriginal candidate interesting himself in aboriginal needs once the election is over, until another election begins to impend.[19]

Taking the case of the Central Provinces and Berar, Grigson pointed out that under the Government of India Act, 1935, only one seat was reserved for backward areas and tribes. In contrast, the numerically commensurate Scheduled Castes had been given twenty reserved seats and were 'far more intelligent and politically minded than the aboriginals'. Only two other Gond candidates won from other seats in the 1937 elections. Thus, their representation (three seats) in a House of 112 was highly inadequate. However, Grigson opined that with the exception of Mandla, where there was a definite move to secure Gond votes for their own candidates,

> Generally speaking, aboriginals went to the poll because they were persuaded that it was a Government order that they should do so and that they would be fined if they did not, and in order to put a vote in 'Gandhiji's box'. The election in fact differed little from a totalitarian election for a list of approved candidates.... It is of course arguable that the desire of the Gond to vote in 'Gandhiji's box' meant that he had imbibed enough political propaganda to believe that a vote for the Congress would bring in a new era; as to the features of this new era or the means by which it would be achieved he was ignorant, and he never understood that the result of putting papers into the box would be that a certain Hindu gentleman from a distant town would be constituted his representative in the chief council of the province.[20]

The aboriginal representation in local institutions of self-government was similar. Grigson offered numerous instances to argue that all the district councils or local boards in the partially excluded areas of C.P. and Berar had neglected 'aboriginal uplift'.[21] These bodies were constituted 'without any effective aboriginal voice and without any members appointed to watch over

[19]Grigson, *The Aboriginal Problem*, p. 371.
[20]Ibid., p. 373.
[21]Ibid., p. 375.

aboriginal interests.'[22] Concerning the state of affairs in local self-governing bodies, he wrote,

> ... as they stand there is little hope of assistance for the aboriginal since he has little chance of securing election, and few aboriginals who are elected are seldom of sufficient influence, education and intelligence to be able to understand District Council and Local Board powers and procedure or to influence the other members to pay due attention to aboriginal needs.[23]

From here, Grigson linked the issue of education to that of effective aboriginal representation. He quoted with approval Pandit Ravi Shankar Shukla, the Premier of C.P. and Berar, who had said that 'unless the representatives are sufficiently educated their mere presence will not result in increasing interest being taken by the District Councils in the welfare of the aborigines.'[24] Grigson noted that most of the non-official witnesses answering his questionnaires had 'suggested that franchise itself teaches voters its meaning and that an elected member even if uneducated is preferable to a nominated member, perhaps on the principle of *kursi kam sikha deti hai*'.[25] However, he disapproved of this notion and suggested that for some time to come, the aboriginal representatives would have to be nominated ones. For the aboriginal areas, Grigson recommended that independent local boards should replace the district councils as the latter were inevitably biased towards the demands of the 'voters of the open country', who were 'bound to retain for a long time far more political influence than the voters of the backward areas.'[26]

Nandini Sundar has shown that Grigson was the progenitor of the Panchayat scheme in Bastar State, which was purportedly based on the idea of tribal customary laws.[27] We have seen how, in the early and mid-1930s, Hutton was vigorously pushing this idea forward as the main pivot of the differential treatment of predominantly tribal areas. In the C.P. and Berar report, too, Grigson comes back to this idea, which was based on the notion

[22]Ibid., p. 387.

[23]Ibid., p. 382.

[24]Ibid.; emphasis in the original.

[25]Ibid., pp. 382–383; emphasis in the original. 'The chair/seat (of power) itself teaches the work' (translation mine).

[26]Ibid., p. 383.

[27]Nandini Sundar, *Subalterns and Sovereigns: An Anthropological History of Bastar*, New Delhi: Oxford University Press, 1999.

of the distinctiveness of these laws from those codified as Hindu Law. Grigson rued the fact that most lawyers, judges, and magistrates were quite oblivious to aboriginal law and custom. The existing literature on these laws was very thin and sketchy. Realising the difficulties, Grigson nevertheless suggested a scheme of codification of these customary laws and wrote,

> It is not an easy matter to arrive at a consistent body of tribal customary law. It would involve throughout the province a detailed anthropological enquiry conducted over a number of years by trained enquiries making use of the genealogical and other methods, supplementing the notoriously defective memory of the average aboriginal as to his immediate ancestors from the records of the various settlements that have taken place since the Central Provinces came under the British rule.... From my own experience I know the difficulties of such an enquiry even when confined to one tribe in one place; for the whole province, with its varying degrees of hinduisation amongst the various tribes and in the various tracts, the task would involve enquiries spread over years; so rapid is the change in the tribal outlook under the impact of modern conditions that at the end of the enquiry what was true at the beginning of the enquiry might have ceased to be true. That is why I stress the desirability of greater recourse to reference to arbitration panchayats of civil cases involving a decision on tribal law and custom.[28]

While Grigson was extremely supportive of the 'village or purely local tribal panchayat', which was essential for indigenous institutions to survive, he was also keen that as a check on the possible arbitrariness of these local bodies, 'group panchayats' with powers of appellate jurisdiction must exist.[29] According to Grigson, it was these bodies that should be cultivated for both justice and administration, as 'regular elections by ballot would be too advanced at the present stage'. Grigson wrote,

> In time no doubt nomination of candidates and voting would become more formal operations as the people come gradually to appreciate their power of choosing members of these group panchayats and the advantage of the group panchayat being at hand to give decisions in petty civil and criminal cases for which they now have to go to distant courts.[30]

[28]Grigson, *The Aboriginal Problem*, pp. 388–389.
[29]Ibid., p. 391.
[30]Ibid., p. 392.

Grigson recommended the Union Board system of Bengal as the best pattern of local government institutions suitable for backward areas. He remarked that such an organisation was better geared for the 'political training of the backward tribes than in the ineffective scattered Village Panchayats'. The small compact areas of these units would provide a reasonable chance to acquaint voters with the candidates, and this system was 'particularly sound for areas where the tribal organization has broken down'.[31] Ultimately, Grigson argued that the Union Board system would provide the pool of electors for the district councils as well as the provincial legislatures, which

> would ensure that the backward tribes through the experienced elders selected by them as members of the Union Boards or group panchayats selected their representatives in the legislature and the larger local bodies by an intelligent vote, instead of at present flocking like sheep into a pen to put pieces of paper into a box for no purpose intelligible to them.[32]

Lastly, Grigson recommended that in all schools and training colleges in the aboriginal areas, pupils should be given training in the meanings of local bodies and adult franchise. This should be done through their own school panchayat and elections, as well as by providing practical instruction in civil duties and responsibilities.[33]

Another major point of departure from the views of Hutton and Mills was the issue of education. While the frontier administrators had noted that education was undesirable, Grigson believed it was a crucial area where massive State intervention was much needed. He noted that it was 'lack of education that leaves the aboriginal so much at the mercy of his exploiters and prevents him from using his numerical superiority to control local bodies and properly influence Government through Provincial Legislature'.[34]

Grigson recommended that tribal children be given instruction in their own languages, such as Gondi and Korku. Although this was a challenging task as they lacked a script, he was of the opinion that this problem could be overcome. Other major recommendations concerned the special training of aboriginal teachers, who would then be recruited to work in these areas. In fact, in Hyderabad, along with Christoph von Furer-Haimendorf,

[31] Ibid., p. 393.
[32] Ibid., p. 394.
[33] Ibid., p. 395.
[34] Ibid., p. 396.

Grigson had already begun work on a pioneering scheme of education. He approvingly quoted the full text of Elwin's reply to his questionnaire on aboriginal education.[35] Elwin had written that the aims of any scheme of aboriginal education should be:

> (a) to conserve and develop aboriginal culture, religion and tribal institutions; (b) so to equip the aboriginal that he will be able not only to defend himself against those elements of civilisation that threaten to destroy or degrade him, but also to take his place in this rapidly changing world and make his contribution to it; and (c) to improve his economic condition.[36]

Elwin's note ended with the following words:

> The matter is very urgent. If the schools of the existing type are opened on a large scale and with rules of compulsion, the result will be disaster to the aboriginals, disaster comparable to that which has decimated similar people in the Pacific and elsewhere. Only by the application of scientific research, by the utmost caution, by centralized control, can this unhappy result be avoided.[37]

Coming towards the end of the C.P. and Berar Report, the above extract is symptomatic of the continuities and changes between the views of Hutton and Mills versus those expressed by Grigson and Elwin. While the former group viewed education with unabashed disdain, the latter viewed it as a necessary pre-requisite for the true evolution of modern representative democratic consciousness among the Central Indian tribes. However, there is a striking continuity in the idea of the depopulation of primitive communities, as evident in the recurring example of the Pacific Islands which continued to hold appeal for both groups. The two groups also shared the paradigm of 'culture contact' as developed by Rivers and Balfour, in which their emphasis was on the pursuance of a policy of 'protection' that would enable the tribal communities to maintain their cultural distinctiveness. From other pieces of evidence mentioned above, it is also clear that although the notion of tribal cultures being distinct from Hinduism was shared by the two sets of ideologues, the latter (Grigson–Elwin) attached less importance to it. Both Grigson and Elwin were uneasy with Hutton's notion of 'Tribal Religions'. The continuity, however, is stark on the issue of 'tribal

[35]Ibid., pp. 399–405.
[36]Ibid., pp. 399–400.
[37]Ibid., p. 405; emphasis mine.

customary law', which both groups regarded as central to their conception of the cultural distinctiveness of Indian tribal communities.

Among the other notable departures which the C.P. Report establishes was Grigson's advocacy of increased communications. While Hutton and Mills were vehemently against the 'opening up' of aboriginal areas, Grigson was less antithetical to the idea. As we have seen earlier, he drew a sharp distinction between the tribal areas on the North-East Frontier and those in the Central Indian belt. Grigson wrote,

> It may certainly be conceded that it would be premature to open up to the outside world by all-weather roads the most backward tracts of the province in their present stage of educational and economic development. At the same time our aboriginals as a whole have been more exposed ... and [they are] working to[wards] contacts with the modern Indian world, and the time has come perhaps in their own interests to make the outer world more accessible to them and their villages more accessible to the protecting officials. The very backward areas not yet ready to be exposed to all that the all-weather road and the motor-bus bring in their train.... But elsewhere better communications are essential, and if the reforms advocated in this report are pushed through, there will be no undue danger of accelerating exploitation.[38]

In the last segment of the report, Grigson undertakes a survey of the various measures and studies on the aboriginals in various British Indian Provinces and a few Indian states. He argued that, with the exception of D. Symington (author of the Bombay Report), the overwhelming assumption belying these activities was that there was little difference between the Scheduled Caste and the aboriginal problem. Grigson was against this understanding and remarked that the 'problems of the aboriginals are entirely distinct'.[39] Consequently, any piecemeal approach towards their welfare was unreasonable. For the Central Provinces, Grigson recommended that a senior ICS officer designated as the 'Protector of Aboriginals' should be put in charge of all the activities to be conducted for their welfare. He also recommended the establishment of a special 'Aboriginal Tribes' department,[40] if the special officer was 'to effect a real

[38]Ibid., p. 413.
[39]Ibid., p. 423.
[40]Ibid.,p. 427.

sustained improvement of aboriginal conditions.'[41] Elaborating his stance, Grigson wrote,

> The important thing about the aboriginal problem is that it cannot merely be treated along with other rural welfare problems, but is a thing *sui generis* which, without a special organization of its own, will once more be relegated to the pending shelf or to the record-room where it has lain for so many years.[42]

Lastly, Grigson made a few important remarks about the concurrent debate on the partial exclusion of predominantly aboriginal tracts. In an attempt to defend a policy that was increasingly coming under nationalist attack, Grigson wrote,

> It was not the purpose of Partial Exclusion to label or stigmatize for all time any areas of any province as backward: these provisions of the Government of India Act merely drew attention to an existing state of affairs. In the province almost every era of civilisation from the Stone Age to the twentieth century can be seen in the life of different communities in different districts. Can it be asserted that a Kamar or a Bharia-Bhumia or a Maria can by a stroke of pen be transformed into an intelligent citizen and voter in a commonwealth? Partial Exclusion came therefore only to protect the interests of tribes not yet fit to hold their own under the stress of modern civilisation until they have been fitted to hold their own. All that has been said before in this Report makes it quite clear that even the more intelligent of the Gond and Korku need protection, which they have not had in the past. The aboriginals as a whole have lost, or are losing, their language, their culture, their dancing, their tribal solidarity, their lands and their laughter, and are sinking to the status of a depressed class of landless labourers.[43]

Grigson argued that little legislative attempt had been made in the past to obviate the negative influence on tribal communities. Laws that were suitable for the advanced areas were clearly unsuitable for predominantly aboriginal tracts, 'especially when different treatment is necessary in reality for different sections of the aboriginals themselves.' The excise and prohibition laws were made to address the social reform movements of the 'advanced plains.' Also,

[41]Ibid., p. 422.
[42]Ibid., p. 424.
[43]Ibid., p. 425.

there was a 'wholesale neglect of specialized nation-building activities in all the backward areas'.[44]

According to Grigson, the controversy on partial exclusion had been immensely beneficial, as

> Partial Exclusion really for the first time threw the aboriginal problem into the limelight and made it through the Ministers the concern of the whole legislature and of the provincial public. It thus associated enlightened public opinion with the solution of the problem, for in the long run the only true safeguard of the aboriginal is an enlightened public opinion alive to, and ready to tackle the problem, and the position was that the aboriginal, by the constitutional changes, was brought face to face with an overwhelmingly Hindu and Muslim electorate actuated mainly by self-interest of its most influential landholders, businessmen and townsmen. Without Partial Exclusion and Special Responsibilities the new Ministers might have found it politically very difficult to resist the clamour of the vocal portion of the new electorates for the spending of Government revenue mainly on amenities and improvements for the towns and villages where the voters are most advanced.[45]

Finally, Grigson lauded the powers to tweak laws unsuitable to aboriginal areas under the provisions of partial exclusion as 'most valuable'.[46] He also opined that for the aboriginals of the Central Provinces and Berar, isolation was not 'practical politics'.[47] In his concluding paragraph, Grigson referred to the ongoing debate as 'somewhat sterile', because there were no 'out-and-out isolationists'.[48]

Conclusion

This chapter has tried to show that Grigson was influenced by the anthropological ideas advanced by Hutton and Mills. Like them, he believed that the aboriginal communities were a distinct element of the Indian population and that 'culture contact' had had a degenerating influence on

[44] Ibid.

[45] Ibid., pp. 425–426.

[46] Ibid., p. 426.

[47] Ibid., p. 428.

[48] Ibid., p. 429.

them. There is evidence to suggest that Hutton visited Bastar State during the course of the 1931 Census operations, when Grigson was nearing the end of his term as its Administrator. Grigson had also contributed some ethnographic pieces in the main report of the 1931 Census. Like Hutton and Mills, Grigson saw himself as the spokesperson for espousing and articulating the interests of the tribal communities. He also saw the necessity of preserving and encouraging tribal customary laws as the key to fostering the cultural autonomy of these communities. However, there are important differences as well. Most notably, from the time of the excluded and partially excluded areas debate, Grigson favoured the provisions of partial exclusion for the predominantly aboriginal areas of Central India. By the early 1940s, he had also discarded the notion of 'tribal religion' as separate from Hinduism. In the 1940s, Grigson became well-known for his tremendous acumen in administering predominantly aboriginal areas, through a deft handling of popular demands and the simultaneous introduction of reforms. More scholarly work on understanding the contributions of this fascinating personality needs to be conducted.

The tribe, in all these debates, emerges as a conceptual category with a series of competing imaginations. In this respect, Grigson occupied a middle-of-the-road position between the likes of Hutton and Thakkar. In contra-distinction to total exclusion (Hutton) and complete assimilation into the Hindu 'mainstream' (Thakkar), Grigson forcefully argued that partial exclusion was preferable to total exclusion.

Linked to this was Grigson's advocacy of increased communications in tribal regions. While Hutton and Mills were vehemently opposed to the 'opening up' of aboriginal areas, Grigson desired better communications and infrastructure related to travel. Finally, a major point of departure is represented by Grigson's views on the issue of education. While Hutton deemed modern education undesirable, Grigson held that it was one crucial area where massive State intervention was needed. He stressed the need for aboriginal education by arguing that 'Political and General Education' were prime 'Nation-Building' activities. Grigson also recommended that tribal children be given instruction in their own languages.

It is clear from the evidence presented until now that the theoretical cohesion of the knot of men was beginning to break open. While Hutton deployed the Neo-Diffusionist arsenal to great effect and secured a massive expansion in the areas scheduled under the categories of excluded and partially excluded areas, the discursive scene witnessed a relative vacuum after he left for Cambridge in 1937. Moreover, when individual figures applied Huttonian ideas to their respective regions and landscapes, a divergence of opinion emerged. Consequently, we have in Grigson a figure who, being well-versed in the socio-political dynamics amongst the Central Indian tribal communities, took recourse to a significantly different set of interpretations and policy measures. Even while the island imagery developed—for the primitive communities in the Melanesian Islands continued to dominate the discourse ('large or small islands in a sea of Hindus')—the main theoretical challenge to the Huttonian paradigm was to emerge soon from within its own ranks.

This figure, whose articulations in the 1940s were to precipitate a decline and the eventual disintegration of the main planks of the anthropologists, was Verrier Elwin. Elwin shifted positions several times in the 1930s and 1940s and, in his manoeuvres, useful fault-lines were revealed. Emerging as the second hinge of the late colonial discourse, Elwin's inconsistencies and ambivalences provide a very useful window to understand the tumultuous 1940s.

7

Re-examining the Ghurye–Elwin Debate

The Aboriginal Tribe as 'Backward Hindu'

For decades, the intellectual history of the discourse on tribal populations and their future in independent India has been trapped within the binary limits of the Isolation/Protection *versus* Intervention/Assimilation debate. In order to move away from this divide and scholarly consensus, some fundamental and well-established notions need to be re-examined. To begin with, no scholar seems to have asked a few fundamental questions which undergirded these conceptual frameworks: Protection from whom? Isolation from what? Assimilation into whom? Intervention into what? Were these terms and epithets neologisms, or were they merely old wine in a new bottle? What were the intellectual continuities and changes between the earlier variant of the discourse vis-à-vis the 1940s, when these seemingly new terms burst forth on the discursive terrain of the tribal question in India?

The preceding chapters have already traced the earlier history of the emergence of these catch-all terms and how another key associated term in this discourse on tribal futures, that is, 'civilisation', really stood for the combined forces of law, democracy, and organised religions. This chapter argues that the tone and tenor of the discourse on tribal populations was not set by the debate between Verrier Elwin and G. S. Ghurye, as has often been claimed. In fact, the much vaunted Ghurye–Elwin debate never really took place and the real intellectual battle happened between Thakkar and Elwin. This chapter will also analyse the role played by Verrier Elwin in recasting the discourse on the scheduling of predominantly tribal areas. After the departure of Hutton, it was Elwin who emerged as the hinge of the discourse on tribal communities and their future in an independent India. This changeover was set to have a long-lasting impact on the entire discourse in an India on the cusp of political independence from British rule.

Image 7: Sketch of Harry Verrier Holman Elwin

Source: By permission of Oxford University Press Archive.

Caught between extreme adulation and professional disdain in the times he lived through, Harry Verrier Holman Elwin remains an enigmatic figure in Indian anthropology even today. Elwin was an Oxford-educated Englishman whose remarkable life has been captured in a much celebrated biography by Ramachandra Guha.[1] However, as we shall see, Guha's portrayal of Elwin is quite monochromatic and an intellectual enquiry into this Christian missionary turned Congress nationalist turned 'Philanthropologist' reveals the many fault-lines that characterised the milieu that the 'Mr. Elwin' of Ghurye attempted to navigate through. We shall also analyse the famous book by G. S. Ghurye which marks the high watermark of nationalist position on the tribal question in India.

[1]Ramachandra Guha, *Savaging the Civilized: Verrier Elwin, His Tribals, and India*, New Delhi: Oxford University Press, 1999. However, there are many problems with the book, as established by Virginius Xaxa in 'Elwin's tribals,' *Economic and Political Weekly* 36 (18), 5 May 2001, pp. 1519–1520.

Elwin and the Indian Tribes

Elwin was introduced to the plight of the tribals in Central India by none other than A. V. Thakkar.[2] The two seem to have come in contact in Pune and worked together closely while conducting an enquiry into police atrocities in Gujarat. Jamnalal Bajaj also played an instrumental role in Elwin's move towards social service among the Gonds of Central India. When Bajaj died in 1942, Elwin remembered,

> The death of Seth Jamnalal Bajaj took from us one of our oldest friends in India. It was from his lips that I first heard the words 'Gond'. In 1931 I was planning to work in Gujerat but I met Jamnalalji in Ahmedabad and he urged the claims of largely neglected aboriginals and offered us the freedom of his house and all the support that great hearted generosity could give. On his advice we explored the Betul and Chhindwara districts and finally found our present home in Mandla.[3]

In Mandla, Elwin established an organisation called the Gond Seva Mandal (later renamed as Bhumijan Seva Mandal). He was joined by Shamrao Hivale, whom he first met at the Christa Seva Sangh. Together, they started doing humanitarian work amongst the tribals. It was here that Elwin started undergoing a profound philosophical metamorphosis vis-à-vis the tribal communities, which finally compelled him to shun the Congress nationalist position.

In 1936, the Government of India had issued the Order-in-Council of the final list of excluded and partially excluded areas. The entire district of Mandla (barring Mandla town) was declared as a partially excluded area. Even earlier, given Elwin's closeness with the Congress nationalists, the local administration had interfered with his work constantly. With the tag of partial exclusion, local government officers in Mandla became even more powerful, theoretically, and it became imperative for Elwin to negotiate a truce with the government. Therefore, for Elwin, it was not just an ideological parting of ways, but a pragmatic necessity as his own work in Karanjia was being regularly stifled by petty local government officials. By cutting his perceived association with the Indian National Congress, he

---

[2]Verrier Elwin, *The Tribal World of Verrier Elwin*, New Delhi: Oxford University Press, 2002, pp. 61–62. Also see Guha, *Savaging the Civilized*, pp. 53–54.

[3]Verrier Elwin, 'Appeal for Help: Bhumijan Seva Mandal', *The Rural India*, August 1942, p. 348.

tried to mend his strained relationship with the local representatives of the colonial State.

In 1936, perhaps owing to his past record as a Christian missionary, Elwin enlisted the support of William Paton of the International Missionary Council. Paton was well-connected with the India Office and requested them to offer Elwin a chance to clear the air. Paton forwarded a letter to the India Office in which Elwin had written of 'steadily increasing differences' between himself and the Congress nationalists. For the aboriginals themselves, he could 'conceive of no greater disaster ... than the coming to power of a nationalist government'. Expounding his opposition, Elwin wrote,

> For example, it seems to be the aim of the Congress politicians to bring the aboriginals within the Hindu fold and then to treat them as though they had no special claims; they resent the establishment of Excluded and Partially Excluded Areas; they dread the claims of Anthropology to guide the administration of these areas. This company of vegetarians and teetotalers would like to force their own bourgeois and puritan doctrines on the free wild people of the forests.
>
> On the other hand, I myself consider the aboriginals to be Pre-Hindu and that the adoption of popular Hinduism will be a major disaster for them; I welcome the Excluded Areas, and only wish that there were many more of them; I consider that scientific anthropology should guide and regulate the administration of all primitive peoples and that they should not be handed over to the mercies of elected politicians who have no knowledge of their special problems and I think that the social and moral outlook of the Congress would cut the tap-root of the votality [*sic*] of aboriginal India.[4]

Thus, besides breaking away from the nationalist ranks, Elwin identified completely with the theoretical outlook of the anthropologically-minded administrators. Significant here is Elwin's formulation of aboriginals as 'Pre-Hindu', which was nearly a complete espousal of Hutton's views as postulated in the 1931 Census. It is precisely on this issue that Elwin made a major theoretical intervention which changed the course of the debate on the tribal question.

Nonetheless, such a complete ideological retreat earned Elwin an audience with the India Office. After hearing him, the officials were convinced

---

[4]Copy of a letter from Verrier Elwin to William Paton of the International Missionary Council, dated 28 October 1936, F. No. P&J 5395, 1930, in IOR/L/PJ/6/2013.

that he was a 'repentant sinner', eager to mend his relationship with the colonial State in India. Hyde Gowan (the Governor of C.P. and Berar) and R. Peel, in particular, were assured that Elwin was now completely devoted to his work among the Gonds, and that he should be given 'all the help of which we are capable'.[5] In fact, very soon Elwin was made an Honorary Magistrate in Mandla, which greatly eased his fortunes.

The timing of this truce could not have been better for Elwin had started working on multiple fronts. However, his troubles continued even after switching sides. This was the time when the Government of India Act, 1935, was being made operational and the debate in the British Parliament, particularly Churchill's controversial statement, had politicised the issue of exclusion and partial exclusion. The Congressmen had started mobilising around the issue and there was a strong chance of their coming to power in the Provinces after the elections in 1937. At the same time in his own Mandla district, a Raj-Gond movement for the Hinduisation of tribals was rapidly gaining ground. Life at Karanjia was becoming difficult and towards the end of 1936, Elwin had decided to move his base by 15 miles to the more amenable Sanhrwachhapar village in Dindori tahsil of Mandla.

In such a context, Elwin consciously began positioning himself with the anthropologists in India. In his 1936 trip to England, besides gaining an audience with the India Office, Elwin met with a number of anthropologists, such as Hutton, Seligman, Raymond Firth, and Bronislaw Malinowski. He gave a lecture at the Royal Anthropological Institute and published an article on 'Baiga Dreams' in the *British Journal of Medical Psychology*.[6] That same year also saw the publication of his book on the Central Indian tribes. Titled *Leaves from the Jungle: Life in a Gond Village*, it was based on his experience in Karanjia and won him considerable accolades and scholarly attention.

Thus, by the late 1930s, Elwin's most important achievement was gaining the trust of a few key anthropologists like Grigson, Hyde, and ultimately Hutton as well. Elwin came in contact with W. V. Grigson who in turn introduced him to others such as Edgar Hyde, who was then

---

[5]P&J 5031/36, Letter from R. Peel to R. M. Maxwell, Secretary to GoI, Home Department, dated 8 December 1936, and Personal and Confidential letter from Hyde Gowan, Governor, C.P., to Sir Findlater Stewart, Parliamentary Under Secretary of State, dated 3 January 1937, in ibid.

[6]Personal letter from Verrier Elwin to E. S. Hyde, dated 16 December 1936, Box III, Hyde Papers, CSAS, Cambridge.

serving as the Administrator of Bastar State (1933–1939). Elwin regularly corresponded with them and gradually earned their confidence through his charm, articulation, and undoubted scholarly potential. From time to time, he reiterated his commitment to the cause of the tribals. For instance, he wrote to Hyde in 1936 that 'I believe we are going to have to fight for the Gonds and other tribesmen one day, and I want to be sufficiently equipped to take anyway a little part in the battle'.[7] Elwin knew that his past was likely to haunt him and that it was important to dispel the mistrust of the sceptical and reticent English bureaucrats. In one of his earliest letters to Hyde, Elwin wrote,

> I think that I ought, for your conscience sake, tell you about my political position, because four or five years ago I made a very stupid excursion into politics, as a result of which I am still suspect! But, as a matter of fact, my interests have never really been political, though I have friends among politicians (but such friendships are not built on politics) and I came here partly to escape from all that.... I am writing this so that you needn't feel anxious that I will let you down.[8]

Alongside his humanitarian work among the Gonds, Elwin was conducting research and collecting material for a book on the Baigas. However, conditions in Mandla were rapidly worsening for him and by early 1937, his letters to Hyde constantly mention dullness, boredom, depression, disappointment, and being 'in the dumps'.[9] He opined that Congress propaganda had 'taken the life out of our Gonds'. Elwin also felt a lot of hostility as a non-official Englishman and wrote of a 'dark future' as power shifted to the hands of Hindu Congressmen who were quite ignorant of the aboriginals and treated them as mere objects for religious and political propaganda.[10]

In such a frame of mind, Elwin was toying with the idea of leaving Mandla altogether. He began looking towards Bastar as a potential field for ethnographic studies after completing his book on the Baigas. Elwin asked Hyde if he could be made the Honorary Ethnographer of Bastar State,

---

[7]Personal letter from Verrier Elwin to E. S. Hyde, dated Mandla, 9 February 1936, Box III, Hyde Papers, CSAS, Cambridge.

[8]Ibid.

[9]Personal letter from Verrier Elwin to E. S. Hyde, dated 28 October 1937, Box III, Hyde Papers, CSAS, Cambridge.

[10]Personal letter from Verrier Elwin to E. S. Hyde, dated Mandla, 20 June 1937, Box III, Hyde Papers, CSAS, Cambridge.

where they could 'work together a very fruitful partnership.'[11] Moreover, Grigson apparently encouraged Elwin to take up Bastar as a field of study, especially among the Murias.[12]

By the end of 1938, Elwin had finished his book on the Baigas. In his Referee's Report, Hutton waxed eloquent about Elwin's work, calling it the 'greatest thing of its kind that has yet been done.'[13] Hutton also agreed to write a Foreword to *The Baiga*. This was a much needed shot in the arm for Elwin, who was trying desperately to fashion himself as an anthropologist.

The year 1939 saw the publication of Elwin's first major anthropological work, *The Baiga*. It is here that he first clearly articulated his stand. Elwin argued that the provisions of the Government of India Act, 1935, which wholly or partially excluded certain areas from direct operation of legislative control, were not sufficient to prevent the degeneration of tribal groups. Instead, he advocated the establishment of a 'National Park, in which such groups could take refuge.'[14]

However, despite some rave reviews, the book failed to generate the attention that Elwin had hoped for. He went to his home country the same year and met a 'good many anthropologists.' However, England was reeling with anxiety at the possibility of a war with Germany, which seemed sure to engulf the whole of Europe. In such an atmosphere of war-mongering, Elwin returned to India 'with a deep sense of failure and disappointment.' He admitted to have tried to 'put forward the "gospel" which Hutton and Grigson and you and I' believed in. But instead of the 'hearing' he had hoped for, all that Elwin received was 'sympathy.' In the charged atmosphere of England, 'People simply were not concerned. The left-wing people were absorbed in Spain: the right wing in A.R.P. [Air Raid Precautions].'[15]

Meanwhile, Elwin was busy with other projects such as a monograph on the Agarias, an iron-smelting tribe of Central India which was steadily losing its livelihood under the double impact of heavy taxation on their

---

[11]Ibid.

[12]Personal letter from Verrier Elwin to E. S. Hyde, dated 28 October 1937, Box III, Hyde Papers, CSAS, Cambridge.

[13]Report by J. H. Hutton on 'The Baiga,' attached to a letter from Verrier Elwin to E. S. Hyde, dated Mandla, 12 December 1938, Box III, Hyde Papers, CSAS, Cambridge.

[14]Verrier Elwin, *The Baiga*, Oxford University Press, 1939.

[15]Personal letter from Verrier Elwin to E. S. Hyde, dated 12 July 1939, Box III, Hyde Papers, CSAS, Cambridge.

kilns and the infusion of cheap mill-made iron implements. Early in 1939, D. N. Majumdar gave the Presidential Address to the Anthropology Section of the Twenty-sixth Indian Science Congress at Lahore on the theme of 'Tribal Cultures and Acculturation'.[16] Both Elwin and Majumdar were interested in doing a detailed study of the institution of the *Ghotul* (youth dormitory) amongst the Murias of Bastar State. Majumdar's paper had provided a preliminary foray into the working of this institution, and Elwin must have felt it urgent to carry out a full-length study before others like Majumdar took the lead.

About this time, Elwin's *alma mater*, Merton College in Oxford, conferred upon him a research student status enabling a grant to study the Muria *ghotul*.[17] The next month, the Resident of the Eastern States approved Elwin's appointment as the 1941 Census Officer for Bastar State. This was immediately after the outbreak of World War II, which was set to change everything for the British Empire.[18]

Elwin, Bastar State, and the Loss of Nerve

In January 1940, Elwin came to Bastar 'on a longish preliminary visit especially in the Muria country'.[19] The scenic landscape of Bastar 'burst into a song' and completely overwhelmed Elwin, who was accompanied by his wife Kosi. He loved the people, who were generally poor but lived happy and content lives. Expressing unbridled praise for Hyde's work as Administrator of the State, Elwin wrote,

> It was bracing and thrilling experience, for me who am used to hearing everywhere one long tale of complaint and woe, to hear in Bastar of the love and gratitude with which you yourself and the Darbar are regarded. Bastar in the last ten years has been the brightest spot in the

[16]Presidential Address of the Section of Anthropology by D. N. Majumdar, 'Tribal Cultures and Acculturation', *Proceedings of the Twenty-Sixth Indian Science Congress, 1939*, Calcutta: Asiatic Society, 1939.

[17]Personal letter from Verrier Elwin to E. S. Hyde, dated 7 August 1939, Box III, Hyde Papers, CSAS, Cambridge.

[18]Personal letter from Verrier Elwin to E. S. Hyde, dated Mandla, 21 September 1939, Box III, Hyde Papers, CSAS, Cambridge.

[19]Personal letter from Verrier Elwin to E. S. Hyde, dated 8 December 1939, Box III, Hyde Papers, CSAS, Cambridge.

> aboriginal situation. I am wondering how to bring this home, how to apply its example, both to Congress people and the administration in British India. If only I had a stenographer I would write reams![20]

The desire expressed by Elwin in the penultimate sentence of the above extract holds the key to a nuanced understanding of his ideological evolution. How he brought 'home' the example of Bastar is well-known to the world. Undoubtedly, this was done through the pamphlet *Loss of Nerve*, wherein he juxtaposed the dire straits of the aboriginal condition in the Central Provinces (C.P.) with the mirth and gaiety he witnessed in the Bastar tribes.[21] However, before we analyse some of the ideas in this oft-quoted polemical article, it is essential to reconstruct how this pamphlet came to be written. The Hyde Papers collection at Cambridge holds the key to this riddle.

Late in 1939, Elwin wrote to Hyde, saying that he had been trying to write an essay for the Wellcombe Medal contest, possibly for some scholarly attention as well as monetary reward for conducting his Bastar research.[22] After initial difficulties due to incessant bouts of malaria and also possibly because of other work-related preoccupations (as the Honorary Ethnographer and Census Officer of Bastar State), Elwin completed this essay and submitted it in 1940. However, Elwin failed to win the award later that year (the award went to Darryl Forde[23] of the London School of Economics, who was 'practically invincible'). A jealous Elwin rued that despite getting an 'honourable mention' ('the examiners said it was of "outstanding merit"'), the essay would not be printed. Nonetheless, he expressed his intention to 'revise it and send it in again'.[24]

---

[20]Personal letter from Verrier Elwin to E. S. Hyde, dated Mandla, 11 February 1940, Box III, Hyde Papers, CSAS, Cambridge.

[21]Verrier Elwin, *Loss of Nerve: A Comparative Study of the Result of the Contact of Peoples in the Aboriginal Areas of Bastar State and the Central Provinces of India* (1941), Verrier Elwin Papers, Mss Eur D950/76, British Library.

[22]Personal letter from Verrier Elwin to E. S. Hyde, dated Mandla, 11 November 1939, Box III, Hyde Papers, CSAS, Cambridge.

[23]Forde became a noted anthropologist in Africa and later headed the Africa Institute.

[24]Personal letter from Verrier Elwin to E. S. Hyde, dated 18 September 1940, Box III, Hyde Papers, CSAS, Cambridge.

This unsuccessful essay was titled 'The Cause and Cure of the Failure of Nerve Among the Aboriginals of the Central Provinces of India'.[25] I would argue that this essay was the foundation from which emerged the iconic *Loss of Nerve*. However, before we compare the two essays, it is essential to analyse a note which Elwin prepared at the request of Edgar Hyde, which I believe is the bridge between the two texts. This five-page note, titled 'Appreciation of the effects of the present policy of the Bastar Administration on the primitive population by Mr. Verrier Elwin, M.A., Anthropologist, drawn up on February 11th 1940',[26] was most probably written in connection with the proposed reforms scheme in Bastar. In essence, it was possibly meant to be forwarded to the higher colonial bureaucracy as part of the lobbying which Hyde, Grigson, Mills, and Alfred Norvall Mitchell had embarked upon to block the introduction of a slew of administrative reforms in the Bastar State's administration. Elwin wrote that during four tours, 'preliminary to more serious research there', he was struck by the 'character of the Bastar aboriginal'.[27] Elaborating their 'special characteristics', Elwin wrote,

> They are happy and content. The standard of human enjoyment, the quality of the life they live, is comparatively high.
>
> In spite of their obvious poverty, they are of fine physique, strong and agile.
>
> Their religious and cultural institutions are flourishing—agricultural festivals, the gotul dormitory system, tribal legal and social organisation, dance and song, are still in good state of preservation.
>
> Their indigenous industries have not been destroyed. Their sense of beauty, especially the art of personal decoration, remains keen.
>
> They have a most remarkable devotion not only to the Maharaja Saheb, whom they regard as divine, but also of the Diwans, Mr. Grigson and Mr. Hyde. In the course of many years of touring and living among simple people, I have never heard administrators spoken of with such great affection and gratitude. As an intelligent Bastar Gond once told me, 'In Chhattisgarh, the people are ruled by the District Council which is full of our oppressors, the banias and money-lenders, but here we are protected and loved by the Diwan Saheb who saves us from our enemies'.[28]

[25] Typed MSS, Box III, Hyde Papers, CSAS, Cambridge.

[26] Typed MSS, File B, Box IX, Hyde Papers, CSAS, Cambridge.

[27] Ibid., p. 1.

[28] Ibid., pp. 1–2.

The above statement is remarkable because it suggests that the indicators earmarked by Hutton ('fine' physique, 'flourishing' tribal religious and cultural institutions, 'tribal legal and social organisation', a distinctive aesthetic 'sense of beauty', etc.) during the constitutional discourse on excluded and partially excluded areas in the 1930s still provided the yardstick by which to measure the state of 'tribal health'. Elwin stresses this point (reinvigorating Hutton's paradigm) when he claims as an 'anthropologist' that the above characteristics were 'symptoms of tribal health, in marked contrast to the tribal degeneracy in other parts of India and the world'.[29] Elwin had referred to the 'depopulation' phenomenon in the Pacific Islands, a pet theme of Hutton's. Also, the statement by the anonymous 'intelligent Gond' was provided as proof of the benefits of 'direct rule', which was preferable to that of the district councils dominated by the exploiters of tribal people (banias and moneylenders).

Elwin further contrasts the state of Bastar Gonds with their brethren in the Central Provinces. While the latter were experiencing 'a sense of frustration and dismay, a certain loss of nerve, depression, degradation and a decay of tribal institutions', among the former, 'tribal life and organisation still retains its old vitality'.[30] Significantly, it is at this point that Elwin asked the question: 'What is the reason for this difference?' By resorting to a comparative study, Elwin was hoping to identify a set of reasons that could explain the stark differences in their respective tribal predicaments. He identified the following factors:

> The loss of land.... The loss of the freedom of the forest.... Contact with courts and lawyers ... a (unsuitable) system of education ... economic exploitation.... The disturbance of primitive jurisprudence.... Internal reforms (by greedy self-interested leaders).... Exploitation by politicians and agitators....[31]

Incidentally, this list is almost an exact replica of the theoretical paradigm which Elwin explicated upon in the 1940 essay submitted for the Wellcombe Medal.[32] With minor changes in classifications and terminology and one major theoretical intervention, these factors also provided the framework of

---

[29]Ibid., p. 2.

[30]Ibid.

[31]Ibid., pp. 2–3.

[32]The exact list in the essay provides nine causes for the 'Depression' of the Central Provinces aboriginals. These were:

the argument espoused in *Loss of Nerve*.[33] Giving the reasons for the better conditions of the Bastar aboriginals, Elwin wrote,

> I am convinced that the reason why the Bastar aboriginal is so much happier and better than his fellow-tribesmen outside is that the Bastar administration during the last ten years has adopted prophylactic and remedial measures with regard to these very matters, which have caused such decay and confusion under popular Governments.... For example, the aboriginals in Bastar have been confirmed in their possession of land, and where they have lost it, it has often been restored. This one thing has kept them a dignified and noble people. The forests have been preserved in such a way that the aboriginals have not lost their sense of freedom and have been allowed to continue many of their traditional occupations. The establishment of the panchayat system has saved the people from the worst effects of a civilised legal system wholly unsuited to their temperament, and has preserved the tribal 'chiefs' and tribal sanctions in something of their traditional authority.... Finally, in Bastar the administration has taken effective steps to protect the tribesmen from economic exploitation, from so-called reformers, from agitators, from all others who would disturb and dislocate tribal life. The tribesmen themselves are far from taking this happy state of affairs for granted: again and again, I have heard them compare their condition in the old days before Mr. Grigson initiated the policy that has since been followed. I have never once heard any desire for change—except in regard to compulsory service

---

(1) Loss of Land (p. 10); (2) Loss of the Freedom of the Forest (p. 14); (3) Contact with Courts and Lawyers (p. 14); (4) Depression caused by an Unregulated System of Education (p. 16); (5) Depression caused by Economic Exploitation (p. 17); (6) Administrative Interference in Tribal Custom (a) Shifting Cultivation (p. 21), (b) Hunting (p. 29), (c) Distillation of Liquor (p. 29); (7) Depression caused by Excessive Taxation (p. 31); (8) The Disturbance of Primitive Jurisprudence (p. 32); (9) Decadence caused by Internal change and Reform (p. 35).

[33]The corresponding headings in the 'Causes of Depression' mentioned in *Loss of Nerve* were:

(1) Loss of Land; (2) The Loss of the Freedom of the Forest; (3) The Disappearance of Ritual Hunt; (4) Prohibition on Distillation of Liquor; (5) Nervous and Moral Exhaustion from Contact with the Law; (6) The Effect of an Unregulated System of Education; (7) Depression Caused by Economic Impoverishment; (8) The Collapse of Tribal Industries and Frustration of the Creative Impulse; (9) The Effect of External Contacts on Tribal Religion; (10) Organised Movements for Reform.

> on the roads—nor any demand for representative institutions on the lines followed in the Central Provinces.[34]

The transformation from the 1940 essay to *Loss of Nerve* (1941) is well-encapsulated in the above extract. In the latter, Elwin contrasted the Bastar tribals with the aborigines living in the Central Provinces and elaborated how measures taken by its Princely State administration followed sound anthropological principles, particularly from Grigson onwards. Through such juxtaposition, Elwin was trying to nuance the contemporary debate on scheduling around the effective regulation of 'culture contact' between aborigines and non-aborigines. The successful policy had enabled the Bastar tribals to keep their way of life comparatively free from the degenerating influences of 'civilisation'. In Elwin's narrative in *Loss of Nerve,* the Bastar aboriginal became the archetype of the 'Pure/Uncorrupted/Ideal' primitive tribal who led a happy life, thanks largely to the policy of 'protection' based on the principles of applied anthropology. In a nutshell, 'Anthropology in Administration' had come of age!

On the fundamental issue of the unsuitability of representative institutions in predominantly aboriginal tracts, Elwin shared his concerns and objections with the official knot of men. For instance, one of the reform proposals in Bastar was the introduction of representative institutions through the mechanism of elections, which was opposed tooth and nail, particularly by Grigson and Hyde. Basing his arguments on the experience of the partially excluded areas of British India, especially the Central Provinces, Elwin argued that even the Gonds chosen to represent aboriginals in the C.P. Assembly were 'all moneyed men, long since Hinduised, with no knowledge of the tribal religion, customs or necessities'. He opined that the C.P. tribals would 'infinitely prefer the direct rule of the Deputy Commissioner'.[35]

Nevertheless, the main theoretical intervention in *Loss of Nerve* was on the issue of tribal religion. Before we analyse the significance of his formulation, it can be emphasised that after Elwin broke with the nationalist ranks around the mid-1930s, he adopted the position held by Hutton and Mills which stated that in their religious beliefs, aboriginal tribes were absolutely distinct from the Hindus. As early as the first year of his Bastar study, a letter to Hyde reveals what Elwin thought on the issue.

[34]Typed MSS, File B, Box IX, Hyde Papers, CSAS, Cambridge, pp. 3–4.
[35]Ibid., p. 5.

The following letter reveals the disparaging views that Elwin held about a group called the Gond Maha Sabha, one of whose chief patrons was Jawahir Singh, the Raja of Sarangarh. Elwin wrote,

> While there (Sarangarh) I heard a lot of the inside work of the Gond Maha Sabha. This is a rather pompous term for a group which actually consists of twelve people who frame all the resolutions and such yes-men as they are able to gather from time to time.... In what possible way these people can represent the Gonds I cannot say; I would think that the interests of most of them conflict directly with the people we are concerned for.
>
> The Mahasabha has drafted a Memorial to the Governor which is so bad that Sarangarh has given it to me to re-write. The real aim of these people is to make themselves into a strong caste of Hindus which will be classed among the military races. Under Sarangarh's influence they are now saying they don't want to be Hindus; what they mean is they don't want to be low-caste Hindus. I have every sympathy with these well-to-do Gonds wanting to be classed as Rajputs, but I doubt very much if Hinduisation will benefit the poorer Gonds who will never establish their claim to be a high jat. I doubt if even any of the Gond Maha Sabha people would eat with our Dindori Gonds, for example. We must not be taken in by Wickey and Co's diatribes against Hinduism: that has all come from Sarangarh, who is a Hindu to the core, as they all are. A Hindu surely is one who worships Hindu gods, holds Hindu beliefs and follows Hindu social practices.
>
> I was depressed at Sarangarh because I felt that a Congress Government of the future is going to pay primary attention to these people who have no sort of claim to represent the real Gonds and whose influence, like all Hindu influence, is bound to be pernicious. I agree with you absolutely that 'it is all a question of protection'—but who is going to give it to them? All our efforts and love and knowledge will be swept away in a few hours when the Nationalist Hindu Governments come back to power.[36]

[36]Personal letter from Verrier Elwin to E. S. Hyde, dated Camp Sadhawan Bastar State, 6 November 1940, Box III, Hyde Papers, CSAS, Cambridge. An invitation letter to Hyde from Jawahir Singh, the Raja of Sarangarh, confirms Elwin's arguments. Drafted the very next day after Elwin's letter, Jawahir Singh called for a meeting at Sarangarh between 9–14 January 1941, which would be attended by Grigson, Furer-Haimendorf, Elwin, Archer (the Census Commissioner of Bihar), Symington (author of the Bombay Report), Bell (Census Commissioner of Orissa), R. K. Ramdhyani (Census Commissioner of C.P.), Raja of Raigarh, and zamindars

This letter suggests that, even at the end of 1940, Elwin essentially believed (or at least projected to others that he did) that the few affluent Raj-Gonds constituting the Gond Maha Sabha were false representatives of the Gonds in general. The former formed a highly Hinduised group and had little in common with their poor brethren. Much like Hutton, by categorising 'all Hindu influence' as 'pernicious', Elwin also suggested the distinctiveness of tribal religious beliefs from the Hindu mainstream. However, Elwin's attitude towards tribal religion shifted decisively in the light of his Bastar experiences. Exactly a year from the letter quoted above, Elwin wrote to Hyde that,

> I was afraid that you would not agree with what I wrote about the Hindu character of aboriginal religion, but I have been forced to that conclusion very largely, curiously enough, by a study of Bastar and the religion of the Palace in Jagdalpur. Hinduism is itself an aboriginal religion. Of course, what I call Animism, if you like to call it that, belongs to the Hindu family that puts it alongside Buddhism and Jainism. I think the members of the family are undoubtedly more attractive than the parents.[37]

The above letter was possibly written shortly after Elwin completed *Loss of Nerve*. Here, one can clearly see that Elwin's stance had changed profoundly. Tracing this metamorphosis, Elwin's biographer Ramachandra Guha has written that while in Mandla, Elwin, the social reformer, developed a 'strong dislike of Hinduism'. However, Bastar led him to discover that 'Hinduism as a theological system was not that far removed from aboriginal thought'.[38] This decisive shift towards accepting the aboriginal religion as part of the Hindu family was a major theoretical break which Elwin propounded through *Loss of Nerve*. When one compares the 'causes of depression' as outlined in this text vis-à-vis its 1940 precursor (see fns 32 and 33), the only major addition was 'The Effects of External Contact on Tribal Religion'. Under this sub-head, Elwin wrote,

---

of Phuljhar, Harai, and Palasgarh. Jawahir Singh promised 'an excellent duck shoot and a very pleasant setting to what might be rather a unique occasion when we could discuss quite informally the status and future of the ancient tribes of India and *specially their classification at the coming census*'. Jawahir Singh's letter to Hyde, dated 7 November 1940, Box III, Hyde Papers, CSAS, Cambridge; emphasis mine.

[37]Personal letter from Verrier Elwin to E. S. Hyde, dated Jagdalpur, 8 November 1941, Box III, Hyde Papers, CSAS, Cambridge.

[38]Guha, *Savaging the Civilized*, p. 137.

> The religion of the Indian aboriginal outside Assam should be regarded as a religion of the Hindu family, with a special relation to the exciting, dangerous, catastrophic Shaivite type, but as having a distinct existence of its own. For purposes of the Census, all aboriginals should be classed as Hindus by religion, but separate returns of their numbers by race should be provided. Much resentment has been caused by official, missionary and even scientific attempts to separate the tribesmen from the Hindus on religious grounds, and some of the hostility to the Census in Nationalist circles is due to this. In earlier years, the Census classified tribal religion as 'animist'; later the expression 'followers of tribal religion' was used. The test proposed was to ask a person whether he worshipped Hindu or tribal gods.
>
> This distinction was meaningless. On the one hand, the aboriginal is always willing to worship a few more gods if by doing so he can gain some material or social benefit; on the other, the Hindu has no objection to including tribal gods in a pantheon of thirty-three crores of deities. Among the Gonds Bhera Pen is easily translated into Bara Deo and then to Maha deo. It is hard to understand why the Census of India continues to record statistics or religion which every one knows are scientifically valueless and are used or misused only for political purposes. At every census there is an outbreak of Hindu missionary activity to persuade the aboriginals to return themselves as Hindus. This is a perfectly legitimate activity, and in fairness it must be said that Mohamedans and Christians are equally anxious to inflate their numbers. Any effort to prevent this does more harm than good.[39]

The above extract is significant because it was a frontal attack on the theoretical unity on the issue of 'Tribal Religion', which Hutton had achieved after much effort. He was also implicitly attacking past Census operations, which had been conducted on the principle of establishing the distinctiveness of tribal faiths from those of their 'Hindu' neighbours. Elwin reprimanded the colonial State's demographic mapping efforts to divide the Indian population on unscientific lines.[40] For him, clearly, the distinctiveness

[39]Elwin, *Loss of Nerve*, p. 35.

[40]Although there is no direct evidence in the Elwin papers, we must remember that since 1940 Elwin had been serving as the Honorary Ethnographer of Bastar State, assisting the 1941 Census operations. As such, it is highly likely that to fulfil his role adequately, Elwin studied the Census reports of 1921 and 1931, where he would have come across the debunking of the Hinduism *versus* Animism distinction as articulated by L. J. Sedgwick and J. T. Marten in the 1921 Bombay and all-India reports, respectively. For details, see Chapter 2.

of the tribes emerged from the factor of 'race'. His argument also drew a distinction between the aboriginal tribals in Assam and the rest of India. Slowly but surely, others like Grigson were converted to Elwin's argument. How crucial Elwin's Bastar experience was in enabling him to make this break becomes clearer when he wrote,

> The real problem, however, is not whether Gonds or Murias are Hindus or not, or whether they call themselves Hindus or not, but how far contact with Hinduism has affected tribal religion. Here is a very curious question. Why is it that the Gonds, Pardhans and Baigas of Mandla, who live along the main Hindu pilgrim route to sacred Amarkantak, have hardly any religion at all, either Hindu or tribal, while the Murias who live in Bastar far from Hindu influence have a highly developed, authoritative, and richly furnished system of worship that is actually, while wholly tribal, far more akin to real Hinduism? The Mandla aboriginal is completely Hinduised, yet he knows nothing of religion; the Bastar aboriginal is quite un-Hinduised, yet his care of the gods, his beautiful little shrines, his sacrifices and festivals, his priests and pilgrimages have much in common with Hinduism.[41]

Thus, Elwin created a principle on the basis of which he differentiated tribal communities whose religious faith had been eroded as a result of contact with Hinduism from those (such as in Bastar) who had evaded such corrosive effects and were at least able to maintain a cultural distinctiveness. Based on this formulation, which became his basis for assessing the state of 'tribal health', Elwin postulated a three-fold division of the four million-odd aboriginals of Central India.[42]

The first class consisted of the old Gond aristocracy, which included 'a few great Binjhwar landlords, Korku noblemen and a number of tribesmen, mainly Gonds, who by their enterprise and education have made a position for themselves in Government service or in business'. This group retained their old tribal name, observed their clan and totem rules, and retained elements of tribal religion. In general, this group had adopted 'full Hindu

---

[41]Elwin, *Loss of Nerve*, p. 36.

[42]Here again, Elwin does not recognise or acknowledge the source of this idea in *Loss of Nerve*. However, this tripartite division of aboriginals is very similar to, and most likely stemmed from, J. T. Marten's all-India Census report for 1921. See J. T. Marten, *Census of India, 1921, Volume I, India, part-I, Report*, Superintendent Government Printing, Calcutta, 1924, p. 111. For my analysis of the same, see Chapter 2, this volume.

faith and live(d) in modern and even European style'. Elwin cited the Raja of Sarangarh (Raja Jawahar Singh) as an example of this numerically miniscule class.[43]

The second class of aboriginals was 'most numerous' and included those who had begun to lose 'their hold on tribal culture, religion and social organisation' owing to external contact. In Elwin's inimitable words, aboriginals of this class were '"Hinduised" without being Hindus. Some have received a little education; some have been to the Tea Gardens of Assam and have brought back new ideas and customs; all are suffering from a sense of frustration and dismay, a certain loss of nerve.'[44]

The third and final group of aboriginals were those who had exhibited the 'greatest power of resistance to the alien cultures that have pressed upon their borders'. They primarily resided in the Satpura mountains, Abujhmar hills, woodlands of the Maikal range, Melghat, zamindaris of Chhattisgarh, the jagirs of Chhindwara, Sironcha tehsil, and the plateau of Bastar.[45] By implication, the inaccessibility of these areas had acted as a check upon the influence of outsiders (mostly civilised caste Hindus).

In Elwin's opinion, the first group had by and large 'won the battle of culture-contact'. The legacies which they inherited, such as an aristocratic tradition, economic stability or affluence, an arrogance and self-confidence combined with outside encouragement, had enabled them to 'assimilate the blessings of civilization without injury to themselves'. Elwin outlined the central problematic of the tract as 'why the second class has suffered moral depression and decay as a result of contacts from which the third class has largely been free.'[46]

Before Elwin began his analysis of the factors responsible for the 'loss of nerve', he took an important detour into the question of exclusion and partial exclusion under the Government of India Act, 1935. While he lauded the provisions under which the areas so declared were placed under the control of the Governor, Elwin also deplored their inadequacies as 'no Governor would have time or opportunity to keep himself informed of the affairs of the tribesmen so difficult of access and so obscure'.[47] The panacea to this problem lay in the appointment of 'Special Officers' in the Provinces

---

[43]Elwin, *Loss of Nerve*, p. 1.

[44]Ibid.

[45]Ibid.

[46]Ibid., p. 2.

[47]Ibid., p. 6.

which had such notified areas. Such officials were supposed to work 'as an adviser in regard to these areas with the special duty of keeping Government and the Governor fully informed of their needs'. Elwin rued the fact that this suggestion, 'so vital, so essential to the welfare of the tribesmen', was unacceptable to the provincial governments.[48] This was a direct continuation of the line formulated by Hutton and Mills.

Outlining his analysis of the debate around the excluded and partially excluded areas, Elwin wrote that the 'reservation of aboriginal areas caused the worst possible impression in India'.[49] As a case in point, he cited Rajendra Prasad's speech[50] on the issue and the resolutions of the Indian National Congress at Faizpur (1936) and Haripura (1938), which denounced the move to exclude and partially exclude predominantly tribal areas in British India. A highly controversial remark by Winston Churchill added fuel to the fire and 'further exacerbated Nationalist opinion'. An Excluded Areas Association was formed and the Indian Legislative Assembly and some provincial assemblies also passed resolutions against the move to exclude and partially exclude these areas. In these debates, Elwin remarked that 'otherwise intelligent persons declared that the excluded areas were a trick of the anthropologists to preserve the aboriginals as museum specimens for the exercise of their "blessed science"'.[51] Disappointed at the form and content of the exclusion debate, Elwin wrote that the discourse as conducted thus far had destroyed 'any real chance of protecting them at all'. In the partially excluded areas of the Central Provinces, the aboriginals lived under 'very little advantage' as the 'ordinary system of Government (prevailed) and is exposed to every form of political and social propaganda'. Here schools,

---

[48]Ibid.

[49]Ibid., p. 7.

[50]Prasad had reportedly said,

> One of the worst features in the Government of India Act is the provision dealing with the so called Excluded Areas. While nobody objects to safeguarding the rights of the aboriginal people and all of us would be happy to see everything done to raise and uplift them educationally, socially and economically, we are not persuaded that the provisions contained in the Act will really tend to improve their position or make their lives better. There is indeed reason for suspicion that the aborigines only furnish an excuse for excluding some of those tracts which have rich mineral and other natural resources from the jurisdiction of Ministers who, though puppets, may still have some little power to show. (Ibid., p. 7)

[51]Ibid., p. 8.

roads, cattle pounds, and wells were controlled by the district councils, 'which often contain a majority of the very people who have risen to some kind of position by exploiting him (aboriginal)'. Some of them had the right to vote, but were unaware of how to utilise this. The three elected Gond representatives were 'less representative of the aboriginal population than a sympathetic European would be. None of these members were able to effect anything of value in the Assembly, for they were not aware of the fundamental problems of the people.'[52] Thus, Elwin showed an absolute distrust of the modern representative democratic institutions in tribal majority areas. Outlining precisely how his archetypal 'anthropology in administration' model in Bastar was better than the one then being followed in C.P. and Berar, Elwin wrote,

> On the whole, political and administrative questions have little effect on the aboriginal. Yet when, as in Bastar, there is an administration specially adapted to the needs of the tribesmen, it has a remarkably good effect. The Bastar administration is highly centralised and for the last ten years has been in the hands of admirable officials borrowed from the Central Provinces cadre; here the tribesmen are at least saved from the futilities and nepotism of the District Councils, the corruption of the electoral machine and the fads and extravagances of the political theorists. A former administrator has declared his belief that the model for a largely aboriginal State like Bastar should be the principle of indirect rule associated in Nigeria with the name of Lugard and in Tanganyika with that of Cameron, and already considerable devolution of rule has been achieved in favour of clan and village panchayats....[53]

In the concluding section of *Loss of Nerve*, Elwin stresses that it was 'an essay in diagnosis, not of cure'. He also argued that the tribal situation was 'past remedy; there is much that could be done if there is the will to do it'. What was fundamentally required was a 'change of attitude' that will naturally pave the way for 'all the details of administration and protection'. Pitching strongly for the role of anthropologists in devising suitable administrative models for tribal areas throughout the Indian subcontinent, Elwin wrote, 'The future of the aboriginals, not only in the Central Provinces but throughout India, depends largely on the attention that is given to the recommendations of scientific observers.' In his view, an 'application of universally recognised

[52]Ibid.

[53]Ibid., pp. 8–9.

anthropological principles would solve the problem'.[54] Elwin propounded three principles which should be the basis of all reform and uplift activities:

> The first principle that will help the aboriginal is the recognition of the fact that he has his own life to live and that customs and ideas which may seem ridiculous to the 'civilized' reformer are a necessary ingredient of his existence. Tribal life is still vital and energetic in the remoter districts. It is all of one piece, a living whole, an organism. You cannot, whether by reform, by missionary propaganda or by administrative interference, deprive the people of part of their life without impairing the whole ... even if you check quite obviously bad customs without providing some substitute, you will inevitably initiate a process of degeneration. Every proposed interference and reform must therefore be subject to the closest scrutiny before it is permitted.
>
> Another vital point will be the recognition that there are three distinct types of aboriginal ... and that while the first type can look after itself, entirely different treatment is needed for the second type and yet another treatment for the third.... Most projected schemes of betterment or enlightenment for the aboriginals are applied to all three types indiscriminately, and thus do more harm than good. It should be added that the aboriginals of the first class are quite unfitted to represent the aboriginals of the second or third classes in the Legislatures, for they know little about them.
>
> A third principle which I believe to be of great importance is that economic improvement should precede any schemes of reform, education, or political representation. 'It would be barbarous', says Rousseau, 'to twist a child's nature and kill his joy in preparing him for a future which may not be his.' Yet many schemes of education prepare the aboriginal boy to hold positions which will never be vacant and to enjoy a life that he can never afford. Culture contact and 'civilisation' do not harm to those who can afford it [*sic*]: acculturation must be based solidly upon an income. Our mistake is to force our schemes and our new expensive life on the poorest of the poor.[55]

Lastly, Elwin stressed that he did not support the policy of 'absolute isolation'. Instead, he preferred one of 'isolation from debasing and impoverishing contact'. Elwin added that for the moment, it must be recognised that it was

[54]Ibid., p. 49.

[55]Ibid., pp. 49–50.

the 'tribesmen's right to live his own life according to his own laws' and that 'any wanton interference with his customs may be disastrous'.[56]

From the above evidence, it is clear that for Elwin, Bastar provided a model administrative regime aptly suited to the conditions of the aboriginals living within its confines. What was most significant was that Bastar provided a frame of reference for Elwin, under which the monolithic category of 'aboriginal' was effectively broken up into three sub-categories on two grounds. The *first* was 'class', through which Elwin delineated the more affluent amongst the aboriginals who could hold their own in the battle of culture contact with civilisation better than their poor brethren. The *second* vital marker for Elwin was 'cultural autonomy'. In the light of his Bastar experiences, Elwin removed the category of 'Tribal Religions' from his framework, arguing that tribal religious faiths were part and parcel of the Hindu religio-cultural paradigm. In Elwin's argument, the tribal groups that stayed in 'remoter districts' were relatively little influenced by the degenerating contact of caste Hinduism. Thus, 'inaccessibility' helped these groups to maintain their own distinctive belief systems. Therefore cultural autonomy became the marker to distinguish the largest mass of aboriginal tribes, who were nearly all poor. As we shall see, nationalist scholars such as G. S. Ghurye took a leaf out of Elwin's formulation of aboriginals as *not* distinct from Hinduism and went a step further to argue that they were no more than 'Backward Hindus'. Perhaps, much more than the substance of Ghurye's argument, the tone and tenor with which the Brahmanical sociologist lambasted the lapsed Christian missionary has led to the widespread impression that there was a so-called 'Ghurye-Elwin Debate'. Nevertheless, Elwin's views also enabled him to create a bridge with the Congress nationalists, with whom he had been in staunch opposition in the latter half of the 1930s.

Finally, by laying stress on the need to distinguish these three groups within the aboriginal tribes, Elwin laid the ground for further theoretical work on the subject. By making economic betterment the main thrust of all 'uplift' activities, he was pre-empting the nationalist rhetoric on tribal welfare in independent India. Thus, Elwin emphasised tribal autonomy, a graded differentiation of the monolithic category of 'aboriginal', and finally, that economic improvement must precede all other schemes of reform.

[56]Ibid., pp. 50–51.

Thakkar versus Elwin: Re-Framing the Protectionist versus Interventionist Debate

As highlighted earlier, the intellectual history of the discourse on the tribal populations and their future in independent India has been trapped within the binary limits of the Isolation/Protection *versus* Intervention/Assimilation debate. Verrier Elwin and G. S. Ghurye have often been represented as the faces of these two warring camps. I will now systematically outline evidence that conclusively proves that there was neither any debate nor even an exchange that ever happened between the two supposedly chief protagonists of their so-called schools of thought.

Despite their initial closeness in the arena of social reform with its focus on aboriginal tribes, Elwin and Thakkar had steadily grown apart since the mid-1930s. In private correspondence with Thakkar and his associates like D. J. Naik of the Bhil Seva Mandal, Elwin used to call himself the 'chela' of 'Guru' Thakkar.[57] However, their positions differed widely on many issues such as prohibition,[58] shifting cultivation,[59] the nature of sexual relations,[60] and the role of customary laws in tribal communities.

In 1939, after the publication of Thakkar's Orissa Report, which supported a complete ban on Podu cultivation, and Elwin's own work, *The Baiga*, the two had been at loggerheads with each other on a variety of issues. By 1940, Elwin had started calling himself a 'Protectionist' in preference to the term 'Isolationist', which was given by social workers to people favouring the colonial 'man on the spot' model of administration. In contrast, he christened the likes of Thakkar as 'Interventionist' and also lambasted the philosophy of 'uplift', as defined by the Poona-based social workers-cum-reformers.

[57]Copy of Verrier Elwin's letter to A. V. Thakkar, dated 7 July 1941, Mandla, C.P., Subject File No. 8, P. Kodanda Rao Papers, PMML.

[58]A. V. Thakkar, 'Bhil and Drink: To the Editor', *The Times of India*, December 1944.

[59]See the section on the Orissa Partially Excluded Areas Report in Chapter 5.

[60]Thakkar was a puritan Vaishnavite who condemned what he perceived as sexual licentiousness in the case studies in Elwin's book on the Baigas. Elwin, on the other hand, was non-judgmental about the fleeting nature of these escapades.

In September 1940, A. V. Thakkar wrote to W. G. Archer, the Census Superintendent of Bihar.[61] Here, he referred to his work among the aborigines as 'my old love', to which, because of his preoccupation with the Gandhian programme of Harijan welfare, he had been unable to give much attention. Having first mooted this idea in 1927,[62] Thakkar remarked that the time had come for an organisation that would bring together 'all the workers working in all parts of the country on non-political lines for the improvement of the lot of aborigines and for their all-round uplift'.[63]

In letters written to a number of anthropologists and social workers, Thakkar proposed forming an association tentatively called the 'Indian Aborigines Friends Society', which would 'meet once a year, exchange experience and ideas, discuss all the subjects connected with the various groups of Aboriginal people and evolve, as far as possible, a co-ordinated policy and programme'.[64] To initiate this process, he suggested the following three-point agenda:

(1) To study the living conditions of the members of the Hill and Forest Tribes who live an isolated life, to bring them nearer to

---

[61]This was an important moment in time as the Adibasi Mahasabha, under the leadership of Jaipal Singh Munda, had been formed in 1939. The Mahasabha was making rapid inroads into the predominantly tribal regions of Chota Nagpur and Santal Pargana and demanded the bifurcation of Bihar to create a separate province of Jharkhand. By the mid-1940s, Jaipal Singh Munda and his associates had emerged as one of the biggest political challengers to the Congress Party in Bihar. See Saagar Tewari, 'Framing the Fifth Schedule: Tribal Agency and the Making of the Indian Constitution (1937–1950)', *Modern Asian Studies* 56 (5), 2022, pp. 1556–1594.

[62]A. V. Thakkar, 'The Aboriginal Tribes of India', *The Modern Review* XLI (2), Whole No. 242, February 1927, p. 131.

[63]Letter from A. V. Thakkar to W. G. Archer, dated Bombay, 12 September 1940, Correspondence with A. V. Thakkar, W. G. Archer Papers, Mss Eur F236/11, British Library.

[64]Letter from A. V. Thakkar to W. G. Archer, dated Bombay, 12 September 1940, Correspondence with A. V. Thakkar, W. G. Archer Papers, Mss Eur F236/11, British Library. Thakkar was perhaps hoping to create an all-India body for social work amongst aboriginal tribes on the template of his parent organisation, the Servants of India Society. After independence, Thakkar did create this organisation, but interestingly junked this earlier name, 'Indian Aborigines Friends Society', and chose to call it Bharatiya Adimjati Sevak Sangh. 'Aborigines' had turned into 'Adimjati'! See the last section of Chapter 8.

their own tribals living in the plains and to be familiar with other customs and manners.

(2) To organize, coordinate and assist welfare work conducted for their benefit, such as schools, dispensaries, sanitation and hygiene, which it is always understood, is conducted along humanitarian lines only.

(3) To represent to the Provincial Government concerned their disabilities and to suggest schemes for their moral, cultural, economic and political uplift with a view to bring them on a par with the advanced classes in the community.[65]

Thakkar's letter elicited a detailed response from Verrier Elwin. While Elwin called the proposal for the Aboriginals Association 'attractive',[66] he thought it 'essential' that such a venture not be 'confined to Congress minded Hindus' alone. Instead, the 'broad-based' model that Elwin espoused was that of the 'Africa Society ... with some weight of scholarship behind it that will earn it the widest respect'. In that vein, he proposed that scholars such as Sarat Chandra Roy, W. V. Grigson, and J. P. Mills also be included in the association.

In the same letter, Elwin referred to a 'divergence of opinion' between what he termed the 'Protectionist' and 'Interventionist' lines of thought. By providing these new catch-all categories, Elwin was in fact recasting the debate between Anthropologists (now called Protectionists) and Nationalists (now called Interventionists) in terms of their policy prescription towards the aboriginal tribes. However, despite its obvious focus on the British Indian Empire, Elwin claimed that this divergence was not specific to India, but could be seen in relation to aboriginal cultures in Africa, America, and the South Seas as well. Detailing his views on the Protectionist stance, Elwin wrote,

> The Protectionist is mainly occupied with the problem of social and cultural change. He has examined the fate of the aboriginals in Africa, Australia and North America. He has watched the decay of tribal religion, the collapse of ancient forms of village organisation, the extinction of village industries, the weakening of moral fibre which follows the contact of simple and primitive people with civilisation.... Well meaning and kindly people, such as missionaries and 'reformers'

[65]Ibid.

[66]Copy of letter from Verrier Elwin to A. V. Thakkar, n.d., Correspondence with A. V. Thakkar, W. G. Archer Papers, Mss Eur F236/11, British Library.

> have often done as much harm as the exploiter. The Protectionists long to see the Indian aboriginal saved from the fate that has befallen his brethren elsewhere.
>
> Moreover, the Protectionist regards the aboriginals with love and reverence. He does not regard him as a being on a lower level. He recognises that his honesty, his courage, his simplicity, his truthfulness are far superior to the normal level of honesty and truth in 'civilised' society. He regards as intolerable the suggestion that he should 'uplift' him. He admires his culture and religion and would like to preserve all of it that has survival value. He recognises, of course, that tribal society has great evils, but he knows that even these must be so cured that they do not leave a torn and jagged rent in the fabric of the society of which they have been a part.[67]

About the Interventionists, Elwin wrote,

> The Interventionist, on the other hand, is all for uplift. He would not say so, but in his heart he looks down on the aboriginal—otherwise why should we use the word 'uplift'?—and regards him as being on a lower social and cultural level than himself. He has cut-and-dried ideas about what is good for people and he applies these indiscriminately....
>
> The Interventionist has very rarely lived among the aboriginals so as to understand what they really think, though he has often visited them in order to do them good. He regards their customs as trivial, he ignores their tribal organisation, and he wants to bring them into line with the rest of the population as soon as possible. He would forbid their ancient methods of cultivation, bring them down from the hills which have been their immemorial home, and attach them (though hotly denying that he is a proselytiser) to whatever religions or social sect he may happen to belong.[68]

After this theoretical elaboration, Elwin declared himself to be an 'out-and-out Protectionist' who believed in gradual change. Suitable men had to be picked, methods had to be carefully worked out, and, most importantly, 'economic advance' had to be put before education and social change. As should be evident, Elwin is phrasing anew the arguments made by Hutton and others about the dangers of culture contact. His articulation represents a mature stage of the debate, where positions such as Protection/Isolation *versus* Intervention/Assimilation could be counter-posed. Also, re-reading these lines, one can clearly see that Elwin had recast the anthropologists

[67]Ibid.

[68]Ibid.

(anti-civilisation) as the desirable 'Protectionists' while the nationalist social reformers (pro-civilisation) were termed 'Interventionists' and deemed undesirable. Hence, in Elwin's attempt to re-define these camps, an ethical/moral edge was provided to the Protectionists over the Interventionists. The anthropologists were far superior to the narrow-minded nationalists!

With regard to the proposed Association, the chief question for Elwin was on which side it would stand. He expressed grave reservations about Thakkar's suggestions to bring the aboriginals 'nearer to their tribals living in the plains', calling it a 'disastrous' policy that would compel the Protectionists to 'stand aside from the organisation.'[69] Elwin also cautioned Thakkar that if his Association followed a wholly Interventionist policy, his name 'would go down as one of those who contributed to the destruction of the people you love'. In order to avoid such a calamitous course, it was desirable that the two sides evolve a combined programme, which Elwin suggested could be on the following lines:

> (1) To study the traditional organisation, social customs and economic condition of the aboriginals in order that everything proposed for their advantage may be based on knowledge and not on sentiment or preconceived ideas.
> (2) To study above all the conditions of social and cultural change and to devise means to ensure that the progress of the aboriginals in India may be achieved with the minimum of distress and disaster to themselves.
> (3) During this interim period to afford special protection for the aboriginals against oppressive landlords, grasping money-lenders, corrupt officials, ignorant politicians, proselytising missionaries of any religion, and to free them from any legal or administrative measures that tend to their psychological or economic depression.
> (4) To organise, co-ordinate and assist welfare work for their benefit.
> (5) To represent to Governments the disabilities and needs of the aboriginals and to suggest schemes for their advantage.
> (6) To do everything possible to revive and encourage all that is good and that has survival value in the traditional tribal culture. This will include the revival of aboriginal village industries, restoration of hunting rights, stimulation of dancing and singing and worship of the ancient gods.[70]

[69]Ibid.
[70]Ibid.

W. G. Archer,[71] himself a scholar-administrator of repute, was enthused by Elwin's reply to Thakkar. He wrote to Thakkar stating that Elwin had discussed the position admirably, and also asked him to regard Elwin's letter as an expression of 'our joint views'.[72] In his own earlier, independent reply to Thakkar, Archer had written that what the aborginals required were conditions where 'their economic worries are mitigated but their tribal way of life is firmly and strictly protected'. Living in the plains would involve a disintegration of the 'tribal way of life', in most cases reducing tribals to the status of serfs. For this reason, Archer wanted the phrase in the first point of Thakkar's proposal ('to bring them nearer to their own tribals living in the plains') to be deleted from the aims of the Association.

Archer also opposed Thakkar's proposal calling for 'moral and cultural uplift' of the tribals. He wrote that this phrase implied the inferiority of tribal culture as well as a 'wish to tamper with it.' On the contrary, he argued that tribal culture was replete with poetry, riddles, music, and dancing, which were 'beautifully adapted to tribal needs'. Archer wrote,

> I do not think that there is any chance of ever bringing the tribes on a par with other classes—in a sense of making them as clever and as self-resourceful. Their whole psychological make-up is against it. No Uraon can ever be a Kayastha. But what does seem important is to obtain from other classes the recognition that the tribes have an equal right to live in their own way. It is not the tribes that should be modified so much as the attitude of other classes to them. Unless this is done, the tribes have no future and are doomed.[73]

Thakkar responded with irritation. This was understandable as both Elwin and Archer had effectively punctured his proposal. At the same time, this reply provides evidence of Thakkar's tenacity and his unwillingness to cede ground. Thakkar positioned himself as a 'social worker' and not an anthropologist 'like you and Mr. Elwin'. He wrote that he was not in favour of revolutionising the life of the aboriginals, but believed 'that by slow degrees it

---

[71]A senior I.C.S. officer belonging to the Bihar cadre, Archer made several anthropological contributions, especially in the realm of tribal folklore. After the death of Rai Bahadur S. C. Roy, Archer and Elwin took over the editorship of the journal *Man in India*.

[72]D.O. No. 215-C, dated Hazaribagh, 31 October 1940, From: W. G. Archer to A. V. Thakkar, Correspondence with A. V. Thakkar, W. G. Archer Papers, Mss Eur F236/11, British Library.

[73]Ibid.

is bound to change and that cannot be resisted too strongly'. On the question of culture contact, Thakkar did not think that it was possible any longer 'to confine the hill people to their hills and make them live their isolated life which they have done upto some time ago.' Agreeing that no 'tribal culture is inferior because it is tribal', he also agreed that the poetry, dance, and riddles of these communities were worthy of preservation. Replying to Archer's jibe ('No Uraon can ever be a Kayastha'), he added, 'but is it not desirable to make a Uraon a more clever man, more intellectual, more resourceful than he at present is? If the tribes continue to live in their own way without any change whatsoever, they are sure to go still lower down in the society.'[74]

Apart from marking the mature stage of the debate on the 'tribal question', this exchange is extremely interesting because it provides evidence that the nationalist articulation vis-à-vis the tribes was neither unquestioned nor remained un-critiqued. Thakkar's argument highlights the flaws and problems in the nationalist position on tribes. For instance, Thakkar, being a staunch Gandhian, was quite puritanical on matters such as sex and the consumption of alcohol, which were hardly taboo subjects in most tribal societies. There is also a desperate attempt in the emergent nationalist line to co-opt tribal people in the grand narrative of the nation. However, this was not to be done on terms agreeable to the tribes, but was rather to be based on a set of moral and cultural norms intrinsic to the religiously informed Indian nationalism of the late colonial period.

Perhaps it was this heated exchange that compelled Thakkar to provide a more theoretical response, one which outlined the nationalist position on aboriginal tribes. In 1941, Thakkar delivered the fifth R. R. Kale Memorial Lecture at the Gokhale Institute of Politics and Economics. Titled 'The Problem of Aborigines in India', this tract authored by A. V. Thakkar should be considered the ideological kernel of Thakkar and his band of nationalist social workers.[75] Here, the nationalist ideologue attacked the Protectionist position and, in a tit-for tat move, called it the Isolationist argument, which was favoured by 'anthropologists, and British members of I.C.S. and other government officers'. He defined Isolationism as the philosophy of 'keeping

[74]Ibid.

[75]A. V. Thakkar, L.C.E., 'The Problem of Aborigines in India', R. R. Kale Memorial Lecture 1941, Gokhale Institute of Politics and Economics, in T. N. Jagadisan and Shyamlal (compiled and edited), *Thakkar Bapa: Eightieth Birthday Commemoration Volume*, Madras: Diocesan Press, 1949, pp. 354–377.

the aborigines in their areas untouched by the civilisation of the plains.'[76] Lambasting the Isolationists (read Anthropologists), Thakkar argued against their contention, saying that contact with civilised areas would not necessarily introduce bad customs and social evils such as untouchability, purdah, early marriage, and taboos regarding food (for example, against beef-eating) into tribal societies. Instead, safeguards such as the non-alienability of land were needed, which would protect the aborigines from potential exploitation by more advanced sections of the plains. He declared, 'But to keep these people confined to and isolated in their inaccessible hills and jungles is something like keeping them in glass cases of a museum for the curiosity of purely academic persons.'[77] Here, we clearly notice that in Thakkar's conception, civilisation emanated from the 'plains' while the 'inaccessible hills and jungles' of India were the abode of Indian aborigines. This is the most clinching archival evidence which show that, at least until 1941, for Thakkar the answer to the question 'Who was an Aboriginal?' lay in the Huttonian framework. The autocthonous population living in the hills and forests of India were the quintessential Aboriginals or the original inhabitants of India.[78] Therefore, just like his anthropological counterpart, the leading nationalist ideologue too identified predominantly aboriginal areas with the geographical metaphors of hills and forests.

Nevertheless, what makes Thakkar's lecture stand out is the heavy emphasis on the discourse of backwardness that was infused into the analysis of the tribal question in India. According to Thakkar, the chief challenge lay in enabling the aborigines to realise their state of backwardness and to work for their own social, economic, and political progress. Isolationism/Protectionism prevented tribal contact with advanced sections of the surrounding plains society, hindering their development. A 'healthy comradeship' between aborigines and non-aborigines was needed, where 'each should profit culturally from the other and in course of time work hand in hand for the welfare of India as a whole.' He strongly advocated 'reservation of seats, but in a general electorate, for the Adivasis in the legislatures and Local Boards for some time to come.'[79]

---

[76]Ibid., p. 370.

[77]Ibid., p. 371.

[78]See Chapter 2 for a detailed discussion of the Hills versus Plains paradigm set up by J. H. Hutton.

[79]Thakkar, 'The Problem of Aborigines in India', p. 371.

Thakkar expressed confidence that indigenous social workers and nationalist politicians were well-educated, and hence aware of the pitfalls of social evils like untouchability. He objected to the anthropologists' argument that increased detribalisation only turned aboriginals into part of the Depressed Classes. On the contrary, Thakkar opined that the practice of untouchability was 'dying in the plains'. Hence, the possibility of it taking root amidst the aboriginals was non-existent.[80] He took issue with the Isolationists not objecting to 'Christian Missionaries' close and uncontrolled contact' with aboriginals, which was used to spread 'Christian Propaganda and even Roman script for tribal dialects'.[81] Through such articulations, Thakkar was pointing fingers at the collusion between the colonial State/anthropologists and the Christian missionaries working in aboriginal areas with the chief aim of converting them.

In the same lecture, following Elwin (who had self-defined the anthropological position as the Protectionist one), Thakkar junked the label 'Interventionists' and instead self-defined the nationalist position by the term 'Assimilation'. Thakkar also put up a staunch defence of the Assimilationists and tied it to the fate of the nation. Thakkar, the staunch nationalist, remarked:

> In fact, it is unjust and wrong to call the indigenous social workers 'interventionists'. It would be proper to call them advocates of the policy of 'assimilation'. The aborigines should form part of the civilized communities of our country, not for the purpose of swelling the figures of this religion or that, but to share with the advanced communities the privileges and duties on equal terms in the general, social and political life of the country. Separatism and isolation seem to be dangerous theories and they strike at the root of national solidarity. We have already enough communal troubles and should we add to them instead of extinguishing the existing ones and seeing that we are all one and indivisible? Safety lies in union and not in isolation.[82]

Nevertheless, despite the formulation of Tribe=Hindu by Elwin in *Loss of Nerve*, his gulf with Thakkar continued to widen. In early 1942, the duo sparred on issues of customary laws and the suitability of modern legal

---

[80] Ibid.

[81] For an early expression of Thakkar's views on Christian missionary activities in the field of education, see A. V. Thakkar, '"Farming out" of Education in the Assam Hills', *The Servant of India* IX (9), 1 April 1926, pp. 109–110.

[82] Thakkar, 'The Problem of Aborigines in India', p. 372.

codes, both civil and criminal, in addressing the conditions prevalent in predominantly tribal communities.[83] This period was perhaps the absolute low point between them. Thakkar passed on copies of his correspondence with Elwin to P. Kodanda Rao, with the snide comment: 'It seems he is bent upon having a fight, though I do not wish to go in for it.'[84] A good window into the relationship is provided in a letter Thakkar wrote to Elwin:

> Thanks for sending me a copy of your article on 'Do we want to keep them in a Zoo?' You say that it may be of interest to me. How can it not be, especially as you have mentioned poor old Thakkar not less than a hundred times therein?
>
> Controversy is not in my line. I do not know how to carry it on. So it is necessary as well as wise for me to restrain myself. But is it fair on your part to hold me responsible for the advertisement in the 'Hitavad'? Is it honest?
>
> You have not acknowledged my letter to you dated Delhi, the 18th last, written in reply to yours of the 6th November. If you have purposefully done so in order to bury the past, I do not mind it. But it seems you are not doing so, as you perhaps want to write several 'Puranas' on what I have written. I cannot omit to mention one fact that I gave my opinion about 20 millions of aborigines, and all the aborigines are lumped together in all Census reports, and now you say that my suggestions and opinions are correct about with regard to 15 million but not to the other 5 millions living in the hills. Is there not less exaggeration in writing about 20, though applicable to only 15, than to criticise on my statement, keeping in view what applies only to 5? However, I will mention nothing more of it.[85]

---

[83]See A. V. Thakkar, 'Reader's Views: Mr. Elwin and Aborigines', *The Times of India*, 30 January 1942, p. 4; Elwin's reply to the Editor of *The Times of India*, titled 'Law and the Aboriginal: A Plea for Tribal Panchayats', 6 March 1942, p. 6.

[84]Letter from A. V. Thakkar to P. Kodanda Rao, dated 31 January 1942, Camp: Beawar (Ajmer-Merwara), Subject File No. 8, P. Kodanda Rao Papers, PMML.

[85]Letter from A. V. Thakkar to Verrier Elwin, dated 31 January 1942, Camp: Beawar (Ajmer-Merwara) in Subject F. No. 8, P. Kodanda Rao Papers, PMML. This file has a typed copy of Elwin's article, 'Do we want to keep them in a Zoo?', which provides a further example and evidence of the fraught relationship between Thakkar and Elwin. This article also has some example of cheap advertisements that Thakkar referred to, which appeared in *The Hitavada*. In the same file, also see a letter from Thakkar to Elwin, dated 9 February 1942, in which Thakkar responds to a challenge posed by Elwin and writes, 'Your challenge means that I have failed

Besides showing the growing strain in the Thakkar–Elwin relationship, the paragraph above is remarkable because it reflects the aftermath of Elwin's formulation of the argument presented in *Loss of Nerve*. Essentially, Elwin's intervention had attempted to shake up the monolithic category of the aboriginal on geographical, economic, cultural, and racial grounds. He *differentiated* the category which had long remained stable, and came up with three (in some expressions, four) separate categories of aboriginals. This classification appears in many reports that Elwin penned in the period after the publication of the *Loss of Nerve* in 1941.[86]

This exchange dates to the period after Thakkar's Kale Memorial Lecture, where he had recognised the aboriginals as the 'original sons of the soil', who were driven 'from the plains to the hills and forests' by the Aryan invasion.[87] Both on philosophical and historical levels, Thakkar was articulating his argument on the turf developed by the long line of colonial scholar-administrators and missionaries. As a sharp debater, Elwin had identified the chinks in Thakkar's argument and was needling him to come out and debate further. Soon after formulating his argument in *Loss of Nerve*, Elwin set about 'having a fight' with the leading nationalist ideologue and social reformer working in predominantly aboriginal areas. In public life, then as now, a valid strategy to enhance one's own reputation and standing is to enter into a public dispute with leading figures in the field. Elwin was a master polemicist; he knew his strength and energetically played out this skill to the fullest in the early 1940s.

On the other hand, Thakkar was a man of action, a trained engineer who had taken up the calling of serving the poorest people. Although endowed with good writing skills, he was no match for Elwin's talents as a wordsmith and his intellectual depth. Therefore, Elwin became a constant irritant for Thakkar. Also, through his untiring energy and prodigious output, Elwin was quickly establishing a name and reputation for himself.[88] Even Thakkar

---

to send the desirable type of teachers into the aboriginal areas under my influence. Will you please quote chapter and verse for the alleged failure also?'

[86]For instance, in reports on Ganjam and Koraput, Orissa; also in the report that Elwin prepared at the instruction of A. N. Mitchell in the princely states of Bonai, Keonjhar, and Pal Lahara.

[87]Thakkar, 'The Problem of Aborigines in India', p. 355.

[88]Frustrated with her workaholic husband not giving her enough attention, Kosi Elwin once remarked, 'I married a man not a typewriter'. See Guha, *Savaging the Civilized*, p. 176.

could not ignore Elwin's challenge for too long. In such a context, my argument is that Thakkar was in search of an ally who could take up cudgels on his behalf. In other words, Thakkar needed a scholar to lambast Elwin on ideological grounds, using the full blast of anthropological vocabulary and theoretical argumentative skills.

For the nationalist social workers in general and Thakkar in particular, this much desired ideological antidote to the anthropologists' position came in the form of a seminal book by Bombay-based sociologist, Govind Sadashiv Ghurye. However, before outlining an analysis of Ghurye's trenchant critique of colonial anthropology, some assessment of his scholarship is necessary.

It must be highlighted that, despite being an orthodox Brahmin trained in Sanskrit, Ghurye, the anthropologist, was not an Indian creation. Like other leading scholar-administrators of the period such as Hutton and Mills, Ghurye too was influenced by Neo-Diffusionism.[89] In fact, he had been trained in anthropology by the undisputed leader of the depopulation thesis, W. H. R. Rivers. No less than M. N. Srinivas (who wrote his first doctoral thesis under Ghurye's supervision) attested that Ghurye suffered from an 'Egypt fixation', so characteristic of Rivers and his followers.[90] In his memoirs, Srinivas recounted that between 1936–1944, Ghurye's main concerns were 'kinship, caste, social organization, and tracing the distribution of cultural traits, all of which were derived from Rivers'.[91] In a piece which contrasts Elwin and Ghurye, A. C. Sinha has argued,

> Ghurye was trained in the Indian classical tradition in Sanskrit for his college and university degree. Once he went to England on scholarship, the theory of cultural contact and the English diffusionist thinkers influenced and converted him completely. He began to believe that 'sociology was nothing but the past history of mankind'. In his own words:

[89] This can be clearly seen in his earliest post-Ph.D. publications; see G. S. Ghurye, 'Egyptian affinities of Indian funerary practices', *Anthropos* 4, 1923, pp. 420–430; also see 'Dual Organization in India', *The Journal of the Royal Anthropological Institute of Great Britain and Ireland* 53, January–June 1923, pp. 79–91.

[90] M. N. Srinivas, 'Practicing Social Anthropology in India', *Annual Review of Anthropology* 26, 1997, pp. 1–24, p. 4.

[91] Ibid., p. 5.

> 'My contacts with Rivers, Haddon, Smith and others had confirmed me in my belief that both archeology and Sanskrit literature, were useful and necessary for sociology.'[92]

Such insights into and perspectives on Ghurye's intellectual influences indicate the curious amalgam which he brought to the discourse on Indian tribes in general, and on scheduling in particular. W. H. R. Rivers was, of course, Ghurye's chief mentor, but the former's death in 1922 necessitated that his Indian pupil latch onto A. C. Haddon, who was close to Rivers. Finally, in 1924, Ghurye submitted his doctorate under the supervision of Haddon at the University of Cambridge. The third name mentioned in the above extract refers to Grafton Elliot Smith, who was based in University College London. George Stocking, Jr. has established that Smith was a very close associate of Rivers, and that after the latter's death, a leading figure of the Heliolithic School ('Children of the Sun', or those who believed that civilisation began in Egypt and 'diffused' slowly to other parts).[93]

Thus, Rivers' depopulation thesis, endorsed by J. H. Hutton (himself an Oxonian) who became its main champion within the ICS 'knot of men', could perhaps be most effectively challenged by someone within the Oxbridge network of anthropology. It is worth remembering that after retiring from the ICS in 1936, Hutton returned home and joined the University of Cambridge as the William Wyse Chair of Anthropology. His predecessor at the Chair, T. C. Hodson, was another ex-ICS officer of the Assam cadre, who adhered to the theory of the debilitating impact of 'culture contact' with civilisation. While Hutton's appointment must have been a shot in the arm of the now struggling Neo-Diffusionists (whose influence rapidly waned after the death of Rivers and the rise of new stars such as Bronislaw Malinowski and Alfred Reginald Radcliffe-Brown), these multiple entanglements, characteristic of academic politics, are highly suggestive and need to be worked out more fully. Nevertheless, these details do suggest that what played out in the early 1940s Indian tribal discourse

---

[92]A. C. Sinha, 'Colonial Anthropology vs Indological Sociology: Elwin and Ghurye on Tribal Policy in India', in T. B. Subba and Sujit Som (eds), *Between Ethnography and Fiction: Verrier Elwin and the Tribal Question in India*, Hyderabad: Orient Longman, 2005, pp. 71–85.

[93]See Chapter 5, titled 'The Revival of Diffusionist Ethnology: Rivers and the Heliolithic School', in George W. Stocking, Jr., *After Tylor, British Social Anthropology, 1888–1951*, London: Athlone, 1996, pp. 179–232.

was not dissociated from the battle going on between anthropologists in Cambridge and elsewhere in Great Britain.

Image 8: Professor Govind Sadashiv Ghurye

Courtesy: A. R. Momin (ed.), *The Legacy of G.S. Ghurye: A Centennial Festschrift*, Mumbai: Popular Prakashan, 2006.

Especially for someone as steeped in the Neo-Diffusionist discourse as Ghurye was, he had a definite academic interest in creating a critique of colonial anthropology. Soon after his return from England, he was appointed in the School of Economics and Sociology, University of Bombay. Several essays in leading journals soon followed. Ghurye remained a die-hard Hindu nationalist throughout his long teaching and writing career. His nationalist credentials were first established after the publication of his seminal book, *Caste and Race in India* (1932), which challenged the claims of Herbert

Hope Risley[94] about the racial origins of caste, 'especially ... politicising of caste, particularly in relation to the census'.[95] According to Nicholas Dirks, Ghurye was the first Indian anthropologist to devise a larger critique of colonial anthropology from the nationalist perspective. Carol Upadhya too outlines British orientalism, nationalism, and diffusionism as the three primary sources of Ghurye's sociological imagination.[96] She argues that Ghurye's perspective on Indian society was intensely Brahmanical, so much so that Indian social history was essentially 'the history of Hinduisation or the assimilation of non-Hindu groups into Hindu society'.[97] Thus, Ghurye's nationalist credentials were beyond doubt and, after the buoyant reception of *Caste and Race*, another academic critique of the colonial category of 'aboriginal tribes' was a natural corollary, simply waiting to happen.

Before proceeding towards an analysis of Ghurye's ideas on tribal communities, an important aspect which needs to be established are his links with the Servants of India Society. Despite being based in Bombay, Ghurye maintained close ties with the city of Poona, which was an important intellectual centre in western India. The growing connections of the scholar with the SIS can be ascertained from several contributions that Ghurye made to its newsletter. The earliest appearance of Ghurye's name dates to 1927, in a co-authored journal article that elicited praise from the editor.[98] Subsequently, Ghurye started contributing articles to the SIS,

[94]For a recent full-length study of H. H. Risley's India career, see C. J. Fuller, *Anthropologist and Imperialist: H.H. Risley & British India, 1873–1911*, New Delhi: Social Science Press, 2023.

[95]For a detailed discussion of this work, see Nicholas B. Dirks, 'G.S. Ghurye and the Politics of Sociological Knowledge', *Sociological Bulletin* 62 (2) (Special Issue on The Bombay School of Sociology: Stalwarts and Their Legacies), May–August 2013, pp. 239–253.

[96]Carol Upadhya, 'The Hindu Nationalist Sociology of G.S. Ghurye', *Sociological Bulletin* 51 (1), March 2002, pp. 28–57. Also see T. K. Oommen, 'Scheduled Caste, Scheduled Tribes, and the Nation: Situating G. S. Ghurye', *Sociological Bulletin* 60 (2), May–August 2011, pp. 228–244; C. N. Venugopal, 'G. S. Ghurye on Culture and Nation-Building', *Sociological Bulletin* 42 (1–2), March–September 1993, pp. 1–13. For a full length study on Ghurye, see S. K. Pramanick, *Sociology of G.S. Ghurye*, New Delhi: Rawat Publications, 2020 [1994], 2nd revised edn.

[97]Upadhya, 'The Hindu Nationalist Sociology of G.S. Ghurye', p. 46.

[98]'The Konkan Agriculturist', *TSI* X (31), 8 September 1927, p. 363.

mostly on the theme of marriage and kinship.[99] In the early 1930s, most of his contributions were short book reviews.[100]

Although the cantankerous scholar had never worked on the aboriginal tribes, some of Ghurye's inclinations can be ascertained from two articles published in the 1930s. While making a case for the study of anthropology in the prestigious journal *Man in India*, Ghurye wrote,

> There are a number of peoples, jungle tribes and others, whose assimilation in our civilization is one of the important problems awaiting solution. In order to be able to solve the problem their past and present condition must be carefully studied, and their cultural affinities fully investigated. No doubt an amount of good material is already available. But the problem has not been authoritatively enquired into in the light of the material. It is time that an expert committee were appointed either by our Congress or by the Government to discuss this problem and to lay down a plan and a programme to be worked out with a view to ameliorate the condition of these peoples who have remained outside the main path of cultural development in our country. It is clear that the District and other officials who have come into close contact with these peoples in the administrative capacities, ought to have good training in Anthropology in general and the ethnography of the specific area in particular.[101]

The nationalist leanings of the Bombay University Professor and his espousal of a social service framework are clearly visible in the above passage. Inside the SIS network, too, Ghurye was rapidly becoming a highly regarded intellectual figure. In 1938, this status found reflection in the invitation extended to him to deliver the Second Annual R. R. Kale Memorial lecture.[102] Organised by the Gokhale Institute of Politics and Economics, an

---

[99]G. S. Ghurye, 'The Marriage Law', *TSI* XII (38), 26 September 1929, pp. 450–451; also see 'Marriage and Family', *TSI* XII (30), 1 August 1929, pp. 354–355.

[100]G. S. Ghurye, 'The Institution of Marriage', *TSI* XIV (2), 8 January 1931, pp. 20–21; 'Problems of Rural Sociology', *TSI* XIV (47), 26 November 1931, pp. 567–568; 'The Home', *TSI* XVIII (4), 24 January 1935, pp. 41–42; 'Early Human Culture', *TSI* XVIII (46), 14 November 1935, pp. 596–597; *TSI* XX (33), 2 September 1937, p. 392.

[101]G. S. Ghurye, 'Anthropology and our Educational System', *Man in India* 15 (2 &3), 1935, pp. 93–107.

[102]G. S. Ghurye, 'The Social Process (in the Light of a Century of Sociology)', Gokhale Institute of Politics and Economics, R. R. Kale Memorial Lecture, 1938. This was a flagship annual event where Ghurye's lecture was followed by

affiliate organisation of the SIS (established in its silver jubilee year), only leading academics and experts were invited to deliver these lectures. Ghurye, by now the Head of the Department of Sociology, University of Bombay, suited the occasion perfectly.

That same year, a precursor to Ghurye's later sociological imagination of aboriginal tribes as 'Backward Hindus' appeared in a two-part essay published in the SIS newsletter. In the concluding part of his article, he wrote:

> We have amongst us a number of groups called tribal castes such as Bhils, Katkaris, Waralis, Badagas, Todas, Mundas, Oraons. Their culture are in varying stages of assimilation with the main culture pattern of the Hindus round about them. Their problems are therefore special to them. Their assimilation or their preservation is a matter of larger policy. But looking to the fact that a large element in the cultural pattern of popular Hinduism is so akin to some of the ideas and practices of these people, it appears to me that *their natural course of evolution lies in their progressive assimilation with the Hindu population surrounding them.*[103]

Thus, the evidence cited above presents several points of congruence between Thakkar's and Ghurye's positions on the tribal question in India. The stereotyping of aboriginal tribes as 'tribal castes' and a desire for their 'assimilation' with the surrounding Hindu population suggests why Thakkar would choose Ghurye in a proxy role for a theoretical battle against Verrier Elwin. Although there is no clinching evidence to show that Ghurye was commissioned to participate in this debate by Thakkar, there are strong indications supporting the conjecture that Thakkar heavily enlisted as well as endorsed Ghurye's scholarship and yoked him to the nationalist cause in the intense tug-of-war with the anthropologists, especially Verrier Elwin. His 1943 monograph, *The Aborigines—'So-Called'—And Their Future*, did come as a panacea for the Assimilationist argument. It is a significant fact that the book was No. 11 in a series published by the Gokhale Institute of Politics and Economics, Poona, established to commemorate the silver jubilee of the SIS. It is also pertinent to mention that at the time of the

---

B. R. Ambedkar (Federation versus Freedom, 1939), K. T. Shah (The Constituent Assembly, 1940), and three years later, by A. V. Thakkar (The Problem of the Aborigines in India, 1941).

[103] G. S. Ghurye, 'Social Work and Sociology', *TSI* XXI (23), 9 June 1938, pp. 285–287; emphasis added.

book's publication, Thakkar was a Vice-President of the SIS. Thus, it makes a case for patronage, with Thakkar facilitating the publication of Ghurye's book for the theoretical ballast it provided to the nationalists against the likes of Elwin and other anthropologists. The following is an excerpt from the annual report of the SIS, for the year 1943–1944:

> During the year under report we published 'The Aborigines, So-Called and their Future' by Dr. G.S. Ghurye. Our series of publications has so far been confined to studies made by workers or students directly connected with the Institute. Dr. Ghurye's subject was, however, so closely related to some of the problems that we have attempted to tackle ourselves and a thorough and scientific review of it was so essential in the present that we were very glad when Dr. Ghurye offered us his work for inclusion in our series.[104]

Thus far, we have established that the real debate on the tribal question was between Thakkar and Elwin, in which Ghurye was set up as a proxy to attack Elwin. Now let us look at the manner of Ghurye's critique as it appeared in the first edition of the book in 1943.

G. S. Ghurye and the Tribal Question

In 1943, Govind Sadashiv Ghurye published his pathbreaking work on the aboriginal tribes, titled provocatively *The Aborigines—'So-called'—And Their Future.*[105]

Ghurye's work was focused on the western and central tribal belts, which extended from the 'Aravalli hills in the West, through the Vindhyas, the Satpuras, the Mahadev hills, the Maikal range, and through Chota Nagpur to the Rajmahal hills, including the plains and plateaus contiguous to many of them.'[106] Territorially, these areas were found in the British Indian provinces of Bombay, C.P. and Berar, Orissa, Madras, Bihar, and Bengal, and were home to about fifteen million aboriginal tribes.

---

[104] Appendix I, Gokhale Institute of Politics and Economics, Poona, 'Report for the year 1943–44', *The Servants of India Society, Report for the Year 1943–44*, Poona, Monday, 12 June 1944, p. 37.

[105] G. S. Ghurye, *The Aborigines—'So-Called'—And Their Future*, Poona: Gokhale Institute of Politics and Economics, 1943; hereafter, Ghurye.

[106] Ibid., p. 8.

Ghurye's book engaged with a detailed survey of the different Censuses conducted by the British colonial State. Regarding the category of 'Animism', which was usually defined 'in contradistinction to Hinduism', Ghurye opined that the 'census authorities were more or less concerned of the unreliable nature of the classification.'[107] In this context, Ghurye picked particularly on Hutton's argument of 'soul substance' being the central criterion for categorising a variety of religious groups under the term 'Tribal Religions'. Ghurye wrote,

> If Dr. Hutton has succeeded in proving his thesis, it provides sound reason for grouping together all the creeds of these people under the single title of 'Tribal Religions' because of the underlying unity running through them all. Yet it does not justify their being separated from Hinduism, in view of the chorus of opinion pointing to the close similarity between them and the Hinduism of some sections of the admittedly Hindu society. Nay, Dr. Hutton's explanation of the genesis of Hinduism strengthens the case of those who have objected to the separate classification of Animists on the ground that their faith is not utterly distinct from some forms of Hinduism. The pre-Aryan substratum, which, amalgamated with Rgvedic religion, gives us modern Hinduism in Dr. Hutton's opinion, must also be a part and parcel of the creed of the so called animists. Just as in modern Hinduism the special features are Rgvedic, so in the creeds of the tribes the peculiar elements are those that have not been incorporated in Hinduism. But the common substratum must subsist in both modern Hinduism and Tribal religions. When, therefore, Dr. Hutton tells us that 'the tribal religions represent, as it were, the material not yet built into the temple of Hinduism,' and that the unused material is similar to the material already taken in Hinduism, he is obliterating one side of the picture he himself has painted. In the light of the opinions and observations quoted above, the only sound conclusion is that the creeds of so-called Animists and the Hinduism of some sections of Hindu society have so much material which is either similar or common or both, that demarcation between the two, being almost impossible, is thoroughly artificial.[108]

Ghurye argued that a major flaw in the Census operations was that, since the categories had been fixed and strictly defined, the varying levels of Hinduisation within the tribal communities were not taken into account.

---

[107] Ibid., p. 1.

[108] Ibid., pp. 6–7.

He wrote, 'even if a tribe has a Hinduized section, and a non-Hinduized one, the whole tribe is included in the category of "Forest" or "Primitive" tribe'. Ghurye pointed out that a single criterion such as religious affiliation or language was insufficient to categorise a community as a 'Forest' or 'Primitive' tribe. In fact, the term 'aborigines', as used by Sir Herbert Risley, was at best a matter of convenience; according to Ghurye, this term 'begged an insoluble question'.[109] He highlighted that the various colonial authorities had used the autochthonous/son of the soil argument to legitimise the use of the term 'aborigine'. It was also commonly said that these population groups had been pushed into the hills and forests by newer inhabitants. However, Ghurye asked, 'But what about those sections of these so-called autochthones, which have refused to be driven into the fastnesses of hills and forests and into the consequent isolation, but have continued to live among the newcomers and have become sufficiently modified to be declared Hinduized?'[110]

The stock argument which Ghurye utilised in his book to demolish the thesis of tribal autochthonous status belonged to Captain J. Forsyth's book, *The Highlands of Central India*. First published in 1871, this work by a nineteenth-century Englishman in India was cited several times by Ghurye to contend that aboriginals were not dissimilar to the Hindus of the surrounding plains. Forsyth called the Central Indian tribal tract the 'cauldron of peoples'.[111] Using other colonial sources, Ghurye argued,

> ... many of the so-called aboriginal tribes have come to their present habitat from somewhere else in India. They cannot, therefore, be considered to be the autochthones of their present tracts. When the history of internal movements of peoples is not known and in the opinion of some is not likely to be known, it is utterly unscientific to regard some tribe or the other as the original owner of the soil.[112]

Not only migration, but the various linguistic families to which tribal languages belonged also suggested that 'the question as to who are the original settlers of India remains still open'.[113] Thus, Ghurye declared that '...

[109]Ibid., p. 9.

[110]Ibid., p. 10.

[111]Captain J. Forsyth, *The Highlands of Central India: Notes on the Forests, Wild Tribes, Natural History and Sports*, Dehradun: Natraj Publishers, 1994, p. 23. Cited in Ghurye, p. 10.

[112]Ghurye, p. 12.

[113]Ibid., p. 13.

science and history do not countenance the practice of calling these tribes aborigines'. If this was accepted, then Ghurye argued that their claim for special treatment becomes problematic as, 'To adjust the claims of different strata of the Indian society on the ground of antiquity or comparative modernity is a frightfully difficult task, which, if undertaken, will only liberate the forces of disunity.'[114] Encapsulating the central argument of his monograph, Ghurye wrote,

> ... the proper description of these people must refer itself to their place in or near Hindu society and not to their supposed autochthonism. While sections of these tribes are properly integrated in the Hindu society, very large sections, in fact the bulk of them, are rather loosely assimilated. Only very small sections, living in the recesses of hills and the depths of forests, have not been more than touched by Hinduism. Under the circumstances, the only proper description of these people is that are imperfectly integrated classes of Hindu society. Though for the sake of convenience they may be designated the tribal classes of Hindu society, suggesting thereby the social fact that they have retained much more of the tribal creeds and organization than many of the castes of Hindu society, yet they are in reality Backward Hindus.[115]

Interestingly, it must be remembered that the argument of tribals as 'Backward Hindus' appeared on the twenty-first page of the first chapter of a work spanning 232 pages. The above argument and Ghurye's much highlighted pot-shots at Elwin were only a few significant aspects of this work. Most scholars end their analysis of the text by highlighting these two points; however, G. S. Ghurye does many, far more important things than establishing his dislike of Elwin, who by the time of the publication of this tract had undoubtedly become the chief proponent of the Protectionist school of thought in the debate on the future of the aboriginal populations in India. Guha's work has shown that despite Ghurye's vitriolic attack, Elwin did not respond in any significant manner. Indeed, Elwin was enraged by Ghurye's invectives and, as an editor, did consider publishing a special issue of *Man in India* which would carry reviews of *The Aborigines—'So-Called'—And Their Future* by W. V. Grigson, Christopher von Furer-Haimendorf, and B. S. Guha, with a view to 'putting Ghurye in his place'. However, Ram Guha argues that upon Archer's advice, the journal took the 'more prudent

[114]Ibid., p. 14.
[115]Ibid., p. 21.

and politic course of ignoring the book'.[116] It must also be remembered that in 1943, Elwin had already begun the process of rapprochement with Thakkar and company by raking up the issue of the Dutch Missions in Mandla.[117]

Ghurye covers a very wide terrain in this book. In Chapters Two and Three, both titled 'So-Called Aboriginals and Hindus', Ghurye outlines a number of reformist movements amongst the tribal communities, which were consciously or otherwise aimed at the Hinduisation of the tribes. Such Hinduisation movements had frequently helped the communities to wean themselves away from evils such as shifting cultivation and the conspicuous consumption of alcohol. By training them in the methods of settled cultivation, the advanced Hindus had improved the economic lot of the so-called aboriginal communities. In fact, Ghurye argued that 'the contact of the aborigine with the Hindus is productive of good to the former, who go so far under that influence as to try to revitalize their crude and worn out creed'.[118] Outlining the positive impacts that contact with the Hindus had had on the aboriginals, Ghurye wrote, 'their religious beliefs have come to include some conception of a supreme God at the least. They have become conscious of the need of education. Reform in some of their customs has been seen by them to be urgently needed.'[119] In a profound passage, Ghurye attacked the anthropologists' idea of a pristine autochthonous 'Aborigine' undergoing a 'loss of nerve' and wrote,

> Altogether the contact has created a desire to level up among the Hinduized sections, the sincerity of which we have no grounds to doubt. The picture thus presented is vastly different from the one that is characterized by moral depression or loss of nerve. That some discomfort to some sections, positive pain to others, and unmitigated loss to some, must have been caused, is quite clear from the accounts. But before we credit all that as a grievance to the account of Hindu contact, we must ponder over the fact that the process of breaking up and remaking of groups had been in progress for many centuries, and that internal migrations had been causing a good deal of wrenching in the naturally pleasant social surroundings. In short, we must

[116]Ramachandra Guha, *Savaging the Civilized*, p. 160.

[117]Nandini Sundar, 'Verrier Elwin and the 1940s Missionary Debate in Central India', in T. B. Subba and Sujit Som (eds), *Between Ethnography and Fiction: Verrier Elwin and the Tribal Question in India*, Hyderabad: Orient Longman, 2005.

[118]Ghurye, p. 51.

[119]Ibid., p. 62.

> remember that the so-called independent or semi-independent tribes of today have not all been tribes in working order as units for a very long time, and that some of them may be merely derelicts from older and more co-ordinated units. Further, within the larger tribes of today, there must have been individuals with differing abilities as there must have been units with varying capacities for adoption.[120]

Ghurye then outlined the four main charges against Hinduisation: untouchability, lowering the position of women, the introduction of child marriage, and the suppression of tribal song and dance. He rubbished the notion that in all cases, when integrated into Hindu society, the tribes would inevitably fill the ranks of the Depressed Classes. On the contrary, Ghurye argued that a large number of tribes had 'obtained status higher than that of the lowest castes' and a 'fair number' were even admitted in the higher castes.[121] Moreover, he pointed out that twentieth-century India was on a progressive march,

> Contemporary Hindu society is no more the Hindu society of the last century. Untouchability is not the sole idea nor the only pattern held up before the Hindus in respect of the lowly strata. The anti-untouchability campaign, though it might have effected only slight modifications in actual practice, has provided a powerful counter-offensive, and a strong alternative concept and pattern. Under such social conditions one need not fear that the tribalists, if Hinduized, will fall into the quagmire of social degradation of untouchability.[122]

With regard to the position of women, Ghurye's defence was that a few specific restrictions that had been placed upon certain tribal communities such as the Hos would lighten their burden of work. Also, similar to the efforts towards prohibition, restrictions imposed upon women on activities such as dancing were designed to 'chasten the sex-morals of the community'.[123] In a similar puritanical vein, while Ghurye agreed that the increase in incidences of child marriage (which he preferred to call 'pre-puberty' marriages) among Hinduised tribalists were 'unfortunately true', they were in effect a deterrent to 'pre-marital sexual intercourse'.[124] Like Thakkar, the aspect of sexual morality was a major obsession for Ghurye,

[120]Ibid., p. 63.
[121]Ibid., p. 67.
[122]Ibid., p. 27.
[123]Ibid., p. 68.
[124]Ibid., p. 70.

who devoted a really long paragraph spanning two-and-a-half pages on the life histories of Baigas as presented in Elwin's eponymous book on the tribe to highlight sexual promiscuity among its individual members. For the Brahmanical Ghurye, the correct and legitimate outlet for sexual gratification was within matrimony, which the life stories of Baigas, marked by promiscuity and incest, thoroughly negated. This becomes the ground on which Ghurye rejects the notion of stable marriage ties among the so-called aboriginals. The charge of the decline of customs like dance was also refuted along the same lines.

Ghurye agreed with the contention that the 'so-called aboriginals' had lost their lands to the Hindus. However, he attributed such land alienation (which was one of the central arguments of the Protectionists/Isolationists) primarily to 'an incident of conquest or a result of the favour of ruling families', and only secondarily to the 'expropriatory tactics of the Hindus'.[125] Ghurye inverted the Protectionist logic to argue that, in fact, the introduction of the British system of revenue and law was the chief factor behind tribal land alienation. In his opinion, '(D)ivested of the potentiality of land-grabbing, Hindu contact would have been nothing but an unadulterated boon to the so-called aboriginal tribes.'[126]

More critically for our purposes, in subsequent chapters Ghurye delves into the genesis of the idea of special administrative regimes for predominantly tribal areas. He gave a detailed account of the work of Augustus Cleveland in the Rajmahal Hills, which led to the formation of a Hill Assembly amongst the Pahariyas and to the first regulations that designated certain tribal tracts as 'non-regulation' areas where a simplified form of administration was followed. It presents a grand sweep of legislative measures from the late eighteenth century, which, according to Ghurye, were instigated by, 'their [tribes'] nature being sullen and on occasions violent, the main purpose of the British policy was to secure peace and not necessarily to help the people to advance on the road to progress either by assimilation with the plains' Hindus or otherwise'.[127] Hence, controlling the recurrent tribal rebellions was the deciding factor behind imposing a separate administrative regime for tribal majority tracts. It was not the 'white man's burden', but rather the need for pacification that was the main imperative behind the British policy towards the tribes.

[125]Ibid., p. 30.
[126]Ibid., p. 63.
[127]Ibid., p. 89.

In his book, Ghurye presented a synopsis of various developments in nineteenth and twentieth-century Chota Nagpur and Santhal Parganas. He drew a link between the spread of British rule in these areas and the enactment of the Scheduled Districts Act of 1874. Furthermore, he connected this narrative with the twentieth-century constitutional developments. He cited various colonial authorities to provide an account of the policy pursued and the results achieved. On the whole, Ghurye's evaluation was quite negative:

> In the earlier period, British arms and British administrative tact both proved useful and successful in settling the more turbulent tribes to a peaceful life devoted more or less to ordinary pursuits, however crudely followed. The more sanguinary and reprehensible customs were put down with a firm hand and generous dealing. Once the turbulent tribes had become peaceful, the method, which proved so useful in subduing and pacifying them and which may be called the method of indirect rule with the help of almost absolute powers vested in the executive head of the district or the tract, was stereotyped and adhered to. The fact that, even after the establishment of almost absolute executive control of the areas, many of the tribes concerned rose in rebellion over and over again, or almost came to the point of doing so in the desperate attempts to redress more or less the same grievances, affords clear proof of the partial failure of the administrative expedient to take proper care of their welfare.[128]

It is clear from the above extract that in Ghurye's opinion, the policy of centralised rule by a 'man on the spot', which nearly all British/European scholar-administrators-cum-anthropologists heavily favoured, had not succeeded in pacifying the tribes. This sort of paternalistic despotic rule in which the executive and judicial functions were concentrated in a single person was a remnant of the late eighteenth and nineteenth-century administrative regimes. According to Ghurye, there was very little evidence to suggest that the model of indirect rule had led to the general welfare of the subject population. The solution lay in greater contact with the Hinduised segments of the population, as such a course would be 'one of the best educative processes, provided it is properly supervised'.[129]

In another long chapter, Ghurye provided a detailed analysis of the constitutional deliberations on the question of Backward Tracts. Starting with the Simon Commission proceedings until the debate in the British

[128]Ibid., pp. 123–124.
[129]Ibid., p. 125.

Parliament, he presented a thorough survey of how the list of excluded and partially excluded areas was massively expanded. The retention of the territorial logic embodied in the system of exclusion and partial exclusion greatly irked Ghurye as for him, it symbolised a return to the situation when the Scheduled Districts Act had been passed. He alleged that,

> This means that sixty years of administration, general and special had not enabled the machinery entrusted with it to do much by way of preparing the people to take care of their interests in a population which ... was largely sympathetic to their cause. This fact should be sufficient condemnation of exclusion as a protective measure.[130]

Ghurye acknowledged that the favourite argument in support of the exclusion and partial exclusion of backward tribes was the 'non-preparedness of the backward peoples for parliamentary institutions'.[131] However, in this context he also raised the issue of usurpation of the legitimate political rights of the non-aboriginals in excluded and partially excluded areas. He argued that the system of territorial segregation disregarded and 'ignored the relevant questions regarding the non-aboriginals in whose midst the protected aborigines live and on whom they depend to some extent for their livelihood'.[132] The non-aboriginal sections of the population were, in many cases, long-term settlers in these tracts, and were not necessarily the classes exploiting the so-called aboriginals. Also, Ghurye argued, 'Because some of them took unfair advantage of the simplicity and ignorance of the aborigines it does not mean that their quota to the socio-economic development can be written off, much less can they be treated as a rightless population.'[133] He pointed out that politically conscious Indians were demanding that the system of administration in Scheduled Districts or Backward Tracts needed reforms on the principle of 'utter separation of judicial from executive functions'. Any delay in meeting these demands of the non-aboriginals segments was 'bound to nurse anger against the aborigines who thus appear to it in the role of a hindrance to its political advancement'.[134]

About the overall efficacy of protectionist policies via the territorial segregation of predominantly tribal areas, Ghurye was of the opinion that

---

[130] Ibid., p. 142.
[131] Ibid., p. 144.
[132] Ibid., p. 146.
[133] Ibid., p. 150.
[134] Ibid., p. 151.

'the device is not such a panacea for the ills of the so-called aborigines that it should have been considered indispensable.'[135] It is clear from a perusal of the evidence presented in this section that Ghurye's monograph constituted an up-to-date scholarly intervention in the debate between the Protectionists and the Assimilationists. The Hindu nationalist views of Ghurye had created a political bias against scheduling, predicated as they were upon the distinctiveness of the aboriginal religious faith, as distinct from mainstream Hinduism. Thus, Ghurye prepared the theoretical ground to nullify the tribal 'aboriginality' argument. Soon enough, the results were visible. Poornima Paidipaty has written,

> Ghurye's intervention unravels the two fundamental assumptions that had guided anthropology in India since its early formation as a frontier science. The first assumption centered around territory and its role in physically locating and enframing India's tribes, and the second concerned the presumption [that] tribals are aboriginals who share a set of historical dilemmas and political struggles were [*sic*] similar communities in Australia and Americas. These assumptions were closely entwined; each was made possible by the other. Ghurye challenges both assumptions, and in so doing, lays the groundwork for a post-colonial social science that takes the developing nation-state as its object.[136]

By the middle of 1945, A. V. Thakkar, the leading nationalist proponent of the Assimilationist school of thought, had adopted Ghurye's sarcastic expression, 'so-called Aborigines'. In one of his public responses to Ambedkar, Thakkar wrote:

> All the people enumerated as Tribes are neither Aborigines, nor are they all Hill Tribes; and that is why I have used the word 'so-called' above. It is very difficult even for scientists and anthropologists who migrated first into Hindustan—either from the North-West or the North-East. In a way, even the large Aryan population may be called Aborigines. Nor are all the tribal people 'Hill Tribes'. A very large percentage of them do, as a matter of fact, live in the plains, and may have come down from the hills in the distant past. At any rate, a very

[135]Ibid., p. 153.

[136]Poornima L. Paidipaty, 'Tribal Nation: Politics and the Making of Anthropology in India, 1874–1967', Ph.D. Dissertation, Graduate School of Arts and Sciences, Columbia University, 2010, p. 112. This is a correct assessment, although a lot of archival spadework needs to be done in this direction.

> small percentage of the Tribals, which may be estimated at between 10 and 20 percent may be called by the name by which they are generally known, namely, Aboriginal and Hill Tribes. So the words 'Tribes' and 'Tribal Peoples' is a more correct description of them, to distinguish them from other communities—Hindus, Muslims and Christians.[137]

This evidence indicates that Ghurye's academic mockery of the term 'Aborigines' did provide a major theoretical break for Thakkar at precisely the time when his views were rapidly gaining political ascendancy in the 1940s. The legitimacy of the earlier term was waning and efforts were underway to substitute it with a new term. This points towards the wider effect that Ghurye's thesis had. In his Kale Memorial Lecture delivered in 1941, Thakkar had repeatedly used the word 'aboriginal' and called them 'original sons of the soil'. Ghurye's work literally splintered the argument of autochthonous status embedded in the concept 'aboriginal', and the Congress nationalists incorporated this logic rapidly into their rhetoric.

Thus, *The Aborigines—'So-Called'* can legitimately be seen as epitomising the nationalist critique of the British policy towards tribal communities. By simultaneously using and critiquing colonial sources, Ghurye mounted a frontal attack on the anthropologists'/Isolationist/Protectionist logic and argued that the category of 'aborigines' was a myth and a colonial construct. As depicted in the title, they were 'so-called' without much factual/historical ground. At best, they could be described only as 'Backward Hindus'. Essentially, Ghurye broke the back of the argument that aboriginals were autochthonous communities.

By the time *The Aborigines—'So-Called'* appeared in print, Ghurye was wielding considerable academic influence. As Rivers' pupil, Ghurye's years of anthropological training at Cambridge had equipped him well to take on the likes of Hutton and Elwin. Having been trained by the undisputed leader of the Neo-Diffusionist school of anthropological theory, Ghurye was also well aware of the strengths and weaknesses of their ideological arsenal. He deployed this knowledge with aplomb and particularly targeted Elwin for his attacks. It is chiefly on the strength of those attacks that a lasting

[137] A. V. Thakkar, 'Education among Tribal People very Backward: State's Responsibility for their Advancement', *Leader*, 11 July 1945, reproduced in *Aboriginals' Cry in the Wilderness: Controversy between Dr. Ambedkar and A.V. Thakkar with Facts and Figures Regarding Aborigines and Hill Tribes, Their Education and Representation in Legislature*, Published by A. V. Thakkar, Servants of India Society, Bombay, n.d.

impression took root: that the early 1940s had witnessed a Ghurye–Elwin debate on the fate of the aboriginal communities.

Paradoxically, however, as should be apparent by now, this supposed vibrant debate never took place, and is an academic myth/misnomer. After the publication of Ghurye's book, Elwin retreated absolutely and unconditionally. The polemicist *par excellence*, who always loved a good fight, had clearly been jolted by the vitriolic nature of Ghurye's opposition. One must also remember that Elwin was not a university trained anthropologist. Of course, his wide reading and years of social work had made him deeply familiar with issues surrounding the future of the aboriginal communities, but the anthropologists based in metropolitan Britain still did not take him very seriously. Quite unlike his style of functioning, Elwin never gave a public reply to Ghurye. In fact, I would argue that Ghurye's book, more than anything else, triggered a shift in Elwin's tactics and strategy, which becomes visible later. He started bridging his differences with Thakkar and the two began collaborating on countering the Christian missionary challenge in Elwin's operational base of Mandla district.

Fortunately for Elwin, the publication of his own pamphlet, *The Aboriginals*, closely followed Ghurye's book. It is hard to say whether this was a deliberate tactical move on Elwin's part. Nevertheless, the pamphlet was eminently accessible, readable, and remained a succinct and brief introduction to the aboriginal issue in India of the 1940s. Also, owing to its reputed publishers and their far wider distribution networks, *The Aboriginals* was much more widely read than either Ghurye's work or Elwin's own *Loss of Nerve*, which had been published two years earlier.[138] In fact, *Loss of Nerve* had a very limited print run and soon went out of print. Elwin used the new pamphlet to broadcast his ideas and its timing also helped to undercut the force of Ghurye's criticism without even once referring to him. Much of the material and paragraphs in the new pamphlet were lifted straight out of *Loss of Nerve*.

---

[138] A careful perusal of Elwin's work suggests that he was intensely competitive and not a very generous scholar as far as acknowledgements were concerned. Even for the *Loss of Nerve* argument, he may have been inspired by N. K. Bose's essay in *Science and Culture*, titled 'The Hindu Method of Tribal Absorption'. Nowhere does Elwin acknowledge Bose. In return, perhaps, no article of Elwin was published in *Man in India* after Bose took over its editorship in 1951. Alas, the long-term nature of academic rivalries!

Nevertheless, in the pamphlet, under the sub-head 'Missionary solution', Elwin echoed the position of scholar-administrators like Mills and Hutton, who spoke consistently against the proselytising activities of Christian missionaries. He wrote that conversion to Christianity 'does not so much solve the problem as substitute another problem for it'. Much to the delight of the nationalist social reformers, Elwin took the position that:

> The religion of the aboriginals, at least of peninsular India, should be regarded as a religion of the Hindu family, with special relation to the exciting, dangerous, catastrophic Shivaite type, but as having a distinct existence of its own. For purposes of the Census, all aboriginals should be classed as Hindus by religion, but separate returns of their numbers by race should be provided'.[139]

This was a huge victory for the nationalist camp epitomised by Thakkar and Ghurye. For now the opposition, that is, the anthropologists, seemed humbled.

Conclusion

By the late 1930s, the debate on the pros and cons of scheduling, also known as the 'tribal question', had scaled up to influence the entire discourse on the aboriginal tribes. The catalyst became, yet again, the upcoming Census operation of 1941, which, if only in retrospect, was destined to be the last colonial decennial Census. At the time, however, the fate of the British Indian Empire was yet unknown and with Viceroy Lord Linlithgow's unilateral declaration of India joining World War II on the side of the Allied Powers (without consulting Indian politicians), the Congress ministries resigned *en masse* in protest. These developments had the effect of placing the provisions of the Government of India Act, 1935, into a state of suspended animation. In such uncertainty and flux, the contours of a post-war power-sharing arrangement would depend upon the success of organised political groupings in claiming and rallying the largest number of constituent subjects under their respective banners.

Therefore, like earlier Census operations, the partial Census of 1941 also became a highly politicised affair whereby religious identity became a primary unit of enumeration. Thus commenced a highly contested series

[139]Verrier Elwin, *The Aboriginals*, Oxford Pamphlets on Indian Affairs No. 14, Humphrey Milford: Oxford University Press, July 1942, p. 25.

of claims, critiques, and counterclaims on the religious status of the Indian aborigines, which sharpened the already existing fault-lines in the ongoing discussions on the future of aborigines in India. While this chapter does not explicitly deal with the conduct of the 1941 Census operations, it focuses on how the question of religious identity stopped being an underlying issue of debate between ICS men, a debate usually confined to the Census reports. At this new juncture, Indians were actively participating in what was fast becoming a public sphere, where religion had emerged as the defining lens for representational politics. Such discussions proliferated at an unusual pace, which accelerated the dismantling of the cognitive framework set up by J. H. Hutton and its substitution by a new one informed fundamentally by the 'Hindu' religious identity of aboriginal tribes. This momentous transformation occurred in three distinct stages: (*i*) Elwin's breakaway from the Huttonian framework; (*ii*) Ghurye's proxy appearance and attack on the category of 'aborigines'; and finally, (*iii*) the setting up of the Isolation/Protection versus Intervention/Assimilation binary, which, I have argued, was an expression of the divide between the anthropologists and the nationalists.

Therefore, this chapter begins with a prolonged discussion of the India career of Verrier Elwin, one of the chief protagonists in the so-called Ghurye-Elwin debate. He began social work amongst the aborigines along the template set up by Thakkar and received patronage from Congress supporters/financiers like Seth Jamnalal Bajaj. However, Elwin's growing sympathy for tribal people, combined with a pragmatic necessity to mend bridges with the English ruling class, led him to embrace the anthropological position. In fact, Elwin crossed camps several times and each shift in ideological posturing was marked by a pressing need to adapt to contingent political conditions. Thus, Elwin's life embodied the shifting fortunes of various factions in the late colonial debate on scheduling of tribal areas. As a participant in a series of often public debates, opportunism did guide Elwin, and he emerges as much a crucial political figure as an intellectual one. While the binding theme in these many crossovers was the tribal predicament, I would single out Elwin's transformation of the idea of aboriginal religion, which changed the contours of the discourse on aboriginal tribes. After critically studying his intellectual metamorphoses, it becomes very hard to think of Elwin's India career in neat 'Philanthropologist' terms. Nonetheless, he was a key figure whose multiple contributions must be analysed in order to understand the continuities and changes in the discourse on tribal people, from colonial to independent India.

The departure of J. H. Hutton for England left a leadership vacuum, which was sought to be filled by Elwin. Being a master polemicist, Elwin knew that to buttress his bid to helm the anthropological bandwagon, he required an innovative strategy that opened public debates with Thakkar, the undisputed nationalist ideologue on Indian aboriginal tribes. Realising that leadership claims often require new labels and slogans, Elwin began recasting the older debate between anthropologists and nationalists. In 1940, when Thakkar sent a proposal to W. G. Archer, the 1941 Census Commissioner of Bihar, for the establishment of an 'Indian Aborigines Friends Society', Elwin critiqued it and came up with a new binary, viz., 'Protectionists' versus 'Interventionists'. While the former, he argued, appreciated aboriginal culture on their own terms and advocated preserving them against rapid changes, the latter derided it and wanted to 'uplift' the aborigine to a level of uniformity with the outside world. In a tit-for-tat response delivered at the Fifth R. R. Kale Memorial Lecture (1941), Thakkar refused to cede ground and accused the Protectionists of being regressive 'Isolationists' who wanted to stop the natural evolution of aboriginals for academic reasons. Thakkar debunked Elwin's expression 'Interventionist' and self-defined himself as an 'Assimilationist'. In Thakkar's articulation, Assimilationist stood as a synonym for the nationalist, who advocated steady assimilation with the surrounding culture.

Besides the ongoing semantic feud with Thakkar, the early 1940s were also the stage for Elwin's intellectual break with Hutton. The moment came while Elwin was serving as the Honorary Ethnographer and Census Officer of Bastar State for the 1941 Census. Earlier, from his base in Mandla district, Elwin had observed the problems encountered by aboriginals in British-administered India. Bastar, being a Princely State, provided a comparative frame of reference for Elwin's analysis of aboriginal tribes in Central India. The experiences gained therein resulted in the publication of *Loss of Nerve*, which marks a turning point for the anthropologists in general and for Elwin in particular. This pamphlet made two important moves. *First*, it discarded the straitjacketed identification of all the hilly and forested areas as quintessentially tribal habitats, thereby critiquing the monolithic conception of the true Indian aborigine based on geographical metaphors. *Second*, Elwin found that the religious practices of aboriginals in inaccessible areas like Bastar were remarkably akin to mainstream

Hinduism, leading him to jettison the bogey of 'Tribal Religion' as entirely distinct from Hinduism. Combining the insights of both these departures from the Huttonian framework, Elwin's intervention went on to shake up the theoretical unity of the 'Aboriginal Tribe'. He proposed an alternative analytical framework based on class and cultural autonomy, using which the Indian aboriginals could be divided into three sub-categories of Hinduised, semi-Hinduised, and those who were geographically far enough from mainstream Hindu influences, to enable the maintenance of cultural distinctiveness. To sum up, I have argued that Elwin played a key role in recasting the discourse on aboriginal tribes in India by foregrounding the theory that the tribes were part of the Hindu religio-cultural paradigm.

Almost simultaneously, Thakkar was mounting a measured and carefully calibrated strategy to nullify Elwin's challenge for an open public debate. Initially, he held back any knee-jerk response to Elwin's consistent (and, at times, below the belt) criticism, aware that he was being baited. Being a man of action (and not of words), Thakkar also realised that such a duel would be an unequal one where Elwin, the litterateur par excellence, held an edge. Thus, Thakkar's ideation in the Kale Memorial lecture should be seen only as an interim response, which paved the way for a final assault. To mount an effective theoretical response, Thakkar needed a sharp ally, someone well-versed in the anthropological vocabulary and willing to play a proxy role. Ultimately, Thakkar sprung a surprise by endorsing and publishing G. S. Ghurye's *The Aborigines—'So-Called'—And Their Future*, which marked the apogee of a theoretical intervention for nationalists.

In this book, Ghurye effectively countered both the central claims of the anthropologists. arguing that any 'proper description' of the 'so-called' aborigines should account for 'their place in or near Hindu society and not to their supposed autochthonism'. As 'imperfectly integrated ... tribal classes' of Hindu society, their true description was 'Backward Hindus'. The strength of Ghurye's thesis came from his use of colonial ethnographic and Census records as the building blocks for erecting the nationalist argument against the anthropological position. Scarred by Ghurye's personal attack, Elwin never responded to his nemesis in either public or private capacity. Subsequently, Elwin withdrew from any identification with a pro-scheduling stance, which the nationalists had used to malign him.

Finally, after a careful analysis of the amalgam of ideas implied in the binary opposition of 'Protection/Isolation versus Intervention/ Assimilation', we can undoubtedly say that it was simply another iteration of the anthropologists *versus* nationalists debate. In these exchanges, while the term or the idea of scheduling was seldom used, substantively speaking, a clear resonance between the two sets of ideas can be seen. The anthropologists, who advocated the widespread scheduling of areas with a demographic majority of aboriginal tribes, were cultural relativists, arguing that civilisation (a metaphor for the combined forces of law, democracy, and organised religions) would spell doom for the future of Indian aborigines. A 'ring-fencing' of such areas would act as a useful check and provide the aboriginal tribes with invaluable time to make the necessary adjustments and survive a possible cultural genocide. Thus, the creation of 'islands' against 'civilisation' was a desirable way forward.

In contrast, the nationalists were cultural universalists, with a firm belief in the pan-India project of a standardised and uniform mainstream 'Hindu' culture that absorbed or 'assimilated' everything in its wake. For them, the metaphor of civilisation with the very same combination of forces (law, democracy, and religion) was a desirable path and since the instrument of scheduling had tried to check the march of civilisation into aboriginal areas, it was deemed as an unmitigated evil that struck at the roots of national solidarity. Hence, despite their seeming freshness, the catch-all terms were no more than new tags or synonyms in the politics of scheduling. Proverbially, it was a case of old wine in new bottles! Undoubtedly, Elwin as well as Ghurye had played an instrumental role in bringing these terms into circulation. In time, these labels attached to these personalities created a false binary that gradually supplanted the ideological one between anthropologists and nationalists.

Nevertheless, the nationalists were far from being totally victorious, for a number of challenges awaited them as World War II came to an end. The Congressmen who claimed to represent all of India were to face several challenges in disparate tribal theatres across the country. These had a catalytic impact on the politics of scheduling, and it is to these diverse regional narratives that we now turn our attention.

8

A Future for the Tribes

The Making of the Fifth and Sixth Schedules of the Indian Constitution

As World War II stretched into mid-1944, the balance of power turned in favour of the Allied forces. Although Britain was on the winning side, her economic and military might had been shattered. The Quit India Movement of 1942 had witnessed an unprecedented upsurge, which could only be suppressed by brute force. Additionally, the working of the constitutional machinery under the Government of India Act, 1935, remained suspended during these years. As the war drew to an end, in anticipation of the transfer of power through a new working Constitution, hectic political mobilisation began on all sides.

An End to Colonial Administrative Discourse: Towards the Constituent Assembly

In this critical phase, Sir Robert Reid, Governor of Assam (1937–1942), was the earliest to advocate an alternative arrangement for administering tribal areas. Sympathetic towards the eastern hill tribes of India and Upper Burma, Reid proposed a 'Crown Colony' comprising the Naga Hills, the North-East Frontier Agency, the Chittagong Hill Tracts, and the Naga-inhabited areas of Burma. Since these areas were inhabited by similar racial groups, he believed it was possible to 'create a nation out of the congeries of tribes'.[1] This

[1]Asoso Yonuo, *The Rising Nagas: A Historical and Political Study*, Delhi: Vivek Publishing House, 1974, p. 139.

radical idea was, however, not made public and only floated in the higher echelons of the colonial State apparatus.[2]

A similar suggestion was made by Sir Reginal Coupland, the Beit Professor of Colonial History at the University of Oxford, in his three-volume report on the constitutional problem in India.[3] In the third volume of his report, titled *The Future of India,*[4] Coupland identified three primary needs of the aboriginal people: *first,* protection of their land and customary life from exploitation and disturbance; *second,* an extension of social services, especially health and education; and *third,* sympathetic administration on the lines of 'indirect rule' as practised in British Africa.[5] Coupland wrote,

> The ultimate responsibility for the welfare of these backward people thus rests at present on the British Parliament. No specific promises have been made about their future; but since their claims must be considered in the framing of the new constitution and since they cannot speak for themselves, the British Government would clearly be entitled to make representations on their behalf.[6]

Drawing on these suggestions, Leopold Amery, the Secretary of State for India, wrote to the Viceroy Lord Wavell in September 1944,[7] impressing upon him the 'moral obligation' of the British to ensure the welfare and protection of these 'primitive and helpless people'. He suggested that 'some extra-constitutional arrangement' for the protection of tribes be 'agreed and included in the Treaty between the new India and His Majesty's Government'.[8] Except in the Assam-Burma tract, a British High Commissioner with a specially trained staff might be vested with powers

---

[2]For the full report by Sir Robert Reid as well as some other plans being mulled over for the North-East Frontier tracts in the 1940s, see David R. Syiemlieh (ed.), *On the Edge of Empire: Four British Plans for North East India, 1941–1947,* New Delhi: Sage, 2014.

[3]IOR/L/P&J/7/6787, pp. 268–269.

[4]Reginald Coupland, *The Future of India: Third Part of a Report on the Constitutional Problem in India submitted to the Warden and Fellows of the Nuffield College, Oxford,* London: Oxford University Press, 1943.

[5]IOR/L/P&J/7/6787, pp. 268–269.

[6]Ibid.; emphasis mine.

[7]Pol. 6301/1944, Leopold Amery's letter to Lord Wavell, dated 28 September 1944, in IOR/L/P&J/7/6787, p. 178.

[8]Quoted in Pol. 9980/1945, Lord Wavell's letter no. 1005, dated 10 October 1945, in IOR/L/P &J/7/6787, pp. 41–43.

of supervision over relations with the backward tribes. Alternatively, he thought the United Nations Organization could be induced to undertake certain responsibilities in respect of the tribes.[9] Wavell, however, was not convinced of the practicability of Amery's proposals and replied that he could not foresee future British governments 'spending large sums or making great efforts for the backward tribes'. Additionally, Indian governments too would be unwilling to accept 'British or international interference or supervision'.[10]

In the last quarter of 1945, Amery's successor Frederick Pethick-Lawrence asked Wavell's advice on the possibility of effective supervision of tribal areas from the Centre. He had been impressed by the proposals of Verrier Elwin and John A. Hubback (ICS, former Governor of Orissa) on the appointment of an Adviser for the aboriginal tribes.[11] Pethick-Lawrence favoured Hubback's idea of having a three-member Board (comprising an anthropologist, an administrator, and a missionary) and suggested that a proposal similar to Articles 73 and 74 of the San Francisco Charter[12] be incorporated in the new Constitution as part of a declaration of minority rights.[13]

Following this, Wavell wrote to the Provincial Governors, laying out the proposal for an Advisory Board and seeking their responses. Foreseeing 'administrative objection to complete centralization', he argued that the balance lay in an arrangement where 'the Provincial Governments retained their administrative responsibility (and) the central government gave special grants, undertook inspections and received periodical reports'.[14] The idea of financial grants from the Centre was also proposed. Thus, a shift away from the earlier Governor-centric paradigm of 'scheduling' was already taking place in the late colonial administrative discourse. These ideas may also be seen as the first rudimentary steps towards the provisions of scheduling that came to be enshrined in the Indian Constitution.

---

[9]Ibid.

[10]Pol. 7378/1944, Extract from Private and Secret Letter of Lord Wavell to Mr Amery, dated 10 October 1944, in IOR/L/P&J/7/6787.

[11]Elwin to Francis, 8 November 1944, Pol. 9169/1945, pp. 103–105, and Hubback's Note on Verrier Elwin's Orissa Report, pp. 45–46, L/P&J/7/6787, IOR.

[12]Articles 73 and 74 of the UN Charter comprise the 'Declaration Regarding Non-Self-Governing Territories'.

[13]Wavell to Governors, 10 October 1945, Pol. 9980/1945, L/P&J/7/6787, IOR, pp. 41–43.

[14]Ibid.

The responses of the Provincial Governors were interesting and varied. They almost unanimously opposed the inclusion of a missionary as the third member of the proposed Central Board, since 'it would arouse the suspicions of over-sensitive Indians'. Instead, they suggested that the third member be chosen on the basis of 'experience and knowledge of the Backward Tribes', thereby allowing 'the missionaries an equal chance of being selected along with other specialists such as doctors and agricultural experts'.[15] On the matter of having a central advisory authority, the Governors were a divided house. While the Provincial Governors of Bombay, Madras, and Bengal favoured the idea, others were emphatically opposed to it on the grounds that advice and supervision from the Centre would be disadvantageous to provincial autonomy. Subsequently, the discussion regarding the establishment of a central supervisory board for tribal areas was unceremoniously dropped.

Constitutional Deliberations on Future Administration of Tribal Areas

It was the British Cabinet Mission statement of 16 May 1946 that paved the way for the final constitutional deliberations on the predominantly tribal areas of India. According to paragraphs 19(iv) and 20 of the Cabinet Mission proposals, an Advisory Committee on the 'rights of citizens, Minorities and Tribal and Excluded Areas' would be constituted. It would contain full representation of the interested parties and would

> report to the Union Constituent Assembly upon the list of fundamental rights, the clauses for the protection of minorities, and a scheme for the administration of the tribal and excluded areas and to advise whether these rights should be incorporated in the provinces, group, or Union Constitution.[16]

At this juncture, the All India Excluded and Partially Excluded Areas Association mounted a stiff resistance against the instrument of scheduling, opposing any attempt 'to make this invidious distinction a permanent feature of the future constitution of India'.[17] Instead, it argued for the abolition of

---

[15]Minute on the subject of 'Backward Tribes', in IOR/L/P&J/7/6787, N.S. 2.

[16]K. M. Munshi (ed.), *Indian Constitutional Documents: Munshi Papers, Volume II*, Bombay: BVB, 1967, p. 30.

[17]20 September 1946, File No. G-59, 1947, AICC Papers, PMML, New Delhi, p. 49.

these barriers so that 'the so called aboriginal races will in common with their other countrymen work out the destiny of a greater and happier India'.[18] A General Body meeting held at Rajahmundry on 12 and 13 September 1946 decided that the Association would relocate its office temporarily to Delhi during the sessions of the Constituent Assembly so as to keep track of unfolding developments. The General Body appealed to the interim Central government and provincial governments to create 'Backward Areas and Tribes Development Departments'. It further called upon the interim Central government to appoint an inquiry committee to look into the conditions of these areas and suggest measures for their development. The Constituent Assembly was asked to elect 'peoples' representatives from the excluded and partially excluded areas to the proposed Advisory Committee.

The Association further organised a conference in Delhi on 20 January 1947. At this event, P. Kodanda Ramaiah, the Chairman of the Reception Committee, made an emotive appeal to members of the Constituent Assembly, 'in the name of humanity, to treat the tribal people on the same footing as others and thereby avoid the creation of another minority'.[19] The Conference was inaugurated by the Congress President, J. B. Kripalani, who in his inaugural address said,

> The greatest injustice done by the British rule to the people of this country was that it tried to keep the Indian society in a fossilized State. Under the plea of preserving the integrity, honesty and purity of the Aborigines, they put them under special rule. The real aim was to prevent the exploitation of the rich mineral resources of the Excluded Areas. Though the Aborigines had a rich democratic tradition and experience of panchayat raj they were not allowed to advance so that they might help the British in their 'divide and rule' policy.[20]

Kripalani assured the conference that as soon as the Congress assumed power, the system of excluded and partially excluded areas would be abolished.

Four days after the conclusion of the conference, on 24 January 1947, the Constituent Assembly decided to elect an Advisory Committee as per the Cabinet Mission Plan. According to the original plan, there would

---

[18] Ibid.

[19] 'Excluded Areas Abolition: Delhi Conference Plea', *The Times of India*, 20 January 1947, p. 9.

[20] Pol. 10329/1947, Information Department, India Office—Telegram B.46 from the Press Information Bureau, New Delhi, dated 20 January 1947, in IOR/L/PJ/10/31.

be thirteen members from Tribal and Excluded Areas who were to decide on the appropriate administrative model for tribal areas. This Committee went on to issue a number of pamphlets on the subject of excluded and partially excluded areas.[21] These documents constitute the first official Indian exposition on the tribal question in the nascent stages of the Constitution-making exercise. They lay down the paradigm within which the nationalists sought to resolve the problem of the 'Backward Tribes' in independent India.[22]

At the same time, the pamphlets cited the concerns of several administrators, conveying the views of the still present 'official block' that continued to feed into the discourse on tribal areas. For example, in the case of Bombay, the pamphlet quoted extensively from the report of D. Symington to discuss the massive under-representation of tribal communities in local self-governing institutions:

> Mr. Symington pointed out that at the time of his report, out of 18 elective seats in West Khandesh District Local Board not one had ever been filled by a Bhil though their population in the district was 35 per cent. The Bhil representatives in the local Board were two nominated members. Similarly in some taluka boards, with Bhils over 50 per cent of the population, there were no elected Bhils out of a total of 63 elective seats. Mr. Symington concluded that there was in practice no local self-government for the aboriginal and hill tribes.

Similarly, in the case of Central Provinces (C.P.), it relied upon the report by W. V. Grigson to analyse local self-governing institutions and various protective legislations. Grigson had criticised the Congress Ministry's move to abolish the nomination of aboriginal members in the local boards and district councils through Act XXXII of 1939, calling it a 'premature and regrettable change'. Like Symington, Grigson, too, was of the view that the representation of the aboriginals through elections was not satisfactory. In his opinion, the existing district councils and local boards had completely neglected the aboriginal areas, and hence should be replaced by independent

---

[21] *Constituent Assembly of India, Advisory Committee (Tribal and Excluded Areas), Excluded and Partially Excluded Areas (I and II)*, Printed by Manager, Government of India Press, New Delhi, 1948.

[22] *Constituent Assembly of India, Advisory Committee (Tribal and Excluded Areas), Excluded and Partially Excluded Areas-II*, New Delhi: Government of India Press, 1948. The next few paragraphs and quotes are based on this source, especially pp. 4, 9, and 21.

local boards with official office-bearers and mostly nominated members for tribal areas other than Mandla. For the backward areas, he held, a system of indirect election was the most suitable model.

As far as Assam was concerned, there were three classes of tribal areas: Sadiya, Balipara, and Lakhimpur tracts were 'Frontier Tribal Areas' which, along with the 'Naga Tribal Area' on the Indo-Burmese frontier, were loosely administered by the Political Officers; the excluded areas of Naga Hills District, Lushai Hills, and the North Cachar Hills; and the partially excluded areas of Garo Hills, Mikir Hills, and Khasi and Jaintia Hills. These areas comprised a bewildering variety of tribes, and the influence of Christian missionaries had also led to the emergence of a small minority of educated tribesmen. In view of the educational advancement witnessed amongst the hill tribesmen, the Advisory Committee remarked that educationally, these areas cannot be said to be backward and even in the excluded areas inhabited by the remote Nagas, 'the general situation does not seem to be as bad as in the Ganjam hill tracts of Orissa'. However, sounding a cautionary note, the Advisory Committee acknowledged that the tribes were 'by no means a single people and the question of finding a limited number of representatives like one or two may present some difficulties'.

As is evident, in the deliberations of the Advisory Committee, the issue of representational democracy for tribal areas emerged as the primary fault-line, which divided the nationalist opinions from those of the anthropologists. The Committee launched a frontal attack on the advocates of tribal isolation and protection, especially Verrier Elwin, whose work was characterised as seeking to 'achieve their [aboriginals] freedom and happiness by shutting them off'.[23] Instead, the Committee gave greater credence to the views of B. S. Guha, an anthropologist whose position approximated that of the Congress. Guha held that the main considerations for tribal areas should be: (*i*) preservation of tribal life and authority, and (*ii*) participation and gradual integration of the tribes in the general life of the country. He pointed out that the United States government had followed a policy of aboriginal segregation in sanctuaries or reservations, but the decline of the Native American tribes had continued to take place on account of their 'lack of adaptability and loss of will to live'.

In its final take on the policy of isolation, the Advisory Committee remarked that the proposals for national parks or isolation were based on an

[23]Several passages from his published works were quoted in a chapter titled 'The Policy of Isolation'.

over-statement of the case for safeguarding the interests of the aboriginals. As the country was moving towards independence and sovereignty, this was irrelevant and did not constitute 'practical politics'. Moreover, the isolation line could not be representative of the aspirations of the tribals themselves, as they did not understand its implications.

At its meeting on 27 February 1947, the Advisory Committee set up three sub-committees: the first to consider the tribal and excluded and partially excluded areas in Assam; the second to consider the tribal areas in the North-West Frontier Province and Baluchistan: and the third to consider the excluded and partially excluded areas in provinces other than Assam.[24] These sub-committees were given a period of three months to tour their respective areas and submit their recommendations. They could also co-opt members from the tribal areas.

By June, however, with the pronouncement of the Partition Plan by the new Viceroy Lord Mountbatten, the North-West Frontier Tribal Areas Sub-Committee was no longer required to undertake its task. Given the complexity of their task and the inaccessible terrain they had to traverse, the other two sub-committees overshot their deadlines. The Assam sub-committee, headed by Gopinath Bordoloi, submitted its report on 28 July 1947. The sub-committee headed by A. V. Thakkar submitted its report in two instalments: the first interim report relating to Madras, Bombay, Bengal, Central Provinces, and Orissa in August 1947, and the second report dealing with Bihar, United Provinces, and Punjab in September 1947.

The reports of these two sub-committees are important documents that formed the basis for the enactment of the Fifth and Sixth Schedules. Before analysing them, a few qualifications are in order. *First*, they dealt only with the British Indian provinces and hence, a third of the Indian landscape comprising the Princely States were outside their purview. *Second*, they were written very hastily during a time of great political drama.

---

[24]The composition of these sub-committees was: (a) *North East Frontier (Assam) Tribal and Excluded Areas Sub-Committee*: (*i*) Gopinath Bordoloi (Chairman); (*ii*) Rev. J. J. M. Nichols-Roy; (*iii*) Rup Nath Brahma; (*iv*) Mayang Nokcha; (*v*) A. V. Thakkar; (b) *North West Frontier Tribal Areas Sub-Committee*: (*i*) Khan Abdul Gaffar Khan; (*ii*) Khan Abdul Samad Khan; (*iii*) Mehr Chand Khanna; (c) *Excluded and Partially Excluded Areas (other than Assam) Sub-Committee*: (*i*) A. V. Thakkar (Chairman); (*ii*) Jaipal Singh; (*iii*) Devendra Nath Samanta; (*iv*) Phul Bhanu Shah; (*v*) Jagjivan Ram; (*vi*) Prafulla Chandra Ghosh; (*vii*) Raj Krushna Bose.

The sub-committee headed by A. V. Thakkar, the leading nationalist ideologue on the aboriginal problem, had as its co-opted members, Khetramani Panda, Sadashiv Tripathi, Kodanda Ramaiah, Sneha Kumar Chakma, and Dumber Singh Gurung. An ICS officer, R. K. Ramdhyani, was appointed the Secretary of the sub-committee. Thus, the members of this body were mainly Congressmen, and the only Adivasi members were Jaipal Singh Munda and Devendra Nath Samanta, both of whom hailed from Chota Nagpur. The latter also owed allegiance to the Indian National Congress.

A prime item on the sub-committee's agenda was the introduction of representational democracy through direct elections. Under the Government of India Act, 1935, the excluded areas were not represented in the provincial legislatures and hence had 'no experience of local self-governing institutions of the modern or statutory type'. On the other hand, all the partially excluded areas were included in the electoral constituencies of the provincial legislatures. With the exception of the Agency tracts of Madras and Orissa, the Santhal Parganas, and Jaunsar Bawar, the partially excluded areas were covered by local boards as well.

The debates over the issue of elections can be seen in some of the representations made to the sub-committee. In March 1947, when the sub-committee visited Bombay, the non-official witnesses whom it examined (D. N. Wandrekar, Parliamentary Secretary to the Prime Minister of Bombay, L. M. Shrikant, MLA V. V. Dandekar, MLC, and J. G. Natawadkar, MLA) submitted that the aboriginal tribes of Bombay Province should be represented in the central and provincial legislature by providing a reservation of seats in joint electorates. On the other hand, the official witnesses (D. Symington, E. W. Perry, M. D. Bhansali, and P. I. Sawe) reportedly told the sub-committee that the aborigines were 'not yet fit to be entrusted with responsibilities since they were in a nursery stage and had to be taught to stand on their own feet'.[25] In Madras, too, similar views were reportedly expressed.[26]

In the Central Provinces, officials as well as ministers expressed divergent views. While Grigson favoured a scheme of indirect elections by means of group panchayats, the C.P. officials were generally sceptical about

[25] *The Times of India*, 17 March 1947.

[26] Interim Report of the Constituent Assembly of India, Excluded and Partially Excluded Areas (other than Assam) Sub-Committee, Manager, Government of India Press, New Delhi, 1947. The rest of the section is based on this source.

elections producing suitable representatives. Wadiwa, a Gond pleader who gave evidence before the sub-committee, said that he could not contest the elections as the expenses involved were prohibitive. The ministers of the Central Provinces did not object to elections, but were strongly opposed to the reservation of seats in proportion to the aboriginal population. They held that increased representation in the various communities would be provided by their scheme of 'demarcating constituencies without the evil of creating a separatist mentality'. Grigson was also opposed to reservation, but opined that if reservations were made for the Scheduled Castes, there could be no justification for not providing similar protection to the aboriginals.

The interim report opposed the provisions of partial exclusion. It argued that ever since the system had been introduced in 1936, the representatives of partially excluded areas had not succeeded in bringing 'sufficient pressure and influence to bear on the Ministry'. Also, some partially excluded areas constituted small pockets in large districts, which often meant that their interests were subordinated 'to those of the larger areas in which they were contained'. Consequently, in these areas, the sub-committee recommended that the 'whole tribal population should be treated as a minority community for the welfare of whom certain special measures are necessary'. On the vital issue of elections, the sub-committee remarked:

> We have given serious thought to the question and have come to the conclusion that the tribals should have reserved seats in a joint electorate based on adult franchise.... The case of the tribals is not essentially different from that of the Scheduled Castes and they are in fact more backward in education and in their economic conditions than the Scheduled Castes. Representation in proportion to their numbers in the legislatures, even if some of them are not vocal or able to argue their case will emphasize the importance and urgency of their problems.... We do not think that the method of indirect election or nomination should be resorted to. The aboriginals have to take part in direct election some time and the sooner their training for this starts the better.

In its discussion on excluded and partially excluded areas, the sub-committee often reiterated the colonial discourse on these regions. Thus, it held that the social system of tribal people differed from those in plains areas. In terms of social customs, tribal laws of inheritance, marriage, and divorce were seen as distinct, a difference compounded by the fact that in several areas, people were 'too primitive to be able to understand or make use of the complicated procedure and law of the civil, criminal and revenue courts'. Consequently, a simplified system of justice was deemed necessary.

The discussion on land alienation also reiterated the colonial discourse. Land was seen as the 'only thing left to the aboriginal' as they did not follow non-agricultural professions. The sub-committee agreed that 'grant of the power of alienation to the tribals is certain to result in his gradual expropriation'. Thus, the report concluded that in certain areas, laws of the provincial legislature (which were likely to be based on the 'needs of the majority') should not apply automatically, at least in respect to certain subjects. Such areas were christened 'Scheduled Areas'.

In the colonial system of exclusion and partial exclusion, the Governor occupied a central position, with a 'special responsibility' that allowed him to over-rule any legislation deemed inimical to the tribal interests. The sub-committee remarked that in independent India, such discretionary powers would be 'undemocratic'. As an alternative mechanism, it recommended the constitution of a provincial body named the 'Tribes Advisory Council' (TAC), whose primary function would be to review the suitability of laws passed by the provincial legislature on 'special subjects', such as '(1) social matters, (2) occupation of land including tenancy laws, allotment of land and setting apart of land for village purposes, and (3) village management including the establishment of village panchayats'. The Council was to have veto rights on these matters. On other subjects, the provincial government could withhold or modify legislation on the advice of the TAC. The establishment of this body for at least ten years was deemed necessary in the provinces of Madras, Bombay, West Bengal, Bihar, Central Provinces and Berar, and Orissa.

Since funds were a major anxiety for Scheduled Areas, the sub-committee recommended a separate statement in the provincial budget that would show the revenues derived from and expenditure incurred in these areas. In the states of CP, Orissa, and Bihar, there was to be a separate minister in charge of the tribal areas, who would ideally be a tribal himself. Further, adequate representation was to be given to tribals in government services at the level of forest guards, constables, excise peons, and clerks. The report also spoke of encouraging tribal panchayats, a temperance propaganda, checking moneylending activities, and eliminating shifting cultivation.

Developmental tasks such as the construction and maintenance of roads, a special allowance for officials, provision of schools, medical facilities, and water supply were also 'dire needs which will doubtless make a heavy demand on the budget'. Although the sub-committee desired that the funds for such schemes should be found 'to the maximum possible extent' from the provinces, it was equally clear that unless the Central government 'provides the necessary assistance', at least some of the provinces may find it impossible to carry out schemes of improvement. Thus, as a solution to the financial needs of the Scheduled Areas, the sub-committee recommended that 'for all schemes of development approved by it the Central Government should contribute, in whole or in part, funds for the implementation of the development schemes'.

On 5 July 1947, the Indian Independence Act was passed by the British Parliament. It received royal assent on 18 July and this marked the end of British rule over India. In August 1947, the two States of India and Pakistan came into being. With this, the Government of India Act, 1935, and its Sections 91 and 92 relating to excluded and partially excluded areas became null and void. However, scheduling soon received a new lease of life when the Constitution of India adapted the protective provisions of these sections to meet the political exigencies of the successor State in independent India. Before moving on to the Constituent Assembly deliberations, it will be useful to survey the political landscape of the tribal question in India over 1945–1950.

Congress, Communists, and the Adivasi Mahasabha: Responses to the Emerging Tribal Political Consciousness

In scholarship, the resolution of the tribal question is often presented as sympathetic non-tribals speaking on behalf of the tribal populations because the tribes themselves were unable to articulate their demands.[27] Contrary to this position, I shall argue that the role played by tribal agency in this period has been inadequately understood, especially the dynamics of Adivasi interaction with the national movement led by the Indian National Congress. The final outlines of the discourse on tribes adopted by the independent Nation-State were predicated upon the negotiation with and eventual appropriation of tribal groups into the body-politic of India. This

---

[27]For an exception, see Prathama Banerjee, 'Writing the Adivasi: Some Historiographical Notes', *Indian Economic and Social History Review* 53 (1), 2016, pp. 131–153.

was a highly tumultuous process that needs to be studied on its own terms, and not from the dominant lenses of standard nationalist historiography.

In 1938, the Adivasi Mahasabha was established to advocate for constitutional rights for the tribals of the Jharkhand region. Subsequently, one of the chief demands of the Mahasabha was for the formation of a separate province of Jharkhand. Many tribal leaders associated with this organisation were Christian converts. They were also sought by Muslim League leaders looking for a possible alliance against the Congress. These developments alarmed Gandhi for he feared that under the influence of the Christian missions, the tribals might become 'de-Indianized' and develop separatist sentiments.[28] He wanted the Congress to take up the challenge to counter this in a strongly Indian manner by working amongst the Adivasis and wrote, 'They provide a vast field of service for Congressmen.'[29] As a counter to the Adivasi Mahasabha, the Congressmen established an Adivasi Seva Mandal headed by B. G. Kher, who was also Prime Minister of the Congress government in Bombay Province during 1937–1939.

To account for the earlier oversight, Gandhi added the (previously absent) topic of 'service of Adivasis' to a manifesto of the constructive programme.[30] He also started using the term 'Adivasi' consistently until his death. David Hardiman argues that Gandhi's usage of the term proves that he rejected the argument of the likes of G. S. Ghurye, who claimed that the tribals were merely 'backward Hindus' who had to be fully integrated into the Hindu mainstream.[31] Hardiman writes that by this stage,

> He [Gandhi] feared, however, that the Adivasis might follow the example of the Muslim League and launch a series of campaigns for separate states. He anticipated that this would happen if the caste Hindus continue to grind the Adivasis under their heels. The only way to prevent this, so far as he was concerned, was for nationalists to work amongst them in a selfless manner. If the government tried to ban

[28]David Hardiman, *Gandhi in His Time and Ours*, New Delhi: Permanent Black, 2003, p. 150.

[29]'On train Bardoli-Wardha, January 9 1942', from *Harijan*, 18 January 1942, in *Collected Works of Mahatma Gandhi*, Vol. 75, pp. 210–211. Available at www.gandhiheritageportal.org (accessed July 2024).

[30]'Constructive Programme: Its meaning and place', 13 December 1941, *CWMG*, Vol. 75, pp. 161–162. Available at www.gandhiheritageportal.org (accessed July 2024).

[31]Hardiman, *Gandhi in His Time and Ours*, pp. 151–152.

> them from Adivasi areas, they should court arrest and be prepared to go to jail. In an address to the Congress workers of Midnapore district in Bengal—an area with a large Adivasi population—he stated: 'The 1935 Act had separated them [the Adivasis] from the rest of the inhabitants of India and had placed the "excluded areas" under the Governor's direct administration. It was a shame that they had allowed them to be treated like that. It was up to them to make the Adivasis feel at one with them'. In the final three years of his life, he emphasized the need for such work in a way he had never done before, and he made a point of channeling Congress funds in that direction.[32]

Subsequently in 1942, the Quit India Movement once again witnessed a considerable swell in tribal support for the Indian National Congress. Although there exists very little secondary literature on the issue of tribal participation in this movement, Biswamoy Pati's article on Laxman Naiko's revolt in the Malkangiri area gives us a good idea about the course such events took.[33]

Malkangiri was under the *mustajari* system, whereby village headmen were in possession of hereditary rights to collect taxes from the tenants and make payments to the estate. Laxman Naiko was a Bhumiya tribal who, having inherited the post of *mustajar* from his father, was in charge of paying the taxes to the estate of Jeypore, a geographically large principality in Orissa. The area had a rich legacy of popular movements and the Rampa uprisings of the nineteenth and twentieth centuries (like that of Alluri Sitaram Raju) had evoked a considerable response. Naiko himself was influenced by Raju's *fituri*, although he did not pick up a gun.

Earlier in the 1920s, the Jeypore estate had witnessed some turmoil during the Non-cooperation Movement, but the local Congress organisation lacked a firm foothold then. This situation changed after Koraput was merged with the new province of Orissa in April 1936. The Provincial Congress Committee (PCC) made serious efforts to entrench itself on the ground. All three PCC candidates (Radhakrishna Biswaroi, Radhamohan Sahu, and Sadashiv Tripathy) from Koraput won in the 1937 elections against representatives of the zamindaris and the Jeypore Maharaja. With

---

[32]Ibid., p. 152.

[33]Biswamoy Pati, 'Storm over Malkangiri: A Note on Laxman Naiko's Revolt (1942)', *Social Scientist* 15 (8/9), August–September 1987, pp. 47–66. The next few paragraphs are based on this article. Quotations have been taken from pp. 58 and 61.

the establishment of a Congress ministry in Orissa, Congress propaganda spread like wildfire in the zamindari, and its recruitment drive gathered momentum. About 300–400 new Congress recruits were sought to be remoulded in line with its politics through a training camp opened at Nuaput (about 5 miles from Jeypore) in November 1938.[34] Laxman Naiko was one of the trainees at this centre and, along with others, 'served to link Koraput to the Congress'.

These new Congress recruits assumed a leadership role in breaking forest rules and taking forcible possession of land. A number of petty riots took place and, in some instances, police officials were attacked as well. Timber was illegally taken and funds were collected to set up Congress ashrams. Rumours abounded; those centred around Gandhi virtually deified him and provided great momentum to the recruitment drive. In Malkangiri, Laxman Naiko had proved his worth in several struggles between 1938–1942, and was made the President of the Congress Primary Committee of Mathili. Pati says that to the people, Laxman was the 'Gandhi of Malkangiri', and his elevation to a leadership position not only alarmed the Maharaja, the estate authorities, and the colonial administration, but also had the effect of spreading the Congress propaganda far and wide.

After the August declaration of the Quit India Movement, the Congress organisation in Koraput was declared illegal. Nonetheless, Laxman organised his 'armed' (with saplings, cudgels, and *lathis*) supporters and went about campaigning in the dense forests for *swaraj*. His band engaged in attacking opium and liquor shops as well as destroying liquor, fermented *mahua*, and other distillation apparatus.[35] Such actions spread Naiko's fame further and he was soon considered the future king of Malkangiri. The climax of the revolt came on 21 August 1942 when an opium shop and the Revenue Inspector's office at Mathili were raided. Under Laxman's leadership, the 'crowd' marched to the police station, where he made a speech expressing their collective aspirations. Pati writes,

---

[34]The three-month training period included instructions on spinning, scouting, village service, farming, animal husbandry, and of course, the prohibition of liquor.

[35]This was in stark contrast to what Pati writes about 'crowd' behaviour. Opium shops were the first targets and the forfeited opium was readily 'distributed' among the crowd, the purpose being to protest against the government 'obtaining revenue from this popular means of relaxation'. The crowds also acted against a few notorious rural elite and liquor shop owners. Finally, the crowds made their way to the *haat* (market), which was also the place where the protests possibly started.

> As he [Laxman Naiko] put it, Gandhi Raj had replaced British Raj and the 'shandy' and forest dues no longer had to be paid. Although portrayed as a 'violent mob' the 'crowd' remained peaceful. Its basic aim was to disobey orders, have a meeting and hoist the Congress flag in the police station as a symbol of defiance and court arrest.

Subsequently, a tussle followed, which gave the police a pretext for lathi-charging and firing, in which about a dozen people were killed. Since Laxman was seen as a possible threat by other elites and the colonial administration, he was made the scapegoat in the incident and sentenced to death.

The remarkable aspect of this movement was that it represented the convergence of Naiko's local revolt with the all-India movement. While it incorporated elements from the earlier tradition of fituri (such as its messianic and millenarian aspects) in the area, it was also characteristically different from it. Pati suggested a 'dialectical interaction of *swaraj* with the popular level'. Analysing the strategy of the PCC, he wrote,

> By adjusting itself to popular pressures in the 1937–42 phase the PCC could not only increase its influence over Malkangiri, but also wrench it to the all-India movement. The support of the PCC, however, imposed certain constraints on the revolt. This was primarily due to its links with the estate, once the 1937 elections were over, and its choice of comparatively affluent allies (i.e. *mustajars*) as the important leaders of the revolt. These implied that although slogans against bethi, goti and other oppressive taxes had been raised they could never become integral component of the revolt. Although the revolt had strong anti-feudal current it was whipped up only as a factor to promote the politics of anti-imperialism. Our evidence indicates a compromise with the feudal structure. Consequently, the association with the PCC (which led the revolt) dampened the social transformative content of the movement.

Pati's assessment certainly has a ring of truth in it. However, the relationship between the Congress and Indian tribes is a relatively under-explored theme in modern Indian historiography. Many scholarly works remain to be written about the role tribals played in the Congress movements of the 1940s.

Nevertheless, politics in India during 1945–1947 stood on the cusp of a sea change. In the preceding decade, the social base of all major political formations had shifted rapidly, especially after the introduction of provincial autonomy and the establishment of Congress ministries. In the 1937 (and 1946) elections, only provincial subjects who met certain financial (land revenue, chowkidari tax, etc.) or educational qualifications were included in the voters' roster. As a result, franchise was restricted to only a tenth (later, one-seventh) of the British Indian population, and only about half actually cast their votes.[36] This gave a definite elitist character to all elections conducted under the Government of India Act, 1935, until Indian independence. This also played a major role in a string of impressive electoral performances by the Congress, because the powerful landlord section had thrown its weight behind the Congress as the main organised political force most likely to replace the British. The top Congress leadership committed itself to universal adult franchise upon independence. But they knew that their hold on State power would be tenuous if every adult Indian were to vote, and this underlined their imperative to find new allies to ensure continued electoral success.[37]

Since the 1930s, the Communist takeover of the Kisan Sabha Movement had established them as the chief opponents of the Congress, who would try to capture political power once British rule came to an end. The Congress leadership was aware of both this challenge and the consequent necessity to expand their social base.[38] Reviling the Communists as 'violent, lawless and anti-Indian', they sought to portray themselves in contrast as 'committed, patient advocates of gradual, peaceful reform who only needed more time to bring positive changes'.[39]

Between 1945–1950, a number of political movements and insurrections erupted in the predominantly tribal areas of the subcontinent. Such movements can be divided into two categories: those occurring in British India (the Warli revolt in Bombay and the Tebhaga Movement in Bengal) and those in the Princely States (the Telangana revolt in Hyderabad and political agitations in Orissa). A crucial feature of these movements was that the majority of them were led by Communists,[40] and in what follows, I will provide an outline of some significant moments of struggle.

Rural Bengal in 1946–1947 was the scene of the Tebhaga Movement, an intense Communist-led struggle by sharecroppers (*bargadars*) to reduce

---

[36]'The Indian Elections—1946', *The World Today* 2 (4), 1946, pp. 167–175.

[37]Deepak Pandey, 'Congress-Muslim League Relations 1937–39: "The Parting of the Ways"', *Modern Asian Studies* 12 (4), 1978, pp. 629–654.

[38]See, for instance, K. K. Sharma, *Agrarian Movements and Congress Politics in Bihar 1927–47*, Delhi: Anamika, 1989.

[39]Leslie J. Calman, 'Congress Confronts Communism: Thana District, 1945–47', *Modern Asian Studies* 21 (2), 1987, p. 330.

[40]See S. R. Chowdhuri, *Leftism in India 1917-1947*, New Delhi: Sage, 2017.

the rent they paid to the *jotedars*, a class of rich farmers, from one-half to one-third.[41] Under the *bargadari* system of cultivation in Bengal, landowning classes such as the zamindars, talukdars, and rich jotedars used the services of tribals such as the Santhals to reclaim forest land for agriculture. However, once the tribals were turned into peasants, they were quickly ousted from the land that they had reclaimed.[42] The Communists had been working ceaselessly since the 1920s in Bengal and during the 1930s, they effectively utilised the Kisan Sabha platform to swell their ranks.

A stronghold of the movement was the Mymensingh district of East Bengal. In the northern Susang region of the district, the Hajong tribals-turned-tenants paid a *tanka* (a fixed quantity of crop) as produce-rent to their landlords. As part of the movement, the tribals held massive demonstrations on 8 December 1946 to highlight their demands. Crops were harvested and carried in stacks to their own threshing floors, instead of to the landlords and jotedars. In January 1947, a procession in Susang attacked post offices and police stations. An office of the zamindars was also seized, which led to clashes with the police. The Hajong tribals openly raised the banner of revolt and roamed the area armed with bows, arrows, and even guns. Similar clashes were reported from Dinajpur and Jalpaiguri districts. A large number of Santhal and Oraon tribals participated in these struggles as well. However, despite their populist character and militant peasant action, the Tebhaga Movement could not be transformed into extensive fighting or large-scale peasant violence.

The Princely State of Hyderabad was the site of the Telangana struggle during 1946–1951, a movement that went through several phases. The trajectories of this struggle have been analysed by several scholars as well as by participants.[43] So long as the Nizam of Hyderabad existed as an independent entity, the Telangana Movement held its own against the massive repression unleashed by the Hyderabad army, police, and the notorious *Razakar* militiamen. At the high point of the movement in mid-1948, *sanghams* were established in 2,000–3,000 villages. Since the ruling

---

[41]For an interesting account of the movement, see the chapter on 'The Tebhaga Movement in Bengal, 1946–47', in D. N. Dhanagare, *Peasant Movements in India: 1920–1950*, Delhi: Oxford University Press, 1983, pp. 155–179.

[42]Ibid., p. 159.

[43]For an analytical study of the movement, see Akhil Gupta, 'Revolution in Telengana: Part I & II', *South Asia Bulletin* IV (1 and 2), 1984. Also see the chapter on the Telangana Movement in D. N. Dhanagare's *Peasant Movements in India*.

elite had fled the affected areas, there was 'no forced labour, debt bondage, or grain levy, and land "distribution" often came in the form of cessation of rent payments, and free access to common grazing grounds, water and forest resources'.[44] It was during this early phase in 1948 that the Communists made inroads into the Hyderabad tribal areas. However, their presence was as yet quite limited.

As far as the predominantly tribal areas in Hyderabad were concerned, Kumra Bhimu's rebellion in Adilabad (in 1940) had led the Hyderabad State to initiate a chain of administrative reforms under the guidance of W. V. Grigson and Christopher von Furer-Haimendorf. In the Gond tracts of Adilabad, some pioneering schemes were undertaken to impart education to the tribals in their own language, along with a massive scheme to distribute land title deeds (*pattas*). The Hyderabad Legislative Assembly had also passed a legislation that 'scheduled' certain tribal tracts in the Nizam's territories, which were to be administered along the lines of the Madras Agency Tracts. However, it was perhaps a case of 'too little too late' for, these ameliorative measures notwithstanding, the Hyderabad tribals were becoming increasingly restive. In January 1948, much before the Communists established their bases in the tribal tracts, the Koyas had rebelled against the Nizam's forces and established panchayati raj in about fifty villages.[45]

After the 'Police Action' of September 1948,[46] the Nizam's rule came to an end. There was hardly any effective resistance and, in less than a week, Hyderabad acceded to the Indian Union. Although the 'internal security threat' posed by the Nizam had been nullified quite easily, the new government had to engage in a long struggle against the Communist rebels. A massive clampdown followed, in which the Indian Army committed several excesses. Their raids decimated the Communist squads and thousands were

[44]Jonathan Kennedy and Sunil Purushotham, 'Beyond Naxalbari: A Comparative Analysis of Maoist Insurgency and Counterinsurgency in Independent India', *Comparative Studies in Society and History* 54 (4), 2012, p. 838.

[45]Ibid., p. 841.

[46]This term is, however, a misnomer for it was a full-fledged military operation. Somehow, quite inexplicably (perhaps the force of nationalism!), it struck root, and most scholars apply it uncritically.

arrested. The squads were forced to either give in or run away, as 'in the plains there was no place to hide'.[47]

Thus, the Telangana Movement entered its next phase in which the Communists expanded into the forested tracts, 'both to the south along Krishna and more dense ones to the east along the Godavari'. The Communists had not planned for this eventuality, but 'they found themselves among forest-people who fled at the sight of them'. Nonetheless, they started working amongst them and within four to six months had won over their confidence. In an article on the contemporary Maoist movement in India, Jonathan Kennedy and Sunil Purushotham have argued that the Telangana insurrection was a direct predecessor of the Naxalbari rebellion of 1967. Evaluating the effects of the entry of Communists into the tribal areas of Hyderabad, they wrote,

> The CPI cadres provided disparate groups of aggrieved *Adivasis* with a unified organizational structure, which channeled previously disaggregated struggles into a common insurgency and allowed for tribal participation despite potential ideological incompatibilities with Maoism. In return, the insurgents provided *Adivasis* with collective incentives that addressed their primary grievances: they chased away Forest Department officials, redistributed land, negotiated higher prices with traders for forest products, and forced contractors to pay fair wages. Above all else, the CPI pledged support for a politically autonomous Koya area and local self-government. Presciently, the director of the Intelligence Bureau saw the potential strength of this union. In 1951 he warned that if the Communists succeeded in setting up base area in the hill and forest areas of northern Telengana and what is now Southern Chhattisgarh, it would 'be difficult to dislodge them'.[48]

Undoubtedly, entry into these forested regions provided the Telangana Movement with a fresh lease of life. However, jungle warfare extracted its price as the cadres were ill-fed and often unwell. Their morale was also low

[47] Akhil Gupta, 'Revolution in Telengana 1946–1951 (Part One)', *South Asia Bulletin* IV (1), 1984, p. 19. Recently, Sunil Purushotham has published a major study which has shed important light on the Indian State's approach and strategy to deal with the Communist insurgents entrenched in the tribal belt of Hyderabad. See Chapters 5 and 6 in Sunil Purushotham, *From Raj to Republic: Sovereignty, Violence and Democracy in India*, Stanford: Stanford University Press, 2021, pp. 182–246.

[48] Kennedy and Purushotham, 'Beyond Naxalbari', pp. 841–842.

as contact with the State Party Centre was lost and they were constantly on the run. Meanwhile, the government adopted the 'Briggs Plan' in which tribal people were 'evacuated to "camps" outside the forest areas and their hamlets razed to the ground'. By mid-1949, the Communists had regrouped again 'along strict lines of Maoist guerilla warfare, and began to spread to new areas', such as among the Chenchu people in the Nallamalia forests of the Krishna River Forest Area and in the north among the Gonds in Adilabad. Subsequently, a combination of factors, including State repression, counterinsurgency measures, depletion in the Communist ranks, and an ideological split at the national level brought the struggle to an end. The stiff resistance put up by the tribal people of Telangana (under Communist leadership) carried on simultaneously with the proceedings of the Constituent Assembly of India. Devised under the Cabinet Mission Plan in 1946, this august body had the mandate to devise the future administration of predominantly tribal areas and its members were thus faced with a question that had long troubled their colonial predecessors—how to keep the recalcitrant tribes pacified. The challenge before the CA was to devise a formula which appeared to 'protect' the tribes while also allowing 'development' of the forest and mineral resources necessary for the nation's progress. In the instrument of scheduling, they had a tried and tested legal technology with proven effectiveness.

A third important theatre of struggle was Thana district of Bombay Presidency, where in 1944, the Warli tribal community first went on a wage strike in a resistance prompted by K. J. Save, a government servant who tried to raise consciousness about a just wage. However, this attempt failed and B. G. Kher[49] and the Adivasi Seva Mandal[50] managed to convince the strikers to return to work. Thus, the Congressmen and its tribal welfare wing worked 'to end the agitational method, not to win for them [tribals] their demands'.[51]

However, the education of tribals in modes of political activity had begun. In December 1944, Shamrao and Godavari Parulekar began organising the tribals to end the practices of forced and bonded labour. After

[49]The first Indian Premier of Bombay Province, a local Congress stalwart who took an active interest in 'uplift' work with tribal communities.

[50]A nationalist-oriented tribal welfare organisation of Bombay Province.

[51]Leslie J. Calman, 'Congress Confronts Communism: Thana District, 1945–47', *Modern Asian Studies* 21 (2), 1987, pp. 329–348. The following paragraphs about the Warli rebellion are based on this article.

three weeks of agitation, the landlords agreed to a wage rate of 12 annas per day. Emboldened by these successes, the Communists started mobilising the Warlis for a wage increase for grass-cutting in October 1945. Soon after the 1946 elections, control of the Bombay administration passed into the hands of a Congress government headed by B. G. Kher, with Morarji Desai as the Home Minister. This government, Leslie Calman writes, was 'even less sympathetic to Communist organization than the British had been'. When the Kisan Sabha controlled by the Communists started mobilising Warlis in the grass-cutting season of 1946, another crisis unfolded. The Special Officer for Tribal Welfare, A. H. Khan, brokered a deal between the Timber Merchant Association and the Kisan Sabha for a wage increase for cutting trees. Apparently, the strike was called off and the Association too ratified the agreement.

Unfortunately, this agreement was not put into effect and as a result, massive unrest spread amongst the Warlis of the region. On 14 November, the Bombay government declared a state of emergency in Thana. Within a week, scores of agitating tribals were arrested and the Communists leading them were externed. These measures did not have the desired effect, for the agitation spread to new areas in January 1947. The government dispatched a company of the Maratha Light Infantry to Dahanu on 6 January, but owing to a public outcry in sections of newspapers, it was withdrawn. Such military measures led to an increase in anger and acts of violence by bands of Warlis.

Citing the response of Morarji Desai (who had said, 'anything which helps the communists in their nefarious activities will not be tolerated'), Calman has argued that evidence suggests that the primary concern of the government was to end the Communist influence. During this phase, the Adivasi Seva Mandal worked as a *de facto* state agency to pacify the area. By April 1947, the rebellion had been quelled.

In her evaluation of the Warli Movement, Calman wrote,

> Despite the undeniable justice of the struggle for Adivasi welfare and the modest size of the Thana movement, the Congress ministry that governed Bombay understood that local victories would strengthen the Communist Party's long term goals. Congress believed that the Communists were using the Adivasis as tools with which to build revolution, and it soon matched the Communist Party in its opportunistic use of these tribals. The true agenda of the 1945–47 movement in Thana, and the Congress's response to it, were not the struggle for Adivasi uplift but rather the broader questions of the way

> in which change should occur, who should initiate it, and which classes and parties should benefit from it as Indian independence neared.[52]

Despite the fact that the last lines were written specifically in the context of the Warli revolt, I would argue that Calman's judgement seems an equally valid assessment of all three Communist-led movements. Barring the case of Bengal (which had a Krishak Praja Party government), the Congress governments in both Hyderabad (after the 'Police Action') and Bombay saw to it that the Communist-led protest movements among the tribals were brutally crushed. It has been established that the landlords constituted a formidable social base for the Indian National Congress. In areas where tribals predominated among the population, an irreconcilable conflict of interest existed between them and the landlords. Land alienation had been the single biggest issue in the protectionist discourse during the last three decades of colonial rule.[53] Where the Congress only paid lip service to ensuring that land did not pass from tribals to the non-tribals in these areas, the Communists made it a central issue in their agitations.[54] Despite their calls to ensure 'social justice' to the tribals, in each of these cases of conflict, the Congress leadership ultimately favoured the local interest groups (landlords, etc.) who had, materially and electorally, supported them in the 1937 and 1946 elections.

Contemporary to and juxtaposed against these Communist-led movements was the tribal autonomy movement in Chota Nagpur, which was led by the charismatic tribal leader Jaipal Singh and genuinely challenged the Congress. The distinctiveness of this movement vis-à-vis the Communist-led insurrections in tribal areas is worth underlining. The Communist Party of India, under the sway of the B. T. Ranadive line, theoretically viewed the tribal question as one of 'peasant' unrest, which required organisation, mobilisation, and violent resistance.[55] They harped on the need to overthrow the Indian State, but never provided an organic idiom to tribal identity. Such a limited approach was to perhaps proscribe a wider dissemination of their politics.[56] Another weakness in the Left's

---

[52]Calman, 'Congress Confronts Communism', p. 329.

[53]V. Raghavaiah, 'Background of Tribal Struggles in India', in A. R. Desai (ed.), *Peasant Struggles in India*, New Delhi: Oxford University Press, 1979.

[54]D. N. Dhanagare, 'The Politics of Survival: Peasant Organisations and the Left-Wing in India, 1925–46', *Sociological Bulletin* 24 (1), 1975, pp. 29–54.

[55]Personal communication with Professor Bhagwan Josh.

[56]Personal communication with Dr Rakesh Ankit.

approach to the tribal question was its overreliance on 'class' analysis. Hence, while the Communist challenge in predominantly tribal areas raised some meaningful demands on behalf of the tribals, they also exemplified the limitations of a politics based purely on economic considerations, which lacked any powerful emotive appeal for autonomy or self-determination. In this respect, the development of an Adivasi identity under the aegis of the Adivasi Mahasabha heralded a new era of democratic power politics. Under the leadership of Jaipal Singh Munda, the Mahasabha went on to play an important role in the regional power politics of eastern and central India.

Historians have often spoken of a lack of tribal voices in the archive. The evidence is, however, not altogether absent, for a new middle class was emerging within tribes, especially in Chota Nagpur and North East India. Some of these voices were heard in a debate conducted in the Bihar Legislative Council in April 1939 on the demand for a separate tribal state of Jharkhand to be carved out of Bihar.[57]

During this debate, Ignes Beck, an Indian Christian representative in the House, put forward a version of the history of tribal communities, claiming their autochthonous status. He said that the current aborigines were the descendants of the 'ancient *Adibasis,* the aristocracy of India', and that several of the depressed classes, too, were descendants of the Adibasis.[58] Beck claimed that despite the efforts of the tribal people to align themselves to nationalist forces, Gandhi and the Congress high command remained unsympathetic. In contrast, they acknowledged the case of the Harijans as an all-India problem because the latter had 'threatened to move away'. The object lesson for the tribes was that they could not trust anyone and 'must stand on [their] own legs'. While Beck agreed that seclusion was harmful for the tribes, he reiterated the need for protection thus:

> We feel we have been exploited and are left neglected due to our poverty and small number and specially because we have no political organization, because we have no political force behind us. Having seen all these, we have happily started our own movement—the Adinibas Movement.... I would request my Bihari friends, all the same, not to

---

[57] See S. M. Bosu, 'Jharkhand Movement: A Historical Analysis', in Mrinal Miri (ed.), *Continuity and Change in Tribal Society*, Shimla: Indian Institute of Advanced Study, 1993.

[58] 3 April 1939, File No. 137/40-R, Secretariat of the Governor General (Reforms), GoI, 1940, p. 33. The next two paragraphs draw from this report, pp. 35–36, 39.

> misinterpret this movement as being anti-national or anti-Congress. It is not a conspiracy; it is not a missionary tactics. It is a sincere move for self-determination. If we have kept ourselves back from generously following into the Congress fold, it is not out of malice. It is for you to win our confidence. You must know that these aborigines are moving fast and that they are meant to live and live powerfully, whether you like it or not. This question of self-determination, this question of separation of the province must not be so confused or interpreted as to say that they are anti-national. This is the view point, this is the fear, this is the feeling that we, aboriginals, have with regard to the old Government and also with regard to the present Ministry and it is for the present Ministry to create full confidence in us. We do not want to be secluded. Seclusion will be harmful to us: we want protection and if that protection comes from our own brethren, we will be the happier for it.

Bonifice Lakra, the other tribal representative who spoke during the debate, also minced no words in criticising the Congress government. He said that while Congress paid lip service to the idea of giving special protection to the minorities, in reality, its attitude had been 'rather cold, unkind and unsympathetic towards the aborigines.' If there was a clash of interest between the aboriginals and non-aboriginals, the ministry would invariably rule in favour of the majority. Before ending his speech, Lakra warned the Congress ministry that if it continued to disfavour the Adibasis and be 'hostile to our interest,' the tribals of Bihar would claim a separate province.

Lakra's use of the majority-minority framework was significant for it pointed to the self-identification of tribes as a distinct segment of Bihar's population, which required a separate autonomous homeland for protection and freedom from exploitation. At a symbolic level, by pitching for statehood, such articulations reiterated the essential link between tribal identity and territoriality/land. Both these tribal representatives were Christian converts, but the manner in which they articulated their frustrations, aspirations, and a distinctive sense of pride in their history suggests that the political landscape had begun to change. At least in Chota Nagpur, the politics of indigeneity and ethnicity had begun to percolate down to the consciousness of the tribal elite. It heralded a new age of modern associational politics within the Chota Nagpur tribes, who consciously started identifying themselves as Adibasis. The concerns of 'self-determination,' so finely articulated by Ignes Beck and Bonifice Lakra, were soon to take the form of a vigorous agitation for a separate Jharkhand province under the leadership of Jaipal Singh Munda.

Jaipal, alias Pramod Pahan, was born in Takra village to a Munda family of priests on 3 January 1903. He was admitted to St. Paul School at Ranchi, whose Principal Canon Cosgrave took an interest in him and converted him to Christianity. In 1918, Cosgrave took him to England. In 1926, Jaipal Singh graduated from St. John's College at Oxford University with honours in Economics. Besides being good in academics, he was a star orator and an excellent hockey player. He led the Indian hockey team to the finals of the 1928 Amsterdam Olympic Games, where it won its first ever gold medal. In 1937, he returned to India to take up the post of Vice-Principal of Rajkumar College at Raipur. The next year, he joined Bikaner State as a minister and was soon promoted to the position of Foreign Secretary. Upon his return, Singh tried to join the Indian National Congress but was apparently snubbed by Rajendra Prasad, which led him to join the Adivasi Sabha instead. With his wide-ranging experience and effective oratory, he quickly rose to lead the organisation, rechristening it as the Adivasi Mahasabha in 1939. His stated goal was to achieve a separate 'homeland' for the Adivasis—a future Jharkhand, which would include Chota Nagpur, the Santhal Parganas, as well as several Princely States from Orissa and Chhattisgarh.[59]

Meanwhile, these Princely States were rapidly becoming a hotbed of nationalist activity. Since 1933, they had been administered as the Eastern States Agency and enjoyed direct relations with the Government of India. As independence neared, these States tried to consolidate themselves as a unified Eastern States Union. Through deft machinations, Vallabhbhai Patel and V. P. Menon at the State Department managed to scuttle these plans, forcing the States to accede to the Indian Union in December 1947. With effect from 1 January 1948, the States of Kharsawan and Seraikella were to be amalgamated with the state of Orissa. Jaipal Singh Munda, however, wanted Kharsawan and Seraikella to become a part of the Bihar Province. With the tacit support of the rulers of these States as well as the Bihar government, he began fomenting a strong agitation in support of his demand. On 1 January 1948, a clash ensued between Jaipal Singh's tribal supporters and the police, in which several people were killed and hundreds were injured. Munda raised the issue in the Constituent Assembly and held the Orissa government responsible for the bloodbath. However, Patel dismissed these allegations and rejected Jaipal Singh's demand for an enquiry committee.

[59]Nivedita Mohanty, *Oriya Nationalism: Quest for a United Orissa 1866–1956*, Jagatsinghpur, Cuttack: Prafulla Pathagar, 2005, pp. 339–349.

Image 9: Group photograph of all the members of the Constituent Assembly of India

Courtesy: Photography Section, PMML, New Delhi.

The decision to merge Seraikella and Kharsawan into Orissa was put on hold and the issue referred to a tribunal under Chief Justice Baudekar of the Bombay High Court. However, this tribunal did not take off and the matter was ultimately referred to the States Ministry. In May 1948, the Government of India overturned its award and decided, for reasons of administrative convenience, to merge Seraikella and Kharsawan with the Singhbhum district of Bihar. Instead of being placated by the award, Jaipal Singh became even more vociferous. He relentlessly pursued the goal of a larger Jharkhand by all possible means, stepping up the political tension by demanding the return of 'nine other Chotanagpur States, viz., Changbhakar, Jashpur, Korea, Surguja, Udaipur, Bamra, Bonai, Gangpur, and Keonjhar'.[60]

The Jaipal Singh Munda-led Jharkhand Movement was viewed with grave suspicion by top nationalist leaders. R. S. Shukla, the Premier of Central Provinces, wrote a letter to Patel placing certain 'extra-judicial' considerations before him:

> The Adibasi problem is already proving to be a serious headache. The agitation to merge Surguja and Jashpur with Bihar is really connected with Jaipal Singh's movement for the creation of a separate Jharkhand. Jaipal Singh wants all his Adibasis under one provincial government so that he may have to fight only on one front.... His Adibasis are spread over the four provinces of West Bengal, Bihar, Orissa and the CP. If Jashpur and Surguja are merged with Bihar, Jaipal Singh will be in a strong position and his movement may prove too strong to be dealt with by Bihar. It is obvious whether in the larger national interests of the country this separatist tendency should be encouraged by concentrating the Adibasi population in one province....[61]

These words seem to have had their intended effect and all further demands of Jaipal Singh were resolutely set aside. The merger of Seraikella and Kharsawan with Bihar was the only concession that the movement for Jharkhand received from the not so benevolent Patel, and the lid was effectively clamped on the agitation in subsequent years.

My main concern in recounting these instances of disturbance and revolt in predominantly tribal areas is to establish a link between them and the Constitution-making process for tribal areas. In this context, it will be

---

[60]Harekrushna Mahtab to Vallabhbhai Patel, 21 May 1948, in Durga Das (ed.), *Sardar Patel's Correspondence: 1945–50, Vol. VII*, Ahmedabad: Navjivan, 1973, pp. 517–518.

[61]Ibid., 12 May 1948, R. S. Shukla to Patel, pp. 546–547.

pertinent to mention that at least one of these disturbed areas was toured by the Excluded and Partially Excluded Areas Sub-Committee. These were the Umbergaon and Dahanu talukas of Thana District, which the Sub-Committee visited in March 1947, soon after the Warli disturbances had been quelled. The Sub-Committee asked the Warlis present about the wages they received and their land yield. Some women were also questioned about their food and cloth requirements, to which they replied that they had to sell chicken to procure cloth. Enquiries were also made about caste, panchayats, and the settlement of disputes.[62] Dr Bhise, Secretary of the Adivasi Seva Mandal in Umbergaon, provided an account of the work done by the organisation, and also introduced the Sub-Committee to his team of social workers who were 'carrying on propaganda among the Warlis bringing them back to normal life'. When questioned about the needs of the aboriginals, he replied that they wanted 'four freedoms': freedom from fear, from ignorance, from superstition, and from disease. The Communist activists of the Warli Movement, being externed from the district, did not meet the Sub-Committee.

As a vocal tribal representative of this Sub-Committee, which comprised a majority of Congressmen, Jaipal Singh told a journalist that after touring a few of the Warli villages and meeting a number of villagers, he felt they were the 'most neglected people in the country'. Singh had asked

> ... the Warlis to narrate their grievances and demands. He said that the British were quitting India shortly and the Indian Government would redress their grievances. If the aboriginals did not speak now their rights would be overlooked. He asked the Warlis if they wanted seats on District Boards and the Legislative Assembly. A representative of the aboriginals came forward and asked for ameliorative measures like the grant of land, timber for building houses, the opening of schools, hospitals and the digging of more wells as they had to drink stream water, resulting in the spread of disease.

It is interesting to note that it was the lone tribal member of the CA Sub-Committee who asked the Warlis whether they wanted reserved seats in representative institutions. The only Warli response expressed no interest in tribal representation in democratic politics; instead, he asked for the fulfillment of more everyday needs.

---

[62] *The Times of India*, 17 March 1947, p. 7. The next two paragraphs and extracted quotes draw from this report.

In its final report submitted to the Advisory Committee in September 1947, the Thakkar Sub-Committee dealt with the issue of Jharkhand in some detail. It remarked that Bihar contained 'the largest compact block of territory comprising any scheduled area in India'.[63] Here, again, the issue of the Christian tribals featured prominently. They were educationally and economically advanced when compared to non-Christian tribals, as well as more organised politically. The second important aspect which the Sub-Committee reported concerned the general feeling among the inhabitants of Chota Nagpur that they had 'little share in the administration commensurate with its area, population and industrial importance'. Their role in the 'separatist' Jharkhand Movement was also discussed, as an 'extreme expression of the discontent prevalent in Chota Nagpur', and it was conceded that the movement was 'capturing the imagination' of the tribals.

Jaipal Singh added a note of dissent to the Thakkar Report. He expressed dissatisfaction about a large portion of previously declared partially excluded areas being de-scheduled. Singh claimed that all the witnesses examined by the Sub-Committee were 'emphatic that the Chota Nagpur Division as a whole should be scheduled and no district or territory should be excluded from the scheduled status'. In his opinion, the veto power of the Tribes Advisory Council was essential to protect the one-and-a-half million Adibasis of Manbhum, Hazaribagh, and Palamau districts, which had been de-scheduled. He also proposed that the Indian government should reclaim the Chittagong Hill Tracts from East Pakistan and that the tribal tract in Mirzapur district of the United Provinces should be transferred to the scheduled areas of the Chota Nagpur plateau. In his reply to Jaipal Singh's note of dissent, Thakkar side-stepped him by asserting that none of the witnesses examined by the Sub-Committee were told that their task was to recommend the 'scheduling' of certain areas in different provinces.

The Final Framing of the Fifth and Sixth Schedules

On the suggestion of Sardar Patel, a joint meeting of both the Sub-Committees headed by Bordoloi and Thakkar was held on 25 August 1947.

[63] B. Shiva Rao (ed.), *The Framing of India's Constitution: Select Documents, Vol. 3*, Delhi: Universal Law, 1967; reprint 2004, p. 774. The next two paragraphs draw from this report, pp. 764–772.

This meeting summed up the problem of backward areas in the following manner:

> The areas inhabited by the tribes, whether in Assam or elsewhere, are difficult of access, highly malarial and infested also in some cases by other diseases like yaws and venereal disease and lacking in such civilizing facilities as roads, schools, dispensaries and water supply. The tribes themselves are for the most part extremely simple people who can be and are exploited with ease by plainsfolk, resulting in the passage of land formerly cultivated by them to money-lenders and other erstwhile non-agriculturists. While a good number of superstitions and harmful practices are prevalent among them, the tribes have their own customs and way of life with institutions like tribal and village panchayats or councils which are effective in smoothing village administration. The sudden disruption of the tribals' customs and ways by exposure to the impact of a more complicated and sophisticated manner of life is capable of doing great harm. Considering past experiences and strong temptation to take advantage of tribals' simplicity and weaknesses, it is essential to provide statutory safeguards for the protection of the land which is the mainstay of the aboriginal's economic life and for his customs and institutions which, apart from being his own, contain elements of value.[64]

Here, we can see that the Constitution-makers were employing almost exactly the same language, stereotype, and imagery for tribals as the colonial State had in its paternal avatar. The proverbial 'inaccessibility' (difficult of access), 'promiscuity' (yaws, venereal diseases), and 'unhealthiness' (malaria, ecological frontier) become yet again the standard tropes for the construction of a 'frontier imagination'. The word 'aborigine'/'aboriginal' was also deliberately avoided in these discussions, which may be termed as the 'Ghurye effect'. Ghurye's articulation had certainly enabled the nationalists to debunk the autochthonous status implicit in the term 'aboriginal'. Instead, the favoured term of the nationalists became 'tribe', whose backwardness was defined in educational, economic, sanitary, social, and even moralistic terms.[65] Perhaps, in these deliberations, Jaipal Singh was often the lone dissenting voice, articulating the aspirations of his constituency by the consistent

---

[64]Ibid., p. 774.

[65]In time, the Central and state governments became the final arbiter of which community was to be given the status of a 'Scheduled Tribe', which would enable its members to benefit from the affirmative action framework of the Indian State.

application of the term Adivasi. The term emphasised the autochthonous status of localised communities and gave them a sense of rooted territorial identity in the domain of representative democracy.

The joint meeting acknowledged that protection of land, backwardness, illiteracy, medical aid, and communication were common issues and concerns in these different regions. Nevertheless, certain fundamental differences existed between the tribal areas in Assam and those situated in other provinces. The Assam Hills and Frontier Tracts were distinctive as they were:

> divided into fairly large districts inhabited by single tribes or fairly homogeneous groups of tribes with highly democratic and mutually exclusive tribal organization with very little of the plains leaven which is so common a feature of the corresponding areas, particularly the partially excluded areas of other Provinces. The Assam Hill districts contain, as a rule, upwards of 90 per cent of tribal population whereas, unless we isolate small areas, this is generally not the case in other Provinces. The tribal population of other Provinces has moreover assimilated to a considerable extent the life and ways of the plains people and tribal organizations have in many places completely disintegrated. Another feature is that some of the areas in Assam like the Khasi Hills or the Lushai Hills, show greater potentialities for quick progress than tribes in the other Provinces. They may also be distinguished by their greater eagerness for reform in which they have a dominant share than the apathy shown by the tribals of some other Provinces. Having been excluded totally from the ministerial jurisdiction and secluded also from the rest of the Province by the Inner Line system, a parallel to which is not to be found in any other part of India, the excluded areas have mostly been anthropological specimens: and these circumstances together with the policy of officials who have hitherto been in charge of the tracts have produced an atmosphere which is not to be found elsewhere.[66]

This extract is helpful in delineating the decisive factors which accounted for the inclusion of tribal areas in North-East India under the provisions of the Sixth Schedule of the Indian Constitution. *First*, the areas so selected had 'homogeneous' populations of above 90 per cent. *Second*, these areas had maintained their distinctive 'tribal' organisation. The 'inner-line' policy of the colonial administrators had managed to stave off the migration of outsiders into these 'isolated' tracts, which of course was instrumental in

[66]Rao (ed.), *The Framing of India's Constitution*, p. 774.

maintaining the homogeneity of their population as well as the continuance of their tribal organisation. *Third*, the 'greater eagerness for reform' might be attributed to the influence of the work of Christian missionaries, which over a course of time had produced a local educated elite amongst the tribes. The meeting argued that unparalleled conditions such as these necessitated the proposals for the establishment of special local councils, which 'in their separate hill domains will carry on the administration of tribal law and control the utilization of village land and forest.'[67] These decisive factors lay behind the creation of the Sixth Schedule of the Indian Constitution.[68]

Subsequent to this, on 5 September 1949, the draft Fifth Schedule was tabled before the Constituent Assembly by the Chairman of the Drafting Committee, B. R. Ambedkar.[69] Ambedkar introduced three important changes to the original draft. *First*, the provision for a Tribes Advisory Council in every state having scheduled areas or Scheduled Tribes was amended and the matter was left to the discretion of the President. A *second* amendment converted the Council into a toothless body as it gave the Governor the discretion to overrule the Council's advice on laws made by Parliament or the Local Legislature. Ambedkar said that it was 'much better' that 'his [Governor's] discretion should not be controlled absolutely'. *Third*, the original draft did not allow for amendments to the Fifth Schedule. An amendment was moved to this effect, enabling Parliament to do so with a simple majority at a later date. Ambedkar deemed that the Parliament should have this power as 'it is no use creating a sort of a State within a State.... (The situation) should not be stereotyped for all times and it should be open to Parliament to make such changes as time and circumstances may require.'[70]

These amendments drew the ire of Jaipal Singh Munda, especially the second amendment converting the Tribes Advisory Council into a shadow

---

[67]Ibid., p. 772.

[68]On Assam, see Suryasikha Pathak, 'Tribal Politics in the Assam: 1933–1947', *Economic and Political Weekly* 45 (1), 2010, and Sriram Ananthanarayanan, 'Scheduled Tribe Status for Adivasis in Assam', *South Asia: Journal of South Asian Studies* 33 (2), 2010, pp. 290–303.

[69]Apparently, the amendments were made rather surreptitiously and Jaipal Singh was not kept in the loop. The modified Fifth Schedule was sent to the CA members on Friday, 2 September 1949, and the final discussion was conducted on Monday, 5 September 1949.

[70]*Constituent Assembly Debates*, Book 4, Vol. IX, 30 July 1949–18 September 1949, Lok Sabha Secretariat, New Delhi, 2014 (Sixth Reprint), p. 969.

of its original image. While moving a series of five amendments that would restore the potency of the Tribes Advisory Council, Jaipal Singh gave a scathing speech:

> I find that this new proposed Fifth Schedule has, somehow or other, perhaps without meaning it, emasculated the Tribes Advisory Council. The whole pattern of the original draft was to bring the Tribes Advisory Council into action. It could initiate, originate things, but somehow or other, the tables have now been turned. The initiative has been placed in the hands of the Governor or Ruler of the State. I regret this is a situation I cannot accept, and, while I say this, Mr. President, I would like to state it is a matter of regret I have to tell the House that, for the last days secret talks and conferences have been going on among certain people. I have not been consulted. It cannot be said that all parties were consulted. I certainly was not brought to any of those conferences. Suddenly a bomb shell is thrown by way of the new proposed Fifth Schedule. I do not grumble about the Fifth Schedule. But what I say is there is plenty of scope for improving the Fifth Schedule. I as an Adibasi had and must have the first claim to be consulted in the proposed change.... I want that the Tribes Advisory Council should be effective and have a real say in what is being done.... As I have already stated, there are only two principles involved in my five amendments: first that the Scheduled Tribes, all of them, should be benefitted by the provisions of the Fifth Schedule and, secondly, that the Tribes Advisory Council should be a reality and not a farce. Let us not give it a big name, without any powers to do things.[71]

K. M. Munshi of the Drafting Committee offered two reasons for revising the Fifth Schedule. *First,* the earlier draft was a 'uniform stereotyped code for the whole country', while in every province, the tribal problem showed specific variations. *Second,* while the earlier draft only related to the provinces, the political set-up had undergone a massive change as a result of the accession of Princely States into the Union of India. Several of them had large populations of tribal people, and it was essential to have one scheme for the whole country.[72] Of such a persuasion, Shibban Lal Saksena said,

> The existence of scheduled tribes and the scheduled areas are a stigma on the Hindu religion. That these brethren of ours are still in such a sub-human state of existence is something for which we should be ashamed. Of course, all these years this country was a slave of the

[71] Ibid., p. 978.

[72] Ibid., p. 999.

> British, but still we cannot be free from blame. I therefore think Sir, that these scheduled tribes and areas must as soon as possible become a thing of the past. They must come up to the level of the rest of the population and must be developed to the fullest extent.... I only want that these scheduled tribes and scheduled areas should be developed so quickly that they may become indistinguishable from the rest of the Indian population and that this responsibility should be thrown on the Union Government and on the Parliament.[73]

In a paper titled 'Exploitation in Chota Nagpur: The Nemesis', A. K. Dhan, former Vice-Chancellor of Ranchi University and former member of the Union Public Service Commission (UPSC), said that

> injustice to the tribals had been done even by the Constituent Assembly which drafted the country's constitution. When matters pertaining to tribals came for discussion anticipation and interest decreased out of total membership of 324 to only 103 members. Even out of 103, no less than 66 spoke only once or twice. Thus only 33 members spoke on more than two occasions, which was just 9 per cent of the total membership of this august body. Mr Jaipal Singh and Mr Samanta had given dissenting reports with regard to recommendation of sub-committees on tribal issues. But their views were not considered at all.[74]

Nevertheless, the 1940s witnessed the emergence of Jaipal Singh Munda as *Marang Gomke* (Supreme Chief/Leader) of the Adivasis in central and eastern India. In an odd sense, he was both an insider and outsider in the political drama being played out.[75] Undoubtedly, the Oxford-educated superstar of Indian hockey was also the most vocal 'tribal' representative of the Constituent Assembly. After his return to India, he donned a political hat and straddled many roles. Jaipal Singh heralded a truly modern, representative, and associational mode of doing politics, especially amongst the Adivasis of the Chota Nagpur region. In that core territory, he helped to construct a distinct regional identity by leading a tribal autonomy movement centred around the demand for a separate state of Jharkhand. This movement was a landmark political stir, and was innovative at all levels

---

[73]Ibid., p. 981.

[74]Janak Singh, 'Jharkhand Mukti Morcha: Past, Present and Future', *The Times of India*, 8 December 1989, p. 11.

[75]Unlike Birsa Munda, on whom see K. S. Singh, *Birsa Munda and His Movement 1872–1901: A Study of a Millenarian Movement in Chotanagpur*, Calcutta: Seagull, 2002.

As a first step, he established the Bharatiya Adimjati Sevak Sangh (BAJSS) on 24 October 1948. This move was perhaps the culmination of a long-held dream of establishing an all-India body dedicated to the uplift of aborigines. This was the very same idea that had sparked a controversy between him and Elwin (referred to in Chapter 5). Rajendra Prasad, who subsequently became the first President of the Indian Republic, was chosen as the Founder-President of BAJSS.[82] By then, Thakkar had already served as the executive head of the Harijan Sevak Sangh, since 1933–1934. He had amassed years of experience of running a pan-India network of donors, social workers, and a propaganda mechanism working for uplift activities for the Harijans. Now, in the autumn of his life, Thakkar probably wished to leave behind an institutional legacy that would undertake similar work amongst the aboriginal and hill tribes. Here, it is interesting to note the term 'Adimjati' that Thakkar used for the target group of his ameliorative action. The term could be loosely translated as 'Primitive Caste' and indicates that Thakkar, even late into his life, imagined these groups as castes that had to be uplifted and given a proper place in the Hindu social order. After Thakkar's death, his followers started a journal and called it *Vanyajati* or 'Forest Castes', again with similar moorings.

Aside from establishing the BAJSS, Thakkar concentrated his energies on canvassing for the creation of the Backward Classes Commission as outlined in the draft Constitution of India (then under discussion in the CA as Article 301). He started publishing articles in leading newspapers, which provide an important window to his peculiar vision of social reform through affirmative action, backed by State policy and funding. Thakkar was certainly one of the founding fathers of the Indian Constitution, and hence how far his ideas worked is an important issue to ascertain historically.

In these newspaper articles, Thakkar complained that the Indian State was not offering universal and compulsory primary education to all its citizens. The idea had only been accepted as a Directive Principle of State Policy, which was at best a moral and normative ideal. As a lifelong

[82]Rajendra Prasad served as BAJSS President from 1948–1962, followed by U. N. Dhebar (1962–1964) and Morarji Desai (1964–1986). The organisation played a highly influential role in tribal welfare policy as enunciated in independent India. See https://bajss.in/about.php and https://bajss.in/former.php (accessed 31 July 2024). An institutional biography of the BAJSS can shed significant new light upon the discourse and practice of 'tribal welfare' in independent India.

activist for the educational uplift of the exploited and marginalised sections of society, Thakkar had hoped for its recognition as a Fundamental Right, which would make it a mandatory and legally binding commitment on the part of the Indian State. For a variety of reasons beyond the scope of this chapter, his hopes were belied and the CA opted for the former route of adopting the Directive Principles with respect to education.

For Thakkar, this meant that the existing social inequities were likely to continue. He argued that the numerically insignificant Advanced Classes (10 per cent) will 'always be at the topmost rung of the ladder in Government services, in trade and industries and in administration'. The Intermediate Classes (50 per cent) would continue to struggle 'to work their way up and thus try to compete with the people above them and take away a part of their monopoly in services and industries'. However, the worst affected would be the Backward Classes (40 per cent), who were 'very far behind in the race of life and it will take them many decades to come up to the level of the people of even the second class, not to mention the first'.[83]

Thakkar admits that the term 'backward' was ambiguous at best and writes that '(I)n a country like ours, it is very difficult to say which are the advanced and which the backward sections in society. These are comparative terms.' However, he provides the example of Bombay where the Starte Committee (of which he was a member) Report of 1930[84] delineated the category of 'Backward Classes' as constitutive of (*i*) depressed and 'untouchable' castes; (*ii*) aboriginal and hill tribes; and (*iii*) other backward castes of Hindus and Muslims. As a result of its recommendations, in 1931, a Backward Classes Department was also constituted, which carried out welfare work for all three groups, particularly in the field of education.

Thakkar was appreciative of the work done by the Backward Classes Department in Bombay. Nevertheless, he felt that it was unfortunate that 'no other province, not to speak of any State, has copied the example of Bombay in this respect'. However, since the victory of the Indian National Congress in the 1946 elections, the Central Provinces, Bihar, United Provinces, and Orissa had started 'either departments for either one or two categories of

[83]A. V. Thakkar, 'How are the Backward Classes?' (From *The Hindustan Times*, 26 December 1948) in *TBCV*, pp. 336–339. The next four paragraphs, including the quote below, are based on this source.

[84]Thakkar was a member of this Committee. For details, see Chapter 4 on the discourse of backwardness in this book.

their backward classes'.[85] In fact, Bihar had even started a 'department for its backward Muslims also, formerly called Julahas or weavers, and now Momins'. But several Provinces such as Assam had done very little, while East Punjab and West Bengal were 'doing some work for Harijans only'. Despite such a sorry state of affairs, Thakkar argued,

> But now the time has come when all backward classes in all the provinces, in Hyderabad, in Rajputana, and even in the backward regions like Himachal and Vindhya areas, must be taken care of by the Union as a special obligation imposed upon it by the new Constitution.

Thakkar referred to a recent CA discussion on Article 10, which constituted one of the Fundamental Rights for citizens. The central point of debate was that if equal opportunity was to be given to 'all citizens in State service without any discrimination', should there be an exception made 'in favour of the backward classes of citizens who are not adequately represented in the services at present'? Thakkar wrote:

> During the discussion it was brought out that the word 'backward' was undefined and that the listing of any caste as backward and recruiting higher services from among such castes under this article might create inefficiency and even chaos in the administration.... However, the article has been adopted and now forms a part of the constitution.

This discussion was the genesis of Article 340 (Article 301 at the time that Thakkar wrote his opinion piece) of the Constitution of India, with three sub-clauses:

> 301. (1) The President may by order appoint a Commission consisting of such persons as he thinks fit to investigate the conditions of socially and educationally backward classes within the territory of India and the difficulties under which they labour and to make recommendations as to the steps that should be taken by the Union or any State to remove such difficulties and to improve their conditions and as to the grants that should be given for the purpose to which such grants should be given, and the order appointing such Commission shall define the procedure to be followed by the Commission.
> (2) A Commission so appointed shall investigate the matters referred to them and present to the President a report setting out the facts as found by them and making such recommendations as they think proper.

[85] Here, 'one or two categories' refers to Harijans and tribals.

> (3) The President shall cause a copy of the report so presented, together with a memorandum explaining the action taken thereon to be laid before Parliament.[86]

Thakkar had great hopes from this proposed mandatory exercise of the Backward Class Commission which the CA was to soon commit itself to. He wrote that this proposal 'will, when passed, provide a great charter for all backward classes'. To be appointed by the President of India, its task was to 'go out through the whole of the country including Indian States and find out which castes of Hindus, Muslims, etc. are really backward according to certain standards, educational, social, economic etc'. Based upon its experience and wisdom, the Commission would then recommend 'ways and means to bring them up to the level of other classes, within a certain period and the Parliament of the day shall vote funds required for the purpose'. Thakkar calculated that this massive exercise would take at least five years. Hence, the backward people could hope for State measures 'to uplift them and to put them on the road to equality with more advanced sections'. After witnessing a lifetime of tumult, Thakkar was a tired but still hopeful soul and wrote:

> The writer earnestly hopes that this process of pushing upwards the weakest sections of our society will not be unduly delayed by our leaders on account of political stress or due to any domestic trouble. Inequalities exist everywhere in the world, but nowhere as in a caste ridden country like ours. It is therefore more necessary in India that the welfare of the backward classes, which form such a large section of the population, should be a special charge on the central administration, and not be left to small units of administration unable to find funds for heavy tasks.

The above extract shows clearly that Thakkar's prognosis of the problem was based fundamentally on the category of caste. Elsewhere, he had also stated that caste was as much part of the Muslim society as it was of the Hindus. Additionally, as a seasoned social worker, he knew very well that finding the money for reform action, especially in the field of education, which required sustained activity, could not be effected without State support.[87]

From the perspective of the top-most leadership of the incipient sovereign Indian nation-State, too, the overall situation in 1949 was far more

[86] A. V. Thakkar, 'Protection of Minorities', *TBCV*, 4 December 1948, pp. 339–342.

[87] Evidence has been provided earlier on this aspect of Thakkar's thinking.

conducive to the focussing of energies on the Constitution-making exercise. This was also the last fully active year of Thakkar's life and he fervently wished to have the Backward Class Commission see the light of day.

Thakkar first wrote a letter to Jawaharlal Nehru in which he appealed to him to appoint the Backward Class Commission 'forthwith without waiting for the Constitution coming into force'. Thakkar defined 'Backward Class' as constitutive of (*i*) Scheduled Castes or Harijans among the Hindus (4.5 crores); (*ii*) Aboriginal and Hill Tribes (2.5 crores); and (*iii*) Other Backward Classes of Hindu and Muslim castes (at least 3 crores).[88]

Thakkar wrote that the first two sub-categories were already listed under different schedules of the Draft Constitution. The lists of the third had been obtained from the Provinces by the Education Ministry, Government of India, for the purpose of distributing scholarships. Therefore, barring the information from State Unions or States (ex-Princely Order), the required information about all three divisions was available to the Government of India. As per the 1941 Census, they numbered at least ten crores. In 1949, the estimated total population was about thirty-five crores, of which the Backward Classes constituted at least 11–12 crores. Thus, a third of the Indian people belonged to the Backward Classes, and this was 'a fairly large proportion to be left behind in the race of life and it be rushed forward by all legitimate means'.

Thakkar pressed for an all-India policy which would 'mean a real advance for this weakest section of our population'. He also reminded Nehru that the provision for the reservation of seats by the governments had been planned for only ten years, and would lapse in 1960. Hence, 'unless we have by then fitted them educationally and economically to be on the same level with the advanced classes, they will form a very backward block even after 1960'. Indeed, the citizens from the Backward Classes would also exercise the power of the vote, but serious measures were required 'to elevate them socially, educationally and economically as well as politically as soon as possible'. Thakkar's appeal had an immediacy to it because if the government waited for the Constitution to come into force, the enquiry and its results would drag on for a further three to four years.

---

[88]Letter from A. V. Thakkar c/o Harijan Sevak Sangh, Kingsway, Delhi; To: Honourable The Prime Minister, Government of India, Secretariat, New Delhi, dated 22 May 1949, in F. No. 8/30, February 1947–December 1950, Correspondence with Shri Thakkar Bapa of Harijan Sevak Sangh, pp. 74–75, Sardar Patel Papers, NAI.

The second major point of this letter to Nehru was Compulsory Basic Education, a theme dear to Thakkar's heart. He referred to a very urgent need to educate the masses, especially children in the age group of 7–14. In the Budget of 1949–1950, Maulana Azad, the Education Minister, had asked for a modest sum of Rs 540 lakh from the Cabinet, which was refused. Thakkar presciently warned Nehru that '(U)nless we do something serious, something big, in this direction, it will take several decades before our literacy figure come up to something respectable.' As per the 1941 Census, the male literacy rate in India was 21 per cent, while females stood at a paltry 6.25 per cent. For Thakkar, these figures 'were low enough to put us to shame in the eyes of the World. We must do something big to wipe out our almost universal illiteracy, specially of the female sex.'

Thakkar asked for a short interview with Nehru in connection to both his appeal to wipe out national illiteracy and the appointment of the Backward Classes Commission. We do not know if this interview ever took place. Meanwhile, the CA wrapped up its proceedings and in the last three months gave final shape to the proposals for the enactment of the Fifth and Sixth Schedules. On 26 November 1949, the CA adopted the Constitution of India. Thakkar's labour as a Constitution-maker had ended, but the Assembly continued to function as the Parliament of India.

Here, we may add that a major change in nomenclature in the Constitution of India had been effected at the instance of B. R. Ambedkar. After an amendment moved by him, the category of 'Aboriginal and Hill Tribes' was done away with and in its place emerged the 'Scheduled Tribes.' The Indian State became the final arbiter of which communities were to be clubbed as Scheduled Caste (Article 341) and Scheduled Tribes (Article 342). They were to receive the benefit of State subsidies as well as reservation in educational institutions and government service. These new, apparently secular terms were to be firmly entrenched in the Statist discourse on the most marginalised sections of Indian society. As Parmar points out, the phrase 'Scheduled Tribes,' adopted by the CA in preference to the colonial category 'aborigines' or 'Adivasi' (adopted by Jaipal Singh and the Adivasi Mahasabha), meant that the claims by indigenous people 'were thus effectively written out of the *Constitution*, foreclosing any possibility of a future recognition in the country's law.'[89] This move also 'changed the terms of discourse' as the Scheduled Tribes were now entitled to help and

[89]Parmar, 'Undoing Historical Wrongs,' p. 515; emphasis in the original.

protection from the nation-State on account of their perennial state of 'backwardness', which 'underscores the denial of agency to them'.

In a letter to Sardar Patel written soon after the promulgation of the Indian Constitution, Thakkar reminded the Deputy Prime Minister of the incipient sovereign Indian State about the promise of a Backward Class Commission made under Article 340. Thakkar requested him to 'take early measures for the appointment of such Commission mentioned above at an early date'. He went on to delineate the three categories which together made up the generic category of 'Backward Classes'.[90]

Thakkar also reminded Patel that this enquiry has to be a comprehensive all-India exercise applicable to 'all States enlisted in parts A, B and C of States mentioned in Schedule No. 1 of the Constitution viz. (1) 9 Provinces now called States; (2) 9 State Unions and States forming part B of the Schedule; (3) 10 Centrally administered areas directly under the Government of India.'

Thakkar argued that since 26 January, the Constitution of India had been in 'full working order', and so the Backward Classes Commission 'may be appointed as soon as possible'. According to him, conducting the full enquiry could take up to two years and more time would be required to write the report. Therefore, if Article 340 were to really fulfil its intention of ameliorating the 'conditions of all backward classes', a minimum period of up to three years was required to complete the task of conducting a full study and writing of a meaningful report. Hence, in Thakkar's view, it was imperative to set the ball rolling as soon as possible for the process was bound to take a long time.

Citing 'present financial position' as the chief impediment, Patel dodged any commitment to the endeavour and replied:

> (Y)ou have to take note of the fact that we have many urgent problems of [*sic*] the moment with which we have our hands full.... The Commission which is contemplated is not going to be an ordinary Commission. It will have to be fairly representative and will have to tour extensively. It will also require a substantial staff. There is no compelling urgency about this and I feel that the matter can be allowed

[90]Letter from A. V. Thakkar, M.P. c/o Harijan Sevak Sangh, Kingsway Delhi, To: Sardar Vallabhbhai Patel, The Hon'ble Deputy Prime Minister, Government of India, New Delhi, regarding 'Appointment of a Commission to investigate the conditions of the Backward Classes in India', dated 21 February 1950 in F. No. 8/30, February 1947–December 1950, Correspondence with Shri Thakkar Bapa of Harijan Sevak Sangh, pp. 139–144, Sardar Patel Papers, NAI.

> to rest for the time being. We can take this matter up when we have a little leisure and can better afford to appoint it.[91]

Thus, both Patel and Nehru were non-committal to Thakkar Bapa's request for a Backward Classes Commission. That demand was itself based on an accurate mapping of the complex social reality of India through the Census operations. In fact, Patel, in a conference of government officials gearing up for the 1951 Census operations, had jettisoned the idea of collecting caste data. He said:

> There is also another departure from past. Formerly there used to be elaborate caste tables which were required in India partly to satisfy the theory that it was a caste ridden country and partly to meet the needs of administrative measures dependent on caste divisions. In the forthcoming census, this will no longer be a prominent feature and we can devote our energies and our attention to the collection and formulation of basic economic data relating to the means of livelihood of the people and other economic activities of the individual and the State.[92]

This proves that Patel never had any intention of fulfilling the request of the veteran Gandhian. The three categories therefore remained divided and the Indian State became the final arbiter of which groups were to be clubbed under Scheduled Caste, Tribes, or Backward Classes, which continues to be the case even today.

Conclusion

In this chapter, I have charted the process by which the Constituent Assembly appropriated the colonial ideas of protective provisions for tribal populations and wove them into the fabric of the Indian Constitution. In reconstructing the range of interests, individuals, and ideologies that were involved in this dynamic, I have presented a narrative that shows how

---

[91]Letter from Vallabhbhai Patel to A. V. Thakkar, No. 137, DPN/50, dated 24 February 1950, in F. No. 8/30, February 1947–December 1950, Correspondence with Shri Thakkar Bapa of Harijan Sevak Sangh, p.73, Sardar Patel Papers, NAI.

[92]Speech of the Deputy Prime Minister, Summary Proceedings of the Census Conference held at New Delhi, from 23 February–1 March 1950, Office of the Registrar General, India, Ministry of Home Affairs, Government of India, Manager, Government of India Press, New Delhi, 1950, p. 1.

interconnected events occurring in disparate theatres had an impact on the final resolution. These separate streams have to be woven together to understand the final picture that emerged. Additionally, I have argued that the agency of the tribals themselves was an important factor in achieving the ultimate resolution enshrined in the Indian Constitution through the Fifth and Sixth Schedules.

As curtains were drawn on World War II and the British exit seemed imminent, plans of either the British High Commissioner or the United Nations taking charge of tribal areas in frontier spaces emerged in the administrative discourse. Such ferment and serious discussions around these extraordinary proposals in the highest reaches of the colonial State also indicated that a new post-imperial global order was on the anvil. In a world trying to come to terms with organised and State-sponsored ethnic cleansing projects (including the Holocaust of Jews), the debates on minority rights in what would soon become ex-colonies acquired an immediacy in the international legal discourse. As a future sovereign member of the international community, the Indian nation-State, through its Constitution, had to display elements that were considered legitimate in an impending world order.

In this context, the anxieties of tribals, the Depressed Classes, and religious minorities had to be addressed in the constitutional framework announced under the Cabinet Mission Plan of May 1946. The earlier solution to the tribal predicament advocated by the anthropologists was protection from legislative intervention through a territorial ring-fencing of predominantly tribal areas. Thus, in the late colonial framework, scheduling was an instrument of 'excluding' the notified areas, totally or partially, from the legislative powers of democratically elected assemblies or councils. In response, the nationalists lambasted this administrative device as another expression of the larger British policy of divide and rule. Post the Haripura Congress session in 1938, the nationalists decided to oppose it in an organised manner. Towards that end, the All-India Excluded and Partially Excluded Areas Association, manned and sponsored by the Indian National Congress, received a fresh lease of life. It remained the main platform for voicing the nationalist demand to repeal the provisions of the special administrative regimes contained in the Government of India Act, 1935.

Earlier, from about 1944–1945, in anticipation of the transfer of power through a new working Constitution, hectic political mobilisation had begun on all sides. Through pressures generated by the Communist-led tribal movements in Telangana, Tebhaga, and Warli, the need to address the position of tribes in a future Indian nation-State had certainly acquired an urgent dimension. The Telangana revolt (1946–1951), in particular, continued to loom over the entire Constitution-making process, and even beyond.

While the Communists operating under the far-Left Ranadive line could be dismissed as violent, lawless, and anti-national, the challenge posed by the Jaipal Singh Munda-led Adivasi Mahasabha was of a qualitatively different order. The relentless efforts of their cadres in raising the demand for a separate autonomous state of Jharkhand enabled the Mahasabha to make successful inroads into the electoral politics of the Chota Nagpur region. Potentially, it was a far more serious threat to the long-term political dominance of the Indian National Congress. Through building up a robust organisational structure, deft and tactful mobilisation techniques, as well as its canny decision to support the British war effort, both Munda and the Adivasi Mahasabha had grown in political stature during World War II. In the provincial elections of 1946, held a few months prior to the announcement of the Cabinet Mission Plan, the Adivasi Mahasabha was able to win enough seats (three) to send their Marang Gomke to the CA, even though Munda himself lost the contest for a Bihar provincial Assembly seat to his Congress rival. All this took place in the face of stiff political resistance by the Bihar Congress, in a period of high drama and turmoil. Thus, by the time the CA began deliberating on the future constitutional framework, the Adivasi Mahasabha had emerged as an important pivot of anti-Congress opposition forces in the politically important province of Bihar. Furthermore, the agitations being led by Jaipal Singh in several of the ex-Princely States was galvanising a regional Adivasi political identity across provincial borders, and increasing his sphere of influence.

In this period (1947–1950) of tenuous legitimacy for the independent Indian nation-State, the task of pacifying the often violent tribal autonomy movements in various parts of India fell on the shoulders of the national leadership of the Indian National Congress. Over the three years of constitutional deliberations, they gradually worked out a strategic shift vis-à-vis the Congress's earlier stated position against the scheduling of predominantly tribal areas. When activists become rulers, a different set of demands impinge upon their principles and ideology, which necessitates tactical retreats in order to gain wider legitimacy.

In such a transitional framework, the Congress nationalists were fighting a two-pronged battle: militarily against the Communists and electorally against the Adivasi Mahasabha. With the control over a highly coercive ex-colonial military apparatus just emerging out of World War II, the Congress-led governments in Hyderabad and Bombay managed to violently repress the political challenge posed by the Communists. While the Congress's success over their Communist rivals was a foregone conclusion, the charge raised by the tribal autonomy movement under the leadership of Jaipal Singh and the Adivasi Mahasabha required tricky political manoeuvring. The challenge before the Congress was reining in the Adivasi Movement, especially its attempt to divide the politically important province of Bihar, which was home to many senior leaders of the party, including the President of the CA, Rajendra Prasad. In the bitter tug of war for political dominance, the Congress chose to push back any resolution of the tribal question until the closing months of the CA.[93]

Moreover, in order to strengthen its own rank and file, Congressmen needed to win allies in the Chota Nagpur region. Also, in a promised land of universal adult franchise, the Congress could ill-afford to be seen as working against the interest of the Adivasis. The choice was clear: it could only choose between keeping Bihar as a unified state, or sticking to its long-held principled position of repealing the provisions of excluded and partially excluded areas. Thus, it was pure political expediency that made the Congress chose the former over the latter. It disregarded the demand for Jharkhand and agreed to incorporate the provisions for the Fifth Schedule. However, this incorporation was allowed only on terms dictated by the Congress. As a result, certain key modifications designed to undercut the challenge being mounted by a once Olympic champion-turned-shrewd politician were introduced. It is interesting to note that the amendments were proposed by the Chairman of the Drafting Committee, B. R. Ambedkar, the pioneering leader of the Scheduled Castes. It was a shot that the Congress took from his safe shoulders.

The acceptance of scheduling by a Constituent Assembly dominated by Congressmen should also be seen as a transformation in the political character of the Indian National Congress. Before the British exit, the Congress was essentially a united front of anti-imperialist nationalist forces whose top leadership led an independence movement and aimed at the establishment

---

[93] Although both the Bordoloi and the Thakkar Sub-Committees had submitted their respective reports in 1947, the debates in the CA on provisions for the Fifth and Sixth Schedules happened only in early September 1949. Less than three months later, the CA wound up its proceedings.

of a sovereign, democratic nation-State in India. After a taste of political power during the period of the Congress Ministries (1937–1939), however, the organisation was slowly mutating into a quintessential political 'party' engaged in an electoral number game to capture and maintain State power. In the ultimate resolution of the tribal question through special provisions of the Indian Constitution, the role of tribal agency is discernible in two ways.

First, starting with the Bihar Legislative Assembly and down to the CA debates itself, figures like Ignes Beck, Boniface Lakra, and Jaipal Singh Munda took a leading role. The Sub-committee headed by Thakkar, of which Jaipal Singh was a member, toured important tribal tracts and acquainted themselves with the conditions, which led to its accepting in principle the policy of territorial segregation. *Second,* the various Communist-led movements in tribal areas and the Jharkhand agitation by the Adivasi Mahasabha under Jaipal Singh Munda's leadership gave tribal demands a certain 'visibility' in the constitutional dynamics played out between 1947–1950. Already reeling under large-scale communal genocide after the Partition, the sharpening of the tribal question further pressurised the nationalist leadership, who were stretched thin. The combined effect of these movements played a decisive role in the changed stance of the Indian National Congress on the issue of excluded and partially excluded areas. Under pressure from several sides, the new rulers of the independent Indian nation-State devised a new administrative paradigm for governing tribal areas, which differed significantly from the Governor-centric one enshrined in the Government of India Act, 1935. In this process, almost the entire colonial discourse on tribal people was appropriated, but with one crucial distinction: representational democracy through elections was now given pride of place.

In the final analysis, despite a deficit in a sufficiently broad-based English-educated and vocal middle-class elite, owing to the successful mobilisation campaigns by the Communists and the Jaipal Singh Munda-led Adivasi Mahasabha, the tribes did claim a share of national attention and political visibility in the constitutional deliberations of the late colonial period (1918–1947). Had it not been for these resistances, it was highly unlikely that the Indian National Congress would have agreed to the inclusion of Fifth and Sixth Schedule Areas as a part of the Constitution of India. Although both forces were ultimately dissipated and many of their cadres were absorbed into the Congress, they played a historic role in breaking the Congress hegemony and position in the predominantly tribal areas of the Indian subcontinent.

Epilogue

Almost all these tribes live in the solitude of forests and jungle-clad hills—small pools of humanity without any living connection with the main currents of Indian life and culture. Truants to civilization, their life is an unending series of terrors, terror of man, animals and unknown powers.

V. Thakkar[1]

'Not less than thirty millions'. This is the verdict of Indian scientists on the numerical strength of the most ancient people in this country, Adivasis as they are increasingly coming to be called, the original settlers. Enumeration of Adivasis has been so vitiated at each decennial census that the present figures indicate only the groups which have not been assimilated to the Hindu fold. For centuries the process of acculturation and proselytization has been going on. There are the fully Hinduised Adivasis who have ceased to identify themselves with their original confreres; there are millions who have not been brought into the Hindu fold, and these may be called semi-Hinduised. Besides these two categories there is the outer circle of no-man's-land where the Adivasis oscillate between their ancient status and the apparent lift a new nomenclature offers them. Ethnically, therefore, it would be nearer the truth to say that Adivasis are about one hundred million.

Jaipal Singh Munda[2]

These two quotes juxtapose two distinct understandings of the place occupied by the 'Aboriginal Tribes' in India's cultural matrix. They also indicate the phenomenal transformation the concept

[1]A. V. Thakkar, 'The Aboriginal Tribes of India', *The Modern Review* XLI (2), February 1927.

[2]Jaipal Singh, 'Problems of 30 million Adivasis', *The Times of India*, 26 January 1950, p. B6.

underwent from the 1920s until the foundational moment of the new Indian Republic. Under colonial rule, the quintessential aborigine was a member of any people who were the first to live in a country or region, especially as compared to later arrivals. However, as the curtains fell on the British Raj, the *a priori* historical status of aboriginals, reinvented by political movements as the *Adivasi*, was quietly brushed aside and the new constitutional framework labelled them 'Scheduled Tribes' (STs).[3] Although the Constitution of India remains silent on how it cognised such groups, this study argues that the axis of identification for the aborigines shifted from geographical markers and metaphors to a religious one. In Ghurye's influential formulation, the 'so-called' aborigines were nothing but 'Backward Hindus'.[4]

Following Independence and Partition in 1947, the source of sovereign power was transferred from the British Parliament to the Constituent Assembly of India. In striking a new 'deal' for the tribal people, the Indian ruling elites jettisoned earlier terms such as 'protection' or 'assimilation' and instead sought to facilitate their 'integration'[5] into the 'mainstream' of national life.[6] But as a range of scholars and activists have pointed out over decades, even as the Indian Constitution brought the promise of modern citizenship to the 'Scheduled Tribes', on the ground, many of these promises remain

[3]The amendment to change the constitutional nomenclature from 'Aboriginal and Hill Tribe' to 'Scheduled Tribes' was introduced by Dr B. R. Ambedkar.

[4]Interestingly, all the later editions of Ghurye's 1943 book, *The Aborigines—'So-Called'—And Their Future*, were re-titled and published as *The Scheduled Tribes*.

[5]For Jawaharlal Nehru's own thoughts on the tribal people of India, see 'The Tribal Folk' (Speech at the Opening Session of the Scheduled Tribes and Scheduled Areas Conference), New Delhi, 7 June 1952, in *Jawaharlal Nehru's Speeches*, Vol. 2 (1949–1953), New Delhi: Publication Division, Government of India, 1954, pp. 576–583.

[6]T. S. Wilkinson, 'Isolation, Assimilation and Integration in Historical Perspective', *Bulletin of the Tribal Research Institute, Chhindwara, M.P.*, 2 (1), June 1962, pp. 19–28. Also see Chapter 4, 'The Tribal Problem', in Ezra Rashkow, *The Nature of Endangerment in India: Tigers, 'Tribes', Extermination & Conservation, 1818–2020*, New Delhi: Oxford University Press, 2023, pp. 166–204. For a recent volume with several Adivasi writers, see S. R. Bodhi and Bipin Jojo (eds), *The Problematics of Tribal Integration: Voices from India's Alternative Centres*, Hyderabad: The Shared Mirror, 2019.

unfulfilled. Empirical assessments of the Indian State's policy framework towards the STs reveal a rather tragic record.[7]

The complex and variegated ensemble of groups constituting the 'Scheduled Tribes' together make up for a little over 8 per cent of the Indian population. This translates to over 100 million individuals living in highly disparate landscapes and conditions. On the indicators of human development and access to resources, the STs usually occupy a place far worse than Muslims and Dalits.[8] That such an appalling state of affairs has continued even three generations after independence suggests that the Indian nation-State, for all its welfarist rhetoric on tribal development, has not offered them a square deal. Therefore, scholarly enquiries are required to understand the terms under which tribal communities were to be integrated into the body politic of the Indian nation. This book constitutes one such attempt at historicising a complex and forgotten past.

Today, a key issue in the public discourse surrounding tribal communities is the efficacy of 'scheduling' as an instrument of tribal governance within the constitutional apparatus of independent India.[9] While provisions of the

[7]The noted tribal rights activist, the late B. D. Sharma, has characterised the period since independence as an 'unbroken history of broken promises' for the tribal people of India. See his eponymously titled book, *Unbroken History of Broken Promises: Indian State and the Tribal People*, New Delhi: Freedom Press, in association with Sahyog Pustak Kuteer, 2010.

[8]Virginius Xaxa, 'Protective Discrimination: Why Scheduled Tribes Lag Behind Scheduled Castes', *Economic and Political Weekly* 36 (29), July 2001, pp. 2765–2772.

[9]Namita Wahi and Ankit Bhatia, *The Legal Regime and Political Economy of the Land Rights of Scheduled Tribe in the Scheduled Areas of India*, New Delhi: Centre for Policy Research, 2018. For a complete state-wise list of Scheduled Areas, see Annexure 7 in C. R. Bijoy, Shankar Gopalakrishnan, and Shomona Khanna, *India and the Rights of Indigenous Peoples: Constitutional, Legislative and Administrative Provisions Concerning Indigenous and Tribal Peoples in India and their Relation to International Law on Indigenous Peoples*, Chiang Mai: Asia Indigenous Peoples Pact (AIPP), 2010, pp. 221–245. Both are compact and very useful volumes. The latter also provides details of the Constitutional Orders (hereafter, C.O.) which notified the Fifth Schedule Areas in various states.

The first Scheduled Areas under the Constitution of India were notified through the *Scheduled Areas (Part A States) Order, 1950 (C.O. 9) dated 23–01–1950* and the *Scheduled Areas (Part B States), 1950 (C.O. 26) dated 7–12–1950*. The list was modified *vide* the *Madras Scheduled Areas (Cesser) Order, 1951 (C.O. 50)* and the

Sixth Schedule are often hailed for ensuring robust local autonomy for tribal communities in the North-East region,[10] their counterparts living in tracts notified under the Fifth Schedule have experienced a largely dysfunctional administrative-legal State apparatus.[11] For instance, in areas affected by left-wing extremism (which often overlap with the Fifth Schedule), Adivasi lives are caught in a web of everyday violence between State and non-State actors.[12] The Tribes Advisory Councils in the ten states[13] having Fifth

---

Andhra Scheduled Areas (Cesser) Order, 1955 (C.O. 30). A significant expansion in the inventory of notified Scheduled Areas occurred during the Emergency and its immediate aftermath. See *Scheduled Areas (Himachal Pradesh) Order, 1975 (C.O. 102) dated 21–11–1975; Scheduled Areas (States of Bihar, Gujarat, Madhya Pradesh and Orissa) Order, 1977 (C.O. 109) dated 31–12–1977*, which, rescinding the earlier C.O.s, added new territories. The trend of expanding the Scheduled Areas continued in the 1980s. See *Scheduled Areas (State of Rajasthan) Order, 1981 (C.O. 114) dated 12–02–1981*, and *Scheduled Areas (Maharashtra) Order, 1985 (C.O. 123) dated 02–12–1985*. Scheduled Areas were also transferred from composite to new states after the formation of Chhattisgarh and Jharkhand. See *Scheduled Areas (States of Chhattisgarh, Jharkhand and Madhya Pradesh) Order, 2003 (C.O. 192) dated 20–02–2003*. See Bijoy, et al., *India and the Rights of Indigenous Peoples*.

[10]For an empirical assessment, see Prabhat Kumar Datta and Panchali Sen, 'Governance in the Sixth Schedule Areas in India's North-East: Context, Content and Challenges', *Indian Journal of Public Administration* 66 (2), June 2020, pp. 191–205. Also see H. Kham Khan Suan, 'Salvaging Autonomy in India's North-East: Beyond the Six Scheduled Way', *Eastern Quarterly* 4 (1), April–June 2007.

[11]Pradip Prabhu, 'An Unbroken History of Broken Promises', in V. Srinivasa Rao (ed.), *Adivasi Rights and Exclusion in India*, New Delhi: Taylor & Francis, 2018, pp. 269–296. Also see 'Overview of Scheduled Areas' within the 'Introduction', in Varsha Bhagat-Ganguly and Sujit Kumar (eds), *India's Scheduled Areas: Untangling Governance, Law and Politics*, New Delhi: Routledge, 2020, pp. 1–13. For an assessment by a seasoned administrator, see Bhupinder Singh, 'The Fifth Schedule of the Indian Constitution', *Indian Journal of Public Administration* 59 (2), 2017, pp. 211–227. Available at https://journals.sagepub.com/doi/abs/10.1177/0019556120130201?journalCode=ipaa (accessed 24 September 2024).

[12]Ajay Dandekar and Chitrangada Choudhury, *PESA, Left-Wing Extremism and Governance: Concerns and Challenges in India's Tribal Districts*, Anand: Institute of Rural Management, 2010; Nandini Sundar, *The Burning Forest: India's War in Bastar*, New Delhi: Juggernaut, 2016.

[13]Maharashtra, Gujarat, Rajasthan, Madhya Pradesh, Chhattisgarh, Odisha, Jharkhand, Andhra Pradesh, Telangana, and Himachal Pradesh.

Schedule Areas remain inert, and the implementation of progressive laws duly passed by the Indian Parliament (such as the Panchayat Extension to Scheduled Areas Act, 1996 [PESA] and the Scheduled Tribes and other Traditional Forest Dwellers [Recognition of Forest Rights] Act, 2006 [FRA])[14] has been patchy and highly unsatisfactory.[15] The Governors of states, who enjoy a prominent position in the administrative frameworks of the Fifth Schedule, have been inadequate trustees of tribal interests.[16] By and large, it is believed that the Sixth Schedule model of tribal governance has outperformed that of the Fifth Schedule.[17]

Statistically, out of the 640 administrative districts in India, 104 have Scheduled Areas.[18] Of these, thirty-six districts are fully notified

[14]For PESA and FRA, see Savyasachi, 'Deforestation, Nature and Conservation: An Indigenous Discourse', *Contemporary Perspective* 2 (2), 2008, pp. 279–313, and 'Forests Rights Act, 2006: Undermining the Foundational Position of the Forest', *Economic and Political Weekly* 46 (5), April 2011, pp. 55–62.

[15]See Yatindra Singh Sisodia and Tapas K. Dalapati, 'Decentralised Governance and Implementation of PESA in Tribal Areas', in V. Srinivasa Rao (ed.), *Adivasi Rights and Exclusion in India*, New Delhi: Taylor & Francis, 2018, pp. 332–347; Apoorv Kurup, 'Tribal Law in India: How Decentralised Administration is Extinguishing Tribal Rights and Why Autonomous Tribal Governments are Better', *Indigenous Law Journal* 7, 2008.

[16]For two relatively recent analyses of the theme, see Nayakara Veeresha, 'Governance of the Fifth Schedule Areas: Role of Governor', *Indian Journal of Public Administration* 63 (3), 2017, pp. 444–455; and Virginius Xaxa, 'Governors and the Fifth Schedule: Failing the Constitutional Mandate', *Economic and Political Weekly* 54 (44), November 2019, pp. 10–11. Available at https://journals.sagepub.com/doi/full/10.1177/0019556117720614; https://www.epw.in/journal/2019/44/alternative-standpoint/governors-and-fifth-schedule.html (accessed 14 September 2024).

[17]In many parts of central India, such as the undivided Bastar region, strong demands have been raised by tribal activists and politicians to convert the status of Fifth Schedule Areas into the Sixth Schedule, which would allow far greater levels of autonomy. In more recent times, people living in mountainous frontiers such as Ladakh have raised a vociferous demand for inclusion within the Sixth Schedule. See https://www.samataindia.org.in/right-place-wrong-arrangement/; https://theprint.in/opinion/ladakh-protest-for-sixth-schedule-has-hit-an-impasse-govt-should-propose-middle-ground/2006063/ (accessed 14 September 2024).

[18]For this paragraph, the statistical information has been taken from C. R. Bijoy, 'How a History of Broken Promises has Let Down India's Scheduled Areas', *The Wire*, 9 November 2021. Available at https://thewire.in/rights/

while the rest (sixty-eight) are partially notified ones (see Maps 1 and 2). Approximately 11.3 per cent of the total geographical area of the country has been declared Scheduled Areas and demographically, about 5.7 per cent of India's population—both tribal peoples and otherwise—reside here. Despite covering large swathes of land, only about 35.2 per cent of India's total ST population resides in notified Scheduled Areas. While these enclaves were constituted in order to maintain the demographic majorities of tribal communities in their traditional habitats, owing to a slew of developmental projects and an incessant influx of migrants, today only about 53 per cent of the population in Scheduled Areas belongs to the Scheduled Tribes.[19] Since the 1990s, the growth of neoliberal economic frameworks in these forest and mineral resource-rich areas have accelerated the primitive accumulation of capital, which continue to generate intensive peoples' resistance.[20] More recently, a vigorous and still unfolding movement known as 'Pathalgadi' in

---

how-a-history-of-broken-promises-has-let-down-indias-scheduled-areas. (accessed 14 September 2024). Statistics from census reports are provided in Ajeet Jaiswal, 'Tribes of India: India's Overall Demographic Scene and Demographic Features in Tribal Societies', *Anthropology and Ethnology Open Access Journal* 2 (2). Available at https://medwinpublishers.com/AEOAJ/AEOAJ16000123.pdf (accessed 14 September 2024). For a full-length study on tribal demography, see Arup Maharatna, *Demographic Perspectives on India's Tribes*, New Delhi: Oxford University Press, 2005.

[19]Amita Baviskar, *In the Belly of the River: Tribal Conflicts over Development in the Narmada Valley*, New Delhi: Oxford University Press, 1997. For an in-depth study of the Adivasi-Bengali relationship when the 'displaced persons' from East Pakistan were resettled in the undivided Koraput district of Odisha under the Dandakaranya Project, see Jagannath Ambagudia, *Adivasis, Migrants and the State in India*, London and New York: Routledge, 2019.

[20]For an excellent collaborative study on the effects of the neoliberal economic framework on underprivileged Indians (including tribal people), see Alpa Shah, Jens Lerche, Richard Axelby, Dalel Benbabaali, Brendon Donegan, Jayaseelan Raj, and Vikramaditya Thakur, *Ground Down by Growth: Tribe, Class, Caste and Inequality in Twenty-First Century India*, New Delhi: Oxford University Press, 2018. For a moving study of the impact of the mining industry on Adivasi lives, see Samarendra Das and Felix Padel, *Out of this Earth: East India Adivasis and the Aluminium Cartel*, New Delhi: Orient BlackSwan, 2020 [2010]. For a recent study on the same theme, see Swagato Sarkar, *Democratic Despotism: Politics of Primitive Accumulation in India*, London and New York: Routledge, 2023.

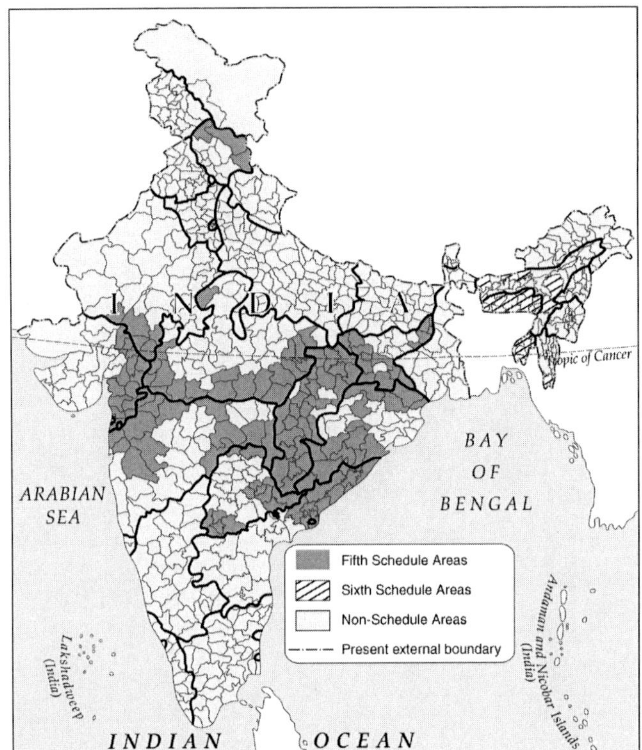

Map 1: Scheduled and Tribal Areas in India

Source: Adapted from Namita Wahi and Ankit Bhatia, *The Legal Regime and Political Economy of the Land Rights of Scheduled Tribe in the Scheduled Areas of India*, Centre for Policy Research, 2018, with permission.

Jharkhand has invited academic scrutiny.[21] Meanwhile, despite consistent efforts by Adivasi rights advocacy groups, the Indian State has resolutely

[21]Anupama Roy and Ujjwal Kumar Singh, 'Pathalgadi Movement, Self-Governance, and the Question of "Weak Statehood"', in Dieter Neubert, Hans-Joachim Lauth, and Christoph Mohamad-Klotzbach (eds), *Local Self-Governance and Varieties of Statehood: Tensions and Cooperation*, Cham: Springer, 2022, pp. 117–113; Also see Chapter 5, 'Echoes from the Graveyeard: Pathalgadi, Birsaites and the Landscape of Memory', in Rahul Ranjan, *The Political Life of Memory: Birsa Munda in Contemporary India*, New Delhi: Cambridge University Press, 2023, pp. 207–257.

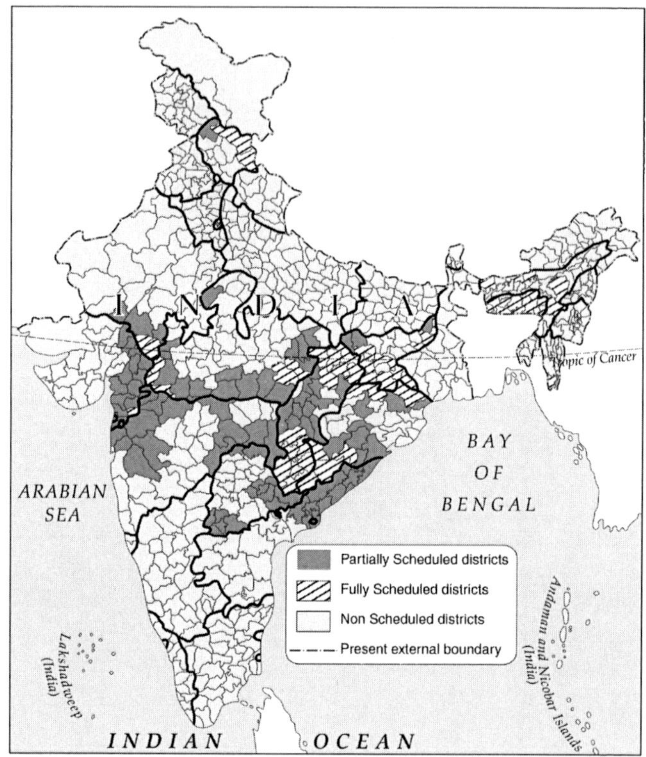

Map 2: Fully and Partially Scheduled Districts

Source: Adapted from Namita Wahi and Ankit Bhatia, *The Legal Regime and Political Economy of the Land Rights of Scheduled Tribe in the Scheduled Areas of India*, Centre for Policy Research, 2018, with permission.

refused to recognise STs as the 'indigenous people' of India, and continues to deny all such claims.[22]

This book, which began as my Ph.D. thesis, sought to respond to many of these contemporary conversations on the Indian tribal people by asking a set

[22]For India's stance in the United Nations, see T. C. James, 'International Discussions on Indigenous People and India', RIS Discussion Papers, 2022; Bengt G. Karlsson, 'Anthropology and the Indigenous Slot: Claims to and Debates About Indigenous Peoples' Status in India', in Bengt G. Karlsson and T. B. Subba (eds), *Indigeneity in India*, London: Routledge and Kegan Paul, 2006, pp. 51–73; Manvir Singh, 'It's Time to Rethink the Idea of the "Indigenous"', *The New Yorker*, 20 February 2023.

of historical questions. While scholarship on Independence, Partition, and Constitution-making[23] has greatly expanded our understanding about the twilight of the British Indian Empire, much spadework remains to be done with regard to analysing forms of representative politics outside the Congress fold. Even as the Indian National Congress evolved as a broad-based anti-imperialist front in the early twentieth century, its claims of representing the interests of all Indians did not go unchallenged. Sekhar Bandyopadhyay, in his remarkable survey of the colonial period, has proverbially termed such alternate imaginaries as 'Many Voices of a Nation'.[24] He highlights five groups (Muslim, Non-Brahmin/Dalit, Business, Working Class, and Women) whose aspirations were not entirely in congruence with the official Congress vision of *swaraj*. Despite their sufficient recalcitrance, the aboriginal tribes do not feature in this list of dissonances with mainstream nationalism. This book offers a corrective by inserting a pan-India discourse on the future of tribal communities, which was vitally shaped beyond the scope of nationalist ideas.[25] In the approximately 400 pages of discourse analysis, however, the genuinely tribal voices are few and far between, even as many claimed to speak *on their behalf*. Nevertheless, with the discourse of scheduling acting as the pivot, this study provides an intellectual and constitutional history of the 'Tribal Question' in the last three decades of colonial rule in India. In a nutshell, it offers a serious academic attempt to revise and redefine the historiography on Indian tribal communities.

There were two main ambitions behind this research work. To begin with, my effort has been to historically understand how terms such as 'Assimilation', 'Protection', 'Uplift', 'Civilisation', etc., came to acquire such immense power in the discourse on the Indian tribal people.[26] Even today, most discussions on tribal development/welfare deploy the very same

[23]Nandini Sundar, '"We will Teach India Democracy": Indigenous Voices in Constitution-Making', *The Journal of Imperial and Commonwealth History* 52 (1), 2024, pp. 181–213.

[24]Sekhar Bandyopadhyay, *From Plassey to Partition: A History of Modern India*, Hyderabad: Orient Longman, 2004, pp. 334–404.

[25]I thank Dr Sourav Kumar Mahanta for this point.

[26]For an important survey of key academic theoreticians and ideas, see Virginius Xaxa, 'Transformation of Tribes in India: Terms of Discourse', *Economic and Political Weekly* 34 (24), June 1999, pp. 1519–1524. Also see Bhangya Bhukya, 'The Mapping of the Adivasi Social: Colonial Anthropology and Adivasis', *Economic and Political Weekly* 43 (39), October 2008, pp. 103, 105–109.

frames within which colonial administrators and nationalist politicians and social workers operated. Despite such evident similarities in the terms of discourse, a historically grounded argument that could explain the continuance of these paradigms in independent India's welfarist rhetoric has not been undertaken. This book addresses the gap by providing the first evidence-based analysis and explanation of the following puzzle: Why, following independence, did the Government of India accept a model of governance through scheduling that the Congressmen had vehemently opposed in the 1930s and 1940s?

Second, I sought to write a monograph that would mark a point of departure from historiographical narratives on Indian tribes, which have often amounted to micro-studies of one tribal insurrection or another. This decades-old legacy has led to the ubiquitous representation of the tribal/Adivasi[27] as an insurgent *par excellence*. Such a research loop has ended up fetishising the local at the expense of regional and para-regional contexts. I have deliberately avoided a localised, tribe-specific paradigm and instead opted for a pan-India framework. If, in doing so, greater weightage has been given to western India, the reason lies in the choice of characters and archives, for the activities of Thakkar, Elwin, Ghurye, et al., were all heavily tied up with the cities of Bombay and Poona.[28]

At the very beginning of my research work, I was struck by the fact that, among all the 'minority' groups within the Indian nation, only the STs were conferred a territorial solution, despite strong nationalist opposition. Thus, the advocates of scheduling were successful in finding a constitutional place in the new Indian nation-State for enclaves that had exceptional status in the legal and administrative framework of British India. Moreover, these enclaves were often situated in the hills, forests, and other relatively inaccessible areas away from the 'civilisation' of the plains. What stoked my interest further was the virtual absence of any genuine 'representative' voice from amongst the tribes until the emergence of Jaipal Singh Munda towards

[27]For an exceptional piece, see Prathama Banerjee, 'Writing the Adivasi: Some Historiographical Notes', *Indian Economic and Social History Review* 53 (1), 2016, pp. 131–153. For a relatively recent survey of the state of Adivasi Studies, see Sangeeta Dasgupta, 'Adivasi Studies: From a Historian's Perspective', *History Compass* 16 (10), October 2018, e12486. Available at https://compass.onlinelibrary.wiley.com/doi/epdf/10.1111/hic3.12486 (accessed 14 September 2024).

[28]It is possible that a different set of characters and/or regions from the same period might yield unique insights into the discourse on aboriginal tribes.

the end of this period. Thus, one was led to ask: What happens to a minority political discourse which does not have an English-educated, middle-class elite to represent its group interests?

Searching through secondary literature was not helpful. While most articles and books had discussions about the 'Ghurye-Elwin debate' (the former a Saraswat Brahmin while the latter had come to India as a Christian missionary) or on 'Assimilation versus Protection', invariably, any attempt to look for chronologically deeper histories of the Fifth and Sixth Schedules within the Indian Constitution were linked with the passing of the Scheduled Districts Act, 1874 (SDA). On closer scrutiny of the evidence, both claims proved to be insufficiently historical, and I hope my research will provide a necessary corrective. Uncovering these layers, however, took copious amounts of time and space, which has resulted in a rather lengthy book. I have refrained from over-pruning extracts as the ones reproduced here have never appeared in academic literature earlier. Recovering these lost voices and making them publicly accessible in a single volume has been the guiding principle behind archival selection.

This book argues that the scheduling discourse acts as a unifying historical paradigm to aggregate and analyse the highly disparate tribal theatres of the Indian subcontinent. It veritably remains the only bridge of State policy that can explain the predicament of tribal communities as they moved from the colonial period into independent India. Consequently, the bulk of the monograph charts a prosopography of the key ideologues to highlight continuities and changes in the terms deployed during debates on the scheduling of aboriginal areas in British India. While doing so, I demonstrate that the story of scheduling has been wrongly framed as a sharp and vigorous (albeit, to my mind, non-existent) debate between G. S. Ghurye and Verrier Elwin—two figures who never actually debated with each other. Instead, a careful analysis of sources reveals the contours of a once vigorous debate conducted not between two individuals but rather between two lobbies, viz., anthropologists and nationalists. Thus, what began as a purely administrative discourse of ring-fencing tribal majority areas or scheduling was reworked on several occasions during a period of recurrent constitutional reforms. While the analysis of the book focuses on British India, a clear influence of the frontier territories (Naga Hills) and the Princely States (Bastar and Hyderabad) can nevertheless also be discerned in the narrative.

Until now, the SDA had been touted as the beginning point in the story of the 'scheduling' of predominantly tribal areas. Unfortunately, the exact legal meaning behind the nomenclature 'scheduled districts' has not been scrutinised, and owing to the use of different forms of the same word ('Schedule'), a thoroughly false assumption has acquired the status of commonsense. In fact, this late nineteenth-century legislation had no 'tribal' connection whatsoever. The term deployed in the early stages of legislative discussions was 'Excepted Districts', and its emergence can only be understood in the context of a power tussle between the executive and judicial arms of the colonial State apparatus. Finally, a legislative route for resolving conflict was found and two sister laws, viz., the SDA and the Laws Local Extent Act, were simultaneously enacted in 1874. They shared an exact same inventory of notified areas or 'schedule', earmarking territories acquired in the later stages of Company rule. The ostensible purpose of these twin legislations was to keep the listed areas as well as laws operational in them outside the powers of judicial review of the High Courts, which were constituted after the upheavals of 1857. Therefore, I have argued that the Scheduled Districts really began their journey as 'Excepted Districts' and, by implication, were 'spaces of exception', a meaning that was reworked during the early twentieth century. It was over forty years later that the Montague-Chelmsford Report (1918) recognised the SDA as the possible source from which 'Backward Tracts' could be carved out. This territorial ring-fencing was duly performed after the Government of India Act, 1919, was passed, and the areas notified as Backward Tracts now constituted 'regimes of protection' for the aboriginal tribes. Consequently, the SDA has long obfuscated scholarly enquiries and to understand its true significance, a separate research lens is required. Hence, it is my contention that the scheduling of tribal areas and the SDA should now be decoupled in academic analysis.

To go over the contours of the narrative, this study sought to identify and interrogate the *first principle* behind the ring-fencing of predominantly tribal areas. When the initial list of 'Backward Tracts' was notified after the operationalisation of the Government of India Act, 1919, the use of scheduling as an instrument to check constitutional reforms in tribal territories was rather limited. The list of 'totally excluded' areas only included Laccadive Islands and Minicoy (Madras), Chittagong Hill Tracts (Bengal), Angul (Bihar and Orissa), and Spiti (Punjab), and the largest block was declared from the Burma Province. The list of areas 'excluded with modifications' had somewhat larger territories and included the Agency Tracts (Madras), Darjeeling (Bengal), Lahaul (Punjab), Chota Nagpur (Bihar and Orissa), Santal Parganas (Bihar and Orissa), Sambalpur (Bihar and Orissa), and the hilly tracts of Assam. As the list makes apparent, no areas from either Bombay or Central Provinces and Berar were included under Backward Tracts. The entire enlisting exercise was done in concurrence with the respective local governments, and at this stage of administrative discourse, only Darjeeling and the Agency Tracts invited debate and discussion. This arrangement continued for almost fifteen years with a few milestones like the Indian Statutory Commission (Simon Commission, 1928) and the Round Table Conferences (early 1930s), with the former especially adding some significant aspects to the discourse of scheduling.

A key to the first principle was revealed in the British Parliament which, as an institution, had the ultimate responsibility for the protection of backward people (including the aborigines) in the British Indian Empire. In the debates that took place in the Parliament between March and May 1935, two key terms, that is, 'homogeneous' and 'self-contained', were deployed by the sparring parties. Interestingly, population figures from the 1931 Census featured prominently in these discussions, providing an extremely useful hint. Thinking through these expressions and the term 'homogeneous' (which was also used in the Shimla–Madras debate over the Agency areas)[29] revealed that they referred to tracts in British India that contained an overwhelming majority of aboriginal tribes, which were finally classed as 'totally excluded'. Following intervention by the British Parliament, in 1935, the first all-India aboriginal enquiry was conducted by Districts Officers and local governments, which also exhibited little deviance about what 'homogeneous' areas were. The final Order-in-Council in 1936 buttressed this convergence of opinion and the numbers of 'excluded' areas did not increase very significantly. Thus, an equivalence was established between 'homogeneous' and 'excluded' areas by participants in the Parliamentary debate on scheduling. The underlying logic of total exclusion was to maintain the majority character of the population. Within this ring-fence, land could not pass to non-aboriginals, disputes could only be settled through custom rather than law, and modern electoral democracy would be completely debarred.

---

[29]The Madras Agency Tracts were classed as excluded with modifications, but the local government insisted that these areas be effectively given the protective cover of the totally excluded status. See Chapter 1.

The phrase 'self-contained' areas evoked considerable dissension in the British Parliament. Two interventions made in the House of Commons debate on 13 May 1935 were significant in understanding the implications of this expression. *First*, Lord Eustace Percy, referring to Rudyard Kipling's famous *The Jungle Book*, said that it tells the story of an 'aboriginal population existing in a semi-settled, semi-nomadic condition in the midst of an ordinary agricultural population'. *Second*, another stalwart of the House of Commons, Winston Churchill, while supporting the Cadogan Amendment, controversially said: '... I should not object indeed to including in it the entire scope of the great Indian peninsula'.[30] The subsequent all-India enquiry and final Order-in-Council dramatically expanded the scope of the areas classed as 'partially excluded'.[31] Thus, a second equivalence was established between areas termed 'self-contained' and areas proposed for 'partial exclusion'. Interestingly, the maximum number of new areas was added to this group from the provinces of Bombay, and Central Provinces and Berar, which had earlier escaped the scope of scheduling entirely. Both these large provinces not only had a significant overall tribal population (Bombay, 12 per cent and C.P. & Berar, 19 per cent), but in certain (self-contained) pockets, the aborigines also enjoyed a demographic majority. In his speech on the subject, Percy also said that aboriginal tracts in the Central Provinces were those where the 'aboriginal element' ranged between 25–60 per cent, and in such areas 'the aboriginal population exists side by side with, generally, an Hindu population'. Taking into account these articulations of Percy, Churchill, and the Districts Officers reporting on the aboriginal tracts in C.P. and Bombay, a framework emerged where the basis of 'partial exclusion' was *territory*, *demographic majority*, and *religion*. This triumvirate constitutes the key to unlocking the *first principle* in the discourse on scheduling.

The above debates provide the context in which the Neo-Diffusionist ideas articulated by W. H. R. Rivers (who worked them out in the Melanesian Islands of the Western Pacific) provided the ideological kernel informing

[30]House of Commons Debate, 13 May 1935, Vol. 301, Columns 1411–1412. See Chapter 1 for details of this parliamentary discussion.

[31]The original Government of India Bill had a draft Schedule Six attached to Clause 91, which proposed four areas for total exclusion and eleven areas for partial exclusion; the extension clause in the Cadogan Amendment of May 1935 proposed twenty areas to be excluded and thirty-one to be partially excluded; and the final Order-in-Council of 1936 notified eight areas in the excluded category while twenty-eight were partially excluded.

the constitutional protections that tribal communities were first guaranteed under the Government of India Act, 1935. In the Riversian paradigm, the rapid 'depopulation' of aboriginal communities in island ecologies was argued to be a work of the variegated forces of 'civilisation' (colonialism, disease, the introduction of firearms, etc.). These isolated geographies had long served as autonomous primitive abodes, whereby the surrounding ocean had prevented 'cultural contact' with materially superior forces of civilisation. However, when 'civilisation' arrived in the form of European colonialists, merchants, and missionaries, an accelerated cultural contact began to take shape, which ultimately had a disastrous impact on these aboriginal communities, sapping their ability to physically and culturally reproduce future generations. According to Rivers, the 'loss of interest in life' caused the birth rate to decline and the death rate to spike in native communities. This psycho-social collapse led to an *en masse* extinction of aboriginal tribes, and hence, behind this genocide lay the forces of civilisation. These ideas, originally framed for the Melanesian Islands, were applied by colonial anthropologists to the tribal predicament in British India. Hence, 'Islands Against Civilisation'.

This book has argued that the story of scheduling can only be understood by a close historical examination of the trajectories of anthropological thought and nationalist politics. In this dynamic, both sides deployed varying notions of frontier, isolation, inaccessibility, and (perhaps most importantly) 'backwardness'. Their intersections produced a series of imaginations about the aboriginal tribes, sharing points of both similarities and contrasts. Initially, these representations were expressed uniformly, using geographic and spatial metaphors (read 'hills and forests', as expressed by Thakkar at the beginning of this chapter), which provided a consensus for both lobbies. Hence, the concept of 'aboriginal tribe' remained intact so long as both anthropologists and nationalists viewed them as the truly autochthonous element in Indian demography, and as people who inhabited the peripheral regions marked by hilly and forested terrain.

The protagonist who set up the 'tribal question' as a great battle of ideas was John Henry Hutton, who spent most of his career in the Naga Hills. Hutton's worldview was deeply informed by the notion that the interests of 'aboriginal' hillmen were in complete opposition to those of the 'civilised' plainsmen. In the Huttonian paradigm, hills and plains were not merely different topographies, but rather represented two entirely distinct and contrary ways of life. While the plainsmen believed in the 'rule of law' as embodied in written 'codes' and enforced by courts, judges, and lawyers, the hillmen were people of 'custom', to be held in sacred trust and interpreted by the elderly. The plainsmen eulogised representative democracy through elections as a way of balancing interests, but the hillmen, being 'backward', were unaware of the power of the vote and needed local autonomy to protect their ancestral land from passing into the hands of outsiders. Finally, in the realm of religious beliefs and practices, plainsmen were followers of organised faiths such as Hinduism/Christianity/Islam, while the hillmen were mainly 'animists' who believed in propitiating the spirits and reposed their faith in ancestor worship.

In an era of rapid Indianisation of services and devolution of powers to Indian political representatives. Hutton believed that the sympathetic European 'man on the spot' was the last bulwark protecting the interests of hillmen against plainsmen. He deeply mistrusted nationalists and particularly the class of lawyer-politician, for whom electoral success in local or legislative bodies was the chief route to political power. To succeed in elections, ambitious politicians would necessarily attend to the interests and demands of the far more numerous voters from the plains, thereby compromising the interests of tribal people from the hills. Moreover, there was a strong fiscal argument that the hills were permanently deficit areas needing large subventions from provincial and Central governments to meet the cost of administration. Thus, in a democratic set-up where governmental spending would be decided by politicians from the plains (which also contributed far more substantially to revenue collection), it was highly likely that the hills would be starved of funds.

Consequently, Hutton's chief objections were against the interference of legislative bodies and the jurisdiction of the High Courts, which would certainly follow if the scheme of constitutional reforms was introduced in aboriginal tracts. In effect, he argued that the legislative and judicial functions of the State should remain permanently suspended until the aborigines chose to integrate themselves fully into the provinces. From the 1920s onwards, when the discourse on scheduling was still largely confined to the colonial administrative domain, Hutton repeatedly wrote representations and gave evidence before constitutional experts/committees, stating that the simple aboriginal tribes residing in the hills and forests should be entirely excluded from all possible contact with the wily plainsmen. Hence, Hutton should be seen as the first hinge of the 'Protectionist' school of thought, who advocated the widest possible ring-fencing of areas with a demographic majority of aboriginal tribes. His chief motivation was to insulate the tribal cultures of hills and forests from the forces of civilisation embedded mainly in the plains.

Already a reputed anthropological expert, Hutton became the All-India Census Commissioner for the exercise scheduled in 1931. In this influential position, he created a unique blend of Riversian ideas on the depopulation of aboriginal communities in the Melanesian Islands with his long-held dichotomy of hills against plains. When the 1931 Census reports were published, they showcased the most extensive tables and data-sets on the castes and tribes of the British Indian Empire, including Princely States. Special arrangements were made to enumerate tribal people living in the remotest corners of the subcontinent. Within this monumental report—which remains the last complete caste and tribe census undertaken in India—Hutton made liberal use of Neo-Diffusionist anthropological theory to predict a demographic and cultural genocide of Indian aboriginal tribes if immediate corrective steps were not taken. Using this superimposed hybrid model, Hutton developed an argument which sought to re-establish the legitimacy and distinction of tribal religion vis-à-vis Hinduism, identifying hills and forests with the former and plains with the latter. Blaming vigorous Hindu and Christian conversion movements for a significant fall in the numbers of 'followers of Tribal Religions' in the 1931 Census tables, Hutton argued that an 'Acquisitive Hinduism' had accelerated detribalisation and turned aborigines into members of the Depressed Classes. Such detribalised aborigines were rapidly losing their land and cultural autonomy, and faced an existential threat as Hindu migrants continued to stream into tribal territories.

According to Hutton, the only solution was to completely exclude the hilly and forested tracts from constitutional reforms. This logic privileged the identification of hills and forests as the natural abode of the aboriginal tribes, which needed to be safeguarded from the forces of 'civilisation'. Thus, in the Huttonian argument, 'civilisation' became a metaphor for the combined forces of law, democracy, and organised religions. In extending the hill-plain binary across the Indian subcontinent, Hutton pushed the island imagery to its furthest limits; this also helped him to mask essentially religious differences through a geographical metaphor. In the Huttonian framework, once cordoned off, hills and jungles would act as safe havens for followers of tribal religion. Territorial segregation through scheduling would create 'islands', insulating Indian aboriginal tribes from outsiders, and thereby check the threat of extinction which Hindu civilisation posed to them. It is significant that Hutton, as well as his close associate Mills, did not attack mainstream Hindu bodies alone; rather, owing to their administrative experience, they were also equally against Christian missionaries, whose proselytising activities were similarly threatening the tribal cultures of the Naga Hills.

In contrast to Hutton, the ideological fountainhead of the nationalist opposition to the instrument of scheduling was the resilient social worker Amritlal Vithaldas Thakkar. Raised as a puritanical Vaishnavite, Thakkar was a vegetarian teetotaller who trained as a civil engineer and went on to play an extremely significant role in the discourse on aboriginal tribes. He disliked the Christian missionaries who sought religious conversion, yet also admired the efficacy of their model for social reform, which focused on education, temperance, and healthcare. Using the same template but giving it a distinctive 'Hindu' turn, Thakkar successfully ran the Bhil Seva Mandal for more than a decade.[32] While working in western India, Thakkar also toured other tribal areas in the 1920s, and gradually developed an understanding of a potential pan-India Hindu Mission which would facilitate the absorption of aboriginal tribes into the Hindu fold.

In the theatre of constitutional reforms, Thakkar continued to interrogate Hutton's moves and objected to the nomination of British 'officials' as representatives of aboriginal interests, instead of electing real tribesmen to the legislative bodies. He also advocated that the tribes be guaranteed seats in proportion to their demographic share at both provincial and national levels. Although Thakkar seemed ideologically opposed to the instrument of scheduling, as the author of an important report on the Orissa Partially Excluded Areas Committee, he did not recommend the complete abolition of scheduling.[33] In fact, in opposition to the Gandhian economic framework, Thakkar's policy recommendations included the promotion of modern industrial development and mining, as well as better communication infrastructure for the aboriginal tracts of Orissa.

It is important to mention that Thakkar also helmed the Harijan Sevak Sangh, which had been formed by Gandhi after his famous pact

[32]Established in 1922, it remains the oldest nationalist Hindu missionary organisation working amongst tribal communities, and has trained generations of social workers in a highly puritanical project of sanskritising the tribes.

[33]Thakkar's position may partly explain why the Congress agreed to maintain Scheduled Areas in the Indian Constitution.

with Ambedkar at Poona. By the early 1940s, Thakkar had gathered a truly all-India cadre and personal experience of running a dense network of social welfare institutions. These organisations contributed significantly to mobilisation campaigns aimed at admitting marginalised groups of the 'untouchables' and aboriginal tribes within the fold of a reformed Hinduism. Essentially, Thakkar saw no fundamental difference between the problems of 'Depressed Classes'/'Harijans' and those of 'Aboriginal Tribes'. In his worldview, both were backward sections of Hindu society which needed education and guaranteed representation to enable them to voice their aspirations and become a part of mainstream national life. For Thakkar, the operative words were 'uplift' and 'assimilation', which had emerged from the vocabulary of social workers like Vithal Ramji Shinde and institutional frameworks such as the Servants of India Society. In practical terms, 'uplifting' aborigines signified their 'Hinduisation' through a multi-pronged socioeconomic, religious, and cultural reform. Such a reformist agenda stressed the propagation of education, temperance, cleanliness, and standardisation of tribal customs.

A separate stage in Thakkar's project came in 1948 when a pan-Indian organisation named the Bharatiya Adimjati Sevak Sangh was established, which received State patronage for making targeted interventions in tribal areas across India. The idea seems to be that when primitive tribes (*Adimjati*) made progress along the Hinduisation track, their 'primitive' (*Adim*) traits would be sanitised, facilitating a complete assimilation into the caste (*jati*) framework. Therefore, the organisation's project, as envisaged by Thakkar, was to remove the fault-lines that weaken Hindu national identity. In a nutshell, Thakkar's social work paradigm was a form of religiously informed nationalism in which marginalised Dalits and Adimjatis must be recognised as part and parcel of the Hindu civilisational matrix.[34]

With Hutton and Thakkar as the archetypical personalities for the anthropologist and nationalist lobbies, respectively, a clash was imminent. In stark opposition to Hutton, Thakkar demanded that the aboriginal tribes be included in the scheme of devolution of powers to the Indians. However, they did not engage in any public debate because the discourse had not

---

[34]It is highly likely that many variations of such ideas were later incorporated by the Rashtriya Swayamsevak Sangh's own model while running Vanvasi Kalyan Ashrams in various parts of the country. For a brilliant ethnographic account of RSS activities in the North-East of India, see Arkotong Longkumer, *The Greater India Experiment: Hindutva and the Northeast*, New Delhi: Navayana, 2022.

reached its tipping point yet. As the evidence presented shows, barring a few exceptional individuals like Thakkar, the nationalists did not display much interest in the issue of aboriginal representation in the future Indian body politic. It seems that British anthropologists such as Hutton, Mills, and Grigson were more concerned about their fate than Indians themselves. While the issue evoked due consideration in administrative ranks, the virtual apathy among nationalists stood in stark contrast. It was only after the Cadogan Amendment and the notorious speech by Winston Churchill in the British Parliament that Congressmen were sufficiently alarmed and decided against any further complacency on the matter. The subsequent nationalist outrage led the administrative discourse to spill over into politics. Conversely, by expressing their strong and organised objection to the authority exercised by the British Parliament, the nationalists converted the 'tribal question' into a political theatre of contest. Since this development coincided with the growing representation of Indians in legislative assemblies and councils, a new wave of resolutions and debates began. Therefore, the period after 1936–1937 was marked by intense anti-British fervour, whose trenchant critical tone overshadowed all previous political opposition. Subsequently, for both anthropologists and nationalists, the idea of 'civilisation', which aboriginal tribes were either to be protected from or assimilated into, became a Hindu idea. Similarly, the word 'mainstream', too, started carrying Hindu overtones and connotations.

Both conceptually and politically, the 1940s provided a temporal stage for perhaps the most important period of debate on the 'tribal question' in India. This decade demands careful perusal as the catch-all terms of Isolationists/Protectionists *versus* Assimilationists/Interventionists began to make an appearance. In addition to anthropological works, several provincial reports on the partially excluded areas of Bombay, Central Provinces, and Orissa were appearing at regular intervals, placing a lot of material on Indian tribes into the public domain.

After the departure of J. H. Hutton, Verrier Elwin became the second hinge of the anthropologists who carried forward the baton of Riversian ideas on depopulation and cultural genocide. Paradoxically, however, Elwin's articulations were to precipitate a decline and an eventual disintegration of the main planks of British anthropologists' advocacy for the scheduling of tribal tracts. As is evident in this book, Elwin shifted positions several times in the 1930s and 1940s, and his navigational tactics reveal ideological fault-lines. His inconsistencies and ambivalences provide a useful window to understand the tumultuous 1940s, during which the discourse on aboriginal tribes in India took on a religious colour.[35] While Elwin continued to advocate the ring-fencing of predominantly tribal areas, his experiences in Bastar state led to a change in his position on the religious character of tribal religion. In his long stint as the state's Honorary Ethnographer during the 1941 Census operations, when Elwin was also researching his famous book on Ghotuls, he began to argue that tribal religions were part of the Hindu family. Taking off from this idea, Elwin published a reworked thesis titled *Loss of Nerve*, in which he propounded a theory dividing the monolithic conception of aboriginal tribes into three categories: 'fully Hinduised', 'semi-Hinduised', and those who were still at a distance from mainstream Hinduism, enabling them to remain culturally autonomous. Through this intervention, Elwin had diluted the conceptual cohesion of 'aboriginal tribes' and paved the way for a critique of the anthropologists' position. Two central tenets of the Huttonian framework: (*i*) the monolithic 'aborigine' living in the hills and forests of peninsular India, and (*ii*) the distinctiveness of tribal religion as entirely distinct from Hinduism, were thus critiqued and left exposed to nationalist attacks. As a result, the axis of identification became unhinged from geographical metaphors (hills and forests) and began moving towards a Hindu religious identity. The endgame had begun, which accelerated quickly thereafter.

Meanwhile, Elwin's efforts to raise his stature in the ongoing debate on tribal futures also boomeranged. Initially, he was trying to engage in debates with A. V. Thakkar and, in response, Thakkar sprung a surprise by endorsing and publishing G. S. Ghurye's *The Aborigines—'So-Called'—And Their Future*, which marked the apogee of nationalist theoretical intervention on the tribal question. Ghurye's critique of colonial policy vis-à-vis Indian tribal communities, that is, scheduling and their characterisation as 'Backward Hindus', greatly appealed to the nationalists. Thakkar played a key background role in first propping Ghurye as his proxy against Elwin and then enthusiastically endorsing his ideas. This prepared the ground for the eventual de-legitimisation and erosion of the category of 'Aboriginal and Hill Tribes' from the future constitutional fabric of India. This was soon to be substituted by the term 'Scheduled Tribe', which points to the taxonomical impact of Ghurye's thesis.

---

[35]Ramachandra Guha, 'Between Anthropology and Literature: The Ethnographies of Verrier Elwin', *Journal of the Royal Anthropological Institute* 4 (2), 1998, pp. 325–343.

It is reasonable to ask why the colonial anthropologists desired a territorial solution rather than one predicated on rights and representation. Perhaps they could not foresee the subterranean developments that had laid the ground for the mass mobilisation of tribal people by political forces as diverse as the Congress, Communists, and the Adivasi Mahasabha. What differentiated this new moment from an earlier era of *fituris* and revolts was the fact that tribes were willing and eager to engage with forms of modern associational politics. The Congress, the Communists, and the Adivasi Mahasabha were organised political entities with a distinctive reading of the identity of aboriginal tribes, their place in the cultural matrix of India, and the desirable agenda for future politics. Tribal participation with these forces gathered visible momentum *after* the departure of J. H. Hutton, who had ensured that the provisions for exclusion and partial exclusion were enshrined in the Government of India Act, 1935.

Another reason for preferring a territorial solution lies in the rapid dissipation of an earlier congruence of opinions. As stated earlier, both anthropologists and nationalists began reading the tribal question from common vantage points. Two developments disturbed the uneasy equilibrium and eventually contributed to the demolition of this shared analytical framework. The *first* was the introduction of a 'provincial autonomy' under which elections became the sole legitimate route to access State power; and the *second* was the partial Census of 1941, which became a highly politicised affair.

The effect of provincial autonomy and the 1937 elections turned Indian politics increasingly competitive, with many politicians and parties jumping into the fray. The ensuing political battleground simultaneously emboldened and weakened the Indian National Congress. While its movement towards an all-India party machinery with a high-command structure of control was strengthened, the Congress's position as an anti-imperialist 'united front' faced a steady decline in the wake of competition from other political forces.

The effect of the 1941 Census was more subdued, but eventually far more consequential than party politics. Owing to war-time austerity and curbs on official expenditure, this last colonial Census was a truncated one and did not focus on generating elaborate caste and tribe data. As a result, religious identity became the primary unit of enumeration, which triggered a highly contested series of claims, critiques, and counter-claims on the religious status of the Indian aborigines. This sharpened the already existing fault-lines in ongoing discussions on the future of aborigines in India.

Therefore, by the early 1940s, the question of religious identity stopped being an issue of debate between ICS men, a debate usually confined to the official files and Census reports. At this new moment, Indians were actively participating in a public sphere where religion had emerged as the defining lens for representational politics. Such discussions proliferated at an unusual pace, further accelerating the dismantling of the cognitive framework set up by Hutton, and its substitution by a new one, informed fundamentally by the 'Hindu' religious identity of the aboriginal tribes.

In addition to competitive party politics (fuelled by elections) and the increasing prominence of religious markers of identity (induced by the Census), a third factor which vitally affected the discourse on tribes was the parallel discourse on educational 'backwardness'. In the colonial context, the ability of any elected 'representative' to successfully manoeuvre through the corridors of power was crucially dependent on literacy and education. So long as the reins of State power remained in the hands of the British, a *sine qua non* for the successful Indian representative-politician was dexterity in the English language. When the ability to speak for or 'voice' collective aspirations became a necessary condition for conducting politics, it commenced a process of classifying groups on a scale of educational attainment. In this context, aboriginal tribes were seen as backward. Without education, they had no jobs and no vocal middle-class elite, which also adversely affected their visibility and agency in national politics.

Unfortunately, there is an absence of historically grounded studies of what the concept 'Backward' stood for in the late colonial period. Essentially, it is a relational idea and, as Thakkar pointed out, a 'comparative' concept. For someone to be considered backward, there has to be someone either ahead of them (horizontally) or above them (vertically). Also, the larger the distance between 'advanced' and 'backward' segments of the demography, the greater the space it offered social reformers to try and bridge the gap. That is why the idea of 'uplift' was central to the agenda of the socio-religious reform movements that were appropriating the social groups traditionally at the margins of Hindu civilisation.

British anthropologists and Indian nationalists both held that the 'backwardness' of aboriginal tribes was a huge challenge that had to be overcome. Yet again, in this shared paradigm, the strong link between education and representation generated synergies that were most visibly at work in western India. Social reformers in this region worked to spread literacy and education amongst underprivileged groups such as aboriginal tribes, Depressed Classes and Intermediate Castes, who together constituted the category called 'Other Backward Classes'. The guiding criterion of this umbrella category was the level of educational backwardness of groups that were nevertheless a part of mainstream Hinduism.

Nationalists like Thakkar saw great merit in the scheme of 'backwardness' derived from a differential level of literacy and education among Hindu social groups. Such a measurable and non-anthropological basis provided the ideological edifice for a nationalist, socio-political and religious imaginary. It also placed caste groups in a core-periphery model for ameliorative State action. Targeted State intervention in the arena of education could thus potentially remove the disabilities of peripheral social groups by enabling *sui generis* educated elites to voice the interests of their respective political constituencies. Thus, even if the Constitution of India is silent on the civilisational nature of the Indian subcontinent, it assumes that groups such as Scheduled Castes, Scheduled Tribes, and Other Backward Classes are essentially part of a distinctive 'Hindu' civilisational matrix.

As a result of cumulative developments, by the mid-1940s, the idea of the 'aboriginal tribe' in India had emerged as a conceptual category under immense stress. It is clear from the evidence presented that the theoretical cohesion of the 'knot of men' was beginning to break down. While Hutton deployed the Neo-Diffusionist arsenal to great effect and secured a massive expansion in areas scheduled under the categories of excluded and partially excluded areas, the discursive scene witnessed a vacuum after he left for Cambridge in 1936. Moreover, when individual figures applied Huttonian ideas in their respective regions and landscapes, a divergence of opinion emerged. Consequently, we have in Grigson a figure who, being well-versed in socio-political dynamics amongst the central Indian tribal communities, took recourse to a significantly different set of interpretations and policy measures.

In this respect, Grigson occupied a middle-of-the-road position between Hutton and Thakkar. In contra-distinction to total exclusion (Hutton), and complete assimilation within the Hindu 'mainstream' (Thakkar), Grigson forcefully argued that partial exclusion was preferable to total exclusion. He reasoned that the aboriginal problem in the Central Provinces was characteristically different from the North-East frontier. Grigson advocated increased communication in tribal regions, and his position stood in contrast to Hutton and Mills, who were vehemently against the 'opening up' of aboriginal areas. Besides better communications and infrastructure related to travel, Grigson also differed from his colleagues in North-East India on the issue of education, as he was of the view that massive State intervention was needed to overcome the 'challenge of backwardness'. Regardless of these distinctions, for the 'knot of men', the Scheduled Areas were 'islands against civilisation', the last bulwark to ensure that the rising tide of standardisation and uniformity did not lead to a cultural genocide, as had been experienced in the Melanesian Islands.

In recent academic production of knowledge on modern India, a term that has generated wide-ranging conversation and literature is 'decolonisation'.[36] Regrettably, though, the task of historicising it has mainly focussed upon the 'political' transition from the colonial State to successor States in India and Pakistan (and, later, Bangladesh).[37] The stress on political aspects has undermined scholarly enquiries into how transitions were made in the 'epistemic' structures of power inherited from the colonial past. Arguably, without such investigations, any meaningful decolonisation will continue to remain a pipe dream.[38] While conducting this study, an initial engagement with anthropological literature alone proved inadequate, and an attempt to historicise the discipline itself in the period of constitutional reforms became imperative. Nevertheless, this work only offers a peep into one such limited period, and many other studies on the history of anthropology in India are waiting to be written.

For instance, given the current debate on a caste-based Census, understanding the cognitive lenses and vocabulary of the colonial Census exercise becomes unavoidable. After all, contemporary statist frameworks in the subcontinent are far from decolonised and continue to ascribe fixed and immutable identities upon their citizens in much the same manner as was done on colonial subjects.

---

[36]Felix Padel, 'Decolonising Tribal Research and Education in India', Lecture at the Centre for Culture and Development, 17 April 2021. Available at http://ccdgujarat.com/wp-content/uploads/2024/07/4th-Foundation-Day-Lecture.pdf (accessed October 2024).

[37]For a representative volume with exceptional essays, see Sekhar Bandyopadhyay, *Decolonisation and the Politics of Transition in South Asia*, New Delhi: Orient BlackSwan, 2016.

[38]For an earlier period of colonial rule, pertinent epistemic enquiries were made by the late Professor Bernard Cohn. See Bernard S. Cohn, *Colonialism and its Forms of Knowledge: The British in India*, Princeton, NJ: Princeton University Press, 1996.

Three major absences characterise this book in terms of the archives I have accessed. *First,* I could not factor in the influence and dynamics of Islamised tribal areas in the North-West Frontier. For instance, an evaluation of the role of an individual like Khan Abdul Gaffar Khan in regional tribal politics could be very insightful. *Second,* while I have engaged with and analysed the administrative, anthropological, and nationalist frameworks of ideas on aboriginal tribes, I was unable to incorporate sources and cognitive frameworks concerning Christian missionaries, many of whom were working actively in tribal regions. Last but not the least, much work remains to be done on the relationship between Princely States and their tribal populations in late-colonial India. Taken together with themes such as franchise, agency, and democracy, future scholarship will hopefully be able to work out the histories of tribal people outside the orthodoxies of nationalism and development. Forays into these domains are bound to yield valuable insights into the forms of democratic politics in South Asia which emerged in the aftermath of the transfer of power. If this book inspires other researchers to undertake further work in the crucial period of 1937–1950 with regard to tribal areas in the Indian subcontinent, the purpose of my effort will be adequately served.

Bibliography

Primary Sources

Asia and Africa Reading Room, British Library

IOR/L/PJ (Public & Judicial)
IOR/Q/RTC (Round Table Conference)
IOR/Q/IDC (Indian Delimitation Committee)

Private Papers

W. G. Archer
Verrier Elwin
Chelmsford
David Symington
ICS (District Officers)
Templewood (Sir John Simon)

British Parliamentary Debates (House of Commons and House of Lords). Available at https://hansard.parliament.uk/ (accessed September 2024).

Special Collection, SOAS

James Philip Mills

Centre for South Asian Studies, University of Cambridge

Edgar Stanley Hyde

Museum of Archaeology and Anthropology, University of Cambridge

John Henry Hutton

National Archives (earlier Public Records Office), KEW

1933 White Paper on Indian Constitutional Reforms (Excluded and Partially Excluded Areas)

Journals

Man in India
Modern Review
Science and Culture
Indian Journal of Social Work
The Eastern Anthropologist
The Indian Social Reformer
The Servant of India

Newspapers

The Times of India

Prime Ministers Museum and Library

Institutional Records

All India Congress Committee
Federal Papers

Private Papers

Purushottamdas Thakurdas
P. Kodanda Rao
Verrier Elwin

National Archives of India, New Delhi

Department of Home (Legislative)
Reforms Office
Political Department
Legislative Department
Cabinet Secretariat Papers

Private Papers

Sardar Patel Papers

Colonial Era Reports

Report of the Depressed Classes and Aboriginal Tribes Enquiry Committee, Bombay Presidency, March 1930, Government Press Kolhapur (reprint, 1950).

Symington, D., *Report on the Partially Excluded Areas of Bombay Province*, 1939.

Thakkar, A. V., *Report of the Partially Excluded Areas Enquiry Committee (Orissa)*, Superintendent, Government Press, Cuttack, Orissa, 1940.

Grigson, W. V., *Notes on the Aboriginal Problem in the Mandla District*, Government Printing, C.P. & Berar, Nagpur, 1940.

———, *The Aboriginal Problem in the Balaghat District: A Preliminary Report*, Government Printing, C.P. & Berar, Nagpur, 1941.

———, *The Aboriginal Problem in the Central Provinces & Berar*, Government Printing, C.P. & Berar, 1944.

Reid, J., *Final Report on the Survey and Settlement Operations in the District of Ranchi 1902–1910*, Bengal Secretariat Book Depot, 1912.

Government of India Act 1935, Excluded and Partially Excluded Areas (Section 91) Recommendations of the Provincial Governments and the Government of India, His Majesty's Stationery Office, London, 1936.

Indian Franchise Committee, Volume I (Report), Central Publication Branch, Calcutta, 1932.

East India (Constitutional Reforms), Indian Franchise Committee, 1932, Volume V, Published by HMSO, 1932.

Joint Committee on Indian Constitutional Reform, Minutes of Evidence taken before Sub-committee D, Die Lunae 16 Octobris, 1933, His Majesty's Stationary Office, London, 1933.

Report by Mr. L. Littlehailes, M.A., C.I.E., Educational Adviser to Baroda State, Baroda State Press, 1934.

Naik, J. P., *Compulsory Elementary Education in the Province of Bombay: A Historical Review*, first published in the Progress of Education, Poona, December 1940.

Report of the Committee appointed by the Government of Bombay to consider and report on the question of the introduction of free and compulsory primary education into the Bombay Presidency, Yeravda Prison Press, Poona, 1922.

The Legislative Assembly Debates (Official Report), Volume I, 1936 (3 February to 14 February 1936), Third Session of the Fifth Legislative Assembly, 1936, Government of India Press, New Delhi, 1936.

Census Reports

Dracup, A. H., and H. T. Sorley, *Census of India, 1931, Vol. VIII-Part I, Bombay Presidency, General Report,* Government Central Press, 1933.

Hutton, J. H., *Census of India 1931: With Complete Survey of Tribal Life and System,* Gian Publishing House, Delhi, 1989 (reprint).

Lacey, W. G., *Census of India, 1931, Vol. VII, Bihar and Orissa, Part I-Report,* Government Printing Bihar and Orissa, Patna, 1933.

Marten, J. T., *Census of India, 1921, Vol. I, India, Part I, Report,* Superintendent Government Printing, Calcutta, 1924, p. 110.

Mills, J. P., 'The Effect on the Tribes of the Naga Hill District of Contacts with Civilization', in J. H. Hutton, *Census of India (With Complete Survey of Tribal Life and System), Vol. III,* Gian Publishing House, New Delhi, 1991 (reprint), pp. 147–149.

Mullan, C. S., *Census of India, 1931, Vol. III Assam, Part I Report,* Government of India, Central Publication Branch, Calcutta, 1932.

Porter, A. E., *Census of India 1931, Vol. V, Bengal & Sikkim, Part I, Report,* Central Publication Branch, Calcutta, 1933.

Sedgwick, L. J., *Census of India, 1921, Vol. VIII, Part I, General Report,* Government Central Press, Bombay, 1922.

——, *Census of India, 1921, Bombay Presidency, Vol. VIII, Part II, Tables (Imperial and Provincial),* Government Central Press, 1922.

Shoobert, W. H., *Census of India, 1931, Vol. XII, Central Provinces & Berar, Part I Report,* Government Printing, C.P., Nagpur, 1933.

Secondary Sources

Ahuja, Ravi, '"Opening up the Country"? Patterns of Circulation and Politics of Communication in Early Colonial Orissa', *Studies in History,* New Series 20 (1), 2004, pp. 73–130.

Alavi, Seema, *The Sepoys in the Company: Tradition and Transition in Northern India, 1770–1830,* New Delhi: Oxford University Press, 1998.

Ambedkar, B. R., *Ranade Gandhi & Jinnah*, Bombay: Thacker & Co., 1943. Available at https://franpritchett.com/00ambedkar/txt_ambedkar_ranade.html (accessed January 2025).

Appadurai, Arjun, *Fear of Small Numbers: An Essay on the Geography of Anger*, London: Duke University Press, 2006.

Arnold, David, 'Rebellious Hillmen: The Gudem Rampa Rising 1839–1924, in R. Guha (ed.), *Subaltern Studies, Vol. I*, Delhi: Oxford University Press, 1982, pp. 88–142.

Asad, Talal (ed.), *Anthropology and the Colonial Encounter*, London: Ithaca Press, 1973.

Bajpai, Rochana, 'Constituent Assembly Debates and Minority Rights', *Economic and Political Weekly* 35 (21/22), 2000, pp. 1837–1845.

———, *Debating Difference: Group Rights and Liberal Democracy in India*, New Delhi: Oxford University Press, 2011.

Baker, D. E. U., *Changing Political Leadership in an Indian Province: The Central Provinces and Berar (1919–1939)*, Delhi: Oxford University Press, 1979.

———, '"A Serious Time": Forest Satyagraha in Madhya Pradesh, 1930', *Indian Economic and Social History Review* 2 (1), 1984, pp. 71–90.

Balfour, Henry, 'The Welfare of Primitive Tribes', *Folklore* 34 (1), March 1923, pp. 12–24.

Banerjee, Prathama, *Politics of Time: 'Primitives' and History-writing in a Colonial Society*, New Delhi: Oxford University Press, 2006.

———, 'Writing the Adivasi: Some Historiographical Notes', *Indian Economic and Social History Review* 53 (1), 2016, pp. 131–153.

Barrier, N. Gerald (ed.), *The Census in British India: New Perspectives*, New Delhi: Manohar, 1981.

Bates, Crispin, 'Congress and the Tribals', in Mike Shepperdson and Colin Simmons (eds), *The Indian National Congress and the Political Economy of India, 1885–1985*, Dartmouth Publishing, 1988.

———, 'Race, Caste and Tribe in Central India: The Early Origins of Indian Anthropology', in Peter Robb (ed.), *The Concept of Race in South Asia*, New Delhi: Oxford University Press, 1995.

———, 'Human Sacrifices in Colonial Central India: Myth, Agency and Representation', in Crispin Bates (ed.), *Beyond Representations: Colonial and Post-Colonial Constructions of Indian Identity*, New Delhi: Oxford University Press, 2006.

Bates, Crispin, and Alpa Shah (eds), *Savage Attack: Tribal Insurgency in India*, New Delhi: Social Science Press, 2014.

Baviskar, Amita, 'The Politics of Being "Indigenous"', in Bengt G. Karlsson and T. B. Subba (eds), *Indigeneity in India*, London: Kegan Paul, 2006.

Bayliss-Smith, Tim, 'Colonialism as Shell-Shock: W.H.R. Rivers' Explanations for Depopulation in Melanesia', in Edvard Hviding and Cato Berg (eds), *The Ethnographic Experiment: Rivers and Hocart in Island Melanesia, 1908*, New York and Oxford: Berhahn, 2014, pp. 179–213.

Benton, Lauren, *A Search for Sovereignty: Law and Geography in European Empires, 1400–1900*, New York: Cambridge University Press, 2010.

Beteille, Andre, 'The Concept of Tribe with Special Reference to India', *European Journal of Sociology/Archives Européennes de Sociologie/ Europäisches Archiv für Soziologie* 27 (2), 1986, pp. 297–318.

——, 'The Idea of Indigenous People', *Current Anthropology* 39 (2), 1998, pp. 187–192.

Bhagat-Ganguly, Varsha, and Sujit Kumar (eds), *India's Scheduled Areas: Untangling Governance, Law and Politics*, London and New York: Routledge, 2020.

Bhagwan, Manu, *Sovereign Spheres: Princes, Education and Empire in Colonial India*, New Delhi: Oxford University Press, 2003.

Bhatia, Udit (ed.), *The Indian Constituent Assembly: Deliberations on Democracy*, London and New York: Routledge, 2018.

Bhukya, Bhangya, *Subjugated Nomads: The Lambadas under the Rule of the Nizams*, New Delhi: Orient BlackSwan, 2010.

——, *The Roots of the Periphery: A History of the Gonds of Deccan India*, New Delhi: Oxford University Press, 2017.

Bijoy, C. R., Shankar Gopalakrishnan, and Shomona Khanna (eds), *India and the Rights of Indigenous Peoples: Constitutional, Legislative and Administrative Provisions Concerning Indigenous and Tribal Peoples in India and their Relation to International Law on Indigenous People*, Chiang Mai: AIPP, 2010.

Blunt, E. A. H., *The I.C.S.: The Indian Civil Service*, London: Faber and Faber, 1937.

Bose, N. K., 'The Hindu Method of Tribal Absorption', *Science and Culture* 7 (2), 1941, pp. 188–194.

Brown, Judith, *Gandhi's Rise to Power: Indian Politics, 1915–1922*, London: Cambridge University Press, and Bombay: Blackie and Son, 1972.

Cadogan, Edward, *The India We Saw*, John Murray, 1933. Available at https://archive.org/details/in.ernet.dli.2015.279094 (accessed September 2024).

Calman, Leslie J., 'Congress Confronts Communism: Thana District, 1945–47', *Modern Asian Studies* 21 (2), 1987, pp. 329–348.

Cederlof, Gunnel, *Landscapes and the Law: Environmental Politics, Regional Histories, and Contests over Nature*, New Delhi: Permanent Black, 2008.

Chakravarty, Kalyan Kumar (ed.), *Tribal Identity in India: Extinction or Adaptation*, Bhopal: Indira Gandhi Rashtriya Manav Sangrahalaya, 1996.

Choudhry, Sujit, Madhav Khosla, and Pratap Bhanu Mehta (eds), *The Oxford Handbook of the Indian Constitution*, New Delhi: Oxford University Press, 2016.

Chaudhuri, B. B., and Arun Bandopadhyay (eds), *Tribes, Forests and Social Formations in Indian History*, New Delhi: Manohar, 2004.

Chowdhuri, S. R., *Leftism in India 1917–1947*, New Delhi: Sage, 2017.

Chandra, Uday, 'Liberalism and its Other: The Politics of Primitivism in Colonial and Postcolonial Indian Law', *Law and Society Review* 47 (1), 2013, pp. 135–168.

Choksi, Nishaant, 'From Language to Script: Graphic Practice and the Politics of Authority in Santali-Language Print Media, Eastern India', *MAS* 51 (5), 2017, pp. 1519–1560.

Cohn, Bernard S. *An Anthropologist among the Historians and Other Essays*, New Delhi: Oxford University Press, 1987.

____, *Colonialism and its Forms of Knowledge: The British in India*, New Delhi: Oxford University Press, 1997.

Corbridge, Stuart, Sarah Jewitt, and Sanjay Kumar, *Jharkhand: Environment, Development, Ethnicity*, New Delhi: Oxford University Press, 2004.

Coupland, Reginald, *The Future of India: Third Part of a Report on the Constitutional Problem in India Submitted to the Warden and Fellows of the Nuffield College, Oxford*, London: Oxford University Press, 1943.

Das Gupta, Sanjukta, 'Peasant and Tribal Movements in Colonial Bengal: A Historiographical Overview', in Sekhar Bandyopadhyay (ed.), *Bengal: Rethinking History. Essays in Historiography*, New Delhi: Manohar, 2002.

____, 'The Tribal Issue, 1964–1984', in Aditya Mukherjee (ed.), *A Centenary History of the Indian National Congress, Vol. V: 1964–1984*, New Delhi: Academic Foundation, 2011.

Das Gupta, Sanjukta, *Adivasis and the Raj: Socio-economic Transition of the Hos, 1820–1932*, New Delhi: Orient BlackSwan, 2011.

——, '"The Eye of a *Diku* is Like Eye of a Dog": Changing Role of *Dikus* in an Adivasi Society of Chotanagpur Under Colonial Rule', in Lata Singh and Biswamoy Pati (eds), *Colonial and Contemporary Bihar and Jharkhand*, New Delhi: Primus Books, 2014, pp. 39–57.

Das Gupta, Sanjukta, and Raj Sekhar Basu, *Narratives from the Margins: Aspects of Adivasi History in India*, New Delhi: Primus Books, 2012.

Dasgupta, Sangeeta, 'Reordering a World: The Tana Bhagat Movement, 1914–1919', *Studies in History* 15 (1), 1999, pp. 1–41.

——, *Reordering Adivasi Worlds: Representation, Resistance, Memory*, New Delhi: Oxford University Press, 2022.

Dasgupta, Shomik, *Ethics, Distance and Accountability: The Political Thought and Intellectual Context of Rammohun Roy*, New Delhi: Oxford University Press, 2021.

Datar, Abhay 'Defining Backwardness: Debates in Bombay/Maharashtra', *Economic and Political Weekly* LII (51), 23 November 2017, pp. 89–96.

Devalle, S. B., *Discourses of Ethnicity: Culture and Protest in Jharkhand*, New Delhi: Sage, 1992.

Dewey, Clive, *Anglo-Indian Attitudes: The Mind of the Indian Civil Service*, London: Hambledon Press, 1993.

Dhagamwar, Vasudha, 'Tribals and the Law', *India International Centre Quarterly* 13 (3/4), 1986, pp. 95–114.

——, *Role and Image of Law in India: The Tribal Experience*, New Delhi: Sage, 2006.

Dhanagare, D. N., 'Social Origins of the Peasant Insurrection in Telengana (1946–51)', *Contributions to Indian Sociology (ns)* 8, 1974, pp. 109–134.

——, 'The Politics of Survival: Peasant Organisations and the Left-Wing in India, 1925–46', *Sociological Bulletin* 24 (1), 1975, pp. 29–54.

——, *Peasant Movements in India: 1920–1950*, Delhi: Oxford University Press, 1983.

Dirks, Nicholas, *Castes of Mind: Colonialism and the Making of Modern India*, Princeton: Princeton University Press, 2001.

——, 'G. S. Ghurye and the Politics of Sociological Knowledge', *Sociological Bulletin* 62 (2) (Special Issue on the Bombay School of Sociology: Stalwarts and their Legacies), May–August, 2013, pp. 239–253.

Dube, B. K., and F. Bahadur, *A Study of Tribal People and Tribal Areas of Madhya Pradesh*, Indore: Government Regional Press, 1967.

Dube, S. C., 'Tribal Development: Illusion and Reality', *Bulletin of the Tribal Research and Development Institute* 12 (1), 1984.

Elwin, Verrier, *The Baiga*, London, 1939. (Reprint from New Delhi: Gian Publishing House, 1972.)

____, *Loss of Nerve: A Comparative Study of the Result of the Contact of Peoples in the Aboriginal Areas of Bastar State and the Central Provinces of India*, Bombay: Wagle Press, 1941.

____, *The Aboriginals*, Oxford Pamphlets on Indian Affairs No. 14, Humphrey Milford: Oxford University Press, July 1942.

____, *Maria Murder and Suicide*, Oxford University Press, 1943 (reprint, New Delhi: Vanya Prakashan, 1991).

____, *The Muria and their Ghotul*, Oxford University Press, 1947 (reprint, New Delhi: Vanya Prakashan, 1991).

____, *A Philosophy for NEFA*, Shillong, 1957.

____, *The Tribal World of Verrier Elwin*, New Delhi: Oxford University Press, 2002.

Embree, Ainslie T., and Mark Juergensmeyer (eds), *Frontiers into Borders: Defining South Asian States, 1757–1857*, New Delhi: Oxford University Press, 2020.

Fisher, Michael H. (ed.), *The Politics of British Annexation of India, 1757–1857*, New Delhi: Oxford University Press, 1993.

Forsyth, Captain J. *The Highlands of Central Asia*, New Delhi: Natraj Publishers, 1994 [1871].

Fox, Richard G., *Kin Clan, Raja and Rule: State-Hinterland Relations in Preindustrial India*, Bombay: Oxford University Press, 1971.

Fuchs, Stephen, *The Aboriginal Tribes of India*, London: Macmillan, 1977.

____, *Godmen on the Warpath: A Study of Messianic Movements in India*, New Delhi: Munshiram Manoharlal, 1992.

Fuller, C. J., *Anthropologist and Imperialist: H. H. Risley and British India, 1873–1911*, New Delhi: Social Science Press, 2023.

Furer-Haimendorf, Christoph von, *Tribes of India: The Struggle for Survival*, Berkeley: The University of California Press, 1982.

Galanter, Marc, *Competing Equalities: Law and the Backward Classes in India*, New Delhi: Oxford University Press, 1991.

Gautam, O. P., 'The Indian National Congress and Nation Building', *The Indian Journal of Political Science* 46 (4), 1985, pp. 487–505.

Ghurye, G. S., 'Egyptian affinities of Indian funerary practices', *Anthropos* 4, 1923, pp. 420–430.

Ghurye, G. S., 'Dual Organization in India', *The Journal of the Royal Anthropological Institute of Great Britain and Ireland* 53 (January–June), 1923, pp. 79–91.

——, 'The Konkan Agriculturist', *TSI* X (31), 8 September 1927, p. 363.

——, 'The Marriage Law', *TSI* XII (38), 26 September 1929, pp. 450–451.

——, 'Marriage and Family', *TSI* XII (30), 1 August 1929, pp. 354–355.

——, 'The Institution of Marriage', *TSI* XIV (2), 8 January 1931, pp. 20–21.

——, 'Problems of Rural Sociology', *TSI* XIV (47), 26 November 1931, pp. 567–568.

——, *Caste and Race in India*, Bombay: Popular Prakashan, 1932.

——, 'The Home', *TSI* XVIII (4), 24 January 1935, pp. 41–42.

——, 'Early Human Culture', *TSI* XVIII (46), 14 November 1935, pp. 596–597.

——, 'Anthropology and our Educational System', *Man in India* 15 (2&3), 1935, pp. 93–107.

——, 'The Social Process (in the light of a century of Sociology)', Gokhale Institute of Politics and Economics, R.R. Kale Memorial Lecture, 1938.

——, 'Social Work and Sociology', *TSI* XXI (23), 9 June 1938, pp. 285–287.

——, *The Aborigines—'So-Called'—And Their Future*, Poona: Gokhale Institute of Politics and Economics, 1943.

——, *The Scheduled Tribes*, Bombay: Popular Book Depot, 1959 [1943].

Gilmour, David, *The Ruling Caste: Imperial Lives in the Victorian Raj*, London: John Murray, 2005.

Govind, Rahul, 'The King's Plunder, the King's Justice: Sovereignty in British India, 1756–1776', *Studies in History* 33 (2), 2017, pp. 151–186.

Grigson, W. V. *The Aboriginal Problem in the Central Provinces and Berar*, Nagpur, 1944 (reprint, Bhopal: Vanya Prakashan, 1993).

——, *The Maria Gonds of Bastar*, Oxford University Press, 1938 (reprint, Bhopal: Vanya Prakashan, 1991).

——, *The Challenge of Backwardness*, Hyderabad: Government Press, 1947.

Guha, Ramachandra, *Savaging the Civilized: Verrier Elwin, His Tribals, and India*, New Delhi: Oxford University Press, 1999.

Guha, Ranajit, *Elementary Aspects of Peasant Insurgency in Colonial India*, Delhi: Oxford University Press, 1983.

—— (ed.), *Subaltern Studies*, Vols I–VI. New Delhi: Oxford University Press, 1982–87.

Guha, Sumit, *Environment and Ethnicity in India, 1200–1991*, Cambridge: Cambridge University Press, 1999.

Guite, Jangkhomang, and Thongkholal Haokip, *The Anglo-Kuki War, 1917–1919*, New Delhi: Routledge, 2019.

Gupta, Akhil, 'Revolution in Telengana: Part I & II', *South Asia Bulletin* IV (1 and 2), 1984.

Hardiman, David, *The Coming of the Devi: Adivasi Assertion in Western India*, New Delhi: Oxford University Press, 1995.

____, *Gandhi in his Time and in Ours*, Ranikhet: Permanent Black, 2003.

____,'Assertion, Conversion and Indian Nationalism: Govind Giri's Movement Amongst the Bhils', in R. Robinson and S. Clarke (eds) *Religious Conversion in India: Modes, Motivations, and Meanings*, New Delhi: Oxford University Press, 2003, pp. 255–284.

____, *Histories for the Subordinated*, Kolkata: Seagull Books, 2007.

Hunt, Roland, and John Harrison (eds), *The District Officers in India*, London: Scholar Press, 1980.

Hutton, J. H., *The Sema Nagas*, Bombay: Oxford University Press, 1968 [1921].

____,'Depopulation of Primitive Communities', *Man in India* II, 1922, pp. 220–227.

____,'Assam and the Pacific', *Man In India* IV (1 & 2), 1924, pp. 1–9.

____,'Anthropology and Administration', Presidential Address to the Section of Anthropology in 'Proceedings of the Fourteenth Indian Science Congress, Lahore, 1927' (Second Circuit), Asiatic Society of Bengal, Calcutta, 1927, pp. 286–299.

____,'Census of India, 1931', *Journal of the Royal Society of Arts* 80 (4154), 1 July 1932, p. 794.

Inden, Ronald, *Imagining India*, Oxford: Basil Blackwell, 1990.

Jagadisan, T. N., and Shyamlal (compiled and eds), *Thakkar Bapa: Eightieth Birthday Commemoration Volume*, Madras: Diocesan Press, 1949.

Jha, J. C., *The Kol Insurrection of Chota-Nagpur*, Calcutta: Thacker, Spink, and Co., 1964.

Jhala, Angma Dey, *An Endangered History: Indigeneity, Religion and Politics on the Borders of India, Burma and Bangladesh*, New Delhi: Oxford University Press, 2019.

Jones, Kenneth W., *Socio-Religious Reform Movements in British India* (The New Cambridge History of India, Vol. III-1), New York: Cambridge University Press, 1989.

Jordens, J. T. F., 'Reconversion to Hinduism: The Shuddhi of Arya Samaj', in G. A. Oddie (ed.), *Religion in South Asia: Religious Conversion and Revival Movements in South Asia in Medieval and Modern Times*, New Delhi: Manohar, 2020, pp. 145–162.

Karlsson, Bengt G., *Unruly Hills: Nature and Nation in India's Northeast*, New Delhi: Social Science Press & Orient BlackSwan, 2011.

Karlsson, Bengt G., and T. B. Subba (eds), *Indigeneity in India*, London: Kegan Paul, 2006.

Katyayan, Rashmi (ed.), *Lo Bir Sendra: An Autobiography*, by Marang Gomke Jaipal Singh, Ranchi: Prabhat Khabar Publications, 2004.

Kela, Shashank, *A Rogue and a Peasant Slave: Adivasi Resistance, 1800–2000*, New Delhi: Navayana, 2012.

Kennedy, Jonathan, and Sunil Purushotham, 'Beyond Naxalbari: A Comparative Analysis of Maoist Insurgency and Counterinsurgency in Independent India', *Comparative Studies in Society and History* 54 (4), 2012, pp. 832–862.

Kipgen, Ngamjahao, and Doungul Letkhojam Haokip (eds), *Against the Empire: Polity, Economy and Culture During the Anglo-Kuki War, 1917–1919*, New Delhi: Taylor & Francis, 2020.

Klingensmith, Daniel, *One Valley and a Thousand: Dams, Development and Nationalism*, New Delhi: Oxford University Press, 2007.

Kopf, David, *British Orientalism and the Bengal Renaissance: The Dynamics of Indian Modernization, 1773–1835*, Berkeley: University of California Press, 1969.

Kuklick, Henrika, *The Savage Within: The Social History of British Anthropology, 1885–1945*, New York and Cambridge: Cambridge University Press, 1991.

Lally, J., 'Crafting Colonial Anxieties: Silk and the Salvation Army in British India, circa 1900–1920', *MAS* 50 (3), 2016, pp. 765–807.

Langham, I., *The Building of British Social Anthropology: W.H.R. Rivers and his Cambridge Disciples in the Development of Kinship Studies, 1898–1931*, Dordrecht: D. Reidel Publishing Company, 1981.

Leach, Edmund, 'Notes on the Mythology of Cambridge Anthropology', *The Cambridge Journal of Anthropology* 9 (1), 1984, pp. 1–12.

Legg, Stephen, 'Dyarchy: Democracy, Autocracy and the Scalar Sovereignty of Interwar India', *Comparative Studies of South Asia, Africa and the Middle East* 36 (1), 2016, pp. 44–65.

Lowie, R. H., *The History of Ethnological Theory*, New York: Rinehart and Company, 1937.

Major, Andrew J., 'State and Criminal Tribes in Colonial Punjab: Surveillance, Control and Reclamation of the "Dangerous Classes"', *MAS* 33 (3), 1999, pp. 657–688.

Maheshwari, Malvika, 'Collective Conservatism and the Constituent Assembly Debates: The Case of Free Speech in India', *Studies in Indian Politics* 5 (2), 2017, pp. 218–232.

Malhotra, S. G., 'Tribal Autonomy Undermined', *Economic and Political Weekly* 49 (13), 2014, pp. 221–225.

Menon, V. P., *Integration of the Indian States*, Hyderabad: Orient BlackSwan, 2014.

Metcalf, Thomas R., *Ideologies of the Raj* (The New Cambridge History of India, Vol. 2.4). Cambridge: Cambridge University Press, 1995.

Mills, J. P., *The Lhota Nagas (with an Introduction and Supplementary Notes by J.H. Hutton, C.I.E., Hon. Director of Ethnography, Assam)*, Published by direction of the Government of Assam, London: Macmillan and Co., 1922.

———, 'The Lesson of the Red Man', *Man in India* III, 1923, pp. 221–222.

———, *The Ao Nagas (with a Foreword by Prof. Henry Balfour and Supplementary Notes and Bibliography by Prof. J.H. Hutton)*, Published by direction of the Government of Nagaland, Delhi: Oxford University Press, 1973 (first edition, London: Macmillan & Co., 1926).

Miri, Mrinal (ed.), *Continuity and Change in Tribal Society*, Shimla: Indian Institute of Advanced Studies, 1993.

Mishra, P. K., 'J. H. Hutton and the Colonial Ethnography of North-East India', in T. B. Subba (ed.), *North-east India: A Handbook of Anthropology*, New Delhi: Orient BlackSwan, 2012.

Mishra, Prabhu Lal, *The Political History of Chhattisgarh (1740–1858): Chhatisgarh under the Marathas*, Nagpur: Vishwa Bharti Publications, n.d.

Misra, Sanghamitra, *Becoming a Borderland: The Politics of Space and Identity in Colonial North-eastern India*, New Delhi: Routledge, 2011.

Mitra, Subal Chandra, *Isvar Chandra Vidyasagar: A Story of his Life and Work*, New Delhi: Rupa, 2008 [1902].

Momin, A. R. (ed.), *The Legacy of G. S. Ghurye: A Centennial Festschrift*, Mumbai: Popular Prakashan, 2006.

Mukerji, B., and P. K. Bose (eds), *Indian Science Congress Association (with Life-Sketches of General Presidents), 1914–1963*, Calcutta: Indian Science Congress Association, 1963.

Munda, R. D., and S. Bosu Mullick (eds), *The Jharkhand Movement: Indigenous People's Struggle for Autonomy in India*, Copenhagen: International Works Group for Indigenous Affairs, 2003.

Munshi, Indra (ed.), *The Adivasi Question: Issues of Land, Forest and Livelihood (Essays from EPW)*, New Delhi: Orient BlackSwan, 2012.

Munshi, K. M. (ed.), *Indian Constitutional Documents: Munshi Papers, Vol. II*, Bombay: Bhartiya Vidya Bhawan, 1967.

Murali, Atluri, 'Alluri Sitarama Raju and the Manyam Rebellion of 1922–24', *Social Scientist* 12 (4), April 1984, pp. 3–33.

Nathan, Dev (ed.), *From Tribe to Caste*, Shimla: Indian Institute of Advanced Studies, 1997.

Nathan, Dev, and Virginius Xaxa (eds), *Social Exclusion and Adverse Inclusion: Development and Deprivation of Adivasis in India*, New Delhi: Oxford University Press, 2012.

Nongbri, Tiplut, 'Tribe, Caste and the Indigenous Challenge in India', in Bengt G. Karlsson and Tanka B. Subba (eds), *Indigeneity in India*, London: Kegan Paul, 2006, pp. 75–95.

Nilsen, Alf Gunvald, 'Subalterns and the State in the *Longue Durée*: Notes from "The Rebellious Century" in the Bhil Heartland', *Journal of Contemporary Asia* 45 (4), 2015, pp. 574–595.

O'Hanlon, Rosalind, *Caste, Conflict and Ideology: Mahatma Jotirao Phule and Low Caste Protest in Nineteenth Century India*, Ranikhet: Permanent Black, 2002 [1985].

O'Malley, L. S. S., *The Indian Civil Service, 1601–1930*, London: John Murray, 1931.

Omvedt, Gail, *Dalits and the Democratic Revolution: Dr. Ambedkar and the Dalit Movement in Colonial India*, New Delhi: Sage, 1994.

——, *Building the Ambedkar Revolution: Sambhaji Tukaram Gaikwad and the Kokan Dalits*, Mumbai: Bhashya Prakasham, 2011.

Oomen, T. K., 'Scheduled Caste, Scheduled Tribes, and the Nation: Situating G. S. Ghurye', *Sociological Bulletin* 60 (2), May–August, 2011, pp. 228–244.

Padel, Felix. *Sacrificing People: Invasions of a Tribal Landscape*, New Delhi: Orient BlackSwan, 2011.

Padel, Felix, and Samarendra Das, *Out of this Earth: East India Adivasis and the Aluminium Cartel*, New Delhi: Orient BlackSwan, 2020 [2010].

Pandey, Deepak, 'Congress-Muslim League Relations 1937–39: "The Parting of the Ways"', *MAS* 12 (4), 1978, pp. 629–654.

Pant, Rashmi, 'The Cognitive Status of Caste in Colonial Ethnography: A Review of Some Literature on the North West Provinces and Oudh', *Indian Economic and Social History Review* 24 (2), 1987, pp. 145–162.

Pooja Parmar, 'Undoing Historical Wrongs: Law and Indigeneity in India', *Osgoode Hall Law Journal* 49 (3), 2012, pp. 491–525.

Pati, Biswamoy, 'Peasants, Tribals and the National Movement in Orissa (1921–1936)', *Social Scientist* 11 (7), July 1983, pp. 25–49.

____, 'Storm over Malkangiri: A Note on Laxman Naiko's Revolt (1942)', *Social Scientist* 15 (8/9), 1987, pp. 47–66.

____, *Resisting Domination: Peasants, Tribals and the National Movement in Orissa, 1920–50*, New Delhi: Manohar, 1993.

____, *Identity, Hegemony and Resistance: Towards a Social History of Conversions in Orissa, 1800–2000*, New Delhi: Three Essays Collective, 2003.

____ (ed.), *Adivasis in Colonial India: Survival, Resistance and Negotiation*, New Delhi: Indian Council of Historical Research & Orient BlackSwan, 2011.

____, *Tribals and Dalits in Orissa: Towards a Social History of Exclusion, c.1800–1950*, New Delhi: Oxford University Press, 2019.

Pawar, G. M., *The Life and Works of Maharshi Vitthal Ramji Shinde*, Sudhakar Marathe (trans.), New Delhi: Sahitya Akademi, 2013.

Peabody, Norbert, 'Cents, Sense, Census: Human Inventories in Late Precolonial and Early Colonial India', *Comparative Studies in Society and History* 43 (4), 2001, 819–850.

Pramanick, S. K., *Sociology of G.S. Ghurye*, Jaipur: Rawat, 2020 (rev. second edition).

Prasad, Archana, *Against Ecological Romanticism: Verrier Elwin and the Making of an Anti-Modern Tribal Identity*, New Delhi: Three Essays Collective, 2003.

Purushotham, Sunil, *From Raj to Republic: Sovereignty, Violence and Democracy in India*, Stanford: Stanford University Press, 2021.

Radhakrishnan, Meena, 'The Criminal Tribes Act in Madras Presidency: Implications for Itinerant Trading Communities', *Indian Economic and Social History Review* 26 (3), September 1989, pp. 269–295.

____, 'Surveillance and Settlements under the Criminal Tribes Act in Madras', *Indian Economic and Social History Review* 29 (2), June 1992, pp. 171–198.

Radhakrishnan, Meena, *Dishonoured by History: 'Criminal Tribes' and British Colonial Policy*, Hyderabad: Orient Longman, 2001.

—— (ed.), *First Citizen: Studies on Adivasis, Tribals, and Indigenous Peoples in India*, New Delhi: Oxford University Press, 2016.

Raghavaiah, V., 'Background of tribal struggles in India', in A. R. Desai (ed.), *Peasant Struggles in India*, New Delhi: Oxford University Press, 1979.

Rajan, S. Ravi, *Modernizing Nature: Forestry and Imperial Eco-Development, 1800–1950*, Hyderabad: Orient Longman, 2006.

Rangarajan, Mahesh, *Fencing the Forest: Conservation and Ecological Change in India's Central Provinces 1860–1914*, New Delhi: Oxford University Press, 1996.

Ray, Reeju, *Placing the Frontier in British North-East India: Law, Custom and Knowledge*, Oxford: Oxford University Press, 2023.

Risley, H. H., *The People of India*, Calcutta: Thacker, Spink, and Co., 1908.

Rivers, W. H. R., 'A Genealogical Method of Collecting Social and Vital Statistics', *Journal of the Anthropological Institute of Great Britain and Ireland* 2, 1900, pp. 74–82.

——, 'The Government of Subject Peoples', in A. C. Heyward (ed.), *Science and the Nation*, Cambridge: Cambridge University Press, 1917.

——, 'The Concept of "Soul-Substance" in New Guinea and Melanesia', *Folklore* 31 (1), 30 March 1920, pp. 48–69.

——, 'The Dying Out of Native Races', *Lancet* 98, 1920, pp. 42–44, 109–111.

——, 'The Psychological Factor', in W. H. R. Rivers (ed.), *Essays on the Depopulation of Melanesia*, Cambridge: Cambridge University Press, 1922, pp. 84–113.

——, *Medicine, Magic, and Religion*, London: Kegan Paul, Trench, Trubner & Co., 1924.

Rivers, W. H. R., and H. Head, 'A Human Experiment in Nerve Division', *Brain* 31, 1908, pp. 323–450.

Rizvi, B. R., 'J.P. Mills and India's North East', in T. B. Subba (ed.), *North-East India: A Handbook of Anthropology*, New Delhi: Orient BlackSwan, 2012, pp. 79–98.

Rodrigues, Shaunna, 'Excluded Areas as the Limit of the Political: The Murky Boundaries of Scheduled Areas in India', *The International Journal of Human Rights* 25 (7), pp. 1126–1147.

Roy, S. C., 'Anthropological Research in India', *Man in India* 1, pp. 43–44.

Rustomji, Nari, *Enchanted Frontiers: Sikkim, Bhutan and India's North-Eastern Borderlands*, New Delhi: Oxford University Press, 2008 [1971].

Said, Edward, *Orientalism*, New York: Routledge and Kegan Paul, 1978.

Samarendra, Padmanabh, 'Classifying Caste: Census Surveys in India in the Late Nineteenth and Early Twentieth Centuries', *South Asia: Journal of South Asian Studies*, n.s., XXVI (2), August 2003, pp. 141–164.

Savyasachi (ed.), *Tribal Forest-Dwellers and Self-Rule: The Constituent Assembly Debates on the Fifth and Sixth Schedules*, New Delhi: Indian Social Institute, 1998.

Sen, Rahul, 'Tribal policy of India', *Indian Anthropologist* 22 (2), 1992, pp. 77–89.

Scott, James C., *Seeing Like a State: How Certain Schemes to Improve the Human Condition have Failed*, New Haven: Yale University Press, 1998.

——, *The Art of Not Being Governed*, New Delhi: Orient BlackSwan, 2010.

Sen, Asoka Kumar, *From Village Elder to British Judge: Custom, Customary Law and Tribal Society*, New Delhi: Orient BlackSwan, 2012.

Shah, Kantilal, *Thakkar Bapa*, New Delhi: Bharatiya Adimjati Sevak Sangh, 1955.

Shani, Ornit, *How India Became Democratic: Citizenship and the Making of the Universal Franchise*, Gurgaon: Penguin Viking, 2018.

Sharma. B. D., *Tribal Development: The Concept and the Frame*, New Delhi: Sahyog Pustak Kutir, 1978.

——, *Planning for Tribal Development*, New Delhi: Prachi Prakashan, 1984.

——, *Whither Tribal Areas? Constitutional Amendments and After*, New Delhi: Sahyog Pustak Kutir, 1995.

Sharma, K. K., *Agrarian Movements and Congress Politics in Bihar 1927–47*, New Delhi: Anamika, 1989.

Shukla, H. L. *Tribal Heritage of Madhya Pradesh: An Annotated Bibliography*, New Delhi: B. R. Publishing House, 1986.

——, *History of the People of Bastar*, New Delhi: Sharada Publishing House, 1992.

Singh, K. S., *Dust Storm and Hanging Mist: Birsa Munda and His Movement*, New Delhi: Oxford University Press,1983.

——, 'Foreword', in J. H. Hutton, *Census of India 1931: With Complete Survey of Tribal Life and System*, New Delhi: Gian Publishing House, 1989.

—— (ed.), *The Tribal Situation in India*, Shimla: Indian Institute of Advanced Studies, 2002 [1972].

——, *Tribal Society in India: An Anthropo-Historical Perspective*, New Delhi: Manohar, 1985.

Singh, K. S., 'Tribes, Partition and Independence', in S. Settar and Indira B Gupta (eds), *Pangs of Partition*, Vol. I, New Delhi: Manohar, 2002, pp. 259–276.

——, 'G.S. Ghurye, Verrier Elwin and Indian Tribes', in A. R. Momin (ed.), *The Legacy of G.S. Ghurye: A Centennial Festschrift*, Bombay: Popular Prakashan, 2006, pp. 39–45.

Sinha, A. C., 'Colonial Anthropology vs Indological Sociology: Elwin and Ghurye on Tribal Policy in India', in Tanka B. Subba and Sujit Som (eds), *Between Ethnography and Fiction: Verrier Elwin and the Tribal Question in India*, New Delhi: Orient Longman, 2005, pp. 71–85.

Sinha, Shanshank S., 'Adivasis, Gender and the "Evil Eye": The Construction(s) of Witches in Colonial Chotanagpur', in Biswamoy Pati (ed.), *Adivasis in Colonial India: Survival, Resistance and Negotiation*, New Delhi: Orient BlackSwan, 2011, pp. 112–136.

Sinha, Surajit. 'State Formation and Rajput Myth in Tribal Central India', *Man in India* 42 (1), 1962.

——, *Tribal Polities and State Systems in Pre-Colonial Eastern and North Eastern India*, published for Centre for Studies in Social Sciences, Calcutta, by K. P. Bagchi & Company, Calcutta, 1987.

Sivaramakrishnan, K., *Modern Forests: State Making and Environmental Changes in Colonial Eastern India*, Stanford, NJ: Stanford University Press, 1999.

Skaria, Ajay, *Hybrid Histories: Forests, Frontiers and Wildness in Western India*, New Delhi: Oxford University Press, 1999.

Spangenberg, Bradford, *British Bureaucracy in India: Status, Policy and the I.C.S. in the Late 19th Century*, Columbia, MO: South Asia Books, 1976.

Srinivas, M. N., 'Practicing Social Anthropology in India', *Annual Review of Anthropology* 26, 1997, pp. 1–24.

Stevens, John A., *Keshab: Bengal's Forgotten Prophet*, New York: Oxford University Press, 2018.

George W. Stocking, Jr., 'The Ethnographer's Magic: Fieldwork in British Anthropology from Tylor to Malinowski', in George W. Stocking, Jr. (ed.), *Observers Observed: Essays on Ethnographic Fieldwork*, History of Anthropology Vol. 1, Madison: The University of Wisconsin Press, 1983.

——, *Victorian Anthropology*, New York: The Free Press, 1987.

——, *After Tylor: British Social Anthropology, 1888–1951*, Madison: University of Wisconsin Press, 1995.

Stokes, Eric, *The English Utilitarians and India*, New Delhi: Oxford University Press, 1982 [1959].

Subba, T. B. (ed.), *North-east India: A Handbook of Anthropology*, New Delhi: Orient BlackSwan, 2012.

Subba, T. B., and Sujit Som (eds), *Between Ethnography and Fiction: Verrier Elwin and the Tribal Question in India*, New Delhi: Orient Longman, 2005.

Sundar, Nandini, 'The Dreaded Danteswari: Annals of Alleged Sacrifice', *Indian Economic and Social History Review* 32 (3), 1995, pp. 345–374.

____, *Subalterns and Sovereigns: An Anthropological History of Bastar (1854–2006)*, New Delhi: Oxford University Press, 2007 [1997].

____, 'Verrier Elwin and the 1940s Missionary Debate in Central India', T. B. Subba and Sujit Som (eds), *Between Ethnography and Fiction: Verrier Elwin and the Tribal Question in India*, Hyderabad: Orient Longman, 2005.

____ (ed.), *Legal Grounds: Natural Resources, Identity and the Law in Jharkhand*, New Delhi: Oxford University Press, 2009.

____ (ed.), *The Scheduled Tribes and their India: Politics, Identities, Policies and Work*, New Delhi: Oxford University Press, 2016.

Syiemlieh, David R. (ed.), *On the Edge of Empire: Four British Plans for North East India, 1941-1947*. New Delhi: Sage, 2014.

Tewari, Saagar, 'Developing Bastar: The Dandakaranya Project', in Ravi Kumar (ed.), *The Heart of the Matter-Development, Identity and Violence: Reconfiguring the Debate*, New Delhi: Aakar Books, 2010, pp. 115–134.

____, 'Spaces of Protection, Regimes of Exception: Anthropologists, Administrators and the Framing of the Late Colonial Discourse on Tribal Regions (1920–1950)', *Karatoya: North Bengal University Journal of History* 12, March 2019, pp. 114–130.

____, 'Kasht Nivarak Thakkar Bapa: Samaj Seva ko Samarpit Jivan par ek Vihangam Drishti', *Pratimaan: Samay Samaj Sanskriti* 5 (2), July–December 2017, pp. 278–296.

____, 'Framing the Fifth Schedule: Tribal Agency and the Making of the Indian Constitution (1937–1950)', *MAS* 56 (5), 2022, pp. 1556–1594.

Thakkar, A. V., 'Famine Tour in Panch Mahal', *TSI* II (10), 10 April 1919, pp. 117–118.

____, 'Compulsory Education', *TSI* II (44), 4 December 1919, p. 519.

____, 'Bhil Seva Mandal Dohad', *TISR* XXXIII (47), 21 July 1923, p. 763.

____, 'In the Land of the Aborigines: Savars, Binjhwars and Halbas', *TSI* IX (6), 11 March 1926, pp. 69–71.

Thakkar, A. V., 'Education in Baroda: Neglect of the Aborigines', *TSI* IX (8), 25 March 1926, pp. 98–100.

——, '"Farming out" of Education in the Assam Hills', *TSI* IX (9), 1 April 1926, pp. 109–110.

——, 'In the Land of the Aborigines: Assam Hill Tribes', *TSI* IX (11), 15 April 1926, pp. 137–139.

——, 'The Aboriginal Tribes of India', *The Modern Review* XLI (2), No. 242, February 1927, p. 131.

——, 'Representation of the Aborigines', *TSI* XV (23), 23 June 1932, p. 192.

——, 'The Problem of Aborigines in India', R. R. Kale Memorial Lecture 1941, Gokhale Institute of Politics and Economics, in T. N. Jagadisan and Shyamlal (compiled and eds), *Thakkar Bapa: Eightieth Birthday Commemoration Volume*, Madras: Diocesan Press, 1949, pp. 354–377.

——, 'V.R. Shinde', *TISR* LIV (31), 8 April 1944, pp. 246–247.

——, 'Education among Tribal People very Backward: State's Responsibility for their Advancement', in *Leader*, 11 July 1945, reproduced in *Aboriginals' Cry in the Wilderness: Controversy between Dr. Ambedkar and A.V. Thakkar with Facts and Figures Regarding Aborigines and Hill Tribes, Their Education and Representation in Legislature*, Published by A. V. Thakkar, Servants of India Society, Bombay, n.d.

——, *Five Year Plan for the Betterment of the Condition of the People in the Backward Areas of Central Provinces & Berar*, n.d.

Tolen, Rachel J., 'Colonizing and Transforming the Criminal Tribesman: The Salvation Army in British India', *American Ethnologist* 18 (1), 1991, pp. 106–125.

Trautman, Thomas R., *Aryans and British India*, Berkeley: University of California Press, 1997.

Uberoi, Patricia, Nandini Sundar, and Satish Deshpande, *Anthropology in the East: Founders of Indian Sociology*, Ranikhet: Permanent Black, 2007.

Upadhya, Carol, 'The Hindu Nationalist Sociology of G.S. Ghurye', *Sociological Bulletin* 51 (1), March 2002, pp. 28–57.

Venugopal, C. N., 'G. S. Ghurye on Culture and Nation-Building', *Sociological Bulletin* 42 (1–2), March–September 1993, pp. 1–13.

Vidyarthi, L. P., *Rise of Anthropology in India: A Social Science Orientation Vol. I, The Tribal Dimensions*, New Delhi: Concept, 1978.

Visvanathan, Susan, 'S. K. Rudra, C. F. Andrews and M. K. Gandhi: Friendship, Dialogue and Interiority in the Question of Indian

Nationalism', *Economic and Political Weekly* 37 (34), January 2002. pp. 3532–3541.

Wagoner, Philip B., 'Precolonial Intellectuals and the Production of Colonial Knowledge', *Comparative Studies in History and Society* 45 (4), 2003, pp. 783–814.

Woodruff, Philip, *The Men Who Ruled India: The Founders*, London: Jonathan Cape, 1953.

——, *The Men Who Ruled India: Vol. II, The Guardians*, London: Jonathan Cape, 1954.

Xaxa, Virginius, 'Transformation of Tribes in India: Terms of Discourse', *Economic and Political Weekly* 34 (24), June 1999, pp. 1519–1524.

——, 'Tribes as indigenous people of India', *Economic and Political Weekly* 34 (51), December 1999, pp. 3589–3595.

——, 'Elwin's Tribals', *Economic and Political Weekly* 36 (18), 5 May 2001, pp. 1519–1520.

——, 'Tribes in India', in Veena Das (ed.), *The Oxford Companion to Sociology and Social Anthropology in India*, Oxford: Oxford University Press, 2003, pp. 373–408.

——, 'Politics of Language, Religion and Identity: Tribes in India', *Economic and Political Weekly* 40 (13), March 2005, pp. 1363–1370.

——, *State, Society, and Tribes: Issues in Post-Colonial India*, New Delhi: Pearson, 2008.

Yagnik, Indulal, *The Autobiography of Indulal Yagnik* (in 3 vols), New Delhi: Manohar, 2011.

Yonuo, Asoso, *The Rising Nagas: A Historical and Political Study*, Delhi: Vivek Publishing House, 1974.

Zachariah, Benjamin, *Developing India: An Intellectual and Social History, c.1930–1950*, New Delhi: Oxford University Press, 2005.

Unpublished Thesis/Dissertations

Gokhale, Nishant, 'Re-Negotiating Tribal Property Rights in India', *LLM* Writing Requirement, Harvard University, 2018.

McEldowney, Philip Frederic, 'Colonial Administration and Social Developments in Middle India, The Central Provinces, 1861–1921, Ph.D. Dissertation, Cocoran Department of History, University of Virginia, 1980.

Paidipaty, Poornima L., 'Tribal Nation: Politics and the Making of Anthropology in India, 1874–1967', Ph.D. Dissertation, Graduate School of Arts and Sciences, Columbia University, 2010.

Prasad, Archana, 'Forest and Subsistence in Colonial India: A Study of the Central Provinces, 1830–1945', Ph.D. Thesis, Centre for Historical Studies, Jawaharlal Nehru University, 1994.

Index